Turkey

Edited by Marianne Mehling

Turkey

A Phaidon Cultural Guide

with over 470 colour illustrations
and 18 pages of maps

Phaidon

Contributors: Gerd Glassen, Maria Paukert M.A., Heinrich Schöttler, Pitty Schöttler, Dr Rainer Warland, Joachim Willeitner M.A.

Photographs: Joachim Willeitner, Heinrich Schöttler, Pitty Schöttler, Gerd Glassen, Dr Rainer Warland, Turkish Ministry for Culture and Tourism, Norbert Dallinger

Phaidon Press Limited, Musterlin House, Jordan Hill Road, Oxford OX2 8DP

First published in English in 1989
Originally published as *Knaurs Kulturführer in Farbe: Türkei*
© Droemersche Verlagsanstalt Th. Knaur Nachf. Munich 1987
Translation © Phaidon Press Limited 1989

A CIP catalogue record for this book is available from the British Library

ISBN 0 7148 2530 1

Translated and edited by Babel Translations, London
Typeset by WM Print Limited, Walsall
Printed in West Germany

Cover illustration: Agia Sofia, Istanbul (photo: The *Telegraph* Colour Library)

Foreword

An old proverb suggests that 'anyone who has drunk from the Bosporus will always be thirsty for it'. Nowadays, like many other waterways of our times, the Bosporus is hardly attractive as a source of drinking water. But this important stretch of water, a former river valley, twenty miles long and 723 yards wide at the narrowest point, not only connects the city of Istanbul with the rest of Turkey, but also joins two seas and two continents: the Sea of Marmara and the Black Sea, Europe and Asia.

Turkey has an area of 30,491 square miles, and consists of a European section (East Thrace, 9,228 square miles) and an Asiatic section (Anatolia). It borders on such culturally and politically different lands as Bulgaria, Greece, the USSR, Iran, Iraq and Syria; and has a coastline on the Black Sea, the Sea of Marmara, the Aegean and the Mediterranean.

The country contains wonderful, unspoilt scenery and people whose hospitality remains unchanged. The further one travels through the wild and varied landscape of Anatolia, with its veiled women and streets full of men, the more one has a sense of being in the East. Those who look more closely will realize that many sights which at first may seem picturesque and romantic in fact show a people living in real poverty and struggling to survive. Compared to those in the north of the country, these people are still far removed from the 'Europeanization' favoured by Kemal Atatürk. It is not difficult to see why many of them leave their homes, families and accustomed territory to make a living elsewhere.

There is a wealth of fascinating and important sites to visit in Turkey. The most important city is Istanbul. A bridge between East and West, it was once the capital of the Eastern Roman Empire of the Byzantine emperors, the 'second Rome', and later became the centre of power for the Ottoman Empire, which extended into Europe and North Africa. Buildings like the Hippodrome, and Byzantine churches, fortresses, mosques and palaces still bear eloquent witness to past greatness. A Western lifestyle is paired with Islamic tradition to make the city a 'corridor' between the two cultures. This is also largely true of East Thrace and its towns such as Edirne, Abydos and Iznik.

In Western Anatolia the trail of the ancient Greeks may be followed in Pergamon and Troy. There are other examples of Ionian architecture and culture at Ephesus, Priene, Miletus, Didyma, Geyre (Aphrodisias) and Bodrum (Halikarnassos). The stalactite terraces of Pamukkale are a natural architectural masterpiece, and should also be visited.

On the Mediterranean coast is Termessos, and the ruins of ancient Pamphylian cities (Perge, Aspendos, Side). Issos is renowned for Alexander's famous battle in 333 BC; he founded Alexandretta, now known as Iskenderun, after his victory. Antakya, formerly Antioch, is associated with early Christendom; it was once the capital of the Seleucid Empire, and the largest city in the Orient.

There are many other important sites in Turkey. The present capital of the country, Ankara, is in Central Anatolia; here may be found the vast mausoleum of Kemal Atatürk, the 'father' of modern Turkey. Then there is Çatal Huyuk, on the plain of Konya, one of the oldest sites in the world; Gordion, where Alexander the Great undid the legendary Gordion knot with a bold stroke of his sword, to become ruler of all Asia; Göreme, with its strange valleys and gorges, curious 'rock mushrooms' and the world-famous Byzantine rock churches with mosaics; Trabzon, on the Black Sea coast, the ancient metropolis of Trebizond; and Sinop, famous as the birthplace of Diogenes. On the border with the USSR and Iran lies Ağrı Dağı, better known as Mount Ararat, where Noah's ark is said to have landed. And in the extreme east of Taurus is the tomb and cult site of Antiochos I of Commagene at Nemrut Daği, an impressive testimony to the pomp with which rulers were once buried and honoured.

Of course, this is just a selection of the most renowned sites of interest. This book will provide further information about mosques, churches, ancient Byzantine and Ottoman buildings and museums in more than 700 places. As with the other guides in the series the text is arranged in alphabetical order of place names for easy reference. The link between places which are geographically close but separated in the text because of the alphabetical arrangement is provided by the maps on pages 564-79. They show all the principal towns mentioned in the text, and also those subsidiary places mentioned in the environs section at the end of each entry.

The heading to each entry gives the name of the town, its region and reference to the map section with page number and grid reference. Within each entry the main sights are printed in bold type: less significant objects of interest appear under the heading **Also worth seeing** and places in the vicinity under **Environs.**

The appendices at the end of the book include a chronological table, an alphabetical survey of the peoples of Asia Minor, a glossary of important Turkish and Arabic terms, and an index of places mentioned in the text.

View of old Istanbul ▷

Adana

Adana   p.574□L 6

Adana is the fourth-largest town in modern Turkey, and thanks to its position in the middle of the fertile Çukorova plain, ancient Cilicia, it has been an important centre of trade and commerce for centuries and a subject for dispute between the surrounding great powers. This is still clear today from the fact that the province of Adana has about 40 surviving castles and fortresses dating from the Hittite to the Ottoman period. Particularly advantageous sites have been used on numerous occasions.

History: According to legend, the town was founded by Adanus and Sarus, sons of the Greek god Uranus. Cilician myths ascribe its origin to the Luwian god Santas. At the time of the Hittite empire (2nd millennium BC), *Adaniya*, as the town was known in the cuneiform texts of the time, was the centre of the border province of Kizzuvatna. In the first half of the first millennium BC the town was often under Assyrian rule and in the 6C BC was their vassal town of *Que*, under a local native dynasty.

In 401 BC Adana was a satrapy of the Persian Achaemenids, then Macedonian under Alexander the Great and under his

◁ *Adana, Ulu Cami, entrance*

successors, the Diadochi, was part of the Seleucid empire, and known as *Antiocha ad Sarum*. It was part of the Roman province of Cilicia from the latter's foundation in 102 BC. After the division of the empire the town was part of Eastern Rome, then subsequently disputed between the Omaiyads and their Islamic successor dynasties and the Byzantines, until in 1077 the Seljuks under Süleyman Shah occupied the whole of Çukurova. In the 14C it was ruled by Egyptian Mamelukes. In the 15 & 16C it flourished under the local dynasty of the Ramazan Oğlu, from whom the Ottoman Sultan Selim I took over in 1516.

Adana remained Turkish, apart from a brief period of foreign rule in the mid-19C by Mohammed Ali of Egypt, until it was occupied by France in the First World War. The French were compelled to return it to Turkey by the Treaty of Ankara (5 January 1922).

The picturesque old town on the W. bank of the Seyhan has survived, forming a striking contrast with the spacious new town on both banks of the river.

Taşköprü (Stone Bridge): This bridge over the Seyhan dates back to the Roman Emperor Hadrian (1st third of the 2C AD). It is 43 ft. wide and was originally 340 yards long. 14 of the original 21 round arches have survived. The largest, at the apex of the curved bridge, is decorated with a lion relief.

Ulu Cami (Great Mosque): Built in 1507 by Halil, a prince of the local Ramazan Oğlu dynasty. The buildings include a mosque, a Koran school (medrese), a mausoleum (türbe) and a Koran reading school (ders-hane), grouped around an arcaded courtyard within a defensive wall. The buildings are particularly interesting because of the variety of styles they represent: generally speaking they are in the Syrian tradition, decorated with Seljuk ornaments and also Ottoman faience tiles.

The site is entered from the W. through

a gatehouse with a conical stalactite dome. It is one of the most recent examples of this building style, usually found only further to the E. The dragons facing each other at the top of the domes are Seljuk in both motif and style. A building inscription in the elongated and crenellated gateway niche shows that it dates from a later extension under Mustafa Ramazan Oğlu (1541).

The *courtyard* is paved in marble, and bordered by rows of columns, threefold in the N. and double in the W.; the arcades are domed in the rear, and surrounded by the rooms of the medrese. The slender, polygonal *minaret*, in Syrian style with lavish polychrome marble encrustations, is N. of the mosque, which in its turn is entered through the magnificent E. façade. The minaret also has a building inscription placing it in the period of Halil Ramazan Oğlu. Three gates with pointed arches and lavish moulding lead into the interior of the mosque. The E. wing is dominated by the *türbe*, with its onion-shaped dome. In front of the türbe is a building with groin vaulting and a small columned vestibule. The colourful *prayer niche* (mihrab) of the türbe is particularly striking; its base is

covered with blue Iznik faience tiles (mid 16C). The tiles on the three tombs are coloured to tone with them, but date from a later restoration in the 18C. This is the burial place of Halil (d. 1510), Piri Paşa (d. 1534) and Mustafa (d. 1552), all rulers of the Ramazan Oğlu family, father, son and grandson respectively. The *ders-hane*, (built 1540) opposite the W. façade of the mosque was, like the lavishly decorated public bath (Carsi Hammam) outside the complex (built 1529), endowed by Piri Paşa.

The small *mesçit* (house of prayer) by the Ulu Cami was built in 1495 by Halil Ramazan Oğlu and is thus the oldest surviving building of those endowed by this dynasty in Adana.

Yağ Camii (Butter Mosque): The origins of this house of prayer cannot be established precisely. A restoration inscription in the narthex of the mosque of Halil Ramazan Oğlu shows that the buildings must have been here before 1501. Ibrahim, one of Piri Paşa's sons, undertook further restoration in 1552, and the medrese by the mosque also dates from this period. This is confirmed by the

Adana, Ulu Cami, exterior view

Adana, Roman bridge

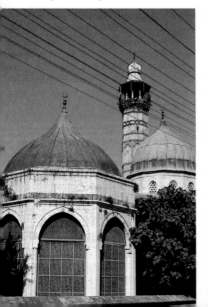

bipartite inscription above the main entrance to the buildings, a gateway flanked by side niches and small decorative columns. It is sited within a raised entrance section with crenellations and Gothic vaulting. It leads into the courtyard, which has the medrese in the E. and the mosque in the S.

The individual rooms of the *medrese* are built in and decorated with brick. The domed iwan in the middle is, however, a delicately ornamented stone building.

Adjacent to the mosque in the E. is a medieval former church, used as an extension of the prayer room. The minaret rises between the two buildings; its upper section has been rebuilt.

Archaeological museum (*Bölge Müzesi*): This museum directly adjacent to the bus station was established in 1972 and has two storeys showing finds from prehistoric times to the Moslem period, with the Hittites and their successor states taking up an important part of the collection. The most important item from this era is a figure of a king or god in dark hard rock found in Tell Halaf, the ancient Guzuna, and dated from the early 1st millennium BC. Numerous clay tablets from the period of the Assyrian trading colonies in Asia Minor (1st half of the 2nd millennium BC) and Egyptian finds confirm wide-ranging trading links. Also outstanding are the Urartian relief bronzes (900−600 BC) and a large Orpheus mosaic (3C BC).

Also worth seeing: *Ethnographic Museum* (Inönü Caddesi, not far from the Tourist Office). This former church houses a remarkable collection of Islamic folk art from the Ottoman period to the most recent past.

Clock tower (Büyük Saat): In the town centre on the road between Ulu Cami and Yağ Cami. The building is over a hundred feet high and was built in 1882 under Governor Abidin Paşa by Haci Bekir Sirri Efendi. S. of here is the picturesque covered *bazaar* (bedesten or Kapali Çarsi).

Hasan-Kethüde-Mosque: This house of prayer was the work of the famous Ottoman architect Sinan, responsible for many 16C mosques, particularly in Istanbul.

Eski Cami (Old Mosque): This building on the Ali Münif Caddesi was a Christian church before being turned into a mosque.

Environs: Karataş (49 km. S.): This seaside resort and small harbour town at the entrance to the Gulf of İskenderun and not far from the mouth of the Pyramos, known in ancient times as **Magarsa** (also **Magarsus, Megasos** etc.), still offers the possibility of bathing in the Mediterranean. On the spit a little to the S. of the town (Cape Karataş) there are still some ancient ruins to be seen, in all probability dating from the times of the Crusades for the most part. Alexander the Great is said to have sacrificed to the gods here before the battle of Issos (333 BC). Sparse remains of a fortress (Mollas Kale).

Adıyaman

This town 168 km. E. of Karamanmaras, today the administrative centre of the province of Adıyaman, was founded in the 7C AD, and was then known as *Hisn Mansur*. The *citadel*, which dominates the modern town, probably also dates from this early Omaiyadic period. It was restored by the Abbaside caliph Harun al-Rashid (786–809) and rebuilt under the Seljuk Turks. The most notable building in the town centre, walled with three gates, is the 14C *Ulu Cami*.

Modern Adıyaman is at the heart of the terrain known to the ancients as *Commagene*. The capital of what was then an important kingdom was Samosata, the modern Samsat, 40 km. away.

History: The area is first in evidence in the annals of the Assyrian King Salmanassar III (858–824) under the name Kummuhi, as one of several tributary states. As the Urartian kingdom strengthened under King Sardur II, the Assyrians lost their eastern provinces to their opponents, then regained their influence when the Urartian kingdom was defeated. It was,

however, not until the reign of the Assyrian King Sargon II that Kummuhi lost its status as a small state in its own right and became part of the Assyrian empire.

Later the area was part of the Persian Achaemenid empire. The Commagene general Aroandas (also Artasuras; usually Orontes in Greek) made such a reputation for himself in the conflict between the Persian King Artaxerxes III (404–359) and his brother Cyrus, who was in revolt, that he was given the victorious Artaxerxes' daughter Rhogune as his wife. The ruling house of Commagene is known as the Orontid dynasty after this founding father. The first ruler was Samos I, in the early 3C BC, who had the title of king, and founded the future capital of the empire, Samosata (now Samsat), which was named after him. His son Arsames (mid-3C BC) is said to have founded the towns of Arsamaeia on Nymphaios (now Eski Kâhta) and Arsamaeia on Euphrates (now Gerger), which were likewise named after him. He also gave shelter to the Seleucid Antiochos Hierax, who was fleeing from his brother.

Ptolemaios, Arsames' grandson, tried in vain to extend the empire N. of the Taurus. His son Samos II (c.130–100) was probably buried in Arsameia on Euphrates (Gerger) and had a relief of himself carved on the castle rock. Persistently smouldering conflicts between Commagene and the neighbouring Seleucid empire were brought to an end by the marriage of Mithridates I Kallinikos, the son and successor of Samos II, to Laodike, the daughter of the Seleucid King Antiochos VIII Grypos (Eagle Nose; 125–96). Their son Antiochos I (69–34) was to become the most famous ruler produced by the Commagene dynasty.

The Armenian King Tigranes the Great, who claimed lawful succession within the Seleucid empire, and also rights in Commagene, through his marriage with

Arsameia on Nymphaios (Adıyaman), relief at base site III ▷

Cleopatra, daughter of the equally power-ful King Mithridates VI of Pontus, had become an even more threatening oppo-nent for Antiochos I. The danger was allayed, however, by the victories of the Roman general Lucullus, and subse-quently Pompey, over both Tigranes and Mithridates.

After his death (36 BC), Antiochos I was buried in the hierothesion on the Nem-rut Dağı. The ruler, who, as the reliefs on his tomb show, was legitimized both by Alexander the Great and the Achae-menid Persians, had demanded that he be worshipped as a god even in his lifetime. He was succeeded by his son Antiochos II, with whose reign the decline of the Commagene empire began.

A brother of Mithridates, Antiochos II, was summoned to Rome for overstepping his responsibilities and executed there in 29 BC. The son of another, anonymous brother finally succeeded to the Com-magene throne as Mithridates III.

Commagene troops were integrated into the Roman army. The horsemen and archers in particular were a feared and powerful fighting unit. The last member of the ruling Commagene house we hear of, at the time of the Roman Emperor Hadrian (117–138), was Gaius Julius Antiochos, who had the name Philopappos (Grandfather-Loving). He was Roman consul and lived in Athens, where he had his mausoleum built on the Hill of the Muses, opposite the Acropolis (see Phaidon Cultural Guide *Athens and Attica*, p. 88 under *Hill of the Muses*). The pictorial decoration on his tomb shows him with his grandfather Antiochos IV and the father of the race, Seleukos I.

A better base than Adıyaman for a **tour** of the most important Commagene sites is the little town of **Kâhta**, 44 km. fur-ther E. It has recently acquired a number of hotels. To make it more easily distin-guishable from the site of the ruins of the

Arsameia on Nymphaios, Antiochos inscription (left), castle rock (right)

ancient town of Arsameia on Nymphaios, now known as Eski Kâhta, the modern town is also known as *Yeni Kâhta* (New Kâhta).

The best time to start is the early morning, visiting the archaeological sites in the following order: from Kâhta to Karakuş, on across the Chabinas bridge, stopping on the way at the Yeni Kalle, to Arsameia on Nymphaios, modern Eski Kâhta, then visiting the Nemrut Dağı at midday or in the early afternoon.

Environs: Arsameia on Euphrates (*Gerger; c.*65 km. N. of Kâhta): The **castle rock** with Commagene inscriptions and a large-scale relief of the ruler was discovered in 1838 by Count Helmut von Moltke, later Field Marshall Moltke, when he was still a young captain in the service of the Turks reconnoitring military supply lines for use in the conflict of the Ottoman empire with Mohammed Ali of Egypt. The Prussian Academy of Science sent an expedition as a result, led by the archaeologists Puchstein and Sester. Thanks to the inscription that had already been discovered, they were able to establish that the place had been founded by King Arsames in the mid-3C BC. But it was not until exactly 100 years after the discovery that an exact survey of the site was made by another German team under Dörner and Naumann.

According to the long Greek foundation inscription on a gatehouse to the E. of the castle, the precinct was dedicated to the goddess Argandene. Other ancestors of Antiochos I were probably buried here as well as King Samos II, of whom there is a representation in relief on the W. peak of the castle rock.

Approaching on the road from Kâhta a *relief* is seen on the W. peak of the towering castle rock. It is a front view of a standing figure, with head turned to the left. According to the associated inscription at the figure's feet this is a representation of Samos II, the grandfather of Antiochos.

Arsameia on Nymphaios, base site II ▷

Below the relief, three windows in the rock can be made out. They belong to a chamber in the rock, now plundered and inaccessible. It is possible to get closer to the relief, roughly 13 by 9 ft., and the only Commagene relief cut directly into the rock, by following a narrow path which begins at the N. foot of the castle rock, and is recommended only to those with a head for heights.

Access to the interior of the fortress is from the S. peak, where an artifically deepened ditch separates the approximately diamond-shaped castle rock from the surrounding area. The visitor keeps to the E. slope, and after the entrance gate passes another wide opening before arriving at the third gate, with the inscription which has already been mentioned, now severely weather-worn. The beginning of this is missing. This is also the point of transition from the lower castle, the plateau of which is covered with the rubble of more recent buildings, to the upper castle. In the centre of the lower castle is a covered cistern, and another, larger one is let into the N. peak. The castle is difficult to find, in particular because there is another place called Gerger only 9 km. E. of Nemrut. The

approach (from Kâhta) is on the same stretch of road which leads to Nemrut Dağı (signposted). Ten km. after Narince, turn left off the stretch leading to Nemrut Dağı along a track leading to a village with extremely poor roads from which it is still 17 km. to the castle of Gerger, already visible from this point.

Arsameia on Nymphaios (*Eski Kale;* 23 km. NE): As its name suggests, the town was founded by King Arsames (mid-3C BC). The ruins, not striking at first sight, are set on a steep slope. At three salient points, which mark the course of a former procession road which zigzags up the mountain, and which are known as 'base sites', are *reliefs*, among the finest products of Commagene art. The sharp corner, diagonally on the left from the tour already suggested, shortly beyond the Chabinas bridge and another Seljuk bridge, and leading steeply upwards to the ruins, is easily overlooked. This approach can only be used in dry weather; otherwise access is only on foot.

The first feature to be reached is *base site II*, with a relief almost 15 ft. high depicting the god Mithra-Helios. This was originally part of a group of two, showing the

Chabinas bridge (Adıyaman)

god shaking hands with King Antiochos I. This motif, by which the Commagene king places himself confidently on the same plane as the gods, is to be found on almost all representations in relief of Antiochos I. These pictures are known as the 'dexiosis scene' (Greek for 'offering the right hand'). The surviving representation of the god was found a little at a time, and it was the discovery of the upper part by local people which drew archaeologist Karl Dörner's attention to this important site. In the course of excavations started in 1951 it became clear that what had been found was the Hierothesion, the tomb and place of worship of King Mithridates I Kallinikos. Exhaustive information about this is provided by an inscription in five columns with letters about an inch high, placed at *base site III* by Antiochos I, the son of Mithridates. Below the inscription a man-high tunnel in the rock, in several stages provided with steps, leads to a total depth of 520 ft. into the rock. Dörner used miners from the Ruhr to assist with the clearing of the last section of this passage. The original function of this blind corridor is still unclear. At the entrance to the tunnel by the inscription is a square area cut into the rock, crowned with the finest and largest of all the Commagene reliefs: almost 11 ft. high and 6 ft. wide, representing one of the Commagene kings, either Mithridates, who is buried here, or his son Antiochos, who extended the complex, in state robes before the god Hercules, identified by the artist by his club. The relief was discovered in 1953.

From base site III a path leads to the summit plateau. Here foundations of buildings with mosaic floors were found, but to protect the tiny stones these were either covered up again by the archaeologists or taken to the museum in Ankara. Stylistically the mosaics seem to date from the late 2C BC, roughly the time of Mithridates. Dörner suggested, on the basis of sculptural fragments discovered, that the tomb of Mithridates was located on the mountain plateau, and decorated with colossal statues. Other archaeologists place the tomb of this ruler in the great *chamber* hewn in the rock at the W. corner of the processional way between base sites II and III: a vestibule, open at the front and visible over a considerable distance.

Arsameia on Nymphaios, tunnel entrance, base site III (left), Nemrut Dağı, lion (right)

14 steps lead down into the hall, almost 30 ft. high, and approximately 28 by 29 ft. in area. This site is known as *base site I*, because of the relief fragments found here and set up in front of the rock hall. They probably represent Mithridates and his son Antiochos. Dörner sees the rock hall as a place of worship of the god Mithras, who is present in relief at base site II, lower down the hill.

Chabinas bridge (20 km. N. of Kâhta): This crossing point of the Cendere Suyu, ancient Chabinas, near the village of Kil-lisik was built by the XVI Flavia Firma Roman legion stationed in Samsat (Samosata) between AD 198 and 200. They used stone blocks transported from the grave mound of Karakuş, about 10 km. S. The bridge has a single arch with a span of 112 ft., and is over 390 ft. long over-all. There are inscriptions relating to its foundation and consecration, both on a stone block in the stepped parapet, and also on the columns, over 30 ft. high. There was originally a pair at each end of the bridge, and three of them have sur-vived. The two columns to the S. have an inscription relating to the Emperor Sep-timius Severus, in whose reign (193–211) the bridge was built, or his wife Julia Domna. The two columns at the N. end also had texts naming the Emperor's two sons Caracalla and Geta. After Caracalla, who succeeded his father as Emperor, had his brother murdered, the column with the Geta inscription was removed.

Fragments of milestones found here show that this must have been an important river-crossing point even before the build-ing of the bridge, which is still in full use, and has to be crossed to reach nearby Yeni Kale and Eski Kale (Arsameia on Nymphaios).

Horis Kale (castle of Kores; 94 km. S. of Adıyaman): This fortress, of which little has survived, is between Gerger (Arsameia on Euphrates) and Samsat (Samosata). It stands directly on the Euphrates, which

Nemrut Dağı (Adıyaman), heads of statues ▷

borders the almost triangular site (sides just over 400 ft. long), on its steep NE side. The NW flank, on which parts of the pavement have survived in the S. section, is protected by an artificial moat. Remains of vaulting can still be seen on the inside of the castle wall that runs past this point. There is a little brook at the foot of the S. slope. Access is opposite this at the N. extremity. The site is reached by going from Adıyaman via Kâhta to the village of Akincilar, where a track on the right leads to the Euphrates in the S.

A relief fragment with Commagene inscription was found in the nearby village of Ancoz by F.K.Dörner in 1938; he was also responsible for investigating the castle of Kores with R.Naumann.

Karakuş (12 km. N. of Kâhta): This tumulus, about over 100 ft. high and built of small local stones, is directly to the left (W.) of the road to the Chabinas bridge. It is easy to miss the access road, but the characteristic columns surrounding the grave mound are conspicuous as you drive past. Originally there were three pairs of columns, set up in the S., NW and NE. 4 specimens have survived more or less intact.

Nemrut Dağı, Zeus Oromasdes

They all supported figures. The eagle which is still perched on the surviving S. column gave its name to the whole place (Karakuş: Black Bird). A complete pair has survived only in the N. One column is topped with a bull, and the other has an important inscription. This text was discovered in 1882, and recorded and translated a year later. It supplies the information that the tumulus was built by a King Mithridates for his mother Isias, his sister Antiochis and her daughter Aka, the king's niece. The text is known as the 'Isias inscription', after the mother mentioned in it. Puchstein considered that Mithridates I, the father of Antiochos I, commissioned the entire complex.

This view persisted until 1979, when J. Wagner succeeded in deciphering another inscription that F.K. Dörner had noticed in 1938. It stands at a height of 26 ft. on the abacus of the surviving NW column. This text, approximately 18 inches high, also mentions Laodike, the second daughter of Antiochos I, who was married to the Parthian king Orodes. Thus the building could be ascribed to Mithridates II, the son of Antiochos I. Visitors will recognize this column by the dexiosis relief at its apex. This representation is the only one found so far to show a female member of the royal household, probably Laodike.

The grave chamber was not discovered until F.K. Dörner, despite technical difficulties, detected it by drilling in 1967. Unfortunately the chambers were plundered in ancient times, so that no grave goods were discovered.

Nemrut Dağı (90 km. NE of Adıyaman): The highest mountain in the N. of the Land of the Two Rivers (7,053 ft.), with its famous colossal statues, was discovered by the German civil engineer Karl Sester in 1881, and investigated by him with Puchstein for the Prussian Academy of Science in May of the following year. On their way to the site they also discovered the Karakuş tumulus and the Chabinas bridge. In 1883 more detailed research was started by Puchstein, Karl Humann (who took the Pergamon altar to Berlin) and Felix von Luschan. Hamdy Bey, the director of the Imperial-Ottoman Museum, had already turned the relief-slabs round, revealing the images upon them. In 1951 an American team under Theresa Goell started new investigations on Nemrut Dağı, in the course of which the relief terraces were completely cleared in 1953–6. Since May 1984 a group of German archaeologists under F.K. Dörner has undertaken restoration work on the mountain. It has so far proved impossible to find the grave chamber of Antiochos I, which must be under the tumulus, an artificial mound of small stones which added another 164 ft. to the height of the mountain at its summit.

The final place to be reached is Narince. Here the road forks: to the right (S.) a good stretch leads rapidly to the main Diyabakır–Adıyaman road, which enables a quick run back from Nemrut Dağı to Kâhta. The left-hand road leads to the mountain. Bear left again after about 10 km. (then about 16 km. further; Gerger is signposted to the right). The road up to Nemrut Dağı is steep, but reasonably passable, as it is cobbled over long stretches to provide a good grip. The final climb to the summit has to be on foot, from a cafeteria with car park; this takes about a quarter of an hour.

The first point reached is the so-called East Terrace. Apart from the fact that it has additional sacrifical altars, it is similar in design to the West Terrace on the other side of the artificial grave tumulus. On the N. flank of the tomb, between the two relief terraces, is a row of steles, (originally over 260 ft. long; they are no longer upright); in ancient times space for access to the hierothesion was probably left free between them.

East terrace: Here the row of seated deities with their backs to the tumulus has survived almost complete. All that is missing of the statues, which are carved not from single blocks of stone, but from 8 layers of ashlar, is their heads, but these are displayed on the ground.

Until quite recently the head of the goddess Commagene was still on the appropriate torso, but fell off in a severe storm. With heads the statues were between 26 and 29 ft. high. The group on the extreme left, originally a lion and an eagle on a plinth, has now been completely des-

Nemrut Dağı, head of Heracles (left), the goddess Commagene (right)

troyed. On the right next to this the seated figure of Antiochos I has survived to shoulder height, and next to this is the goddess Commagene, patron goddess of the empire, with her cornucopia in her hand. In the centre of the row, conspicuously larger than the other deities, is Zeus-Oromasdes (Ahura Mazda); he is followed on the left by a male deity, in whom elements of Apollo-Mithras, Helios and Hermes are mingled. This figure was for a long time thought to represent Mithridates, and the figure now thought to be the king was considered to be the mixture-god. The next statue is also a syncretic deity: Heracles-Artagenes-Ares with characteristic club. Finally, as formerly at the other end of the row, come an eagle and a lion. The bird's legs can still be distinguished. Below the enthroned deities and directly to the side of them there were originally relief slabs, showing mainly dexiosis scenes. The N. and S. side of the terrace was bordered with altars and rows of plinths, also originally supporting relief steles, which are now to be seen on the site in a more or less fragmented condition. The front side represents a person

Sesönk (Adıyaman), Karakuş, pair of columns

in each case, named on the rear of the slab. It was thus possible to establish that these figures were Antiochos' ancestors, the paternal line to the N. going back to the Persian royal house of the Achaemenids, and the maternal line to the S., going back to Alexander the Great via the Seleucids. In the open section of the terrace at the front, bordered on the other three sides by thrones of deities and rows of steles, a large altar platform was set up, missing on the West Terrace.

West Terrace: Here the tumulus statues have almost all been destroyed, but the heads have survived intact, both in number and condition. They have been set up again on the terrace, which is significantly lower than its eastern counterpart, in front of the rudimentary torsos. The same deities appear in the same sequence as on the East Terrace, but the ascription of the heads is still disputed. Antiochos is shown as a godlike, beardless figure with a headdress flattened at the side. The cheek flaps have been pushed away to reveal the lower part of his ears. When the light is good it is possible to discern a rosette pattern on the forehead band under the broad bulge of the headgear. Mithras is also beardless, but his ears are covered, and the broad edge of his head-dress is set directly on his forehead. The goddess Commagene is easily identifed. Her braided headgear, beautifully placed and rather like hair, is made up of fruit and ears of corn, and positioned alongside the collapsed blocks of the torso. The face with full beard behind one of the two eagles' heads is said to be Hercules, and thus the other head with a full beard, roughly halfway between the heads of the two birds of prey, with headgear set rather lower, can only be Zeus-Oromasdes. He is similarly represented, although broken off below the lower lip, on the East Terrace. On the West Terrace the row of enthroned gods is continued by a series of relief slabs, showing Antiochos with various gods, in a manner typical of the dexiosis scenes. The four slabs show (from left to right) the naked Hercules with his club, Zeus the father of the gods seated (this slab is larger in size), Apollo in an aureola and finally, very badly damaged, the local goddess Commagene. The relief between the seated statues of gods and the dexiosis scenes is of particular interest. This is the so-called 'lion horoscope', which is also repeated, though in very poor condition, on the East Terrace. The relief slab is almost six ft. high and almost eight ft. wide, and shows a prowling lion wearing a crescent moon around its neck. Its body and the background of the stone slab are covered with a total of 19 stars, of which three above the animal's back are clearly emphasized by their size. According to the accompanying inscription, these are the planets Jupiter, Mercury and Mars. Astronomers believe that this a particular configuration in the heavens said to have occurred on 7 July 62 BC. It is not clear whether it coincides with the date on which the buildings were founded. The date could also, however, be connected with the Princes' Congress of Amisos, at which Antiochos was not only granted enlarged territories, but also considerably enhanced his 'international' status.

Like the East Terrace, the West Terrace is bordered on one of its sides (the S. in this case) by a row of ancestors. It represents the paternal, Persian genealogy, but is badly damaged, and has survived only in part. The maternal ancestors are not depicted on the corresponding N. side, but instead the relief slabs were placed in the W., in sight of the enthroned gods.

Pirin (Perre; 3 km. NE of Adıyaman): The most striking monument in this little place, founded in Roman times as *Perrhe*, are the 208 *burial caves*, probably dating from antiquity.

Samsat (*c.*40 km. SSE of Adıyaman): This village, insignificant in modern times, was the ancient **Samosata**, capital of the Commagene kingdom. The name makes it probable that the residence was established here by King Samos I in the early 3C BC. Although the site was measured and investigated by Puchstein on his second Turkish journey in 1883, a Turkish group is again working on the ruins, under pressure of time, as ancient Samosata will be submerged in the artifical lake created by the new Euphrates dam.

Until this happens, Samsat is very easy to reach. The road from Adıyaman curves steeply down into the Euphrates valley

Sesönk (Adıyaman), tomb tumulus of Karakuş

Sesönk (Adıyaman), eagle column of Karakuş

shortly before Samsat. The hill with its ruins, formerly topped by a castle of which little remains, towers conspicuously above the river plain. The access road is flanked on both sides by the surviving fragments of aqueduct arches and channels, once used to supply the residence with water from over 30 km. away. The system was built under the Roman Emperor Septimius Severus *c.*AD 200. Its course was established by Nöldecke in 1917. Before the present village is reached, the hill with ruins, about 150 ft. high, can be seen on the left; a small twisty path leads up the W. side to the summit plateau.

Two famous personages called Lucian were born in Samosata, firstly the sophist philosopher (125–192), and later the Christian martyr (b. 235; killed 312 in Antioch). From about AD 640 the town was disputed between Byzantine Christians and Muslim Arabs and Turks. In the 10C Samsat belonged to the emirate of Aleppo. In 1070 it was reconquered by Byzantines, who had also owned the town *c.*700 and *c.*860. After the Armenian Philateros the counts of Edessa became the new lords of the town in 1098, but soon lost it to the Aijubids, who were followed by Turkish Seljuks.

Sesönk (*c.*60 km. SW of Adıyaman): The name Sesönk (Three Columns) goes back to the archaeologist Puchstein, who discovered the site by chance on 1 July 1882, on his way back from his first Turkish journey. Its official name is now **Dikilitas**. A great similarity with the Karakuş tumulus, which like Sesönk (Three Columns) was surrounded by three pairs of columns, leaves little doubt that the place was a royal tomb, in all probability that of Mithridates II and his queen. All that now survives complete on the site is a single pair of columns in the S., connected by an architrave. The *grave chamber* was for a long time inaccessible, until in 1984&5 grave robbers cleared the passage (dromos) leading to it, revealing the vaulted chamber with its three burial places. The rear grave on the longitudinal axis of the dromos was destroyed by the grave robbers as they tried to tunnel into the rock behind it. It is assumed that this was not the chamber of the royal coffin, which has still not been discovered if this is the case, but a secondary burial place.

The tumulus has a maximum diameter of 377 ft. and is almost 20 ft. high, making it the smallest Commagene tomb. From Kâhta, travel via Adıyaman in the direction of Gölbaşı. About 61 km. beyond Kâhta and directly after the little town of Sambayat, turn off to the left towards Basli and Gemüsli, crossing three shallow watercourses (no bridge!) within three kilometres. Here the tumulus of Sesönk, with its characteristic pair of columns, towers up. After 8 km. there is a small village with police station, after 4 km. another watercourse, and after another 10 km. the village of Zormagora, from which there are 4 km. to be covered on foot.

Yeni Kale (Eski Kâhta, Adıyaman), Mameluke fortress

A few kilometres before Sesönk are the remains of a *Roman bridge* over the Göksu, the ancient Singas. It formed part of a Roman military road running parallel to the left bank of the Euphrates. Only two arches of the bridge remain on either side of the river; the central and larger arch over the river collapsed.

Sofraz Köy (*c.*40 km. SW of Adıyaman): This place 15 km. SE of the larger village of *Besni* no longer has any monuments which are worth seeing, but it was here that in 1947 J. Wagner discovered one of the best-preserved Commagene *reliefs*, which had been pulled out of a well shaft by local people shortly before. The piece is identifiable by incription (text on the back and the two narrow sides) and shows Antiochos I before Apollo Helios. It is now in the museum in Gaziantep.

Süpürgüç (about 80 km. SW of Adıyaman): About 3 km. from the point at which the Karasu flows into the Euphrates from the W., at a sharp bend on the larger river, the Karasu makes a striking bend around the lower edge of a tongue of rock. At this point there is a *rock relief* dating from the period of the late-Hittite principalities. The relief is quite shallow, on a rock surface about 6 ft. 6 ins. high and just over 5 ft. wide, and faces the river. It is best seen in the morning light, and depicts a stag striding to the left, with a god, armed with sword and bow, standing on its back. The scene is surmounted by a winged disc of the sun, a motif based upon an Egyptian device. The relief dates from the period between 950 and 850 BC. It is named after the village of Süpürgüç, which is about 1.5 km. away. A path leads from the stone block with the relief, which is on the steep, rugged slope a little towards the river valley. The path consists partly of rock steps, partly of limestone slabs, and leads to the plateau on the tongue of rock.

One kilometre W., upstream on the Karasu, there is a *Roman bridge* over the river. 2 arches have survived intact, and three more in part. This bridge, like the one in Sesönk, was part of the Roman military road to the W. of the Euphrates, and was also built under Septimius Severus.

Yeni Kale (Eski Kâhta; 67 km. NE of Adıyaman): Coming from Kâhta, after crossing the Chabinas bridge, the route turns off to the right, and shortly before Arsameia on Nymphaios crosses a Seljuk bridge over the Kâhta Çayı, a tributary of the Chabinas. On the other hand, if you turn left from the route immediately after the Chabinas bridge, you reach the village of Eski Kâhta, passing the long and impressive fortress of Yeni Kale (New Castle) on the right.

It is a historical certainty that an earlier version of the present castle was conquered and destroyed by Kara Sonkar, governor of Aleppo, in AD 1286. The present fortress goes back to the Mamelukes. The inner building contains building or restoration inscriptions by Sultans Kala'un (1270–90), Ashraf Chalil (1290–3 and Nasr Mohammed (1293–1341).

In 1965, F.K. Dörner excavated the main entrance to the castle, in the NW, and the outer ward behind it, leading to the lower castle. The upper castle is adjacent to the NE, and to the S. a narrow, slightly curving corridor leads to the outwork. There is also a steep flight of steps leading down from the lower castle to the so-called 'water gate', boldly placed below a massive overhanging rocky spur. The building has two storeys, with battlements and arrow slits, and was used to supply not only Yeni Kale with water, but the precious liquid was also transported from here across the Kâhta Çayı on a light bridge to nearby Eski Kale (Arsameia on Nymphaios). There was also a room apparently used for housing carrier pigeons in the upper storey of the water tower. Evidence of this is the large rectangular hole to allow them to fly in, and the 32 niches used as

nesting boxes. These pigeons, first used for this purpose by Sultan Nur ed Din (1146–1173) were also of great use to Sultan Kala'un, who probably also set up the Yeni Kale pigeon station. They brought him rapid information about troop movements of his Mongol opponents before the decisive battle of Homs (1281).

Afyon

The town is dominated by the ruins of a large citadel on a cone of black trachyte. It has been known since the 17C as *Afyon-Karahisar* (Black Opium Castle) because of the important opium crop (poppies) in the area.

History: The citadel is presumed to have been the Hittite fortress of Chapanuva (mid-2C BC). The original inhabitants were said to have been the Arzavers under Hittite hegemony. There is evidence of a settlement in the Phrygian period. The *Akroinos* of the kingdom of Pergamon later became Roman, then from AD 395 a Byzantine fortress, at which Emperor Leo III bloodily defeated an Arab invasion in 740. The town was conquered by Seljuks in the late 12C (inscription on the Altogöz Köprüsü), and they extended it considerably under Alaeddin Kaykobad I. In 1428 the town finally became part of the Ottoman empire.

Ulu Cami (in the upper part of the old town): This is the most important of the numerous mosques. It was built in 1272 by Hasan Nusretüddin, and is one of the few outstanding examples of Seljuk wooden mosques in Anatolia. The wooden beamed roof of the prayer hall with low ceiling, nave, eight aisles and no arches is supported by 40 wooden columns with skilfully carved stalactite capitals. The ceiling in the broad nave is slightly raised to empahasize the central axis, but this is not immediately apparent. The forest of

Afyon, view of old town

columns, here still clearly performing a supporting function, is an impressive spatial experience (→ also Beyşehir).

Kuyulu Camii (Fountain Mosque): This mosque has a minaret decorated with glazed tiles, a notable example of Seljuk architecture.

Kubbeli Mesçit: The 'little domed mosque' dates from 1330.

Kara Hisar: Significant ruins of the mountain fortress with powerful walls, towers, cisterns, seray and small mosque.

Museum: Archaeological finds from the bronze age and the Phrygian, Hittite, Hellenistic, Roman and Byzantine periods; also Islamic art and folklore.

Also worth seeing: Fine *old houses* in the picturesque old town, and in the main square the *victory monument,* in memory of the decisive victory under Kemal Atatürk over Greek troops in 1922.

Ağlasun
Isparta   p.574□F 5

This village in the Pisidic Taurus is 28 km. S. of Isparta, below ancient **Sagalassos**, from which the modern name is derived. The old, steep mountain road leads in a few kilometres to the ruins of Sagalossos, magnificently sited at a height of between 5,250 and 5,580 ft. Ancient written sources are scant. The settlement is said to date from the third millennium BC. There is definite evidence from the period of Alexander the Great, who conquered Sagalossos on his

Afyon, Ulu Cami, interior with mihrab niche and pulpit

Persian campaign in 334 BC after fierce fighting. The later Greek historiographer Arrian described the battle in detail in I,28, calling the people of Sagalossos the most belligerent of the warlike men of Pisidia. The short reign of Antiochos III was ended by the Romans in 189 BC, and Marius Vulsus extracted the enormous tribute of 50 silver talents and 40,000 measures each of wheat and barley from the town. After uneasy changes of power, Sagalossos achieved increasing prosperity under Augustus. According to Livy (38;15) it was 'rich and fertile in every kind of fruit'. The large ruined buildings that can still be seen date from this period. Two temples converted into churches and recorded names of bishops confirm the existence of a Christian community until the 10C.

Ancient town: In the S., on a high piece of level ground, is a *temple precinct* surrounded by columned halls with the imperial temple of Antoninus Pius, a Corinthian peripteros with 6 x 11 columns. To the left of this the S.–N. axis of the town led to the *lower agora*. W. of the agora is the *temple of Apollo Klarios*, later converted into a church. To the E. is a large, partially flooded *thermal bath*, to the N. a *nymphaeum*, a *odeion* or *buleuterion*, and the *upper agora*. To the NW are the high walls of a Doric *temple in antis*, and near this relief slabs with representations of dancing girls in robes reaching to their feet were found (in the lapidarium in the village). The large *theatre* in the NE (late 2C AD) is still in the state to which it was reduced by a major earthquake.

The town is surrounded by interesting *necropolises*: tombs in the N. rock wall, magnificent funeral buildings in the NE

Ağlasun, Sagalassos theatre

and a large number of sarcophagi on the mountain slopes to the S.

Ağri
Ağri   p.570□T 3

This town, occasionally also called *Karaköse* or *Karakilise*, is the administrative centre of the province of the same name, and is about 230 km. N. of Van in the valley of the Murat Nehri, the largest tributary of the upper Euphrates. The enormous Ararat massif which towers over the town to the NE is called Ağrı Dağı in Turkish, after the town. The volcanic cone of Ararat, which last erupted in 1840, is the highest mountain in Turkey (16,945 ft.); the next highest is Küçük Agrî Dağı at 12,877 ft. Geologically Ararat consists of alternating layers of lava and tufa. The mountain still catches the imagination as the possible landing-place of Noah's Ark, and visitors who know their Bible are always keen to claim that they have found timbers from the boat, despite the fact that serious Old Testament research has established that the sites involved in the early history of Israel are to be found much further S.

Environs: Doğubayazıt (96 km. E.): Because of its proximity to Ishak Paşa Sarayı this town has recently built hotels and developed into a tourist centre and starting point for excursions to Ararat (lasting several days).

İshak Paşa Sarayı (102 km. E.): About 6 km. SE of Doğubayazıt, on a 7,283 ft. high promontory of a rocky plateau, the world-famous palace towers over the surrounding countryside. From here the silk road, which brought the local lords large incomes from tolls, was controlled. Even at the times of the Urartians (1st half of the 1st millennium AD) there was a fortress here. The Seljuks also built a castle here, and so did the Ottomans. Their ruler Beyazıt I Yıldırım (Lightning; 1389–1403) fell into the hands of the Mongol prince Timur-Leng (Tamerlane) at the Battle of Ankara, and was banished by him to the fortress of Doğu Bayazıt. The earlier settlement, destroyed on the withdrawal of Russian troops in 1914 (in an unoffical version in 1939 by Turkish troops putting down a Kurdish rebellion), is at the foot of the castle rock on the opposite side of the road.

The palace in its present form dates from the time of the Kurdish ruler İshak Paşa; its high walls give it a fortress-like appearance which offers little to suggest the lavish interior decoration, in which a wide range of differing stylistic influences can be traced. Armenian and Georgian design elements exist alongside Ottoman, Seljuk or Persian ones.

A lavishly decorated *portal* leads to the rectangular front courtyard, where unfortunately the buildings are in a poor state of repair. To the side of the entrance is a niche with a pointed arch and a little fountain. A second portal leads to another, smaller, likewise rectangular courtyard. The complex of rooms at the end of the courtyard has survived in good condition. Only the ceilings of the rooms are missing now. The monumental entrance in the middle of the façade gives an idea of the splendour of the rooms behind it. An iwan-like pointed arch leads into a rectangular corridor flanked with little columns. Adjacent and at right angles on the right is the *selamık*, the 'courtyard of greeting'. Here the prince received his guests and pronounced judgement. On the left, after going through a little passage, you reach the mosque, the most striking parts of which are the black round dome running to a point at the top and the red and white, transversely striped, slender minaret. There is still some ornamental painting within the dome.

On the left of the entrance to the entire building, which was reserved for men, is the strikingly slender *mausoleum* of the prince. The octagonal building is surrounded by little columns in its central area, between which, in slightly sunken niches, tiny stylized trees sprouting from small round pots have been carved. The türbe is topped by a pointed roof, which can be opened. The two low, hut-like stone buildings with gable roofs mark the entrance to the underground grave chambers.

W. of the courtyard the most magnificent of the three portals leads into the most extensive set of buildings in the palace. These contained the *women's rooms* (harim), arranged around an inner ambulatory, which itself surrounds a central salon. The central room still has most of its white stone paving. The base of the wall is also covered with rectangular stone slabs, this time alternating black and white. Above this, the wall is pierced by rectangular windows in round-arched niches. Two anterooms on the narrow ends of the ceremonial room are each separated off by two pairs of reddish polygonal columns. Both the outer sides of the arches on the columns and the framing around the window niches are decorated with skilfully interwoven ornamental bands. On the upper strip of the wall is a frieze of triangular mouldings pointing downwards. The longitudinal rooms in which the ladies of the court spent their time still have the open fireplaces, standing by the walls, round, like columns, with pointed smoke hoods. Opposite the palace, on the slope to the NE, is another Ottoman *domed mosque* in good condition. In the steep rocks behind it are the massive walls of a *fortress*, the most striking features of which are the massive semicircular *towers*. To the left of this defensive building and behind the domed mosque is chiselled the only Urartian *rock relief* on Turkish soil. The two human figures represented are on either side of a rectangular opening

Ağrı, Mount Ararat ▷

Doğubayazıt (Ağrı), Urartian rock chamber near İshak Paşa Sarayı

leading into a rock chamber. This is probably the tomb of an Urartian prince.

The rock relief was noted by Charles Texier, who discovered the Hittite capital of Hattuşa/Boğazköy. The scenes on the approximately 16 ft. by 10 ft. smoothed surface probably date from the 9C BC. The figures are best made out in the late afternoon, in an oblique light. The figure on the left, probably male, is standing on a plinth and extending his arms to an animal across the passageway. This section is interpreted as a worshipper with sacrificial beast. The figure on the right-hand side of the entrance, larger in size and better carved, is often wrongly described as the god accepting the gift. This is not possible, however, as this figure is turning in the same direction as the figure behind, whereas the god would have to face the person offering the sacrifice.

Malazgirt/Manzikert (116 km. SW): This once important Armenian town is reached by the road from Ağrı to Van, travelling as far as Patnos (80 km.). There the road to Malazirk (another 80 km.) branches off. When the famous council took place here in 726, at which the Armenian church, which represented the Monophysite point of view (Christ only had one nature, a divine one, and never 'became man') separated itself from the Byzantine imperial church (which supported the divine and human natures of Christ), the place was already under Arab rule. Christians were allowed to practise their religion undisturbed, however. In the 9C Malazgirt became the capital of an Arab emirate. In 996 the united armies of the king of Kars and the head of the Armenian province of Theodosiopolis (Erzerum) David of Taik succeeded in taking the town, which they also successfully

İshak Paşa Sarayı (Ağrı), palace

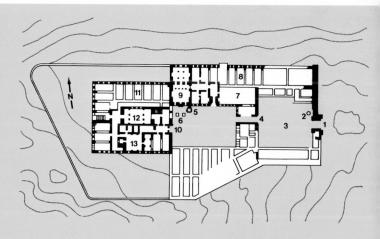

İshak Paşa Sarayı (Ağrı) 1 Entrance **2** Fountain **3** Guards' courtyard **4** Portal of 2nd courtyard **5** Türbe **6** Entrances to crypts **7** Courtyard of greeting (Selamlık) **8** Men's quarters **9** Mosque **10** Entrance to harem **11** Women's quarters (harem) **12** Central common room of harem **13** Kitchen

defended against the advancing army of the emir of Azerbaijan, Mamlun. In 1001 the emperor Basileios incorporated the town, which was besieged by Toghrul Beğ in 1055, into the Byzantine Empire. On 11 August 1070 the Seljuk Alp Arslan finally succeeded in conquering the town, and this was confirmed by a victory over the Byzantine emperor Romanus IV Diogenes (whom he actually took prisoner) outside the gates of the town. With the fall of this settlement which was blocking their way, the Seljuks were free to march to Asia Minor.

The town wall with its towers is still a reminder of the period in which the town flourished, as are also the numerous Armenian spoils built into the dwelling houses, easily seen on a walk around the town.

Ahlat

Bitlis   p.578☐S 4

This culturally and historically important site is 42 km. from Tatvan, on the N. bank of Lake Van.

Eski-Ahlat appears in Roman source material as *Hilyat*. In Armenian times it was called *Kelath* or *Chlath*. At that time the emir of Malazgirt ruled over an Arab enclave among the surrounding Christian-Armenian kingdoms. In 993 the Byzantine emperor Basil II tried in vain to storm the town, which became Seljuk in the course of the 11C. At that time Ahlat was the most important town on Lake Van. A freed slave of the Seljuk emir of Choi (Azerbaijan) named Sukman succeeded in establishing an independent small empire in the early 12C. From his residence in Ahlat he was able, after taking the title of King of Armenia, to extend his power rapidly from Muş and Bitlis W. of Lake Van to Choi in the E. In 1209 came the Aijubids, the Mongols ruled between 1245 and 1335, but they resigned their power to the Georgian princess Thamata. In

İshak Paşayı, relief, türbe (left), harem (right)

1467, Ahalt was finally conquered by Turkmen of the White Sheep tribe, and remained Kurdish until 1513. Ismail I then won it briefly for Persia, before it became part of the Ottoman Empire under Sultan Selim I in 1517 (other sources say 1433).

Castle (*Kale*): This is 2 km. from the modern village at the E. extremity of the site, which extends over several kilometres directly on the bank of Lake Van (5,643 ft.). It was founded in 1554 by Süleyman II, and completed by Selim II in 1568. The latter date features in the inscription E. of the two entrance gates in the outer wall, which has round and square towers. The actual fortress (Iç Kale) within these walls has its own ring wall. Opposite the S. gate of this is one of the two mosques built between the two castle walls, the Iskender Paşa Çamii, built between 1564 and 1570 by the town governor of the same name. Not far from this, between the SE corner of the inner castle and the bank of the lake, is a second place of prayer, the Kadi Mahmut Çamii, dating from 1584 and, like the first, a domed mosque with narthex.

İshak Paşa Sarayı, 2nd courtyard, türbe

Iki Türbe (Two Mausoleums): These are 2 grave towers close by the castle to the N., directly by the path leading from the modern village to the W. The mausoleum was built in 1279 for Hasan Takin and used again by Hasan Timur in 1729. The mausoleum next to it was built for Emir Buğatay Aĝa in 1281.

Emir Ali Kümbet: One of the 3 mausoleums adjacent to Iki Türbe group a few hundred yards away to the W., by the edge of the path. The lower section is massive, and the pointed arch, flanked by stepped walls with saddle roofs, does not entirely overcome the impression of clumsiness. The construction is topped with a roof supported by a strip of masonry.

Ulu Kümbet: The mausoleum W. of the castle not far from the bank of the lake is the largest, over 60 ft. high. It has two storeys and consists of a round grave chamber in the cellar and the prayer chamber above this. There is a strip of inscriptions running below the stalactite frieze on the outside.

Bayındır Türbesi: The foundation inscription runs under the roof and shows that this mausoleum, which also has a rectangular meşit with a flat roof, was built in 1491&2 for the governor of Roha, Bayındır, and his son. The building is not far from the old Islamic cemetery. Two thirds of its upper storey are designed like a monopteros: small columns with stalactite capitals support arches which in their turn support the roof. Only the rear wall to the N., where the meşit joins on, is solid masonry. There are small pots at the top of the vault which served to increase resonance.

Hasan Padişa Türbesi: This mausoleum is the only one W. of the Islamic cemetery, some way from it and separated from it by the somewhat higher rocky area of the Tacht-i Suleiman (Suleyman's Throne). The building dates from 1275 and is not in good condition.

Local museum (*Müze*): This collection

Ahlat, Iki Türbe ▷

Ahlat, Bayındır Türbesi

Adılcevaz (Ahlat), Ulu Cami

in a modern building between Bayındır Türbesi and Ulu Kümbet (dating from 1971) is well worth seeing. It includes a folklore collection and also a series of finds from the Urartian period; the Urartians dominated the area around Lake Van in the first half of the first millennium BC.

Environs: Adılcevaz (26 km. E.): The history of this little town on the N. bank of Lake Van goes back to the Urartian period. Numerous blocks covered with cuneiform inscriptions by this ancient people were discovered in the medieval citadel which towers over the town by the bank of the lake (only a few remains of walls today). These inscriptions indicate that there was an Urartian fortress here in the first half of the first millennium BC. Two significant Urartian finds were made in the ruins of the castle, firstly a relief, spread over several basalt blocks and

showing a god standing on a bull in front of a palmetto with heavily stylized lance-shaped leaves. The relief was probably originally a door jamb, completed by a corresponding relief on the other side, and is now in the courtyard of the Van museum. The second object is a cubic stone base weighing about two tons, with the same representation in relief running round all four of its sides, a fortress with battlements and small windows forming the background to a winged god, this time standing on a lion. This monument is now in the museum in Ankara.

Below the castle, directly on the bank of the lake, is the *Uli Cami*. The central part of the building, with 3 x 3 shallow masonry domes in dark stone has a transversely placed raised narthex with three smaller vaults above in front of it.

About 300 yards from the lake an Urartian *necropolis* with rock tombs was dis-

Ahlat, Islamic graveyard, steles

covered in the lava rocks at the foot of Süphan Daği, which dominates the N. of Lake Van. At the N. end of the village, on the way to Kefkalesi, is a school with some Urartian finds exhibited in the yard. **Kefkalesi** (10 km. N. of Adılcevaz): The remains of the Urartian *fortress*, at a height of 7218 ft., are reached from the N. along a rubble track, on which you have to walk the last section (about 30 mins. climb). It was built by Rusa II in the second quarter of the 7C on a gigantic plateau. It is possible that this is the site of Qallania, which was a stopping-place on the Assyrian king Sargon II's eighth campaign in 714 BC. The site is surrounded by a wall of massive blocks and was dominated in the N. by a citadel and in the NW by a bastion on a rocky promontory. On the S. slope were storerooms, as yet not excavated. The shoulders of large supply vessels can be seen sticking out of the loose, sandy ground, and shards of pottery decorated with reliefs can be found strewn throughout the area. There are about 30 rooms in the residence inside the walls. The most striking relics still to be found on the site are the numerous little towers, built of carefully cut basalt blocks. They have the corner projections typical of Urartian architecture. It is possible that they were the supports for piers; some of them are decorated with reliefs.

Below the castle mound to the S. are the remains of the Armenian *'Miracle of Ardguzi' monastery church*, dating from the 8 or 9C BC, and cruciform in plan.

Aksaray

Niğde   p.574☐K 4

The town still has a number of important

Seljuk buildings. The view to the SE is dominated by the twin Hsandağ volcano. Büyük Hasandag is 11,903 ft., Küçük Hasandağ 10,069 ft., while the surrounding Melendiz mountains are 'only' 6,227 ft. high.

History: This can be traced back at least to the Roman period, where the town is mentioned in documents as *Garsaura*. Because of the similarity of the name it has so far been customary to identify the place with the ancient oriental town of Kursaura, whose prince Tisbinki is said to have formed a league against the south Mesopotamian Accadian king Naramsin (second half of the third millennium BC). In the Byzantine period the town was called *Archelais*. It was conquered by the Seljuks in the 11C AD. The ruined castle which dominates the modern town dates from this period. In the 13C the town became Mongol, a century later the local Karaman dynasty ruled here.

After the fall of Constantinople, part of the population was compulsorily deported to this new metropolis of the victorious Ottomans, to whose empire Aksaray now also belonged. The new arrivals called their new settlement after the place from which they came, and there is still a part of İstanbul called Aksaray.

Ulu Cami: The house of prayer in the main square goes back to the time of the Seljuks and inside there is still a fine timber dating from this period, but rebuilding and restoration have meant that little of the original design remains.

Also worth seeing: *Nakaşli Cami:* The lavishly decorated *minaret* (16C) is a notable feature of this mosque. *Zinciriye Medrese:* This Koran school was built under the local Karaman dynasty in 1345. *Ibrahim Kadiroğlu Medrese:* The original Seljuk building was restored in the early Ottoman period (15C).

Environs: Ağzıkara Hani (16 km. NE): This Seljuk building dating from AD 1238 is the best-preserved of the three caravanserais that are all to be found directly by the road from Aksaray to Nevşehir (→ Öresin Hanı and Alay Hanı). The finest features are the magnificent portal with stalactite vaulting and the seven-sided corner towers.

Akhisar (12 km. SE): This village is dominated by a Byzantine *fortress* set on a steep rock. 7 km. E. of Akhisar is a site with the ruins of several cave monasteries and the remains of Çanli Kilise (also: Çanlik Kilise, Church with the Bell Tower), which have survived in relatively good condition. This Byzantine centrally planned building has three apses and dates from the 10 or early 11C. The two-storeyed narthex, however, was added in the second half of the 11C. The polychrome arches give a weak impression of the former pictorial decoration, and the frescos in the main part of the church have disappeared almost completely.

Alay Hanı (35 km. NE): This Seljuk caravanserai on the road to Nevsehir has a striking access gate leading to the lavish main portal.

Gelveri (30 km. SE): In ancient times this was in all probability the town of *Karbala*, in which St. Gregory of Nazianzus was born in 328. The Byzantine church at the foot of the rock, riddled with cave churches, was dedicated to him before it was turned into a mosque in 1896. The remarkable monastery of *Yülsek Kilise* is SW of the village on a rocky cone.

In the last century Gelveri had a large Greek colony, but its inhabitants were driven out at the beginning of the present century.

Helvadere (about 45 km. SE): The best way to reach this out-of-the-way site is via Taşpinar and Tokariz. 5 km. further on you reach the Anatepesi (→ Sivrihisar), and after another 5 km. Kargin (from where there is another route to Aksaray, via Akhisar). After another 4 km., Helvadere itself is reached. S. of the town in a crater is the extensive site of the ruined monastery of *Viranşehir* (Destroyed Town), where remains of two churches

Aksaray, old Turkish bath

have survived, among other things. The churches are *Kenerli Kilise* (Church with the Arches), cruciform in plan, built of heavy, regular trachyte blocks, and *Kara Kilise* (Black Church), a single-aisled basilica not far S. of Kemerli Kilise. There are isolated stretches of Byzantine fortress walls all over the area. The site was well chosen, because the access point to the present ruins is through a narrow gateway in the rock, the *Demikapi* (Iron Gate).

Mamasun (about 20 km. E.): About 2 km. before Ağzikara Hans a track leads off to the right (E.) of the road from Aksaray to Nevşehir, and from here it is 7 km. to Mamasun.

There are several monasteries and a church, the *Köy Ensesi Kilisesi*, set on the rocky slopes of the narrow gorge in which the village is so picturesquely sited. The church is a centrally-planned building with nave and two aisles and central apse (i.e. on a Greek cross plan). The interior still has remains of late-10C frescos. They represent Christ and the 12 Apostles and also the Archangels Michael and Gabriel. Parclose and altar are cut out of the rock. The present name of the village is derived from St. Mames, a shepherd martyr from Caesarea, whose remains are kept in the village mosque because he is said to have been a secret convert to Islam.

Nenezi (*c*.30 km. SE): This town, the ancient **Nazianzus**, can be reached only with difficulty. Take the road to Gelveri up the Melendiz Suyu valley. Shortly after crossing the river at the village of Göstük (18 km.) you reach the village of Kızılkaya. At the end of the village turn left to Ağlaçi, from where it is 9 km. to Nenezi. The only monument is reached before the village. It is a tomb (türbe) dating from the Seljuk or Mongol period, octagonal in plan, with a stalactite frieze made of brick, and a Kufic inscription. The pyramid roof has unfortunately collapsed in part.

Öresin Hanı (20 km. NE): Unfortunately only ruins have survived of this Seljuk caravanserai dating from the late 13C, between the Ağzikara Hanıand the Alay Hanı, on the left-hand side of the road to Nevşehir.

Peristrema valley (32 km. SE): The wild and romantic valley combines, similarly to the Göreme region, beautiful landscape and important cultural and historical monuments in an almost unique fashion. The deep gorge with its steep rocky sides was formed by the Melendiz Suyu (and is for this reason sometimes known as the Melendiz valley). The river does not dry up even in the summer, and in places it flows over massive blocks of rock.

Here, between the little towns of Selime, the ancient *Salamun*, in the N. and Ihlara in the S. Christian hermits wishing to renounce the world withdrew to this isolated valley, where they hollowed about 50 chapels and churches, monasteries and cells out of the rock or built them in front of it. The number of monuments increases in the S. section of the gorge, between Ihlara and Belisirama. Also concentrated around these two villages are the two styles of wall painting according to which the Christian buildings can be classified: in the N., around Belisirama, the churches are decorated almost exclusively in the Byzantine imperial style, but further S., around Ihlara, there are wall paintings only in the local Capadocian style, showing oriental (Persian, Syrian) influence. The churches around Ihlara, despite their sometimes naïve and provincial style, are significant in terms of history of art because they were partly painted in pre-iconoclastic style, that is to say in the period in which the dispute about whether it was permissible to represent God pictorially (which reached its climax in the so-called iconoclastic controversy of the 8&9C) was of no concern. As new wall paintings continued to be added at later periods, the continuing development of Christian painting in the area can be studied in a unique fashion.

The most important churches around Ihlara include:

Eğri Taş Kilise (Church with the Slanting Stones): The wall paintings include scenes from the childhood of Christ, such as the Flight to Egypt or the Three Kings, portrayed in oriental dress.

Ağaç Alti Kilise (Church under the Tree): This church is difficult to reach. It is T-shaped in plan, with two small aisles. The apse is set immediately at the end of the aisles, replacing the fourth transverse arm. The wall painting are in the local Capadocian style.

Yilanlı Kilise (Snake Church): Despite its concealed entrance this is probably the most interesting building in the valley. The church is cruciform, and the rear arm has a striking horseshoe-shaped apse. The finest paintings are in the narthex, including the scenes in hell, with the monsters that gave the church its name.

Also worth seeing are the *Kokar Kilise* (Fragrant Church) with magnificent scenes from the life of Christ on the vault of the nave, and the *Pürenli Seki Kilise* (Terrace Church), two single-aisled chapels and apse with fragmentary wall paintings in the local Capadocian style.

The *Sümbülü Kilise* (Church with the Hyacinth) forms a link with the N. style around Bilisirama, influenced by the Byzantine imperial style. The wall paintings in this T-shaped church with apse placed directly at the point of intersection of the nave and aisles are of the best Byzantine standard. They have survived above all in the S. aisle. On the other hand the rhythmically articulated, stately outer façade shows oriental-Persian influence.

The churches around **Belisirama**, whose ancient name Peristrema gave its name to the entire valley, show the upsurge of religious painting after the area was reconquered by the Byzantines. Only the *Açikel Ağa Kilise* (Church of the Lord of the Open Hand) has any pre-iconoclastic painting. All the other houses of prayer are decorated in Byzantine style:

Koyunağul

YAPRAK HISAR

Güvercinlik Davullu

Gelveri

Zığa

Ala

BELISIRAMA

Direkli

Bahattin Samanlığı

Eski Baca

St. George's

Bezir Ana

Karagedik

Yılanlı

Sümbülü

Karanlık Kale

Ağac Altı

Pürenli Seki

Kokar

Eğri Tas

Peristrematal (Aksaray)

Kemer

IHLARA

Gelveri

Helvadere

St. Michael's

Peristrema valley, cave church, frescos

Direkli Kilise (Columned Church): This cruciform domed church with nave and two aisles was built under Basileios II (976–1025). The paintings show saints and martyrs. Directly by it is the *Bahattin Samanlığı Kilesi* (Church of Bahattin's Storehouse), a simple building in the form of a single-aisled, rectangular hall with a semicircular apse at the rear. The paintings are in subdued colours, and show scenes from the life of Christ.

Ala Kilise (White Church): The most striking feature of this cruciform domed church with nave and two aisles is the magnificent façade, which, similarly to Sümbülü Kilise, shows oriental influence, while the interior decoration, unfortunately rather badly damaged, is in the Byzantine imperial style.

The remains of frescos in the *Karagedik Kilise* (Church with the Black Collar),

built in the 11C of brick and trachyte blocks, but badly damaged by a rock fall in later years. The time at which Christian architecture and painting flourished came to an end when the Seljuks assumed power in the late 11C. Nevertheless a little Christian community lived here until at least the 13C. This is borne out by the *church of St. George* (Kirk Dam Alti Kilise) in Belisirama, founded between 1283 and 1295 by the emir Basileios and his wife Thamar. They were Christian vassals of the Moslem sultan of Konya. As Constantinople was providing no new Christian impulses at this time, this last evidence of individual Christian life in the Peristrema valley is only a pale imitation of older models.

For several centuries there is no evidence of the a Christian presence, then in the 19C Greeks living here began to make new churches in the rock.

About 2 km. N. of Belisirama, in the direction of Selime, is **Yaprak Hisar**, where there is a *monastery* with a particularly striking façade. The buildings in the village itself are largely churches and cells from abandoned monasteries.

The Peristrema valley is reached from Aksaray by proceeding for 12 km. along the road to Nevşehir, then taking a right turn to Ihlara, which is 20 km. further on. It is advisable to check on the condition of the roads. A local guide makes it easier to find the buildings in the rocks, some of which are partially hidden.

Sivrihisar (40 km. SE): Driving from Gelveri on the road through the town leading towards the SE, which also crosses a 6,500 ft. pass, 55 km. before Niğde you reach the little town of Sivrihisar with numerous cave dwellings and sparse remains of a small Byzantine fortress. 2 km. beyond the settlement to the left of the road on the hill called Anatepe is a church in good condition built of dark red trachyte, the *Kizil Kilise* (Red Church). It dates from the 5C, and is cruciform in plan. The central dome has an octagonal drum with four squinches between it and the dome proper.

Sultanhanı (Aksaray), caravanserai

Sultanhanı (40 km. SW): This modern town on the road to Konya takes its name from the most significant monument in the centre of the present settlement, the *Sultanhanı caravanserai*. It dates from the time of the Seljuk sultan Alaeddin Kaykobad I, who had it built in 1229. It is considered to be one of the most beautiful inns in Turkey. As it is on an important trading road leading from E. to W., probably used in pre-Roman times, and secured in the Seljuk and Ottoman periods by a dense network of military bases, the Sultanhanı was also surrounded by fortifications shortly after its completion. Camel caravans moving from the harbours of Ephesus or Smyrna via Konya and Aksaray to Kayseri and points E. could pause here, exactly a day's journey from Aksaray. The buildings are entered through a massive gate with stalactite niches and delicate ornamentation. In the middle of the

courtyard is a small mosque on four piers. The rooms on the left contained sleeping accommodation and also kitchens, two baths and shops.

Akşehir

Konya   p.574□G 4

Byzantine *Philomeion*, a lively small town in central Anatolia, was the home of Nasreddin Hocas, the great master of tricks and jokes, a prankster who was one of the best-known personalities in old Turkey. He was born in Horto near Sivrihisar, lived for more than 50 years in Akşehir, and died here at an old age in AD 1285. His türbe in a little park on the outskirts of the town was restored in 1905, and is still lovingly cared for today.

Philomelion, presumably founded under

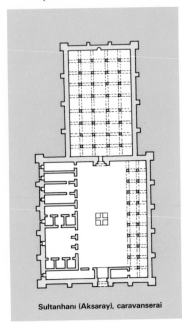

Sultanhanı (Aksaray), caravanserai

the Macedonian prince Philomelos in the 3C BC, was an important town in Phrygia, later Pisidia. In 51 BC Cicero passed sentence on mutinous troops from the Roman army here. In 1190 Frederick Barbarossa came to Akşehir via nearby Sultan Dağlari, on the third crusade. In 1403 the unhappy sultan Yıderım Beyazıt died here after a year's imprisonment by Timur-Leng.

Worth seeing: The *Ulu Cami* and *İplikçi Cami* mosques. In the NW, the *Taş Medrese*, built by Sahib Ata in 1216, with fine portal, 2 rows of Roman-Byzantine pillars in the inner courtyard and a massive Seljuk minaret built of brick, with some glazing remaining. This early medrese with iwan has been restored and used as a museum since 1986. It is surrounded by an extensive ancient lapidarium. From here the fine street through the

old town leads up the slope to the octagonal *tomb-türbe* of the mystic Seyğit Mahmut Hayrani, dating from 1224 originally, in the SW of the town. By the türbe is a little *meşit* (prayer chapel) built of ancient stones.

Environs: Bolvadin (60 km. NW): Ancient *Polybotus* was heavily fortified against the Seljuks by the Byzantine Emperor Manuel Comnenus, but conquered by the Seljuks shortly afterwards. The fine Alaça Çeşmesi *Seljuk fountain* with large gabled roof and the Ottoman *caravanserais* of Kuşunlu Han and Seljuk Han have survived. The originally Seljuk *Kirkqöz Köprü* (bridge) was rebuilt and restored by Sinan.

Çay (48 km. NW): The ancient *Julia Ipsus*. The Seljuk *Taş Camii* (1278) has a large tree in front of it and a lavishly decorated portal. Nearby is an old fountain with Seljuk motifs. The Seljuk *caravanserai* (1278) has partially fallen into disrepair, but hall and portal have survived in good condition. The hall is used for storage purposes, and is locked up. The interior is dark and blackened with soot. Each of the outer walls of the hall has two massive pointed towers and two corner towers. The plan of the hall is similar to that of the Sultandaği (see below). This Seljuk Külliyen precinct founded by Emulbek ibn Mohammed also includes the ruined domed medrese with faience tiles. Outside the town is an *old bridge* with 40 arches.

Sultandaği, formerly İşaklı (27 km. NW): Immediately to the W. of the road are the ruins of *İşaklıHan*. It was built by the famous Sahib Ata, who was responsible for many famous buildings, including some in Konya and Akşehir (Taş Medrese), Kayseri and Sivas. İşaklıHan was his chief concern. It was completed in 1249, and sited on the caravan road from Afyon to Konya. The hall, 69 x 69 ft., has five aisles, with a large courtyard in front of it. In the middle of the courtyard is a beautifully built mosque with a fine courtyard portal, 6 ft 6 ins. wide, set forward of the

Akşehir, türbe of Seyğit Mahmut Hayrani

wall and very elegantly articulated, with finely worked ornamental strips meeting at a point in the half dome of the niche. The square mosque has two storeys, the upper one with eight sections of groin vaulting and a stalactite dome (mukarnas) admitting light through a circular opening. 5 pairs of arbours used to stand by the N. wall of the courtyard, and 2 pairs have survived. Their arches lead to two tunnel-vaulted bays. The central aisle of the hall is wider and higher. The *Ulu Camii*, dating from 1458, is also worth seeing.

Alabanda/Araphisar

Aydın   p.572☐D 5

This Carian town is 4 km. W. of the Marsyas (Çine Çayı). a tributary of the Meander. The foundation legend speaks of a King Car who, after a victorious cavalry battle (in the Caric language *ala* = horse, *banda* = victory) called his son Alabandos, and also named the town after him. Alabanda is mentioned in various documents, but it is hard to establish a continuous history. It is certain that from the 3C BC it possessed a declaration of inviolability issued in Delphi, valid for the town and the territory which belonged to it. In the commercial field the town was known for its hemp, and also for a reddish marble suitable for glass manufacture, and a precious stone like a garnet.

Agora: 394 x 262 ft. of open space between the council chamber and the theatre.

Aqueduct: A small section survives outside the town (Kemerderesi).

48 Alaca Hüyük

Necropolis: Outside the town to the W., with hundreds of rectangular box sarcophagi, often recording the profession of the buried person.

Council house: Rectangular building with semicircle of seats (85 x 118 ft.); in the E. on both sides are steps leading up to the seats at the back.

Temple of Apollo Tsotimos ('of equal honour' = ranking with Zeus?): Ionic pseudodipteros with 8 x 13 columns over three feet thick. The columns were set at double distance from the cella. Basic measurement: 71 x 113 ft; the frieze shows a battle between Amazons and Greeks.

Temple of Artemis (?): On an artificial terrace, with 6 x 11 columns in Doric order, pronaos and cella.

Theatre: Only a section of the supporting wall has survived, with vaulted access to the diazoma on each side.
There is scarcely any evidence to support the fact that Strabo held the town to be particularly given to luxury.

Alaca Hüyük

Çorum   p.566☐K 2

This town and the imperial capital Hattuşa, 30 km. away, are the most important Hittite sites; objects from the period before the Hittite immigration have also been found. Alaca Hüyük's archaeological importance has been known since 1836, when it was rediscovered by W.J. Hamilton, but it was not until 1906 that the ruins were first excavated by H. Winkler and T. Makridy. H.H. von der Osten carried out further investigations in 1926&7. The most spectacular results were not obtained until the most recent excavations, carried out by the Turkish archaeologists H.Z. Koşay and R.O. Aruk in 1935&6 and 1962. The mound of ruins, 360 yards in diameter, was found to contain 4 large settlement horizons (I–IV), which could then be subdivided into 14 distinct layers (1–14). The finds suggest that settlement began around the middle of the fourth millennium BC, in other words in the early stages of the Bronze Age (layer 14 in horizon IV).

At this period Anatolia was settled by a non-Indo-Germanic, pre-Hittite tribe (the so-called 'Hattians'), whose power was concentrated particularly in Alaca Hüyük. Evidence of this is given by the **13 tombs of princes** containing lavish grave goods discovered on the site of the town. They date from the late third millennium BC (layer 7; early Bronze Age II/III), consisted of single or double burials of man and wife, and numerous gold and silver vessels, gold jewellery and weapons, including a dagger with an iron blade, then the most valuable metal. Several so-called 'standards' were also discovered, i.e. discs with filigree geometrical patterns or carvings of animals (stags, oxen), all in bronze, some with gold and silver inlays, and all with a fastening device. These strange objects are now considered to be decorations for the funeral chariots on which the dead princes were carried to their tombs. They were interred with the dead men and women to accompany them into the next world. The wooden part of the vehicles has now rotted away, only metal sections have survived. After burial the rectangular, 10–26 x 6–16 ft. graves, clad in stone and covered with sturdy wooden planking, were covered over. It is not clear whether the ox bones found among the rubble used to fill the graves came from the animals which pulled the funeral cars and were then sacrificed for the dead. Almost all these grave goods are now in the museum in Ankara, only a few were retained in the local museum in Alaca. The graves on the site (on the left behind the sphinx gate) have been concreted for reasons of conservation, in order to fix the stone blocks used for the cladding. Some wooden beams recently placed in position are intended to give an impression of the ancient covering.

Alaca Hüyük, Hittite temple and palace

The history of the town is unclear in the early stages of the second millennium BC, at the time of the Assyrian trading colonies and the immigration of the Indo-Germanic Hittites, which was certainly not achieved without some violence. Archaeologists have established that the town was destroyed by fire, which could be connected with the arrival of the Hittites. There is no basis whatsoever for the supposition that Alaca Hüyük, whose ancient name is still unknown, could be identical with Kuššara, the place of origin of the conqueror prince Anitta, who conquered and destroyed the subsequent Hittite capital of Hattuša (now Boğazköy) from his seat of Kanesh (now Kültepe). The assumption that the place was called Tavinia in the Hittite period has also not yet been proved decisively.

At the time of the Hittite empire (1600–1200 BC) Alaca Hüyük was cer-

tainly overshadowed by the capital, Hattuša, not very far away. Despite this the settlement was extended at the time to become a fortified town with at least two gates. Only the lower sections of the **W. gate** have survived. It has been proved, however, that there was a small tunnel here, similar to the one under the Yerkapı in Boğazköy.

The more important entrance, for its relief decoration alone, is the **Sphinx Gate** in the S., named after the two figures on either side, looking outwards and intended to protect the city from evil. The heavy wigs worn by the sphinxes, with strands of hair flowing down to the chest, are a clear sign of Egyptian influence. The Egyptian goddess Hathor as well as the sphinx has hair like this. Ever since small ivory sphinxes were found in Açemhüyük, 18 km. NW of Aksaray, it has been assumed that the Hittites became familiar

Alaca Hüyûk, princes' tombs

with the motif from figures of this kind. The right-hand gateway block, as well as a sphinx, has an additional relief of a double-headed eagle with outspread wings on its inner side. This ancient oriental motif appeared on seals from the Assyrian trading colony of Kanesh (now Kültepe). The animals that the eagle of the sphinx gate is holding in its talons could be hares, but are not readily identifiable.

The monumental stone blocks of the walls on either side of the sphinx gate are also decorated with reliefs. On the site these are casts of the originals, which are in the museum in Ankara. When they were discovered these relief blocks were in a state of chaotic collapse. Only the lower band of the pictorial friezes that used to be on the lower part of the twin towers on either side of the sphinx gate, and that was certainly originally in two layers, has been reassembled.

The principal scene on the front of the E. section shows an enthroned goddess receiving a group of worshippers. The relief cycle on the front of the W. tower is more interesting. It shows a procession moving towards the weather god, who appears here in the shape of his emblem, a bull on a pedestal. The procession, which is facing to the right, is led by king and queen in typically regal costume, followed by sacrificial animals and a group of priests. Finally there is a mysterious group either climbing a ladder or playing musical instruments (?; they could also be sword swallowers), known to archaeologists as the juggling scene. The final block at the extreme left has an incomplete portrayal, with two round shapes only roughly cut out of the stone on either side, of the outline of a bull. At right angles to this series of pictures is a ritual scene on the right, bordering the access passage.

Alaca Hüyük, figure from sphinx gate (left), tunnel system (right)

In the museum in Ankara are several more blocks showing hunting scenes with lances, bow and arrow pursuing stags, boar, bulls and lions, some with assistance from hounds. These come from the upper frieze, and their relationship to each other is unknown. There is also a striking corner block with a vivid representation of a lion tearing a bull calf to pieces.

The sphinx gate opens on to a little square from which, via another courtyard with portal, a path leads to a long courtyard originally flanked by piers on its E. side. The rectangular bases which bore these supports can still be discerned at regular intervals. This colonnade also formed the show façade of a building placed directly on the courtyard that may have been either a temple or a palace. The matter is still disputed.

A large wooden viewing tower has been set up on the site, and this provides the best view of the complcated architecture of the ruins and also the foundations of the other buildings adjacent to the large main building in the W.

When the Hittite empire went into decline when stormed by 'peoples from the sea and from the North', settlement in Alaca Hüyük came to a temporary end. As in neighbouring Hattaşa, there was a short period of settlement by the Phrygians in the first half of the first millennium BC.

Local museum: A new building in the modern village of Alaca, to which the finds from the nearby ruined site were transferred from an older museum in 1981. Although the most important objects are housed in the museum in Ankara, this lovingly presented little exhibition is well worth a visit.

Environs: There are numerous settlements from the Copper Age (fourth millennium BC) around Alaca Hüyük, all of which have produced similar finds. This culture is known as the 'central Anatolian Chalcolithic period'. It includes places like **Büyük Güllücek** (about 17 km. NE), which has its own characteristic ceramics, or **Kaletepe** (about 15 km. N.), where excavation by Turkish archaeologists showed that this was a Phrygian as well as a Chalcolithic settlement.

Eskiyapar (6 km. W.): Important jewellery, now in the museum in Ankara, was found in this early bronze age hill in the course of excavations by R. Temicer from 1967 onwards. There are no significant remains on the site.

Alahan Monastir

11 km. N. of Mut in the Göksu valley a steep path leads E. to a small monastery on a narrow Taurus terrace 2 km. away, at a height of just under 4,000 ft. Extensive sections of the establishment have survived. Visitors arrive at the W. end of the terrace, by the so-called *Evangelist church* dating from the first building period in the late 5C. E. of the narthex, of which little has survived, is the beautiful frame of the monumental *church portal*, dating from the early building period. The stone reliefs beneath the portal lintel show the four symbols of the Evangelists, and those on the W. side show two angels carrying the head of Christ. Inside on the right-hand jamb is a winged St. Michael above two women with Phrygian caps. Opposite is the Angel Gabriel standing on a bull, perhaps representing the triumph of the angels over the heathen? The nave of this basilica was supported by two rows of ten columns, some of which have survived. The adjacent *second church* was built later; it has a single aisle, and is much smaller. Parts of the first basilica, including the apse, were incorporated in it.

Alaca Hüyük, orthostat reliefs on sphinx gate

At the E. end of the terrace is the domed basilica, which is in excellent condition. Architectural historians place this important building on the border between late ancient domed buildings and the beginning of the Justinian-Byzantine building period. In the centre of the nave is a square bay with corner piers, opening on to the aisles with triple arches. These are supported on Corinthian columns, and borne by elegant arches to the E. and W. Above this is a row of similar triple arches forming the lower section of the drum, and above that a dome with squinches. Two delicate windows in the conch-shaped apse and two more transverse rectangular bays to the W. with corner piers and slender columns give the space its particular effect. The left-hand aisle is bordered by a smooth wall of steel-blue rock on the mountain side. There are fine fish and ten-

dril ornaments on the stone frames of the three entrance portals. The impressive architecture of the church is the work of first-class masons, and artfully decorated. There is a splendid view of the extensive Göksu valley.

Environs: Aloda (2 km. N. of the Alahan monastery turning, steeply down to the left): **Cave church** in a cliff with large apse to the E. and a smaller one to the SE. Ornamental **painting** on the ceiling and in the E. apse: hatched circles linked inside and with each other. On the upper part of the W. wall is a badly damaged Entombment and Resurrection. The *floor mosaic* is unique, probably older than the painting. This cave church is difficult to get to, but important as an example of ornamental painting from the early period of the iconoclastic controversy.

Alanya

Antalya   p.574☐H 6

Skylax places the existence of an earlier settlement under Persian rule in the 4C BC. Ancient *Korakesion* became known in the 2C BC when the notorious pirate ruler Diadotos Tryphon (Libertine) established a pirate fortress on the protected peninsula. In 67 BC Pompey conducted a lightning war on behalf of Rome against piracy on the Mediterranean coast of Asia Minor. He completely destroyed the pirate fleet in a naval battle off Korakesion and had the fortress razed to the ground. After the Romans (Korakesion was for a short time one of the morning gifts made by Antony to Cleopatra) and Byzantines, who called the town *Kalonoros* (Beautiful Mountain), the Armenian kings of Cilicia

Alahan Monastir, entrance façade of basilica

ruled Kalanoros for 150 years. After a futile siege the Rumseljuk sultan Alaeddin Kaykobad I took over the town in peaceful exchange from the Armenian Kir Farid, called it *Ala Iya* and made it his second winter residence. He built the fine fortifications which can still be seen on the marble foothills of the mountain range and made Ala-Iya into an important naval base. In 1471 the town fell to the Ottoman empire.

Red tower (*Kizil Kule;* by the harbour): The tower is the work of the famous architect Ebu Ali of Aleppo. It is one of Kaykobad's earliest buildings, octagonal, each side is just under 40 ft. long and 115 ft. high, and battlemented. It forms an effective link between the land and sea walls. There are five floors in the interior. A large cistern in the central pier extends to the fourth floor. 200 yards to the S. is

the famous Seljuk **dockyard** (tersane), unique in design and state of preservation. The ships of the fleet were built in 5 spacious vaulted tunnels connected with each other by arched openings, and they were launched through the pointed arches, and also repaired and stored here. Adjacent to it and facing the sea is the 'Tophane', a defensive tower and arsenal.

Town walls (above the buildings on the shore): The walls wind up the rocky slope, surrounding the houses and gardens of the old town. In the section running from the Red Tower to the W. is the main gate *Kale Kapisi* with two gate sections in the outer and inner wall. Further up the hill at the N. end of the wall is the *Ehmedek* fortress, also the residence. S. of this are remains of the Seljuk to early Ottoman *old town*; especially interesting are the ruins of an extensive caravanserai, of a *mosque*, of a

Alahan, basilica, apse with domed bay   *Alanya, red tower*

bazaar (bedesten) in relatively good condition and further W. of this of the
interesting *Akşebe* Türbesi, a burial place
with meşit.

Citadel (in the W. at the highest point
of the castle rock): Heavily fortified and
spacious group of buildings (içkale: inner
castle) with an interesting *Byzantine
chapel*, untouched and tolerated by all
Islamic groups. The view from the 'terrace of execution' is magnificent.

Environs: Alarahan: Seljuk *caravanserai*, built 1231&2 under Alaedin
Kaykobad I. The han is upstream on the
Alara Çay, between Alanya and Side,
beyond the village of Okurcalarköy on the
left bank of the river near the old fork in
the road for Alanya–Antalya and
Alanya–Konya. The ground plan of the
han is unique, differing from the S.

Anatolian courtyard han (set around a
usually square open courtyard with all
rooms placed symmetrically). Alarahan is
built to an improvised design, and is thus
unlike any other Seljuk caravanserai. The
exterior dimensions are 167 x 128 ft., but
the inner courtyard is only 88 x 16 ft., and
has 7 rooms on both the right and the left,
of which 3 on each side are open iwans.
Between the main and courtyard portals
are individual rooms and access to the two
vaulted aisles along the outer walls and the
transverse aisle at the rear; it is inaccessible directly from the courtyard, unlike
a courtyard han. The Alarahan had a
spring, a mosque and all the comforts
which a merchant could expect in practically every caravanserai at the time. At the
same time the han was well fortified and
secure. The familiar opening ('the sultan
ordered the building of this blessed han')
to the inscription above the entrance por-

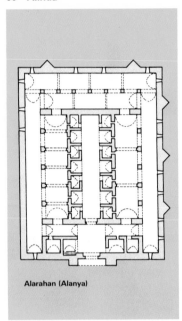

Alarahan (Alanya)

tal is missing in this case. The inscription runs: 'the great, the sublime Sahanaḥ, owner of the necks of the people, lord of the sultans over Arabs and non-Arabs, the lawful sultan, the conqueror of the lands of the world' etc.

The romantically sited castle of *Alara-Kale* above the han was the W. outpost of the kings of Lesser Armenia and fell to Alaeddin Kaykobad I shortly before the han was built.

Hamaxia (2 km. W. of Alanya on the right to Elikesik, ask there for Sinek Kalesi, as the ancient town is now known): The ruins, mainly from the Byzantine period, are heavily overgrown. They include remains of the *town wall*. At the foot of the hill upon which the town is set is an *ancient well* near a spring. The *necropolis* is on the N. slope. From the top there is a beautiful view over Alanya and the distant coast. The port of Hamaxia is

said to have supplied Cleopatra with cedar wood, her preferred material for shipbuilding.

Laertes (about 15 km. E. of Alanya from Mahmutlar): Ancient town, first mentioned by Ptolemy. There are the remains of a *building* with rows of seats, a *shrine to Zeus*, a *necropolis*, *Byzantine church*, *exedra*.

Mahmutlar Kasabasi: The village is close to a *ruined Byzantine town*; the towering remains of its walls can be seen from a considerable distance.

Sarafşa Han (15 km. W., on the right, near the road): 1236–46 is given as the building date. This is a sturdy Seljuk hall with 24 wall towers and battlemented walls. The interior dimensions of the hall are unusually in the proportion 203: 29 ft. Eight blind arches support a shallow, slightly pointed tunnel vault. There are arched windows in the rear wall of each bay, narrowing to slits on the outside. In the E. is a smaller portal leading to the adjacent mosque, which cannot be reached from inside. The mihrab is strikingly slender and tall.

Syedra (35 km. SE of Alanya): Immediately on the right of the road in a little bay with a sandy beach are the ruins of a *harbour thermal bath* and remains of a *necropolis*. The lower town of Syedra, first mentioned in the Hellenistic period, stretched some way up the hill. Further up, high in the mountains, is the *acropolis* with the public buildings of the town. On the rocky coast is a little mountain stump with clearly visible remains of walls.

Alinda

Aydın   p.572□C 5

The ruins are 22 km. SW of Çine near the village of Karpuzlu. Alinda is a Carian foundation, and only a phase of its history is known: when Ada, the sister of King Mausolos, was driven from the throne of Halikarnassos by her brother Pixodaros *c.* 340 BC she withdrew to Alinda and extended the typical Carian castle settlement on a lower second hanging terrace into a Carian-Greek double town with defensive system. It is well worth visiting the settlement on its 525–656 ft. high terrace from the point of view of landscape alone. On the lower terrace the principal buildings are the agora, market hall and theatre, i.e. the business quarter, and on the terrace 98 ft. higher is the former residential quarter, where Ada's palace was probably also sited. When Alexander the Great was approaching in 334 BC, Ada went out to meet him and handed Alinda to him. The conqueror set her up as ruler over the whole of Caria, with the exception of the Greek cities, which remained autonomous.

Agora: This is Hellenistic, about 98 ft. wide, and was once surrounded by columned halls.

Second acropolis: 98 ft. above the lower terrace, after an intervening saddle. The living quarters with cisterns are set behind ashlar walls over six ft. thick. Below the acropolis are remains of an *aqueduct.*

Market hall: This Hellenistic building has survived in remarkably good condition. It is 328 ft. long and 49 ft. high, with three storeys, immediately by the agora. The rooms on the ground floor were arranged in such a way as to make shops accessible through twelve doors on the outside, and storerooms at the rear. The central storey was divided by a row of rectangular piers with double half columns, and was probably used for storing goods. The upper storey formed the S. limit of the agora and little of it has survived.

Town wall: Ashlar, in good condition, probably dating from the 4C BC. The two-storey *tower* above the theatre and joined to it by a tunnel, was probably part of the wall.

Theatre: Hellenistic building with *c.*35 rows of seats and a diazoma, reached by two vaulted passages. The stage buildings have collapsed; the stage itself is 16 ft. wide and paved with stone slabs.

Amasra

Ancient **Sesamos** was founded by Miletians in the 6C BC. From the 3C BC it was known as *Amnastris*, after the niece of Dareios III, then queen regent of Herakleia Pontika. In the Roman campaigns against Mithridates, Amastris was occupied by Lucullus in the 1C BC and destroyed because of his partisanship. After the town was rebuilt along with its fortifications under the Byzantines it became a Genoese possession in the 14C, until it was taken by Mehmet the Conqueror in 1459.

The whole town is well worth seeing, as a Black Sea resort with two harbours and for its general appearance.

Citadel: The buildings and massive *fortifying walls* date from the Byzantine period, but were extended by the Genoese, who fortified the peninsula, which is attached by a narrow tongue of land. The peninsula is linked by a *Roman bridge* and an *ancient tunnel* to a densely populated island. Near the W, gate in the wall on the peninsula is the *Kilise Mecidi*, the fortress commander's chapel. There are *Roman necropolises* on the SE slope of the former acropolis and above the SW beach.

Museum: Well-presented collection of finds from antiquity and Turkish culture.

Amasya

The capital of the province of the same name is about 335 km. from Ankara on

the S. edge of the Pontic mountains on the plain of the Yeşilırmak (Green River), the ancient Iris, carved by the waters into the surrounding mountain landscape. The river divides the town into two distinct areas: the little old town is on the N. bank, and behind it towers the citadel on the summit of the castle rock, almost 1,000 ft. high, with tombs cut into it. S. of the river is the centre of the present town, known as the 'new town', but nevertheless containing the majority of the almost 50 Seljuk and Ottoman monuments to which Amasya owes its fame.

History: When the Parthian empire moved west, Mithridates took the title King of Pontus *c.*250 BC, and under the name *Amaseia* the town even became capital of the Pontic empire for a time. In the third Mithridatic war, in which Mithridates VI Eupator suffered defeats by the Roman generals Lucullus and Pompey, the town was conquered and destroyed by the latter. The geographer Strabo was born here in 64/63 BC. He was later to write the famous 'Oikomene', a description of the then known world in 17 volumes. In the Christian period Amaseia was the centre of a diocese, and one of its bishops, Eulalios, was present at the Council of Nicaea. The emperor Phocas was born here in 547. In 712 the town was occupied briefly by the Arabs under their caliph Walid, but they soon lost it again to Emperor Leo III (717–741). After the defeat of the Byzantines at Malazgirt (1071) the town, which was now ruled by the Bagratid Gagik Abas, became Seljuk and was given its modern name. The Seljuks handed the town over to the Turkish Danishmendid dynasty (→ Tokat) under their regent Tailu, but took it back after disputes with the crusaders in the early 12C, under Kiliç Arslan II. In the 13C the town came into the sphere of influence of the Mongols, in the late 14C they were succeeded by the Ottomans under Beyazıt I. The town was the starting point for

◁ *Amasra, ancient bridge, town gate*

the Ottoman reconquest of Asia Minor, when Mehmet Celebi withdrew to the castle of Amasya after the Ottomans lost the battle against Timur-Leng (Tamberlaine; see İshak Paşa Saryı under Ağri) in the year 1402. In 1467 Sultan Selim I, son and successor of Beyazıt II, was born here. In the Middle Ages the town was so rich that it was compared with Baghdad. Severe damage was caused by earthquakes in 1734, 1825 and 1935; almost all of the S. part of the town was destroyed by fire in 1915.

Beyazıt Camii ve Medrese (mosque and Koran school of Beyazıt II): This complex of buildings was built in 1486 by Prince Ahmed, one of Beyazıt's sons. The mosque is on the left-hand side, with a large and a small purification well in front of it. It has two domed halls, each with a narrow annexe with three small domes. In front of the building is a portico with five domes. The two pencil minarets are differently decorated. On the left of the mosque, the largest in the town, is the *library* with about 20,000 volumes, including ancient manuscripts of the Koran, to the right of the mosque is the *medrese*, with a *grave türbe* behind it.

Burmalı Minare Camii (mosque with the twisted minaret; by the road to Zile): The twisted tower from which the muezzin calls to prayer, and which gave its name to the entire mosque, is to the right of the façade. The house of prayer was built in 1242 by the Seljuk bey Necmettin Ferun for Sultan Keyhusrev II. Beside it are the sparse remains of the *Taş Hanı*, a caravanserai built in 1698.

Fethiye Camii: This mosque is not far from the Burmalı Minare Camii, a little further towards Zile. It was badly damaged in the fire of 1915, so that only the apse and some walls have survived. It is still worth seeing because the building was originally a Byzantine church, changed into a Moslem house of prayer in 1117. The minaret was not added until 1812.

Amasya, Beyazıt II Camii

Yörgüç Paşa Camii: This set of buildings commissioned by the tutor of Sultan Mehmet I, the visir Yörgüç Paşa, contains three tombs (to the right of the anteroom to the mosque) as well as the house of prayer, and also a medrese and a hospital. It is at the W. end of the town (on the road to Çorum) near to the Gök medrese, but on the other side of the road, almost on the bank of the river.

Gök Medrese: This former Koran school at the W. end of the town immediately S. of the road to Çorum now houses the *museum* of Amasya. The medrese was founded in 1266 by the governor Torumtay, who is buried in the adjacent *Torumtay türbe* (1278) under a slab of black marble. The school was also used as a mosque. The nave and three aisles of the prayer room each have five domes, and are separated by two rows of four piers of cruciform cross-section. The pointed-arched *stalactite portal* which forms the N. entrance to the building is striking. E. of the mosque is another tomb with octagonal cross-section. Its conical roof has collapsed.

Büyük Aga Medresesi: (also *KapıAg âsi Medresesi):* This large building dating from 1488 on the left (N.) bank directly by the Kuş Köprüsü (Bird Bridge) has only survived as a ruin (restored), but is nevertheless striking for its unusual octagonal ground plan (each side *c.*62 ft. long). The entrance is not placed precisely on the axis set by the raised iwan with central dome and two side half domes at the rear of the courtyard, but placed slightly to one side. All the other segments which join to form the octagon were formerly topped by three round domes, and the inner ambulatory, also octagonal, had oval vaulting.

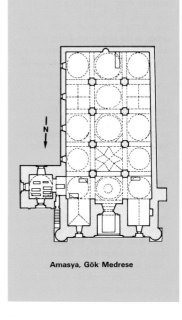

Amasya, Gök Medrese

Amasya, minaret of Beyazıt II Camii

'Türbe district': There are a number of tombs on both sides of the main road through the town on the S. bank, between the transverse streets leading N. to the Meydan Köoprüsü (Square Bridge) and to a wooden bridge without a name. The *Şehzadeler türbesi* was built in 1410 under Sultan Mehmet I for several Osman princes. A son of Sultan Bayazıt I is probably buried in the nearby *Şehzade türbe*. A narrow alleyway opposite the first of these tombs leads to a parallel road with three more mausoleums on the left: the *Halifez Gazi Türbesi* is named after the visir of the Danishmendid dynasty who is buried there and dates from 1145/6. The octagonal grave chamber is set on a high square base and topped with an octagonal pointed roof. The **Şadgeldi Türbesi** beside it was built in 1381, and the Seljuk *Sultan Mesut Türbesi* also dates from the 14C.

Kızlar Sarayı (Maidens' Palace): The remains of the former ruler's palace at the foot of the citadel hill in the N. part of the town are between the Alçak Köprüsü, the middle of five bridges over the river, and the rock tombs. The square is sited impressively above the town, and in the Hellenistic period was chosen by the Pontic kings for their residence. In Islamic times the Seljuk and Ottoman regents settled here. Unfortunately very little of the building has survived.

Rock tombs: Five tombs of Pontic kings are cut into the steep cliffs on which the citadel stands behind the Kızlar Sarayı. Three of the tombs are close together on the little hill to the left of the valley, bounded on the left-hand side by the supporting walls of the Pontic palace (→ Kızlar Sarayı). The other two, rather further apart, are at the front of the rock which rises to the left of the Pontic palace. Access in every case is by steps cut in the steep rock. The façades of all five tombs were formely covered with coloured marble, as the numerous dowel holes indicate. They vary in height between 10 and 40 ft. Two of the tombs are cut out of the rock in such a way that it is possible to walk right round them. Inside a tunnel vault has been hollowed out, and outside they have segmented gables. The westernmost of the tombs was turned into a Christian burial place in the Byzantine period. Pharnakes I (185–159) was probably to have been buried here.

Citadel: This is reached by a steep path with hairpin bends on the E. side of the castle rock. In the Hellenistic period it is said that there was a shrine here of the god of light Ahura Mazda, ancient Persian in origin, who was also worshipped by the Pontic royal household. The sparse ruins of walls were part of an Ottoman fortress. A total of three tunnels with steps lead down towards the river, but their lower exits have never been discovered. The most impressive of them is the one S. of the group of three Pontic tombs. It is pos-

sible that the tunnels were all blind, and used for the cult of Mithras or other gods of the underworld. The ancient heart of the Hellenistic-Pontic settlement was probably once surrounded by a wall that, exploiting the steep castle rock, stretched E. and SW from the citadel to the river, there surrounding the approximately triangular settled area along the bank.

Bridges: There are five bridges over the Yeşilırmak within the town. In the W. the *Meydan Köprüsü* (Square Bridge) leads to Istasyon Caddesi, the road to the station, on the N. side. E. of it is a wooden bridge without a name, then comes the *Alçak Köprüsü*, which leads to the castle rock. This is followed by the *Hükümet Küprüsü*, and at a slightly greater distance the road to Samsun passes over the most beautiful of the bridges, the *Kuş Köprüsü* (Bird Bridge), dating from the Seljuk period.

Also worth seeing: Close to each other to the SE on the Samsun–Çorum road by the river near the Hükümet Küprüsü is the *Gümüşlüzade Camii* (1485) and adjacent to the N. the *Darüşşifa Hanı* (also *Timar Hanı*), built in 1309 under Sultan

Amasya, Halifet Gazi Türbe

Mahmut Olcaytug. In plan it is more like a Koran school than an inn. After it comes the *Mehmet Paşa Camii* (1486). *Kileri Süleyman Ağa Camii* (1485) is not far from Taş Hanı and the Burmalı Minare Camii. On the N. bank, and therefore in the oldest part of the town, between the wooden bridge and the Alçak Köprüsü to the W. are the *Enderun Camii* (also *Loğ Minari Camii*, founded by Sultan Baibar's wife, who had the same name).

Environs: Aynılı Mağara (2 km. N.): This ancient *rock grave* with Greek inscriptions is on the left bank of the Yeşilırmak. Its façade is completely detached from the rock and decorated with corner pilasters and a window with ledge strips.

Eupatoria Magnopolis (about 70 km. E.): The N. route from Amasya to Niksar follows the valley of the Yeşilırmak to Taşova (56 km.), then crosses it a few km. beyond the town. 5 km. N., not far from the confluence with the Kelkit Çayi, is a *bridge* dating from the Roman period, the only significant surviving feature of ancient Eupatoria Magnopolis.

Göynücek (about 55 km. SW): If you take the direct route to Çorum and after a few km. strike off from this road to the SW, following the course of the Cekerek, the ancient Skylax, you reach the village of Göynücek, where, on a rock dominating the gorge, are the remains of a *citadel* and two *staircase tunnels* cut into the rock.

Havza (also *Havca*; 50 km. N.): This little place on the road to Samsun owes its existence to thermal springs, known in ancient times. Two *baths* have survived from the Seljuk period (13C), and a 15C *mosque*.

Kapukaya (*Vezirköprü*; about 80 km. NW): NE of the village of Vezirköprü, which is about 29 km. NW of Havza, is Kapukaya with a Paphylagonian *tomb*. It is decorated with four façade columns in the manner typical of this culture. Further N. on the bank of the Kızıl Irmak are more tomb caves, rather less lavish.

Merzifon (49 km. NW): Some notable Ottoman buildings have survived in the town: in the centre is the *Kara Mustafa Paşa* Camii, a mosque built 1666&7 in characteristic Ottoman provincial style, with a square prayer chamber and dome with four pendentives. The *Murat Camii* was built 1426&7 by Murat II. Not far from it is the *Sultan Mehmed Medresi*, built

Amasya, gatehouse tower and Gök Medrese

Anemurion, mosaic in thermal bath

in 1416 under the emir Unmur and named after Mehmet II. The building, which is in need of restoration, is entered through a door from the E. leading into the square inner courtyard. Symmetry is preserved in that the other sides of the courtyard have central raised and domed iwans, which also jut out from the outer wall. The ancient heating system has survived in some of the classrooms which surrounded the courtyard on all sides.

Anemurion

Mersin   p.574□H 6

Anemurion (Greek: Windy Place) is on Cape Anamur, the southernmost point of Asia Minor on the Mediterranean. The history of the town goes back to the late Hellenistic period, when it was part of Commagene. The last Commagene king, Antiochos IV, was removed from his throne by Vespasian in AD 72, and *Anemurium* became part of the Roman province of Cilicia. The town, later the seat of a bishop, flourished through trade on land and sea, disturbed to a greater or lesser extent by raids from northern mountain tribes, until *c.*AD 650 it declined in the Arab wars of plunder. The Armenian kings settled the town again in the 12&13C, fortified the cape and also included the massive castle of Anamur, 6 km. away, in the defensive system.

Ancient town: Anemurion is like a ghost town. Ruins of large and small buildings, some of them quite close together, extend for over 1,500 yards along the sandy beach and 500 yards towards the mountains. They are in remarkably good condition. On the cape to the S. is the dominant

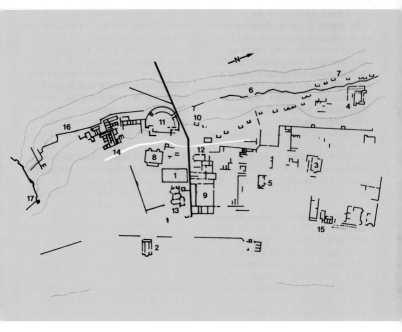

Anemurion, town layout (according to T.Boyd)
1 Apsidal building 2 Basilica 3 Basilica 4
Basilica 5 Church 6 Burial ground 7 Burial ground
8 Odeion 9 Palaestra 10 Town wall 11 Theatre 12-15
Thermal baths 16 Lower aqueduct 17 Citadel

citadel, with the high medieval *defensive walls* running from it to the lower town. Anemurion has been excavated and documented by the Canadian archaeologists Elizabeth Afŏldi-Rosenbaum from 1966, and James Russell from 1970.

In the residential town W. of the path is a large *theatre*, and to the E. an *odeion* with decorated floor. The special feature of this intimate little theatre, (probably used as a buleuterion for council meetings) is a corridor with tunnel vaulting. It was designed to be the lower part of the auditorium, and was used by the public as a passageway, as is shown by the wall painting and floor mosiac, which has survived in good condition throughout its length. Nearby is a *building* with exceptionally fine, carpet-like *floor mosiac*. The mosaic in the apodyterium (changing room) of the ancient Roman *bath* in the NE of the town is of similar quality.

The extensive *necropolis* covers the upper part of the low town, and because of its size and the varied nature of the tombs is a most interesting feature. Many generations from the 1–4C AD built *c.*350 tombs, according to their means. Thus building and decoration range from plain, tunnel-vaulted chambers to magnificent buidings with two storeys, anterooms, side halls and walled courtyards in front of them, floor and wall mosaics, and frescos. There are many mosaics in the town, some of them most attractive, representing fish, birds, hens or people. They have been covered by the custodian for protection, but he will uncover them for a tip.

The most impressive *thermal bath* in this

once famous spa is below the path NNE of the odeion. It has an extensive palaestra, in which the *floor mosaic* with inscription has survived in good condition. The space was used for gymnastic exercises. The bath and palaestra had a total of more than 3,000 square yards of mosaic. S. of the palaestra is another large thermal establishment, and there is yet another S. of the Greek theatre.

The public buildings in this central part of the town date from the late 2C or 3C AD. There are more baths and several churches in the N. W. of the town two *aqueducts* run parallel to the ridge of the cape.

Environs: Anamur (Turkish: **Mamure Kalesi**; 6 km. E.): One of the largest castles in Asia Minor, in excellent condition. It was first mentioned in the 3C AD as a Roman fortress, later notorious as a pirates' lair, then. included in Lesser Armenia's extended defensive system. In the Armenian period alliance with the Crusaders brought a Frankish touch into the castle buildings, which also show Venetian and Islamic elements. After the decline of Lesser Armenia in 1375 the castles belonged to Cyprus for a time, then to the Seljuks, the emir of Karaman and finally to the Ottomans, who extended it again in the early 19C and used it until their empire came to an end. The striking castle is set directly on the sea and is surrounded by a massive wall with battlements and 36 towers in good condition. Inside are two extensive baileys with mosque, stables, keep, baths and well house. From the first bailey, stairs lead to the massive tower of the outer rampart. It is worth walking round the extensive battlements, as they offer a varying view from a considerable height of the entire castle. The finest view over land and sea is from the large tower.

Ani

Kars   p.570□T 2

You need permission from the local police in Cars (Emniyet Müdürlügü; application forms in the tourist information office (Danisma Bürosu) round the corner oppoosite) to visit this ruined town. It is worth the effort. Photography is forbid-

Anemurion, odeion

Anamur (Anemurion), castle

den on the site itself (pictures available in the Kars museum), and an accompanying soldier prescribes a permitted route. It is not possible to visit the citadel and the area behind it, as an observation post has been set up here.

The city, said to have had 100,000 inhabitants and 1,000 churches (there would in fact not have been room for them on the plateau) at the height of its power, is beautifully sited on a triangular plateau, bordered on two sides by the deep valleys of the Arpa Çayı and its tributary the Alaca Suyu. Thus only the open N. side had to be artificially protected, and for this purpose the *land wall*, almost a kilometre long, was built under Smbat II (977–990) and later improved by Georgians and Seljuks.

In the first eight centuries AD the territory was owned by the Armenian Kamsarakan family, who established a castle here in the 5C. In 722 the family was so weakened by a defeat by the Arabs that the Bagtarids were able to take over the area. Their ruler Ashot Msaker also established a small settlement in front of the citadel and is thus the actual founder of Ani, which in 961 under Ashot III replaced Bagaran, also on the Arpa Çayı, as the Bagtarid capital. Subsequently six kings resided here, until 1045. The last but one, Hovhannes Smbat III, was hard pressed by his brother, who had ascended the throne in Kars as rival king under the name Ashot IV, and also by the princes of Vaspuragan. The Byzantines did not withdraw their initial support for Smbat III's two opponents until they were promised that after Smbat's death the kingdom would fall to Byzantium. In 1045 Gagik IV finally had to yield to pressure from Byzantium and abdicate. After isolated Seljuk raids the vassalls of Toğrul Beğ succeeded in conquering the territory around Ani in 1055, and in 1064 the city itself fell into Seljuk hands and was destroyed. David II, King of Georgia, was able to secure his influence over the city, and gave it in fief to one of his noble families; Ani was then ruled by Kurdish emirs. After an initial victory by a Georgian army over the emir of Erzurum in 1126, George III reconquered Ani for a short period in 1184. The population of the town declined rapidly after a Mongol raid in 1250, and in 1319 it was finally destroyed by a severe earthquake.

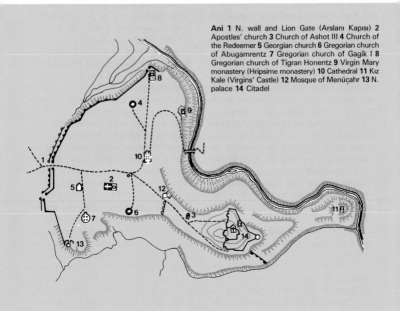

Ani 1 N. wall and Lion Gate (Arslanı Kapısı) **2** Apostles' church **3** Church of Ashot III **4** Church of the Redeemer **5** Georgian church **6** Gregorian church of Abugamrentz **7** Gregorian church of Gagik I **8** Gregorian church of Tigran Honentz **9** Virgin Mary monastery (Hripsime monastery) **10** Cathedral **11** Kız Kale (Virgins' Castle) **12** Mosque of Menüçahr **13** N. palace **14** Citadel

N. wall: The principal entrance to the town in the wall built by Smbat I and later restored is the *Aslanlı Kapısı* (Lion Gate), named after the relief decoration. The *Kars Gate*, 200 yards away, has two massive round towers, for which reason it is also known as Cifte Beden Kapısı. The *Hıdrellez Kapısı*, three hundred yards to the left, is worth seeing for its chess-board-like stone ornamentation.

Church of the Apostles: This church built in 1013 is rectangular in external plan, with entrances in the N. and S. It is only from the inside that it can be seen to be based on four conches. The spaces between the main apses and the corners of the outer walls are skilfully filled in with domed spaces, each with its own apse.

Church of Ashot III: This was the prin-cipal church in the town until the building of the cathedral.

Church of the Redeemer: This church was founded by the Pahlavuni family in 1036. It is a centrally planned building with eight apses and access from the S.; the entire E. half has collapsed. The 13C wall paintings have been painted over in white, but can still be made out.

Georgian church: Only part of the S. façade with relief decoration (Visitation of Mary and Annunciation) has survived of this church dating from 1218.

Gregorian church of Abugamrentz: This twelve-sided centrally-planned building with dome on a high drum was built in the 10C. In the interior are six horseshoe-shaped conches, and the E. apse has two side rooms which also break from

Ani, Gregorian church of Tigran Honentz (left), church of Ashot III (right)

the regular pattern of the building's exterior.

Gregorian church of Gagik I: This large circular building with small apsidal chapel to the E. and entrances in the N. and S. was built between 1001 and 1010 as a copy of the then famous church of Zwartnotz (now in the Armenian SSR). However, the house of prayer collapsed three years after its completion, and was never rebuilt.

Gregorian church of Tigran Honents: This church dates from 1215, and is set right on the edge of the Arpa Çayı gorge. The ground plan is cruciform, with a narthex with two aisles in the W. The central dome with a tall, finely-decorated drum has survived. Wall paintings showing Byzantine influence can still be made out in the interior.

Monastery of the Virgin (Hripsime monastery): This centrally-planned building with six apses and a 'lemon-press' roof is in good condition. It, too, was founded by Tigran Honents.

Cathedral: The main church in the centre of the town was built 989–1001 by Tiridates for Smbat II. After being plundered by the Seljuks in 1064 it was first turned into a mosque, and then reactivated by the Georgians. The dome and drum of this church with nave and two aisles have collpased. The lower part of the building consists of three levels, and the entrance leads down through them. Blind arcades with plain, slender responds articulate the exterior walls. In the interior the building method can be clearly seen, with niches and the apse breaking through to the outer skin. The raised sanctuary has survived.

Kız Kale: This building on a promontory at the tip of the plateau, where the two river valleys meet, is known as the Virgins' Castle, but is also a church (13C).

Mosque of Menüçahr: This Islamic house of prayer with hexagonal minaret was built in 1072 by the first Moslem governor.

North palace: This building (12 or 13C) affords a fine view of the Alaca Suyu. The red and black chess-board pattern over the portal is a striking feature.

Citadel: This building, which unfortunately cannot be visited, contains the remains of the old Bagtarid palace, which in its final phase had two storeys with underfloor heating, baths and a stage for theatrical performances. Next to it is the palace church, founded by Prince Kamsarakan in 622. It is a single-aisled building with apse and simple figurative relief decoration.

Environs: Kızıl Kilise (Red Church): This is the old Armenian Karmir Vank, and it is reached on the approach to Ani by turning off to the left at the reservoir on the Arpa Çayi, then left again by the lake in the direction of Beşgedikler. The *church*, now part of a farm, has survived in good condition, and is visible for miles. **Magarsbert:** The 10C castle has survived in good condition. It is set on a steep slope of the Arpa Çayı valley SW of Ani, and is about an hour's walk from there.

Ankara

If a visitor to Turkey wishes to form an impression of the history of Turkey, a stroll through İstanbul will show him the last two thousand years. Modern history then begins in 1923 with the Turkish Republic and the new capital, Ankara. Developments after this date are incredible to anyone who is aware of earlier circumstances. An insignificant little town of 30,000 inhabitants on marshy ground in the high steppes of eastern Anatolia expands in half a century into a modern metropolis with over two million inhabitants. However fascinating the new districts of Kavaklıdere and Yenişehir may be, with the magnificent architecture of parliament building and ministeries, the splendid embassies and luxury hotels, the university area, gourmet restaurants and modern residential areas—the area around the citadel and stretching to the Ulus, the archaeological museum and the Arslanhane Camii shows a vital connection with the cultural history of the last three millennia. The connection of these two worlds on either side of the railway line is the Atatürk Bulvari, over four km. long. It symbolizes the dynamism and superhuman strength with which a single man set himself against the power, influence and property of established castes from earlier centuries. A massive mausoleum has been built to him, the Father of Turkey, on nearby Anıt Tepe. Atatürk wanted to give the modern state a modern capital. He succeeded. Ankara is the political centre of the country, and also the focal point of road, rail and air transport. From here the traveller can reach famous destinations like the Phrygian Gordion and Midasşeri, Balhisar/Pessinus in the W. and the Hittite area around Hattuşa, Yazılıkaya and Alaca Hüyük in the E.

History: The Hittites are said to have settled on the hills of Ankara and built a fortress there. The Phrygians came *c.*1200 BC. Necropolis finds at the station suggest a city of some importance. Settlement hills on the plain of Ankara are evidence of this period. They were followed by the Lydians, whose lost battle (under Croesus) with the Persians introduced the Achmaenid period in *Ankyra*. Ankyra was first mentioned in particular as a staging post on the great Persian

Ankara, Temple of Augustus ▷

imperial road from Susa to Sardes. Alexander the Great conquered Ankyra in 334 BC. The Tectosages, a tribe of Celtic Galatians who had immigrated from the Pontus, made Ankyra their capital in 278 BC and called it *Galatia*. They built the fortress, the lower part of which still forms the base of the citadel. In 74 BC Mithridates the Great was defeated after a reign of fourteen years by Pompey at Ankyra. The kingdom of Galatia, founded by the Romans was incorporated into the Roman Empire by Augustus after the death of Amintos in 25 BC, and Ankyra was declared capital of the rich Roman province of Galatia. The town showed its gratitude by changing its name to the Greek *Sebaste* (= Augustus).

Sebaste developed, helped by its favourable position on great long-distance roads, developed during the Roman imperial period into a rich town of merchants and craftsmen with an estimated 200,000 inhabitants. In the 3C AD the town became the seat of a metropolitan, with eight suffragan bishops under him. In the late 7C it was conquered for the first time by the Arabs. Sassanids, Seljuks, Danishmendids and Crusaders (Raymond IV of Toulouse in 1101) and Mongols followed each other as owners and plunderers of the town, which was finally incorporated into the Ottoman Empire by Murat I in 1361, who called it *Engüriye*; for Europeans it remained *Angora*. The Mongol Timur-Leng defeated Sultan Bayazıt I here on 2 July 1402.

In 1893 the town on the NW Anatolian high plateau was linked to üsküdar opposite İstanbul by railway. This meant the decline of local crafts, as cheap goods could be imported. In 1920 the 'Grand National Assembly' met here for the first time, summoned by the Young Turks. On 13 October 1923 Ankara became capital of the new state of Turkey (Kemal Atatürk).

Mosques

Arslanahne Camii: This is the oldest and largest mosque in Ankara (early 13C), built by Emor Şerf et Tin using quarry stone and Roman and Byzantine spoils. It is a forest mosque, so called because of its many columns, and one of the few examples of a Seljuk building with wooden columns on a basilican pattern: it has a clearly defined nave and four aisles. The

Ankara, Atatürk mausoleum

flat ceiling is made of artfully jointed, lavishly graded wooden beams and is supported by 24 wooden columns (4 rows of 6 columns), mostly with Roman-Byzantine capitals. The *mihrab* made of faience mosaic and pierced stucco and the *mimber* carved in walnut dating from AD 1209 are masterpieces of craftsmanship. Opposite is the **tomb of Şerf et Tins**.

Ahi Elvan Camii: 14C mosque, founded by the Ahi brotherhood. The flat wooden ceiling is supported by 3 rows of 4 wooden columns. Mimber and window shutters are also fine examples of wood carving.

Alaeddin Camii (in the inner citadel ring): Built under the Seljuk sultan Izzedin Kiliç Arslan II, and later much restored. The mimber of this mosque is also an outstanding example of wood carving.

Mosque of Hacı Bayram (near the Temple of Augustus): Built in 1427, later restored. Hacı Bayram is buried in the türbe. He founded the Bayrami Dervish order here, and is still worshipped as a popular saint.

Ancient monuments, secular buildings

Atatürk mausoleum (*Anıt Kabir* = tomb of honour; on the Anıt Tepe): At present the largest building in Republican Turkey, with *Atatürk Museum*.

Temple of Augustus (*Ogüst Mabedi*): This is the most important ancient building in Ankara, originally built in the 2C BC as an Ionic dipteros for the worship of the Phrygian deities Men and Cybele. When Ankyra became the capital of the province of Galatia in 25–20 BC it was rebuilt by the Emperor Augustus and dedicated to his cult of 'Rome and Augustus'. On the outer wall of the temple is the famous inscription concerning 'the deeds of divine Augustus', the Emperor's political legacy, in Greek; the Latin version is inside. The first version of this 'Testament of Augustus' on bronze tablets was fixed to the walls of the Emperor's mausoleum in Rome and at the same time carved on the walls of every temple of Augustus in the Roman world. It has only survived in completely legible form in Ankara. The German Carl Humann made

Ankara, citadel hill with old town

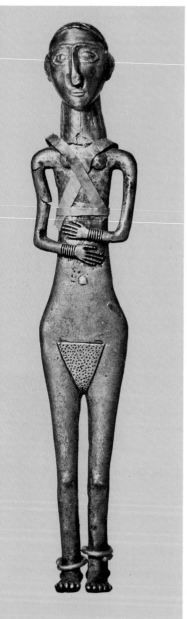

plaster copies of the inscription as early as 1882. Augustus also ordered the census mentioned by St. Luke, which caused Mary and Joseph to travel to Bethlehem. The temple was rebuilt as a Christian church in the 4C. Immediately adjacent are the mosque and türbe of Hacı Bayram Velis.

Citadel (*Hisar*): The oldest houses in Ankara still snuggle against the Akkale castle at the top of the hill, which has afforded protection to the settlement from its earliest years. But however strongly citadels, ring walls and towers were built, and however durable the ancient building materials were, the town was constantly taken by storm and passed from one conqueror to the next. Today, on passing through the massive gate towers in the inner, upper ring wall, armed with 42 towers along its W. wall, and then strolling through the striking old town to the heart of the citadel, the 'white fortress', it is possible to look down from the fire lookout point over the broad plain and its historic battlefields.

Roman baths: These are a few hundred yards W. of the Temple of Augustus beyond the Çankırı Caddesi. The lower storey has survived in relatively good condition. The thermal baths built under Caracalla (212–217) had about 10 large bathing chambers for baths at various temperatures from cold (frigidarium) to hot (caldarium) and changing rooms. There are only a few statues and stone fragments on the palaestra, which was used for over 300 years by bathers for their exercises in the open air.

Column of Julian (*Hkümët Meydanı*; near the Temple of Augustus): This was probably erected in AD 362 to commemorate the visit of Emperor Julian the Apostate. It is almost 50 ft. high.

◁ *Archaeological Museum, statuette, Hasanoğlan*

Ankara, Atatürk monument (left), Arslahane Camii, mosaic tiles on the mihrab (right)

Museums

Museum of Anatolian Civilizations/Archaeological Museum (also called Hittite Museum, Turkish *Eti Arkeoloji Müzesi*; Saraçilar Sokaği): This world-famous, unique museum, in a restored bazaar building, the 15C Mahmut Paşa Bedesteni, is the major attraction of Ankara. In the central room are stone statues by the Hittites and late Hittites, and small finds from the palaeolithic to classical periods.

Entrance hall in the N.

In the right showcase 1: palaeolithic finds from the Karain cave near Ankara: skeletons, skulls and teeth of Neanderthal men, stone tools. These are the oldest finds in Turkey.

W. hall

This is the cult hall of Çatal Hüyük with bulls' heads, reliefs, frescos. Cases 2–8: Çatal Hüyük, neolithic period (6500–5650 BC): Earth Mother statues, tools, pottery. Cases 9–11: Haçılar (5700–5600 BC): female statues, polished ceramics, implements. Cases 12–21: Chalcolithic period (copper age, 5000–3000 BC): Haçılar, Canhasan, Alişar, Alaca Hüyük, Tilkitepe (Van): copper implements, stone tools, pottery with geometrical patterns, female statuettes, animal figures. Cases 22–49: early Bronze Age (from 3000 BC): world-famous finds from the tombs of the 13 kings and princes in Alaca Hüyük: unique cult symbols and statues of stags, bulls and sun in bronze and electrum. Human figures and idols, jewellery and household goods in bronze, gold, silver, copper lead and iron.

S. hall

Early Bronze Age (3000–1950). Cases

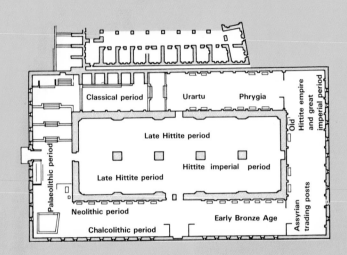

Ankara, Museum of Anatolian Civilizations

50–54: Ališar III, Kültepe, Beycesultan: alabaster fertility symbols. Cases 55–69: Assyrian cuneiform script, seal cylinders, clay goods, pitchers with spouts, animal-shaped rhytons, teapot with strainer, gold jewellery, moulds. The Assyrians sustained 9 great trading centres, carums, administered from Kanesh (= Kültepe). They maintained an exchange of goods and culture between Anatolia and Mesopotamia. Cases 70–88: The ancient Hittites: the Old Kingdom and the Empire (1750–1200 BC).

E. hall

Cases 89–105: Phrygian (1200–700 BC); including finds from Gordion: bronze vessels, ivory reliefs, wooden furniture, stone with Phrygian inscriptions. Case 107: Lydian art. Cases 108–117: Urartian culture, flourished 9–8C BC: large bronze vessels, bronze weapons and shields. Finds from: Toprakkale, Patnos, Altıntepe,

Adılcevaz. Cases 120–125: late-Phrygian art (5C BC). Cases 128–130: classical period.

Central hall

There are large Hittite statues from the period of the Empire (1450–1200 BC) to the late-Hittite period (1200–700 BC) orthostatic reliefs from palaces, temples and town walls, monumental statues of lions, bulls, sphinxes. The reliefs from Alaca Hüyük are particularly notable: royal couple with bull, acrobats' performance, 3 priests at worship. The haut-relief of the weather god Tešub with horned helmet, morning star and curved sword came from the King's Gate in Hattuša and is one of the finest of the period of the Empire. Notable orthostatic reliefs from the late-Hittite period are the 4 children of King Araras (Karkamıs) playing, the mourning procession of the three women (Karkamıs), the goddess Kubaba

Ankara, Archaeological Museum, late Hittite reliefs, Kargamis (9C BC)

on the back of a lion, King Sulumeli before the weather god and 4 other gods, the fighting charioteers running over a dead man (Karakamıs, 9C BC) and the famous profile of the goddess Kubaba. The statue of the basalt lion from the portal in Sakçagözü and the colossal statue of the King of Milid in this group should also be singled out. Also striking are the Phrygian/Hittite orthostatic reliefs in the NE corner of the central hall: horse, bull and lion.

Ethnographic Museum (*Etnografya Müzesi*; by the Talat Paşa Bulvari): In the courtyard is the monumental *equestrian statue of Atatürk*. On the base: reliefs of scenes from the War of Independence and rebirth of the Turkish nation.
Inside the museum is a fine collection of *Turkish folk art* from the Seljuk period onwards: carpets, rugs, textiles, costume, calligraphy, household implements, weapons.

Atatürk's house (in the Çankaya quarter): Atatürk lived here in the early years after Ankara became capital.

Environs: Beypazarı (100 km. W. of Ankara): This is the ancient *laganaia Anastasiopolis*. Several *mosques*, including the 15C Ala et Tin Camii are to be found here.

Gâvur Kalesi (Palace of the Unbelievers; 60 km. SW near Hatmana, the ancient Therma): This Hittite shrine for the cult of the dead and of burial, comparable in purpose with the cult shrine of Yazılıkaya, is set on a rocky plateau almost 200 ft. high, and 115 by 115 ft. square, formerly fortified with cyclopean walls. On the top was a monumental *tomb* from the period of the Hittite Empire, of which the 13 x

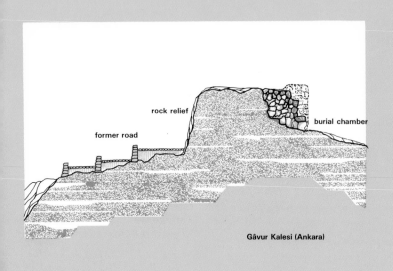

Gâvur Kalesi (Ankara)

former road

rock relief

burial chamber

10 ft underground chamber with a 'false vault' has survived. This was an ossuary, as described in Hittite texts on the ritual of the dead. According to this, dead bodies were cremated, and the remaining bones placed in a underground burial chamber as their last resting place. The rock above the processional road facing the valley was decorated with reliefs, which survived in good condition. They show 2 gods striding to the W., presumably the weather god and his son, with a goddess sitting opposite them. The number of horns on the cap establishes the rank of the gods. The shrine is reached by a processional road secured to the valley wall by supports.

Hasanoğlan (also Hasanoğlu; turn left 33 km. E. of Ankara, then 4 km.): Single early Bronze Age find of the famous female *statuette* in electrum and bronze, dated *c.* 2000 BC, shown in case 34 in the Archaeological Museum in Ankara. This find, considered to be a fertility goddess or Hittite princess, was found in an individual tomb by a farmer, and caused a considerable stir. Near the village are some heavily weathered *rock reliefs* (1C BC?), directions in the village. *Roman milestones* of the same period in the village.

Kalecik (83 km. E. via turning for Hasanoğlan, Elmadağ): This is possibly ancient *Acitoriciacum*. On the conical rock is the *castle of Kalecik* (former acropolis?), built in the 11C AD as a border fortification between Byzantium and the Danishmendid sultanate, and also to secure the nearby ford over the Kızılırmak. Supporting walls of the bulwark terrace and foundations of the older part of the building, made of massive volcanic ashlar blocks, have survived.

Ankara, Archaeological Museum, stag standard (left) and bird-bill jug (right) from Alaca Hüyük

Antakya/Antioch

Hatay   p.576☐M 6

History: The town was founded in 307 BC on the left bank of the ancient Orontes by Antigonos, one of Alexander the Great's generals, and first called *Antigoneia,* after him. After Antogonos' defeat by Seleukos I Nikator at Issos the victor refounded the city in 300 BC and gave it the name *Antiochia.* It became the capital of the Seleucid empire.

Seleukos II established another new settlement, *Epiphania,* immediately next to it. Together with two other small settlements, including a large Jewish colony, it developed under Seleukos IV into *Tetrapolis* (Four Towns), as the settlements grew together. The whole town was walled, and so were each of the four

smaller settlements. In 190 BC Antiochos III was defeated by the Roman general Scipio at the battle of Magnesia, and political decline began. Nevertheless Antioch expanded further. It is estimated that it had half a million inhabitants in the 2C BC. Antioch was in competition with Alexandria, in Egypt, for the reputation of being the second largest city in the world, after Rome.

The town went into temporary decline as a result of an earthquake in 148 BC, being conquered by the Artaxid king Tigranes the Great (83 BC) and destroyed after the town was taken by Pompey, who defeated the last Seleucid king Antiochos XIII in 64 BC. The new Roman overlords undertook extensive building, however, and the town began to flourish again.

In the imperial Roman period Antioch developed into an important base for the

Christianization of the East and subsequently became one of the most important theological centres of early Christendom. Peter is said to have founded the first Christian community here, and to have coined the name 'Christians' for those practising the new religion. Paul's missionary journeys also started from here. Antioch was the seat of a patriarch, and ten councils and church assemblies took place here.

When the town was reconquered by Justinian, after Christianity had long been accepted in the Roman Empire, Antioch was renamed *Theoupolis* (God's Town). After the battle of Yarmuk in 637 the town became Arabian and was extended as a border fortress, then Byzantine again after being reconquered by Nikephoros II Phokas in 969, then taken by Turkish Seljuks in 1084. Crusaders under Bohemund took the town by storm in 1098, after a siege of nine months. From this time the town became a local Frankish principality for 170 years, but it was so weakened by disputes with Byzantium that it was conquered by the Mameluke Sultan Baibar I in 1268. In 1517, under Sultan Selim I Yaviz, Antakya became part of the Ottoman Empire, and remained so until the end of the First World War. In 1918 France established a protectorate on the basis of the Treaty of Mondros. In 1939 the town and the entire province of Hatay became part of Turkey. Very few historic buildings have survived in the town, which covers about a quarter of the area of ancient Antioch.

Aqueduct: Remains of the water supply system, once 9 km. long, are to be found by the town hospital. The system was built under the Roman Emperor Trajan (early 2C AD) and brought water from the springs of Daphne/Harbiye to the town. The arch is known locally as Memikli Cöprüsü.

Roma Köprüsü (Roman bridge): This bridge with four arches over the Asi/Orontes was built in the 3C, at the time of Diocletian. It has retained its original form despite frequent restoration.

Justinian town wall: Sections of the old town fortifications dating from the mid-6C have survived on Mount Silpius (now Habib Neccar) to the E. of the modern town. The citadel (see below) is also to be found here. The wall is built of limestone blocks, and is said to have been so wide that a carriage drawn by four horses could drive along it. The *Bab el Hadid* (Iron Gate) on the Denirkapi hill E. of the citadel was once part of the system of defensive walls. It also had the function of controlling a winter torrent.

Habib Neccar mosque (Kurtuluş Caddesi): This former Byzantine church was turned into a mosque in the 13C. The minaret with striking pointed roof is a 17C addition.

Citadel: This fortress SE of the town on the Habib Neccar can only be reached from the rear, which necessitates a 17 km. drive. It was not completed until the turn of the millennium, under Nikephoros Phocas, and restored under Basileios II and the Crusaders in the early 11C. Little has survived of the walls, formerly fortified with 360 towers, as Mohammed Ali used the citadel as a source of building stone in 1831. Nevertheless there is a fine view of the town from the top.

Cave of Peter (2 km. N.): The Apostle Peter is said to have gathered the first Christian community around himself here on his first missionary journey (between AD29 and 40). The sacred site is reached by the road to Reyhanlı.

In the 12&13C the Crusaders built an early-Gothic façade in front of the cave and created a church with nave and two aisles 31 ft. wide, 43 ft. deep and 23 ft. high behind it. The mosaic floor, made of relatively coarse stones, has survived in part,

Antakya, Archaeological Museum, mosaic ▷

and may well date from the 5C AD. To the right of the altar a basin set in the floor is fed by a spring said to have healing powers. To the left of the altar there used to be an escape tunnel, now filled in, for early Christians fleeing from persecution by the Romans. A solemn memorial service in honour of the saint is held here on 29 June each year.

Archaeological museum: The building was opened in 1948 and extended in 1973, and contains one of the most important *mosaic collections* in the world. The works of art were largely discovered at excavations carried out in 1932–9 by a team from Princetown University and the Musées Nationaux de France. The majority of the exhibits are floor decoration from public buildings or noble villas in Antakya, Daohne, Seleukeia and İskenderun. There are also important Hurrian and Hittite finds, largely from Tell Açana/Alalach and Tell Taynat (see below).

Environs: Demirköprü Köy (15 km. E.): Despite its name, the medieval Iron Bridge over the Orontes is built of lime-

Antakya, Archaeological Museum, mosaic

stone. It was refortified by Balduin IV in 1161. The two towers on the bridge collapsed in an earthquake in 1837.

Harbiye (8 km. S.): This villa suburb is on the site of ancient *Daphne*, where the nymph Daphne is said to have been changed into a laurel to protect her from the wiles of Apollo. The 'Grove of Daphne', already famous as a pleasure garden in ancient times, contains numerous laurel bushes, as well as cypresses and oaks. It was from here, where there is still a picturesque waterfall, that Antioch was supplied with water at the time of Trajan. Ancient texts report the existence of numerous temples, of which only sparse remains of pillars have survived.

What was probably the most important *mosaic find* in the province came from Yakto near Harbiye. The work dates from the late 5C AD (now in Room IV of the museum in Antakya: cat. 1016) and consists of a central medallion with a representation of the 'Megalopsychia', the embodiment of ideal human behaviour. It is surrounded by mythological heroes, identified by name (Adonis, Narcissus, Tiresias, Actaeon, Hippolytus and Meleager).

Kürşat (16 km. S.): This *crusader castle* is on the road to Yayladağı near the village of Sofular. Despite the fact that the fortress was destroyed by Sultan Baibar in 1275 the towers on the SW side have survived in good condition, although the rest of the building is somewhat dilapidated. The entrance is in the NW.

Reyhanlı (about 45 km. E.): This little town on a slope is near to numerous ancient *rock tombs*. It is on the road to Aleppo, and only 8 km. from the Syrian border post at Cilvegözü.

2 km. S.of Reyhanlı is **Yenişehir**, the Roman *Emma* (also Imma). As Emma was at the entrance to the gorge on the Roman road from Antioch to Aleppo it was often the scene of military clashes. The Roman Emperor Aurelian defeated the Palmyrenic Queen Zenobia here in AD 272, and King Balduin III defeated the Arabs here in 1134.

The *fortress* at this strategically important place was destroyed by fire in AD 1139, was rebuilt, then ruined again by an earthquake only 32 years later. Only a few sections of wall survive; the castle was never rebuilt. There is an interesting *caravanserai*.

Samandağı (26 km. SW): This is now a retreat for the Alavites, a sect which split from the Shiites in 874. This group live in the heavily wooded Akra mountains (Kurdish mountains) S. of Antakya, in houses which are half underground, like those in Armenia. The colourful women's costume of this religious minority is an interesting feature.

There is an important Alavite shrine in **El Hidr,** about 3 km. SW of Samandağı. 5 km. NW of Samandağıis the village of **Magaracık** with the ruins of the ancient harbour town of **Seleukia Pieria,** which once had 30,000 inhabitants. The settlement at the mouth of the Orontes was founded as an export harbour for the residence city of Antioch by Seleukos I. Nikator in the 3C BC. The surviving ruins, parts of the town wall and fragments of a nymphaeum and of an aqueduct date from this period. N. of the acropolis are the remains of a gatehouse. The most impressive monument is undoubtedly the *Gariz tunnel,* a cleft in the rock extended into a tunnel about 1.3 km. long in the reigns of Titus (75−81) and Vespasian (69−79). There are inscriptions relating to both emperors in the tunnel. It and other recorded 1&2C AD hydraulic projects were intended to prevent the harbour basin silting up with mud from the Orontes. Today, however, the remains of the ancient harbour mole are on dry land.

Tell Açana (22 km. E.): The remains of ancient **Alalach** were excavated from the mound 150 yards from the road by the English archaeologist Sir Leonard Woolley from 1936−49 (interrupted during the Second World War). Woolley identified a total of 17 layers, going back to the fourth millennium BC. This town on a bend in the Orontes was formerly capital of the principality of Mukiş, which dominated the plain of Amuq, and was important as a reloading point for long-distance trade and as a supplier of wood from the Amanus mountains on the edge of the plain of Amuq. This was a focal point for Mesopotamian, Egyptian, Aegean and

Antakya, Archaeological Museum, mosaic

Demirköprü Köy (Antakya), stone bridge

Syrian influences, and also some from Asia Minor.

Yarimlin, who ruled the kingdom of Yamchad from Aleppo, built a state palace in Alalach *c.*1785 BC. An extremely fine diorite head found here, now in the museum in Antakya, is said (probably incorrectly) to be a portrait of this ruler. The extensive palace archives on clay tablets in cuneiform script gives us useful insights into the power structure of the times, for Yarimlim was a contemporary of Hammarubi and Zimlirim, the rulers of Babylon and Mari respectively.

Shortly afterwards the Assyrian King Shamshi-Adad I conquered the town. In the 17C BC Alalach was Mitannic, and was taken by the Hittite king Mursili I on his Babylonian campaign *c.*1600 BC. Between 1525 and 1460 the town came within the Egyptian sphere of influence. Alalach flourished for the last time during a new period of Mitannic influence under Prince Niqmepa, whose palace was also excavated. The *foundations of the palace building* can still be clearly discerned on the site. Its state entrance was once supported by 2 columns, and their bases have survived.

The entrance to a temple from the town which had carved basalt lions on either side can be seen in the museum in Antakya.

Finally (from *c.*1370 BC) the town was part of the Hittite empire, and in 1275 BC, after the battle of Kadesh on the Orontes, fought between the Hittites and the Egyptians, it was plundered by Pharaoh Rameses II, and finally fell before the storm of the maritime nations *c.* 1200 BC. From this time onwards it was no longer inhabited.

Tell Taynat (about 25 km. E.): The finds were made not far from Tell Açana

Tell Açana (Antakya), entrance to Niqmepa palace

directly N. of the road from Antakya to Aleppo on the Orontes. The settlement hill, 680 yards long and 550 yards wide was excavated by the American archaeologists McEwan and Braidwood for the Oriental Institute Chicago in 1935–8.

The place has been inhabited from the earliest times (so-called Ǧemdet Nasr period, *c.*3000 BC) throughout the entire third millennium.

The *citadel* was revealed at the highest point of the hill. Decorated column bases from the entrance to one of these palaces can now be seen in the museum in Antakya.

Behind the 95 x 190 ft. S. palace was a long *temple* 38 x 83 ft. with an open portico supported by two columns. Both the stone *column bases* from this temple entrance, which were each supported by two beautifully carved lions, are exhibited in the museum in Antakya.

There are, however, no significant remains of any of the buildings on the site.

A similar situation obtains in nearby **Tell Cüydeyde,** where an uninterrupted sequence of layers from 4500 BC to AD 600 was discovered. The ceramics discovered in 1933 and the finds from Tell Taynat enabled archaeologists to establish a chronology of the plain of Amuq which goes back to the discovery of pottery in the neolithic period.

Turfanda (29 km. S.): The three-storey *rock tombs* connected with steps are reached by taking the main road to Yayladağı to the little village of Şenköy (22 km.), then turning off for Tufanda (another 6 km. ESE).

Yayladağı (also **Ordu:** 51 km. S.): This village, which still has the ruins of an old church, is now an important frontier crossing point, corresponding with the Syrian frontier town of Kessab, from which it is possible to reach the Syrian coastal town of Lattayike.

Approaching Yayladağı from Antakya the road passes the *Gebel Aqra* (also *Çebeliakra* in Turkish; 5,705 ft.), the ancient **Mons Casius**. This landmark, visible for miles, was considered a holy place particularly by Greek and Roman seafarers sailing into the harbour of Seleukeia (→ Mağaraçık). It is said that it was here that Seleukos I Nikator, while making a sacrifice, was ordered by the gods to found the port of Seleukeia. In the imperial Roman period, when Jupiter Casius was worshipped on the mountain, tradition has it that Trajan and Hadrian paid visits and made sacrifices. However, the place was probably already an important place of worship in the Hittite period. According to the Byzantine historian Malalas, the mountain is named after the Greek hero Kasos, who ruled here with his consort Amyke, and brought prosperity to the region by settling it with Cypriots and Cretans.

Yoğun Oluk (26 km. W.): Here the ruins of a 13C Crusader church have survived. The little place is reached by taking the road halfway to Samadağı from Antakya,

and after about 15 km. following a track that branches off on the right via Bityas (after 8 km.), along the S. slope of the Musa Dağı for 11 km..

If you remain on the main road to Samandağı, 5 km. after the turning to Yoğun Oluk you reach the starting point for the summit of the Saman Dağı, where there is a *basilica* of St. Simeon Stylites the Younger.

Antalya

Antalya   p.574□F 6

History: A garrison was established by the Pergamene king Eumenes I on the site of the town in the mid-3C BC. The founder of ancient *Attaleia* was Attalos II in the 2C BC. This king of Pergamon needed a harbour on the S. coast of Pamphylia, in order better to realize his intended expansion into this province. He gave his name to the town. He was not in a position to capture an existing town in this fertile province, as they had bought their freedom from Rome, and stood under her protection.

Antakya, Archaeological Museum, column base with double lion from Tell Taynat

This newly-founded harbour town which soon assumed Side's mantle as premier port in the area, made little impact on history. Pompey made it the principal base in his campaign against pirates in 67 BC. After St.Paul and Barnabus the next prominent visitors were the Emperor Hadrian and his wife Sabina (AD 130). Attalaeia decided that it should smarten itself up for the occasion, and the Gate of Hadrian with its three openings was one of the new buildings. Hadrian later built an effective defensive system and made the town and surrounding area into an independent Roman province. The Byzantine Emperors Leo VI (886–912) and Constantine VII (913–959) reinforced the defences against the Arabs and built a second wall. In 1084 the town acquired a bishop, under Emperor Alexios I Commenos. In 1207 the Seljuks took Attaleia from the Byzantines for a second time. Under the name Antalya the town became the winter residence of the Seljuk sultans and a flourishing harbour and trading town. Murat II made it part of the Ottoman Empire in the late 14C.

Alaeddin Camii: This mosque was built in the 7C as a Byzantine church. It was destroyed, then rebuilt by Alaeddin Kaykobad, who retained the original ground plan. As the church faced E., the mihrab (facing SE, towards Mecca) had to be displaced from the axis. The *Yivli minaret* belongs to this mosque, and is an emblem of the town which is visible from a great distance, one of the oldest and most beautiful Seljuk minarets in Anatolia. The fluted, round tower is built of red brick and decorated with turquoise faience.

Kesik Minare: Originally a 5C Panaghian basilica, this is one of the most interesting of the Seljuk and Ottoman mosques in Antalya.

Karatay Camii (1250): This is a typical Seljuk mosque.

Seljuk buildings in the centre below the *bell tower. Türbe of Nigar Hatun and Mehmet Bey* (with pyramidal roof), *Alaeddin Camii* (see above), *Koran school (medrese),* the former 'university' of Antalya, built in the 13C by vizir Karatay, with scientific, philosophical and philological faculties. The 131 ft. *Yivli minaret* (see above;

Antalya, Hadrian Gate

with viewing platform) towers over this district.

Gate of Hadrian (→ History): This was built of marble, with lavish relief ornamentation.

Defensive wall: The most striking remains of the massive fortifications built by Hadrian and from the late pre-Turkish period are the towers, including one by the Gate of Hadrian.

Towers: The *bell tower* in the centre is the most interesting. The *Roman tower* to the left of the Gate of Hadrian (looking from from the outside) and the *Hıdırlık tower*, S. of the wall, which has survived in very good condition (2C AD), are also worth seeing. The latter is 46 ft. high, with a rectangular lower and circular upper storey. It was probably also used as a lighthouse.

Archaeological Museum: This spacious modern museum has a fine collection of finds from Antalya itself and the cities of Pamphylia and Lycia, for example Limyra and Xanthos. Outstanding items include statues of emperors and gods from Perge, including a Roman copy of an Aphrodite by Praxiteles, and a fine sarcophagus with reliefs of the labours of Hercules. An inscription confirms the building of the second wall in the 10C. There are votive reliefs of 10 Lycian gods and muses.

Environs: Beldibi cave (near Beldibi-Köy, 10 Km. W. of Antalya): Here there are prehistoric cave drawings and mesolithic finds. **Belbaşı cave,** mesolithic finds. (For *Thermesos* (and **Evdir Han),** *Incir Han* and *Perge* see under separate entries.
Karain cave (27 km. NW on the limestone slopes of Şam Dagi): Interesting finds from all palaeolithic periods from 200,000 BC to the mesolithic period are to be found here, for example bones, jaws and teeth of Neanderthal man. The attached small *museum* is also unquestionably

worth seeing. (→ also Museum of Anatolian Civilizations in Ankara, case 1).

Antiochia in Pisidia

İsparta   p.574□G 4

The ruins of the ancient city are 5 km. above Yalvaç, W. of Akşehir.

History: The city was probably founded by the Antiochos I Soter of Macedon (280–261 BC). After the victory over Antiochos the Great at Magnesia on Siplyos in 190 BC the Romans conferred the status of a free city. The Emperor Augustus settled a colony of veterans nearby and gave the town the name *Colonia Caesarea Antiochia.*
Antiochia was notorious in its early history for its excessive cult of the Pisidian god Men-Askaénos, for which a large priestly shrine was built. The priests kept numerous temple slaves (hierodules) for their sometimes gruesome orgies. The high priest was a eunuch. St.Paul and Barnabus conducted a mission here (Acts 13, 14–15), but were driven from the town by the Jews. Later, as capital of N. Pisidia and seat of a metropolitan, Antiochia produced 13 distinguished bishops up to the 6C. The town then began to go into decline, and this was sealed by complete destruction by the Arabs in the 8C.

Ancient city: The following ruins of the once very large city, shown on a clear plan on site, can be seen. In the upper town there are remains of the *acropolis propylaeum* from the period of Augustus, where in 1912 a Latin version of the so-called 'Testament of Augustus' was found (→ Temple of Augustus in Ankara). From here there is access to the Square of Augustus, bordered in the E. by a vertical semicircle of rock. Two-storey walks, with Doric and Ionic columns, were built against this wall of rock, and gave the

Antalya, Yivli minaret ▷

Antiochia in Pisidia, temple precinct

space considerable architectural attraction. At the central point is the *Temple of Augustus*, probably on the site of a former shrine of the Men god.

In front of the propylaeum is the Square of Tiberius, and W. of this the ruins of a Byzantine basilica. In the E. are the remains of a large *theatre*; its marble seats were transferred to Yalvaç in the early 19C. Some arches of the massive aqueduct have survived, a little distance away.

In **Yalvaç** are a *museum* and a *mosque* built almost entirely of ancient spoils.

Aphrodisias/Geyre

Aydın   p.572☐D 5

On the road from İzmir to Denizli (Meander valley), 15 km. beyond Nazili a road leads off to the right across the Meander to the valley of the Vandalas Çayı, and after a drive of about 45 km. it reaches the old village of Geyre and the ruins of Aphrodisias, not far from Baba Daği (7,572 ft.), which is snow-covered for a large proportion of the year. The city's changing names, culled from the geographical dictionary Ethnika by the Byzantine grammarian Stephanos of Byzantium (6C) give an insight into its history. The early name *Ninoe* may suggest an early Assyrian settlement (Assyrian trading colony?), possibly with a shrine to Ishtar, the goddess of love and the planet Venus in the Land of the Two Rivers, who under the Greeks became Aphrodite, hence the name Aphrodisia; excavations in the 66 ft. high theatre hill have revealed layers of settlement, like Troy, going back to the 3rd millennium BC.

Aphrodisias flourished under the Romans from the 3C BC, and this period is histori-

Aphrodisias, view of Baba Dağı

cally easier to pin down. The town was granted particular privileges under the emperors of the 2C AD in particular; long before this Mark Antony granted right of asylum in the precinct of the temple. Under the post-Julian emperors Aphrodisias became an artistic and spiritual centre, with a school of sculpture which was known throughout the Roman Empire: marble quarries on the slopes of Baba Daği, 2 km. E. of the town, provided white, blue and grey marble; annual sculpture competitions also brought sculptors to the town from elsewhere. There are records of a philosophical academy and a medical school. The town's life tended, however, to be concentrated around the Temple of Aphrodite and its sacred precinct. It is not known which aspects of the Greek goddess of beauty, originating in the east, and including features of Ishtar and the Magna Mater of Asia Minor, were

particularly worshipped in Aphrodisia; her cult, administered by priestesses and temple servants (hierodules) could included temple prostitution (as in Corinth, and Monte Erice in Sicily).

In the Byzantine period, in the 7C, Aphrodisias was called *Stauroplis*, (City of the Cross), and was first the seat of a bishop, then of the metropolitan of Caria. As the capital of Caria it was finally called *Caria*, which then became Geyre in Turkish.

After it was conquered by the Seljuks, then the Ottomans, the extensive town declined to become the village of Geyre. It is an outstanding example of a rise (because of a mixture of cultures) and decline (incompatibility of cultures) of a culture. Intensive excavations have been carried out since 1961 by Professor Kenan Erim under the patronage of the University of New York.

Agora: 12 Ionic and Corinthian columns in rows give an impression of 2 squares, still to be excavated, separated by a hall (portico of Tiberius, AD14–37), of which the one to the N. served as an agora.

Bishop's residence (W. of the odeion): A room with three conches and a peristyle (courtyard surrounded with columns with 7 column re-erected) have survived.

Christian churches: Three ruins give evidence of the numerous churches of the bishops' city (competing with the temple of Aphrodite): a *basilica* with nave and two aisles (328 x 98 ft.), 3C, S. of the square containing the portico of Tiberius; about 150 yards S. of this are the ruins of of a small 6C *Byzantine church*, probably a 'martyrion': a square, domed space with a narthex; SE of the square in front of the theatre is a *columned basilica* with nave and two aisles.

Heroon: Circular tomb near the odeion for one of the notabilities of the town, a platform reached by three steps, for a sarcophagus, an altar and an octagonal seat.

Odeion: (2C BC): 2 tunnel-vaulted access passages at the sides led into a semicircle of 12 tiered rows of seats with lions' feet; the top row is missing. The orchestra with marble mosaic is surrounded by a high balustrade.

Propylaeum (at the beginning of the circular tour of Aphrodisias, shortly after the museum): This is a monumental gate (2C, probably built under the Emperor Hadrian, 117–138 AD), with 8 spirally-fluted columns, 4 on each side of the gate. It may have been the entrance to the temple precinct, and has a tunnel-vaulted passage.

Sebasteion (not far from the museum): This is a shrine built *c.*50 AD for the worship of the emperor. Three-storeyed halls surround a courtyard (to the N., W. and S.). The S. hall has examples of the three column orders, Doric, Ionic and Corinthian, one above the other. Between them on the ground floor are mythical reliefs, and historical reliefs on the first floor (Augustus to Nero). In the E., at the top of a flight of steps, was a podium temple for the cult of the emperor.

Aphrodisias, Temple of Aphrodite

Stadium (1C): One of the best-preserved ancient stadia, on the edge of Aphrodisias, 286 yards long, 64 yards wide, with 22 rows of steps to accommodate 30,000 spectators. Originally there were blind arcades at the top; there is an entrance tunnel at each of the rounded ends. To the E. a circular wall was included, forming an area for gladiatorial combat. In the middle of the N. side was the imperial box. The stadium was most frequently used for athletics, wrestling and boxing.

Town wall: Generally in good condition; the W., N. and E. gates have survived. The ring wall is 3.5 km. in length, and is quite late, as the spoils show, 4C AD.

Temple of Aphrodite (1C BC): The earliest foundations date from the 6&5C. 14 columns of the Ionic pseudodipteros (13 x 8 columns with double distance between the columns and the cella wall), two of them with architrave. The cult image in the cella, reached through a pronaos, showed the goddess in a severe and rigid pose with her lower arms outstretched (cf. Artemis in Ephesus). The temple was surrounded by the sacred precinct, with columned halls 39 ft. away from the inner sanctuary and 11 ft. wide. The precinct had right of asylum. In the Byzantine period, probably as early as the 4C, the temple was rebuilt as a church.

Theatre (on the E. slope of the 'acropolis' hill made up of the various settlement layers): This Hellenistic building with 25 surviving rows of seats below a broad central passage (diazoma; the upper rows of seats and a second passage are missing; an inscription even mentions a third passage) is in excellent condition. The wall of the stage has survived to a height of sixteen ft., with three passages opening on to the stage; in front of this are the half columns of the proscenium. Under Marcus Aurelius (161–180) the orchestra was set lower down (for animal fights?). The seats of honour with hollowed-out backs are around the orchestra. The large square in front of the theatre was paved with marble slabs in the 4C; the theatre baths are adjacent to it.

Thermal baths of Hadrian: These were built opposite the agora under the Emperor Hadrian (AD 117–138). The

Aphrodisias, stadium

complex has not yet been completely excavated, but the series of rooms include 5 large vaulted rooms, also with a hypocaust system, and a palaestra surrounded by columns.

Museum: By the ruins of Aphrodisias is a museum showing outstanding work from the sculpture school in Aphrodisias.

Environs: Before you reach Aphrodisias on the road from İzmir to Denizli it is possible to turn off to Tralles, above Aydın (about 120 km. from İnzmir) and to Nysa above Sultanhisar (30 km. after Aydın). **Nysa** (about 70 km. NW): This 'double town' (Strabo) 2 km. up from Sultanhisar on the slopes of Mount Mesogis, protected to the E. and W. by cliffs, and cut in two by the Tekkecikdere torrent, was probably formed as a Hellenistic town in the 3C BC by combining several settlements. The Seleucid foundation was given the name of one of the ladies of the ruling house. In the 1C BC (about 50–45) the famous Greek historian and geographer Strabo of Amasya (64 BC–AD 23) studied grammar and rhetoric here with his teacher Aristodemos. He describes the place where he studied very precisely in his 'Geographika' (XIV, 1,43 ff.).

Among the extensive ruins of Nysa (the town was destroyed by the Turks c.1300), predominantly Roman, those in the E. town are the most distinctive:

Agora: Recognizable by erect column drums in the area which is used for agricultural purposes.

Amphitheatre: This was built across the Tekkecikdere torrent, using its steep banks for the 30 rows of spectators' seats. The race track was in the roofed area over the watercourse, and could be used for water games when flooded in the spring.

Library: (2C BC): This was a rectangular building at least two storeys high with outer and inner walls. The inner walls were used to protect the books against damp. Book rolls were stored in the 2 rows of vaulted niches set one above the other;

the central room has another room on either side of it.

Bridge: This joined the two halves of the town above the amphitheatre.

Gerontikon (near the agora): This circular room, conceived like an odeion with 12 rows of raised seats and 5 flights of steps was used for sittings of the council of elders. There were 3 entrances between 4 piers, leading directly to the speaker's platform. The semicircle was within a rectangle of 66 x 75 ft.

Town wall: Very little remains of the Byzantine town wall.

Theatre: The theatre had 48 rows of seats and a horizontal passage (diazoma) in the middle. The stage building had five doors and its façade was 361 ft. wide. The stage in front of it was a platform above a tunnel 328 ft. long, 33 ft. high and 29 ft. wide, with a bend in the middle. It was used to carry water from the mountains through the town.

Thermal bath (Katip Ören): The building is in the W. of the town, and 98 x 43 ft., with Roman-Byzantine walls 10 ft. thick and still 16 ft. high, with a propylaeum on the N. side.

Apollonia/Apolyont

Bursa   p.564☐D 2

The ancient Greek town of Apollonia on the Ulubat or Apolyont Gölu (lake) is now a village known partly as *Apolyont* and partly as *Gölyazi*. In the 5C BC it was famous for its temple cult in the shrine of Apollo. In ancient times the town was partly on the island, partly on the mainland, now connected by a causeway.

In and around the picturesquely-sited island village are remains of *ancient* and *Byzantine* buildings and *walls*. The *mosque* on the causeway was built almost completely with stone from the Roman colossal walls. In the part of the village on the mainland is a large neo-Byzantine *ruined church*, and above the village the shape of an large ancient *theatre* can be discerned.

Aphrodisias, theatre

Artvin

Çoruk   p.570□R 1

The provincial capital is on the periphery of the triangle formed by Hopa, Erzerum and Kars, and unofficially known as Turkish Georgia. The surrounding area has numerous early Christian churches, though most of them are in ruins.

Artvin itself, also known as *Lazin* or *Çoruh*, like the province, is set on picturesque terraces above the valley of the Çoruh Nehri. Tea is grown on the terraced slopes, as well as fruit and vegetables. Only a 15C *fortress* has survived in Artvin itself. Also of interest is the *Salih-Bey-Mosque* in *Cayağzi*, built in 1793 under the governor of Sivan of the same name.

The most interesting collection of old *Christian churches* is in the *Imerhevi Nehri* valley. This tributary flows from the NE,

and joins the Çoruh Nehri S. of Artvin. So many churches and monasteries sprang up along its course and in its numerous side valleys that the area was once known as the Georgian Athos. Many of the institutions were founded in the 9C by Grigor Chandsteli and his pupils. Before embarking on a visit it is advisable to check on the condition of the tracks on which the buildings stand. Many of them can also only be reached by walking for a considerable distance. The little hotel in the village will assist in finding a local person who knows the area well.

Environs: Ardahan (130 km. E.): This little place on the right bank of the Kura Nehri can be reached either via a northern route which goes through Şavşat, or a route to the S. over the Yalnız-Çam pass (8,694 ft.) beyond Tütünlü. The destination, formerly known as **Artan**, has a mas-

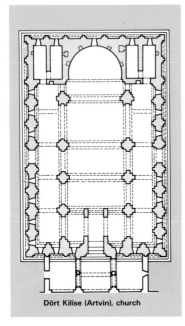

Dört Kilise (Artvin), church

sive *citadel*, which in its present form goes back to Sultan Selim I. The village is at a height of 5,840 ft. and was occupied by Russia from 1873–1921.

Ardanuç (25 km. SE): This village on a S. tributary of the Imerhevi is now insignificant, but was once capital of the principality of Tao Kalrdshetin. Its founder, and also most important ruler, was the Bagtarid Ashot Bagrationi the Great (780–826). He took the title Kuropalat (Keeper of the Palace), and had several churches founded in his empire. The area was already Christian, but had to pay tribute to the emir in Tblisi (Tiflis). By means of skilful manoeuvring between Byzantium and the caliph, Ashot led his little empire into a period in which it flourished greatly. All that has survived of this period inside the fortified area is an Armenian church. The citadel, set on a massive rock, towers over a canyon-like

gorge a few km. SE of the present town, but only the outer walls and a few tower stumps remain. The building can be reached by stairs and ladders.

Çıldır (48 km. E. of Ardahan): This little place, also called *Zurzuna*, is on the NW tip of a lake (Çıldır Gölü) at a height of 6,430 ft. on the road from Artvin to Kars via Ardahan. 14 km. NE is the medieval **Rabat castle**, popularly known as Çeytan Kalesi (Devil's Castle). Because it is so near the Russian border the fortress, which dominates a long valley, can only be visited by permission of the local military command. The last 4 km. have to be traversed on foot.

S. of the NW tip of the lake is **Urta** (also **Gölebelen**) with a Georgian *domed basilica*, now used as a mosque. Further S. on the W. bank of the lake is **Pehreşin**, which can only be reached in a cross-country vehicle. Here are the ruins of a *double church* and a remarkable *Kurdish cemetery*. On the lake island of **Agenkale** are the ruins of a *castle* and a *church*. Ornithologists will find numerous colonies of interesting water birds.

Dolişhane (now **Hamamliköy**; 31 km. E.): This building is the most important of the monasteries which have survived on both sides of the road to Şavşat, in the Imerhevi valley. The *cruciform domed basilica* has an extended W. arm, and dates from the time of King Smbat I (923–985), son of Ardanese II. It has survived in good condition because the lower storey was used for stabling and the upper as a mosque. There is a relief on the dome with an inscription commending the founder to God's protection. The S. window shows the archangels Michael and Gabriel.

Dört Kilise (Ochta Eklessia: four churches; 98 km. S.): To reach this place, remain on the road to Erzerum for 72 km. until the confluence of the Oltu Çayi and the Çoruh, where a side road branches off to Yusufeli (another 11 km.). The way from here to Ispir, which follows the valley of the Çorul upstream for long stretches, leads in about 15 km. to a castle with a chapel on the bank of the river. In the next village keep to the right, and the destination is reached after another 8 km., following the course of a brook. Only one of the four churches referred to in the name of the village has survived. The *basilica* with nave and two aisles is rectangular in plan, and has a stone-slab roof that has survived in part.

Işhan (Ichkhane; 80 km. S.): Again take the road to Erzerum, as for Dört Kilise, but avoid the turning to Yusufeli. This time, turn of to the E., a few km. after crossing the Çoruh. The individual stages of building are still clearly to be seen in the *church* which has survived in Işhan. The horseshoe-shaped E. apse, decorated with rosettes and flowers in relief, has survived from the oldest place of worship, which was probably a four conch building dating from the first half of the 7C. The first rebuilding seems to have taken place *c.*828. More radical rebuilding followed in 1032, when the church was transformed into a domed building with extended W. arm. The drum of the dome with its twisted columns now soars free above the piers of the crossing, as the roof of the nave and aisles has disappeared. Traces of *painting* can still be discerned in the arches of the windows in the drum. The picture in the dome is rather clearer, and shows a cross held by hovering angels. In the N. aisle the painted medallions in the window arches show saints and founder kings. The outer side of the windows is in the typical Georgian tradition framed with guilloche patterns and stylized plant motifs. The outer walls are articulated with stepped arches. The great golden processional cross (height just over 1 ft. 6 ins.), commissioned by bishop Illarion of Işhani for his monastery church in 973, is now in a museum in Tblissi (Tiflis) in the USSR.

Opiza (Opisa; 30 km. E.): The ruins of this village are on a slope in the valley of the Imerhevi Nehri. The monastery itself is said to have been founded by hermit monks in the 8C. In the 9C, Ashot I built the church of St. John here, and this was rebuilt in the 13C. The church and

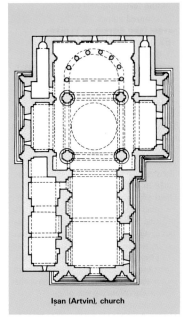

Işan (Artvin), church

associated buildings are now in a very poor state of repair, and the dome has also collapsed.

Parchali (Parhal, Barhal; 90 km. SW): Yusufeli (W. of the road to Erzerum) is again the starting point for this visit, as in the case of Dört Kilise, leaving the village in a north-westerly direction, towards Sarigöl. The *former church* is directly on the road, which runs beside a tributary of the Çoruh. The building is now used as a mosque, which explains its good condition. According to the foundation inscription it was founded in the 10C by David Kuropalat. The nave and two aisles are separated by four pairs of piers. In the little rooms on either side of the apse there are still traces of earlier painting. Some of the windows are decorated with ornamental relief strips, with some figurative motifs such as pairs of peacocks or a lion. Further attempts to decorate the building were made by the use of different coloured stones.

Şavşat (also **Zavsat** or **Yeniköy**; 77 km. NE): This little mountain village (3,281 ft.), dominated by the *ruins* of a massive Georgian *castle* in a rocky promontory E. of the village, was formerly the residence of the prince of Chavchetien, one of the small empires into which Georgia split in the 9C. It enjoyed a period of unity under Bagrat III (late 10C), but split up again as a result of Mongol invasion (1236–1386). NE of the village is the *Tbeti monastery*, and there are remains of several Christian buildings in the region, particularly in the S.

Tbeti (80 km. NE): If you turn left off the road which leads E. through the Imerhevi valley before reaching Şavşat (see above) to Veliköy, you reach a *ruined church* hidden among trees in a little valley. There are still *paintings* in the choir of this building, which is in an extremely poor state of repair, and they suggest that very strong colouring was originally used. The paintings show Christ with outstretched arms, surrounded by angels and saints.

Yeni Rabat (Schatberdi; 40 km. SE): This *monastery* is 15 km. E. of Ardanuç, hidden in a wooded trough. It was built in the 9C by Gregory (Grigol) Chandsteli. As in most Georgian churches the window frames are lavishly decorated. There was once a famous monastery school of book illumination here. Evangelistaries dating from the 9&10C can now be seen in various museums in Tblissi (Tiflis) in the USSR.

Arykanda

Antalya   p.572☐F 6

The remains of this ancient town are half way between Finike and Elmalı near the modern village of Arif.

History: The oldest finds made by Turkish archaeologists go back to the 5C BC.

They are Periclean coins from Akuwami and Arykanda. Persian supremacy was broken by Alexander the Great. He was followed by the Seleucids and, after the peace of Apamea, Arykanda was ruled by Rhodes. The ruins of a shrine of Helios are the only remains dating from this period. It is said that the people of Arykanda's extravagance, idleness and inclination to unbridled pleasure led them to attach themselves to Antiochos III in 1970 BC, in the hope that this would release them from their obligations to the Ptolomeys. In the 2C BC Arykanda became of member of the Lycian Confederacy and struck its own coins. In AD 43 Claudius made Lycia and Arykanda into a Roman province. In the 11C AD the town, then under the Byzantine name *Akalanda*, faded into insignificance. Even in ancient times Arykanda was known as an extraordinarily beautiful town because of its position on a steep, terraced mountainside, surrounded by rushing mountain streams.

Ancient town: The charming *stadium* dating from the Hellenistic period is on one of the upper terraces to the N. The arena in the W. is 52 ft. wide. Part of it was buried by a landslide, the remaining section is 262 ft. long. Only five rows of seats survived, on the mountain side. The *theatre* on the terrace below it, completely excavated by the University of Ankara, is entirely Greek in style, and in good condition. On the next terrace is an *odeion*. On the S. entrance side was a *columned hall* with mosaic pavement 246 ft. long and 26 ft. wide: above the entrances in the outer façade is a coffered frieze with figures. S. of this 'stoa' is the *agora*. W. of this area at the same level as the theatre is the *buleuterion* of the town, with a long stoa leading to it. The walls up to the second storey have survived of a large *thermal bath* further S. of the agora by the *gymnasium*. Two important necropolises and remains of other buildings complete this picture of a ruined ancient town of some importance.

Arykanda, Roman thermal baths

Aspendos

Antalya   p.574☐ G 6

History: According to ancient tradition the town was founded, like Perge and Side in Pamphylia, by the famous seers Mopsus and Calchas. They were retreating with units of the Greek army after the battle for Troy (*c.*1200 BC) and settled here. The Lydian king Croesus also took Aspendos in the early 6C BC. After Cyrus' victory over Croesus in 546 BC the city became Persian. In the early 5C Aspendos struck its own silver coins.

In the Persian wars Xerxes assembled a large army and an enormous fleet outside Aspendos in 469 BC, against Athens and the Delian League. The Athenian general Cimon won a brilliant double victory over fleet and army near Aspendos at the mouth of the broad river Eurymedon, then navigable. In 386 BC, after Athens lost the Peloponnesian War against Sparta, the Persians were once more lords of all the cities of Asia Minor.

In 333 BC Alexander the Great took over from the Persians. Ambassadors from Aspendos went out to meet him, offered to submit and asked that they might not be occupied. They reached an agreement on payment of 50 gold talents and horses. Outside Sillion Alexander learned that Aspendos did not intend to keep to the agreement. To the amazement of the people of the city he immediately turned round and finally took the town, along with fifty talents, distinguished hostages and an annual tribute.

Under Roman rule Aspendos became much more extensive and prosperous. The town owed its commercial prosperity to salt from the lake of Crepia, mentioned by Strabo. It dried up in the summer, leaving the salt available for mining. The town finally went into decline because of the silting up of the harbour, the rise of Antalya and later, Byzantine centralism.

Ancient town: The *Roman theatre* is the best condition of any from the classical period and one of the largest ancient buildings in Asia Minor. It was built in the 2C AD by the local architect Xenon for the Curtius brothers in the reign of Marcus Aurelius and, according to the inscription, dedicated to 'the gods of the country and the imperial house'. The Roman building is different from a classical Greek theatre in that it is completely closed to the outside. The semicircular cavea, with a diameter of 313 ft. at the level of the highest row of seats, has a stage façade 98 ft. high in front of it. This 'scena frons', 203 ft. wide is highly articulated and was used as a variable backdrop for the action. It blocks the spectators' view of the countryside, in contrast with the Greek theatre. A broad diazoma above the lower 21 rows of seats makes it possible to move around comfortably. Above the next 19 rows of seats, the top of the cavea is formed by a completely restored arcade passage with groin vaulting, increasing the impression of closed intimacy of the space enclosed within the theatre, which could seat a maximum of 20,000 spectators.

The *upper town of Aspendos* was on a twin hill over 130 ft. high. The theatre is set next to the lower of the two. On the other side of the dip, on the larger hill to the W., was the town centre. The steep hill had to be secured by walls and gates in only a few places. The main entrance gate is S. of the theatre. On the top of the hill are remains of an agora, to the E. is the outline of the basilica, 328 ft. long. Adjacent is a side building with walls over 6 ft. thick and over 52 ft. high. W. of the agora is a long market hall with two-storey shops, in the N. is the 105 ft. long, 49 ft. high façade of the nymphaeum, which provided the water supply. Adjacent to this was probably the council house. The fine *aqueduct* NW of the hill is the most impressive monument after the theatre. Some of the arches have survived in good condition, and the work is a fine example of Roman hydraulic engineering. Here water was brought from far away in the mountains by a system of communicating pipes. There are remains of two water

Aspendos, Roman-Seljuk bridge (below), theatre (right)

Assos, metope frieze and architrave relief

towers by the aqueduct. The former Eurymedon river (Köprü-Çayı) is still crossed by the large Seljuk *humped bridge* on Roman foundations.

Assos/Behramkale

Çanakkale   p.564 ☐ B 3

Assos is even more interesting for its situation than its ancient remains. It is in the NW of Asia Minor, opposite Lesbos on the S. coast of the Troad and at the entrance to the Gulf of Edremit on a steeply terraced trachyte cone (767 ft.). In the second millennium BC the Leleges (a mythical tribe placed in the Troad by Homer) had their capital here. Aeolians from Mlethymna (Lesbos) established a Greek harbour colony *c.*1000 BC. This came under Lydian rule (Croesus) in 560–546, was Persian from 546–479 and then a member of the Attic League until 405 BC. From 350 BC it was in the territory of the eunuch Hermeias, tyrant of Lesbos and the Troad, and from 334 BC subject to the empire of Alexander the Great, then Pergamene from 241–133 BC, and from 133 BC Roman; thus this geographically exposed coastal settlement is a mirror of the patterns of changing rule on the coast of Asia Minor.

For a time the harbour and trading town achieved academic distinction: from 348–345 BC two members of Plato's academy in Athens, Aristotle and Theophrastes, lived and researched at the branch of the academy (biology, botany, zoology) founded by Plato's pupils Erastos and Corsikos. The Stoic Cleanthes (*c.*331–232 BC) also came from Assos. He held the view that the universe is a living being, with the sun as its heart. In AD 58

Assos, Doric capital of Athena temple

Paul sailed S. from Assos on his second missionary journey; his visit to Assos strengthened the early Christian colony there.

The remains of the ancient harbour town which can be seen today were excavated in 1881–3 by the American School in Athens.

Site: The town covers an area of just under a square mile. The remains are largely Hellenistic and Roman, and a clear example of the type of settlement favoured by the earliest Greek colonists: an acropolis with inner defensive wall, a lower town with an outer wall 3 km long and 62 ft. high, with necropolis ouside it; the harbour is below the lower town. At the centre of the acropolis was a Doric *temple of Athene*, dating from *c.*530 BC. The remains of the stylobate and of some columns and capitals give an impression

of the original building. Material from the temple and from a Byzantine church was used again in the construction of an early Ottoman *mosque* (probably under Murat 1). Its ruins are also to be seen on the acropolis. A massive *gatehouse* in a section of the *town wall* which has survived relatively intact leads into the centre of the lower town, with recognizable outlines of buildings such as the *agora, theatre, gymnasium, buleuterion* (3&2C BC). The *necropolis* outside the town gate (more recent excavations) contains Greek and Roman sarcophagi; Assos was famous for the manufacture of sarcophagi.

Aydın

Aydın is at the foor of the Gevizli Dağı

(Mlessogis) at the N. extremity of the Büyük-Menderes valley on the little Tabak Çay (Evdon) river, which flows into the Menderes. The Islamic history of the town was remarkable; it was occupied by the Seljuks after the battle of Malazgirt in 1071 (victory of Alp Arslan over the Byzantine emperor Romanos IV Diogenes). Aydın was ruled by numerous overlords until it finally came under the Turks in 1280, and was given the name *Güzel Hisar*. First it was Seljuk, in 1310 a Turkish prince of the Aydınoğlu family ruled here, and thenceforward the town was known by its present name. Aydın became Ottoman for the first time under Mahmut II in 1249. It burnt down in the Graeco-Turkish war in 1922, and became provincial capital under Atatürk in 1924.

Alihan Kümbeti (Üveys-Paşça quarter): This is a 14C building. There is a tomb with dome, with a tile mosaic over the door; four graves inside.

Üveys Paşça Camii (in Köprülü mahallesi, Sakatya Caddesi): built 1568.

Ramazan Paşça Camii (in Ramazan Paşça mahallesi, in the market place): originally built in 1594.

Bey (Süleyman Bey) Camii (near the station): This is one of the finest buildings in Aydın, built 1683. Şadırvan with pyramid dome.

Cihanoğlu (Cihanadze) Camii (in Köprülü mahallesi): This was built in 1756, in square plan. Its style is Turkish baroque, and there is a pretty şçadırvan with 12 columns and marble pool. 15 steps lead into the mosque.

Environs: Tralles (100 yards NW): This was the home town of Anthemius of Tralles, one of the two architects of Hagia Sophia in İstanbul, and the place where the Ephebos of Tralles was found, now in the Archaeological Museum in İstanbul. The site is not worth visiting for the ruins alone, but for the combination of ruins and landscape. However, special permission is necessary as Tralles is in a military zone.

Tralles is an elliptical settlement almost 2,000 yards long and over 1,000 yards wide, first mentioned as a Persian military colony in the second half of the 5C BC. It is set about 300 ft. above Aydi'n on a mountain terrace (Güzel Hisar: 'beautiful castle') that falls away sharply on three sides (W.,E.,S.). As **Seleucia** it was for a time part of the Seleucid empire, belonged to Pergamon until 133 BC, then fell to Rome with the rest of the Pergamene empire. The Emperor Augustus rebuilt the town completely after an earthquake, and it was thus known as *Caisareia* until the end of the 1C AD. It became the seat of a bishop c.AD 100. Under the Seljuks (13C) it was the residence town of a principality, and the Karaosmanoğlu dynasty ruled here until 1822.

On walking around the site it is possible to discern the outline of a *stadium*, a *theatre* on the acropolis hill with a subterranean tunnel in the orchestra, a *shrine of Dionysos* (about 200 ft. from the stadium), an *agora*, three arches (known as üç göz: 'three eyes') that were part of a *gymnasium; two Byzantine churches* are still in evidence in outline. There is a little museum showing finds from Tralles.

Ayvalık

Ayvalık, ancient **Cydonia,** is a little town on the Aegean coast set on a peninsula in the Gulf of Edremit opposite the island of Midilli (Lesbos). The group of islands in the gulf is called Yund Adaları, Hecatonnesoi in ancient times. Ayvalık was completely destroyed in the Greek War of Independence.

The Greek population was exchanged for Turks from Midilli, Crete and Macedonia as a result of the treaty of 30 January 1923 concerning the exchange of population. The town has no historical monuments, but is a popular resting place for tourists in transit. There are pretty fish restaurants by the harbour.

Balıkesir

Balıkesir   p.564□B 3

Balıkesir (Balıkesri; the name is formed from Palaeo Kastro Eskihisar) is in NW Anatolia in the old Mysia territory. It was founded by the Turkish emirs of the Karası (Karesi) in 1303 and conquered by the Ottomans in 1363. The town played an important role in the Wars of Liberation. Mobilization against the Greek invasion of 1919 took place in Balıkesir, which was still known as *Karası* (Karesi) until 1926.

Karesi Bey Türbesi (in Mustafa Fakıh mahallesi, near the Paşa Camii): tombs of the founder Karası Bey (d. 1330) and his 5 sons. There is a Kufic inscription on the sarcophagus.

Paşa (Zağnos Paşa) Camii (near the türbe): This was built in 1461 by Mehmet Fatih's tutor. Atatürk preached for freedom in this mosque on 7 February 1923. Next to it is the *türbe* of Zağnos Paşa (d. 1466).

Yıldırım Camii: This was built in the late 14C and was restored on several occasions.

Bandırma

Balıkesir   p.564□C 2

This was a port on the Sea of Marmara (Greek name *Panormos*), inhabited principally by Greeks and Armenians under Ottoman rule. There was a major fire here in 1874. It is now an active trading centre. There are ships to İstanbul.

Environs: Erdek (about 20 km. NW on a peninsula): This is a small resort, connected to the mainland by a narrow tongue of sandy land; the wooded Kapıdağ (Dindymos).
About 7–8 km. before Erdek near Belkıs is the trading town of **Kyzikos**, founded in 756 BC from Miletus, and capital of the province of Hellespontos under Diocletian. Ruins (town wall, theatre, amphitheatre, temple of Zeus). The podium and lower section of the temple have survived; it was once considered one of the wonders of the world. Hadrian had it rebuilt.

Beyşehir

Konya   p.574□G 5

This is a 13C Seljuk foundation, capital of the feudal lord and founder Emir Eşref, standing at a height of 3,773 ft. at the S. extremity of Lake Beyşehir (Beyşehir Gölü). Beyşehir is on the site of the Byzantine *Karallia*, and is probably also the successor of the ancient city of *Parlais*.

Eşrefoglu mosque: Built in 1296 by the son of the founder, this is one of the most important and beautiful wooden mosques in Anatolia. It and the great mosque in Afyon are fine examples of this type of columned hall without arches and with flat

Eflatun Pınar (Beyşehir), Hittite fountain shrine

wooden ceilings. As usual the ceiling in the nave is slightly raised, in the shape of a gable, and the columns are set slightly farther apart, but without the desired effect of emphasizing the nave. The description 'forest mosque' is apt. The massive ceiling beams are examples of the finest carpentry; it is supported by 40 slender wooden columns (knotty pine trunks) with skilfully carved stalactite capitals. The space is majestic and beautiful. The mihrab has fine old *faience* in dark turquoise. The large singers' pulpit in front of it, the minbar and the small singers' pulpit are also fine specimens of wood carving. The founder's *türbe* is on the E. side. Opposite this beautifully maintained mosque is the great *Seljuk bedesten*, rebuilt to house the *new museum*. In late 1986 other buildings dating from the Seljuk period were still in a state of disrepair.

Environs: Eflatun Pınar (14 km. N. in the direction of Isparta: turn off to the right following the narrow metalled road for 5.5 km., then take the track on the left for another 1.5 km.): This is an important *spring shrine* from the period of the Hittite Empire (1450–1200 BC). The spring emerges from the bottom of the dip with the force of a fully-fledged river and forms a pool almost 100 ft. in diameter. The 23 ft. wide ashlar shrine is on the N. bank. Each block is decorated with a relief on the S. side. Clearly this construction was assembled at a later date from the remains of the original shrine. In the upper row is a winged sun, supported at the side by double creatures. On the left is an enthroned god with pointed headgear, and on the right a goddess with platelike Hathor hair. Scholars are in dispute about the significance of the shrine. J. Mellaart considers it to be an Arzawa shrine with

Kubadabad (Beyşehir), summer palace of Alaeddin Kaykobad I

thunderstorm god and sun goddess. Kurt Bittel sees it as a Hittite victory monument dating from the time of Tudhaliya IV (1236–1219 BC). E. Laroche suggests that the left-hand figure is a mountain god and the one on the right a spring goddess; he interprets the complete work simply as a symbol of the life-giving elements sun, earth and water.

Fassılar (Misthia; 10 km. SE of Beyşehir): In the village is a **large sculpture** 24 ft. high on an ancient site about which little detail is known. The monumental statue may have been in the stadium, but academics differ about its origin and meaning. It is thought to originate from the period of the Hittite Empire or the late Hittite period. It is also thought to be associated with the spring shrine in Eflatun Pınar 40 km. away, and may have been intended as decoration for it. The position of the principal figure above the

smaller central figure and flanking lions suggests a god, and so do the horns on his headgear.

Kubadabad: Near the village of Gölyaka on the W. bank of Lake Beyşehir archaeologists have excavated the Kubadabad summer residence, built by the Seljuk sultan Alaeddin Kaykobad I of Konya (1219–36). The road to the site is poor.

Beyşesultan/Civril

Denizli   p.572☐E 4

The hill (tepe) of Beyşultan is 65 km. SE of Uçak, 10 km. S. of Civril. S.Lloyd and J.Mellaart excavated a *prehistoric settlement* here, completing the work in 1959. The important finds are in the Archaeological Museum in Ankara. Beyşultan was

Işıklı (Beyşesultan), rock tombs

inhabited from the late chalcolithic to the Byzantine period, with a break of *c.*400 years after the New Bronze Age (13C, Level II). 21 cultural levels were discovered for the chalcolithic period alone, to a thickness of 36 ft. From the Old Bronze Age a double shrine of a god and a goddess was found, built up over 4 cultural levels. Each cella contained dedicatory horns and sacrificial vessels. One cella contained images of the Magna Mater. The god's symbol was a pole set upright in the cella. An altar for blood sacrifices was also found. This double cult continued to Level II. In Level V (*c.*1900 BC) interesting remains were found of a spacious palace with astonishing parallels with Mallia on Crete. In the late 18C the palace, presumed to be that of the Hittite king Labarna, was destroyed. The extensive excavation shafts in the hill allow the sequence of levels to be studied. On another hill is the solitary tomb of an Ottoman dignitary.

Environs: Işıklı (10 km. E.): The ancient name *Eumeneia* derives from the brother of Attalos II (159–138 BC), who founded the town. There are striking caves in the rocks above, suggesting an older cult customary in this area. Near the modern village of Işıklı there are ancient *rock tombs* above the road, also some remains of ancient buildings in the village. There have been no excavations.

Bileçik

Bileçik   p.564☐EF 2

Ancient **Agrilium** and Byzantine **Belikoma** are NW of Eskişehır.
No significant evidence is extant about their early history. Belikoma was one of the first places to be conquered by the Oğuz clans around Ertogrul *c.*AD 1300, who exercised their fief in the pastureland around Sögüt (see below). Edebali was a comrade-in-arms and Gazi (faith hero) of the Ottoman founding father Ertogrul.

Orhan Camii: This is a plain, early Ottoman single-roomed mosque (early 14C) with one dome, a perfect example of the type. It is to be found in the dip below the town. It is much respected by the Turks as a mosque from the time of the founding fathers. This beautiful site also contains the **Edebali mausoleum** (14C) and the resting place of other 'Osmangazini' and Hatun, in a lower beehive tomb.

Karasu Köprü: This bridge with 8 arches was designed by Sinan. Little remains of the acropolis and Belikoma castle.

Environs: Demircihöyük: Early Bronze Age settlement mound (1st half of the 3rd millennium BC), excavated by the German Archaeological Institute. Pots, figurines and other finds are to be seen in the Eskişehir museum.

Osmaneli (35 km. N.): This is ancient *Leukä*. In the part of the town W. of the main road there are the complete ruins of a Byzantine church, of indeterminate date. Closer examination suggests that it was probably a neo-Byzantine building (19C historicism) associated with the Greek population of the town, which was probably formerly quite large. Nearby there is also a large and impressive Greek silk factory with the villa of the former proprietor. **Geyve** (30 km. NW of Osmaneli, 3 km. to the right): this is the ancient Tataion. In the village there is an Ottoman *bridge* in good condition over the river Sakarya. It was built under Sultan Beyazıt II (1481–1512). About 30 km. N., immediately before reaching **Adapazarı**, after the turning for İstanbul, W. of the road, is the most famous building in Byzantine-Bithynia: the *Justinian bridge* over the Sakarya river (Sangarios in ancient times). The bridge is almost 500 yards long, and dates from AD 560. The bridge has 12 massive, squat arches, and today spans a dry valley, as the Sakarya has long since changed its course. Adapazarı is a modern industrial town with no historic sights.

Söğüt (29 km. SE of Bileçik): In the middle of the 13C AD the Oğuz leader Ertogrul, who was passing through with about 400 families on his way to Anatolia, intervened in a battle near this little town. Because of him the battle was won won by the Seljuk sultan Alaeddin Kaykobad I, who was hard pressed by the Mongols. Ertogrul was given the pasture land around Söğüt for himself and his Turcomen as a thanks-offering. Ertogrul had instinctively helped the weaker party, without knowing the combatants. The basis for the Ottoman Empire was established. Ertogrul led other campaigns for the sultan and on his own behalf against Byzantines near the frontier, and his originally modest clan fief grew as a result of further gifts from the sultan and his own conquests between Söğüt and Bursa. His

Bileçik, Orhan Camii

son Osman distinguished himself particularly as a warrior. Ertogrul died in 1289. The father of the Ottoman dynasty was buried in a türbe 2 km. N. of Söğüt. It was rebuilt by Mehmet I in the early 15C in the beautiful old Ottoman style, and often rebuilt, though with little improvement. The tomb is surrounded by 13 more tombs of members of the clan, and is one of the national shrines of Turkey (illuminated at night). In honour of their Gazi (faith hero) Ertogrul, Yürüks of the Karakeçeli tribe assemble here from great distances every year on the last Sunday in September and celebrate their patron's birthday with prayers, mounted games and a mass meal (Şölen) in which bulgur is eaten from 6 enormous cauldrons. The Oğus families were still Shiities in their adopted country, Persia, and originally celebrated the feast of Ertogrul on a Shiite feast day, the equinox on 9

March. The Yürük festival was transferred to the autumn under Hamid II.

Vesirhan (10 km. N. of Bileçik): 17C *Ottoman caravanserai*. The outer walls of the han, to the W. of the road, have survived in good condition and enclose a hall with a surface area of 22,389 sq ft. The façade is 262 ft. wide, and faces the street. 3 portals with ogee arches and well carved and jointed jambs lead into the central hall, 66 ft. wide and 85 ft. deep. From here there is access to the side halls, each 98 ft. wide.

Birgi

Manisa   p.572☐D 4

Birgi, 45 km. SE of Sardes (metalled road), is a typical Turkish country town of the kind now found only in out of the way places. The town has a great range of 18&19C buildings with flat hipped roofs. The largest, the Çakirağa Konağı, is particularly impressively built and decorated, and worth careful examination. The *Ulu Cami* (Great Mosque) in the upper part of the town is an unusual building from the period of the emirate of the Sarukhanids. The building incsription contains the date 1312, which is very early for the W. coast. The large rectangular prayer room with the kibla wall on the wide side is of the old Seljuk kufa type. The wooden flat roof is supported by monotonous rows of columns under supporting arches. The minbar is a famous masterpiece of Seljuk wood carving. It is not executed using pure Kündekari technique, but in one of the techniques which succeeded it, consisting of very skilful flat carving.

Bitlis

Bitlis   p.578☐S 4

The capital of the province of the same name is picturesquely sited on the slopes

Bitlis, citadel

which the Bitlis Suyu has carved into the mountainous surroundings. Originally called *Balaleson*, is said to have been founded by Badis, a legendary general of Alexander the Great's in the last third of the 4C BC. In 641 the town was conquered by Arabs under Caliph Omar. It became Seljuk in the 11C and Mongol in the 13C. The important medieval trading centre was used from the 16C as the residence of the 'Begs', Kurdish feudal lords who were able to maintain their independence of the Ottoman Empire until 1848, when they became part of it.

Citadel: This dominates the town with its thick walls and massive polygonal towers. Its date is unclear, but the core of the building must be Byzantine, rebuilt and extended in the Ottoman period. In 1911 it was partially pulled down so that

the stone could be reused, but despite this is still an impressive building.

Also worth seeing: *Ulu Camii,* founded in 1126 by an Ortokid emir. *Alemdar Camii* (1198). *Gökmeydani Camii,* a Seljuk building (1216). *Şerefı Camii* (1528). *Ihâsihe Şerafhan Medresesi* (1592) is fortress-like in appearance. *Alaman Hani* (1502): This is a complex with inn, medrese, mosque and baths.

It is worth simply walking round the residential area, where the stone houses are often beautifully decorated, particularly the windows, which makes a charming impression. There are hot sulphur springs below the town on the left bank of the river.

Environs: Garzan (also **Zok**; about 65 km. SW): This town was called **Arzan** in the Middle Ages, and the ruins of a citadel

dating from this period can still be seen there. The town is reached on the road to Diyarbakır. After 57 km., in Haydar Köprüsü turn SW to reach Garzan.

Hizan (40 km. SE): A trip to the monasteries around Hizan should be undertaken only with a local guide. From Bitlis take the road which runs along the S. bank of Lake Van, but leave it and head SE in Kotum, on the W. extremity of the lake. The medieval *fortress* of Eski Hizan (Old Hizan) is about 10 km. NE of the present village. The *monastery ruins* in the area date from the 10&11C. *Our Lady of Hzar* is 4 hours' walk from Nizar Köprü (=Pira Nizar). The *Holy Cross of Hizan* (Chinitzor) is near the village of Bereket Köyü. The third monastery is the *Göçimen Kilisesi* (Our Lady of Baritzor).

Malabadı bridge (*Malaberd bridge;* 125 km. SW): This elegant saddleback bridge has crossed the Batman Suyu, a tributary of the Tigris, since AD 1146. It is today no longer part of the important E.–W. connection between Diyarbakır and Van, but is S. of the modern long-distance road. The large pointed arch, built under the Ortokids, has a span of 115 ft. The curved approaches are supported by several round arches flanking the central arch. There used to be small rest rooms for travellers at each end of the bridge. Only the look-out posts and relief decoration and the carefully laid stone blocks have survived.

Siirt (99 km. SW): This is the principal town of the province of the same name near the Syrian and Iraqi border. In the Abassid period the town, which now has a population of about 47,000 inhabitants, was an important trading and cultural centre. The surrounding countryside, through which numerous tributaries of the Tigris flow, has a notoriously cold and snowy winter, but provides grazing for a breed of goat with particularly fine hair from which the famous Siirt blankets are made. There were recorded Babylonian and Assyrian settlements in the 2nd millennium BC, followed by Urartians, Medes and Persians. In the Roman period this was the border with the Sassanid Empire. Their successors, the Byzantines and Arabs also fought for possession of the town, which became part of the Ottoman Empire after the victory of Sultan Selim I over the Persian Safawids. From Bitlis, take the road in the direction of Diyarbakır to Haydar Köprüsü (57 km.), then branch off to Siirt (another 42 km.).

The *Ulu Cami*, built by the Seljuk sultan Muheddin Mahmud in 1129 was restored in 1129. There is a wooden pulpit from this mosque in the Ethnological Museum in Ankara.

Also worth seeing are: *Cumhuriyet Camii* (Mosque of the Republic), probably founded in the Abassid period in the 8C. *Kavam Hamamamı*, a Seljuk bath dating from the 11C. *Sokul Ayn*, an 11C Seljuk well. *Mesudiye Medreses. Zinciriye Medreses. Archaeological Museum*.

About 8 km. NE of Siirt in **Aydınlar** (*Tillo*) is the *mausoleum* of Ibrahim Hakkı,

which now accommodates a local private astronomical museum.

Tatvan (26 km. NE): This little town is at a height of 5,643 ft. at the W. extremity of Lake Van. There are no notable build-ings in the town itself. The suburb of Tat-van Tuğ is the terminus of the railway from Malatya and departure point for the ferry to Van (rail and car). Tatvan is a good base for a trip to *Nemrut Daği* (not to be confused with the mountain of the same name near Adıyaman with the famous Commagene colossal heads). To do this continue towards Ahlat, leave the road which subsequently runs along the N. bank of Lake Van, but turn off to the left after 4 km.. It is possible to cover the 15 km. in a cross-country vehicle, and there is also a footpath to the cone of the former volcano (active in 1141) from the NE. The crater has a lake at a height of 9,278 ft. The mountain is formed of obsidian of a glassy dark-green colour.

On the journey from Bitlis you pass 3 *caravanersais* one after the other, all in a poor state of repair. First, on the left, comes the **Papsin Hanı,** then (14 km. from Bitlis) on the left of the road through the village of the same name the Ottoman **Başhan** and finally, this time on the right, just before the turning to Elâziğ and Erzurum, the Ottoman **Alaman Hanı.**

Ziyaret: This place, little visited by tourists, is on the road to Batman and Diyarbakır, a few km. beyond the turn-ing to Siirt. Despite the lack of attention from the outside, the Islam local saint buried in the *Veysel Karani Hazretleri Türbesi* plays an important part in the lives of the local people. The mausoleum, on the right near a plain domed mosque with pencil minaret of a later date, consists of a square domed main room, in front of which is a low, slightly narrower narthex with a flat roof. The two entrances in the façade, one for each sex, have round arches and doors flanked with quarter columns with ornamented capitals within a larger, rectangular niche which is hardly recessed at all. The actual tomb behind it, today protected by glass walls and an iron grille,

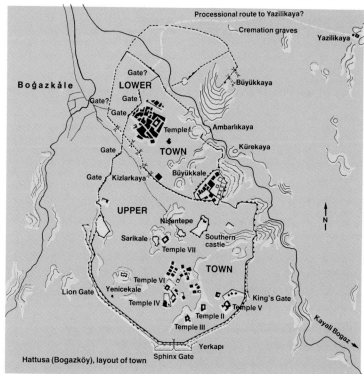

Hattusa (Bogazköy), layout of town

Labels on map: Processional route to Yazilikaya? · Cremation graves · Yazilikaya · Boğazkâle · Gate? · LOWER · Büyükkaya · Gate? · Gate · Gate · Temple I · Ambarlıkaya · Gate · TOWN · Kürekaya · Gate · Kizlarkaya · Büyükkale · UPPER · Nişantepe · Sarikale · Southern castle · Temple VII · TOWN · Temple VI · Lion Gate · Yenicekale · King's Gate · Temple IV · Temple V · Temple II · Temple III · Yerkapı · Sphinx Gate · Kayali Bogaz · N

is placed under a limestone baldacchino supported by 4 columns. The saint buried here is said to have been one of the first people converted to Islam in the region, and to have attempted, when himself a great age, to visit Muhammad in person, in order to be instructed by him. He died before he could carry out his intention. There are some blocks with ornamental reliefs built into a derelict wall of limestone ashlar by the tomb.

Boğazköy

Çorum   p.566☐K 2

This extensive archaeological site of the old Hittite capital of **Hattuşa** is directly

behind the modern village of **Bogâzkale**, 200 km. E. of Ankara. The site was rediscovered on 28 July 1834 by Charles Texier, who was unable to date the remains. A.H. Sayce made the suggestion that they were associated with the Hittites, whose existence was known from the Old Testament (e.g. Genesis 23). In 1992 C. Humann made the first plan of the site. 2 years later E. Chantre found the first clay tablets with cuneiform writing. There were some texts in Accadian, and some in a hitherto unknown language which V. Scheil recognized as Hittite.

The first systematic excavations were undertaken in 1906&7 and 1911&12 by H. Winckler, T. Makridi and O. Puchstein. In the first year of excavation the great royal palace archive was discovered, containing 2,500 cuneiform tablets. These confirmed that the town was the Hittite capital Hattuşa. The name of this town was known in earlier days, as it was frequently mentioned in the so-called 'Amarna correspondence', the state archive of the pharaoh Echnaton from his capital of Achet-Aton in Egypt.

The Czech linguistic researcher B. Hrozny, who had been working on the Hittite clay tablets since 1915, succeeded in proving in 1920 that the Hittite language was a member of the Indo-Germanic family. Since 1931 the German Archaeological Institute and the German Oriental Society have been working in Boğazköy, at first under K. Bittel and R. Naumann. Work stopped at the beginning of the Second World War then started again in 1952, and is still continuing. Peter Neve is at present in charge of the excavations (1986). The lavish range of finds which have appeared over years of work on the Hittite metropolis are now largely in the museum in Ankara and the little local museum at the N. end of the village of Boğazkale. The majority of the clay tablets with cuneiform script are in East Berlin.

As the excavations show, the site of the subsequent Hittite capital was inhabited at a time (just before 2000 BC) when the Hittites had not yet immigrated into Asia Minor. This pre-Hittite population is known to academics as Hatti. At Boğazköy the Hatti occupied the area of the later Büyükkale acropolis mound (Level IV e) and also an area which stretched for a further 650 yards to the NW below the citadel rock (lower town Level V f–c). After Assyrian merchants from what is now N. Iraq settled in Anatolia in order to found trading colonies around a centre in Kültepe near Kayseri (q.v.), a similar foreign settlement came into being in Boğazköy, a so-called karum. It was immediately adjacent to the living quarters of the Hatti to the NW, roughly where the Great Temple (Temple I) was sited in the Hittite period.

Although the correspondence of these foreign merchants, in Assyrian cuneiform script on clay tablets, is the earliest written source material from Asia Minor, it has not so far been possible to prove conclusively whether the Hittites had already settled in Anatolia at the time of the Assyrian trading colonies (19C BC), or whether they were just starting to immigrate. The original homeland of the Hittites is also still disputed. The most probable theory is that destruction of the kind which can be seen in most Assyrian settlements was caused by the Hittites as they forced their way into the territory. In the late period of Assyrian colonization the Hittites had established a firm foothold in Central Asia and, restricted by the ravines and gorges of the Assyrian uplands, had founded numerous principalities which jockeyed for power with each other and undertook military campaigns.

In the late 18C BC a dynasty from the city of Kuşşara, the site of which has not yet been precisely identified, under their most important ruler Anitta, succeeded in achieving a degree of dominance. First Neşa (the principal settlement of the Assyrian merchants, and known as Kanesh) was conquered and extended as a residence, and after this Pijuşti, king of the local Hatti empire, was defeated. However, Anitta was only able to take his capital Hattus because the population was already weakened by a previous famine. The victorious king destroyed the early Hittite competitor town and placed a curse on the site. Archaeologists believe that a thick layer of burnt material in the lower town and citadel (Level IV d) is associated with this event.

Despite the curse Labarna (also Tabarna), who recognized the strategic usefulness of the site, founded a new town here (late 17C ΙBC) and made it his residence. Its name was the same as that of the previous settlement: Hattuşa. Labarna also changed his own name to Hattusili (Man from Hattuşa). He rapidly extended his power base and even undertook a campaign against Alalach (now Tell Açana near

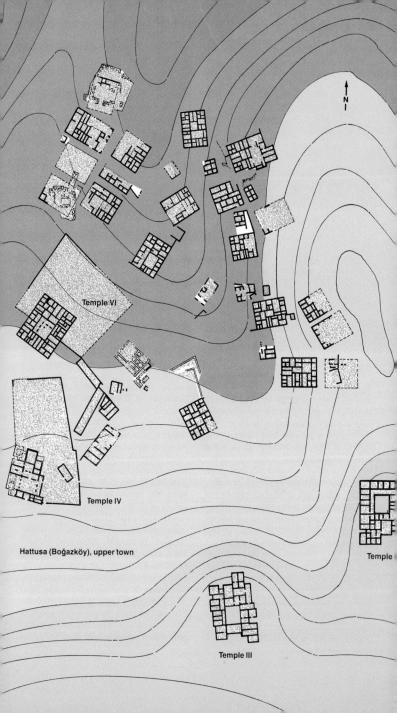

Temple VI

Temple IV

Hattusa (Boğazköy), upper town

Temple

Temple III

Boğazköy, Yerkapı, tunnel

Boğazköy, Sphinx Gate and tunnel

Antakya), and destroyed the town. In a later military campaign by his successor Mursili, Aleppo (then Halpa) and even Babylon were destroyed in the early 16C. Mursili I's murder by his brother-in-law Hantili and his son-in-law Zidanta led to a weaker period for the empire, during which the Black Sea coast was lost, along with other territory, in a raid, probably by the Cashkaeians. Hantili claimed to have extended the fortifications of Hattuşa and built a series of fortifications against the Cashkaeians, but so far no archaeological evidence of this has been found.

Before King Telipinu (late 16C BC) clarified the situation with a regulation of succession, all of his predecessors were violently removed by their successors. When he ascended the throne, Telipinu found a small state that had shrunk to the Anatolian core territories. This ruler was responsible for the oldest Hittite treaty text

known so far, concluded with King Išputsahu of Kizzuwatna (now Cilicia). The new blossoming of the Hittite Empire introduced by Telipinu is occasionally referred to as the Middle Empire. The sequence of rulers in this period is sometimes disputed. One of its representatives, King Zidanta II, renewed the treaty with Kizzuwatna, ruled at the time by King Pilija, also known for a further treaty with Idrimi of Alalach (now Tell Açana near Antakya). The Hittite Empire was obviously weak at the time, as Idrimi managed to conquer some towns which were still subject to Huttaşa under King Hattusili I.

From the mid-15C BC Hittite history was dominated by clashes with the Hurrites, whose strength was increasing, and the Mitannic empire, which they supported. The influence of the Hurrites at the Hittite court must have been very strong, as

the queens and princesses have Hurrite names from the time of King Tudhaliyas II. However, it was also at this time that the dispute with the Hurrites over the strategically important town of Halpa (now Aleppo) reached one of its peaks. Hattisili II, the next king but one, also had to resubjugate the rebellious town.

The power of the Hittites gradually waned. The Egyptian pharoah Amenophis III finally established contact with one of the Hittites' arch enemies, the empire of Arzawa in SW Asia Minor, and under Hattusili's successor Tudhaliya III the capital Hattuşa itself was destroyed by an enemy raid, probably by the Cashkaeians in the N.

The final period of Hittite glory began with Suppiluliuma I (He of the Pure Spring), around the mid-14C BC. Under him the N. section of the upper town of Hattuşa was brought within the ring wall.

This ruler, the son of Tudhaliya III, after he had secured his internal position, undertook a campaign against the Hurritic Mitannic empire. At the same time he established close diplomatic contact with Egypt: about 40 years into hise reign he experienced the Egyptian regency of Amenophis III, the confusions of the Amara period under Echnaton and his queen Nefertete and the period of restoration under the boy pharoah Tutankhamun and the subsequent dispute over the empty throne of the pharoahs. Hittite tradition holds that the widow of an Egyptian pharoah asked Suppiluliuma to send her a Hittite prince as a husband, in order to secure Hittite-Egyptian friendship by a dynastic marriage. His son Zananza, finally sent to Egypt by the Hittite king after much hesitation, was murdered on the way, and Suppiluliuma felt obliged to undertake a campaign of revenge. It is most probable that it was Anchesenamun, the widow of Tutenkhamun, who made this request, even though the letter to the Hittite court is occasionally attributed to Nefertete. Suppiluliuma's successor Arnuwanda II brought the plague to the Hittite empire from a military campaign. This epidemic, which finally killed the king himself, must have decimated the population of Hattuşa and checked the Hittites' activities for almost two decades.

Although Mursili II came to the throne while he was still a child, he quickly restored the old hegemony of his empire with swift and accurately targetted camapaigns. Under the next king, Muwatalli, Hattuşa was abandoned as residence, either to avoid a possible attack by the Cashkaeians in the N., or to be closer to the threatened S. frontier of his empire, so that he could intervene personally if necessary. The new seat of government was Dataşşa, S. of the traditional capital. Its site has still not been found.

In the meantime the Mitannic empire had been eliminated, and the two great powers of the period, the Hittites and the Egyptians, were immediately juxtaposed.

A quarrel about the strategically important town of Kadesh on the Orontes on the S. Becca plain in modern N. Syria led to direct military confrontation between Mutawilli and Rameses I. It is probable that the Hittties won, although Rameses claimed the campaign as his own victory, for purposes of propaganda at home.

Finally both opponents yielded in the face of the increased strength of the Assyrians as the third great power. Under King Hattusli III, who had previously removed Urhi-Tešub, who was entitled to the throne (and who had ruled briefly as Mursili III), a peace treaty was finally signed with Rameses II. This was the first treaty binding by international law in the history of mankind. Reconciliation was finally sealed when 2 Hittite princesses were sent to the court of the pharoahs, and in the 34th year of Rameses' reign one of them was raised to the rank of chief royal consort.

Under Hattusili the capital was moved back to Hattuşa, and the king also extended the acropolis of Büyükkale and probably also commissioned the great main temple in the lower town on the site of the former Assyrian trading colony. He

Boğazköy, Yerkapı, entrance to tunnel from inner town

is also credited with the foundation of the new town to the S. and the building of the town wall with gateways decorated with reliefs.

In order to meet increasing threats from the Assyrians, Hattusili's successor Tudhaliya IV agreed a trade embargo against their common enemy with the Amurru king Şauşga-muwa: no Assyrian merchant was permitted to set foot on the territory of either party to the treaty. The pharoah Merenptah, son and successor of Rameses II, was able to stave off a famine in the Hittite empire by sending grain. This was the point at which the final extension of Hattuşa took place: supplementary gates and halls were built on the acropolis, and the courtyards were paved. The upper town achieved its final appearance. The rock shrine of Yazılıkaya, about 3 km. from Boğazköy, also dates in the main from this period.

The last Hittite king about whom authenticated source material is available was Suppiluliuma II. He became involved in fierce fighting, above all at sea, with invaders from the island of Alašja (now Cyprus), the first emissaries of the so-called Peoples of the North and of the Sea. The Hittite empire finally collapsed *c.*1200 BC under the storm of these attackers, who then thrust down the coast of Lebanon and Palestine, and were finally prevented from entering Egypt by Rameses II in a combined land and sea battle. This wave of destruction is documented by a thick layer of burnt material in Boğazköy.

Some authorities suggest that a small Hittite state with its capital in Boğazköy/Hattuşa was still in existence after Suppiluliuma II. In terms of cultural history the end of the Hittite empire and the invasion of the Peoples of the Sea marks the beginning of the Iron Age. The entire Hittite period was in the Bronze Age.

After a break of about three centuries, the area was settled again in the 9C, this time by the Phrygians, who appeared as Muski in old texts. They refortified the citadel in the late 8C and built a temple to the goddess Cybele, whose cult image just over 4 ft. high was found in a niche of the city gate in the course of excavations.

Archaeologists established that the little Phrygian town was again abandoned in the late 6C BC. It is probable, as Charles

Boğazköy, upper town, temple foundations

Boğazköy, thresholds of storerooms of Temple I

Texier, who discovered Boğazköy, has pointed out, that it was the heavily fortified town of Pteria, mentioned by Herodotus and conquered and destroyed by the Lydian king Croesus in 547 BC. The city, the continous capital of the Hittite kings, with the exception of a brief episode in the 13C BC under King Muwatilli, appears to the modern visitor as a large field of ruins. Only the limestone blocks which formed the foundations have survived of the old buildings, with the exception of the town gates, decorated with reliefs, in the walls of the upper town. Nothing at all remains of the upper part of the buildings, for which a kind of timber-frame technique using clay bricks and wooden beams was used.

The mountainous landscape in which the Hattuşa site is set seems at first entirely unsuitable for a capital city. However, this concealed position, difficult to reach, must have protected the royal residence from destruction by advancing enemies on many occasions. Also the Hittites, talented fortress builders, made maximum use of the topographical situation. Individual exposed rocky eminences like Yenicekale, Şarikale and Nişantepe were fortified separately, and probably contained smaller palaces for the royal family.

The largest hill, Büyükkale, right on the edge of the city, was artificially terraced by the removal of rock, and made into a strongly fortified royal castle with residential palaces and adminstrative buildings including the royal state archive. A bridge, a technical masterpiece for the time, used to span the gorge between the castle hill and Büyükkaya, the hill adjacent to the E. (13C BC). Now only the levelled rock surfaces which once supported the span of the bridge have survived.

At the same time the acropolis marked the

Boğazköy, storage vessels from storerooms of Temple I

dividing line between the lower town in the N. and the upper town in the S.; the site rises steeply by over 800 ft. to the S. There is now a clearly signposted metalled road, several km. in length, leading past all the important monuments in the ruined town, which has an area of about 425 acres, comparable with medieval Nuremberg. In the final building phase, Hattuşa was surrounded by a wall, double in the S., 6 km. long, and an average of 16 ft. wide and 20 ft. high, further fortified every 80 ft. with towers and bastions. Hittite terracotta vessels shaped like fortresses (there is a particularly fine specimen in the museum in Ankara) show that the walls formerly had rounded battlements.

Great Temple (Temple I): This is the only devotional building so far discovered in the lower town. It is also the only one dedicated to two gods, the weather god Teshub and the sun goddess Arinna. Temple V in the upper town also has two sanctuaries, but these are clearly not of equal status. Another unusual feature of Temple I vis-à-vis the other temples is that it is surrounded on all sides by long, extended storehouses, in some of which huge storage jars, known as pithoi, are buried up to their shoulders in the ground. The protruding sections are often decorated.

The modern route round the site leads along the SE façade of the temple, and the sacred precinct is then entered by passing through the foundations of an ancient gatehouse. The first striking feature is the so-called *lion pool*, a large stone basin formerly decorated with a lion at each of its corners. Despite very poor condition, the carved beasts of prey that gave the pool its name are still recognizable. Its function

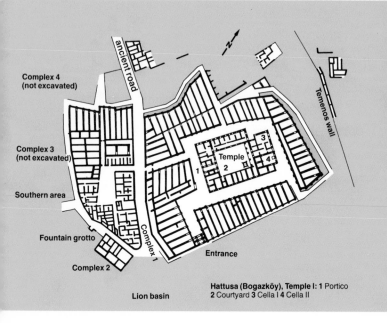

Complex 4
(not excavated)

ancient road

Temenos wall

Complex 3
(not excavated)

Temple
2

3

4

1

Southern area

Fountain grotto

Complex 1

Entrance

Complex 2

Lion basin

Hattusa (Boğazköy), Temple I: 1 Portico
2 Courtyard **3** Cella I **4** Cella II

is unknown. Recently it has been suggested that it was not used for purification, but as a container for the urns containing the mortal remains of rulers. The temple itself, 138 x 210 ft., which doubtless once towered over the surrounding storerooms, probably dates from the time of King Hattusili II (1st half of the 13C BC), and is the best example of the characteristic Hittite temple plan: a monumental portico on the narrow side of the building leads to an inner courtyard, 62 x 85 ft. in this case, which was colonnaded on at least one side. The foundations of an approximately square building of unknown function, thought by some archaeologists to be a tower, have been found in the corner of some courtyards. An extension of the entrance axis leads to the sanctuary, though not in a straight line, but by a twisting route through the groups of rooms at the rear. In contrast with other

oriental cults, the sanctuary was not steeped in mystic darkness, but brightly lit by large windows. The light slits often extended almost to the floor, and can still be discerned in the foundations. In Temple I, with foundations, like those of all the other temples, made of limestone blocks (which supported the timber-frame walls), the foundations of the sanctuaries for the sun goddess and the weather god were in granite.

Another feature typical of a Hittite temple is that the outer walls of the rooms arranged around the courtyard do not run straight, but protrude or are set back according to the different sizes of the various rooms which are juxtaposed apparently randomly, thus producing an irregular ground plan.

NW of the main temple with its storehouses are numerous residential buildings, possibly accommodation for priests and

Boğazköy, stone basin in storerooms of Temple I

other persons associated with the cult. Half a millennium before the building of the temple this was the area inhabited by Assyrian merchants.

SW of the temple precinct and separated from it by an ancient, paved road is is another enclosed, approximately trapezoid area with storage and residential rooms. In its S. corner is a little *spring grotto*, which still provides water. This building has a false vault, and is reached by four steps.

Lion Gate: This is the westernmost of the three town gates decorated with reliefs in the walls of the upper town, double at this point. It takes its name from the two lions' torsos on the outer side of the gate, which was once vaulted in the manner of a Gothic arch. The lions' heads, originally intended to keep evil away from the town with their snarling mouths, are very life-like, in contrast with their stylized manes in a flame pattern with close internal hatching, and with their legs, even more stylized, like unnatural stilts. An extremely shallow scratched inscription can be made out on the body of one of the lions, but only in oblique early-morning light. The text is the the so-called Hittite hieroglyphic script, which probably came into being under Mediterranean influence (c.f Linear A script on Crete), and was used parallel with Hittite cuneiform. At the front entrance with the two lions' heads, as at the other gates of Hattuşa, is a gateway, the full width of the wall, here lined with coarsely cut, but carefully assembled, limestone blocks. At the corners it is still possible to make out the sockets for the great wooden bolt with which the doors (wooden with metal furnishings) could be locked. At the other end of the gateway was a portal with pointed arch with crooked limestone pillars, from the end of which it was possible to look directly across to the fortified hill *Yenicekale*.

Like the other gates of the upper town this building is ascribed to King Hattusili III, after he had moved the capital back from Hattuşa.

Yerkapı and Sphinx Gate: At the southernmost and highest point of the town the wall continues along a massive artificial embankment. This earthwork is carefully covered with limestone blocks on the outside, and has a tunnel opening in its base. The tunnel is impressive: 233 ft. long, and lined with stone blocks leaning inwards like a genuine vault, with wedge-shaped keystones at the apex.

For a long time this tunnel was considered to be an auxiliary exit to be used by defenders of the town for surprise attacks against enemies outside the walls. The tunnel itself would be readily defensible. More recent excavations have completely refuted the military nature of the Yerkapı: the land outside the town at this point is so inhospitable and entirely unsuitable for an approaching army, so that Hattuşa would never have had to contend with an attack from the S. at this point. Also the tunnel exit is not even disguised, but clearly marked and recognizable by massive piers and a limestone lintel. Also 2 flights of steps have been excavated, running equidistant from the tunnel on either side up the artificial slope to the walls. which make a complete mockery of any military or strategic function.

It seems that the only function of the Yerkapı with its tunnel and steps must have been religious.

Just above the tunnel opening, at a height of about 40 ft., at the apex of the artificial embankment, is the *Sphinx Gate*, unfortunately in very poor condition. Outside the building on the W. of the two gateposts, now the only one on the whole site left standing, slight traces can be discerned of one of the sphinxes from which the gate took its name. It is

Boğazköy, Lion Gate

suspected that the lower body and legs of the sculpture were similarly stylized to the Lion Gate. In favourable lighting it is even possible to make out the spiral headdress which once decorated the high pointed headgear of the sphinx figures. The two sphinxes on the other side of the gate looking into the town were different in design. Here not only the the front part of the body, but almost the complete rump with raised wings on the long sides are carved from the stone. Although the sphinxes were found in fragments it was possible to reassemble them. There is one in the museum in Istanbul, and one in the Pergamon Museum in East Berlin.

The tracts of wall to the left and right of the Sphinx Gate are particularly good examples of Hittite building technique. The box masonry consisted of 2 runs of wall reinforced at regular intervals with rectangular towers, whose lower sections

are still recognizable as protruding rectangular bastions. The towers in the main wall and the second wall in front of it were staggered.

King's Gate: The easternmost of the 3 gates with sculptural decoration was named after a relief on the N. gatepost, at first wrongly considered to be a representation of one of the Hittite kings. The figure, very shallow, but modelled throughout, is on the front of the curving pier, made of a single limestone block, and looks inwards, towards the passage through the wall. Details, in particular the crown of horns, show that this must be a god. The relief on the site today is a plaster cast, which is noticeably weathering. The original relief has been taken to the museum in Ankara and still clearly shows the short, hip-length loincloth worn by the figure, with a fine feather pattern,

the only garment which the god is wearing with the exception of the helmet-like crown with cheek flaps. The figure carries a pickaxe in his left hand and the left is raised like a clenched fist. The rolled tip of a sword or dagger quiver rises behind the figure. Despite its heavily stylized nature the successful reproduction of the muscles is impressive, particularly on the legs. On the outside of the gateway it is easiest to imagine how the crooked piers once formed the approximately 20 ft. high gateway, flanked here by two towers 32 by 49 ft. Each gate arch was edged with a broad, protruding strip. Access was by a relatively steep ramp, which ran parallel to the town wall up to the gate.

Temples in the upper town: The other temples of Hattuša are enclosed within the wide outward sweep made by the double

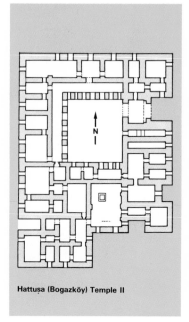

Hattuša (Bogazköy) Temple II

Boğazköy, King's Gate

wall of the town fortifications, set very close to each other. Until recently only 5 such sacred buildings were recognized (Temples II–VI). Excavations in recent years have brought to light a large number of other foundations that the excavators consider must largely be temples. Thus archaeology would confirm the picture of the Hittites as the 'people of 1,000 gods', as they were known in antiquity. The best point from which to see this section of the site is the Yepkapı rise from the Sphinx Gate.

Nişantepe (Nişantaš): This rocky dome in the centre of the upper town is different from the other higher ground, fortified by massive walls, within the town boundary, in that on its E. wall there is a smooth surface with a chiselled text of ten lines of hieroglyphs. It is a memorial inscription for King Suppiluliuma II, the last of the

Hittite rulers. Each line of text is just over 1 ft. high.

Büyükkale: The Hittite kings chose the largest hill in the area as the site of the *citadel* and *palace*. It is on the E. edge of the town, but in the best position strategically, as it is protected by a gorge over 300 ft. deep on the two outer sides.

The oval, or approximately trapezoid site is about 820 ft. long by 460 ft. wide, at the point where the upper and lower towns meet. In order for it to be possible to build the palaces, administrative and domestic rooms within the massive wall which once surrounded the hill on all sides, an artificial plateau had to be created in several terraces, which in places also required supporting walls for the individual stepped levels. As the limestone blocks used for these auxiliary constructions have largely slipped down the hill and as the citadel

in particular, because of its exposed position, has been particularly subject to weather damage, it is hard for the visitor to form an impression of the former building from the combination of areas where rock has been removed (marking the course of the former walls) and from foundation blocks which have survived.

The settlement on the acropolis was conceived as a sequence of several courtyard systems, around which in each case individual, usually multi-storeyed buildings were grouped, with each of the courtyards partially enclosed with columned halls and colonnades. One of the two access gates, each reached by steep flights of steps, is pierced in the defensive wall with towers in the SW. From here to the NE the level of the individual courtyard terraces becomes consistently higher. Each of the units was separated from the one below it by a portal. This division made

for strong defence because a potential attacker was compelled to conquer the fortress in sections. After going through the gate at the SW extremity a path with red sandstone paving led directly to the long lower courtyard. The two courtyards were once separated by a transverse hall 181 ft. long by 23 ft. wide.

The function of the buildings (formerly at least two storeys high) that stood around the edges of the lower courtyard (G and M), is not known. Building J, which is built into the castle wall is related to the water basin, which according to finds must have had religious significance, and to building G. N is probably another gatehouse, through which it was possible to enter the lower courtyard by an older path up the hill.

A monumental portico with three openings led from the lower to the middle courtyard. Immediately to the right is the

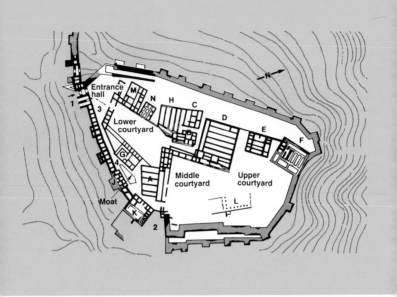

Hattuşa (Boğazköy), Büyükkale 1 SW castle gate
2 SE castle gate **3, 4** Smaller gates

archive building (A), in which about 3,500 clay tablets were found. The NW façade of the central courtyard is formed by building D, 128 x 157 ft., with a long run of storerooms in the lower storey and the royal audience hall, formerly supported by 25 piers, in the upper storey. Access was formerly possible from the middle courtyard. Because of the slope this led directly into the upper storey, and as well as this a passage led down from the lower courtyard W. of the portico to the rooms at ground level, passing the complex formed by buildings H, B and C on the left. In the middle of the latter there was once an open courtyard with basin. This ground plan, and objects found in the building such as dedicatory and votive gifts, suggest that this was once a shrine.

Buildings E and F, which were at the extreme NE, the highest point of the citadel, were palaces for the royal family, i.e. the ruler's private living quarters. Only the points at which the builders cut into the rock can still be seen.

There was another access point to the citadel in the SE, E. of building K, which was set directly by the defensive wall and in which a small clay tablet archive was discovered. This entrance gate made it possible to penetrate directly into the middle and upper castle courtyards, and was possibly reserved for the king. The narrow connecting passage on the inside of the wall between the two entrances to the castle could in case of danger be sealed off by two gates set between these entrances.

Local museum (at the N. end of the modern village of Boğazkale, immediately

Boğazköy, Büyükkale

on the left-hand side of the road from Sungurlu): In the entrance wall ground plans provide information about the development of the town. The exhibition room contains several relief blocks, numerous ceramic vessels and other finds from the ruins, including a small stone head of a goddess with hollow eyes, and typical round, funnel-shaped headgear. This head was found in the lower town, and is particularly notable. The finest pieces are in the museum in Ankara, however.

Bolu

Bolu   p.566□G 2

The city was called **Bithynion**—founded by King Prusias I of Bithynia (AD 125–185)—*Claudiopolis, Hadriana* and *Honorias* in ancient times, and was the birthplace of the beautiful Antinous, the Emperor Hadrian's favourite and travelling companion. Hadrian also favoured Bolu, and encouraged building there, and after almost 1300 years of changing fortunes there was again new building of distinction under Beyazıt I Yılderım. The *Great Mosque (Ulu Camii)* is a reminder of this period (1389–1403). The *Şemsi Paşa mosque*, the *Orta Hamam* and the *Tabaklar Hamam* are the few buildings to remain from the Ottoman period before 1668. In this year Bolu was destroyed by a severe earthquake. In the Ulu Camii (also Karakadi Camii) are remains of ancient sculptures and inscriptions.

Environs: Akçakoca (Greek Diapolis): Black Sea resort with ruined *Genoese fortress*. The Genoese bought special privileges from Byzantium in the 13C.

Mudurnu (54 km. SW): This is a pretty little town in beautiful Pontic countryside with fine Greek domestic architecture. There is an interesting ancient Ottoman hamam.

Üskübü (70 km. NW): This is the ancient **Prusias ad Hypium,** like Bolu founded by Prusias. It is also known as *Konuralp*. The pleasant modern village of üsübü occupies a small part of the formerly rich and flourishing town. In the S., E. of the road, is a large theatre, saved from being plundered for its stone as it was so overgrown. A path now runs through the scena, and there are houses above the edge of the cavea. A few hundred yards above the theatre are remains of a formerly impressive Roman *aqueduct*. Next to the mosque is an Ottoman *well house* with ogee arches. The *Atkapi* (Horse Gate) below the theatre W. of the road has an enormous ancient architrave above it.

Buçak

Burdur   574p.□F 5

This little town 44 km. S. of Burdur has

no sights of its own, but is a good starting point for excursions in the region.

Environs: Incir Han (1 km. N. of the turning for Buçak on the main Antalya-Burdur road turn off to the W., after 1.5 km. turn right, 1.5 km. from there): Formerly a magnificent example of Seljuk han architecture. The low building stands in the hilly landscape in majestic isolation. Apart from the condition of the building nothing has changed as far as the eye can see. The fig trees from which it took its name grow into the smallest chinks and crack of even the most massive masonry. But the han still has a service to perform, although there are no more caravans to break the silence. The courtyard has disappeared, with the exception of the W. foundation walls. The wide entrance in the high arched niche over 6 ft. deep crouches beneath its basket arch. The niche arch is fluted like a shell inside and rests, as in the Susuz han, on small columns with double acanthus capitals, a lion relief with a human face on its back above each column. On the pediment is the building inscription and year of building: 1238&9. On the right and left of the

Mudurnu (Bolu), Greek house

central aisle 7 transverse aisles with tunnel vaults supoported by pointed arches run to the side wall.

Kremna, now **Girme** (2 km. S. of Buçak turn left, it is then 8 km. to thee little village of Girme): The way leads up to the ancient *ruined town* on a high plateau, which drops steeply several hundred feet on the S. side. There is a wonderful view over the Pamun Ovasi (cotton plain) and over to the distant Taurus massif. Little is known of the history of this town excavated by the Turks. Alexander the Great stationed a garrison of archers here in 333 BC because of its importance as a mountain stronghold. There are still extensive remains of buildings confirming the existence of a Roman town, apparently on a square plan. The public buildings are near the S. wall above the steep drop. There a steep path leads through the impressive double gate into the town. On the left is a large ashlar building with tunnel vaulting , and adjacent to the N. the *Forum of Longus* (inscription). About 130 yards E. of this is the *theatre*, with stoa in front of it. On the same line as the stoa to the NE is the *gymnasium* and adjacent to that a *forum* opening to the S. and over

240 ft. wide. W. of the ashlar building, at the level of the S. gate, is a long flight of steps with statue bases near a covered street. All around are houses, shrines, arcades, cisterns, sarcophagi and ruined basilicas of later date. Large numbers of dressed stones of all sizes with reliefs and ornamentation of a high standard can be found lying around, suggesting a wealthy and artistically sensitive population. The wonderful site alone makes this ruined town worth seeing.

Milyas (turn left 25 km. S. of Buçak in the village of **Melli** immediately before the cemetery, then 1.5 km. on foot up the hill): In the *ancient town* there are remains of early Hellenistic walls, predominantly using the polygonal building technique, and remains of the theatre in the NE below the acropolis hill. There is a large ruined building with several entrances near the scena. The large necropolis on the W slope of the hill originally had a large number of sarcophagi and various rock tombs, but is now severely damaged. The remains of this ruined town on its lonely height are surrounded by bushes, and reached only with difficulty after a long climb. Although the situation is

Kremna (Buçak), ancient quarter

Susuz Han (Buçak), overall view

attractive, a visit is not to everybody's taste.

Susuz Han (proceed 10 km. S. from the Buçak turning on the main Burdur-Antalya road, then 1 km. E. in the village of Susuz-Köy): There is a mid-13C Seljuk *caravanserai*. As there is no building inscription, the name of the builder is unknown. The date has been arrived at by analysis of the style. The portal, set in a vestibule almost 25 ft. wide is particularly lavishly and finely ornamented, and surrounded by broad strips of ornamentation. The tranverse wall with inscription has not survived. Above the pointed mukarnas niche is a pointed arch supported by columns with double acanthus capitals. The small side niches to the left and right of the doorway are lavishly decorated and repeat the portal motif. The interior of the hall is in good condition, with just two pits in the

floor dug by robbers. As a result of this the han is now locked, and the key for the tiny padlock is available in the villa 400 yards away. The hall is 85 ft. square. The four barrel vaults of the central aisle are above five arches stretching towards the rear wall, with an elegant dome which from the outside towers over the hall like a massive central tower. Muted light is admitted through the little round-arched windows in the dome cornice and through 5 oculi in the dome. Five transverse aisles run to the side walls on each side of the central aisle. Nine arched windows in the transverse aisles and one in the rear wall, all narrowing to slits on the outside, are further sources of light. The outer walls are supported by 8 massive towers with four different basic designs. The caravanserai is well cared for, and in excellent condition. Building technique and decoration are of outstanding quality.

Haçılar (Burdur), Burdur Museum, neolithic twin vessel

Burdur

Burdur p.572☐F 5

Ancient *Arkania Limnae* is on the E. bank of Lake Burdur. A Hittite settlement has been confirmed on this site on the Afion-Bursa-Antalya N.-S. axis. It is said that the Arzawa princely house came into being in this lakeland area. They were subject to the Hittites and mentioned in Hittite historical sources in 1600 BC. Given its exposed situation Burdur must have been involved in the turbulent history of Anatolia. No particular historical events are known, with the exception of repeated razing to the ground. In 1391 Burdur finally became Ottoman under Beyazıt I.

The earliest signs of building which are still visible date from the late Seljuk period: a small *hamam*. The *Ulu Camii* built by Dündar Bey is early Ottoman (14C). Evidence of the more distant past is only to be found in the museum.

Museum: Exhibits include a fine bulbous jar with twin necks and small handles from nearby Haçılar, and dating from the neolithic period. A statue of a bear and a fine bowl were made in nearby prehistoric Kuruçay-Höyügü *c*.5000 BC. The various representations of the Pisidian-Lydian god Kakasbos on horseback, mythologically comparable with Herakles, are particularly interesting. In the courtyard is a Roman sarcophagus with a peacefully resting couple in the Etruscan style on the lid. There is also a fine Ethnological Section in the building.

Environs: Haçılar (25 km. SW on the road to Tefenni): Here there is a *prehistoric settlement mound* (about 1.5 km. from the

Kuruçay-Höyügü (Burdur)

exuberant female statuettes which abandoned the customary stiff posture of female idols of the period and lay on the floor in casual attitudes. The vertical body axis normally customary in early Anatolian idols is not used here. The curved posture is typical of Haçilar. The significance of these recumbent naked female figures has not yet been established. Fortified villages were discovered in Levels II and III, and a fortress (royal residence) with surrounding buildings was found in Level I, the top layer (*c.* 4975 BC) .

Kuruçay-Höyügü (turn left at yellow sign after about 15 km. on the way from Haçilar-Tefenni, 2 km. from this point): This is a *prehistoric site* which has been excavated and secured in an exemplary fashion. The visitor is standing on the oldest level, from the neolithic period (5500–5200 BC) with foundation walls and implements in their original position. There is also a small lapidarium with stone troughs and pestles. A column of levels to the level of the hill has been left as it was before excavations started, and it is possible to see the vertical stratigraphic sequence of the culture layers going back to the chalcolithic period. Prof. Refik Duru of the University of İstanbul worked here for eight years from 1978, and the site is well worth a visit.

Tefenni (to the SW near the village 45 km. W. of Haçilcar) is the site of the *Kaya Kabatmaları*, fine rock bas-reliefs with representations of the Pisidian-Lydian god Kakasbos, riding a horse. This god is identical with Herakles, always brandishes a club and carries no other weapon. Kakasbos is usually shown in rectangular niches, often with a pediment, as here.

village) dating from the late neolithic period (after 7000 BC), excavated by the British Archaeological Institute in Ankara. The site is now a severely weathered pit, but produced large numbers of the oldest prehistoric finds from the hill cultures, along with Çatal Hüyük (6500–5750) SE of Konya and Çayönü (7250–6750 BC) near Diyarbakır. Tombs were found in 8 of the 9 building levels—with the exception of Level V—and all the levels produced quantities of ceramics. Architectural phases can be clearly distinguished. Neolithic ceramics are monochrome, chalcolithic work has geometrical decoration. 22 small terracotta statues were found at level VI, some of which caused academic dissension. They were dated 5500–5400 BC by the radio carbon method. They are made of clay, and partly fired, partly covered with a paint-like substance. The finds included

---

Bursa

History: Legend has it that Hannibal, whilst fleeing from the Romans, advised

Bursa, Yeşil Türbe ▷

Bursa, Ulu Cami, prayer hall

his host King Prusias I of Bithynia to found a city at the foot of Mount Olympos in Bithynia (8,343 ft.). According to Pliny the Younger, Prusias founded ancient **Prusa** on the mountain terrace above the fertile river plain a little later, in 186 BC. The site is strategically favourable, and there are also hot springs at temperatures from 37–82C, which gave Bursa a reputation as a thermal spa even in ancient times. Emperors and kings used the spa facilities, but this was all that gave the town a historical reputation. In 74 BC Nicomedes III of Bithynia left Prusa to the Romans, and Byzantium took it over from them. In 950 the town was destroyed by Arabs. After another short period of Byzantine rule (with the Seljuks in between) Bursa finally became Ottoman in 1326 after a 10 year siege by Sultan Orhan, thus fulfilling the dream of his father Osman, the first sultan of the young

state. Bursa remained his radiant capital until 1368. Neither Christians nor Jews were allowed to live in the old town, within the city walls, the present castle precinct. In 1368 Murat I moved the residence to Edirne, to be nearer his eastern European sphere of interest; this was also a remnant of the old nomadic mentality. The Mongol Timur-Leng laid Bursa waste in 1402, and in 1413 only the citadel withstood pillaging by the Karamanids. Bursa reached the peak of its achievement under the art-loving Mehmet I (1413–21). Bursa was harder hit economically by the population exchange of Greeks and Turks under Atatürk after 1922 than by the fire of 1801 or the earthquake of 1855. The modern town, however, is developing in a striking fashion.

Ulu Camii (Great Mosque; in the bazaar

Bursa, Yeşil Türbe, carved door

quarter): This mosque was started in the late 14–early 15C by Murat I, continued by Beyazıt I and probably not completed until 1421 by Mehmet I. This work of three generations is not a sultan's mosque, it is a city mosque for daily prayer. The large rectangular building, the largest of the Ottoman piered mosques, has 20 domes set over 5 x 4 bays on twelve piers, hence the term multi-domed mosque, which was followed by the open Arab courtyard mosque. Because of the harsher climate of Anatolia the originally open courtyard was covered with a flat roof, and then vaulted in the subsequent building period, with its tendency to large domes. As a remnant of the Arabian courtyard we find in the Ulu Camii an open dome over the well within the mosque. The spatial impression is dominated by the massive, squat piers, which make it impossible to grasp the disposition of space. The similarity with the Seljuk 'forest mosque' (afyon) must formerly have been even more marked because of the floral decoration under the domes and on the upper sections of the piers.

Yeşil Camii (Green Mosque): This is part of the Yeşil-Külliye complex with Yeşil türbe and the medrese that houses the *Museum of Ethnography and Islamic Art*. The mosque was completed by Mehmet I in 1412 and is the finest example of the so-called Bursa or double-domed mosque: 2 linked domed spaces, with 2 smaller, lower domed spaces on either side. Another typical feature is the domed spaces in front of the mosque, with entrance hall and school rooms at the side, and here in the Yeşil Camii there is also access to the upper galleries for the sultan and his wives. Thus the suppliant has the impression of being in a self-contained

Bursa, Yeşil Türbe, faience

large space with a double dome. The transition from the square walls to the circular dome is achieved with a 'Turkish triangle'. As well as in the dome, stalactites are also used for decoration and as part of the arch in the magnificent *entrance portal*. The interior entrance wall is dominated by three large *galleries*, with the sultan's gallery raised in the middle above the portal. They are completely covered and surrounded by *faience tiles* in the ancient Persian enamel tradition. The enamel technique (→ also Kubadabad) involves applying a mixture of paint and glaze and firing it. The mihrab was decorated using very finely worked tiles in Cuerdeseca technique, only paralled in the mausoleum of Sah-i-Zinda in Samarkand.

Yeşil Türbe, the Green Mausoleum of Sultan Çelebi Mehmet I (d. 1421) is an octagonal building 84 ft. high. In the interior the sultan's *sarcophagus* and the *mihrab* are both magnificently decorated with *enamel faience*.

Mosque of Murat I (Gazi Hunkiar Camii; in the suburb of Çekirge, above Eski Kaplica): This mosque built in 1365 is the oldest of the surviving large buildings from the early Ottoman period. Murat I used it for the first attempt at accommodating mosque and medrese in a single building. The realization of this idea was unique in the history of Ottoman architecture. The ground plan of the mosque is in conformity with the Bursa type. The mosque is surrounded to the N., W. and S. by a two-storey rectangular building containing rooms for study and students' cells. The large façade surfaces are broken up and articulated with materials of many colours, and galleries, double-arched windows with miniature columns and blind pointed arches suggest the influence of Italian architecture, even though the much-travelled Çelebi writes of a 'Frankish' architect. Murat's Külliye complex also includes a school, kiosks and fountains, toilets and even a kitchen for the poor. Murat I was murdered after his victory on the Amsel Field in Serbia in 1389, and later interred in his türbe opposite the entrance to the mosque. On the occasion of the funeral 'great men of Serbia' were beheaded and buried here near the türbe.

Yıldırım Beyazıt Külliyesi: This foundation by Beyazıt I, built 1398–1403, is the first example of a complete set of külliye buildings. Building was interrupted by Beyazıt's year of imprisonment by the Mongol ruler Timur-Leng and his death, but was later completed on a smaller scale by his son Musa. The whole complex was badly damaged and in part destroyed by the earthquake of 1855. The great wall originally enclosed mosque and türbe, 2 medrese, hospital, saray, Dervish monastery, kitchen for the poor and hamam, an aqueduct and a well. Mosque, türbe and one medrese, now used

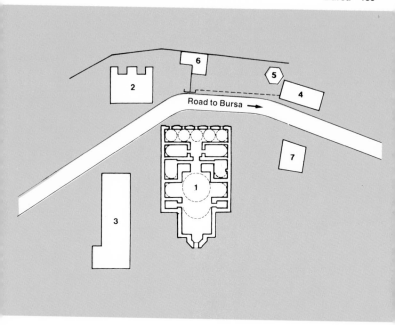

Bursa, Külliye of Murat I. **1** Mosque of Murat I **2** Türbe of Murat I **3** Kitchen for the poor **4** School **5** Fountain **6** Kiosk **7** Toilets

as a hospital, have been restored. The mosque is a somewhat older specimen of the Bursa type than Yeşil Camii. The Bursa scheme of Beyazıt Camii has a monumental narthex with 5 bays and high arches in front of it.

Orhan-Gazi mosque (next to the unusual Bellediye building near the Ulu Camii): This is the oldest of the Bursa mosques, built in 1339 by Orhan I, the conqueror of Bursa. The basic design is like that of Yeşil Camii. The principal prayer room with minbar and mihrab was connected throughout its width to the twin-domed space by a single arch.

Sultans' tombs: These are reached by following the Altı Parmak Caddesi N. around the citadel hill beyond the Djilimbos river on the left, after 1.5 km. In an atmospheric walled garden are a

mosque of Murat II, the *Koran school (medrese)* which he founded and his *mausoleum* with an impluvium, so that the rain can fall upon his plain coffin. There are 9 more polygonal domed *türbe*, some of which have overhanging roofs over their entrances, standing in the shade of cypresses and planes, and surrounded by roses. This is the resting place of Musa, son of Beyazıt I, strangled in 1430 by his own brother, Mehmet I, princes and sons of sultans, and also Mehmet II's brother Cem, who was reached as far away as Naples by the poison intended for him. This is a refreshing place in which to rest from turbulent Ottoman history.

Byzantine citadel: This old building on

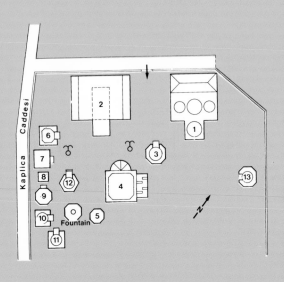

Burse, sultans' tombs 1 Mosque of Murat II 2
Medrese 3 Türbe of Ahmet, Korkut 4 Sultan Murat
II 5 Mustafa 6 Sirin Hatun 7 Güllüh 8 Ebe Kadin 9
Madmut 10 Mukerreme Hatun 11 Gülsah Hatun 12
Cem 13 Hatici Hatun

the hill upon which the town was founded,
and which accommodated the whole of the
ancient settlement, was also Orhan's
residence after Bursa was taken. Orhan
also built the first mosque and the first
Turkish bath within the defensive walls.
At the top of the hill are the mausoleums
of Sultan Osman and his son Orhan, both
honoured as gazi, heroes of fighters for the
faith. The türbe destroyed by the great
earthquake of 1855 were rebuilt. There is
a splendid view from the clocktower
terrace of the town and the sweep of the
plain. There is access to the sultans' tombs
beyond the hospital.

The **baths** used by Roman and Byzantine

emperors in Bursa have long since
crumbled away. The hot springs continue
to flow into newly-built hamams, of which
many sustain Bursa's fame as a spa. Bathing as an aspect of culture is, however, one
of the habits of the townspeople which is
taken for granted. In the 'great washing'
prescribed in the Koran no part of the
body may remain dry. Thus many of the
faithful visit the hamam. Many founders
of such public baths found thanks and
recognition. Worth seeing are:
Eski Kaplıca (Old Thermal Bath, in the
W. suburb of Çekirge, near the mosque
of Murat I): This is the oldest bath in
Bursa, founded in its present form by
Murat I. Ibn Battuta is said to have bathed
here in 1333. The basic shape of the
Ottoman hamam was always: vestibule
with two domes for undressing and dressing placed transversely in front of a domed
hall maintained at a moderately high

temperature in preparation for the main hall, an octagonal building with dome and surrounding small niches in which the water at various high temperatures flowed out of marble fountains. Below these were marble benches on which one could sit or be massaged. In the centre of the hall was the circular steam bath, in which one was only allowed to 'swim' after thorough preparatory washing. Only one immersion in running water counts towards ritual purification. After the bath it was customary to rest on couches in the large entrance hall in separate rest rooms, wrapped in white sheets. Eski Kaplıca, with its colonnades, marble niches, domes and ornamentation, is one of the most interesting examples of early Ottoman bath architecture.

Yeni Kaplıca (New Thermal Bath): Founded by Rütem Paşa, the Grand Vizier of Süleyman the Magnificent. Since 1533 sulphurous vapour from the water at a temperature of 82°C has severely affected the beauty of the painted tiles. Despite this, the baths, on the same ground plan as Eski Kaplıca, have a great deal of marble and faience and are most worth seeing among the countless baths in Bursa.

Bazaar quarter (N. of Ulu and Orlan Camii): This is an attractive district best appreciated at a leisurely pace. This area is still the working heart of the city, with its narrow bazaar streets, market halls and hans, craftsmen, baths and mosques. Great damage, some of it now set to rights, was caused by the earthquake in 1855 and a devastating fire in 1957. Some of the old buildings survived, but much had to be rebuilt or renovated.

The *bedesten of Beyazıt I* (N. of the Ulu Camii) is a bazaar dating from 1400 with 14 domes in two rows, and is well worth seeing. Other sights in this quarter are the Ottoman *caravanserais*. The Ottomans did not take over the Seljuk tradition of monumental hans, architecturally and ornamentally lavishly decorated. An Ottoman caravanserai is a purely functional building and was adapted to the

Bursa, old town, Koza Hanı

rapidly growing demands of trade and commerce in the Ottoman empire. The urban han was the only kind of accommodation available for travellers in the Orient, and was at the same time the market and goods exchange for businesses and guilds. This new han tradition began in Bursa, and quickly became successful, hence the large number and size of the hans in the town. As stopping places on the great overland routes, their design is governed by their function. An Ottoman han in Anatolia usually has two storeys and is built around a rectangular courtyard. Entrance portals lead into the courtyard from outside, but the guest rooms on the second floor can be reached only from the courtyard. Steps led to the galleries with domed bays and arcades facing the courtyard that surrounded it on all four sides. Each of the rooms around it had a fireplace. In the middle of the courtyard was a place of prayer marked with kibla and next to this to the well for washing. The Ipek han in Bursa is one of the Ottoman hans with a mosque, which was the rule rather than the exception in the Seljuk hans. Particularly worth seeing are:

Emir Han (NE of and near the Ulu Camii) dating from the time of Orhan. Four wings with arches on piers.

The beautiful *Koza Hanı* (NW of the Orhan Camii) is a square building with large inner courtyard and a mesçit in the inner courtyard.

Geyve Hanı W. of Fidan hanı.

Pirinç Hanı, built under Beyazıt II (*c.* 1500), one of the three largest and very impressive han buildings in Bursa.

Archaeological Museum *(Arkeoloji Müzesi):* This is a large modern building in the cultural park W. of the city centre on the Altı Parmak Caddesi. The impressive collection in this traditional and ancient provincial museum (formerly in the Yeşil Medrese) extends from the early Bronze Age (from 3000 BC) in Kültepe until predominantly the 3C AD, but does show some coins struck by Byzantines and Venetians.

Environs: İnegöl (44 km. E.): The town is set partly on a hill which produced evidence of settlement going back to the third millennium BC (ceramics). İnegöl was known as *Angelecome* in the Byzantine period. The 15C Ottoman *Işak Paşa Camii* with large five-arched portico and the *türbe* of this Grand Vizier under Mehmet II Fâtih is worth seeing. After the foundation of the Ottoman empire İnegöl grew into an important stopping place for caravans, as the large 14C Ottoman *caravanserai* indicates. The vaults of the inner rooms are raised by drum domes and tower high over the cornice of the hall. Tall chimneys signal the comfort of a Turkish guesthouse from afar to merchants seeking rest. Each guest room, on the second floor, had its own fireplace and for reasons of safety was only accessible from the courtyard.

Mudanya (30 km. NW): This is a small port on the gulf of the same name in the Sea of Marmara, founded as **Myrleia** by Myrlus in the 7C BC. In the late 3C BC Myrleia was destroyed by Philip III of Macedon. Prusias I of Bithynia rebuilt the town and called it *Apameia* after his queen. In 70 BC it suffered in the battles between Mithridates and the Romans, and it was finally razed to the ground by the Goths in the 2C AD. The house in which the Greek-Turkish armistice was signed on 11 October 1922 is now a museum. There are remains of the ancient city 1 km. SE near the villages of Hisarlik and Eskiköy. Best preserved of these is a 5C BC tomb with dromos.

Çanakkale

Çannakale is on the Dardanelles/ Hellespont/Çanakkale boğazi on the Asian side. The ferry journey from *Eceabat* takes 30 mins.

The heart of the town is the *Boğaz Hisarı* (fortress built in 1452 by Mehmet Fatih (1451–81) near ancient Abydos). The name Çanakkale is said to derive from the fact that the fortress is like a bowl (çanak) or that the town was famous for its ceramics (and bowls in particular). Nearby, *heroes* of the First World War are commemorated. It is possible to visit →

Troy (Turkish Truva) from Çanakkale.

Çankırı

Çankırı is 130 km. NE of Ankara on the site of ancient *Germanicopolis*, Byzantine *Gangra*, on a hill with the remains of a Byzantine citadel on Roman foundations, later extended by the Ottomans. A polychrome relief vase of Hittite origin dating from the 16C BC was found in nearby Inandik, but there is no further evidence of connections with nearby Hattuşa. In AD 1135 John II Comnenos succeeding in recovering the once flourishing town and citadel from marauding Turkish tribes, and held it for just about a century. In 1459 the Ottomans finally took Çankırı from the emirs of Kastamonu.

Worth seeing: *Ulu Camii* (in the centre)

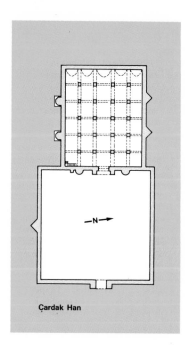

Çardak Han

was built in 1522–8 by the famous architect Sinan. In the part of the town on the other side of the river is the *Taş meçidi*, a medrese in the Seljuk style with hospital and türbe intended for its builder Atabeg Cemaleddin Ferruk (1235). Portal and stairs are original, but heavily restored. In the ruins of the citadel is the *türbe* of the Danishmendid emir Karatekin. The *cave tombs* on the citadel mound date from the Roman period. The relatively large *Provincial Museum* in the main street has an interesting and wideranging collection of finds from the area around the town and the province as a whole.

Çardak Han

The Çardak han is about 65 km. E. of Denizli on the W. Açi Göl (salt lake). The caravanserai, which has survived in good condition, is between the village of Çardak and the railway line. It is a Seljuk hall building with parallel barrel vault running to the rear wall. The courtyard is wider than the hall by almost 15 ft. on the left and just over 8 ft. on the right. According to the building inscription it was built by Emir Raşhideddin Iyaz, an officer of Sultan Alaeddin Kaykobad. The date is given as 627 H (Islamic calculation = 1230). This interesting han is the first example of a hall with five aisles of almost equal width, with tunnel vaults running on 6 arches to the rear wall. The arches are 11 ft. wide and supported by massive, stubby piers just over a yard square. Some of the capitals have bas-reliefs of human and animal heads. The interior of the hall is 75 ft. wide and 89 ft. deep. Above the entrance portal is a niche with pointed arch, containing the building inscription, with a seated lion with a long tongue on either side. The wide portico has a semicircular tower to its right and left. Apparently the left façade is the main one, as it is much more carefully crafted, using

Yılanlıkale (Ceyhan), medieval castle

better materials than the long side on the right. The main façade is supported by two massive pentagonal towers, and there are less elaborate triangular ones on the right.

Ceyhan

Adana   p.576□L 5

This local administrative centre 50 km. E. of Adana on the E. bank of the river Ceyhan, formerly called *Hamidiye*, has no notable buildings of its own, but is a good base for excursions into the surrounding area.

Environs: Anavarza: The extensive ruins of **Anazarbus**, including a town gate and Armenian church, lie to the E. of the road from Ceyhan to Kozan, 4 km.

before Cukurköprü. Exhibits in the local *museum* has include a famous *mosaic* with fine representations of fish (3C AD).

The castle of Anazarbus, together with the more northerly fortress of Sis once formed the political backbone of the Armenian ruling house in Cilicia, from the point when its Prince Thoros I (1100–29) wrested the fortress from the Byzantines with the assistance of the Crusaders. When Prince Leon, brother of Thoros (1129–37), was drawn into territorial disputes with the neighbouring rulers of Antioch, the Byzantines under Emperor John II Comnenus exploited this period of weakness and won the castle back. Leon's son Thoros II (1145–69) managed to reconquer the fortress for the Armenians, but finally had to bow to the supremacy of Byzantium. Despite an alliance with the son of Genghis Khan, which protected the Armenian Empire

Toprakkale (Ceyhan), medieval castle

(from 1199 ruled by kings, rather than princes) from destruction by the Mongol hordes, King Hetum (1289–97), his nephew Leon III and 40 Armenian noblemen were murdered at a banquet in Anazarbus by a Mongol khan who had been converted to Islam.

The Armenian kingdom came to an end when its last ruler Leon V, who only ruled for a few months (from 1374), was defeated by Egyptian Mamelukes. The fortresses of Sis and Anazarbus were the last to fall.

Ayaş (33 km. S.): The Roman town of **Aegeae** is on the gulf of İskenderun/Alexandretta. At the time of the Lesser Armenian Empire, Ayaş took over from Tarsus as the principal harbour in Cilicia. In ancient times, Tarsus was not far from the Mediterranean, but by this time it had moved inland because of the expanding flood plain of the rivers Seyhan and Ceyhan. Ayaş appears as Layaze in Marco Polo's journal. It was much used as a port at one time because of its position at the beginning of the road through Anatolia to the Mongol kingdom. The little fishing village of **Yumurtalık** is now within the ruins of the medieval fortress.

Feke (about 110 km. N.): Follow the road N. from Kozan to Tufanbeyli for about 55 km..

Here, on the river Göksu, was ancient **Vahka** *(Wakka)*, formerly a heavily fortified outpost of a Byzantine garrison. After Prince Ruben, the founding father off the Armenian Rubenids, had successfully detached himself from the Byzantine Empire, his son Constantine (1095–1100) took even this mighty castle and was thus able to force the Byzantines further back into Cilicia. The Byzantine emperor John

II Comnenos (1118-453) was the first to be in a position to strike back. He besieged the Armenian prince Leon I (1129-27), already severely weakened by conflict with Raymond of Poitiers, Prince of Antioch, first in Anazarba, from which Leon managed to escape. It was not until he had reconquered Vahka, where Leon had entrenched himself, that the Byzantine emperor was able to capture his rival and two of his sons.

Kizlar Kalesi (Maidens' Castle): This fortress between Misis and Yumurtalık/Ayas is at a height of about 1,000 ft. in the foothills of the Nur Dağı, the mountains at the heart of the Amanos. It was built either by French crusaders or Armenians.

Kozan (55 km. N.): Kozan, on the site of ancient **Sisium**, can also be reached directly from Adana (72 km.). The Hellenistic/Roman name persisted into the Middle Ages, when the Byzantine *fortress* of Sis, which still dominates the town, was built.
With the support of Prince Raymond of Antioch the Armenian prince Thoros II (1145–69), son and successor of Leon (1129–37), succeeded in capturing numerous Byzantine fortresses, including Sis and Anazarba. On 1152 he confirmed his power base by a victory over the Byzantine emperor Manuel I Comnenus (1134–80).
Sis became the seat of the new ruling house in 1199, when the Kingdom of Lesser Armenia was created by the coronation of Leon I Rubenian as king in Tarsus cathedral. Leon I organized the court and state apparatus on Western lines and pursued skilful expansionist policies until his death in 1219. Trading agreements concluded with Genoa and Venice in exchange for payments to the Armenian court led to the introduction of Italian trading posts in Cilicia. The foreign merchants also built churches.
The last ruler of the Kingdom of Lesser Armenia, Leon V de Lusignan and his

queen, Margaret of Soissons, were crowned in the church of Sophia in Sis in September 1374. However, the king ruled for only a few months. In 1375 Egyptian Mamelukes, who at the time of Leon V's accession already held all the Armenian fortresses with the exception of Anazarba and Sis, also took parts of Sis. Despite an assurance of safe conduct, on the granting of which the fortress of Sis was handed over completely to the Mamelukes, the king and his family were taken prisoner and interned in Cairo. Leon V was not freed until 1382, with ransom payments from Europe. The fall of Sis marked the beginning of a period of decline in Cilicia, and it never rose to such a height again, either under the Seljuks or the Ottomans.
Despite Islamic supremacy it remained the seat of the head of the Armenian church, the Catholicos. After the former kingdom of Armenia had been divided between the Ottomans and the Mongol Timur-Leng (Tamerlane), it was decided at the Council of Etchmiadsin in 1441 to move the seat of the Catholicos to Etschmiadsin. The Catholicos of Sis refused to give up his residence, which led to a split in the church and double occupation of the office.
Sis remained the seat of the Catholicos until 1921.

Toprakkale (Clay Castle; 28 km. E.): This dark basalt castle, built by the Byzantines and insignificantly extended by either the Crusaders or the Armenians in the 12C, is on a steep conical hill which today towers over the junction of the Adana-Gaziantep-İskendrun roads. The building is visible over long distances, and has underground passages and a total of 33 rooms, in particularly good condition in the SE and N. It has a double, rectangular defensive wall which includes a little moat. The two-tier inner wall has embrasures in its upper section. The place was formerly known as *Til Hamdun*.

Ceyhan-Sirkeli, Hittite rock relief ▷

Çorum, Ulu Cami

Yılanlıkale (Snake Castle; 11 km. W.):
This Armenian fortress and Crusader
castle probably goes back to Leon II, the
late 12C Armenian king. Locally it is also
known as *Sahmiran Kale*, derived from the
ancient oriental queen Semiramis. The
building is high on the right bank of the
Ceyhan on a rock, with the actual castle
buildings occupying the NE section. The
massive walls and two solid towers with
entrance between them can also be seen
clearly from the Sirkeli (→ Misi: Environs)
rock relief. The castle is named after the
legendary snake-man Meran, who is said
to have built and lived in it. Tradition has
it that he was killed while bathing in
Tarsus with the intention of abducting the
king's daughter.

Islam Kalesi is another Armenian and
Crusader fortress in the area which is
worth a visit.

Cilician Gates/Gülek Boğazı
Adana   p.574□K 5

This important natural passage through
the Taurus mountains was until the very
recent past the principal connection
between Tarsus and the Anatolian highlands in the N. The new road to Kayseri
opened in 1977 now by-passes the bottle-
neck of the Cilician Gates. Neverthless it
is worth making a detour from the new
road to the traditional route which, now
no longer overloaded with through traffic,
is an impressively lonely gorge with
inscriptions and scribblings from all
periods bearing witness to its former
importance.
Even in ancient times this was an important military road, used among others by
Darius I on his Scythian campaign, and
also by Alexander the Great and various
Roman generals. German troops retreated
along this route from Mesopotamia in the
First World War.
The actual Cilician gates begin about 50
km. N. of Tarsus at *Gülek (Çamalan)*. 5
km. further on the road crosses the Tepir
Tepesi pass at a height of 4,160 ft. The
N. end is 16 km. further on, in *Pozantı*,
ancient *Podandos*.
The ancient road was on the opposite side
of the extremely narrow gorge. It was a
maximum of 6 ft. 6 ins. wide, and partly
cut into the rock or carried on protruding
wooden structures. At the narrowest point
of the pass the Roman Emperor Caracalla
placed a small inscription. This can still
be seen today, and records road-widening
carried out in AD 217.

Environs: Namrun (56 km. SW): Here
on the first slopes of the Taurus are the
remains of the old *Castle of Lambron* (also
Lampron), overlooking and dominating the
upper reaches of the Tarsus Çayı.
It was founded in the late 11C AD by the
Armenian prince Oshin, the first ruler of
the Hetumid dynasty. In 1097 he was able
to extend his sphere of influence to Adana,
but was only able to hold it against the

Turks with the assistance of the Crusaders under their Prince Tancred. The Hetumids subsequently asserted their position against the Rubenids, who (from *c.*AD 1080) ruled a rival Armenian principality from Pazerpert. The most important representative of the Hetumids was Hetum of Lampron (1226–70) who became the successor of the Rubenid king Leo I by marrying his daughter Isabella. After the Rumenids had thus been replaced as kings of Lesser Armenia, the Hetumid dynasty remained on the throne as the last ruling house of Armenia into the 14C.

The history of Namrun probably goes back to the pre-Christian era. It is presumed that this was the site of *Illubra*, whose King Kirua dared to rise against the Assyrian king Sanherib in 696 BC.

Namrun can be reached from Tarsus (72 km.) but the road is bad. It is better to use the road about 18 km. S. of the Cilician gates, still N. of Çiftlikköy, where a linking road goes off to the W. (38 km. to Namrun).

Clavos, see Klavos

Çorum

Çorum   p.586☐K 2

Excavations have shown that Çorum, the present provincial capital and in all probability the site of ancient **Euchaita**, was inhabited at least from the chalcolithic period.

In the early stages of the 2nd millennium BC it was within the catchment area of the Assyrian trading colonies. Records show that there was one in Boğazköy/Hattuşa, only about 85 km. away. The Phrygians were defeated by the Cimmerians in 676 BC, and they were replaced by the Lydians and in 612 BC by the Medes. From 546 BC the settlement was part of

Çorum, Saat Kulesi (clock tower) ▷

the Achaemenid Persian empire. The area came under Western influence for the first time after the victory of Alexander the Great in 332, under the Seleucid dynasty which follwed him. After an interlude with Celtic Galatians from 276 BC Roman rule bagan in the 1C AD, and after the division of the Roman Empire the town became Byzantine. It acquired its modern name after being conquered by the Danishmendid ruler Ahmed Gazi in AD 1075, soon replaced by the Seljuks under Kiliç Arslan II. Then came the Mongol Ilkhana and in 1343 the Eretna (Ertana) dynasty, before Beyazıt I Yıldırım incorporated Çorum into the Ottoman Empire in 1393.

Saat Kulesi (Clock Tower): This slender 19C building is in the middle of the Hürriyet Meydanı (Square of the Republic), the centre of the town.

Ulu Cami: This mosque is slightly concealed, but not far NW of the Hürriyet Meydanı. The way to it leads through the bazaar area. The mosque, also known as *Muradi Rabi Camii*, was built under the Seljuks in the 13C, but was much restored in the last century.

Kale (castle): The fortress dominates the town from the SE. Its almost square defensive wall with round corner towers and two rectangular bastions in each stretch of wall has survived on all sides, and within it are houses which are still occupied. The gate is set forward, and built of limestone blocks with a round brick vault. There are numerous spoils here, particularly in the left-hand jamb of the gate. The *Kale Camii*, which has no minaret, is immediately on the left beyond the gateway, which can still be closed off by two iron-clad gates. The lower part of the defensive wall is made of large limestone blocks, and again between them numerous spoils such as column drums or tombstones (some with inscriptions and ornamentation) are to be found. Above this base the wall consists of smaller quarry stones. The impressive rear of the fortress

has been kept free of buildings, and can be seen on the left from the main Ankara-Samsun road.

Museum *(Müze):* On the SW edge of the town above the roundabout outside the bus station, with a small collection of Hittite, Phrygian and Islamic pieces, the latter mainly from the realm of folklore. The finest exhibits are a striking model of the former Hittite capital of Hattuşa near the modern village of Boğazköy and the Friday pulpit (minbar) from the Hamit Camii.

Also worth seeing: *Inayet Camii* (17 or 18C) NE of the main square. *Ali Paşa Hamamı,* 16C baths.

Environs: Cemilbey (29 km. S.): Not far from this village on the river Çorum, ruins of a fortress that may have been founded in ancient times have survived. It has been much rebuilt subsequently, and is surrounded by old *tombs* and *rock cisterns.*

Işıklar (39 km. E.): On the direct road

Firakatin (Develi), rock relief of Hattusili III and Puduchepas (cast in the Kayseri Museum)

to Amasya off the main Ankara-Samsun stretch, after 34 km. you reach *Meçitözü*, probably ancient *Etonea*. 5 km. SW of here is Işıklar, with numerous Roman *rock tombs*.

Pazarlı The road from Cemilbey runs past a site on which in 1937 the Turkish archaeologist Hamit Kosay excavated remains of buildings dating back to the chalcolithic period (4th millennium BC). The most important period, however, was that of Phrygian settlement, when a fortress was built here *c.*500 BC. Mosaics and terracotta reliefs were found in the house of a Phrygian nobleman. Very little remains on site, as most of the finds have been taken to the museum in Ankara, and some to the local museum in Alaca Hüyük (q.v.), 30 km. away. The most famous find is a terracotta slab with a series of striding, bulbous-nosed warriors with round shields and drawn swords. There are also representations of prowling lions or centaurs (creatures with the body of a horse and torso of a man), all in the museum in Ankara or in the collection at the archaeological faculty of the university. Not far from Pazarlı, near the village of *Mustafa Çelebi*, is the Karapinar spring.

Develi

Kayseri   p.576□L 4

Ancient *Everek* is on the S. slope of Erciya Dağı, the ancient Mount Argaeus which, at a height of 12,848 ft., also dominates the provincial capital Kayseri, 52 km. away. It is best to avoid the direct N.-S. road between the two towns, which runs between the E. side of the mountain and its 6,890 ft. neighbour Koç Dağı. The alternative is the much longer route leading S. from Kayseri in the direction of

Tarsus towards the Mediterranean. After 52 km. there is a crossroads at which a road branches off to the W. for Nevşehir. At this crossroads turn E., and proceed for another 35 km.. Develi is dominated by a ruined medieval castle on a rocky promontory of volcanic origin. The only monuments of real interest are the *Develi Camii* (1821), the *Seyit* Şerif Türbesi (1276) and a *ruined church* of St.Cosmas and Demian. The town is, however, a good starting point for a day's excursion taking in 4 Hittite rock reliefs.

Environs: Firaktin (17 km. SE): This is the nearest and best-known of the *Hittite reliefs,* and also the only one which is sign-posted from Develi. The carving was discovered by Ramsay and Hogarth in 1892, and a cement casting of it has been set up in the garden in front of the museum in Kayseri.

The original is S. of the road from Develi to Tufanbeyli, which you leave after 12 km.. Before reaching Firaktin, the second village on this side road, turn off to the left at an acute angle, almost back in the direction in which you have come. You then pass a striking enclosed poplar grove

on the right, and cross a small watercourse to reach the bank of the Zamantı Su (also Jeniceirmak), the largest tributary of the Göksu. On the other side of the river (there is no bridge at this point) the relief, 20 ft. wide and 4 ft. high, is carved into the rock. Also the smooth background to the relief stands out from the brownish-grey, 20 ft. high, steep trachyte wall as a reddish-brown strip. Above the cliff is a plateau. The long relief falls into three sections. On the extreme left a male worshipper facing left, identified in the accompanying inscription in Hittite hieroglyphs as King Hattusili I, is sacrificing to the water god, who stands facing him, by pouring a drink offering from a pitcher with a spout. The monarch is not wearing the customary round cap, unlike his predecessor Muwatalli in the Sirkeli rock relief near Misis (q.v.), but self-confidently assumes the same pointed headgear as the god. In the scene which follows on the right, showing Queen Puduchepa sacrificing to the goddess Hepat, worshipper and worshipped are also depicted in almost identical clothing, so that the queen is also given enhanced status.

Imamkulu (Develi), Hittite rock relief

Hanyeri (about 75 km. SE): This is the most distant of the *rock reliefs*, 29 km. beyond Taşı directly on the road to Tufanbeyli.

The side of the rock with the picture faces E., towards the village, and is thus only clearly discernible in the early morning. It is 6 ft. high and 11 ft. wide, and shows a prince armed with lance and bow worshipping a bull, in its turn carried by 2 mountain gods. Between them are two groups of Hittite hieroglyphs. The prince's name also appears behind him to the right. The relief was discovered by Ali Riza Yalgin in 1939, and dates from the 13C BC.

Imamkulu (45 km. SE): This relief is an a rock N. of the road to Tufanbeyli. After crossing the bridge 8 km. beyond Taşi (Bakırdağı) turn immediately left on the side road leading to Imamkulu, just beyond the village of Köseler Köyü. E. of the upper reaches of the Zamantı Su (=Jeniceirmak), just before the settlement, there is an isolated house on a slope just under 300 yards from the road to the right. The relief, on a large single rock, is just behind this. It dates from the period of the Hittite Empire (14 or 13C BC), and

for stylistic reasons is so far assumed to have been commissioned by King Tudhaliya IV.

The complicated scene can be broken down into three sections: the central motif is a god on a carriage drawn by bulls. The inscriptions identify the figure as 'weather god of the heavens'. He is facing to the right, and driving over the bowed heads of three mountain gods, each supported by a demon with human body and bird's head, arms raised. On the right is a goddess who has opened her mantle wide, and may therefore be the love goddess Ishtar. She has turned towards the weather god and is offering him her hand. At her feet is a stylized tree in the form of an oak leaf. On the left behind the weather god is another striding warrior with bow and staff. The hieroglyphic inscription is very difficult to make out, but is said to be the same as the one on the Hanyeri/Gezbeli rock relief (see above), suggesting that both the reliefs might have been commissioned by the same royal personage.

Taşı (Bakırdağı: 36 km. SE): This village on the Zamantı Su (also Yeniceirmak) cannot be missed, as the metalled section of the road to Tufanbeyli

Didyma, Medusa on Temple of Apollo

ends here, although the subsequent rubble surface is perfectly adequate. Leave the main road and drive into the village, which is on the right, and take the path which climbs S. from the main square. After 2.3 km. you get back to the river. Here, on the opposite bank on the slope, which is covered by vegetation, are 2 rocks about 35 yards apart, into which the scenes are carved. The very shallow *reliefs* are only in sunlight for a few minutes before mid-day. Then it is possible to make out a group of three people in an attitude of prayer on the right-hand rock. So much soil has been washed against the rock that only the upper parts of the bodies are above ground. The figure in front has hardly survived. The scene can be dated from the cartouche of King Hattusili III (mid-13C BC) on the left-hand edge of the relief. The praying figures are also accompanied by hieroglyphs.

Didyma

Aydın   p.572□C 5

Temple of Apollo: This was once the centre of a Miletian sacred precinct, 19 km. outside the city gates and connected to it by a processional road (via sacra) lined with statues, lions and sphinxes. Greek settlers derived the pre-Greek name from the Greek didyma tekna (twins), meaning that the temple was built at the place where Zeus and Leto conceived the twins Apollo and Artemis (place of birth: Delos; Artemis also had a smaller temple in Didyma). In return Apollo granted visionary gifts to a shepherd who looked after the spring there, and thus began the famous Greek oracle on the site of an ancient temple of Gaia also used for prophecy. The fresh-water spring was enclosed within a laurel grove *c.*700 BC, and from the 7C received votive gifts from throughout the then-known world, signs of its rapid rise to fame.

Didyma, Temple of Apollo ▷

Work on a temple started c.550 BC, and this was destroyed by the Persians in 494 BC. The Miletians decided to rebuild it c.300 BC. At about this time the Diadochid Seleukos I brought the cult image stolen by the Persians back from Ekbatana to Didyma. After a good 650 years (cf. the Temple of Artemis in Sardes) building ceased on the temple, which was still not complete, in the 4C AD; the reason was cost: a column cost 39,000 drachmas, and a specialist worker earned 1–2 drachmas per day.

In the 15C the temple, which from the 5C had housed a Christian basilica, was reduced to rubble by an earthquake. There were Turkish houses and a windmill on the site until excavations started under the German archaeologist Theodor Weigand in 1905–13 and 1924&5.

Didyma was important for three reasons: it was the Delphi of Asia Minor: Apollo gave advice to believers asking about the future through a seer possessed by the god. It was the scene of a religious festival: the feast of the great Didymeia took place every four years (athletics, oratoricalï contests, drama, music). It was a treasury and credit institution (votive gifts were melted down and lent as money for interest; Croesus is said to have deposited a large sum in Didyma). The temple affords the modern visitor a glimpse of an ancient architectural workshop: uncut columns, stones with their transport burls still attached and rough internal walls show a building in the making, above all since the Munich engineer L. Haselberger discovered scratched drawings for the temple on the scale 1:1.

The complex is enormous: 360 ft. long by 196 ft. wide by 78 ft. high, expressing Hellenistic ability to think on a grand scale. It is a dipteros with 122 columns on a stylobate measuring 167 x 357 ft., accessible via a base with seven steps; 108 of the Ionic columns surround the sanctuary in double rows, concluding at the top with an architrave with a frieze of tendrils and gorgons' heads above it (3 heads on the site!) with a toothed fringe, with 10 façade columns and 21 on the longer sides; each columns is 64 ft. high, with a diameter of 8 ft.

From the front one proceeds from the surrounding colonnade to a columned hall with 12 columns in antis. From here, two covered galleries lead to the inside of the

Didyma, Temple of Apollo, column base

temple: an open courtyard (instead of a roofed cella) of 71 x 175 ft., with an little Ionic temple over the sacred spring for the purpose of prophecy. The 82 ft. high walls have a 16 ft. base, then strict surface articulation with pilasters and griffin capitals. Between the outer columned hall and the inner courtyard, formerly planted with laurel bushes, is an intermediate area with two columns to support its roofing: a 78 ft. high staircase leads up from the inner courtyard to a great gate (lintel made of stone blocks 45 ft . high and weighing 70 tons) to a ramp which is open on the outside, but not accessible from there.

Divrigi

This town, the Byzantine *Tephrike*, set at a height of over 4,000 ft. on the Calta Irmak, a tributary of the Euphrates, is 60 km. E. of Kangal, via which it is reached. In the mid-9C, when the town belonged to the Abbasids, members of the Christian Paulican sect found refuge here from Byzantine persecution (particularly under the Empress Theodira). However, their spiritual leader was murdered when the town was occupied by Byzantium in 872. Seljuks took the town in 1071. The emir Mengücek, who ruled on their behalf, was able to establish a certain degree of independence and founded a dynasty which remained in power until 1252 and also included Erzincan in its little empire. It declined in importance when plundered by the Mongols in the second half of the 12C, and became part of the Ottoman Empire in 1516.

The ruined *castle*, which towers over the little town, probably dates from the Byzantine period. Inscriptions confirm restoration by the Mengücek dynasty between 1236 and 1252. The *Ulu Cami* with adjacent *hospital*, the whole complex covering 206 x 104 ft., is one of the most important Seljuk buidings in Turkey. It was built for Emir Ahmed Şah and his consort Turan Melik, daughter of Emir Behram Şah, in 1229, by two probably Armenian architects from Ahlat and Tiflis. 3 magnificently decorated portals, a large one in the N. and 2 small ones to the W. and E. (the latter now walled up) lead into the rectangular mosque with prayer room with five aisles supported by 4 x 4; piers. The hospital wing to the W. (called Sifaiye or Dar üs-Şifa) is entered from the W. A vestibule leads into the central hall, which has octagonal piers ringed with cylindrical columns on its left-hand side. There is an upper storey over the entrance hall.

Other notable buildings in the town include: *Sahanşah Camii* (1181) and the *Sitte Melik Türbesi*, built for the founder of this mosque in 1196, *Kamer ed-Din Türbesi* (also 1196) and *Kemankeş* Türbesi (1240).

Diyarbakır

This formerly important staging post on the   Mosul-Kayseri-Constantinople

Divriği, Ulu Cami, north gate

caravan route is now the provincial capital. It is set amidst the steppe landscape of SE Anatolia on the W. bank of the Tigris (Turkish: Dicle Nehri), on a basalt plateau towering above the river. The basalt was used for the dark, threatening town wall, which has survived almost intact.

History: Diyarbakır was known in Roman times as **Amida**, and may also be the *Amedi* known from Egyptian cuneiform texts and the Seleucid *Annaia*. A relatively shallow basalt block with carving on three sides showing people in Assyrian clothing (fragment of a stele?) has been found within the area covered by the town (now in the local Archaeological Museum). Diyarbakır was persistently involved in conflicts between the Romans and their Iranian neighbours in the early centuries AD. The Roman emperor Trajan defeated the Parthians here in AD 115. Galerius, co-regent of the Roman emperor Diocletian, was defeated by Harran of Persia, where the Parthians had been replaced by the Sassanids, but the important cities of Amida and Nisibis remained within the Roman Empire under the terms of a subsequent treaty.

In 359 the Sassanid ruler Shahpur II conquered the town despite the fact that Constantine II (337–361) had surrounded it with a massive defensive wall, admittedly only enclosing a small area. In 363 Julian the Apostate reconquered it for Byzantium, though he lost his life in the battle. His successor Jovian had to make a new treaty with the Sassanids, and Nisibis was conceded. The Christian population had to leave the lost town within 3 days, and the stream of refugees passed through Diyarbakır, whose population doubled. The area enclosed within the defensive walls was quickly increased. to the W., because of proximity to the Persian Empire. Constantine's original wall had been skilfully adapted to the landscape, but the new wall, intended to protect the refugees from Nisibis as well, was rigidly 'pushed through' on the basis of a fixed plan. In 381 Bishop Mara of Amida took part in the Council of Constantinople as a supporter of the Nestorian and Monophysite doctrine. The town was conquered in an advance by the Sassanids under Kavad II (488–531) in 502, but was returned to Byzantium under Anastasius in the treaty of 505. Chosrau II (591–628)

Diyarbakır, Tigris bridge

took the town again, but lost it to Herakleios (610–641). A turning point was the Arabs victory over Byzantium in the battle of the Yarmuk (636). They occupied the town in 639, which became part of the Osmayid empire 660–750, then came to the Abassids. Byzantine attacks in 856 and 957 were unsuccessful. The town wall was thoroughly restored under the local Marvanid dynasty, who detached themselves from the Abbasids in 990 and styed in power until 1096, although they lost the town to the Seljuks in 1085. In 1183 it was part of the Ortokid empire, then fell victim to the Mongol storm under Hulagu in 1259. In the late 14C the Akkoyunlu (White Sheep) extended the town as their residence. In 1507 it was conquered by Shah Ismail of Persia, and became part of the Ottoman Empire under Selim I Yavuz in 1515. As the centre of the Turkish part of Kurdistan the town has been involved in clashes between Kurds and Turks right up to the present day. The 1925 uprising was particularly bloody.

Town wall and citadel: In its final form the massive wall around the old town surrounds an area 1.6 km. in length (E.–W.) and 1.1 km. wide (N.–S.). The two intersecting streets that divide the town into four also follow these axes (N.–S. street: Gazi Caddesi; E.–W. street in its E. section Yenikapı Caddesi, in its W. section Melek Ahmed Paşa Caddesi). The wall is 5.5 km. long and has a total of 72 towers. With the exception of a parallelogram-like bulge in the SW corner its run is almost oval and includes in the NE corner the *citadel* (İç Kale), itself oval. The walls of the citadel are fortified with 16 towers and pierced by 5 gates, with the main entrance in the W. The citadel is on a mound about 130 ft. higher than the surrounding area because of rubble from previous settlements and deliberate addition of material. It is known as Büyük Tepe, and must be the site of the oldest settlement, although until the time of writing excavations have revealed only the foundations of the Ortokid palace. Finds include walls with raised faience inscriptions, an octagonal, once gilded water basin, ceramic shards and an Ortokid representation of a double eagle. The Ortokids lived in a smaller citadel here in the 12C (Süleyman the Magnificent was responsible for the present building).

Diyarbakır, town fortification

Diyarbakır, Ulu Cami, relief on main portal

Town gates: In the N. part of the
fortifications, at the beginning of the road
to Elâziğ, is the *Dağ Kapısı*, also known
as *Harput Kapısı* (after the once important
earlier settlement of Elâziğ). In the Middle
Ages it was known as Bab el-Armen
(Armenian Gate). The opening is flanked
by two protruding semicircular towers. In
the lower part of the left-hand tower is a
block mentioning the Roman emperors
Valentinian, Valens and Gratian, suggesting that this was also the site of a Roman
gate. The relief representations of 2 lions
and a bird probably date from the Abbasid
period (*c*.900). There are also Arabic
inscriptions on the gate towers.

The front section of the wall adjacent to
the W. that leads in 1.2 km. to the W. gate
(Urfa Kapısı), was pulled down in 1931,
along with its 5 towers. Adjacent is the
town rampart, in good condition and
fortified roughly every 50 yards by a
polygonal or semicircular tower. The
ninth tower has a Seljuk sphinx relief, and
according to an inscription was restored
in 1237. Shortly after it is the *W. gate
(Urfa Kapısı)*, known in the Middle Ages
as Bab er-Rum (Roman Gate). The
keystone in the gate arch has a relief of
an eagle with outspread wings above a
bull's skull. There is also a winged dragon
on either side of the gate inscription. 2 of
the original 3 openings were walled up by
the Ortokid Mohammed. The doors with
iron ornamentation probably also date
from this period. A path leads from here
along the outside of the wall (unfortunately
through a rubbish dump) to the
trapezium-shaped protruding section at
the SW corner of the walls. Its W. tip is
formed by the *Ulu-Badan-Bastion (Ulu
Badan Burçu)*, a tower 82 ft. thick with
a ruined upper section. It has relief decoration (eagles, sphinxes) and also Kufic

Eğil (Diyarbakır), castle rock with Assyrian relief

inscriptions and was rebuilt *c.*1208 on the basis of a Byzantine bastion. The lower casemate storey is still accessible. The other tip of the protruding section is protected by the *Yedi Kardeş Burçu* (Seven Brothers Bastion), dating from the same period. It has a lion relief and inscriptions. The next tower but one in the wall is called *Nur Burçu*, and is 7 towers before the S. gate. Its inscription, next to the relief ornamentation, places it in the Seljuk period (1088). It is possible to go up the inside of the *S.gate (Mardin Kapısı)*, known in the Arabian period as Bab el-Tell (Hill Gate). The view over the Tigris valley is very fine. Only the easternmost of the gateways is still open. An inscription records restoration under Caliph Muktadir (909). Immediately to the E. is a little bastion protruding at an obtuse angle. Its point is formed by the *Kiçi Burçu tower*, dating from 1029–37

according to the inscription. The third tower after it was completely rebuilt in 1052. The *Findik Burçu* halfway between the S. and E. gates can also be dated to the Seljuk period (1098). From here the town is naturally protected by the Tigris, above which it towers on its basalt plateau. Thus there was no need for a moat, which was otherwise provided in front of the defensive wall. At this point a few hundred yards of the ancient wall are missing. The various names which the *E. gate (Yeni Kapı)* was given by the Arabs (Bab ed-Dicle: Tigris Gate; Bab el-Mail: Water Gate; Bab-el-Schatt: River Gate) are all allusions to the fact that it is possible to go down into the river valley from here. Even today the gate is popularly known as Dicle Kapısı (Tigris Gate). The *Kral Kizi Burçu* protects the gate to the N., and dates from 1067. The next section of wall joins almost seamlessly with the oval enceinte of the citadel, which was also connected to the river valley, this time by a tunnel, the *Oǧrun Kapı*.

Ulu Cami: This mosque is conspicuously placed in the centre of the old town on the W. side of the main N.–S. road (Gazi Caddesi). It is not certain whether it occupies the site of the former church of St. Thomas (built 628&9 under Emperor Herakleios), which must itself have had a predecessor, mentioned in 403. In any case a Christian church on this site was rebuilt as a mosque in 639, making it one of the oldest Muslim houses of prayer in Turkey. Records show that in 770 Christians and Muslims were sharing the building, with the latter using two thirds of it. An inscription on the façade of the prayer room, S. of the mosque courtyard, records rebuilding by the Seljuk sultan Melik Çah. At that time there must have been a mosque with columns here, as the Armenian historian Matthew of Edessa reports that 200 collapsed columns were found here after the building was burned down as the result of an earthquake in 1115. The mosque was rebuilt, then much altered in the subsequent period.

Eǧil (Diyarbakır), Euphrates valley

The arch of the entrance portal has the same motif on either side: a lion attacking an ox. In the courtyard behind this are two wells for washing, placed off-centre. One is rectangular and one hexagonal, and each has a pointed roof. The S. side is formed by the façade of the prayer hall, which is raised in the middle and corresponds with the raised bay with saddleback roof behind it, however, the nave has a flat ceiling in the interior.

The courtyard is surrounded by arcades on the other 3 sides. The slightly pointed arches on the broad side (opposite the prayer hall) are supported directly on columns with capitals, but the 9 arches on the narrow side are supported by piers with columns in front of them. The upper storey is articulated by a second row of columns exactly above the first, and pierced with windows. The *Masudiye Medrese* is accommodated in the E. of the two wings, built in 1198. The SE side wings in particular show the mixture of styles for which the mosque is famous. Column shafts of an astonishing variety of designs are topped with reused ancient capitals with acanthus decoration, contrasting with the plain design of the colonnade on the broad side of the courtyard and the façade of the actual mosque opposite.

Behram Paşa Camii: This is the largest mosque in the town, named after the 13th Ottoman governor, who built it in 1572. It is in the centre of the SW quarter and is of interest for its lavish interior decoration and windows.

Fatih Paşa Camii: This was founded in 1522 by Bıyıkıı Mehmed Paşa, Sultan Selim I's general who conquered the town for the Ottomans and became its first governor. The faience panels in the interior of the eight-domed building are a striking feature. The founder's tomb is in the courtyard. The building is on the W. side of the street connecting the Yenikapı Caddesi (leading to the E. gate) with the citadel.

Hazreti Süleyman Camii: This mosque built in 1160 and subsequently much rebuilt is inside the citadel, for which reason it is also called *Kale Camii*. According to the inscription on the minaret, which contrasts in style with the present Seljuk building, it was founded by Abul Kasil Ali.

Hüsrev Paşa Camii: According to the inscription on the S. gate this foundation of the Ottoman governor Hüsrev (1522–58) was originally planned as a medrese. The minaret is in the Seljuk style, is built of black basalt, and has an ambulatory with stalactite deoration. It is on the S. side of the side street which branches off from the main street (Gazi Caddesi) on the left of the Deliller Hanı near the Mardin gate.

İskender Paşa Camii: This mosque was also founded by one of the Ottoman governors. It dates from 1551 and is built of alternating strips of black and white stone. It is in the middle of the NW quarter.

Kasim Sultan Camii (also *Kasim*

Padişah Camii or *Çeyh Muhattar Camii*): This mosque built in the 15C by Sultan Kasim, one of the princes of the Turkoman branch of the Akkoyunlu (White Sheep) is famous for its rectangular minaret supported by 4 columns, and hence known as *Dört Ayakli Minare*. It is on the S. side of the Yenikapı Caddesi just beyond the post office.

Melek Ahmet Paşa Camii: This mosque on the N. side of the Melek Ahmet Paşa Caddesi not far from the Urfa gate was commissioned by Melek Ahmed in 1591. The faience mihrab is notable. The minaret with square lower section and relief-like mosaics with arabesques has two staircases up to the middle of its round shaft.

Nebi Camii (*Peygamber Camii*): It is not known why this domed mosque built under Süleyman in 1524 is known as the 'prophet's mosque'. According to the inscription the minaret was endowed by a wealthy citizen in 1530 and was recently moved 16 ft. in the course of restoration work. Behind the mosque (just beyond the N. gate) there is also a mausoleum.

Lice (Diyarbakır), Tigris tunnel

Safa Camii: This mosque in a side road N. of the Melek Ahmed Paşa Caddesi near to the Ziya-Gökalp Museum dates back to the Turkoman White Sheep dynasty. Restoration in the 16C is confirmed by inscription. When its slender minaret with lavish faience decoration was built, aromatic herbs were mixed with the mortar and until very recently they released a fragrance.

Senceriye Medresesi: This Seljuk Koran school built in 1198 close by the Ulu Cami is, after the Masudiye Medrese inside the mosque, the second most important building of its kind in the town. At the rear of the central courtyard is a large iwan, and at the sides are the pupils' and teachers' classrooms and common rooms. The building was used for teaching until the First World War, then the building was turned into an orphanage and from 1934–82 housed the Archaeological Museum, now in a new building outside the town gates.

Caravanserais: Directly opposite the Ulu Cami on the E. side of Gazi Caddesi is the Hasan Paşa Hanı, built in 1575&6 and named after its founder. It is the largest and finest caravanserai in the town, with a well in the middle of the courtyard around which is the former sleeping accommodation, now used as shops. Further S. on the same side of the road is the *Deliller Ham* (Leader's Caravanserai) also called *Hüsrev Paşa Ham* after its founder. The building dates from between 1522 and 1528, and was extensively restored *c.* 1927.

Baths: Of the 23 baths recorded in the 19C 9 have survived and are in use. Of interest are the *Deve Hamami* in front of the Behram Paşa mosque on the Gazi Caddesi and the *Melek Ahmed Paşa Hamami* in the street of the same name (also called *Çensu Hamami*), not to be

◁ *Diyarbakır, Ulu Cami, decorated column*

confused with the *Paşa Hamami* in on the N. side of the central section of the Yenikapi Caddesi. Halfway between the N. gate and the town centre is the *Vahap Aga Hamami*. The *Çardakli Hamami* is hidden away in the NE quarter of the town.

Meryem Ana Kilise (St.Mary's): This church and the dilapidated church of *St.George* (church with crossing dome, possibly 5C) are the only two of the numerous Christian churches to have survived from the Byzantine period, when the town was the seat of a bishop. Today part of the church, originally dedicated to the Blessed Virgin and probably dating from the second half of the 6C, is used by the Jacobites. The original church was probably a large, centrally-planned building with side walls curving outwards in the form of semicircles and a trefoil naos in the interior, to the E. of which was a large rectangular sanctuary with apse.

Archaeological Museum: This is outside the town, not far E. of the road to Elâziğ. The pink buildings that have housed the finds since 1987 are outside the town walls. A few hundred yards beyond the N. gate is a sign indicating the Tourist Information Office in the Lice Caddesi to the W. The museum is on the other side of the road at the far end of a site with no buildings on it, immediately adjacent to a military heliport.

Atatürk Museum: The memorial is in the rooms in the citadel in which Atatürk lived during his period as town commandant in the years after 1916. The building is not to be confused with the *Atatürk Köşku*, a little palace built in the 15C under the White Sheep on a picturesque site in the Tigris valley S. of the town.

Ziya Gökalp Museum: A memorial to the Turkish philosopher Ziya Gökalp has

Lice, relief of Salmanassar I, Tigris temple ▷

Eğil (Diyarbakır), Assyrian king

been established in his former house not far beyond the Ulu Cami. As well as his private rooms it houses an extensive library.

Kültür Müzesi (Folk Museum): This charming collection is housed in the former house of the poet Cahit Sıtkı Taranci, also not far from the Ulu Cami.

Tigris bridge: 2 km. S. of the Mardin gate directly E. of the access road there is a ten-arched bridge in dark basalt over the Tigris. The inscription, which stands out clearly because it is on long white inset limestone slabs, records that the building in its present form goes back to the year 1065. It probably had a first predecessor in the Roman period. It is certain that the Metropolitan Johannes Sarâ, who was allotted the diocese of Amida in 512 under Emperor Anastasios, had a bridge built

here, but it is not clear whether it was completely rebuilt in 1065, or merely restored.

Environs: Eğil (45 km. NW): Take the road to Elâziğ, turn right after 27 km., through the villages of Oyali (6 km.) and Kazkan (9 km.), reaching Eğil 22 km. from the turning. On the W. edge of the village on a steep rock is a *citadel* dating from the Assyrian period (1st millennium BC). Originally there were passages cut in the rock leading down to the Tigris, but these have now been filled in, though the entrance can still be seen among the ruins. Carefully worked and smoothed areas of rock appear all over the castle area. There is also a magnificent view down into the steep-sided river valley. Below on the bank of the Tigris are remains of *tombs*, also identified as Assyrian. On the narrow side that faces the village of the long castle rock, here almost 40 ft. high, at a height of just over 20 ft. is an Assyrian *relief*, which only emerges from the shadow just before sunset. It was discovered by J.G. Taylor in 1862. It covers an area of just over 6 ft. by 4 ft. 6 ins., enclosed within a double frame. The upper corners of the inner frame are rounded. On the extreme left-hand edge of the relief is a god looking to the right with axe and sword, and raising his right hand. In front of his face, immediately below the upper edge of the relief, is a series of symbols of gods. The rest of the area is empty. It once contained a representation of the king, probably Sargon II (722–705) into whose reign the relief should date for stylistic reasons, facing the god and sacrificing to him. For some inexplicable reason it was later carved away, as can clearly be seen from the marks on the rock. The relief cannot have been left incomplete because, as it stands up from the background, an uncarved raised section would have been left where the king should be. On the opposite slope an enormous block of rock has come away from the rock base, into which a clearly visible staircase has been carved.

Ergani (55 km. NW): This little town is in the middle of the Maden Dağlari (Ore Mountains), where copper is mined, for which reason Ergani has also developed as a centre for copper crafts. On the side road leading SW to Çermik is *Kaplikan*, with its hot mineral springs, and also *Hauburman* with a bridge dating from the Ortokid period.

Lice (70 km. NE): Near this little town are the Tigris tunnel and the source of one of the two rivers which combine to form the actual Tigris further to the S. To reach it take the road to Bingöl, which branches off from the main road to the N. a few km. E. of Diyarbakır. 53 km. before Bingöl and 1 km. before a bridge over the Sebenet Su, to which the road descends in hairpin bends, is a little shallow pool formed by the Tigris on the right-hand side of the road. From here steps cut in the rock lead up the steep mountain slope. These steps are usually considered to have been cut by the Urartians. After passing through a natural gateway in the rock and going downhill for a short distance you reach the entrance to an extensive *cave* on the left. To the right of the cave entrance is a relief, not in very good condition, of King Salmanassar III (858–824). The accompanying cuneiform text is also badly weathered. From here it is possible to risk a complicated climb down the slope opposite to the source of the Tigris. It is simpler to return to the departure point, and from there go round the shallow pool formed by the Tigris immediately after emerging from the rock tunnel. At the rear, at the point at which the Tigris flows into the tunnel, you can climb down to river level again and see two more Assyrian *reliefs* on the rocky cliff. The one on the left is clearly made out. King Tiglatpileser I (1112–1074) stands in front of a long cuneiform text. The representation not far to the right of this, again showing Salmanasar III, can only be discerned in favourable light. The numerous caves in the region are grouped under the general title Birklin Mağaralan. The other branch of the river, which joins

(E. of Eğil) with the river rising in Lice to form the actual Tigris, rises in Hazar Gölü S. of Elâzığ (q.v.).

Silvan (Miyafarkin; 91 km. E.): It is a matter of dispute whether the place through which the road from Diyarbakır to Van runs, is the site of the ancient Armenian capital Tigranokerta. It is however certain that in the 5C BC Bishop Marutha founded the town on the site of a martyr chapel of the hermit Epiphanus, and that it was originally known as **Martyropolis**. This bishop, who convened the Synod of Seleuceia on the Tigris, also achieved tolerance for Christianity in the then adjacent Sassanid empire under King Yezdegard I. The town was then conquered by the Sassanids in 502, it returned to the Byzantine Empire in 591, and became Arabian in 640. The Seljuks, who ruled here in the late 11C, were replaced by the Ortokids in 1121, though they in their turn were subject to the Aijubid empire. In 1260 severe damage was caused when the town was stormed by the Mongol prince Hulagu. The settlement was rebuilt and became part of the Ottoman Empire in 1515. Remains of the old *town wall* have survived, particularly in the E. and the NW corner. The houses there are to a large extent incorporated into the ancient fortification. The *Ulu Cami* in the town centre dates from the year 1227, but numerous post-1913 buildings around it make this difficult to recognize. The *Selaheddin-i Ayyubi Camii* (Saladin Mosque) is also of interest. This mosque built in 1185 by the famous opponent of the Crusaders using columns from a Byzantine basilica has a striking entrance: the rectangular door with two leaves is set inside a much higher niche with a graduated round arch.

Siverek (89 km. W.): On joining the road to Urfa you leave Diyarbakır airport to the left. Here, in bleak countryside, is Siverek, now quite a large town. It formerly protected the road to Amida (now Diyarbakır). Its only interesting monument is a Byzantine *citadel*.

Edirne

Edirne, formerly *Arianopolis*, is at the confluence of the Meric Nehri (Maritza, the principal river of Thrace, Hebros in ancient times) and the Tunça (ancient Tonso), not far from the Greek and Bulgarian borders. Until the fall of Constantinople, from 1367–1453, the modern provincial capital was the second Ottoman residence (the first was Bursa, 1326–67, the third İstanbul, from 1453) and the assembly area for armies preparing for Balkan campaigns. The garrison town of Hadrianopolis, founded in AD 125 by the Emperor Hadrian, probably on the site of the Thracian city of Uskadama on the old military road from the Danube to the Bosporus (later a stop for the Orient Express, now the busy trans-European road E 5), was on numerous occasions a focal point of European history. Here the Emperor Constantine established himself as universal ruler of the entire Roman Empire by victories against his co-regent and Emperor of the West Licinius in 314 and 324, after these commissioning the extension of Byzantium to be his residence Constantinopolis (consecrated 331). It was here that the Visigoths, forcing their way W. during the migration of the peoples, managed to break through into the Roman

Edirne, Selimiye Camii ▷

Empire. In the long struggle for Thrace between Bulgars and Byzantium the town was conquered by the Bulgars on numerous occasions—814, 911, 1002—and the Turks inherited this struggle: the Bulgars occupied the town in the First Balkan War in 1912 (recaptured 1913). The crusaders forced their way in in 1101 and 1147 and took their revenge by plundering and burning. In 1189&90 Frederick Barbarossa made Edirne his winter quarters before crossing the vast expanse of Anatolia. In 1360 Sultan Murat I conquered the town as part of the encircling manoeuvre for the siege of Constantinople. On two occasions, in 1929 and 1878, the border town was occupied by the Russians; it also played the fatal role of being the place where the Ottoman Empire was compelled to ratify its loss of power in the Balkans: in 1829 in the Peace of Adrianople the Greeks were granted freedom and the Danuble principalities placed under Russian rule.

Bayazıt mosque: This was built on the W. edge of the town right by the River Tunça 1484–88 under Sultan Bayazıt II with money exorted on the Moldau campaign. The architect Hayreddin took the ground plan from the Yeşil Camii in Bursa: the square, domed prayer hall with its two attached side rooms for medrese and a mosque courtyard is of the early Ottoman type. The camii is part of a külliye: a collection of buildings with a common purpose, following an Ottoman tradition which started in Bursa. It shows the mastery of its architect Hayreddin in an unusually extensive space. On the right of the mosque is the *hospital*, with hospice (octagonal building with domed central hall and 6 sick rooms), lunatic asylum (with seven cells for the sick behind an arcade) and school of medicine. Sources suggest that numerous doctors worked in the hospital: a chief doctor supervised two senior doctors, two ophthalmic doctors, two surgeons, one pharmacist; music therapy was also practised here (for pain and madness), and ten musicians were employed. To the left of the mosque are *poor kitchen, bakery* and *domestic buildings*. The mosque confirms that Edirne was more than just the favourite second residence of Beyazit II.

Bedesten: This is a bazaar in the town centre built under Mehmet Celebi by the Eski Camii, and intended to support it. It is a market hall with two aisles, 207 x 105 ft., roofed with three rows of domes, and impressive testimony to the flourishing commerce of Edirne, which in the early 16C had 16 large markets and trading areas. Another fragment of these buildings survives in the *Bazaar of Semiz* (= the Fat) *Ali Paşa*, a grand vizier under Süleyman, built by Sinan in 1568.

Eski Cami (Old Mosque): The oldest mosque in Edirne, built 1403–14 as the first Ottoman building in the town, early Ottoman in style, with piered hall with 9 domes in three rows on 4 piers. The building follows the design of the Ulu Cami in Bursa (cf. also the calligraphy) and together with the Beyazıt mosque shows both the consistency of early mosque design and the architectural continuity maintained when transferring a residence. This also applies to the **seraglio** on the Tunça island in the N. of the town, begun by Murat II (1421–51) and completed by his son Mehmet II (1451–81), the conqueror of Constantinople. Only a ruined tower has survived: it was destroyed by departing Turkish troops in 1878.

Selemiye Camii: Built by Sinan 1569–75 for Sultan Selim II, this mosque, set on a hill above the town and dominating it from afar, was the peak of its architect's life's work, and stands as the pinnacle and point of perfection of Ottoman architecture (Sinan called the Prince's Mosque in İstanbul his apprentice work, the Süleymaniye his journeyman work and the Selimiye in Edirne, which he completed at the age of 85, his masterpiece). The building has a central dome, completely harmonious in the balance of its vertical and horizontal dynamics. It is built around an octagon on eight piers set in a retangle 118 x 148 ft. A light transitional area with half dome leads to the 148 ft. high *dome* (diameter 103 ft.). The four *minarets* immediately adjacent to the mosque are 262 ft. high, each with three galleries, and reinforce the strong upward movement of the building, while the *mosque courtyard* with its arcades roofed with 18 domes stresses its breadth, but even here the slightly raised narthex with three large and two small arches introduces the notion of vertical movement.

The Selimiye too is the central building of a küliye with covered *bazaar* under the mosque terrace (now restored and used for business purposes), *medrese* and *hospital* in the rear of the complex.

Rüstem Paşa caravanserai: This was built *c.*1560 by Sinan for the grand vizier and son-in-law of Süleyman, Rüstem Paşa (cf. the magical Rüstem Paşa Camii in İstanbul). The wide, two-storey complex is built around two arcaded courtyards, the smaller used for stabling camels and horses

and the larger as accommodation for travelling merchants. The atmospheric tourist hotel which used to be run here is now unfortunately closed, and the building is not open to the public at the time of writing (1986).

Üçşerefeli Camii (mosque with three galleries on the last minaret to be built; by the Cumhuriyet Meydanı): Built 1437–47 under Murat II, with central dome and rectangular ground plan with inset hexagon as basic support (formed by two hexagonal piers and their corresponding features in the entrance and mihrab wall) for the dome, 79 ft. in diameter. The central hall has side rooms each with two domes. The awkward area at which the the central and side rooms meet show the difficulties found at the high point of the early Ottoman mosque, of which this is one, of creating a totally coherent space. This was not achieved until the mosques of İstanbul were built, after coming to terms with Hagia Sophia.

Yeldirim Beyazıt I Camii: This mosque is an unusual variation on the Bursa scheme. It was built in 1390–1400,

Edirne, Eski Cami

probably as an imâret (poor kitchen), as the building is not oriented towards Mecca (mihrab in the W. iwan). Three wide, tunnel-vaulted iwans run to the SW and N. from the central domed hall. The narthex is supported on 4 Byzantine columns with capitals.

Also worth seeing: Remains of the *town walls* renewed by the Byzantines and the *clock tower* formerly at the entrance to the citadel survive from the Roman town founded by Hadrian. The Ottoman residence city lives on in the numerous sultans' mosques, in the *Muradiye* founded by Murat II in 1435; together with the *tekke* (monastery) it was a centre of the Mewlana Dervishes (principally found in Konya), and in the Murad I mosque area dating from 1361. The bridges over the Tunça are also of Ottoman origin: the 13C *Mihal Gazi bridge*, rebuilt in the 17C; the *Mehmet II the Conqueror bridge* and the *Süleyman bridge*, built by Sinan in 1554. Numerous older buildings, e.g. the *hamam of Sokollu Mehmet Paşa*, built by Sinan in 1579 opposite the Üçşerefeli Cami, can be found on a stroll through the town. The *Museum of Antiquities* and the *Museum of Archaeology and Ethnography*, with finds from the Roman period and Turkish applied art are both in the Selimiye (medrese), and both are worth seeing.

Environs: If you have time on your journey through the granary of Thrace there are other mosques by Sinan to be seen on the 230 km. route from Edirne–İstanbul: in **Havsa** the *Kasim Paşa Camii*, in **Babaeski** the *Semiz Ali Paşa Camii*, in **Lüleburgaz** the *Sokullu Mehmet Paşa Camii*, built in 1549. All the towns on the route, including Corlu, were staging posts on the Roman Via Egnatia, paved throughout its length and running from Durazzo in Albania through Macedonia and Thrace to Byzantium. The towns were later permanent quarters for the Ottoman army. In 507–512 a wall 45 km. long, 16 ft. high and 11 ft. wide was built from Silivri on the Sea of Marmara to Skyllaion on the Black Sea. This was the so-called *Long Wall*, built by the Byzantines as a defensive wall against the Bulgars.

Eğridir, türbe of Baba Sultan

Edremit

Balıkesir   p.564☐C 3

This town, 8 km. from the Gulf of Edremit on the low foothills of the Paşadağ looks over the fertile plain to the S.

Ancient *Adramyttion* was on the coast near Karataş, 4 km. W. of Burhaniye near Kemer, 13 km. SW of Edremit. There are some ancient remains. It is not clear when the town was moved to Edremit. Edremit often changed hand between the Byzantines and the Turks, had a Genoese fortress in the 14C, but soon fell to the Turkoman princes of Karası (Balıkesir).

Şehir Müzesi (*Municipal museum* in the town library): Here there are archaeological finds and a large collection of weapons.

Kurşçunlu Cami (Kurşçunlu Caddesi): This was built in 1231 by the Seljuk Yusuf Sinan, there is a *türbe* next to it.

Environs: Antandros (S. of the Kazdağı, between Altınoluk and Avcılar): This is a town set on a hill, founded by the Pelasgians, later under Byzantine, Hellenistic then Roman rule, an episcopate in the Byzantine period. On the hill is a *fortress* (kale), on the W. slope a cemetery (mezarlık). Coins bearing the image of the mythical founder Artemis have been found.

Eğridir

The town's name is derived from the Greek settlement Akrotiri. It is at the foot of a mountain range, which ends in a peninsula with two islands beyond, on the SW extremity of Lake Eğridir. The picturesque town was called **Prostanna** in the Byzantine period, fell to the sultanate of Rum in the 13C and belonged to the Hamifoğlu emirate for almost 100

Eğridir, overall view of peninsula

years. Eğridir flourished at this time, and is described as the most important town in the region in Persian sources. It was part of the Ottoman Empire from 1381.

Dündar Bay Medrese: This is a conservative example of Seljuk medrese architecture of the period of the emirate, built in 1281 (possibly 1302) under the Hamidids. The entrance iwan has a surprising high Seljuk ornamented *portal*. This fine masonry, largely in marble, was cannibalized from the Eğridir han (built between 1229 and 1236 as one of the 4 great sultans' caravanserais in Anatolia). The cells are grouped around an open central courtyard with arcades in which the arches are supported by columns, some with striking spoil capitals. The building has been restored in an exemplary fashion, and the cells now house shops.
Opposite the entrance iwan is the main iwan. Immediately adjacent is the 15C **Ulu Camii**.

Seljuk citadel: This ruined building towers over the top of the peninsula hill. Remains of portal ornamentation from the Eğridir han were used in a later restoration

of the gate. This beautiful Seljuk masonry gives an impression of the former splendour of the caravanserai, now in ruins. It is 3 km. uphill from the road. From the citadel there is a view of the islands of Tavşçan and Nisç, with ruined Byzantine churches.

Türbe of Baba Sultan (on the N. edge of the town on the right by the lake in the little Kültüs park): This is an impressively plain, small Seljuk building.

Environs: Anamas (7 km. SE of Eğridir, then 3 km. E.): The modern name of this town is *Aksu*. It is situated up river to the right beyond the village before the river. At the end of the narrow gorge is a small Roman *bridge*, behind that a large *cave*, and to its left another one, half walled up with precisely placed ancient stones. These were presumably ancient cult caves, probably associated with a water cult. Ancient stones all around, 3 with inscriptions in various scripts and an animal head.
Barla (2 km. off to the left after 35 km. on the W. bank of the lake): This is a mountain village with an imposing Seljuk *minaret* decorated with glazed tiles. Next to it is the village mosque, Çesçnigir Pasça Camii.
Ertokuş Han (about 27 km. E. in the direction of Gelendost, about 100 yards from the lake): This is a Seljuk *caravanserai*, built in 1213 or 1223 by Mübarizeddin Ertokuş, a great worthy of the time of Alaeddin Kaykobad I. A three-aisled hall 52 ft. wide and 72 ft. deep, with 5 arcades with tunnel vaults running to the rear wall. The hall portal is just over 6 ft. wide and set in an arched niche with the building inscription on its pediment. The outer walls of the hall have three triangular, rather clumsy supporting towers which were clearly a later addition, as they are not connected with the wall. The courtyard is 59 x 88 ft., with 4 tunnel-vaulted rooms with broad arched entrances on either side. The gate façade is in ruins and thus difficult to categorize, and the

whole building is rather crude in execution. It is on the old Denizli-Isparta-Beysçehir-Konya camel caravan route.

Elâzığ

The capital of the province of the same name is on a plain S. of the great artificial lake formed by damming the Euphrates at Keban (see below). When nearby Harput, the traditional centre of the region, was no longer capable of expansion, Sultan Abdül Aziz (1861–76) decided to move the settlement. The present name Elâzığ, official from 1923, developed from *Mamuret el-Aziz* or its shortened form *Alaziz*. It is possible that the new foundation was on historic ground, as many researchers consider this to be the site of ancient Mazara, known for its strategic importantance, and therefore much fought over from the Urartian period. The *Archaeological and Ethnographic Museum* is worth seeing. It was built in 1965, and houses a collection of antiquities from prehistoric times to the Byzantine period, and also folk and ethnographic exhibits from the Islamic period. This museum will soon have competition from a building that is being constructed to house the numerous finds made between 1968 and 1974 in the area flooded after the Keban dam was built. These pieces are at present stored in the local Technical University.

Environs: Habibursaği (52 km. SW): A path leads N. from the road to Malatya after 49 km., a few yards before the old Euphrates bridge. After about 750 yards to the right of the path is the Kömur Hanı (Coal Caravanserai), built under Sultan Murat. 2 km. upstream on the Euphrates is the village of Habibursaği, about 200 yards beyond which the path to the castle branches off on the right. To the right of a rock gate in a small, slightly sunken rectangular niche 6 x 4 ft. 6 ins. is a text carved in Urartian cuneiform script in which King Sardur II (*c.* 760–730) proclaims his victory in 754 BC over the king of Malatya. On the rear side of the castle hill about halfway up is the entrance to a tunnel with steps, and not far from this is a cave. In the next years the hill and its inscription, discovered in 1839 by Moltke and Mühlbach, will disappear in the Euphrates lake. Plans have been made to remove the text and place it elsewhere.

Harput (6 km. NNE): Harput, on a hill (4,166 ft.) on the edge of the plain of Elâzığ is the previous settlement to the present relatively young provincial capital, but it has considerably decreased in importance. The site of the fortress was inhabited in the 16C BC. Urartians, Romans and Byzantines built citadels here when the town was called *Ziata*. In the 10C AD Arabian Hamdanids lived here, to be followed by Seljuks in 1070. The Armenian Philaretes reigned here for a short time, but was driven out by Malek, the Shah of Persia. He was followed by Turkoman Ortokids. Their Prince Balak of Aleppo held the noblemen Balduin of Jerusalem and Jocelyn of Edessa prisoner

in Harput (then Khartapirt), and they were freed by a stratagem by Christian Armenians in 1123. Balduin was then brought by Balak as a prisoner to Haran (until 1124). In 1174 Imaeddin Abu Bakr, son of the Ortokid Kara Arslan, founded an independent local principality here, with Khartapirt as residence. After Eretnids from Sivas and the Timurids, power finally fell to Turkomen of the White Sheep tribe (Akkoyunlu). One of their emirs, Usun Hassan, married Katharine of Trapezunt, daughter of Emperor John IV. She spent the twilight of her years in Harput castle with her two daughters from 1475, and died there in 1485. After a short interlude under Ismail of the Persian Safawid race (1507–15) the town became part of the Ottoman Empire under Selim I. Worth seeing are: *Ulu Cami*, built 1166 under the Ortokids, restored and altered in the Ottoman period. *Arapbaba Camii. Sarâ Hatun Camii* (15C). Since 1960 the Seljuk *Alaca Camii* has had a small *archaeological collection* (mainly Urartian and Roman finds) with exhibits from the immediate surroundings.

Hazar Gölü: This lake 25 km. S. of

Elâzığ, Keban dam

Elâzığ, slightly salty and with many fish, is the source at just over 4,002 ft. of one of the arms of the 1,950 km. long Tigris (for the other arm, the Sebenet Su, → Lice near Ditarbakır).

Içme (18 km. E.): This settlement, now of little importance, is at the S. extremity of the Keban reservoir on the road to Bingöl and Van. In antiquity as **Arsamosata** on the S. bank of the Murat, the ancient Arsanias, it was an important staging post on the route from Melitene (now Malatya) to Amida (now Diyarbakır). In Arabian sources the town is called Samsat. When the artificial lake is completely full, Içme will disappear beneath the water.

Keban (50 km. NW): Keban, which can be reached on a road branching off to the W. via Poyraz, gave its name to the nearby artificial lake on the Euphrates (Keban Baraji). The dam was built by a Franco-Italian consortium and is used for generating electricity (1,249 megawatts) and also to store water for pleasure and irrigation. The dam wall is 680 ft. high and 1,200 yards long at the crown and is causing a lake to form on the Euphrates (Turkish Firat Nehri) with a surface area of 187,500 acres and a cubic capacity of 31 billion cubic metres.

Kiği (185 km. NE): About 30 km. beyond the first turning for Palu on the main road to Bingöl and Van is a side-road leading N., following the Perisuyu valley. It leads in about 90 km. to the Kiği, which is dominated by the ruins of a medieval *citadel*.

Mazgirt (about 120 km. NE): This little place with a ruined medieval *castle* is reached via the road which branches off the main road to Bingöl and Van at Palu to the N. in the direction of Erzincan or Erzurum. At the point where the road runs close to an inlet of the Keban reservoir, the track to Mazgirt goes off to the NE.

Palu (73 km. E.): After about 65 km. on the road to Bingöl the road to Palu goes off to the right in Konvancilar (another 8 km. to Palu), passing the Pinartepe on the right, which produced finds from the chalcolithic age, then the Urartian to medieval periods. Immediately upon reaching Palu a path leads sharply left to the ruins of Eski Palu and the castle hill. The steep citadel rock is surrounded on three sides by the Euphrates or its source

Harput (Elâzığ), medieval fortress

river the Murat, and cannot be climbed on the unprotected N. side. The originally Urartian *citadel* has suffered badly at the hands of stone thieves. Today the ruins of a *church* and two *mosques* are still to be found on the ridge. The entrance to a tunnel with steps dating from the Urartian period has survived on the NW slope. On coming up from the W., a narrow path leads to a *memorial inscription* carved into a free-standing rock. It commemorates the Urartian king Menua, is in a rectangular niche, and can be clearly seen even from below. Beyond this text in cuneiform script in the N. side of the castle hill there are three *grave chambers*, hardly accessible now, cut into the steeply falling rock. From the top there is a good view into the Murat valley, crossed by a railway bridge with a Seljuk bridge next to it. The ruins of *Eski Palu* are to the W. at the foot of the castle rock. They have still not been excavated, and it is possible that there may still be the Urartian lower town below them.

Pertek (to the NE): Until the bridge that is under construction reopens the direct route (now flooded by the Keban reservoir) to Pertek, which is only 25 km.

away, it is necessary to make a tiresome detour (150 km.) around the S end of the lake to see the *ruined castle (Pertek Calesi).* It was built *c.* 1367 and once controlled an important passage over the Murat, which here forms the boundary between the provinces of Tunceli and Elâziğ. In the modern village of Pertek (3,362 ft.) a *mosque* (1650) and an old *caravanserai* (18C) are worth seeing.

Elbistan

Kahramanmanasç   p.576☐N 4

This town 126 km. W. of Malatya is dominated by a ruined medieval fortress, the *Kız Kalesi.* No interesting buildings have survived in the town, but it does have thermal baths.

Environs: Afşin (16 km. W.): The modern town is not far from ancient **Arabissos** on a side road which branches off to the N. a few km. after leaving Elbistan on the main road to Göksun. Here there are a Seljuk *mosque* and *caravanserais* of the same period. Ancient

Hazar Gölü (Elâzığ)

Arabissos was the crossing point of two old roads, of which the one from Kayseri made a loop to the S. in the direction of Antioch (Antakya) while the other coming from Cilicia, led further E. via Melitene (Malatya). The latter stretch of road has a series of Roman *milestones* near the Kurt Tepe.

Göksun (68 km. W.): This town on the Göksun Çayi, the W. of the two sources of the Ceyhan Nehri, is on the site of ancient *Cocosus*, but very little of this has survived.

Karahüyük (6 km. NW): This *settlement hill* is the most important site to have been excavated in the Elbistan plain. The antiquities, including pieces with inscriptions in Hittite hieroglyphics, found here in 1947 by the Turkish archaeologist couple T. and N. Özgüç are now in the museum in Ankara. The most remarkable single find is a terracotta horse's head which decorated a rhyton (drinking horn) at the time of the Hittite Empire (before 1200 BC).

Elmalı

Antalya	p.572□E 6

Elmalı, the 'apple town' and centre of N. Lycia lies on a large fertile plain where fruit and grain are grown. The great Karagölü (lake) outside the town was drained in the 1950s. The *Ömer Paşça Camii* was built in the 15C.

Environs: Karataş-Semayük (5 km. E.): American *excavations* under Machteld J.Melling in the 1960s uncovered the remains of a prehistoric settlement dating back the the beginning of the 3rd millennium BC, including traces of a building of the megaron type of this epoch, known from the same period in the oldest level in Troy: one large room or two, one behind the other, with walls in antis extending forwards to produce an antechamber. The Karataş megaron has an oval courtyard.

In **Kizilbel** and **Karabarun** (near the Karagöl) *wall paintings* which caused quite a stir, were found in 2 tumulus tombs. They date from the 6–5C BC, and confirm the high standard of wall painting in Lycia. The works had been badly damaged over the millennia, but were carefully restored by Machteld J. Melling, so that it is again possible to imagine the beauty of their original colouring. The walls are decorated with scenes from Greek mythology and the life of the buried man: hunting scenes with lions, a battle, farewell to members of the family, battle chariots, horse and warrior in helmet and armour, all in the most beautiful detail.

Ephesus/Selçuk

İzmir	p.572□C 5

The fate of this Graeco-Roman town is mirrored in its foundation myth. Before Androcles, the son of Codros, King of Athens in the 11C BC, set sail with farmers and seafarers willing to emigrate to Asia Minor, he consulted the Delphic

Ephesus, view of Arcadiane and the harbour area

oracle. It replied that he should found a new town at a point indicated by a fish and a wild boar. When they had landed somewhere near Ephesus and were grilling fish, a burning fish jumped out of the fire and set a bush on fire with a piece of burning charcoal which jumped out with it, upon which a boar leaped out of the bush and ran away. In the same way Ephesus was refounded in various different places in the extensive area at the mouth of the Little Meander (Küçük Menderes; ancient Kaystros). There were geographical and geological reasons for this: the continuing silting up of the Kaystros (Ephesus is now 5 km. from the sea), the marshiness of the site and the associated danger of disease, and political reasons: rebuilding after destruction when conquered, and belonging to a new sphere of political influence. At the same time the town kept a firm hold on its central position on the W. coast of Asia Minor: it was not surpassed by Miletus until the 2C AD. The 'Star of Asia' was a traffic centre: because of its protected harbour and as a starting point for the royal road via Sardes to Nineveh. It was also a cult centre for traditional worship of the

female, first Cybele, then Artemis, and finally Mary in the Christian epoch.

Sequence of settlements (→ the large landscape relief on the acropolis at Selçuk, which should be the starting point for a visit to Ephesus).

Ephesus I: Selçuk acropolis, 2nd millennium BC; inhabited by ancient Anatolians, Carians and Leleges, associated with a shrine for their fertility goddess, Cybele of Asia Minor, on the W. slope of the hill.

Ephesus II: Panayir Dağı, N. slope. Achaeans settled on the Kurutepe hill *c.* 1250 BC, then still an island, 1,300 yards W. of Ephesus I. 11C BC: Ionian Greeks under Androcles (see above) settled on the mainland on Panayir Dağı (on which only a fragment of polygonal wall has survived). The ideal settlement conditions: acropolis hill, harbour, fertile land in the surrounding area, caused the city's rapid rise to prosperity, joining the Ionian League. 500 years of history ended with destruction by the Cimmerians in the 7C BC.

Ephesus III: The Lydian king Croesus besieged and conquered the city in the context of his expansionist policies in the mid-6C BC, and compelled it to be

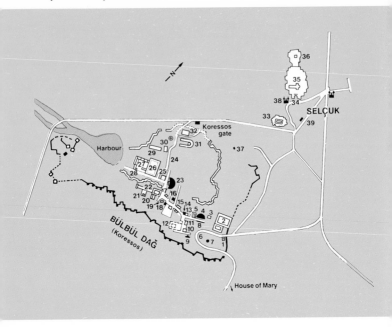

Ephesus 1 Gate of Magnesia **2** E. (girls') gymnasium **3** Varius bath **4** Odeion **5** Prytaneion **6** State agora **7** Burial ground ('Tomb of Luke') **8** Hall of bull-head columns **9** Fountain of Laecanius Bassus **10** Pollio nymphaeum **11** Pollio monument **12** Domitian temple **13** Memmius monument **14** Fountain **15** Nymphaeum **16** Scholastica thermal baths **17** Brothel **18** Octagon **19** Nymphaeum **20** Celsus library **21** Serapis temple **22** Lower (trading) agora **23** Theatre **24** Marble street **25** Theatre gymnasium **26** Verulanus halls **27** Harbour gymnasium **28** Arcadiane **29** Council church **30** Byzantine bath **31** Stadium **32** Vedius gymnasium **33** Artemision **34** Persecution gate **35** Basilica of St. John **36** Seljuk castle **37** Seven sleepers **38** Isa Bey mosque **39** Museum

refounded without walls in the S. (as yet unexcavated) precinct of the Temple of Artemis, and also endowed golden statues of bulls and some columns for the new temple building (on the present site). After his death Ephesus again became a member of the Delian League, but this city which lived on trade and was dominated by a few trading families (oligarchy) exercised diplomatic skills reminiscent of Venice,

even managing to avoid war with the Persians.

Ephesus IV: In the 4C BC the harbour threatened to silt up completely. For this reason Lysimachus, the friend and successor of Alexander the Great in W. Asia Minor, with Pergamon as his residence, established a fourth Ephesus 3 km. further up the long valley between Bülbül Dağı (Koressos) and Panayir Dağı (Pion) and on their foothills. This new town was protected by a town wall 9 km. long and 20 ft. thick (still visible today). He forced the inhabitants to move by flooding the former Ephesus by blocking the drainage channels during the rainy season. Under the Romans, Lysimachos' Ephesus was capital of the province of Asia Minor and had a quarter of a million inhabitants in the imperial period. In 88 BC Mithridates of Pontus' uprising against Rome, which included the whole

Ephesus, citadel of Selçuk and Isa Bey Camii

W. coast of Asia Minor, led to a massacre of the Romans (a secret order to kill which went out from Ephesus led to the murder of 80,000 Romans). In 44 BC Mark Antony entered Ephesus as Dionysos reborn, and accompanied by an army of flautists, guitarists, drummers and a wild retinue of young men and women as Maenads, Pan and satyrs. A cloud of incense and herbs hung over the town as the procession moved through the ivy-clad streets. Mark Antony was on his way to Alexandria to his 'holy wedding' with Cleopatra; he took the valuable library of Pergamon with him as a wedding present. *Ephesus V:* Persistent silting up of the harbour and repeated raids by Arabs who wished to conquer Constantinople in the 7C AD led to the establishment of a new, smaller fortified settlement: Ephesus returned to the acropolis hill, where from the mid-6C AD the basilica of St. John

stood, now the centre of the city, as had been the Temple of Artemis in Ephesus III.

Ancient Ephesus

The cult of Artemis, the most popular of the Greek goddesses in a temple which was one of the seven wonders of the ancient world, made ancient Ephesus a much-visited place of pilgrimage. One month per year was set aside for the religious solemnities and was thus a holiday. Temple and sacred precinct were the religious basis of a highly organized priestly state: at its head was a priestly college of eunuchs; priestesses celebrated the cult; priestesses no longer in service trained novices. Other priestly colleges were part of the organization: essenes (essen-queen bee) for the preparation of feasts after the ceremonies, curetes (the mythical curetes attended Leto at the birth of Artemis), acrobats ('those who walk upon their toes').

Between 540–480 BC the philosopher Heraclitus, who was born in Ephesus, lived near the Artemesion. Nietzsche wrote of this thinker, often described as 'dark': 'probably no-one has ever written more clearly or more luminously'. Fragments of his thought which have survived are concerned with the landscape around Ephesus: 'The death of souls is to become water, the death of water to become earth; but from the earth water wins life, and from water the soul also wins life'. Heraclitus was the son of a priest and sacrificial king and chairman of combats in the stadium, thus a member of the ruling class, and lived in opposition to the second dominant group in the town alongside the priests, the world of business: 'May you never lose your wealth, Ephesians, so that it may not be seen how decadent you are'. Thus during a Persian siege of the town he appeared at a lavish dinner given by a rich family and ate a barley porridge made with water. His example made its impact. It was later said that 'the Persians withdrew when faced with Heraclitus' porridge'.

Disaster struck in the year 356 BC. A man known as Herostratus set fire to the temple of Artemis at night, in order to make a name for himself (the roof, coffered ceiling and interior architraves were made of wood). The faithful thought that he was only able to do this because on that night the goddess was in faraway Macedonia, helping Alexander's mother with the birth of her later so famous son.

In 334 BC Alexander the Great wanted to be involved in the rebuilding of the temple. After marching into the town he sacrificed to Artemis, held a great parade, announced peace for the town (the aristocracy had co-operated with the Persians) and the democratization· of public life; he also enlarged the area available for asylum around the temple. His offer to make an endowment for the

Ephesus, Celsus library ▷

temple if he could be mentioned in an inscription inside was diplomatically refused by the priests: it was not seemly for a god to build a temple for another god. But Alexander had brought the painter Apelles with him, who was granted citizenship in Ephesus; he painted Alexander with lightning in his hand, a picture which was placed in the Temple of Artemis. The Hellenistic trading and residential town founded *c.*296 BC by Lysimachos, Alexander's general and successor, between Bülbül Dağı and Panayir Dağı, with an area of 862 acres and shrine of Artemis about 3 km. away as a separate priestly state, survived for about 900 years and in historical terms was central Ephesus. The town taken over by Rome in 133 BC and then much built over by the Romans forms the centre of a visit to Ephesus today.

Agora: The square, marble-paved market place with sides 360 ft. long was probably redesigned in the 3C BC, probably under the Emperor Caracalla (211–217 BC) and extended as a large open square using older building materials. It was surrounded by double Corinthian colonnades, with shops and stores behind

Ephesus, street of the curetes

them. Here the gold and silversmiths had their workshops and shops, there were shops selling fine fabrics and spices, and above all slaves were sold here. Ephesus was famous for the fact that the most beautiful girls in the East could be bought here. The great range of goods available was determined by the fact that ships sailed into Ephesus from the Black Sea, Egypt, Phoenicia and above all Greece. There was a horologion, a sun and water clock, in the middle of the square.

Arcadiane: This show street 580 yards long and 36 ft. wide was built *c.*AD 400 in honour of the Emperor Arcadius (AD 395–408), and led from the harbour to the theatre. It was paved in marble, and had covered channels at either side of the carriageway, and colonnades with shops behind them on both sides of the road. A particular feature of this show street, which was the first thing seen by visitors arriving in Ephesus by sea, was that it had street lighting with fifty lamps. Rents and fees were correspondingly high: a birth announcement cost 1 denarius, proclamation of a victory at the games 6 denarii, a parsley seller paid 1 denarius for his licence. The monument with 4 columns was reserved for statues of the 4 Evangelists; every so often scratch marks for games can be seen on the marble slabs. At the harbour end the street concluded in an Ionic harbour gate with 3 openings between 4 protruding flights of columns, and there was also a gate near the theatre.

Aqueduct: This was built to bring water to Ephesus between AD 4–14 by Caius Sextus Pollio; a restored fragment can be seen 5.5 km. S. of Selçuk.

Artemision/Temple of Artemis: 'But then, when I finally saw the Temple of Artemis,' wrote the rhetor Antipatros after listing the other wonders of the world, 'soaring into the clouds, all the other pale. I said: has Helios' eye ever seen its like, other than high Olympus?'. And a Byzantine commentator later added: 'Now it is completely desolate and wretched through the grace of Christ and John the Theologian'. He is referring to the mysterious forest of columns of the Temple of Artemis within a tree-lined grove as the stone incarnation of the mysterious natural world of the 'goddess of the outside'.

Building sequence

Starting point: a cult site with a rectangular foundation for an altar, in front of it a pedestal for the cult image. Both bases were combined in the early 6C as the basis for a small temple.

First major building: Ionic dipteros with 2 rows of columns on each side and 3 rows of columns in the front and rear façades. It was built c.550–460 BC by the architect Chersiphron and his son Metagenes of Crete, and Theodoros, who built the dipteros at Samos. The area, 180 x 377 ft., is four times larger than that of the Parthenon, and one and a half times that of Cologne cathedral. There was a total of 127 Ionic columns 62 ft. high, with 21 double rows of columns on the long sides and 8 columns in rows of 3 in the front and rear façades. The columns enclosed not a cella, but an open sekos (courtyard; cf. Didyma) with the statue of the goddess. In front of the sekos was a pronaos, with

ceiling supported by 2 x 4 columns. The stone for the temple, marble with a blueish shimmer, came from marble quarries 12 km. inland.

Second major building: c.350–250 BC. The temple rebuilt after the fire caused by Herostratus followed the same ground plan, but it was now set on a 9 ft. high base with 13 steps, and the columns were more slender, and shorter (59 ft). The famous sculptor Scopas worked on the reliefs (column reliefs on 36 columns), and Praxiteles on the altar relief.

Buleuterion: → government quarter.

Library of Celsus: This library between the Agora-gate of Mazaeua and Mithridates and an auditorium at the point at which the street of marble meets the street of the Curetes was built for 25,000 denarii between AD 114 and 140. It has been rebuilt. The façade was laid out on the ground in the agora from autumn 1970 under the direction of the Austrian Archaeologican Institute. Archaeologists searched over a wide field for remains (some were found as far away as İzmir), and found 700 fragments of the façade ashlar and columns. Then work began on the anastylose using a reinforced concrete

Ephesus, reliefs in marble street

frame capable of withstanding a scale 9 earthquake.

The core of the library is the mausoleum of Tiberius Julius Celsus Polemaeanus, who after a military career became proconsul of the province of Asia with his seat in Ephesus in AD 105. He also spent the last years of his life here, and died *c.* AD 114. He was probably a friend of the last great Roman historian Tacitus, who was also proconsul of the province of Asia (112&113). Celsius founded the library in his spirit, and it, along with the adjacent auditorium, became the intellectual centre of Ephesus, a sort of university. His son Tiberius Julius Aquila then shaped the library as a memorial to his father. With special permission from the city council to bury Celsus within the city walls (an honour granted only to heroes and a few especially worthy citizens) a small vaulted *grave chamber* was created for the marble coffin (the coffin was still untouched when the building was excavated in 1904). Above this was a 69 ft. high base with 9 steps, upon which one enters the reading room through a small porch. The marble panelled walls were 49 ft. high, and the reading room 56 ft. wide and 36 ft. deep.

Ephesus, harbour street of Arcadiane

The walls were divided into 2 to 3 storeys by two galleries. The papyrus rolls were stored in 10 rectangular wall niches in each storey, and the library had room for 12,000 books. A podium just over three feet high ran around the bottom of the walls; in the apse in the W. wall stood Athena, the goddess of wisdom and science. However, the Celsus family's masterstroke was the 56 ft. high display wall of the library, as it can now be seen again with its columns, niches and baldacchinos rising through two storeys. The niches of the lower storey contain female figures embodying qualities most valued by Celsus: wisdom, energy, insight and scholarship. Between the tabernacles of the upper storey were 3 statues of Selsus and one of his son Aquila, presented by his daughter and the grandchildren; thus the building is also outstanding testimony of the way in which the Roman sense of family was presented in public. At the sides of the stairs were equestrian statues of Celsus listing his offices in Latin and Greek. The building was used for its original purpose for about 150 years. Then in the mid-3C AD it was destroyed by an earthquake or a raid by the Goths (AD 262). As the Celsus family had died out in the meantime and the city was impoverished it was not until the late 4C/early 5C AD that the building was changed into a well: the doors were walled up, the interior filled with rubble and the space in front turned into a water reservoir. The façade survived as an example of classical style at the time of Hadrian: four pairs of columns support baldacchinos as a base for the upper storey, in which three baldacchinos span the parts of the lower storey which are not roofed. The lavishly carved entabulature has bead and egg and dart moulding, palmettes, leaf tendrils and denticulation. In the 12&13C AD the façade collapsed in an earthquake. **Temple of Domitian:** This was the first temple built for a Roman emperor in Ephesus, in the 1C AD (Domitian AD 81–96), in a centrally-placed terrace 164 x 328 ft. The temple and the sacrificial altar (decorated with relief arms, see Ephesus Museum) 43 ft. in front of it were surrounded by a colonnade. The temple (79 x 112 ft.) was set on a base with six steps. A portico on the E. side with 4 columns and a periastis with 8 x 13 columns led into the cella (30 x 56 ft.) with the statue of the emperor (head and arm in the museum in İzmir).

Doric hall: The hall on the marble street edge of the agora dated from the period of Nero (AD 54–68); it is on a base clad with bossed ashlar on the street side.

Fountain: Large fountain on the S. side of the state agora opposite the odeion and about 100 yards from it. The centrally planned building is rounded at the front with two wings and a tripartite basin for water in front of it. It received water from the Pollio aqueduct and distributed it into a branching system of clay pipes. The building is articulated with niches and statues, and allowed water to cascade into the basin. It dates from the 2C AD, was thoroughly renovated c.AD 250, and used as a mill after it fell into disrepair.

Brothel: This peristyle building dates, with the Scholastica baths and the toilets, from the 2C AD. The large dining room

is decorated with a floor mosaic of the four seasons (winter and autumn have survived in good condition). A mosaic of a love scene has survived in another room.

Gymnasia: Ephesus has 4 gymnasia: *Harbour gymnasium:* This gymnasium in marshy land at the end of the Arcadiane belongs, together with the Great Baths and the Verulanus halls to a generously conceived mental and physical education centre dating from the 2C AD, an extension of the more modest set of buildings from the time of Lysimachos. The educational complex, later built over by Byzantine private houses, was divided into 2: rooms and 2 two-storey marble halls opposite each other at the N. and S. ends, decorated very lavishly with various sorts of marble and with elaborate wall articulation, were set around a small columned courtyard. A gatehouse with 5 openings led to a square 787 x 656 ft. with three rows of columns set around 2 covered halls with an uncovered central track. This is where the various sporting events took place. Under the Emperor Hadrian (AD 117–138) the high priest of the province of Asia, Claudius Verulanus, had the walls clad in marble (hence 'Verulanus halls').

Ephesus, cow heads on upper agora

E. gymnasium: (also girls' gymmnasium): This gymnasium N. of the Magnesia Gate and dating from the 2C AD was called girls' gymnasium because statues of girls were found here (nothing to do with the pupils). The rectangular baths with large calidarium (82 x 98 ft.) in the centre was surrounded by three halls reserved for sport, and in front of the baths building was a palaestra with colonnades with large halls to the E. and W.

Theatre gymnasium: N. of the theatre, in two sections dating from the imperial period: a marble-paved courtyard 230 x 98 ft. surrounded by colonnades on three sides and steps for sitting on the other: the palaestra; behind this are the ruins of the baths, occupying 9,000 square yards.

Vedius gymnasium: This was built near the Koressos Gate by Publius Vedius Antoninus in honour of Artemis and his friend the Emperor Antoninus Pius (AD 138–161) in the mid-2C AD on an artificial terrace of 14,691 square yards. The complex is a mixture of ancient Greek gymnasium and Roman baths. A propylaeum with three doors leads into the palaestra (131 x 164 ft.) surrounded by colonnades with latrines in the SW corner. W. of this were the baths: 6 piers with half columns in double rows led to the great bath hall (65 x 32 ft.), intended for the cult of the emperor. The two storey room was surrounded by rythmically staggered columns with a niche rising through both storeys for the statue of the emperor, with an altar in front of it for the imperial sacrifice. Subsequent rooms were for bathing: the apodyterium with surrounding bench, frigidarium with central well, tepidarium and caldarium, with associated fireplace and hypocaust.

Temple of Hadrian: This was built in the Corinthian style in the first half of the 2C AD by P. Quintilius for the Emperor Hadrian. The present remains, above all the reliefs, date from the renovation of the temple after earthquake and fire in the 4C AD. The complex consists of a decorated

Ephesus, view of library ▷

façade, vaulted vestibule and cella. The main façade has 2 rectangular piers and 2 columns with architrave with tendril frieze. The architrave rises high between the two columns and has a bust of the city's goddess of good fortune in its apex stone; as the corners show, the façade was topped by a pediment. In the pediment above the entrance to the cella a woman grows out of an acanthus frieze, perhaps Acantho, who gave the flower its name, the mother of Helios of Rhodes and thus also symbolically the mother of the Emperor Hadrian as a reincarnation of Helios. 4 *relief slabs* on both sides of the entrance (originals in the museum in Ephesus) can be discerned: Athena with a round shield and other gods, the foundation myth with Androklos hunting a wild boar, Theseus' fight with the Amazons, Dionysos and retinue, Emperor Theodosius and family on either side of Artemis. The cella contained the statue of Hadrian: on the 4 bases in front of the temple were statues of the Emperors Galerius, Maximian. Diocletian and Constantius Clarus.

Houses on the slope: On the S. side of the Street of Curetes and running up the slope of Bülbül Dağı are domestic houses which at the time of writing are not open to the public, as excavation and conservation are still in progress. The blocks are separated by narrow alleys with steps. The houses themselves have several storeys, sometimes constructed on the vault principle with technical installations and artistic décor (well-preserved wall frescos, mosaics) documenting a Roman way of life which at the top end of the scale was luxurious. In front of the residential district on the Street of Curetes was a colonnade with mosaic floor behind which were shops.

Heroes' graves: Opposite the Baths of Scholastica at the beginning of the Street of Curetes is the *octagon:* a building almost 60 ft. high dating from the time of Augustus with a grave chamber under its square 16 ft. high base. It contained the bones of a young woman in a sarcophagus.

She must have been a heroine (as the ban on burials within the closed settlement was raised only for heroes; cf. library of Celsus). The octagonal core of the building was set directly on the base with surrounding bench and Corinthian colonnade.

By the Octagon are remains of a two-storey *tomb* with Doric columns below and Ionic columns above and a fountain basin which was not added until the Byzantine period. *Round building:* This was probably also a hero's tomb, 262 ft. higher up the slope of Panayir Dağı. A two-storey round building with attic storey and stepped pyramidic roof was set on a sqaure base.

Street of the Curetes (in ancient times Embolos: Wedge): This leads between Panayir Dağı and Bülbül Dağı from the Celsus library up to the upper agora (market) and the Magnesia Gate. The street is named after the Curetes, the group of six priests who guarded the holy flame on the hestia (hearth) in the pyrtaneion (council chamber on the Street of Curetes). The carriageway was paved in marble and lined with colonnades on both sides, and paths with steps led from it to the residential buildings on Bülbül Dağı and Panayir Dağı. The street was lined with a large number of statues on bases. It was framed by two gatehouses with three openings, of which bases and pier pedestals have survived. Remains of the gate by the Baths of Scholastica have base reliefs showing a tripod with omphalos (white cone-shaped stone in the temple at Delphi, for the Greeks the centre of the world), both symbols of Apollo, and a hearth, representing Hestia. The upper gate, the Hercules Gate, has 2 herms in front of the piers: the god Hermes with a ram and a youth with a goat.

Gate of Magnesia: Gate opposite the E. gymnasium, through which one reached Magnesia on the N. side of the Meander plain. Three openings, the central one for horses and carts, the two on the sides for pedestrians, set between two rectangular towers. Apotropaic lions stood in front of the intermediate piers. The remains of the central gate date from the Hellenistic period, the side openings are Roman.

Marble Street: This is the street between the theatre and the agora, which after a bend rises between Panayir Dağı and Bülbül Dağı towards the E. exit from Ephesus. It is a section of the sacred way from the Temple of Artemis, which at the same time was a main road from the E., and reserved for wheeled traffic. It was paved with marble in the 5C AD, and ever since then the stretch between the Vedius gymnasium and Celsus library has been known as Marble Street. There is a pedestrian colonnade to the E.and on the W. side is the 6 ft. high base of the Doric Hall (see above) in rusticated ashlar. On the W. side is a graffito, now protected by a grille: a foot pointing S., a heart, a woman's head with crown, as a signpost to the nearby brothel (see above), and suggesting 'If you go in this direction you will find a woman who will give you your heart's desire'.

Mazaeus and Mithridates Gate: The SE gate of the agora, at the moment under reconstruction from its fragments, which have largely survived, was built in 4/3 BC by two freedmen of Agrippa, Mazaeus and Mithridates, in honour of the Emperor Augustus, his wife Livia, his daughter Julia and his son-in-law Agrippa (by then dead). It has three interconnected arched openings. The two outer ones protrude, and all the arches have an architrave with three fascias, a tendril frieze and a cornice with denticulation. Above this was the attica with, large building inscription, in gilded bronze letters, in Latin on the side sections and Greek in the centre, because of the city's mixed Graeco-Roman population.

Memmius monument: Monument for C.Memmius, grandson of the dictator Sulla, dating fron the 1C AD. It is on the Street of the Curetes (turnoff to the Temple of Domitian) and consisted of a base with reliefs, probably of Sulla's family, above it.

Ephesus, portrait of Artemis ▷

Necropolis: A section cut out of the SE corner of the state agora gives an impression of the settlement levels found in Ephesus, in this case an ancient necropolis.

Nymphaeums: Ephesus was also the city of fountains, as is confirmed by numerous remains from various periods (→ also fountain of Pollio):

Byzantine street fountain opposite the stadium, associated with a macellum, or food market.

Fountain of Laecanius Bassus in the SW corner of the agora, dating from the 1C AD. *Hellenistic nymphaeum* (3–2C BC) in the W. terrace wall of the theatre, a well house enclosed by 2 antes with 2 Ionic columns between them and with coffered ceiling. The water flowed into a basin from three marble lions' heads.

Nymphaeum of Trajan: This two storey well house in the Street of Curetes was built in the 2C AD in memory of the Emperor Trajan. A pool 6 x 32 ft. was surrounded on three sides by façades with composite columns in the lower section (23 ft. high) and Ionic columns in the upper storey (16 ft. high). The colossal statue of the emperor was in the central section.

Government quarter: The upper end of the Street of Curetes leads to the administrative quarter. This includes the agora, the shrine of Hestia, the odeion or buleuterion and the prytaneion.

Prytaneion/Shrine of Hestia: The offical building that housed the senior city officials contained administrative rooms, a hall for dining with guests and receptions, the state archives and the sacred hearth. On the street side was a courtyard with colonnades on three sides. The main building , designed like a temple with 6 Doric columns in antis contained a main hall with a masonry table and 4 columns in the middle. The narrow room behind was the shrine of Hestia with the holy fire, guarded by the Curetes.

Odeion/Buleuterion: Adjacent to the prytaneion: Like the Vedius gymnasiumn this was built in the mid-2C AD by Publius Vedius Antoninus and his wife Flavia Papiana on the slope of Panayir Dağı. It could seat 1,400 in two tiers with 23 rows of seats (13 wider ones below, 10 narrower ones above, the lower ones reached by 6 steps, the upper by 11 steps). At the top was a colonnade with red granite columns. The chamber was certainly roofed in wood, and was used for recitation and musical performances, but also, in association with the prytaneion, for council meetings.

Upper Agora: Unlike the lower agora not far from the harbour the upper agora was the political centre. The Emperor Augustus redesigned the rectangular (525 x 239 ft) area with colonnades on three sides, and also the temple in the middle, which became a double temple of Augustus and Roma. Part of the agora covered an ancient cemetery. In the SW corner is the water reservoir built in the 1C AD, now used as an exhibition room for inscriptions, which repay thorough study. In front of this is the Fountain of Laecanius Bassus (see above). A basilica with nave and two aisles divided the agora from the government buildings on the N. side (prytaneion, odeion); its internal columns had capitals with bulls' heads.

Temple of Serapis: About 30 yards W. of the Mazaeus and Mithridates Gate in the SW corner of the lower agora a staircase with eleven steps and flanked by four ashlar piers led to a square 230 x 230 ft. with colonnades on three sides. On the S. side was a temple built in the 2C AD. Three flights of steps 95 ft. wide led to the temple façade, a colonnade with 8 Corinthian columns in front of the cella. The columns were each cut from a single block, were almost 5 ft. thick and 46 ft. high, and weighed 57 tons. The cella had a tunnel vault of large ashlar blocks. The temple was probably endowed by the Serapis community: there were Egyptian corn merchants living in Ephesus (Serapis was the commonest Egyptian god after Isis in the Roman Imperial period). The building was later used as a church (cf. sanctuary added in the E.).

Stadium: The stadium was much rebuilt (under Nero, for example, AD 54–68), and the present remains date from the 3&4C AD. It is to the S. on the Panayir Dağı, on an artificial substructure to the N. The circle at the E. end suggests gladiatorial contests, as does the accommodation for wild animals. In the 5&6C the stadium provided material for the Byzantine fortress on the Seljuk hill.

Town wall (early 3C BC): The town wall, once almost 20 ft. high and 9 km. long, has survived in good condition on the Bülbül Dağı and partially also on the Panayir Dağı. The tower by the former harbour is eagerly (but wrongly) pointed out as St.Paul's prison.

Theatre: The theatre on the W. slope of Panayir Dağı dates in its original form from the time of Lysimachos (3C BC), and is therefore of the Greek type (cavea extending beyond the semicircle), but was rebuilt in Roman times (building period from the Emperor Claudius, 41–54 AD to Trajan, 98–117 AD): the stage, almost 9 ft. above the orchestra, was extended by almost 10 ft., and the stage building, lavishly articulated with columns, piers, niches for statues and reliefs with with baladacchinos, was raised to three storeys. Three tiers of 22 rows of seats with two broad passageways, divided by 12 sets of access steps into 11 wedges, produce a massive semicircle for 24,000 spectators ending in a colonnade almost 100 ft. above the orchestra. In front of all this was the stage building 131 ft. wide, 82 ft. deep with a proscenium 9 ft. above the orchestra, with a high show façade behind it. Here, while the theatre was being rebuilt, the demonstration against the Apostle Paul was held, and here the mayor of Ephesus made the speech that calmed the people down again.

Baths: As well as the baths already mentioned in the context of the gymnasia there are other baths dating from various periods in Ephesus:

Byzantine bath: The three sections of the 6C bath complex between the stadium and the theatre is intricately arranged around a calidarium and a sudatorium in the NE, a formerly domed conchate room in the S. and a hall flanking the full length of both sections with apses and arcades.

Harbour baths: Directly on the harbour at the end of the Arcadiane, now on marshy ground and as yet unexcavated. The complex is 394 x 219 yards and dates from the 2C AD, rebuilt in the 4C AD. In it the harbour gymnasium (see above) is combined with a palaestra and the so-called Great Baths. Three doors led from the Arcadiane into a courtyard with three colonnades and 2 pools (framed with bulls' heads and garland relief), from which steps led to an anteroom with three aisles before the baths themselves, which were on either side of it.

Baths of Scholastica (on the Panayir Dağı side of the Street of the Curetes): A small street between the Fountain of Trajan and the Temple of Hadrian leads to these 2C AD baths. They were restored c. AD 400 by the Christian Scholastica (her statue and an inscription in her praise were found in the entrance hall and are displayed there). The complex between the Marble Street and the Street of the Curetes included toilets and a brothel. The buildings could accommodate c.1,000 people and included rest rooms, a library, storerooms, with the marble-lined bath houses at their heart. The apodyterium leads into the frigidarium with oval swimming pool, then the tepidarium and finally the caldarium, heated by clay tubes and hypocausts coming from the stoves to the left of the caldarium.

Baths of Varius: This 2C AD Roman bath in the NE corner of the State Agora on the slopes of Panayir Dağı has a massive ashlar arch with quarrystone masonry with windows openings above it. Evidence of floor and wall heating suggests a caldarium, for which Damianus, the Sophist who lived in Ephesus, endowed a hall in the 2C.

Christian Ephesus

Christian Ephesus is based on the tradition that Mary and John the Apostle came to

Ephesus between AD 37&48, and died here. From the 2C AD a tomb on the Selçuk acropolis hill was seen as that of John, one of the 3 pillars of the earliest Christian communities, who worked in Ephesus and was martyred under the Emperor Trajan in AD44. He is associated with the New Testament texts attributed to St. John: the Gospel, the Epistles and Revelation. The Catholic church clings to this tradition; parts of the Protestant church postulate another John, John the Theologian, who lived as a presbyter in Ephesus at the time of the Emperor Nero, and was responsible for the writings mentioned above. His name, Hagios Theologos, gives the Turkish name for the acropolis hill, Ayasoluk. As Revelations shows, Ephesus was one of the 7 Christian communities in Asia Minor, and one of the first Christian communities anywhere. Together with the Jewish community in E. the worship of Mary was at the centre of its development (cf. Council in AD 431). Even early representations show Mary with the crescent moon, the ancient attribute of Artemis in Ephesus. The importance of the Christian community is also to be seen in the fact that the Apostle Paul probably spent two and a half years in Ephesus in the course of his third missionary journey c.AD52–55, until a riot forced him to leave the city rapidly. This is documented in the Acts of the Apostles (19, 23–40): a goldsmith by the name of Demetrius provoked his fellow-craftsmen to a public outcry against Paul, with the cry 'Great is Diana of the Ephesians'. The reason for this was that the gold- and silversmiths feared that his sermons against the cult of Artemis and the worship of idols would damage their business, as they earned the best part of their living from pilgrims who came from all over the world to the shrine of Artemis and bought small models of the Temple of Artemis and the statue of the goddess from the local craftsmen.

The legend of the Seven Sleepers takes us to the 3C AD. The Emperor Decius started to persecute Christians c.AD 250.

7 young Christians fled from Ephesus to a rocky cave on Panayir Dağı. When they woke up from their sleep and wanted to buy bread in the town it became clear that they had slept for more than 100 years. Emperor Theodosius II (AD 408–450) came specially from Constantinople for this reason, and felt that the miracle was proof of the doctrine of the resurrection of the flesh. After their death the Seven, as they were incorruptible, were laid in gold-embroidered garments on biers in their cave; a church was built above the site.

In the 5C, in AD 431, 195 bishops from the Eastern and the Western Empire assembled for the third Ecumenical Council, concerned above all with the question of whether Mary bore a man or God, whether Christ was only God or only man or both, with the result that Christ was decided to have a double nature as God and man (a view opposed to that of the Monophysite Nestorians) and Mary was thenceforth to be known as God-bearer (theotokós). In 449 the Monophysites managed to have their way at a stormy Episcopal Synod, branded Robber Synod by Pope Leo I, but in 451 the Council of Chalcedon (now part of İstanbul) finally excluded them from the church, which declared itself in favour of the decision of the Council of Ephesus.

House of Mary (Panaya Kapulu): The stigmatized Augustinian nun Anna Katharina Emmerich, who died in 1884, described her vision of the House of Mary to the German writer Clemens Brentano, who subsequently published it (1852). In 1891, M. Paulus, Superior of the Lazarists, read the vision and found it to correspond with a little building with narthex and square prayer chamber on the Aladag 7 km. from Ephesus. The walls of the building date from the 6&7C, but its foundations from the 1C AD. In 1892 the Archbishop of İzmir gave permission for mass to be said here. It has remained a lovingly cared-for place of pilgrimage

Ephesus, theatre ▷

(Pope Paul VI prayed here on 26 July 1967). No tomb has been found. **Basilica of St. John** (on the lower plateau of the Selçuk acropolis): The Emperor Justinian and his wife Theodora (AD 527–565) founded a great church in Ephesus, as well as Hagia Sophia, and the Apostles and Irene churches in İstanbul. The domed basilica of the (?) Apostle John. The building is 426 ft. long and 131 ft. wide, and with its two storeys and 6 domes (central dome over the tomb; the five smaller domes were probably over the narthex) reached a height of 93 ft. The atrium gave on to a narthex leading to a nave and two aisles with arches on heavy piers separated by 4 columns in each case. The sanctuary concludes in a synthronon, a semicircle for the priests' seats. In front of this the tomb was indicated by a costly marble floor raised by two steps (cf. restoration) and its barriers. It is said that sacred dust rose through an opening behind the altar from the grave chamber as a miracle performed by John. The altar was set above the tomb, and the church was decorated with multi-coloured mosaics. The column capitals were covered with gold and bore the imperial monogram. On the left of the sanctuary on the outer façade were a chapel with remains of frescos and a baptismal chapel. The core of the Justinian building was the tomb in an underground chamber. A mausoleum was built above this, then the church with its wooden roof. The basilica was built in its stead at the same time as the church of the Apostles in İstanbul.

Church of Mary/Double Church: The building in which the third Ecumenical Council was held in 431 and the Robbers' Synod in 449 had a chequered architectural history. It was originally a museion, 280 yards long with 2 large halls with apses on either side and a three-aisled section, probably an academy for lectures and disputations or a money and goods exchange. Within this, probably in the 4C AD, a columned basilica with nave and two aisles, narthex and atrium was built. The baptistery is on the N. side, a domed centrally-planned building with pool for baptism by immersion, which has survived intact (Council Church). In the 7C AD a domed basilica was built in the W. section of the then derelict Council Church. This basilica had massive brick walls, still standing and at the time of writing under

Ephesus, house where The Virgin Mary died

restoration. There was probably second church between its apse and that of the columned basilica, hence the name double church. After the destruction of the domed church the space between the remaining apses of the Council Church and the domed church was extended as a small piered basilica with nave and two aisles with galleries. The ruined domed church functioned as the atrium, and the remainder of the museion to the E. that had not been used in the churches was the bishop's residence. Finally the piered basilica was also altered by having the galleries, which were in need of maintenance, supported by columns.

Seven Sleepers' quarter (NE of Panayir Dağı): A cleft in the rock and a cave-like room with tunnel vault are held to be the tomb of the Seven Sleepers. They are in the middle of a large cemetery with various large mausoleums, individual tombs, grave chambers. In the middle of the complex was a domed church over a catacomb with ten chambers. Petitions to the Seven Youths were found on the walls.

Islamic Ephesus

From the early 12C AD Ephesus was disputed between Byzantium and the Turkic tribes who had been forcing their way W. since 1091. From 1348–90 Ephesus was the residence of the Seljuk Aydınoğlu dynasty, under the name *Ayasoluk*. The town was plundered by Timur-Leng (Tamberlaine) in 1403, fell to the Ottomans in 1426, and from 1914 it was called Selçuk in memory of the Seljuks.

İsa Bey Camii: Friday mosque of the Arabian courtyard type built in 1375 by the Seljuk sultan İsa Bey I. It covers an area of 187 x 171 ft. at the foot of the Ephesus acropolis, and consisted of an arcaded courtyard (the arcades are no longer in evidence) and a triparite mosque chamber with a double dome over the central section. The building has been restored and its polychrome marble and stalactites are good examples of Seljuk ornamentation.

Citadel: The ring wall on the acropolis, reinforced by 15 towers and topped with crenellations dates from the 6C AD, like the double gate built of spoils a little further down the hill leading to the basilica of John. Because of the relief above the gate this is also known as the Gate of

Ephesus, İsa Bey Camii, entrance from courtyard to prayer hall

Ephesus, Isa Bey Camii, prayer hall

The goddess is wearing a cult robe with real and mythical animals and signs of the zodiac, and a fertility symbol that, according to scholars, may represent breasts, eggs or bulls' testicles. The image combines the block-like form of Egyptian statues (base), the right-angled style of ancient Greek statues (arms) and the sensitive expressiveness of Hellenistic/Roman portraiture. Thus in every sense the goddess is the result of a process of cultural integration and is this respect as well the symbol of Ephesus.

History of the excavations in Ephesus: The English engineer J.T. Wood, looking for the Temple of Artemis in 1863–74, found it by investigating from the Magnesia Gate. The temple was then excavated by D.G. Hogarth in 1904, who also found the temple store and the gold. From 1898–1913, 1926–1935 and from 1954 the work, under the aegis of the Austrian Archaeological Institute, was accompanied by oustanding publications. Individual benefactors made restoration possible, for example the American G. Quatman enabled the reconstruction of the basilica of John.

Persecution. The citadel is part of Byzantine Ephesus, resited on the hill of Ayasoluk. This town was then taken over by the Seljuks, who extended the citadel as a mixed Seljuk-Byzantine complex.

Ephesus Museum: The museum was founded in 1929, and finds in Ephesus have made its collection extraordinarily varied. It includes coins, applied art, grave goods, sarcophagi, individual heads and individual statues, largely of the Roman period and also groups of figures like the Polyphemus scene from the Pollio nymphaeum or the relief frieze from the Temple of Hadrian showing the myth of the foundation of Ephesus. The centre of the collection is the hall with the *cult images of Artemis*, above all the Roman copy of the statue in the Artemesion: the goddess as a combination of Cybele-Aphrodite-Artemis with two hinds.

Environs: 13 km. NE of Selçuk, near the village of *Belevi*, are a *tumulus* and the remains of a large *mausoleum*, probably never completed, and similar to the one in Halikarnassos. Dating and attribution by name of the tombs are uncertain, most probably they date from the 4C BC, the Persian period. In the tumulus a passage 65 ft. long led to 2 rectangular vaulted chambers. Passage and grave chambers were cut out of the rock from above and then covered, and surrounded by a ring of stone. The mausoleum extended over 24 square yards: the base was reached via three steps; above it was a cella with a Corinthian peristyle with 8 columns on each side. The entablature had gryphons at the corners on either side of teams of horses. The vaulted grave chamber in the rock base contained the sarcophagus, now in the museum in Ephesus. The dead man is shown on the lid leaning on his elbows, with singing sirens in relief.

Ereğli

Zonguldak/Black Sea　　　　　p.566□G 1

History: Ancient *Herakleia Pontike* was founded by Megaran Greeks in 560 BC. The once extensive local mythography and history of Herakleia has only survived in fragments. The Argive Herakles, whom the inhabitants thought had founded their town, plays a considerable role in this. The town remained continuously Greek until 1922, and only suffered in the 1C BC. Herakleia was on the side of Mithridates in the struggle against Rome for Pontic Greece. Lucullus' general Cotta wrought bitter vengeance on the town by destroying it completely. It became a Roman garrison after it was rebuilt.

Xenephon describes his landing in the major harbour of Herakleia in the course of a Greek retreat in the Anabasis, and mentions among other things Herakles' expedition into the caves of the underworld, which took place from here. 100 years earlier Herakleia was on the lips of the entire ancient world. Pausanias defeated the Persians at Plataea. In his next campaign in Asia Minor he encountered the beautiful Cleonike in Byzantium, and had her brought to his tent. Cleonike came at twilight, and startled Pausanias from sleep, who inflicted a fatal stab wound. Pausanias suffered from this blood guilt until he consulted the famous oracle of death in Herakleia and the priestess made contact with Cleonike in the Underworld. This was possible since Herakles had performed his final labour and dragged the hellhound Cerberus through the entrance to Hades into the light of the sun. The cave through which according to Euripides Herakles descended into the Empire of Tears can still be seen at the NE end of the town, at the point where railway line and harbour road run close together.

Ereğli, cave of Heracles

In the town itself there are numerous ancient spoils but no buildings from the eventful past. The ruined Byzantine fortress is at the top of the hill. The Greek population was resettled in Greece on the basis of the Peace Treaty of 1922.

Caves of Herakles: At the end of the built-up area of Ereğli a small signpost points to the right to the ancient River Acheron, and a few 100 yards upstream are the Caves of Herakles. It is assumed that the first of the three caves, which follow in sequence, was used for a Christian resurrection cult performed before the background of the ancient sagas. The fragments of *floor mosaic* which remain are susceptible only to Christian interpretation. The area is still known as the 'valley of the unbelievers'. Research so far suggests that the second cave is the ancient 'entrance to Hades'. A narrow shaft with steps leads deep into a dark chamber about 160 ft. wide, in which there are traces of work such as quoins, steps, flooring, niches and painting. Part of the cave is flooded. Outside the cave are sections of building and spoils awaiting interpretation after systematic excavation.

Ereğli

Ereğli   p.574□K 5

This town halfway between Konya and Adana on the Koca Çayı was known in ancient times as *Kybistra*, later **Heraklaeia of Cappadocia.** Nevertheless the area on the N. edge of the Taurus mountains, which includes Ereğli, is known as Lycaonia. Cicero is said to have stayed here in 51 BC during his period as proconsul. In Byzantine times there was a fortress here that was conquered by the Arabs in AD 806, and they later achieved a significant victory over the Crusaders near the town. 4 years previously the Crusaders' leader Geoffrey of Bouillon had stopped here. The Seljuk sultans of Rum (=Konya) wrested the fortress from the Armenian king of Cilicia in 1211, but it fell before the Mongol storm shortly afterwards (mid-13C). In 1467 the town and Karaman became part of the Ottoman empire.

The only interesting feature is the little *local museum*, immediately on the road running S. into the town from the Adana-Konya road.

Environs: Ak Hüyük (12 km. N.): Hot sulphur springs rise on the ridge of this long and narrow hill, which is called white hill because the encrustations caused by the springs have created an effect similar to that at Pamukkale.

Ivriz (16 km. SE): At the edge of this town, picturesquely sited at the N. foot of the Taurus mountains, is a *rock relief* from the period of the late Hittite-Aramaic principalities. It shows two figures, and

is close by the source of the Ivriz Su. It is by a long way the best-preserved of all the Hittite rock pictures. Other examples of Hittite monuments at the source of rivers are Eflatun Pinar near Beyşehir or Akpınar/Sipylos near Manisa.

Somewhat higher up the mountain is an exact copy of this relief cut into the rock. The only difference is that in this case, often called the *Amabardaresi relief*, there is absolutely no inscription. Because it is identical with the relief at the source, identifiable by its inscription as King Warpawalas of Tuwanuwa (Tyana), the mountain relief is probably associated with the same ruler. Warpawalas, of whom another representation was found on a broken stele in Bor (now in the İstanbul Museum), appears in the annals of the Assyrian king Tiglatpileser III (745–727) as the latter's opponent in war, so that the reliefs must all date from the second half of the 8C BC. The relief is almost 20 ft. high, and the entire left-hand side is occupied by the god Tarhu, with characteristic grapes and ears of corn, identifying him as the provider of vegetation. Opposite him is the king, in smaller format and therefore standing on a base of uncarved rock, with arms raised in greeting or prayer. In the relief by the source of the river there are also Hittite hieroglyphs in front of the god's face and behind the king's back. Various influences can be detected in the design of the scenes. The king is wearing a robe based on the robes of Assyrian kings. The god's hair and beard suggest Aramaic models, as do the headdress and the way in which the horns are attached to it. On the other hand the god's robe, as the curved lower hem shows, is in the Hittite tradition, as are the pointed shoes worn by both king and god, and the way in which both protagonists hold their arms. It should be noted in particular that the surcoat with decorated edge worn by the king over his lavishly decorated robe is fastened by a

Ivriz, rock relief: Warpawalaş before god
Tarhu ▷

Altıntepe (Erzincan), entrance to Urartian temple

brooch of Phrygian design. Bronze fastenings of this kind for clothes can be seen in the local museum in Ereğli.

The relief copy in the mountains is reached by climbing the slope to the left of the relief wall, crossing the saddle, going down a little way past some stretches of wall. From here a rocky valley can be seen on the left, leading up again and dominated on the right by a natural gateway in the rock which cannot be overlooked. A few minutes up this valley is the replica relief on a rock wall on the right, practically always in the shade because the gorge is so steep. On the opposite slope are ruined brick buildings with remains of rendering and paintings, probably former churches which may have been part of an out-of-the-way monastery complex. On the right-hand slope, in front of the relief, is a wall, now partially in ruins, with attached semicircular well. The wall used to prevent access to a cave in the rock wall.

Ulukışla (about 45 km. E.): This town on the road to Tarsus, at the point where it enters the Taurus mountains, takes its name, which means large barracks, from an extensive 17C *caravanserai*.

The surrounding area was formerly rich in deposits of silver, known in ancient times. This is shown by a large mine inscription in Hittite hieroglyphics in the Taurus foothills of Bolkar Maden not far from Gülek Boğazi (Cilician Gate) and the modern name of the village of Gümüş (Silver), 14 km. SE of Ulukışla.

Erzincan

Erzincan   p.568☐P 3

The principal town of the province of the

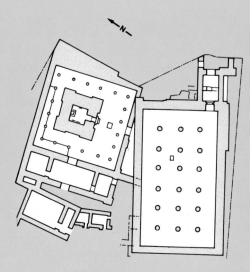

Altıntepe (Erzincan)

same name is an important centre of communications on the Karasu (Black Water), one of the sources of the Euphrates. Carefully planned sugar beet growing in the fertile plain of the upper Euphrates has allowed the town to develop a significant sugar industry.

Erzincan is on the site of the ancient Armenian town of *Erek* (Erez). Little source material exists about its early history. Apparently ancient Persian religious beliefs persisted for a long time here, as tradition suggests that this was formerly the site of the principal temple of the goddess Anahita, who has features in common with the Greek Artemis. Her golden cult image is said either to have been stolen by Cleopatra, consort of Tigranes the Great (95–55 BC, or destroyed by Gregory the Illuminator, who brought Christianity to the Armenians. In the Middle Ages the town

suffered greatly under the Mongol storm, for the first time in 1235. When the Mongols defeated the Seljuks under Ghiat ed-Din Kaikosrau II (1236–45) at Kuzadağ in 1243, Erzincan was destroyed in the fighting. The town was rebuilt and came under the Mongol Ilkhane. From 1916–18 it was Russian, then Turkish again.

Almost all the town's mosques date from recent centuries, including the largest of them on the E. side of the Ordu Caddesi towards the main station, at the S. end of the town.

Environs: Altıntepe (20 km. E.): Important Urartian finds were excavated here. The site is immediately N. of the road to Erzurum. The low wall on the top of the hill, which is climbed from the N. side, is clearly recognizable from a distance.

Altıntepe (Erzincan), Urartian rock tomb

It is no longer known whether the name of the town, which translated means gold hill, indicates that several centuries ago archaeological finds were made. Attention was drawn to the site in 1938, when the railway from Sivas to Erzurum was under construction. When engineering work started on the hill, various vessels were found, and also a large bronze cualdron on a tripod, weapons and furniture fitments in the same metal.

Systematic *excavation* did not start until 20 years later. T. Özgüç investigated the site 1959–66 and revealed the foundations of a palace and a temple, and also Urartian princes' tombs with lavish grave goods. The citadel on the hill is just over 390 ft. long, and was formerly surrounded by two rings of walls. In the early building phase (*Level I*; 2nd half of the 8C BC) a temple stood in the middle of the palace complex. It was square in plan, with walls over 15 ft. thick, though the sides were relatively short, 45 ft. Archaeologists introduced the notion 'Susi temple' for this kind of sacred building with corners protruding rather like bastions, characteristic of Urartian culture. The foundations, made of carefully cut ashlar, which formerly supported the clay brick walls, can be clearly seen on the site. 2 steps lead through the only entrance in the SE façade to the raised square interior chamber, which has masonry benches on all four sides. On the rear wall the base for the cult statue of the Urartian chief god Chaldi stood can still be seen. The sacrificial altar was outside the temple entrance in the open air. The entire sacred precinct was surrounded by a square wall with sides 89 ft. long. The stone *column bases* from the colonnade that used to be within these walls have survived among the ruins. A large number of votive gifts were found under these former arches and inside the temple: principally weapons, such as helmets, large round shields, club ends and arrow and spear tips, also ivory furniture fittings. On the left of the temple precinct and connected with it by an entrance was a long series of buildings. The temple was destroyed in the course of the 7C BC.

Later (*Level II*; 2nd half of the 7C BC) a palace was built beside the temple. Its main section, the so-called audience hall, 144 x 82 ft., was actually built over part of the wall round the temple. The walls were almost 10 ft. thick, and decorated with wall paintings which have survived in markedly better condition than the sparse remains rescued from the temple. At the time when they were revealed it was possible to make out strips with battlement and rosette friezes; also palmettes, winged sphinxes and 'holy trees' flanked by winged genies, showing the influence of Assyrian culture. The palace was not destroyed by force, but abandoned in the late 7 or early 6C, and gradually fell into disrepair.

A large warehouse was also discovered in the citadel, with the great storage vessels still in position.

Outside the defensive wall in the upper third of the the S. slope (facing the metalled road) the *tombs* of local dignitaries were discovered. The grave chambers, built of carefully cut stone blocks without the use of mortar were once set deep in the slope and covered with earth. They are now in the open, although the roof of the larger W. complex is missing. The burial place E. of this is smaller, but has survived almost undamaged. Each of the grave complexes consisted of several chamber vaults. Lavish grave goods were discovered (weapons, horses' harness, beds with ivory carving and decoration) always in the ante-chambers, while each principal chamber contained a sarcophagus.

The rear wall of one of the tombs was adjacent to a remarkable cult site in the open air, probably used for the worship of the dead ruler. 4 tall steles with rounded

tops were set alongside each other in rectangular sockets in an enclosed area 25 x 38 ft. In front of each of these monuments was a round stone basin; so far only one of these has been found. This presumed place of sacrifice is now overgrown and difficult to make out on the site.

All the finds are in the Archaeological Museum in Ankara.

Kelkit (Çiftlik; 76 km. N.): Not far from this place on the road to Gümüşhane and Trabzon is *Sadak* with the ruins of a *fortress* and a Roman *aqueduct*.

Kemah (54 km. SW): Not far from Kemah, formerly known as *Kamakha*, are the ruins of an approximately octagonal Byzantine fortress which, together with → Tercan E. of Erzincan, secured the trade route in the upper Euphrates valley. In Kemah: *türbe* of Sultan Melik (13C); *Gazi türbe*; *Gülalibey mosque*.

Erzurum

Erzurum   p.570☐R 3

Erzurum, capital of the province of the same name and surrounded by high mountains (Palandöken Dağları, 10,253 ft.; Kargaparari Dağları, 10,591 ft.) dominates the basin of the upper Karasu, one of the two sources of the Euphrates. It was once an important staging post on the silk road from Persia to the Black Sea, and is still the most important city in E. Anatolia, with a university since 1958.

The origins of the settlement are obscure, the oldest name of the place seems to have been Kale Arche. After the division of Armenia in AD 387, the boundary between Byzantium and Persia ran in an almost straight line from N. to S. not far E. of the town, now called *Theodosiopolis*, and seat of a bishop. Although the Byzantines extended it as a border fortress it fell to the Sassanids in 502, but was reconquered by Byzantium in 506. The newly fortified settlement was given the name *Anastasiopolis*. In 632 a Christian Synod was called here, at which unification of the Armenian and Orthodox churches was planned. The Arabs, who had been forging victoriously into Armenia since 645, took the town in 655. It was then known as *Qaligala*. Constantine V (740–775) managed to reconquer the town after fierce fighting in 751, but it suffered so much that the remaining population was resettled in Thrace. In 1047 the Seljuks attacked for the first time. After their victory at Malazgirt they soon conquered the whole of Karin, which they rechristened *Arz er-Rum* (Land of the Romans). The modern name of the town developed from this former description of the area. Erzurum was taken by victorious Turks after the battle of Malazgirt in 1071. Timur-Leng (Tamberlaine) conquered the town in 1400 and made it the departure point for his campaigns against the Ottoman sultan Beyazıt I, whom he defeated at Ankara. In 1515 Erzurum became part of the Ottoman Empire under Selim I. The town was occupied by Russia in 1829, 1878 and 1916. Severe damage was caused by earthquakes in 1939 and 1083. The first of these catastrophes caused 40,000 deaths. Rebuilding on this occasion considerably changed the appearance of the town: the streets became wider and the flat-roofed houses were replaced by saddleback roofs on the European pattern. Of the former 65 mosques however only half began to function again or were rebuilt. The earthquake of 1983 came in the winter, notorious in Erzurum for its cold and snow, but international aid helped to alleviate the most severe hardship.

Çifte Minare Medresesi (Double Minaret Koran School): This was built in 1253 by the Seljuk sultan Alaeddin Kaykobad II. The *Hatuniye türbe* on the S. side was built for his daughters and named after them in 1255. It can be visited from inside the medrese, which is now used as a museum. In 1911, when the building was taken over by Europeans for the first time it was used as an ammuni-

tion and weapons store. 4 iwans, of which the southernmost has collapsed, linked by arches, were grouped around a rectangular courtyard 84 x 39 ft. The two eponymous *minarets* are in front of the W. façade. They are built of brick in such a way that the outside, decorated with faience, gives a fluted effect. They frame a tall gate with pointed arch and stalactite decoration. The rest of the building is in dark tufa, decorated at some points with reliefs (vase with leaves. tree with double eagle, ornamental bands etc.).

Ulu Cami (Large Mosque): This mosque is no longer the largest, but in part the oldest in the town. The plain building with 7 piered halls and rectangular courtyard was built in 1179 and badly damaged in the earthquake of 1939, but rebuilt on the old model.

Yakutie Medrese: This Koran school built by the Mongol prince Uljaitu in 1308 is worth seeing for the *relief decoration* on its entrance. It is possible to make out a tree of life, eagles and lions. The building is about 450 yards W. of the Üç Kümbetler, but not always open to the public, as it is in a military zone.

Lala Mustafa Paşa Camii: Beyond the Yakutie Medrese on the same side of the street, probably commissioned by the governor of the city at the time in 1563. Some architectural scholars feel that it could have been designed by Sinan, Süleyman the Magnificent's (1520–66) famous architect.

Üç Kümbetler (Three Mausoleums): These can be seen from the Hatuniye türbe, and are reached via an alleyway leading S. between Çifte Minare Medresesi and Ulu Cami (about 100 yards). The three tombs from which the area takes its name (there is a fourth, very badly damaged, nearby) all date from the 12C. The finest is the *Emir Sultan Türbesi*

Erzurum, Çifte Minare Medresesi ▷

Çifte Minare Medresesi, portal

with reliefs of snakes, eagles and hares' heads. The octagonal building has a round, pointed roof, and the transition from the walls to it is a stalactite cornice immediately below.

Citadel: The fortress was founded by Theodosius I, but constantly altered and extended over the centuries. Today it houses a military unit, so the little mosque and minaret inside cannot be visited. There is a 19C *clock tower* on the base of a Seljuk citadel tower. Not far from this near the wall is the 13C *Gümüşlü türbe*.

Environs: Aşkale (52 km. W.): It is clear from the name of this town at which the roads from Erzurum, Erzincan and Trabzon meet that it has a medieval fortress (kale = castle).
Bana (Pertek/Penek; 177 km. NE): As well as the direct, well-surfaced road to

Kars there is a second route which curves to the N. through Tortum, Oltu and Göle, passing to the N. of the Allahuakbar massif (10,253 ft.). This route makes it possible to visit some of the churches and monasteries of Turkish Georgia, including Bana. After 175 km. the road passes over a little bridge (a few km. beyond Oltu, not far from Kosor) over the Kamli Su. Here turn left, and after 2 km. you come to the village of Penek, beyond which are the ruins of the round *church* of Bana (Penek). It was probably built in the 7C in honour of an anonymous martyr, and was badly damaged in the Turko-Russian war. In the interior are 4 apses on a quatrefoil pattern. Above the corners or spandrels between the circular enclosing wall and the apses were small chapels. This tetraconch was surrounded by a single-storey ambulatory. Records exist of rebuilding under Prince Ardarnase (881–923) and Bishop Kwirike. 2 km. up the valley are the ruins of the *Harap Kilise*, also a centrally-planned building. A climb taking about 2 hours leads to the ruined *Salomonkale* (Solomon's Castle) a little further to the E. Here the castle chapel, a small rock chapel and some remains of wall painting have survived.
Bayburt (125 km. NW): Like Erzurum, Bayburt, which stands at a height of 4,921 ft., has frequently changed its name in the course of its history. It was founded as *Gymnas* by the Scythians. On the site of the massive fortress which now towers over the town on a chain of hills was the Justinian fortress of *Baiberdon* in the Byzantine period, taken over by the Armenian Bagtarids as *Paipert*. In 1361 an emir of *Baiburt* is mentioned. In 1825 the town was destroyed in a Russian invasion. It was the scene of a number of decisive battles like the victory of Alexios II over the Mongols in 1364 or the skirmishes between Mehmet Fatih and Uzun Hassan of the White Sheep in 1462. Some of the original *citadel* building has survived, particularly on the N. side.
Chachuli (Hahul; 90 km. NNE): 82 km. along the road to Artvin (beyond Tortum

Erzurum, Çifte Minare Medresesi, details of portal

and the turning for Oltu) a bridge crosses the Tortum Çayi. From here a path 8.5 km. long leads to the village of Chachuli with its famous yellow sandstone *monastery*. The main church is now used as a mosque and has thus survived in good condition. The domed basilica was originally dedicated to the Blessed Virgin. The monastery was founded in the 10C by David II Kuropalat of the Taik Bagtarid dynasty.

The cruciform ground plan of this centrally-planned building is only discernible from the interior, as the exterior N. and S. sides each have a slightly protrudung portico. Access is from the S. The apse, in which fragments of painting have survived, is flanked by two side chapels. Opposite is a narthex supported by two piers. The lavish *stone carving* is a striking feature: on the drum of the dome an eagle striking a deer, on

the right of the S. portal a lion attacks a bull etc.

N. of the main church is another small *chapel* with three apses, S. of the monastery near the entrance portal are the ruins of three more small chapels, each with a single apse.

One of the altars, the famous *Chachuli triptych*, endowed in the first third of the 12C by King Demetrion I, is now in the museum in Tblissi (Tiflis) USSR.

Cobandede (57 km. E.): There is a *Seljuk bridge* over the Araxes in this place (also called **Köprüköy**; 5,479 ft.) on the main road to Kars (via Sarıkamış).

Hasankale (40 km. E.): The road to Çobandede (see above) passes through Pasinler, very close to which are the ruins of a *fortress* founded by the Armenians and restored under Uzun Hassan. Pasinler itself has hot springs.

Ilıca (17 km. W.): This place at the foot

Euromos, temple of Zeus Lepsynos

of the Dumlu Dağı also has thermal springs.

Ispir (138 km. N.): Beyond the Pontic mountains a little off the road to Rize on the Black Sea is Ispir, the old *Sper*. The modern town in the valley of the Çoruh Nehri at the foot of the Deve Dağı (11,033 ft.) is dominated by a massive castle on a rocky hill. The *bastion* in the NE corner of the *fortress* is impressive. Inside are a ruined mosque and a ruined church. In Ispir itself are three 13C *mosques* (Kadioğlu Medrese, Sultan Melik Mesciti, Togrulşah Camii).

Oltu (115 km. N.): This village on the N. route to Kars (→ under Bana) on the Oltu Çayi at a height of 4,265 ft. is on the site of the Byzantine fortress of **Oukhtik**, capital of the province of Taik. There is scarcely anything in the present insignificant village to recall its days of greatness. Only a *ruined church* in poor

condition has survived. 2 *mosques* are worthy of mention, the Arslan Paşa Camii (1664) and the Içkale Camii.

Öşk also **Oschki** or **Vank** (90 km. NNE): A few km. beyond the turning for Chachuli/Hahul another side road goes off from the road to Artvin at the point where the S. tip of Lake Tortum appears at the side of the road. From here it is 9 km. to Öşk. The *monastery* here is one of the most important of its kind in the former minor empire of Tao Klardshetien. It was completed in 961 by David Taik and his brother Bagrat. A dome on 4 freestanding piers tops the building, which is approximately cruciform in plan. The 'short' arms are formed by three apses, each flanked by 2 side chapels. The 'long' arm, oriented to the W., is preceded by a narthex. As in most buildings of this period there is relief decoration on the outer walls.

Tortum (59 km. NNE): This village at a height of 5,413 ft., in which a bridge leads over to Tortum Çayi is passed through on a visit to Chachuli/Hahul and Öşk. 11 km. beyond Tortum on the road to Artvin is a valley on the left. A two-hour walk into this valley leads to the village of Toryn Kale with a ruined Georgian *castle*.

Euromos
Muğla   p.572□C 5

This Carian town is 69 km. S. of Söke on the road to Milas, 13 km. before reaching Milas.

Temple of Zeus Lepsynos: This peripteral temple 47 x 88 ft. is the Roman temple from the period of Hadrian dating from the early 2C AD in the best condition in Asia Minor. It was built on the foundations of an earlier Hellenistic temple. 16 of the former 6 x 11 slender Corinthian columns of the peristasis are still standing and support sections of the entablature (fascia architrave and bulbous frieze). The 4 unfluted columns suggest that the building was never completed. Stone tablets on the columns record the names of those who endowed them. The cella with three bases for statues can still be clearly seen, and also the door jambs to the pronaos, and finally the altar in front of the E. side of the temple. The masons left their double-axe (labrys) mark in many places.
The temple is outside the walls of the town, which has not yet been excavated. The site is covered with olive groves and maquis. The town was on a hill N. of the temple, and had town walls, a theatre and, a little further off, agora and tombs. The University of Ankara is embarking upon excavation and conservation work.

Fethiye, Amyntas tomb

Fethiye
Mugla   p.572□E 6

The impressive group of more than 20 rock tombs in the steep rock wall above the town is among the last surviving

Fethiye, rock tombs

evidence of ancient **Telmessos**. The tombs are visible from a great distance. Severe earthquakes in 1856 and 1957 completely destroyed the town, and with it the last remains of buildings from the distant past. The new town of Fethiye is a very Turkish port and trading town on the SW Mediterranean coast. The supposition that there were prehistoric and Hittite settlements here may well be true. This is supported by the large and fertile hinterland, harbour protected by islands and a peninsula, as well as proven cave colonies in the Karain caves.

History: In the 5C BC Telmessos was first mentioned in the tribute lists of the Delian League, though not as a Lycian town. Presumably it came to Lycia after the successful siege by King Pericles of Limyra in the 4C BC. Alexander's governor Nearchos is said to have taken

the town without siege again after 334 by a variation of the Trojan horse trick. Members of an all-female orchestra overcame the castle guard in a surprise attack and occupied the acropolis.

After various changes of ruler Telmessos became part of the Roman province of Asia in 133 BC. Membership of the Lycian League is proven, but not the dates of membership. The fact that Telmessos had to pay ten per cent of the total contribution of the 23 members into the federal coffers is certainly an indication of the size and economic power of the town, but perhaps also of its risky position on the W. fringe. This perhaps also explains its interrupted membership of the League. Under Byzantine rule Telmessos was known as Anastasiopolis, and was rechristened Makri, also Megri, in the 9C AD.

Telmessos is said to have had a well-

Kadyanda (Fethiye), tomb with equestrian relief

known shrine dedicated to the Lycian-Pisidian rider-god Kakasbos.

However, there were Lycian and Carian oracles of similar name. The Carian oracle was 12 km. from Halikarnassos. Mausolos of Halikarnassos, former Persian satrap of Caria, assumed temporary overlordship of Caria and Telmessos in 362 BC, after the fall of Pericles. The ambitious Mausolos was able to demonstate his power by enhancing the status of the less famous local oracle of Termissos.

Nothing has survived of the Temple of Apollo and the two theatres in Fethiye. Spratt, Mayer and Texier found a fine theatre with 28 rows of seats in excellent condition in the middle of the last century. Greek influence from the 4C BC later took on the scale of colonization and ended in Fethiye and the surrounding area when the dominant Greek population was repatriated in 1922.

Rock tombs: *Tomb of Amyntas.* This is the most prominent of the Lycian rock tombs in Greek architectural style to have survived in Telmessos. The volutes on the Ionic column capitals are from the Peloponnese. Between the row of columns and the tomb chamber is an anteroom. The roof-supporting 'round timbers' as decorative elements in a Lycian rock tomb are replaced by denticulation. The oldest and best-preserved doors of Greek antiquity are of particular architectural interest. As those in Greece itself were made of wood, no originals have survived. But similar door frames have survived in Greece, and it is reasonable to conclude that the wooden doors would have been similarly ornamented. There are 2 more Greek rock tombs nearby. The other rock tombs are typical Lycian grave houses with flat roofs, similar in decoration to Lycian wooden houses seen today.

The *hyposorion sarcophagus* type occurs in the town. The rectangular hyposorion, in which the servants were laid, stands on a base with steps. This coffin space was covered with a massive slab 20 ins. thick. Above this was the sarcophagus with pointed-arched lid, both decorated with coffers, door ornaments, reliefs and friezes, according to degree of wealth.

According to the Lycian faith the dead were carried into heaven by bird-daemons. Thus the tomb site should be as high above the ground as possible. There is a particularly fine hyposorion tomb near the community centre.

Fortress: The ruins on the acropolis hill are of the 15C building by Knights Hospitaller from Rhodes, and the Genoese.

Museum: A lavish collection of ancient remains of all periods from the town and surrounding area.

Environs: Kadyanda (20 km. N. near the village of Üsümlü; 3,281 ft.): In contrast with Telmessos nothing remains of the history, but a great deal of the old town of Kadyanda, although the buildings have been systematically cannibalized for decades. From the village to the old town there is a climb of 1,400 ft. to be made either on foot or by riding. On climbing the N. side of the hill you pass one of the finest tomb houses in Lycia, of which only a few examples survive. The so-called *equestrian monument* was made from a slab of rock brought down by an earthquake. The relief *c.*6 ft. high, 9 ft. wide and 10 ins. deep on the N. side of the grave house represents a fighting horseman, galloping over a man who has fallen. His lance raised for the fatal thrust is pointed at his opponent, who is kneeling in a defensive position. On the S. side a man lies propped up on a couch, and at its foot are three man facing the one who is lying down. The massive base and the grave house

◁ *Tlos (Fethiye), Bellerophon tomb*

have shifted from the vertical in the course of time. S. of the acropolis almost all of the tombs in the extensive *necropolis* have been destroyed by scavengers. Higher up, on the other side of the town wall, is the *theatre*, parts of which have survived in good condition, overgrown with bushes. 250 yards away on its N. axis is a *thermal bath* in Roman ashlar. Beyond this is the long area of the *stadium*, set transversely in in a W.-E. direction. Inscriptions and statue bases of successful athletes suggest that the town was keen on sport. The stones N. of the stadium diagonally opposite the baths on the left are considered to be the ruins of a Doric theatre.

Kaya, Greek *Levisi*, known in ancient times as **Carmylessus** (4 km. S.): On a slope above a plain, Kaya is now like a ghost town. This was probably where rich Greek citizens of Fethiye lived in large European-style stone buildings in the style of the turn of the century. It was deserted by its inhabitants in 1922 or after the earthquake in 1957.

Tlos (36 km. E. via Kemer-Yakaköy): As you approach the town the acropolis rock towers over the E. hills of the Xanthos valley, with the Akdag massif in the background. This position dominating the valley gave Tlos its outstanding role among the cities of the Lycian League. It had a threefold vote in the League assembly. In Tlos as in the rest of Lycia, research is based on Hittite sources from the 14C BC mentioning the Lukki and connecting the name Tlawa with Tlos. It has yet to be proved that Lycians or Lukki go back to a dispersed group of Hittite refugees. The Lycian castle on the rock has been built over by a Turkish fortress. To the E. the rocky massif falls steeply to a great plain. On the less steep W. and S. sides were the Lycian, then later Roman and Byzantine residential areas, cisterns and other' functional buildings. The remains of town walls on the E. slope are Lycian and run into Roman masonry which has survived in good condition in the W.

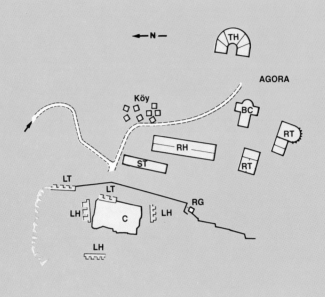

Tlos (Fethiye) C Castle **LT** Lycian tombs **LH** Lycian houses **ST** Stadium **RH** Roman hall **RG** Roman gates **RT** Roman thermal baths **BC** Byzantine church **TH** Theatre

The best-preserved remains however are those of the interesting *tombs* of the Lycian necropolis from NE to N. of the rocky cliff. Outstanding among the known Lycian tomb types is the so-called *Bellerophon tomb* (difficult to reach) far below on the N. side. It is similar to the Amyntas tomb in Fethiye in its Greek-style architecture, size and execution. The two incomplete columns in antis form three openings to the pronaos, into whose outer wall the three doors of the grave chamber are carved. The central one is a decorated blind door. The left-hand door leads into the grave chamber with four couches. The right-hand couch has a stone cushion and a niche for grave goods. The door façade is surrounded by reliefs. On the stone bases under the doors are horses, above the left-hand door a lion, and on the left-hand wall Bellerophon mounted on Pegasus gallops through the air towards the dreaded Chimera. Homer writes of Bellerophon in the 6th Canto of the Iliad: the subsequent local hero of Tlos came to King Proteus in Tiryns as the son of the King of Corinth seeking asylum. There he suffered a similar fate as Joseph with Potiphar. Proteus sent him with a sealed murder commission to his own father-in-law in Lycia. This Iobates had Bellerophon fight against the Chimera, the war-like Solymer and the Amazons, but finally recognized his moral strength and gave him his Lycian daughter as wife. Thus Tlos also had a distinguished ancestor in its history.

Gasipaşa, aqueduct

The centre of the *Roman town* was E. of the acropolis on the plain. It began to expand in the 2C BC as part of the new province of Asia; in the imperial period Tlos, with its magnificent public buildings, was known far afield as a glittering metropolis. Just below the acropolis is the outline of the stadium. W. of this are extensive hall buildings in first-rate Roman masonry with arcaded entrances. S. of the stadium are two large thermal baths in good condition. 7 large windows in the apse of the S. room. The way to the large theatre with more than 30 rows of seats 450 yards to the NE passes through the agora. Halfway, to the left of the ruins, are the ruins of a large Byzantine church. Tlos was the seat of a bishop in the Roman period. Until the late 19C, generations of Turkish Agas ruled in the castle on the hill. One of them, Kanli Ali (Bloody Ali), was a feared bandit chief.

Gasipaşa

Antalya   p.574□H 6

Gasipaşa, ancient **Selinus**, is assumed to have been founded by the Phoenicians. The Emperor Trajan died here on his way home from the Parthian campaign, travelling earlier than planned because of his illness. A large cenotaph was built in his honour and the city temporarily rechristened *Trajanopolis*. The upper town, built on the headland which drops steeply to the sea, stretches a considerable distance on to the plain. There is a ruined *citadel* on the acropolis. The W. slope of the headland drops in terraces, and was fortified with towers and walls extending on to the plain. Water from the mountains was brought on a once considerable aqueduct of which only a few hundred yards of ruins survive. The theatre cut into the rock near the river can only be seen in outline. Numerous ruins have been found in the area, showing the extent of the ancient Roman town.

Environs: Antiochia ad Cragum (18 km. SE of Gasipaşa, then turn off 3 km. beyond the village of Günei): Large *ruined Roman town* high above the ancient Cragus cliff, dropping steeply to the sea by the old harbour. There is little information about its history. The remains of the *acropolis*, some of them imposing, of the massive columns of a former enclosed street in the agora, and other large buildings extend down to the harbour. The *citadel* is above the harbour in a dominant position on a rocky hill.
Jotape (4 km. W.): This is an ancient town, with foundations of old buildings, statues and carefully cut stones, and also a temple dedicated to the Emperor Trajan, who died in the neighbouring town of Selinus, can be seen.

Gaziantep

Gaziantep   p.576☐N 5

The provincial capital is on the Sacır Suyu, a tributary of the Euphrates, between two hills, with a citadel on the one to the E. Here the road from Adana to Urfa intersects with the one from Aleppo/Syria to Maraş. The acropolis, which dominates the fertile valley plain, seems to have been the site of the earliest settlement. The oldest ceramic fragments here are of the chalcolithic coloured type (3700–3500 BC).

In the late-Hittite period there was an important settlement here, incorporated into the Assyrian empire under Sargon II (721–705 BC). In the first years AD the town was called **Ayntab** (Good Spring), and was a source of dispute between Arabs and Byzantines. The latest date for the building of the citadel on the E. hill was after the Seljuks took the town in 1071–98. Next the town came to the county of Edessa. In 1150 it was the scene of a great battle between the Franks and the Turks. It came into the possession of Saladin and fell before the Mongol storm in 1270, three years later the Mameluke Sultan Baibars took it, but continued to reside in Cairo and Ayntab (from which the modern name Antep developed) was ruled by the subordinate emirs of Dulkadir. In 1516 the town passed to the Ottoman Empire under Selim, but was again ruled by Egypt 1832–40. The name Gazi (victorious) was granted to the town when the population resisted occupation by Britain at the end of the First World War, even surviving more than one siege. The subsequent phase of military government by the French ended in 1921.

Citadel: The present fortress on the E. hill goes back to the Seljuks and probably had a Justinian predecessor (6C AD). The entrance with embrasures, protected by a deep moat, has survived in good condition.

Archaeological Museum: The museum in the Karagöz Caddesi has been used for this purpose since 1969. The principal feature of the fine collection, also exhibited in the garden, is relief blocks from the nearby sites in Karkemish, Sakçegözü and Zincirli, dating from the period of the late-Hittite principalities. A sphinx from the Yesemek quarries, in a completely different style, is also exhibited. The Parthian and Roman periods are represented mainly by tomb reliefs. There is also a good collection of old near Eastern roll and stamp seals from the Tell-Halaf to Achaemenid periods.

Environs: Belkis (about 65 km. E.): The village and hill with ruins of Belkis are a few km. from Birecik on a bend of the Euphrates on the W. bank (or S. briefly here) and on the N. slopes of Belkis Dağı. Henderson found numerous Graeco-Roman objects here, including a mosaic cycle showing various deeds of Herakles, but it was investigations in the last few decades by J. Wagner which confirmed that this was the site of **Seleukaia on Euphrates**, known in Roman Times as **Zeugma**.

As the original name of the settlement suggests, it was founded *c.*300 BC by Seleukos I Nikator, Alexander the Great's former governor in Babylon and founding father of the Seleucid race. On the hill (Belkis Tepe) was the acropolis, and there was also a lower town at the foot of the slope. From here the Seleucids dominated an important crossing of the Euphrates, secured on the other side of the river by another of Seleukos' foundations, **Apameia**. Here too, not far from the modern village of *Keskince*, a former acropolis, parts of the town wall, a cemetery and numerous architectural fragments have been found. It is now also known that this important river crossing attracted settlers in the Bronze Age, and Apameia is thus not a genuine Seleucid foundation. As various ancient authors (Strabo, Pliny) confirm, there was a Seleucid pontoon bridge over the Euphrates between Seleukaia and Apameia. It was anchored by masonry piles on the two banks, and these too have been discovered and their remains excavated. The Roman general Crassus crossed the river here in 53 BC, shortly before his total defeat by the Parthians at Carrhae, at which he was killed. The river crossing here was important for trade even in the early Islamic period.

Seleukaia was granted to the Commagene ruler Antiochos I (→ under Adıyaman) at the congress of princes in Amisos in winter 65/64 BC. Substantial income from customs levies brought in by the Euphrates bridge must have made a welcome difference to Antiochos' state coffers, on which heavy demands were made by building the lavish cult sites (hierothesia) on the Nemrut Dağı among other places. 2 heavily weathered fragments of a dexiosis relief (Antiochos with Herakles) from this period were found in 1972 and 1974. They are in the museum in Gaziantep. The relief slab was originally 10 ft. high and 6 ft. 6 ins. wide, and is the souternmost example of its kind. Seleukaia was removed from Commagene under Augustus, and became part of the Roman province of Syria. The Romans extended the town as an important military base. From the time of Tiberius this was the headquarters of a legion, firstly the Legio X Fretensis, withdrawn to Jerusalem in AD 66 and replaced by the Legio IV Scythica, formerly stationed in Armenia. The town flourished again under the Romans, particularly in the 2C AD under the Emperors Trajan and Septimius Severus, and increased considerably in size. The military camp outside the town finally became part of it. The 4th legion left inscriptions in the Ehnes quarry N. of the town and were probably also responsible for the system of tunnels in the chalk cliffs not far upstream from Belkis, part of the military road on the W. bank of the Euphrates. Together with the Legio XVI Flavia Firma in Samosata/Samsat and another army unit in Dura Europs/Syria the 4th legion protected the Euphrates frontier until the time of the Emperor Diocletian (284–305). Nevertheless in AD 256 the Sassanid ruler Schahpur I succeeded in conquering and plundering Assur, Hatra, Dura Europos and also Seleukaia on the Euphrates. The city never recovered from this raid, and the population shrank rapidly from the early 4C. Finally only the citadel seems to have been inhabited. It continued to control the Euphrates crossing until well into the Byzantine period, but yielded in importance to the neighbouring fortress of Birecik at the time of the Crusades.

Birecik (63 km. E.): The road to Urfa crosses the Euphrates on the SW edge of the town. The river is navigable from this point. The bridge was not completed until 1956, and was for a long time the largest bridge in Turkey, with a length of 787 yards. It affords the best view of Birecik's principal attraction, the *citadel*, which was considered to be impregnable. The town itself, and the crossing point from the mountains in the N. to the Mesopotamian plain in the S., is on the left bank of the Euphrates and dominated the river crossing at least from the Roman period. The name *Birtha* conceals the Armenian word for castle, so there must have been a fortress here even in those days. At the time of the Crusades, when Balduin of Bouillon had his residence here, the town was called *Bile*. In 1150 it was sold, along with the county of Edessa's other possessions, to Byzantium, who lost it to the Ortokid Timurtas of Mardin in 1151. Saladin and his armies crossed the Euphrates here in 1183 and 1185. Then the town was ruled by the princes of Aleppo/Syria. The oldest inscription so far discovered in the castle, reporting on restoration work, dates from the time of Elmelik Ezzahir, the first representative of the Syrian dynasty here. In 1259 came the Mongols, then the Mamelukes, under whose leader Baraka Khan (1277–9) the castle was once more strengthened, although most of the inscriptions in the citadel come from Sultan Kait Bey (1482&3) of the same dynasty. From 1516 castle and town, also walled, were part of the Ottoman Empire.

Doliche (10 km. NW): Little remains in the present village of *Dülükbaba*, a little to the E. of the road which three km. further on forks either for Adana via Islâhiye, or Maraş, to show that this is the site of ancient Doliche, which for a long time was more important than Ayntab/Gaziantep. In the Byzantine period this

former seat of a bishop gave its name to the surrounding Teluch area. It was not until it was taken by the Arabs in 637, apparently without a struggle, that Doliche's importance began to wane in favour of Gaziantep. A castle was built here, probably under Harun al-Rachid (786–809), as part of a staggered chain of fortress intended to secure the frontier with Byzantium which ran along the Taurus. Nothing remains of the Temple of Jupiter Dolichenus, which in ancient times had importance beyond the region. All that remains of this period are a few rock tombs.

Elif, Hasanoğlu and Hisar (110 km. NE): These three monumental Roman monuments dating from the turn of the 2–3C AD line the military road along the bank of the Euphrates on the stretch between the two bridges over the ancient Marias (at Rumkale) and N. of this the Karasu (→ Adıyaman, environs), 2 tributaries of the Euphrates, just before their confluence with the major river. All the monuments are supported by square bases taller than a man, made up of a few layers of colossal ashlar and each with an entrance into the grave chamber within. The mausoleum of *Hisar* is 33 ft. high. The base supports a slightly overhanging platform, at the 4 corners of which are piers articulated with projections and concluding in acanthus motifs. They support a sagging pyramidic roof also topped by a cube with acanthus motifs. The *Elif* tomb has masonry above the base pierced on one axis by large arches, and on the other by a comparatively low rectangular door. The roof is missing, but the vault arches can still be seen.

Karkemish/Karkamiş (81 km. SE): The ruins of once-important Karkemish are reached by following the road to Urfa in Nizip, after 48 km., then driving 33 km. S. to the village of Cerablus. Because it is so near to the Syrian border, which runs immediately S. of the ancient settlement, the site can only be visited by special per-

Gaziantep, museum, basalt sphinx ▮

mission of the local military authorities and accompanied by a soldier. It goes without saying that photography is forbidden.

The palace is first mentioned *c.*1700 BC in the cuneiform tablet archives of the town of Mari, further S. on the Euphrates. Even then the town was important principally as a Euphrates crossing, subsequently hotly disputed among the major powers of the area, starting with the Hittite king Hattusili I (second half of the 17C BC). At the time of Pharaoh Thutmosis III, under whom Egypt reached its greatest territorial extent, the section of the Euphrates running N.S. to the S. of Karkemish was the Egyptian frontier with the neighbouring Mitannic empire, and the town itself was in the Egyptian sphere of influence, but then came under Mitannic control. When the Mitannic empire declined in the mid-14C the town became part of the Hittite empire under Suppiluliuma I. The new rulers, anxious to control their Syrian possessions, created the office of viceroy, occupied by high-ranking members of the royal family, and made Karkemish their residence. Numerous cuneiform documents on clay tablets show the important role played by Karkemish in the Hittite empire. When the Hittie empire fell to the Peoples of the Sea, the town was destroyed *c.*1190 BC. Shortly afterwards however it gained in strength again as centre of one of the numerous Hittite successor states, amongst which Karkemish was able to establish supremacy among the surrounding principalities, with the result that its regents for a time assumed the old Hittite title of Great King. Increasing pressure from Assyria at first meant that the allied princes had to hold together, but soon only the payment of tribute permitted a certain degree of independence, and Karkemish became a province of Assyria under Sargon II in 717 BC. After the victory of the Medes and Babylonians over the Assyrians, whose empire was annihilated, a battle was fought outside the gates of Karkemish between the Babylonians and the Egyptians, won by the former under Nebuchadnezzar. The town was an important trading post even under the Greeks, then called *Europs* or *Hierapolis.* It was not until the end of the Roman period that it sank into insignificance.

The British Museum financed excavations in 1911–15 and 1920, in which T.E. Lawrence (Lawrence of Arabia) was involved for a time. The principal discovery was the late-Hittite town, with numerous foundation blocks with reliefs (orthostatic reliefs). These are all in the museum in Ankara. The town was set *c.* 130 ft. above the Euphrates on a hill, naturally protected by the river to the E., and first consisted of a long oval citadel directly on the line of the river. A large walled oval (maximum diameter 656 yards) sharing the wall by the bank with the citadel, made up the 'inner town'. This is where most of the relief blocks were discovered. There was a water gate which gave access from the Euphrates, and two other gates *c.*750 yards apart in the W. and S. There are sparse remains of all three on the present site, but they make little impression without their decorative reliefs. The wall of the 'outer town', partially straight and partially curved, encloses an area of 1,148 yards in an N.-S. direction and 864 yards E.-W., embracing the oval of the 'inner town' like pincers. The only evidence of the Roman period is the foundations of a temple in the citadel area.

Rumkale (also **Kasaba**, 90 km. NE): The impressive medieval *fortress of Rumkale* is high on the bank of the Euphrates nor far from its confluence with the ancient Marsyas, opposite the village of Halfeti on a long tongue of rock with a steep drop on three sides. In the Armenian period the town was called *Hromgla* and was the seat of a patriarch. Thanks to the fortress the settlement was until 1291 the last Christian enclave in Muslim N. Syria under the Mamelukes, until finally it too was conquered.

Gilindere, Roman tomb ▷

Tell Beşir (about 30 km. SSE): The minor road which leads in 46 km. to the frontier town of Akçakoyunlu goes through Til Bahram after 24 km.. About 5 km. ESE of here is the Tell Beşir with the *fortress of Turbessel*, once the preferred residence of the feudal counts of Edessa. By the gate there are still sections of the old walls and some interior buildings.

Gelibolu/Gallipoli
Çanakkale   p.564☐B 2

Gelibolu is on the European bank of the Dardanelles/Sea of Marmara in a strategically important position. The town played an important role in Ottoman history, as naval base and fortress. The Ottomans gained a foothold in Europe here long before the fall of Constantinople. *Gazi Süleyman Paşa*, the conqueror of Rumelia, commissioned the *cami* which bears his name in 1358 (restored). Süleyman Paşa's *türbe* is in *Bolayır* (15 km. NE) on a hill with a fine view of the sea, and next to it is the tomb of the famous Turkish poet Namık Kemal (1840–1888).

Gilindere
Mersin   p.574☐J 6

57 km. E. of Anamur is Gilindere, ancient **Kelendiris**, originally a Phoenician foundation, later colonized by Greeks from Samos. The town figures in the tribute list of the Attic League as in the middle rank of tribute payers. However, under the Roman Empire it was one of the most important harbours in Cilicia, especially as the the shortest sea crossing to Cyprus was from here. There are ruins from this period throughout the bay of Kelendiris, and also Byzantine remains.

Environs: Softa Kalesi: (31 km. W.): The 'scholars' citadel' is above a wedge-shaped rise to the W. The massive ruins of this gigantic fortress, brooding as a threatening presence over the region, date from the Byzantine period. The outer wall with its defensive towers has survived to a large extent.

Gordion
Ankara   p.566☐H 3

The ancient town of Gordion is near the village of Yassıhüyük (17 km. W. of Polatlı, then 12 km. N.). Several tumuli rise over a large area like pyramids in the desert of this upland steppe landscape. The largest is clearly visible from a distance: the so-called tomb of the Phrygian king Gordios. The tumulus used to tower over 250 ft. above the plain. The harsh climate of Anatolia has reduced the height of the man-made colossus to 174 ft., and increased the original base diameter from 820 to 984 ft. Before the tumulus, on the right of the modern Sakara Cay, the ancient River Sangarios, is the acropolis of the ancient city of Gordion, excavated over an area of 546 x 383 yards.

History: Excavations conducted from 1953 under the direction of the American archaeologist Rodney S. Young have proved that the area was inhabited *c.*2500 BC (early Bronze Age). Excavations in Ahlâtlibel S. of Gordion produced finds from the second half of the 3rd millennium BC in 1934. In the 2nd millennium Gordion was within the sphere of influence of the Hittites, and a Hittite tomb area was found under a later Phrygian necropolis.

Shortly after 1200 BC the Phrygian invasion reached the Hittite empire and contributed to its downfall. Indo-Germanic Phrygians from the Balkans and Thrace settled in mid and W. Anatolia. Their period of settlement in Gordion was established among the 18 settlement levels as having been in the mid

9C BC. In the early 8C Anatolian culture began to rise again, indicating the end of the dark ages after the Hittites and associated with the Phrygians. The importance of Hittite cultural elements even at the peak of the Phrygian empire in the 2nd half of the 8C BC is evidence of a typical Anatolian process of mixing two following cultures. At this time Gordion became the capital of the legendary Gordios, king of the empire. He placed the ox cart that according to an oracle took the peasant Gordios straight on to the king's throne in the city temple. A cunning knot (Gordian knot) between shaft and yoke made history another 500 years later.

King Midas, Gordion's son and successor, ruled over the whole of W. Asia Minor. His skill in accumulating gold may have led to the legend that he put wine in the spring of the spring daemon Silenus, caught the drunken sprite and then blackmailed his god Dionysos into granting him the gift that everything he touched should turn to gold. His reputation may also account for the fact that a little later Gordion was particulary thoroughly plundered. In any case the legendary Phrygian treasure was not found in Gordion, nor in any of the tombs, much to the disappointment of archaeologists. The Assyrian king Sargon II (721–705), in his time ruler of the greatest military power in the East, describes Mita (Midas) as a rival to be taken seriously. But Midas was unable to resist the storm of the Cimmerians (700–670 BC) from the Caucasus, followed by the Scythians. They overran Phrygia, and Midas is said to have committed suicide after his defeat by drinking bull's blood.

After destruction by the Cimmerians (685 BC), the Phrygians built a more modest city for their kings on the lower neighbouring hill directly in front of the gates of the town. Phrygia continued to exist within vastly reduced frontiers and circumstances until c.650 BC, then Gordion was occupied by the Lydians. Herodotus writes of the subsequent Lydian empire under King Alyattes (615–560), whose son Croesus was replaced as ruler of Anatolia by the Persian Achaemenids in 546. A little later the Persians covered up the ruins of the old city of Gordion with a thick layer of clay, in order to build a new town of the same size on the old site. Thus

Gordion, excavation with Midas burial mound

Gordion, Phrygian town gate

a wonderfully interesting 'layer of culture' was preserved. The higher level was also strategically more favourable, but ineffective against the severe earthquake *c*.400 BC. Gordion was rebuilt once more.

Alexander the Great chose Gordion for his winter quarters in 334/333 BC because he wished to see the prophecy fulfilled that he who loosed the knot on Gordion's ox cart should be ruler of the world. Alexander finally cut it with his sword. In 278 BC European Galatians laid Phrygia and Gordion waste with such thoroughness that the remainder of the population never returned. Gordion became an unimportant Celtic settlement. Excavations also confirm that any urban or political life worthy of the name was finally extinguished.

Acropolis: This is easily seen on the edge of the excavation crater. It was the centre of the town with its official buildings and accommodation, the king's palace, cult buildings, domestic and storage chambers. The houses of the rest of the population were on the plain outside the town wall. In the Persian period the walls were reinforced and raised, and the Persian Gate was added to the fortifications to secure the garrison and trading town on the imperial road from the Dardanelles to Ankara to Susa.

The Phrygian *town gate* on the W. side of the hill is rated as one of the most monumental buildings in ancient Anatolia, with the finest masonry of the pre-Grecian period. The impressive gatehouse has survived to a height of 31 ft. It was built in the late 8C BC. The 4 *megaron buildings* with vestibule and main chamber with round fireplace in the middle date from the same period. Three of the megara had floors with coloured mosaic. SW of the megaron foundations and on the same axis are 8 foundations of *domestic rooms*, all of equal size. Remains of fine paving have survived in the palace courtyard. The second megaron from the gatehouse is said to have been the hall of the royal palace. The wooden gabled roof was supported by two rows of piers. The 'aisles' were surrounded by galleries. Remains of charred beams were found, also 3 acroteria, which decorated the gabled roof. Here the king is said to have held audience. The floor was paved with fine mosaic ornament in dark red, white and dark blue stones, and a large area of this has survived on the original site.

Large tumulus (by the museum): This is the second-largest of this kind in Anatolia. The highest, at 226 ft., is the tumulus near Bintepe on the Sea of Marmara, near the Lydian metropolis of Sardes, described by Herodotus as the Tumulus of Alyattes. As Alyattes (615–560 BC) also incorported Phrygia into his empire of Greater Lydia, his tumulus had to be bigger. The grave chamber in Gordion was an important

Gordion, burial hill (left), Phrygian vessel (right)

find at the time. The American excavators drove a passage over 200 ft. into the hillside directly into the grave chamber, which they had previously found by sounding. The walls of the inner grave chamber were made of thick pine planks and juniper trunks. The chamber was 20 x 17 ft. The double wooden wall was reinforced by a stone wall. The floor was made up of wooden beams almost a foot thick, with a thick layer of gravel for drainage underneath. The dead man, aged about 65 and 5 ft. 9 ins. tall, lay on a wooden couch covered with several layers of fabric. He lay on his back, his face turned to the E. His clothing was fastened with bronze brooches which survived in good condition at the shoulders and the arms. The brooches were work of the very highest quality, a Phrygian invention and major technical achievement of the period. 175 of them were found in this tomb.

Other finds attesting the high level of Phrygian culture from 750–690 BC are 9 wooden three-legged tables, 2 almost complete wooden screens with excellent light and dark inlay work on a particular pattern, bronze situlae (drinking vessels) with lions' and rams' heads (imports?), bronze omphalos dishes, bronze cauldrons, plates with handles, to be seen as models for Cypriot and Greek objects. 178 bronze vessels of all sizes were found in this tomb, including three large cauldrons.

The controversial question of whether Gordios or Midas is buried here is incorrectly formulated. Old Gordios had long been dead when the tumulus came into being, but Midas was still alive, as he was mentioned as a contemporary by the Assyrian king Sargon II (721–705). Herodotus also places in this period his report about Midas, who had been married to a Greek and who, as the first foreign king sent 'his fine royal throne, on which he sat in judgement' as a votive gift to Delphi. This Midas is said to have committed suicide after the Cimmerian catastrophe (700–670). As the Phrygian kings were from time immemorial called Gordios or Midas alternately, the designation 'king's tomb' is the most precise.

The grave chamber had a saddleback roof with sturdy rectangular beams, carefully insulated, as the whole tomb was protected against robbers with a 10 ft. layer of stones and against dampness with a 130 ft. layer of clay. Rubble was placed on top of this. There was no access to the grave chamber.

So-called **children's tomb** (SE of the museum). Outstanding treasures were found here: lions and bulls carved out of beechwood, ivory reliefs and wonderful wooden furniture.

4 of the largest tumuli excavated in the cemetery at Gordion date, according to their size and furnishings, from the period before the Cimmerian onslaught, probably from the 2nd half of the 8C BC. The objects in the (most recent) of the children's tombs correspond with those in the 7C level, the town that was destroyed. It was thus built c.700 BC, and the oldest of the tumuli c.750, when the hill town to the W. came into being.

Hakkâri

Hakkâri   p.578 ☐ T 5

This town 250 km. from Van, for a long time called Çölemerik, is the centre of the southeasternmost Turkish province, with frontiers with both Iran and Iraq. It owes its present name to the Kurdish Hakkâri tribe, who were driven out of Iraq by the Zengids in the 13C and found a new home here. A small group of Nestorian Christians also used the area as a place to which to retreat because it was so isolated, but this only until the First World War, when they too were driven away. Apart from the citadel and 2 medrese (Seljuk or

16C) the town has no historic buildings of note, but it is in impressive countryside among mountains that are always snow-covered, almost all almost 13,000 ft. The largest (Cilo Dağı) is 13,513 ft., followed by Sat Dağı at 12,526 ft. The Great Zap, a tributary of the Tigris, which has carved itself a deep valley in the surrounding mountain landscape, flows by the town from NE to SW.

The region was inhabited in prehistoric times. Rock drawings with figures on the plateaus of Gevarik (Gevaruk) and Tirsin in the W. of the province, discovered in large quantities over a large area by Múaffak Uyanik, are said to date to a large extent from 5500 BC. Even traces of a stone age settlement have been found in Rasibeyn. Here also tribes of the semi-nomadic Lullubaeans lived, who in the Sumerian and Akkadian periods made great inroads into the fertile Land of the Two Rivers (famous stele of King Naramsin of Akkad on the occasion of his victory over the Lullubaeans; now in the Louvre in Paris). In the first half of the first millennium BC the region was part of the Urartian kingdom, and the important Urartian town of Musasir is held to have been close to Yuksekova (84

Hakkâri, panorama ▷

km. E. of Hakkâri near the Iranian border). Musasir was not conquered by the Assyrian king Sargon II until 714 BC. Reliefs showing the fighting and subsequent plundering found in the Assyrian ruler's palace in Chorsabad/Iraq unfortunately sank in the Tigris while being transported to Europe.

Environs: Albayrak (also **Zapbasi, Şikefti** or **Deir**; 107 km. NNE): A side road turns off to the E. from the road to Van a few km. beyond Başkale near Irishan (106 km. before Van), reaching Albayrak 12 km. later. Because it is so near to the frontier it can only be visited with permission from the authorities, as a military outfit is stationed here. The village consists almost entirely of the monks' former accommodation, who lived not in a walled monastery, but in adjacent individual houses like a village, now taken over by the present population. The *monastery church* which was part of this *monastery of St. Bartholomew* is outside the settlement to the W. on a hill on the right bank of the Great Zap. An earthquake shook the surrounding area (known in the Middle Ages as Aghbak) in 1966, causing the church roof to collapse, and so the interior can no longer be visited. The beautiful tympanum friezes also collapsed partially. Tambour and dome were destroyed as early as 1715. The rectangular building, first mentioned in the 14C and, according to the inscription on the W. façade, restored in the 17C, is 102 ft. long and 56 ft. wide, with the rectangular narthex occupying 50 x 34 ft., with adjacent space under the dome with large apse and two side rooms.

Başkale (95 km. NNE): This place on the road to Van was an important centre of the kingdom of Vaspurakan in the Armenian period, when it was known as *Hadamakert*, and was the capital of the province of Aghbak. The Ardsruni rulers of Vaspurakan were able to hold their ground for a short time against the Bagtarids in the N. and Emir Yussif in the S.

Kotchanes (Qodshanes; 20 km. NE): Until the First World War Kotchanes was the seat of the patriarch of the small group of Nestorian Christians who withdrew to the region around Hakkâri. It is now very difficult to reach. It is possible to reach the pass at a height of 10,171 ft. in a cross-country vehicle from Hakkâri. From the pass it takes about 6 hours on foot, and a local mountain guide is essential. The church of Mar Shalita is outside the modern village of Qodshanes. It is a massive building with very small windows, like a fortified church. It also has a look-out post, and is now used for the storage of dung briquettes.

Soradir (127 km. NNE): Follow the Great Zap for about 20 km. upstream from Albayrak (see above for route). Here, only 15 km. from the Iranian border at a height of over 7,750 ft. on the site of the old Armenian monastery of Etshmiadsin is the village of Soradir. Here, somewhat to one side of a bleak hillock is a *church* which was once part of the monastery of Karmir Vank (Red Monastery), and probably dates from the 6C. The domed church with cruciform ground plan and 4 conches is still in relatively good condition, as it is now used as a grain store. The W. arm and choir opposite have straight outer walls, while on the other sides the internal apses can be discerned from the polygonal outer wall. The church was damaged in the course of clashes between Abbasids and Ottomans. The dome in its present form dates from the 17C.

Halikarnassos/Bodrum

Muğla   p.571☐C 5

The Roman architect Vitruvius (1C BC) described the town as laid out like a theatre, with the agora by the harbour as orchestra, and rows of houses climbing up the semicircular slope like tiers of seats. The town was founded in the 11C BC as a Dorian colony (by Anthes from the mother town of Troezen in the E.

Peloponnese; in order to maintain its link with the mother town Halikarnassos later had a temple of Aphrodite built there) following a Carian settlement. The natural double harbour, easily protected territory for a trading town and acropolis and good agricultural land in the neighbourhood were ideal conditions for a coastal town and ensured its rapid rise. It joined the Delian League together with Knidos, Kos, Lindos, Kamiros and Jasylos, with the Temple of Apollo in Knidos as its centre. Halikarnassos was expelled from the League in the 8C, ostensibly because one of its victorious athletes at a competition took the victor's prize, a bronze tripod, home with him, instead of dedicating it to Apollo in Knidos, as was customary. The actual reason was probably dilution of the Dorian population by Ionians.

In any case the period of political autonomy was short in comparison with the period of dominance from outside. Thus Halikarnassos was part of the Lydian empire in the 7&6C, and of the Persian empire after the defeat of the Lydian king Croesus by the Persians in 546 BC. The Persians instituted a Graeco-Carian dynasty which even had to contribute 5 ships as part of Xerxes campaign against the Greek motherland in 480 BC. The then queen of Halikarnassos, Artemisia I, was commander-in-chief of the little fleet of ships from Halikarnassos, Kos, Nisyos and Kalida. She was a member of the Great King's closest team of advisers, and specifically counselled against a sea battle at Salamis. When the Persian fleet then lost the battle and she was herself in danger she saved herself by running aground her own ship and that of the king of Kalyndos, who was also fighting for the Persians, thus creating a way of escape. Xerxes, admiring this dashing deed from afar, said 'my men have become women and my women men'. The Athenians then placed a price of 10,000 drachmas on the queen's head.

After the Greek world was freed of the Persians, Halikarnassos became a Greek city again from 478 BC, protected by the Delian-Attic League, but in 386 BC fell under Persian dominance again, who established the family of Hekatomnos, who resided in Mylasa, as satraps. His son Mausolos (377–353 BC) transferred his seat to Halikarnassos and set in motion thorough rebuilding of the commercial

Halikarnassos, Roman garland frieze

town as a government capital: he built a wall 5.3 km. long around the extended site, enlarged the population fivefold by compulsory resettlement and built a marble-clad, brick palace for himself (building method taken over from Rome). After his death his sister and consort Artemisia II (the younger) ruled. She built for her brother the tomb famous as the seventh wonder of the ancient world, the Mausoleum. After her death her sister Ada ruled at first, until she was driven out by her brother Pixodaros, who ruled jointly with the Persian satrap Orontobates. In 334 BC therefore Halikarnassos was one of the few actual Greek cities in Asia Minor to resist the advance of Greek-Macedonian Alexander the Great and force him to a time-consuming siege. Alexander then put Ada back in authority over Caria, with the exception of the Greek cities, which were to remain free. In the 3C (c.280–200 BC) Halikarnassos came into the Egyptian sphere of influence (Ptolemy II Philadelphos 285–246 BC), then into that of the Seleucids. When Rome defeated the Seleucid Antiochos III at the battle of Magnesia, Halikarnassos, together with Lycia and Caria, became subject to Rhodes under the patronage of Rome, then to become part of the Roman province of Asia in 129 BC. In 80 BC the notorious Roman governor Verres plundered Halikarnassos' art treasures. Politically the city did not reappear until the 13C, then under the Seljuk emirs of Milas, the Menteşe. In 1402 the Order of St.John (and of Malta) retreating from the Holy Land succeeded in gaining a foothold in Halikarnassos from Rhodes. They established themselves on the peninsula, which was then endowed with a great Crusader fortress, and this was actually recognized by decree as the possession of the Christian Order in 1415 by Mehmet I as compensation for his lost possessions in Smyrna. In 1522 the Ottoman sultan Süleyman I drove the Knights of St.John out of Rhodes, and in 1523 out of

Halikarnassos ▷

Halikarnassos, crusaders' castle

Halikarnassos; the Order then withdrew further W., to Malta.

The most famous citizen of Halikarnassos was Herodotus, the 'father of history', whose 'History' represents the beginnings of this discipline in Europe. He was the son of a leading Carian-Greek family. His work was based on extensive journeys to the Black Sea, Thrace, Macedonia, Greece, Egypt and the lands of the Tigris and Euphrates. He thus made his own experience, impressions and research the basis of historical writing, rather than the passing on of myths, legends and untested tradition.

Very little remains of the ancient town.

Crusader castle of St. Peter: This was built on the rocky peninsula (formerly island) in the 15C, mainly from material from the Mausoleum, which had been destroyed by an earthquake. Work began

on what had previously been a Seljuk fortress, and before that an ancient citadel, from 1402.

The importance of the building can be seen from a papal edict of 1409, according to which anyone involved in construction of the fortress will gain remission of sins. The first fortifications were built by the German architect Heinrich Schlegelholt (1415–37). In 1436 work on the central section of the castle was started. As befitted the international composition of this oldest of the spiritual orders of knights, it has an Italian (Angelo Muscettola) and a French tower. The irregular rectangle of walls and the Snake Tower were started in 1440, the moat in 1476, the English tower was completed in 1480. The final touches were added under the Master of the Order Pierre d'Aubusson 1476–1503, above all the round protruding bastions in the N. and the harbour battery. The chapel was completed last (1520).

The fortress is now used as a museum and contains above all objects discovered by submarine archaeology, including amphoras and large copper ingots recovered from a ship which sank by Cape Gelidonya (E. tip Finike) *c.*1200 BC by a submarine expedition from the University of Pennsylvania under George F. Bassu in 1960. As the ingots are of differing weights (between 35 and 95 punds) it is unlikely that they are a kind of currency previous to the invention of money (1 ingot worth 1 ox).

Mausoleum: Tomb of the satrap Mausolos (377–353 BC), built by his sister and consort Artemisia II, now in the middle of the Turkish town about 100 yards inland. Philo of Byzantium considered it one of the 7 wonders of the ancient world. After destruction by an earthquake in the 15C it was removed to its foundations by the Knights of St. John as building material for their fortress. Excavations by Lord Stratford in 1846 and Sir Charles Newton in 1857 led to the removal of the reliefs and the statues

Herakleia under Latmos, Endymion

which were found of Mausolos and Artemisia to the British Museum in London. An impression of the building can be gained from the admittedly not quite precise description by Pliny the Elder (AD 23–79) in his 'Naturalis historia': above a grave chamber cut into the rock, accessible by 12 steps, was a substructure with five steps supporting a base 108 x 128 ft. Upon this stood a cella with an Ionic peristasis (9 x 11 columns) with a total of 36 columns. A quadriga with statues of Mausolos and Artemisia was placed at the apex of a stepped pyramidic roof (24 steps). Base and cella were surrounded by relief friezes, on which the best-known sculptors of the time worked: Skopas, Timotheos, Bryaxis and Leochares. There were carved lions between the columns. The complete building was about 160 ft., and it stood in a walled square 794 x 344 ft., as recent

Danish excavations have proved. The architect was Pytheos, who also built the fine Temple of Athena in Priene.

Town wall: Some remains, including the Myndos Gate, W. of the town.

Theatre (above the Mausoleum): Despite restoration this has only survived in sketchy outline. It is presumed to date from the 3C BC.

Herakleia under Latmos
Muğla   p.572☐C 5

Originally a 5C BC Carian settlement, which made an annual contribution of 1 talent as a member of the Attic League, it came under the rule of Halikarnassos in the 4C BC. King Mausolos (377–353

Herakleia, Temple of Athena

BC) won the trust of the people of Herakleia by a trick. When they opened their gates to him he marched in with his army and extended the town as a major border fortress on the N. frontier of his kingdom. At that time the town was still at the innermost SE corner of the Latmian Gulf (on which Miletos and Priene also lay), and thus had direct access to the Aegean. Deposits from the Meander did not cut the bay off from the open sea until the 4C AD, forming an inland sea, now the Bafa Gölü, 15 km. long, 7 km. wide and up to 66 ft. deep at the foot of the jagged Beş Parmak Dağı (Five Finger Mountain), the ancient Mount Latmos, a granite massif 4,485 ft. high. For the Greeks this was the home of the legend of Endymion: Zeus fell in love with the beautiful youth, who was involved with his wife Hera. In order to resolve the complications Endymion, when granted a wish by Zeus, wished for eternal youth and eternal sleep; since then he has slept on Mount Latmos, beloved of the moon goddess Selene, who visits him every night, and has already born him 50 daughters. In contradiction to this notion of eternal sleep, Endymion's tomb was shown in Olympia and Herakleia. For the Greeks Endymion was the first man to discover the orbit of the moon. The Christians made him into a mystic who discovered the name of God from the moon and then died. Every year his coffin was opened and the miracle of his humming bones admired: this may be linked with the fact that in the Byzantine period Herakleia and Mount Latmos were popular places of retreat for monks; the ruins on the 4 little islands in the lake are remains of monastic settlements.

Particular features of the site, well worth seeing in its magnificent setting, are:

Agora: Open space upon which the school now stands; Hellenistic pattern withí three-storey market hall in the S. (lower storey survives in part).

Temple of Athena (3C BC): Two columns used to stand in front of protruding side walls of the high cella, which has survived.

Buleuterion: The circular steps NE of the agora indicate an assembly area for the city council.

Rock shrine of Endymion: Rock shrine with four-columned narthex for Endymion; on the way to the lake.

Tombs: These are rectangular chamber tombs of the Carian type, cut into the rocks on the lake shore. They can be closed with lids.

Town wall: The Hellenistic wall is 6.5 km. long, the major sight in Herakleia. It is built on the shell principle, between 7–10 ft. thick and just under 20 ft. high. Steps lead to the parapet at the top, and the entire wall is reinforced with towers 50–100 yards apart. The two arms of the wall climb the cliff to meet at a height of about 1150 ft.

Theatre: The theatre is almost completely overgrown, but its semicircle can be made out on the ground. Summer visitors to Kapıkırı and Herakleia tend to have the place to themselves, as the villagers are out with the flocks on the summer pastures.

I

İğdır

Kars   p.570□U 3

İğdır is at the N. foot of Ararat, not far from the Russian border, formed here by the river Ataxes (Aras). It has no notable sights itself, but in the nearby village of *Malaklu* Russian archaeologists found a late Urartian cemetery (7C BC) in 1913 and took the finds to the museum in Tblissi (Tiflis) in the USSR. Later Turkish excavations (1966 under K.Balkan) revealed relics which are now in the museum in Kars. İğdır is a possible starting point for climbing Mount Ararat, via a route up the Ahira valley leading past Başköy and Koran Kalesi.

Environs: Başköy: This village, reached via a track, is at a height of 6,890 ft. in the Ahira valley, a clinker-filled gorge whose stream is fed by the waters of the great NW Ararat glacier. At the entrance to the valley are 5 *crosses* in the rocks, and above them numerous *caves*, formerly the homes of Christian hermits.

Koran Kalesi: Continuing the ascent of Ararat from Başköy, the route passes coloured tufa cones and mountain lakes with sulphurous fumaroles, then reaches *Lake Kop*, at a height of 13,123 ft. On an underwater terrace is the site known as *Koran Kalesi* with a little fortress and the nearby ruins of an Armenian church.

Tuzluka (about 55 km. W.): The road to Erzurum, which follows the Araxes for long stretches, passes Tuzluka with its unmistakable huge rock-salt caves (some natural, some caused by mining) on the N. side of the road. NW of here on the

Çıldır Çayı, a tributary of the Araxes, is ancient Armenian **Bagaran,** residence in the 9C of the Bagtarid prince Achot the Great (856–890). Special permission is needed for a visit because of its proximity to the border. The only surviving feature of the former monastery of St.John (except a second, very badly damaged church) is the rectangular *main church* with 4 apses. According to the inscription it was built between 624 and 631 and restored in the 13C.

From İğdır it is possible to make an expedition to *Doğubayazıt* with the *İshak Paşa Sarayı* (55 km.). The attractive route leads along the W. slope of Ararat, crossing the Çengel pass (→ environs of Ağrı).

İskenderun

Hatay/Antakya   p.576☐M 6

This town on the gulf of the same name, the former **Alexandretta,** is set on a plain fringed by the Nur Dağları chain. It was founded by Alexander the Great after his victory over the Persians at Issos (333 BC). The town subsequenly came to the Sassanids (AD 260), Arabs (7C) and Byzantines (969). In 1268 it became Mameluke, and in 1515 Sultan Selim made it part of the Ottoman Empire. The French occupied the city and surrounding territory after the First World War and established a protectorate, then returned everything to Turkey in 1939. The port has no notable historic buildings.

Environs: Arzuz (30 km. SW): This little fishing village to the SW with a fine beach and not far from the little river of the same name is probably on the site of ancient **Rhosos** or **Rhosopolis**, a 3C BC Seleucid foundation. Fairly close to the village are remains of an encircling wall and buildings. 15 km. from Arzuz, near **Hınzır,** is a ruined *Crusader castle*, conquered by Saladin in 1188 and later taken over by the Mamelukes.

Bağras: Built by the Crusaders, now in very bad condition, conquered by Saladin in 1188, then later occupied by Armenians and Egyptian Mamelukes. It is possible that this is the site of Pagrae, mentioned by Strabo.

Belen (14 km. SE): This place on the road to Antakya is a popular holiday resort for the people of İskenderun, particularly in summer, when its position at a height of 1,476 ft. makes it cooler than the coastal area. It has remains of an *aqueduct*, a fine *mosque* and a *caravanserai* from the period of Süleyman the Magnificent (mid-16C). Beyond Belen the road to Antakya goes over the Belen pass (2,460 ft.), once controlled by the medieval *fortress of Bagras* (now 4 km. off the road).

Dört Yol (30 km. N.): Not far from this town (the name means 4 Ways) is the site of ancient *Issos,* where Alexander the Great defeated the Persian king Darius III in 333 BC. Dört Yol, at the foot of the Daz Dağı (7,349 ft.), has some fine Islamic buildings such as the *Çin-Kulesi* (Ghost Tower), a *Turkish bath* (hamam), a *caravanserai*, a *medrese*, a picturesque *mosque* and a covered *bazaar*.

Erzin/Yeşilkent (40 km. N.): Not far from here is the extensive ruined site of ancient **Epiphania.** The town was founded by Cicero, and an impressive *aqueduct* in particular has survived.

Payas (17 km. N.): This little place in a bay in the Gulf of İskenderun has a 13C Genoese *Crusader citadel* right on the coast. Behind this Sokollu Mehmet Paşa, Grand Vizier of Sultan Selim II, built a large complex of buildings in 1574. This consisted of a large *caravanserai* in the form of a courtyard surrounded by pointed arches supported by piers. Adjacent to this is a long, single-aisled *bazaar* with tunnel vault and central dome. There are remains of the original stucco decoration. To the right of the bazaar is a domed *bath house* with hot and cold pools. In the W. corner of the complex is a *courtyard mosque* with central domed chamber. All the buildings are in careful ashlar masonry. Syrian influence shows in the decoration of the gates with alternate white, black and red marble bands. The town was at the end of an old caravan road from Mesopotamia, and was a flourishing concern in the mid 18C. It went into a rapid decline, however, under the robber prince Küçük Ali. The surrounding area is now devoted to industry and docks.

Sarı Seki: This is a *mountain pass fortification*, very badly damaged, between İskenderun and Payas, which was improved and rebuilt at various times. The gatehouse, formerly with Gothic vaulting, is Ottoman. The two-line building inscription over the door mentions the years 1543 or 1549, and thus places the building in the reign of Süleyman the Magnificent.

Islâhiye

Gaziantep   p.576□M 5

This town halfway between Antakya and Maraş was called *Niboli* until about 1880. Some academics maintain that this was ancient Nikopolis, founded by Alexander the Great after his victory over the Persians at Issos. It is known that Nikopolis was at an important junction from which it was possible to reach Adana, Antakya, Maraş, Zeugma and Edessa/Urfa.

The metropolis extended by Pompey became part of the Roman province of Syria in AD 21 and was later, together with Rhosos and Anazarbus, conquered by the Parthians. The suggestion that Islâhiye stands on the same site could be confirmed by the fact that its castle probably dates from the 1C BC.

The plain around Islâhiye is important to archaeologists because it has been possible to investigate more than 40 settlement mounds here, populated in the early Bronze Age, according to ceramic finds. This juxtaposition of so many places in a confined space suggests that a flourishing small-scale state must have developed here, probably living on trade with Mesopotamia. It is possible that one of its

Payas, Sokollu-Mehmet-Paşa complex

rulers was 'King Isqippu of the Cedar Mountains', known from cuneiform texts.

Environs: Bektaşlı (67 km. S.): After about 60 km. on the road to Antakya a turning goes off to the village of Saylak (3 km.). Bektaşlı is 4 km. further on, at the foot of the Nur Dağları (Amanos). Nearby are a *ruined Byzantine church* and the *castle*, high on a cliff controlling the Belen pass, in order to anticipate threats to the port of İskenderun from the hinterland.

Gedikli (about 35 km. E.): Excavations (from 1964 under Alkim) revealed numerous finds from a flourishing early Bronze Age trading settlement on the settlement mound of *Karahüyük* near the modern village of Gedikli, within sight of the more important settlement of Sakçegözü. Investigation of the cemetery areas revealed an astonishing juxtaposition

Yesemek (Islâhiye), Hittite quarry and open-air studio

of cremated remains in urns and internments of complete bodies in coffins and chamber tombs, which is held to be the consequence of joint occupation of the site by a long-standing population at the same time as a second group of immigrants, possibly Indo-Germanic (early Hittites). The earliest remains found here go back to the chalcolithic period.

Gündüslü (74 km. S.): About 10 km. before Kırıkhane (destroyed caravanserai) about 900 yards to the l. of the road to Antakya on a rocky promontory are 3 *cave tombs* with a long Greek inscription. The relief above it is badly damaged. A small temple was also found on a little rocky plateau (scarcely any remains).

Sakşegözü (about 30 km. E.): The *ruins* are S. of the road to Gaziantep near the village of Keferdiz. English excavations conducted here in 1908−11 and 1948&9 on the settlement mound known as Coba Hüyük revealed a palace with vestibule and a defensive wall from the most successful period in Sakçegözü's history, when there was an important trade centre here under the Late Hittite principality of Gurgum (with residence in Maraş). The impressive portal lion, other sculptures and stone blocks with reliefs that decorated and protected the wall bases were removed to the museum in Ankara. 12 settlement levels from the chalcolithic period to the 1C AD were discovered as well as these important finds from the first half of the first millennium BC.

Sultankale (Çilvan; 77 km. S.): The *castle* of Sultankale stands guard over the Belen pass about 10 km. W. of Bektaşlı (q.v.). It is impressively set on a rock at a height of 4,101 ft., and probably dates from the Byzantine period. The entrance is now on the W. side. The S. gate with 2 bastions is impressive; opposite it in the N. is a

Yesemek (Islâhiye), Hittite quarry, unfinished lion sculpture

square tower. In the SE a ruined *chapel* with a *cistern* under it are of interest.

Terbezek (58 km. S.): A track leading to the village of Ala Beyli (2 km.) branches off the road to Antakya about 4 km. before Kırıkhane. The *ruined castle*, known at the time of the Crusades as Trapesac, is 1 km. N. of this. It was one of the most important links in the Crusader state of Antioch's defensive chain. It was lost to Saladin after extensive fighting in 1188, then reconquered, then finally fell to the Mamelukes in 1268. Under Baibars it was called Darsak and housed a garison. Only the lower sections of the buildings have survived.

Tilmenhüyük (10 km. E.): Excavations under Alkim, started in 1959, led to the discovery of the foundations of an ancient Syrian palace; the hill had been inhabited since the early Bronze Age. The residence, which is very similar to the contemporary

complex in Tell Açana/Alalalach, was destroyed and rebuilt on many occasions. On approaching the site the *settlement mound* appears at first on the left-hand side, but the road then turns sharply to the left (the road into Yesemek branches off just beyond this point) and the mound disappears behind a long heap of rubble running along the side of the road. Behind this and parallel to it are two more long mounds, and the site is behind this again, reached only by wading through a stretch of water. The first feature to be reached is the lower sections of a gate, built in great basalt blocks using the cyclopean wall technique. It was part of the former town walls, built *c.*1000 BC in the Late Hittite period. The palace precinct was surrounded by a carefully crafted basalt wall built using the so-called saw-tooth technique (i.e the walls do not run straight, but short sections of wall follow each other in such a way as to produce a structure reminiscent of the blade of a saw). When the palace came into being in the 18/17C BC, it was part of the important Syrian kingdom of Yamahad, ruled from Aleppo and made up, according to ancient texts, of about 20 allied principalities. The same documents suggest that one occasion on which the palace was destroyed was during the Hittite king Hattusili's campaign against Aleppo. The palace was extended whilst being rebuilt in the 15/14CBC. The smoothed basalt blocks, standing on end and carefully fitted together to protect the walls, can still be seen on the site. These shallow slabs were secured by the use of pegs, and the holes for these can be seen on the upper sides of the basalt cladding. The most striking monument on the site is probably in the E. of the palace. This is a shallow basalt basin with a long drainage channel, all cut from a single basalt block (just over 11 ft. long). The drain was clearly visible, and ran throught the palace wall to the outside. This construction, known to the excavators as 'bath', though it is more likely to be a shower tub, dates from the 17/16C BC.

Yesemek (22 km. SSE): It is sensible to link a visit to the Hittite *quarry* and open-air sculpture workshop with a visit to Tilmenhüyük, as the somewhat complicated route (local guide!) runs very close to it. The site is beyond the village of Yesemek, and covers an area of about 220 x 330 yards, on a slope on the other side of a little stream. The first of the sculptures which you see here at all stages of completion is to be found immediately on the approach from the village school. Felix Luschan came across this place as early as 1890, but thorough investigation did not begin until 1955 and 1958–61. The Late Hittite sculptors who worked here in the last quarter of the second millennium and beginning of the first millennium provided sculptures and relief slabs for sites in the immediate vicinty and farther afield (such as Dara/Syria, Sakçegözü or Zincirli). Today the site is still strewn with numerous incomplete sphinxes, lions, mountain gods and a so-called 'bear-man'. A particularly attractive work from this workshop, complete and subsequently painted, is a crouching *sphinx* with ringlets, found in Zincirli and now in the museum in Gaziantep.

Tilmenhüyük (Islâhiye), outer wall of palace

Zincirli (9 km. NE): This town was probably founded by the Hittites in the 14C BC, but reached the height of its power after the fall of the Hittite empire, when it became the residence of the principality of Jaadija, one of the numerous states which followed the Late Hittites. At that time it was called *Samal*. The Assyrians incorporated it into their empire under Sargon II (721–705). Asarhaddon replied to an attempt to break free *c.*650 BC by completely destroying the town, which had to be cleared of metre-thick layers of burnt rubbish by the archæologists Humann, Puchstein and Koldewey in 1883 and 1888–1904. Sculptures and relief slabs from the period of the independent small kingdom, in which the most important ruler was Kilamuwa, were taken partly to Berlin (now E.Berlin) and partly to Ankara and İstanbul. On the site are only remains of a flight of steps and the foundations of the massive circular outer walls with more than 100 towers. There were also three equidistant gates, in the S., NW and NE. In the last building phase the wall was double, with the outer wall added some centuries later. Both walls, each over 11 ft. thick, and 25 ft. apart, enclosed an area 787 yards in diameter. In the centre of the town was the egg-shaped citadel, over 300 yards long, with its tip in the NW. Access was only from a double gateway in the S. The palace buildings were in the W. section. It was clear to the excavators that the reliefs on the castle gate were in the Hittite tradition, while the palace reliefs clearly owed a great deal to Aramaic influence.

Yesemek (Islâhiye), Hittite quarry, unfinished group of mountain gods

Istanbul

Byzantium, Constantinople, Istanbul—all three are names for a city with a great past and an interesting present. It was in its time the capital of two world empires which at first glance seem incompatible: the Eastern Roman Empire was Christian, imbued with European and occidental ideals and ideas, whereas the Ottoman Empire was rooted in the traditions and rules of the newest world religion, Islam, born in Asia.

The Islamic conquerors, however, not only took possession of the country, they took over and adapted anything which seemed of value: Byzantine architecture, monasteries as models for their mosques, baths, cisterns, water supplies etc. Thus their capital became a bridge between East and West, and buildings from both eras and both cultures still stand impressively side by side today.

The Bosporus not only divides Europe and Asia, but also the city, which thus becomes a bridge between two continents and cultures. The Ottoman Empire had links and connections with three continents in all—Europe, Asia and North Africa. Kemal Atatürk, the father of modern Turkey, inclined towards Europe, and took his country with him in this direction. This means that Europeans feel

at home yet not at home in this city on the Bosporus and the Golden Horn, but there is nowhere else where buildings, people and general atmosphere make is as easy to understand another world and another culture as it is in İstanbul.

History

Byzantium—Constantinople—İstanbul

'The town is garlanded by the sea; the land thrusts in on the right-hand side. However, it thrusts only so far as to form the last link in the diadem of the sea.' (Procopius, Buildings, 6C).

Procopius' image of the diadem of the sea refers to the unusual site of this capital of two world empires, whose silhouette rises on three sides from glittering water. The Sea of Marmara, the Golden Horn and the Bosporus surround the long ridge of land with its hills and valleys. The old Thracian settlement on the point, where the Saray now stands, took its name from the legendary king Byzas. Little is known of the Hellenistic and Roman town. In 196 Septimius Severus took the town in the course of a punitive expedition, then immediately rebuilt it on a more generous scale than before. The area covered

◁ İstanbul, Topkapı Saray, fountain

Continued on page 250

246 Istanbul

Ancient and Byzantine monuments 1 Palace of Antiochos 2 Arcadius column 3 Binbirderek cistern 4 Palace of Blachernae 5 Palace of Bodrum 6 Palace of Bucoleon 7 Goths' column 8 Hippodrome 9 Theodosius obelisk 10 Snake column 11 Walled obelisk 12 Golden gate 13 Emperors' palaces 14 Constantine's column 15 Land wall 16 Lausos palace 17 Marcian column

Open cisterns 18 Cukurbostan 19 Aspar cistern 20 Mocios cistern 21 Sea walls 22 Tekfur Sarayı 23 Theodosius arch 24 Theodosius column 25 Valens aqueduct 26 Yerebatan cistern

Former Byzantine churches 27 Aya Sofya/Hagia Sophia 28 Bodrum Camii/Myrelaion 29 Fenari Isa Camii, Lips monastery 30 Fethiya Camii/Pammakaristos monastery 31 Gül Camii 32 Hagios Polyeuktos 33 Imrahor Camii/St.John church of the Studios monastery 34 Kalenderhane Camii/Monastery of Maria Kyriotissa 35 Kariye Camii/Chora monastery 36 Koca Mustafa Paşa Camii/Andreas monastery 37 Kücük Aya Sofya Camii/Church of Sergios and Bakchos 38 Sent Iren Kilisesi/Irene church 39 Zeyrek Camii/Pantocrator monastery

Mosques 40 Atik Ali Paşa Camii 41 Azapkapı Camii 42 Bali Paşa Camii 43 Dolmabahçe Camii 44 Firuz Aga Camii 45 Hekemoglu Ali Paşa Camii 46 Kara Ahmet Paşa Camii 47 Kılıç Ali Paşa Camii 48 Lâleli Camii 49 Mahmut Paşa Camii 50 Mesih Paşa Camii 51 Mihrima Camii 52 Murat Paşa Camii 53 Nişana Mehmet Paşa Camii 54 Nuruosmaniye Camii 55 Nusretiye Camii 56 Rüstem Paşa Camii 57 Sehzade Camii 58 Sinan Paşa Camii 59 Sokollu Mehmet Paşa Camii 60 Süleymaniye Camii 61 Sultan Ahmet Camii/Blue Mosque 62 Sultan Beyazıt Camii 63 Sultan Mehmet Fâtih Camii 64 Sultan Selim Camii 65 Yeni Camii

Secular Ottoman buildings

Sultans' palaces 66 Dolmabahçe Saray 67 Topkapı Saray 68 Yıldız Saray

Baths 69 Cagaloglu Hamamı 70 Çemberlitaş Hamamı 71 Mahmut Paşa Hamamı

Bazaars 72 Kapalı Çarşısı 73 Mısır Çarşısı

Fountains 74 Fountain of Ahmet III 75 German fountain 76 Tophane fountain

Buildings 77 Alay Köşkö 78 Bab-i-Ali 79 Çinili Köşk 80 Galata-Kulesi 81 Main post office 82 Şepetçiler Kösk 83 Tophane 84 University 85 Yedikule

Hans 86 Valide Hanı

Museums 87 Arkeoloji Müzeleri 88 Marine Museum 89 Museum of Fine Arts 90 Municipal Museum 91 Turko-Islamic Museum

Also worth seeing 92 Atatürk bridge 93 Atatürk monument 94 Galata bridge 95 Karaköy square 96 Taksim square

Üsküdar Religious buildings 97 Çinili Camii 98 Karaca-Ahmet graveyard 99 Mihrimah Camii 100 Selimiye Camii 101 Semsi Ahmet Paşa Camii 102 Yeni Valide Camii

Secular buildings 103 Çamlıca 104 Kız Kulesi 105 Selim barracks

İstanbul

Rulers and Heads of State

Emperors from Constantine I to Constantine XI

334–337 Constantine the Great
337–361 Constantius
361–363 Julian the Apostate
363–364 Jovian
364–378 Valens
379–395 Theodosius the Great
395–408 Arcadius
408–450 Theodosius II
450–457 Marcian
457–474 Leo I
474   Leo II
474–475 Zeno
475–476 Basiliskos
476–491 Zeno again
491–518 Anastasius I
518–527 Justin I
527–565 Justinian the Great
565–578 Justin II
578–582 Tiberius I Konstantinos
582–602 Maurice
602–610 Phocas
610–641 Heraclius
641   Constantine II and
         Heracleonas,
         Heracleonas alone
641–668 Constantine III
668–685 Constantine IV
685–695 Justinian II
695–698 Leontius
698–705 Tiberius III
705–711 Justinian II again
711–713 Phillipicus Bardanes
713–715 Anastasis II
715–717 Theodosius III
717–741 Leo III
741–775 Constantine V
775–780 Leo IV
780–797 Constantine VI
797–802 Eirene
802–811 Nicephorus I
811   Stauracius

811–813 Michael I
813–820 Leo V
820–829 Michael II
829–842 Theophilus
842–867 Michael III
867–886 Basil I
886–912 Leo VI
912–913 Alexander
913–959 Constantine VII
920–944 Romanus I Lakapenos, first
         co-ruler, then emperor
959–963 Romanus II
963–969 Nicephorus II Phocas
969–976 John I Tzimisces
976–1025 Basil II
1025–1028 Constantine VIII
1028–1034 Romanus III Argyrus
1034–1041 Michael IV Paphlagon
1041–1042 Michael V Kalaphates
1042   Theodora and Zoe
1042–1055 Constantine IX
          Monomachos
1055–1056 Theodora again
1056–1057 Michael VI Stratiotikos
1057–1059 Isaac I Comnenus
1059–1067 Constantine X Ducas
1067   Eudokia Dukaina
1068–1071 Romanus IV Diogenes
1071–1078 Michael VII Ducas
1078–1081 Nicephorus III Botaneiates
1081–1118 Alexius I Comnenus
1118–1143 John II Comnenus
1143–1180 Manuel I Comnenus
1180–1183 Alexius II Comnenus
1183–1185 Andronicus I Comnenus
1185–1195 Isaac II Angelus
1195–1203 Alexius III Angelus
1203–1204 Isaac II Angelus again,
          co-emperor with Alexius IV
          Angelus
1204   Alexius V Murtuzuphlos

Latin emperors:

1204–1205 Balduin I of Flanders
1206–1216 Henry of Flanders
1217   Peter of Courtenay
1217–1219 Iolanthe
1221–1228 Robert of Courtenay
1228–1261 Balduin II (1231–1237 John of Brienne)
1261–1282 Michael VIII Palaeologus (emperor in Nicaea from 1258 on)

1282–1328 Andronikos II Palaeologus (d. 1332)
1295–1320 Michael IX (co-emperor)
1328–1341 Andronikos III Palaeologus
1341–1391 John V Palaeologus
1347–1354 Johannes VI Kantakuzenos (counter-emperor)
1376–1379 Andronikos IV Palaeologus
1390   John VII Palaeologus
1391–1425 Manuel II Palaeologus
1425–1448 John VIII Palaeologus
1448–1453 Constantine XI Dragases Palaeologus

Ottoman Sultans

1451–1481 Mehmet II, the Conqueror
1481–1512 Beyazıt II
1512–1520 Selim I 'Yavuş', the Grim
1520–1566 Süleyman I, the Magnificent, 'Kanuni'
1566–1574 Selim II
1574–1595 Murat III
1595–1603 Mehmet III
1603–1617 Ahmet I
1617–1618 Mustafa I
1618–1622 Osman II
1622–1623 Mustafa I again
1622–1640 Murat IV
1640–1648 Ibrahim
1648–1687 Mehmet IV
1687–1691 Süleyman II

1691–1695 Ahmet II
1695–1703 Mustafa II
1703–1730 Ahmet III
1730–1754 Mahmut I
1754–1757 Osman III
1757–1773 Mustafa III
1773–1789 Abdülhamit I
1789–1807 Selim II
1807–1808 Mustafa IV
1808–1839 Mahmut II
1839–1861 Abdülmeçit
1861–1876 Abdülaziz
1876   Murat V
1876–1909 Abdülhamit II
1909–1917 Mehmet V
1917–1922 Mehmet VI

Heads of State

Presidents of the Republic

Kemal Atatürk 1923–1938
İ. İnönü 1938–1950
M. C. Bayer 1950–1960

C. Gürsel 1960/61–1966
C. Sunay 1966–1973
F. Korutürk 1973–1980
I.S. Caglayangil (interim) Apr.–Sep. 1980
General K. Evren since Sept. 1980

extended to the newly-built Hippodrome
and the square between Hagia Sophia and
the Sultan Ahmet mosque. Constantine
the Great (324–337) pushed the boun-
daries another 3 km. to the W., at the same
time making the city four times larger.
From 324 he systematically extended
Byzantium on its strategically excellent site
and named it after himself at the
celebrations for its refoundation on
5 November 330.

The project of creating a second Rome,
on a par with the old imperial city, could
not be carried out in a single generation.
The city needed an infrastructure as well
as a state resettlement policy and large-
scale artistic projects. A columned road,
known as the Mese, forking in the Aksaray
valley and continuing as the Thracian road
to Adrianople (Edirne) and as the Via
Egnatia, leading along the coast to
Thessaloniki, opened up the city. It ran
through several fora, used equally for civic
and commercial purposes and acting as
points of crystallization for new districts.
The Forum of Constantine opened up a
sequence of squares: Forum of
Theodosius, Philadelphion, Bus, Forum
of Arcadius. Thus the actual burden of
expanding the city was borne by the
Theodosian rulers (379–457). The
Theodosian Wall gave Constantinople an
enduring shield and a frontier which has
lasted until today. Other basic provisions
were the extension of the harbour and an
assured water supply. The Valens
aqueduct and the open cisterns outside the
Constantine wall were part of this plan.
Architects and workshops for the numerous building projects came from the great
cities of Asia Minor. Building from the
imperial era showed the early Byzantine
city the way to innovations in decorative
carving for buildings and vault construction. The Polyeuktos church and Hagia
Sophia were centrally planned buildings
dating from the first half of the 6C, with
a degree of enclosure of space and lavish-
ness of decoration which had never before

Blue Mosque at night ▷

been achieved. Under Justinian I (527–565) new building peaked, then the period of extension of the early imperial city came to an end. Its structure determined the development of the city to the present day.

The centuries of the iconoclastic controversy (717–842) and the rise of the Macedonian dynasty (867–1059) were occupied with extension and maintenance of what was already there. Under the Comnenus emperors, in the mid-Byzantine period (1081–1185) the feudal nobility, who shared imperial authority, played a role as the founders of city monasteries with churches containing tombs. The mausoleum of the Comnenos dynasty was in the Pantocrator monastery. Its typikon, the foundation document of 1137, is a unique piece of cultural history. According to it the complex included a hospital with specialized departments, an old people's home, pharmacies, baths, training facilities and other social institutions. Practicalities were laid down in writing in detail. When Constantinople was conquered by Latin Crusaders the city suffered from catastrophic fires, plundering and desecration of churches. The removal of art treasures hoarded over the centuries was a unique stimulus for the production of art in the West. Goldsmiths' work, panel painting and book illumination stove to equal the Byzantine originals, which left a gap which could not be filled in the old imperial city. After the Latin interregnum (1204–61) Constantinople went through its final period of greatness under the Palaeologus emperors (1262–1453). The Deesis mosaics on the S. gallery of Hagia Sophia, the Chora church and the Pammakaristos monastery are of first-rate quality, and indicate the high level of achievement of late Byzantium. The Eastern Roman Empire had long since shrunk to be a minor state. On 29 May 1453, Mehmet II entered the city on the Bosporus. Yet again it proved possible to raise the city, depopulated and desolate, to the status of metropolis of a world power by means of resettlement policy and building. The infrastructure of the ancient city was restored, the churches were taken over as mosques. The two Saray complexes, the earlier in the area of the present university, the later, which still exists, on the point, and an increasing number of mosques brought the characteristic and

View of Saray point and Hagia Sophia

striking features of the city increasingly close together. The complexes surrounding some of the important mosques, külliye in Turkish, with their constituent poor kitchens, hospitals, schools, baths, wells, altered the appearance of entire districts. Although the great sultans' mosques were not emphasized within the sea of buildings either by squares or the axes of the streets in which they stood, their impact in the overall picture of the city was carefully calculated. The domed Ottoman buildings make their mark on the city from the tops of hills and promontories of land, even more than the Comnenus churches set on raised bases and ridges. The outstanding architect at the height of the Ottoman period in the 15&16C was Sinan (c.1490–c.1584), who had over 400 buildings to his credit, of which most are in İstanbul itself.

After the second fruitless siege of Vienna in 1683, political and economic circumstances turned against the Ottoman Empire, which opened up to Western culture in the 18&19C. Buildings like the Nuru Osmaniye Camii, the so-called High Gate and above all new pavilions in the Saray show the acquistion of the language of baroque design. In the area around the Sirkeci station and the main post office there are some art nouveau façades. On the N. side of the Golden Horn (Greek Pera) the Beyoğlu district grew out of the former embassy quarter as the European reply to the old town, which was felt to be behind the times.

In 1923 Ankara became the capital of the Turkish Republic, but the old metropolis, since then known as İstanbul (probably from the Greek *is tin polin*) lost none of its economic and cultural importance. At the time of writing İstanbul has taken over from war-torn Beirut as economic capital of the Near East and of the Arab oil magnates. In the 1950s and 1960s streets were cut through the sea of houses and a corniche was built along the Sea of Marmara: the modern city is also attacking the infrastructure problem: 1,200 km. of water pipes have been renewed, 2,000 km. of sewerage and heating systems have been laid. The Golden Horn has been redeveloped, and the new Galata bridge, the underground railway and the planned third bridge over the Bosporus will once more change the face of the city on the Bosporus.

Ancient and Byzantine Monuments

Aqueduct of Valens (Bozdagan Kemer): This bridges the tongue of land between the third and fourth hills of the city and has more than 60 arches, some of them on two levels. It is about 1,000 yards long and the slope of the water channels was only 1:1,000. The aqueduct was part of a new water supply system built under Valens (364–378) that flowed into a nymphaeum near the Forum Tauri. This nymphaeum was consecrated in 378 by city prefect Klearchos and suggests a date for the completion of the aqueduct. The arches of the aqueduct had to be repaired even in the Byzantine period, but most of the repairs seen today were made during maintenance work by Ottoman rulers to repair earthquake damage. In 1696&7, under Sultan Mustafa I, 5 arches in the central section were renewed. At the point where it passes the Şehsade mosque the upper section of the aqueduct was not replaced, so that the view of the mosque from a distance would not be spoiled.

Arch of Theodosius (Ordu Caddesi): In 1957&8, while the Ordu Caddesi was

being widened and its level lowered, remains of an arch with three openings were found. This and fragments of the Column of Theodosius in the Beyazıt baths opposite mark the site of the Forum of Theodosius (also called Forum Tauri), consecrated in 393. Its overall dimensions are not known. The two pedestal bases to the side of the central opening each supported 4 columns, the fragments of which now line the edge of the road, together with fragments of the entabulature. The column shafts looked like tree trunks, and their droplet decoration imitated the branch joints of a particularly hard, juniper-like kind of wood. Below the capital, giant hands gripped the column shaft, so that the gateway must have looked as though it was built from Herakles' clubs. The reconstruction of the side openings is contentious.

Binbirderek cistern (Klot Farer Caddesi/Isik Sokağı): Height is the most impressive feature of the drained Cistern of 1,001 Columns (Turkish name), which is smaller in area (210 x 185 ft) than the Yerebatan cistern. The vaulting is sup-

Capital of Goths' Column in Gülhane park

ported by 224 columns in rows of 16 x 14. Each column consists of two shafts rising to a total height of over 40 ft. The cistern, presumably the cellar of a larger building, was built in the 6C.

Bodrum Palace (Sait Efendi Sokağı): This monumental centrally-planned building with a cylindrical section almost 100 ft. in diameter rising out of the present buildings is part of a late antique palace dating from the late 4 or 5C. The S. entrance was connected with a columned way. In front of the N. gate was a spacious square, and its semicircular colonnades were presumably linked with the main street, the Mese. It is possible that it is identical with the Philadelphion, which was known to have had a Tetrach group. It is certainly true that the porphyry foot missing from the porphyry Tetrarch group in the SW. corner of St. Mark's in Venice was found among the rubble of the Bodrum Palace. A cistern was built into the base of the centrally-planned building at a later stage, and this formed a podium for the palace of Emperor Romanos I Lekapenos (920–944), dating from the early 10C.

Bucoleon Palace (Kennedy Caddesi): Remains of a palace façade were found near the sea wall. Once it towered over a little harbour in the the Sea of Marmara. The section of the building jutting out to the left was a monumental wharf opening to the water in a high arch and permitting entrance to the palace by an interior flight of steps. As the later addition of the central door and gallery façade shows, the Bucoleon Palace was built in several phases, though it dates in the main from the 10C. It takes its name from a decorative statue of a lion and a bull (Greek bus kai leon=bull and lion).

Column of Arcadius (Hasekin Kadin Sokağı/corner of Cerrah Paşa Caddesi): Only the monumental base of a column formerly over 160 ft. high has survived of the Forum of Arcadius, built in his honour and consecrated by his son Theodosius II in 421. Numerous fires in the heavily built-up Turkish quarter have severely damaged the surface of the marble, which originally had many reliefs. The base plate on the top and the beginning of the lowest column drum still show fragments of figure-relief. 16&17C drawings and

Hippodrome, reliefs on pedestal of Theodosius obelisk

descriptions suggest a band of distinct reliefs running around the column shaft in 13 coils, and showing the suppression of the Gainas uprising and the triumph of the imperial house of Theodosius. In 740 the statue of Theodosius fell off the lantern-like top of the column, which had an internal spiral staircase. In 1715 the column drums, threatened with collapse by fire and earthquake, were removed.

Column of Constantine (Divan Yolu): Constantine the Great had this column erected in his own honour in the centre of a circular forum in 328. 6 of the original 8 porphyry drums have survived, each with a wreath of honour around it like a ring. The uppermost drum is in small ashlar blocks and dates fron restoration by Emperor Manuel I Comnenus (1143–80) after the statue and three column drums collapsed in the late 11C. Earthquakes and damage by fire made it necessary to fit the column with iron hoops, which gave the

column its Turkish name Çemberlitaç (Hooped Column). The base and the lowest column drum were clad in masonry in 1779. Excavations revealed that the ancient square was nearly 8 ft. lower than the level of the present street, so that the overall proportions of the column are distorted. The imperial porphyry column was for centuries the foundation document of the new capital of the Byzantine empire, especially as Constantine is held by later tradition to have placed a collection of heathen, Jewish and Christian relics under the column. He himself was deified in the statue as Apollo with helmet decorated with the rays of the sun.

Column of Marcian (Kiztaşı Caddesi): The honorific column of the Emperor Marcian was built under city prefect Tatianus in the mid-5C. The dedicatory inscription has survived in negative relief of the bronze lettering, which as been removed. Under this, two striding

Hippodrome, tip of Theodosius obelisk (left), relief on base (right)

victories hold a shield as a sign of triumph. The other sides of the base are decorated with a christogram and wreath, in the manner of barrier slabs. The monolithic shaft of the column, over 30 ft. high is made of pink granite and topped with a Corinthian capital supporting a plinth with eagles at the corners for the statue of the emperor. When the Fâtih quarter was redesigned after the fire in the year 1908 the column, hidden for centuries in private gardens, became the centre of a new square.

Column of Theodosius (Ordu Caddesi): Since the level of the street was lowered, fragments of the column of Theodosius are visible among the foundations of the Beyazıt Hamami. Theodosius I (383–395) commissioned the honorific column in 385 on the model of the column of Trajan in Rome. Reliefs of the emperor's campaigns against the barbarians wound their way up the column. Soldiers marching, in boats

and paying homage can be seen on the surviving blocks. In 1517 the column, which was in danger of collapsing, was removed and the Bayazıt Hamami built on the site.

Golden Gate (*Altınkapı*): The main gate of the city, built in the early 5C at the same time as the Theodosian land wall, was both a fortification and a triumphal arch. The gatehouse with three openings and inner chamber has two almost square flanking towers in front of it, forming a small courtyard, like an outer ward. The buildings are almost completely without windows, and completely faced with light marble ashlar. They also served as a monumental base for numerous statues, including Theodosius, Nike, Tyche and four gilded elephants. The gate took its name from the gilded doors (Greek: chrysai pylai). The central opening was reserved for the emperor. Triumphal processions began here with the

Hippodrome, relief details on base of Theodosius obelisk

Hippodrome, Theodosius obelisk, relief, emperor's box with ruler's family

ceremonial entry of the ruler. In the mid-Byzantine period the N. opening was closed and its jambs used to reduce the size of the central opening. The outer gate was extended in the late period, making lavish use of spoils. The Turkish conquerors used the Golden Gate exclusively as a fortification *(Yedikule).*

Goths' Column (Gülhane Park): This is a granite column almost 50 ft. high, set on a pedestal and topped with a Corinthian capital. The inscription on the restored base deals with a victory over the Goths (presumably Constantine II's campaign against the Goths in 332).

Hippodrome (At Meydanı): The Hippodrome was started under Septimius Severus in 203, then enlarged and re-equipped under Constantine the Great (324–337). The surviving remains give little impression of the dimensions of the original arena. The starting gates (Latin: carceres) for chariot races were on the site of the present Kaiser Wilhelm fountain, donated on the occasion of a journey to the Orient by the Kaiser in 1900. The line of the two parallel race tracks is marked by the two remaining obelisks. They are all that survives of the numerous trophies set up on the central dividing wall (spina) between the two turning points. The Hippodrome continued for a further 410 ft. beyond the buildings at the SW end of the square, and was thus over 400 yards long overall. Substructures on several levels, visible today on the way to the church of Sergius and Bacchus, pushed the semicircular end, the so-called Sphendone, far out over the natural drop towards the Sea of Marmara. The arena had tiered rows of seats with room for about 100,000 spectators. Over the centuries the

View of land walls

Hippodrome was not only the place where the dominant blue and green circus factions competed, but also an important political institution. State occasions were celebrated with great pomp (feast of the city's foundation on 11 May 330), and revolts suppressed with great cruelty (Nika revolt in 552). The Hippodrome fell into disrepair under Latin rule and after the fire of 1203&4. After the Turkish conquest it became a quarry for palaces and mosques.

The **Theodosius Obelisk** *(Dikilitaş)* in the centre of the square was set up in 390 in honour of the imperial house of Theodosius. According to the two inscriptions the technological miracle of its erection was performed in 30 or 32 days under the direction of city prefect Proklos. The obelisk is Egyptian, and came from the Temple of Amon in Karnak. It has hieroglyphs and pictures from the time of Thutmosis I (1490–1436 BC). It is just over 64 ft. high, three fifths of the original height. Four bronze cubes support the enormous weight of the obelisk and form a link with the base, dating from the time of Theodosius and covered with reliefs on all sides, and its substructure. The relief strips are *pictorial tables* showing early Byzantine imperial ceremonial. The imperial family is always shown in a position of supremacy in the imperial box. The 4 sides are not intended as a pictorial sequence, but as static images corresponding axially. On the longitudinal axis of the circus the two miniature friezes of the base show the erection of the obelisk and a chariot race. The reliefs above them show the Theodosian rulers taking part in circus games. On both occasions the same place and situation is depicted. The other pair of reliefs, facing the imperial palace and the stand opposite it, shows the emperor standing holding the victory wreath, accompanied by dancing and music and the ruler enthroned accepting the so-called wreath contribution (Latin: aurum coronarium), the ancient vassals' tribute. Kneeling representatives of subject barbarian peoples from all over the world pay tribute in acknowledgement of Theodosian world rule. The fine modelling of the reliefs and the details of faces, hair and objects are striking features of this state monument.

The modest remains of the **Serpentine Column** *(Burma Sütün)* originally had three snakes' heads protruding from the coiled mass. The column was a votive gift to the Temple of Apollo in Delphi from 31 Greek cities, whose names are engraved on the bodies of the snakes, after the victory over the Persians at the Battle of Plataea in 479. Constantine the Great moved the column to grace his new capital, along with many other works of art of the ancient world.

The **Masonry Obelisk** *(Örmetaş)* at the S. end of the square is made entirely of

Base of Marcian column

limestone ashlar. It was presumably built instead of a monolithic obelisk which did not become available. It has been sheathed in bronze since the timei of Constantine VII Porphyrogenetos at the latest (913–959), whose restoration inscription has survived on the base.The peg-holes intended for securing the sheathing also remained visible after the more recent restoration in 1895&6.

Imperial palaces: Byzantine imperial palaces extended over the whole Hagia Sophia and Hippodrome quarter to the coast of the Sea of Marmara. The extensive complex consisted of successive groups of buildings only loosely connected with each other, also including churches. Thus the famous Chalke, the bronze-doored gatehouse of the imperial palace, became a synonym for the entire palace precinct, to which the general public were not admitted. The site of this gatehouse, not unlike a triumphal arch, is assumed to have been in the region of the present square between Hagia Sophia and the Sultan Ahmed mosque. From the time of Constantine, the oldest parts of the palace were on the site of the Sultan Ahmed mosque, and they were connected with the imperial box in the Hippodrome. The complex below the mosque, the so-called mosaic museum gives the impression of an enclosed palace precinct arranged around a peristyle courtyard. The site of other residential palaces like the famous porphyry-encrusted set of buildings which gave princes born there the name Porphyry-Born (Greek: Porpyrogennetoi) has not been identified.

Land walls: The land side of Constantinople was fortified with a wall about 6 km. long under Theodosius II (408–450) and the city prefect Anthemios. This enormous building project seems to have been completed in less than 5 years. Work on the towers was complete in 413, in accordance with a law in the Codex Theodisianus. The Theodosian wall created a link with the older Blachernae wall over the rising ridge, establishing a closed line of defence from the Sea of Maramara to the Golden Horn.

The land wall is a combination of moats, outer wall and inner wall, staggered both in height and from back to front. The moat in front of the first wall was divided into individual pools and could be filled with water. Also, the ground between the walls is artificially raised. The 96 towers of the 36 ft. high main wall are staggered in relation to those in the front wall, thus effectively halving the distance between individual towers. The visible limestone ashlar covers an interior core. The 5 horizontal lines of brick run the entire length of the walls, forming a base run and decorating and articulating the construction.

The wall is pierced by 7 *town gates*. From S. to N. these are: *Golden Gate (Altınkapı); Xylokeros Gate (Belgrat Kapı); Pege Gate (Silivri Kapı); Rhesium Gate (Yeni Mavlevihane Kapı); Romanus Gate (Topkapı); Pentou Gate (Örülü Kapı); Charius Gate (Edirne Kapı).*

Work continued on the Theodosian wall throughout its period of use in the Byzantine and Ottoman periods. Earth-quakes rather than enemy action consistently made restoration work necessary. Numerous Greek and Turkish inscriptions explain the lack of uniformity of appearance of the wall, which is increasingly falling into disrepair.

Lausos Palace (At Meydanı):The palace of the principal imperial chamberlain Lausos was built in 419&420, close to the adjacent Palace of Antiochos in both space and time. Steps lead to a semicircular portico from which there is access to a circular building with 8 semicircualr niches cut into the thickness of its walls. Later a hall with two apses and an apsidal room 164 ft. long were added to the centrally-planned building. The apsidal room was later itself extended by 3 niches on either side. The characteristic ground plan makes the room's function as a dining hall clear.

Open cisterns: As well as the better-known closed cisterns (Yerebatan and Binbirderek), three open cisterns of considerable size have survived in the city.

The **Aspar cistern** (Yavuz Selim

Tekfur Sarayı, Palaeologic palace

Aya Sofya, Hagia Sophia

Caddesi) near the Selim I Camii is a 500 ft. cube of comparable capacity. It was built for Patriarch Aspar in 459. It is 36–39 ft. deep, with gardens and trees at the bottom, forming a pleasing contrast with the surrounding buildings.

The **Çukurbostan** (Fevzi Paşa Caddesi) near the Edirne Gate is generally considered to be the cistern commissioned by city prefect Aetius in the early 5C. It has an area of 800 x 278 ft. and a cubic capacity of 327,000 cubic yards. It was presumably associated with the nearby Valens water supply system. Today it comfortably accommodates a football pitch.

The **Mokios cistern** (Cevdet Paşa Caddesi) in Altimermer is 558 x 482 ft., and was probably built under Anastasios I (491–518).

Palace of Antiochos (At Maydanı): All that remains of the palace of Antiochos dating from 416–418 are the foundations of the centrally-planned building reused in the 6C as the church of St.Euphemia. Originally the haxagonal domed chamber and other buildings were arranged around a broad exedra. After Antiochos, who had considerable influence at court as tutor of Theodosius II and senior palace chamberlain, was relieved of his post the private palace became the property of the emperor.

Palace of Blachernae (Dervişzade Sokağı): The imperial palace was moved to the Blachernae quarter under the Comnenus emperors. The emperors lived here until the fall of Constantinople in fortress-like residential palaces, connected with the Blachernae wall built in front of them by Manuel I Comnenus. The high substructure of the so-called Anemas

Inside Hagia Sophia

prison and the Tower of Isaac Angelos built of spoils (1185–95) are remains of these palaces.

Sea walls: On completion of the land walls, Theodosius II (408–450) also fortified the 8.5 km. coastline on the Sea of Marmara. Because of the natural protection afforded by the sea itself, a single wall with 188 defensive towers was sufficient. In the mid and late Byzantine period, increasing threats from the sea made it necessary to raise the height of the walls.

There was also a sea wall along the Golden Horn. The older sections, from the Saray point to the Atatürk bridge, built to secure the Constantinian city, were removed when the town was extended. The line of the subsequent section running on to the Blachernae wall is still clearly discernible, despite numerous repairs and gaps.

Tefkur Sarayı (Şişehane Caddesi): It is not known what this probably early-14C palace was called, nor for whom it was built. Its Turkish name means Ruler's Palace. The high section for living accommodation is set transversely between the outer and inner Theodosian walls. The N. side of the three-storey building is lavishly endowed with windows and articulation. The high standard of Palaeologic architecture is shown especially by the colourful treatment of alternating runs of brick and hand-cut ashlar, spandrels with detailed lozenge decoration and the coloured glass tubes in the window arches of the upper storey.

Yerebatan cistern (Hilaliahmer Caddesi, opposite Hagia Sophia): According to Procopius, the best-known and largest of the closed cisterns was built under the Justinian basilica in the 6C. It is 459 x 230

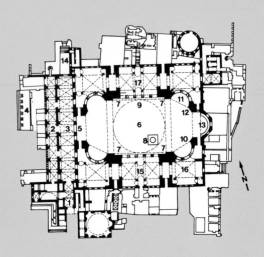

İstanbul, Aya Sofya (Hagia Sophia) **1** Beautiful door **2** Outer portico **3** Inner portico **4** Theodosian portico (remains of excavations) **5** Emperor's door **6** Central aisle **7** Marble balconies for Murat III **8** Emphalos (where Emperors were crowned from 1204 on) **9** Marble pulpit of Murat IV **10** Islamic pulpit **11** 19C balcony for rulers **12** Old balcony for rulers **13** Prayer niche, apse mosaic of Theotekos and two Archangels (9C) **14** Way up to gallery **15** S. side aisle **16** W. upper storey **16** N. side aisle

ft. and has a capacity of 104,640 cubic yards. The 326 columns, arranged in 28 rows, came from abandoned 6C buildings or were faulty items from the marble workshops on the island of Proconnesus. The cistern always contains water, and has been a setting for legends and novels since the 16C. The Turkish name means Sunken Palace.

Former Byzantine Churches

Aya Sofya/Hagia Sophia: The original building commissioned by Justinian I (527–565) has survived from the mid-6C, shored up by buttresses and restored on numerous occasions. The extraordinarily daring domed building was never surpassed in Byzantine architecture and continued to be admired as the principal mosque of the Ottoman city. It has been a museum since 1935. The Justinian church was preceded by two buildings. The 'Great Church' of Constantine was consecrated on 15 February 360. It was followed by a Theodosian building in 415. This was probably a basilica with nave and four aisles. Important sections of a monumental gate arch belonging to it were excavated in 1953. Fragments of entablature with lamb friezes have remained on the excavation site in front of the W. entrance of Hagia Sophia. Other pieces of pediment, vaulting and entablature are displayed in the garden.

Hagia Sophia, mosaic above emperor's gate

The Justinian building abandoned the basilican design of its predecessors in favour of a spacious centrally-planned church with two-storey galleried aisles. The apse in the E. and narthex and exonarthex to the W. provide an axis. Access to the central space is on the narrow side, via the narthex and exonarthex, which are not of equal size. The three high central doors lead into the naos, with the Imperial Gate on the axis of the building. The other six portals lead from the narthex to the aisles. A window, unnoticed at first by the visitor entering from the W., lights the smooth entrance wall, articulated only by bronze door jambs and choice marble incrustation.

In the interior the height of the many-sectioned vaulting is impressive. 4 piers, connected by arches, support the domed square space. 4 pendentives make the transition from the basic square to the circle of the dome, just over 100 ft. in diameter, which supports the dome vaulting. The dome is supported by 40 ribs, with windows between them. On the N. and S. sides the arch openings are filled with tympanum walls. The accuracy and ease with which the load-bearing and filling walls complement each other is deceptive, however. The walls and arches mask a massive system of piers and subsidiary piers. The devices used for abutment of the thrust of the dome are concealed in various ways. The aisles are not aisles in the traditional sense, but independent spaces intended to mask the irregularities and illogicalities of the self-supporting vault compartments, thus contributing to the perfect appearance of the naos. As the aisle columns and vaults are lower than the naos arches, a further optical effect is obtained: the arch positions at the level of the galleries follow precisely the positions on the lower level, separated only by a console cornice. The pediment above originally contained large windows, so that in the Justinian building there was a dramatic contrast between the solidity of the corner piers and the openness of the wall between them. The dome square was extended by half domes to the E. and W. They in they turn are underpinned by a trio of conches and tunnel vaults, with alternating semicircular and triangular niches, as in the Sergios and Bacchus church. The retrogression of the vaulting corresponds to the reduction of the columns, set on pedestals in the semicircular niches. The domed building was designed by a mathematician and an engineer, Anthemios of Tralles and Isidor of Miletus, and it was built in less than 6 years. The Justinian church was consecrated on 27 December 537. In 550 the dome collapsed after several earthquakes, burying the ambo in the middle of the naos. When the dome was rebuilt the statics were improved by raising the height of the apex by 23 ft. In 563 the rebuilt church was consecrated. There is evidence that the vaulting was repaired again in 994 and 1346.

The *mosaics* in Hagia Sophia have survived only as fragments. It is assumed that the Justinian church had no figurative mosaics. The Theotokos (Mary as Bearer of God) apse mosaic and attendant archangels were created when the church was redecorated in the 2nd half of the 9C after the iconoclastic controversy had been settled. In the Palaeologian period there was a Pantocrator image in the dome. The mosaics in the S. gallery were created as individual pictures in the space reserved for the imperial family. Architectural ornamentation and marble incrustation have survived to a much larger extent. The various kinds of marble were brought from the Mediterranean area and made into geometrical and colour patterns. Pier, pilaster and column capitals are in marble from Proconnesus, with acanthus ornamentation.

Bodrum Camii/Myrelaion (Laleli Caddesi): The Armenian Grand Admiral, Romanos Lekapenos, proclaimed emperor in 920, had a residence built on the base of the late antique Bodrum Palace, to which the Myrelaion church was added at the side. In order to achieve uniform

Hagia Sophia, dome (left), mosaic above S. entrance to narthex

levels the church needed a considerable platform, the shape of which dictated the layout of the building itself. It is recorded that Romanos endowed the palace as a monastery and the church as his family tomb. The burial of Romanos' wife in 922 sets a tentative date for the Myrelaion. It is a church with crossing dome; the 4 column were replaced with piers in the Turkish period. The building is tunnel-vaulted with lunettes, and the dome has 8 concave segments. The fire of 1917 was particularly fierce in this district and left only the shell of the building standing, and this has been further distorted by restoration: the N. wall is completely new. The entire building is in brick, and special rounded bricks were produced for the exterior articulation. The rhythm of the articulation and the vaulting of the narthex with two apses show the quality of this mid-Byzantine building. As was the case on so many sites containing un-named ancient ruins with vaults, the subsequent mosque was called Cellar Mosque.

Eski İmaret Camii/Pantepoptes monastery (Haydar Yokusu, Astar Sokagi): The Monastery of the All-Seeing Redeemer was founded in the eighth decade of the 11C by Anna Dalassena, the mother of Emperor Alexios I Comnenus. The monastery was mentioned in documents in 1087. The domed church towers over the sloping site on a high platform. The domed crossing is marked by 4 piers which replaced the original 4 columns in the Ottoman period. Adjacent to the E. is a deep staggered choir with trefoil side chambers. In the W. is a narthex with two apses and a gallery (probably originally with side domes) opening to the nave. A second narthex was added in the late Byzantine period. The original form of N. and S. walls is not quite clear. It is possible that there was access to tne monastery buildings through slender arches with narrow windows above them. The ornamentation on the masonry on the S. side, built using a concealed layer technique, confirms restoration of the exterior in the Palaeologian period. The building has survived because it was incorporated into the Mehmet Fâtih foundation in 1453, and used as a poor kitchen (hence the Turkish name Mosque of the Old Poor Church). Latterly it became a Koran school.

Hagia Sophia, Deesis mosaic

Fethiye Camii (Pammakaristos monastery) with parekklesion

Fenari Isa Camii, Lips monastery (corner of Vatan Caddesi/Halicilar Caddesi): The churches of the Lips monastery are the N. church, dedicated in 908 and the S. church built *c*.1300. The W. entrance of the two churches was then obscured by an exonarthex, continued as a parekklesion to the S. Thus the fine group of apses in the E. affords the best overview of the buildings. The *N. church* (Theotokos church) was founded by the patriarch Constantinos Lips (d.917), who held high office: he became Drungarios (Supreme Commander of the Fleet) in 908. Thus the Emperor Leo VI (886–912) was present at the consecration of the Theotokos church on 20 June 908. Remains of the dedicatory inscription to the Theotokos (the Virgin Mary as the Bearer of God) are to be found on the exterior apse cornice. It was built as a church with crossing dome supported by 4 columns,

replaced by arches in the 17C. The steep proportions of the interior are repeated in the high transenna windows in the exterior of the main apse. This is flanked by two-storey side apses, themselves with chapel-like apsidal chambers. Only the S. apsidiole has survived, as it was used as the side apse of the S. church. Similarly the staircase tower added to the narthex of the older building was incorporated in the narthex of the more recent one. The *S. church*, dedicated to John the Baptist, was founded by the Empress Theodora, widow of Michael VIII (1261–82). She created an important tomb for the Palaeologian imperial family. The S. church is a square domed naos with ambulatory. The exterior of main and side apse has blind niches and ornamental brick decoration. The Turkish name comes from Fenar Isa (d. 1496), who had the two churches turned into Islamic prayer halls. The building's

Pillar capital from Polyeuktos church

poor condition was caused by the fire of 1917.

Fethiye Camii/Pammakaristos monastery (Fethiye Caddesi): The heart of this mosque, which was extended by breaking through walls, is a square naos with dome and ambulatory on three sides. The copy of the lost apse inscription has caused more confusion than enlightenment in dating the building. It names a John Comnenus and his wife Anna of the Duka family as founders, so that John Comnenus who died in 1067 and was married to Anna Dalassena is ruled out. The original building of the Monastery of the Joyous Mother of God is presumed to date from the 12C. Only base walls of the tripartite apse of the Comnenus church have survived. When the church was rebuilt as a mosque it was replaced by a domed building set on the diagonal with

the prayer niche directed towards Mecca. In the Paleologian period the Comnenus core was surrounded by a perambulatory on three sides. The protruding entrance portal in the W. thus served as the bottom storey of a tower.

The most important extension however was the *parekklesion* at the end of the S. hall. According to the metric inscription on the outer cornice this was endowed as a tomb church for the deceased protostrator Michael Glabas by his widow. The exterior and the interior decoration are masterpieces of Palaeologian architecture and art (*c.*1315). The main building of the tall church with crossing dome and two-storey narthex is hidden by a severe three-storey façade to the S. and only detectable from the dense arrangement of windows and niches. The walls are in alternating brick and stone and decorated with ornamentation of various kinds. In

Pillar relief from Polyeuktos church

the interior the horizontal division of the three storeys is repeated in the separation into zones of the *mosaic decoration*. The highest zone, the dome, has Christ Pantocrator surrounded by Old Testament prophets. Below this is a festival cycle, of which only the mosaic of the Baptism of Christ and a fragment of the Ascension have survived. From the four corner sections below this saints, martyrs, bishops and abbots look down into the nave. The apse, in which one would expect to see the Theotokos (Bearer of God) is particularly striking, and shows Christ Enthroned stretching out his hand in blessing. The inscription on a gold background gives Him the title Hyperagathos, the All-Loving. This key concept from the liturgy of the dead explains the intercessionary function of the Deesis group in the sanctuary and the entire pictorial programme in this Paleologian tomb.

After the city was conquered by the Turks, the Pammaristos monastery beame the seat of the Patriarchate until 1591, when it moved to the church of St. George in the Phanar. At that tine the monastery was changed into a mosque, known as the Victory Mosque in memory of the conquest of Georgia and Aserbeijan under Murat III (1574–95). In the course of restoration of the parekklesion, now a separate museum, by the Byzantine Institute of America, remains of a Palaeologian exterior wall painting cycle on the subject of the Blessed Virgin were discovered in front of the funeral chapel.

Gül Camii, Byzantine name unknown (Mektep Sokaği): The 11&12C Rose Mosque is built on a high artificial terrace and towers over the buildings on the bank of the Golden Horn. From the exterior the basic cube of the building and monumental apse façade are dominant, because of alterations made by the Turks to the roof. They raised the top of the wall above the apses and added a mosque dome without drum, and thus the vaulting makes no impression from the outside. Radical alterations can also be seen in the interior, involving the galleries, side screen walls and the W. side. The domed Comnenus building with 4 piers was probably in ruins when it was used as the basis for a mosque in the 16C. It is not certain that this church was part of the Christos Euergetes monastery.

Hagios Polyeuktos (Saraçhane): The church of St.Polyeuktos dates from 524–7, and was an important foundation by by the patrician woman Juliana Anicia, a granddaughter of Valentinian III (425–55). In 1962–9 the foundations of the church were discovered at the spacious junction of Atatürk Bulevard and Şehadze Caddesi. They suggest an almost square galleried church with sides *c.*170 ft. long, probably with a dome. However, these foundations are less interesting than the sections of the building erected in the courtyard of the Archaeological Museum

Pillar capital from Polyeuktos church

and outside the Hagia Eirene. Piers, capitals and niche blocks are completely covered with vegetable and ornamental decoration, detached from the background by undercutting. One of the niche blocks, with the feathers of a displaying peacock in its shell, has a fragment said to be from the building inscription of the Polyeuktos church. The Crusaders of 1204 took two piers from the church to Venice, where they were set up on the S. side of St.Mark's. At that time the Polyeuktos church was already in ruins, perhaps because of an earthquake.

İmrahor Camii/church of St. John of Studios (İmrahor Ilyas Bey Caddesi): In 450–54 the patrician Studios founded a monastery on his estates by the Golden Gate. Its church was dedicated to John the Baptist. The church is on the verge of collapse as a result of fire and earthquake,

particularly in recent times, but shows its late antique design clearly, and is also worth a visit because of important sculptural remains. In the E. section of the atrium, which serves as a narthex, there is a set of four columns with capitals and entabulature in fine-toothed acanthus. The church has nave and two aisles, and is on a square ground plan with polygonal apse. The nave is more than twice the width of the aisles. The centre of the space was further accentuated by sets of seven verd antique columns carrying an entabulature on 3 sides. Above this was a gallery articulated with arches. The proportions of the apse arch suggest that there was originally a clerestory. Thus the church was not only extraordinarily wide, but also remarkably high, showing a clear tendency to central design. Only the fine opus sectile floor covering of the Comnenus period has survived from the interior decoration. The

Imrahor Camii (St. John Church of Studios Monastery), NW corner of ruins

sanctuary, apse and W. wall were altered when the building was turned into a mosque, named after Beyazıt II's master of the horse (İmrahor).

Kalenderhane Camii/monastery of Maria Kyriotissa (Mart Sehitleri Caddesi): This massive church with crossing dome at the E. end of the Valens aqueduct dates from the late 12C. 2 frescos with the words Maria Kyriotissa established the church's name, which had for a long time been uncertain. The exterior is dominated by the wide dome. Originally the building had additional rooms on three sides, some with galleries. This is particularly true of the narthexes on the W. side, which have lost their upper storeys. The exonarthex was added in the Paleologian period, but the esonarthex was part of the the Comnenus design. The high arch in the W. wall, now filled in with a wall con-taining two windows, is explained from the inside as a gallery opening. A stepped tripartite arch of monumental dimensions, as wide as the naos and almost as high as the vaulting, did not close the gallery off as a separate space, as was customary, but made it an extension of the naos. The tripartite arch, from the early Byzantine period the architectural hallmark of the gallery, is thus transformed from a barrier to an architectural frame and reverses the relationship of wall and opening. A high transverse tunnel vault spanned the gallery, and it also had a dome to admit light, on the axis of the naos. The line of the gallery is continued in an encircling cornice as a dividing line between upper and lower storey and emphasizes the cruciform plan of the colourfully encrusted interior. The brickwork is covered with remains of the marble cladding in a decorative system of individually framed

Imrahor Camii

fields. At the side of the apse are high picture frames of the Palaeologian period
intended, like those in the Chora church,
for mosaic icons of Christ and the Mother
of God. The added apse section, adminstered by the Museums' Department,
focuses attention on the early building history of this church, for a long time held
to date from the 9C.

A research team from Harvard and the
Technical University of İstanbul under
the direction of C.Striker and D.Kuban
investigated and restored the building in
1966–78. 7 separate stages of building
were established, starting with a Roman
bath *c.*400, church buildings in the 6&7C,
then the existing church with crossing
dome dating from the 12C and its Palaeologian additions. According to these investigations the apse of the 7C monastery
church forms the basis of the bema. Here
two striking finds were made: a framed

mosaic of the Presentation of Christ in the
Temple, hidden in a wall cavity, probably
to protect it during the iconoclastic controversy. It is probably the oldest mosaic
in Constantinople. It dates from *c.*700 and
is now in a special room in the Archaeological Museum, in which the wall paintings of a St.Francis cycle are also kept.
This was found behind a wall in the S.
side apse in 1967. It is comparable with
Ducento Italian panel painting, with a central figure of St. Francis flanked by small
individual scenes from his life. Francis'
canonization in 1228 and the end of Latin
rule in 1261 restrict the possible range of
dates for the paintings. In the Turkish
period the church was turned into a
mosque, and named after the House of the
Mendicants, a particular Dervish order.

Kariye Camii/Chora monastery
(Kariye Camii Sokağı): Built on 6C

Istanbul, Kariye Camii/Chora church 1 Virgin Mary
with angels 2 Christ Pantocrator 3 Founder Theodor
Metokhites before Christ 4 Wall icon of St.Peter 5
Wall icon of St.Paul 6 Koimesis 7 Wall icon of Christ
8 Wall icon of Maria Hodegetria 9 6C false doors
(reliefs detached) 10 So-called Deesis, with Isaac
Comnenus and Melane the nun 11 Tomb of Theodor
Metokhites 12 Tomb of Michael Tornikes 13 4 warrior
capitals, probably from the 11C building

foundations and including 11&12C
sections, the Chora church dates in the
main from the early 14C. Theodore
Metochites (c.1260–1332), one of the most
famous statesmen and scholars of the
period, extended the basic cruciform
building founded c.1120 by Isaac
Comnenus. The Comnenus apse and
closed cubic naos were given new emphasis by the addition of numerous additional
spaces. Side apses were added in the E.,
a two-storey corridor built in the N. and
two narthexes of unequal size created in
the W. The shorter inner narthex was surrounded by a second, outer one which was
continued around the S. side to open into
the parekklesion. Only the exterior view
of the apses on the slope side shows the
early stages of the building history. The
parekklesion stands out as a separate section of the building among the enhanced
decoration of the S. side. The wall has
coloured strips, and is divided into two
storeys by a cornice. This creates a ten-
sion between horizontal and vertical articulation, the latter provided by windows
and semicircular vertical projections, making this exterior a high point in
Palaeologian architecture. A further
unusual feature of this late Byzantine
church is that the protruding base storey
of a tower has been retained under the
Turkish minaret. Theodore Metochites
spent the last years of his life in the Chora
monastery and exerted considerable
influence over the decoration of his

Kariye Camii (Chora church), Resurrection, wall painting in apse of parekklesion

church. He chose the parekklesion as his funerary chapel.

A unique feature of the Chora church is the *pictorial decoration*, large sections of which have survived. It dates from 1315–21. The two narthexes and the naos were originally completely covered with mosaics, whilst in the separate parekklesion wall painting dominated. The unprepared visitor, confronted immediately on entering the narthex with this complex pictorial world, covering lunettes, wall arches, spandrels and domes, will find difficulty in orienting himself. The habit of considering a museum piece from a fixed point goes very deep. It is essential to move through a Byzantine pictorial programme, however. In the Chora church there are two fundamentally different types of picture on the two principal routes which can be taken. The series on the axis which leads through the narthexes

and forms the shortest route to the naos consists mainly of individual pictures. Above the door from the outer to the inner narthex is Jesus Christ Blessing the Land (Greek: Chora) of the Living, according to the inscription. This is a monumental Pantocrator picture, whose model can be traced back to a 10C dome medallion, and it explains the name of the church. Opposite this, above the outer door, is a Madonna at prayer, with angels paying homage at her side. Its inscription makes a similar play on the name of the church. Continuing along the axis of the building, over the esonarthex is a full figure image of Christ, another customary image for a door lunette, the founder's picture. Theodore Metochites, in contemporary vestments, offers his building to Christ Enthroned. Icons of St. Peter and St. Paul flank the entrance to the naos. This direction of movement is crossed by sequences of pictures of the lives of Christ and Mary in both narthexes. The starting point is the N. dome compartment of the inner narthex, and the end is the equivalent point in the S. The domes which light the windowless inner narthex are thus fixed points in the spatial unfolding of the narrative pictorial programme. In both, ancestors of Christ are grouped around a head-and-shoulder picture in the dome medallion, in the N. around Mary, in the S. around Christ. In the 3 N. bays of the esonarthex the story of the childhood of Mary is told in the surrounding lunettes. At the point at which the sequence is interrupted by the picture of the founder, the run of scenes jumps back to the vault of the previous compartment and continues over the three wall arches and the sections of wall opposite these in the W., until the starting point under the N. dome is reached. The story of the childhood of Christ continues at a comparable point at the N. end of the outer narthex. On the lunettes of the E. wall the events of the Nativity and the Journey of the Magi are narrated. The narrative sequence runs around the SW corner, over the tripartite arch outside the parekklesion and across to the window wall, where much is missing, then returns to its N. starting point. The continuation, Christ's ministry, unfolds across the vaults. The two S. bays outside the parekklesion have a sequence of miracles which then continues in the S. section of the dome of the inner narthex. This strikingly independent section is dominated by a monumental wall mosaic of Christ, the interceding Madonna and a small figure of the founders, Isaac Comnenos and Maria Palaeologina, who as a nun had the name Melane. Its position in the narthex, the antiquated pictorial type, not a Deesis as John is missing, and also the unusual additional name of Chalkites for Christ, suggest an older 12C founder picture, as in the so-called Martorana in Palermo, transferred into a new Palaelogian version. Thus the

Kariye Camii, narthex mosaic ▷

memory of the earlier founders is preserved.

The complete programme did not end in this S. dome section, however. It was enhanced and concluded in the festival cycle in the naos. This explains the gaps in the narrative sequence in the outer narthex. The actual scene of Adoration is missing between the arrival and departure of the Magi. The Baptism is missing at the beginning of the sequence concerned with Christ's Ministry. Adoration and Baptism formed part of the cycle of liturgical festivals in the naos, of which only the Koimesis, the Dormition of Mary, has survived above the entrance. It is also not by chance that the Miracle of the Wine at Cana and the Miracle of the Loaves are placed in the central, particularly wide domical vault of the outer narthex. Bread and wine as anticipatory images of the eucharistic gifts are transferred to the entrance axis. The corresponding vault of the inner narthex shows Mary's Entrance into the Temple. Thus the main and transverse axes knit together on many levels, representative and narrative images become an all-embracing pictorial programme. The high theological standard of the mosaics is supported by the extraordinary quality of their execution. The dense Mary cycle in particular, which takes much of the detail for its 19 individual scenes from the apocryphal Book of James and Pseudo-Matthew, shows the unique qualities of Palaeologian style. Architectural settings, in varying perspective and lavishly draped, are used as elements in the composition. The figures make expressive gestures, using not just hand and head, but the whole body, bent, twisted, elongated, as a means of expression. The light does not model in soft transitions, but sets independent accents and effects in the active internal design of the ever-changing garment motifs.

The pictorial programme in the *parekklesion* is determined exclusively by its function as funerary chapel. The line of the sharply-defined exterior cornice is repeated in the interior, in order to separate the wall zone with icon-like rows of saints and church fathers from the vaults with scenes of the Resurrection and the Life, the Last Judgement, Heaven and Hell and the Mother of God as the Bridge between Heaven and Earth. Again the formal organization of the scenic wall paintings requires to be read in a particular order. The development starts on the left-hand side of the N. wall, then leads back to the entrance on the S. window wall. The contents of facing sections of wall are complementary, however, and form a thematic unit with the vault paintings above them. Thus the domed entrance bay and wall arch deal with the subject of the Mother of God as intercessor. The Old Testament scene of the altar worshipped by Aaron and his sons points forward to Mary, and so does the undamaged town opposite, in front of which an angel sends the Assyrians into flight as the result of a prophecy by Isaiah. In the sequence of Jacob's Ladder and the Burning Bush, a Mariological interpretation beyond the Biblical text is indicated directly by added head-and-shoulder pictures of the Madonna. On the opposite side the Bearing of the Ark of the Covenant and the Dedication of the Temple of Solomon have a similar metaphorical link with Mary. The key to the selection of Old Testament images is the pictures of authors on the dome pendentive above. The Evangelists are replaced by the four most important writers of Marian hymns, in which Mary is praised in an ever-broadening series of metaphors. Furthermore, these hymns, whose opening lines can be read in the wall paintings, were part of the Liturgy of the Dead. Thus in this first spatial unit the tomb of the founder, assumed to be in the lavishly-sculptured niche in the N. wall, was placed under the particular intercession of the Mother of God, who dominates the centre of the dome amidst angels. The next, smaller section has the Last Judgement on walls and vaulting. An angel rolls up the scroll of heaven, while Christ and the Apostles

Küçük Aya Sofya (left), Sent Iren Kilisesi (church of Irene, right)

sit in judgement. On the N. lunette the Just enter Paradise, where they are awaited by Mary and the Just Thief, who was crucified with Christ. Opposite, in the remaining field of the S. lunette. the damned are enfolded in fire and darkness. The last, tripartite unit shows the Resurrection of the Dead. The Waking of the Youth of Naim and Jairus's Daughter are prefigurations of the final resurrection of all the dead. In the apse picture of the Anastais (Resurrection) Christ has broken the Gates of Hell. Satan lies bound.

Kilise Camii, Byzantine name unknown (Molla Semsedin Gräni Sokagi/Katip Vefa Caddesi): The Church Mosque, wrongly identified in older literature as the church of St. Theodore, is made up of a Comnenus church of the 4 pier type and a 13C narthex. However, Palaeologian builders added more to the 11C Comnenus church

than just a second narthex. An independent section was erected in front, doubling the original façade and adding a second storey level and three domes. In the N. the base of a tower was built. The Palaeologian façade is lavishly articulated, Slender blind niches are placed by the tripartite arches in the wall. Balustrade slabs, columns and capitals are older components being used for the second time. Only the stepped arches of the upper window level share the bay division of the interior. Oval vaults were inserted between the dome sections. Early Palaeologian mosaics of the Madonna and the Forbears of Christ have survived in the S. dome.

Koca Mustafa Paşa Camii/Monastery of St.Andrew (Koca Mustafa Paşa Caddesi): This monastery, presumably dating from early Byzantine times, was rebuilt in the 13C as the result of an endowment by Theodora Rauliana, a niece of Emperor Michael VIII Palaeologus (1261–82). The surviving domed naos with ambulatory on three sides and the W. narthex date from this period. The tripartite arch dividing naos and ambulatory between the dome piers has also survived. It is built of reused components. The capitals with shallow acanthus leaves and central medallion are of the 6C type predominant in Hagia Sophia. In the N.–S. axis the corresponding arches have been removed and the space filled with half domes with inserted windows. These are Ottoman alterations to make the church suitable for use as a mosque. Later the Byzantine building was reoriented to the S., towards Mecca. Since then a narthex to the N. made the mosque a broad space with corridor-like halls. The dome was renewed after the earthquake of 1765. The exterior of the present mosque almost completely conceals the original Byzantine building. The surrounding mosque complex still contains the *türbe* of the founder, Grand Vizir Koca Mustafa Paşa (d. 1512) and also the *tomb* of Sümbül Efendi (d. 1529/30), the first sheikh of the attached Dervish monastery. The cemetery, used from the 16–19C, shows in what high honour he was held.

Küçük Aya Sofya Camii/Sergius and Bacchus church (Mehmet Paşa Sokağı): This centrally-planned building dating from 527–536 has, since the 16C, been isolated in a mosque courtyard, but irregularities in the masonry and the ambulatory show that it was originally part of a larger complex. Documents suggest association with a monastery of the Apostles Peter and Paul and the Hormisdas place, dating from the time of Constantine. According to the building inscription the centrally-planned building was dedicated to St. Sergius by Justinian I (527–565) and Theodora. Sergius was a Syrian soldier saint, honoured together

Sultan Ahmet Camii, the Blue Mosque with associated complex of buildings ▷

with St. Bacchus. The internal octagon is supported by 8 piers connected by arches. The arch openings are filled with alternating straight and semicircular walls, opening the interior to the ambulatory and galleries with a two-storey grid of columns. A lavishly carved entablature with the dedicatory inscription as frieze links columns and niches to form a spatial unit opening on to the sanctuary. The inscription probably also continued on the walls of the sanctuary. The sides of the octagon are not of consistent length in the W. and E. The entrance side is longer, and the bema side is longer still. Thus the centrally-planned building tends to the notion of an additional apse. The architrave above the piers makes a caesura in the vertical movement, allowing the ground and gallery floors to be appreciated as two levels of the church. A dome in 16 segments, with windows over the arch apexes and concave sections over the corners, forms the vaulting of the octagon. The articulating stucco strips date from the Ottoman period. Despite the raised floor level, the window openings in the apse and the whitewashing of the capitals, the present mosque contains one of the most important centrally-planned buildings of the Justinian period. The different kinds of marble, green in the flat niches, red in the semicircular ones, the net-like masonry of the vaults and undercut capitals show in the detail the luxury of its decoration. In terms of architecture and ornament it predates Hagia Sophia, and deserves the Turkish name Little Hagia Sophia.

Sent Iren Kilisesi/Hagia Eirene (Topkapı Saray): The origins of this old episcopal and council church go back to the time of Constantine the Great, but knowledge of this oldest church is purely literary. Hagia Eirene continued to be held in high esteem even after Hagia Sophia was built; the two churches and a famous hospice for the needy shared a site. Like Hagia Sophia, the original church burned down in the Nika Revolt of 532. It was rebuilt by Justinian I (527–565), and his church forms the basis of the present building with atrium, narthex and galleried basilica with central dome, nave and two aisles. Justinian's church was so badly damaged by an earthquake in 740 that fundamental sections of the building had to be renewed. The arches in the lower floor were redesigned, and those in the gallery abandoned, to be replaced by screen walls beneath the tunnel vaults over which the great crossing dome soars. Surviving from the 8C furnishings, the period of the iconoclastic controversy, are the cross in the apse and the six tiers of seats for the clergy. Hagia Eirene became part of the Topkapı Saray complex after the Turkish conquest, and so the church was never turned into a mosque, but used as an arsenal and storage depot. It is now a concert hall and museum for temporary exhibitions.

Zeyrek Camii/Pantocrator monastery (Idabethane Sokağı): This early 12C complex, towering over the Atatürk Bulvarı, is one of the most important churches of the Comnenus period. In fact it includes three churches, started before 1124 and completed in rapid sequence by 1137. The best place from which to form an impression of the history of the building is the E. section of the apses. The dominant domed church in the S. was founded by the Empress Eirene (1118–24) as the church of the Pantocrator, and she was buried there. Her husband, John II (1118–43), built the smaller church to the N. The original intention was to link the two buildings with corridors, but this plan was dropped in favour of the single-aisled church of St.Michael. Its broader proportions and twin domes allow it to make an impact as part of the rhythm and movement of the group of buildings as a whole. On the W. entrance side the narthexes of the two main churches join to form a unified double-storey façade, the upper storey of which led as a gallery to the naos of each

Mihrima Camii, by Sinan ▷

church. The S. church soon reasserted itself as the dominant building in the group by the addition of a second narthex. The gallery added behind this was given a central dome. At the same time the church of St. Michael was completed. Late-Byzantine restoration shows in the tripartite gallery window above the narthex of the N. church. The right-hand capital from the division between the windows, discovered in 1966&7 and completed in concrete, is now in the Bode Museum in E. Berlin. In the interior the three naves communicate by means of pierced walls in the adjacent long sides. The church of the Archangel, mausoleum of the Comnenus and Palaeologus dynasties, is the centre of the complex in terms of both space and contents. The fine *marble floor* gives a hint of the lavish furnishings of the church of the Pantocrator. The 4 monumental porphyry pillars, once under the broad crossing dome, were replaced by piers in the Turkish period. Fragments of pictorial stained glass were found among builders' rubble in the apse. This suggests that the apse windows contained stained glass sections, including a representation of the

Pantocrator. A parallel find in the Cora church suggests a similar situation there. During the Latin interregnum, the Pantocrator monastery was the Venetian residence. Numerous art treasures were stored here before being removed. After 1453 the monastery was used first of all as a Koran school, then later as the Zeyrek district mosque.

Mosques

Atik Ali Paşa Camii (Yeniceriler Caddesi): The eunuch Ali Paşa, grand vizier of Sultan Beyazıt II, built this mosque in 1496&7, together with a monastery, a poor kitchen and a school; some remains of the latter can still be seen. This is one of the oldest mosques in the city, and various elements of the domed room with courtyard and side rooms are early Ottoman in style.

Azapkapı Camii (Tersaner Caddesi): This mosque with an unusual minaret is on the bank of the Golden Horn near the Atatürk bridge. It was founded by Sokollu Mehmet Paşa, who served as grand vizier under 3 sultans. It was built in old age by

Rüstam Paşa Camii, faience of the Kaaba

Sinan, the great İstanbul mosque architect, in 1577. The slightly raised substructure once housed shops, and the porch, reached by a flight of steps, is somewhat over-shadowed by the modern bridge. The octagonal room with large central dome and eight half domes makes a spacious impression. The fine tiling was added in the course of far-reaching restoration. The marble pulpit and prayer niche are simple, noble and elegant.

Visitors to the mosque should not fail to notice the fine *fountain* to the N., lavishly decorated with floral patterns. This was endowed by Daliha, the mother of Mahmut I, in 1732, and has been well restored.

Bali Paşa Camii (Bali Paşa Caddesi): This little mosque, founded in 1504, was probably refurbished by Sinan at some time, as it features in his building list. Unfortunately it has been severely damaged by fire and earthquake, and presents a rather sorry picture.

Davut Paşa Camii (Ali Paşa Caddesi): This little mosque was completed in 1485 and named after its founder, the grand vizier of Beyazıt II. It makes a small and modest impression, and is on a square ground plan with shallow dome, columned porch and polygonal mihrab. The founder's *türbe* is in the old cemetery.

Dolmabahçe Camii (Meclisimebusan Caddesi): This little mosque on the bank of the Bosporus was designed by members of the Balyan family of architects, and completed in 1853. The mixture of traditional Ottoman, i.e. oriental, and neobaroque, i.e. what was then modern European architecture, makes this house of prayer look like a baroque garden pavilion with high dome and minarets. The interior also has hints of the European, and this brought it into the firing line for critics of architecture.

Firuz Aga Camii (Divan Yolu): This little mosque, a cubic, domed house of prayr with small domed porch (1491) is a typical example of the pre-classical mosque type prevalent in Anatolia before 1500. The founder's sarcophagus is next to it.

Hekemoğlu Ali Paşa Camii (Heke

Rüstem Paşa Camii, faiences (left), minaret of Sehzade Camii (right)

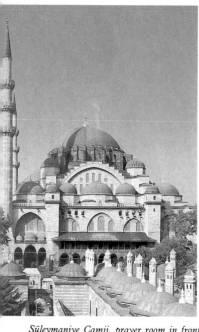 

Süleymaniye Camii, prayer room in front of kibla wall (right)

Moğlu Ali Paşa Caddesi): This complex founded by Mahmut I's grand vizier in 1734 includes a charming garden with fountain, library, the founder's türbe and the mosque, an elegant domed room with apse-like prayer niche, fine glass windows and attractive tiling.

Kara Ahmet Paşa Camii (Topkapı Caddesi): This complex is again the work of Sinan, although it was thoroughly restored at the end of the previous century. It includes the mosque, the residential cells of a medrese, a large classroom, washrooms and the founder's türbe. Rüstem Paşa had the building completed in 1555. It was founded by the grand vizier of Süleyman I, also a leader of the Jannisaries. He fought in Hungary, and later fell victim to court intrigue. Important features are the arabesque *paintings* in red, black, blue and gold and the

tiles. These came from the famous İznik potteries and are a fine and impressive example of late cuerda seca technique.

Kılıç Ali Paşa Camii (Necati Bey Caddesi): Ali Paşa, Calabrian by birth, distinguished himself in the fateful sea battle of Lepanto (7 October 1571), and at least managed to bring the sad remains of the once proud Ottoman fleet back to home waters. He was rewarded for this with the name of Kılıç (Crooked Sword) and the rank of Admiral of the Fleet. Again Sinan was the architect of this complex founded by Ali Paşa, including mosque, baths, şadırvan, medrese and founder's tomb, *c.* 1580, although he was by then very old. The influence of Hagia Sophia is strongly felt in the mosque, a domed room with porch, aisles, two-storey, vaulted ambulatory and rectangular mihrab with İznik tiles.

Sultan Ahmet Camii, interior

Lâleli Camii (Ordu Caddesi): Sultan Mustafa III was the founder and Mehmet Tahir the architect of the Tulip Mosque, built 1759–63. It has two minarets with onion domes, and is thought by connoisseurs to be the most beautiful baroque mosque in İstanbul. The impressive house of prayer with massive drum dome is set on a terrace-like lower storey with a central underground hall with fountain, supported by eight powerful piers. Around this are charming arcades with numerous busy shops and a café. Before entering the mosque itself, one passes a decorative baroque fountain house, the founder's türbe and the poor kitchen. The plain domed room on a rectangular plan with windows in the dome drum has impressive *wall decoration*, using a combination of multi-coloured marble with harmonizing semi-precious stones in the pietradura technique. Mihrab

niche and pulpit with lavish ornamentation and the other equally opulent furnishings complete the luxurious, if somewhat excessive, overall impression.

Mahmut Paşa Camii (Vezir Hani Caddesi): This mosque was founded in 1462/3 by Mahmut Paşa, the important Graeco-Serbian grand vizier of Mehmet I. It has suffered much damage, and was last restored in the present century. Mahmut Paşa was known as an upright, hard-working and exceptionally capable man and politician who also acquired a considerable literary reputation under the pseudonym Adeni. He was an outstanding and discerning patron of the arts. However, he attracted the wrath of his sovereign in old age, and was removed from his position of power and subsequently executed.

The building date, the T-shaped ground

plan and the combination of rooms intended for various purposes show that the mosque is an early Ottoman building based on the Bursa type. Given this, the work of maintenance and renewal carried out by restorers in the plain but dignified interior are not always entirely happy. The baths (→ Mahmut Paşa Camii under Ottoman secular buildings), parts of the han and the founder's türbe have survived from the orignal complex. The *türbe*, octagonal and pierced by double rows of windows, was built in 1474. The elegant, blue and turquoise tile mosaic in the upper section is an impressive feature.

Mesih Paşa Camii (Akşemsettin Caddesi): This mosque on a tall substructure, with octagonal interior, was founded in 1585 by the notoriously cruel and bloodthirsty former Egyptian governor Mesih Mehmet Paşa. In the centre of the courtyard, normally the site of the şadırvan, is the founder's türbe. For this reason the taps and basins for ritual washing are in the domed arcades surrounding the courtyard. It is worth visiting this mosque, probably the work of a pupil of Sinan, for the fine tiles and excellent masonry in the marble mihrab niche, on the minbar and on the grilles on the generously proportioned windows.

Mihrima Camii (Edirnekapı Camii; Sulukule Caddesi): This cubic mosque on the sixth hill of the city, set on a terrace substructure with shops, was built in the middle years of the 16C (scholars dispute the precise date, but the early sixties are usually suggested) by Sinan for Mihrimah, the favourite daughter of Süleyman I, known as the Great or the Magnificent. There are tower-like structures at the four corners of the cube. The drum of the dome has windows all round it. There is a slender minaret to the W. Severe damage by natural disasters has meant that this masterly building has been much restored. The other parts of the complex such as the double hamam and medrese were allowed to fall into disrepair, however.

The courtyard with fine şadırvan leads to an impressive porch with massive columns and seven domes. Only fragments have survived of the second porch, which was a favourite of Sinan. The many windows in the dome drum and the walls flood the interior with light. Galleries, side rooms and the effect of the light mask the essential simplicity of the building. The dome, 121 ft. high and 66 ft. in diameter, is supported by the main walls, and the side rooms each have three domes. The painting in pale, subdued colours is stencil work of a later date, but the minbar, contrasting with the architecture in its lavish ornamentation, is original.

Murat Paşa Camii (Vatan Caddesi): This mosque in the Bursa style with a low porch supported by ancient columns and topped by five domes was built in 1469 for a member of the Palaeologus family who converted to Islam and was taken into the service of the sultan. The main room is divided into two squares each with a dome, and there are two similarly designed side rooms each with two domes, forming the T-shaped ground plan already mentioned under Mahmut Paşa Camii.

Nişana Mehmet Paşa Camii (Fehmi Paşa Caddesi): Sinan or not Sinan? His work list says no, but many scholars contend that only the grand old man could have brought off this interesting and successful tour de force of the late classical period in 1584–8 (the year in which Sinan died). The eight little towers around the outer dome are continuations of the columns supporting the cental dome in the interior. It is surrounded by eight half domes. The interior is successfully composed on a square plan with inset octagon and mihrab apse, and surrounded by galleries except on the kibla side. The marble cladding and two Koran pulpits are interesting features.

Nuruosmaniye Camii (Nuruosmaniye Caddesi): The Mosque of the Sacred Light of Osman dating from 1748–56, the first 'baroque' mosque in İstanbul, is on a small terrace at one of the busiest points if the city, just by the covered bazaar. Signs of baroque influence are the square pilasters topped with domes and the broad wall arches pierced with windows. All the cornices are emphasized. The horseshoe-shaped courtyard with squat archways looking like a wall with small domes from the outside is an unusual feature. The many windows admit a great deal of light into the cubic, domed interior, which also has some baroque decoration. The mihrab apse rises out of the cube like a smaller version of the courtyard horseshoe.

Nusretiye Camii (Meclisi Mebusan Caddesi): This mosque, the Victory Mosque, built in 1826 after the suppression of the Janissaries' Revolt by Kirkir Baylan, the first of the capable and meritorious family of architects that built for the Ottomans in the 19C, is another attractive example of the 'Europeanization' of architecture in this period. Striking exterior features are the bulbous lanterns over the corner projections, the window jambs, the urns at the level of the dome and the bases of the fragile-looking slender minarets, which make the whole building look like a rococo pavilion and stem from the architect's time as a student in Paris. The unusual *square* in front of the mosque with its charming fountain is another interesting feature. The interior has a great deal of marble, and is dominated by French architectural and decorative detail.

Rüstem Paşa Camii (Hasircilar Caddesi): This small but very striking mosque was commissioned from Sinan by the grand vizier Rüstem Paşa, husband of Mihrimah, the favourite daughter of Süleyman the Magnificent, in 1561. Small in comparison with the → Süleymaniye Camii, which towers up behind it, this modest building has an elegant courtyard and two porches. The important feature of the little interior with two galleries are its magnificent and very colourful *tiles*, starting in the porch. They are from the İznik pottery, then at the peak of its fame. Geometrical patterns merge with plant and flower ornamentation to form an imaginative, impressive but never excessive or congested overall impression, making the mosque one of the most beautiful in the city.

Sultan Mehmet Fâtih Camii, fountain in old courtyard

Şehzade Camii (Şehzade Bası Caddesi): In 1543 Prince Mehmet, favourite son and heir apparent of Süleyman the Magnificent, died of smallpox at the age of 22. After his distraught father had got over the first shock he commissioned Sinan, who had been court architect since 1539, to build a külliye in memory of the unhappy heir to the throne. The Prince's Mosque was built 1544–8. He himself called it 'apprentice work', but it was his first great building in İstanbul, and also marks the beginning of his attempt to come to terms with Byzantine architecture, and Hagia Sophia in particular, which forms a thread throughout his work.

As one approaches the W. façade with round-arched windows with grilles and elegant stalactite portal, one is struck by the way the building rises to the main dome, also the highest, and also by the lavish but balanced architectural and ornamental design continuing on the sides, with their domed arcades incorporating the two slender, skilfully ornamented minarets. The square courtyard with surrounding arcades and central fountain makes an elegant impression. In comparison with the lavish ornamentation of the exterior the *interior* is restrained, even bleak. There are no columns. The main dome is supported by four massive piers and flanked by four half domes, each with two further small half domes. The corner niches are also domed. The sparse painting, restricted to the upper areas and the domes, was probably done later. The minbar is the most lavishly and skilfully designed feature.

The foundation also includes a medrese, school, poor kitchen, caravanserai and various türbe in the garden.

Prince Mehmet is buried with his brother Cihangir and his daughter Humaşah in a lavishly ornamented *octagon* with fluted dome. The interior is lit by stained-glass windows and is a truly 'paradisal' symphony of İznik tiles in cuerda seca technique, with the original dome painting and fine baldacchino offering worthy competition. If this is not enough, there is no less splendid and valuable decoration, also from the İznik potteries, in the *türbe* of Rüstem and Ibrahim Paşa and the unusual tomb of Destari Mustafa Paşa. In comparison with these three 'heavenly' final resting places, the three other undecorated türbe make a decidedly 'earthly' impression.

Sinan Paşa Camii (Beşiktaş Caddesi): This was built by Sinan for Rüstem Paşa's brother, Grand Admiral Sinan Paşa, who was already dead when the mosque was completed in 1556. It is a copy of Uç Şerefli Camii, built a good century earlier in Edirne.

Opposite are a türbe built by Sinan and a modern memorial to the notorious Cheireddin (Chair Ad Din; 1467–1546), a Greek converted to Islam also known as Barbarossa, who defeated the imperial fleet in 1538 and also distinguished himself in the service of the Turkish fleet.

Sokullu Mehmet Paşa Camii (Kadırga Caddesi): Sinan built this mosque, impressive above all for the harmony of its interior and exterior decoration, in 1571&2 for grand vizier Sokullu Mehmet Paşa. This harmony begins to make itself felt in the spacious courtyard, in the centre of which is a charming şadırvan. The pupils at the medrese originally lived under the arches of this courtyard, and were taught in an unusually designed dershane. The rectangular interior with main and side domes and gallery on three sides makes a solemn and harmonious impression. The wall decoration in İznik tiles and the sparse painting were skilfully distributed over the walls, restrained in their stone and marble shades, in such a way as to provide a worthy frame for the magnificent kibla wall, which contains relics in the form of stones from the sacred Kaaba in Mecca. Mihrab and minbar are comparatively plain, but executed with style and elegance.

Topkapı Saray, faience in harem ▷

Topkapı Saray, harem

Süleymaniye Camii (Süleymaniye Caddesi): Who other than Sinan could have built such an outstanding and worthy monument to such an excellent ruler as the great Süleyman II (1494/5–1566, sultan from 1520). The second-largest sultan's mosque in İstanbul, built 1550–7, is one of the finest Islamic places of worship in the city, and one of its architect's masterpieces. The obligatory associated buildings, several schools, a caravanserai, poor kitchens and other institutions were not completed until later. The four *minarets*, of equal height in pairs, with a total of ten balconies, are said to have symbolic meaning: Süleyman, the tenth sultan of the Ottoman dynasty, was the fourth ruler of his house to live in İstanbul. The mosque is on a particularly attractive site above the Golden Horn, and is surrounded by a garden with an openwork wall on three sides. Multicoloured marble

columns from the old Hippodrome were used in the elegant rectangular *courtyard* in front of the mosque. The courtyard has 28 domes, and is entered via a stalactite portal in a fine gatehouse. The şadırvan seems small in comparison with the massive arcades.

The spacious, rectangular *interior* with drum dome framed by two half domes, supported by four columns, four ribbed arches and pendentives, with windows in the drum, is lit by more than 130 windows. The central area and aisles are separated by further ancient porphyry columns. The galleries are reserved for important personages on special occasions. particularly attractive features are the fine windows and inscriptions by the great calligrapher Karasihari and also the excellent mihrab niche, the minbar and the pulpit. The successful combination of solemn architecture and skilfully balanced

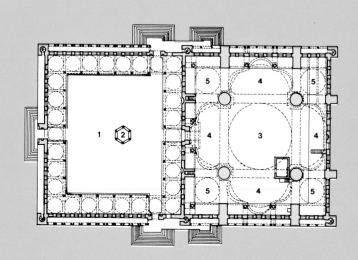

İstanbul, Sultan Ahmet Camii 1 Forecourt surrounded by arcades **2** Şadırvan **3** Interior, almost square, with main dome supported by four broken gate arches on ponderous columns and four pendentives **4** Semi-domes raising the gate arches **5** Small domes spanning the four corner rooms

decorative elements join to make the mosque an impressive and worthy place for the worship of Allah and his prophet Mahomet.

The most important feature of the *cemetery* behind the mosque is Sinan's octagonal *türbe* for Süleyman, with columned surrounding porch and openwork crowning cornice. The tiles, from İznik like those in the mosque, jewelled marquetry and ancient porphyry columns make it a worthy last resting place for the great sultan. The other türbe seem comparatively plain and modest; one of them is that of his favourite wife, Roxelane.

The associated buildings grouped around the mosque are arranged and designed in such a way as to make the entire complex an aesthetically pleasing functional unit. Particularly worthy of attention are the Museum of Turkish and Islamic Art accommodated in the poor kitchen (→

under Museums) and the tomb which Sinan designed for himself, which is not without a charm of its own, but modest in comparison with his other magnificent buildings. It is in the NW corner of the garden wall.

Sultan Ahmet Camii (*Blue Mosque*; At Meydanı): The principal mosque of İstanbul with its six minarets is by the Hippodrome opposite Hagia Sophia. Mosque, medrese, poor kitchen and other functional buildings were built in 1609–16 by Sinan's pupil Mehmet Ağa for Sultan Ahmet I (1590–1617, sultan from 1603), remembered above all for his peace treaties

İstanbul, Sultan Ahmet Camii 1 Forecourt surrounded by arcades **2** Şadırvan **3** Interior, almost square, with main dome supported by four broken gate arches on ponderous columns and four pendentives **4** Semi-domes raising the gate arches **5** Small domes spanning the four corner rooms

with the Emperor and the Persians (1612). The mosque precinct is surrounded by an openwork wall, and the mosque itself follows the traditional building scheme: a large courtyard with domes and arcades also contains the main portal, and the almost square interior with galleries on three sides is centred around the great main dome.

The *tiles*, predominantly in shades of blue and green, in the interior, lit by 260 windows, some of them with stained glass, are from İznik, and have its typical plant and flower ornaments. These and the painting have earned the building its title Blue Mosque. Minbar and mihrab niche are outstanding works in light marble, while the wood of the galleries, decorated with fine marquetry, and the exquisite, largely red carpets complete the picture of a worthy and dignified place of prayer. The pulpit is based on the one at Mecca, and was used to announce the dissolution and annihilation of the feared corps of Janissaries in 1826. In the prayer niche is a stone from the Kaaba in Mecca, formerly the destination of İstanbul pilgrims from the Sultan Ahmet Camii on the hegira. Ahmet died at the age of only 27 and is buried with other members of his family in the *türbe* NE of the mosque.

On the left of the courtyard portal, in the adjacent building, is the *Vakıflar Halı Müezesi* (carpet museum). On the terrace below that is the *Vakıflar Kilim Müezesi* (textile museum).

Sultan Beyazıt Camii (Yeniçeriler Caddesi): Beyazıt II, the son of Mehmet Fâtih, conqueror of Constantinople, commissioned the oldest surviving sultan's mosque from Yakup Şah bin Sultan in 1501–6, thus introducing the epoch of classical Ottoman architecture. An attempt to come to terms with Hagia Sophia, repeatedly taken up by Sinan, was clear even at this early stage. Three fine portals lead into the very elegant courtyard with domed arcades and a 17C şadırvan. The harmonious colours of the various building materials are particularly beautiful. The two minarets with balconies also show a high level of craftsmanship. The interior is relatively restrained in design, and reminiscent of its great Byzantine predecessor with its main dome between two half domes and aisles without galleries. The longitudinal axis directed

Dolmabahçe Saray, part of façade

towards kibla wall and mihrab niche is set against a transverse axis formed by the cruciform side rooms adjacent to the front aisles. The complex also includes a türbe garden with plain tombs of the founder and members of his family and also the more elaborate *türbe* of the grand vizier Koça Resit Paşa, who died in 1857; also the oldest surviving school in the city, the former poor kitchen (now national library) and medrese (now municipal library), also a shopping alleyway by Sinan, the second-hand book market and the ruins of the baths.

Sultan Mehmet Fâtih Camii (Darüssafaka Caddesi): The mosque built by Mehmet II, the conqueror of Byzantine Constantinople, from 1463–70 on the fourth hill of the city on the site of the old Apostles' church collapsed in 1766 as a result of repeated earthquake damage. The present building with two minarets, rising in stages to the main dome, was built as a replacement in 1767–71. The most striking feature of the *courtyard* with unusual ablution fountain are the capitals of the ancient columns, the wonderful tiled decoration on the lunettes and the refined design of the courtyard and mosque portals. The interior, compared with other mosques in İstanbul, is not without decoration, but does not make such a profound impression.

The Conqueror's mosque is also part of a külliye including the usual functional buildings, of which some have survived. In the garden are the *türbe* of Mehmet, with some extravagantly baroque elements and the extremely austere tomb of his consort Gülbahar. It is said of her that she may have been a Christian princess, but more probably she was a slave who never renounced her religion and died an 'infidel'.

Sultan Selim Camii (Yavuz Selim Caddesi): Süleyman the Magnificent completed the mosque of his father, Selim I (1470–1520, sultan from 1512), famous for numerous conquests and known as the Cruel or the Grim. The building is relatively austere, with massive central dome and two minarets, reminiscent of the Beyazıt Camii in Edirne. It is beautifully sited, with a tremendous view over the Golden Horn. The ground plan of the cubic, domed prayer room with rectangular

Topkapı Saray, Baghdad kiosk

Topkapı Saray, Orta Kapı (left), weapon collection (right)

courtyard is enlivened by the square side rooms inserted like transepts at the corners where courtyard and mosque meet. The interior is also plain and dignified, and architectural and colour elements join in a harmonious pattern. Among the türbe, *Selim's monument* is octagonal with a fine tiled porch and interior dominated by a plain sarcophagus decorated with the usual turban.

Yeni Camii (Hamidiye Caddesi): This mosque with two fine minarets with balconies at the old town end of the Galata bridge near the ever-lively Eminönü Square should properly be called *Yeni Valide Camii* (New Mosque of the Sultan's Mother), and has a complex building history. In 1597 Sinan's pupil David Ağa started the building at the bidding of Mehmet III's mother, and over 60 years later, in 1663, Mehmet IV's mother

ordered its completion. In terms of ground plan the mosque is again a variation on Hagia Sophia, with a charming courtyard. The interior, in which striking features are again the well-crafted prayer niche, minbar and small Koran pulpit, is decorated with tiles and paintings. An interesting additional feature is the *Sultan's pavilion*, a complete residence with kitchen, bathroom, toilet and servants' quarters, which not only provided the ruler with pleasant accommodation, but also offered him the possibility of entering and leaving his loge in the mosque from the outside without being seen.

Ottoman secular buildings

Like their Christian predecessors, Constantinople's Muslim rulers did not provide their city only with impressive and dignified buildings for the worship of

Topkapı, Saray, harem

God. Their secular buildings added an oriental touch, and also were impressive testimony of a period of success and prosperity. The most interesting are presented in the following section, arranged in categories. The finest are presented first.

The Sultans' Palaces

Dolmabahçe Saray (Dolmabahçe Caddesi): Sultan Abdül Mecit commissioned a new palace on the site of an old summerhouse on the banks of the Bosporus from Karabet and Nikogos Balyan in 1853. He was able to move into his new residence in the capital two years later. Today the palace is used for state visitors, ceremonies, receptions and other official functions. Otherwise it is open to the public. Kemal Atatürk, the father of the modern Turkish state, also stayed here when he was in İstanbul. He died in the

palace on 10 November 1938 and lay in state here until his funeral.

If the palace is viewed from a boat on the Bosporus, one sees the long façade overlooking the sea, with high central building and two side wings of unequal length, and it is easy, faced with the baroque and neoclassical architectural features it displays, to feel that one is in the Europe of the absolute rulers rather than at the gate of the Orient. This 'sugar icing' style also dominates the land side of the palace, which nevertheless fits in very well with the landscape. However, connoisseurs will recognize, among the lavish display of occidental architecture, native elements such as stalactites and grilles. There is certainly room for dispute about the tastefulness, suitability and beauty of the interior decoration and furnishings (particularly the throne room, crystal staircase and bathroom), but there can be no doubt that the more than lavish use of expensive materials such as marble, porphyry, alabaster, crystal, gold and other precious metals, velvet and silk means that it is of inestimable material value. It also contains fine furniture, paintings and *objets d'art*.

Topkapı Saray (Taya Hatun Caddesi): After the fall of Constantinople, Mehmet Fâtih commissioned a new palace on the site of the old university in 1454&5, more suitable to his wishes and needs than the existing Byzantine residences. About 9 years after he had moved from Edirne to

Topkapı Saray, treasure chamber, pearly throne

the new capital, *c.*1464, he gave orders to build a new seraglio on this gloriously placed spit of land, part of the first hill of the city, and surrounded by the Golden Horn, the Bosporus and the Sea of Marmara. It was intended more for administrative than residential purposes. Süleyman the Magnificent was the first sultan actually to make it his residence. The palace is now used as a museum, and because subsequent sultans altered and extended the palace until 1855 (change of residence to the Dolmabahçe palace), and catastrophic fires in the 16, 17&19C made restoration and rebuilding necessary, it is a fascination reflection of Ottoman architecture from the 15–19C.

It is fair to say that the Topkapı palace was originally a city within a city. As well as the sultan's family, the harem and countless servants, it also housed the divan (supreme imperial council), and a palace

school to train future high state officials. There were stables, storehouses, kitchens and accommodation for domestics, and also all the traders necessary for the existence of a community, from farmers and bakers to the master of the horse.

The modern visitor can only be aware of a fraction of the buildings and treasures that this enormous museum has to offer in the course of a tour, and can only gain a hint of the mind and spirit, so alien to us, which created it.

Thus the route suggested in the sketch map should be seen as a rough guide only. As has always been the case, the palace is entered today through the central arch of the *Bab-i-Hümayun*, under the imperial monogram of Mehmet II. The two side niches were formerly used to display the heads of delinquents beheaded at the sultan's bidding. The upper storey, now removed, served as a treasury, used

Topkapı Saray, items from the collection of miniatures

principally for the examination of property confiscated from delinquents. The *first court* (1) has been much altered over the centuries. Of interest are Hagia Eirene (→ Sent Iren Kilisesi under Former Byzantine Churches), the fountain house, the ruins of the old mint and the Gate of the Keepers of the Maidens leading to the archaeological museum. The museum workshops are also accommodated here. The *Orta Kapı* (Middle Gate, 2) with its two side towers with pointed roofs seems rather more European. Only the sultan was allowed to go through it on horseback, everyone else, even dignitaries of the highest order, had to pass on foot. Condemned prisoners awaited execution in the chambers of the towers, and afterwards the executioner washed himself and his tools in the Cellat Çeşmesi (Executioner's Fountain).

In the spacious, park-like *Second Court* (3),

officials and dignitaries dealt with state business and affairs. The divan (imperial council), the highest administrative body, met in the square *Kubbe Altı* (6), over which rose the tower of justice, with a pointed roof. The grand vizier, highest court official and thus the highest official in the Ottoman Empire, dealt with his business in his own lavishly furnished rooms, much altered and restored over the years. The wide-ranging and valuable clock collection housed here is of interest to non-specialists. An interesting collection of weapons is housed in the former *Treasury* (5), and the former *kitchen*, immediately recognizable by its characteristic chimneys, present a magnificent collection of European and Asiatic porcelain of all kinds assembled by the sultans, and Süleyman the Magnificent in particular. Cutlery and crockery, kitchen equipment and furnishings give

Topkapı Saray, exhibits from the collection of miniatures

an impression of the way in which the bodily needs of the inhabitants of the saray were looked after. In an arcade on the W. side of the court is a collection of inscriptions, of particular interest to experts. The *Court of the Guard* (7), with an unusual mosque and other functional buildings, was reserved for the use of the Sultan's guard, who occasionally also undertook domestic duties in the palace. The Gate of the Dead was used to take out residents and visitors who died in the palace. Adjacent to this are the *stables* (8), which accomodated the ruler's favourite horses and the stable staff. It now houses an exhibition of tack, and sedan chairs and carriages belonging to Ottoman notables. Two entrances, the *Araba Kapısı* (Carriage Gate, 9) and the *Cümlü Kapısı* (12) lead into the *Harem*, the 'forbidden' area of the palace. It was not just reserved for women, but could be called the 'private residence'

of the sultan and his family. Beyond the *guardroom* (10) is the *Courtyard of the Black Eunuchs* (11), a long court with mosque and the modest cells in which the eunuchs lived, in three storeys. The *residence of the Ağa* (13), who ran the harem as Lord of the Maidens, and thus had power and influence, is also by no means large or luxurious.

The accommodation around the *Courtyard of the Women Servants* (14) is also modest. This was used by female servants and slaves of all ranks. This tract also contains the harem hospital. The first high spot, though still restrained, is the *Courtyard of the Sultan Mother* (15), with the *rooms* (16) used by the ruler's mother, who directed women and servants, and often enough her reigning son. The rooms are decorated with attractive faience and painting, and elegantly furnished. The Room with a Hearth leads to the *Rooms of the*

Highest-Ranking Women (17) and those of the *Sultan* (18). The domed Hünkar Sofası, the *Hall of the Emperor* (19), was designed and decorated in the 16&17C, and seems magnificent, lavish, but perhaps a little excessive. Adjacent is the *Fountain Room* (Çeşmeli Oda, 20), with charming tiling and 17C fountain. The *Anteroom to the Salon of Murat III* (21) is also decorated with splendid tiles. This spacious, well-proportioned domed room bears the stamp of Sinan, and tiles, excellent İznik work, the inscription frieze running round the room, discreet polychrome marble fountain, noble fireplace and the remaining furnishings combine to form an impressive unit.

In comparison with this room, the *Library of Ahmet I* (22) with blind windows and stylized decorative inscriptions, seems artificial. The lavish flower and fruit ornamentation in the *Dining-Room of Ahmet III* (23) gave it the name Fruit Room. The *Bedroom of Abdül Hamit I* (24) has lavish baroque design and furnishings. More recent (18&19C) is the *Köşk of Osman III* (25). It is assumed that the *Princes' Chambers* (26), also much more aptly styled 'Cages', were used by the

reigning sultan as accommodation for his brothers, far from the world and everyday events, so that they could not do any unwitting damage to the processes of his government. The official tour ends in a colonnade known as the *Consultation-Place of the Jinn*. The *Courtyard of the Favourites* (27) and the accommodation for the sultan's wives, now falling into disrepair, can only be viewed from a distance. They have remained untouched since the last woman left the Harem at the beginning of the present century.

This is of course not the end of the tour of the Saray. The *Bab-üs-Saadet* (30), designed and decorated as we see it in the 19C, leads from the Second to the Third Court, where the buildings were used largely for the palace school for the training of future high officials and to accommodate the White Eunuchs, who ran the school. The 16C *Audience Hall* (31), decorated in the 17C, and with an attractive wall fountain, was used by the sultan to inform himself about meetings of the divan and to discuss problems of state with court officials. The *Library of Ahmet III*, elegant, with all the hallmarks of a place of relaxation, and still housing valuable

Topkapı Saray, Carriage Museum, Ottoman coach

books and manuscripts, was built in 1718/19 in fine marble on the site of an older pavilion. The main library is now housed in the *Ağalar Camii* (33), formerly the principal mosque in the complex, and also accessible from the Harem. It has been much altered. The former *Hall of Privy Chamber* (museum of calligraphy, 34) leads to the part of the saray most sacred to Turkish and Islamic visitors, the *Pavilion of the Holy Mantle* (relic chambers, 35). The 4 domed rooms with their valuable furnishings are a worthy and by no means excessively lavish setting for the weapons and personal belongings of the Prophet. There are also valuable old editions of the Koran and various objects from the holy city of Mecca. A window with a grille affords a view of the last room, decorated with excellent tiles from the heyday of the İznik potteries. Two golden shrines house the Holy Mantle of Mahomet and the Holy Standard, unfurled to proclaim a jihad, or holy war. The former *Hall of the Commissariat Pages* (36) houses a collection of valuable paintings and miniatures, particularly on historical subjects. Beyond the *Museum Administration* (37) is the *Treasury* (38).

It would be impossible to attempt to do justice to any of the treasures exhibited here, thrones, furniture, crockery, weapons, armour, costume, jewellery, decorations and a great deal more. The visitor will also find it difficult to pay due attention to each of these gems and retain then in his memory.

The former *Hall of the Expedition Pages* in this court is also worth seeing; it combines oriental and occidental architectural features, and houses a splendid costume collection.

The *Fourth Court* (40) is more a terraced garden, from which there are splendid views of the roofs, domes and minarets of İstanbul, and over the Golden Horn, the Bosporus and the Sea of Marmara. The small pavilions here were formerly used for relaxation and leisure. Lovers of the Turkish tiles are offered a particular treat in the *Sünnet Odasi* (41). This was built by Crazy Ibrahim in 1641. He covered it completely in tiles from all over the country, both inside and out. Thus this little building offers an almost seamless and entirely fascinating survey of the history and development of tiles, from the beginnings via the peak of Iznik

Topkapı Saray, harem

Street of shops in Kapalı Çarşısı, the covered bazaar

perfection to the late period, and subsequent ones. The elegant and eccentric *baldacchino* on the marble terrace (42), formerly over a fine throne from which the ruler enjoyed the wonderful view, was also associated with Ibrahim. The pavilion with surrounding colonnade known as the *Bağdad Köşk* (43) was built at the end of the terrace for Murat IV in 1639, in commemoration of the conquest of Baghdad in 1638. The domed interior with several niches is again impressive for its tiles, flawless inscriptions, dome painting and intarsia work. The massive bronze fireplace in the form of a mihrab niche is a striking feature. The large *double hall* (44), an open colonnade with early-Ottoman decoration leads to the *Revan* Köşk (45). This pavilion is similar to the Bağdad Köşk, and was also commissioned by Murat IV, this time in 1635&6 in memory of the conquest of the then

Persian fortress of Revan, now known as Jerewan (Eriwan) and capital of the Soviet Republic of Armenia. The marble and tiles of the walls are again impressive. Ahmet III, the great tulip lover, built the unusual *Sofa Köşk* (46) in the middle of his tulip garden in 1705. Its design and interior décor (1742) make it is exactly like a European rococo pavilion. The remains of the *Başlâla Kulesi* (47), doubtless once proud, also date from the time of Mehmet Fâtih. In 1840, shortly before he moved to the Dolmabahçe Palace, Abdül Mecit built the most recent of the Topkapı palace buildings, the *Mecidiye Köşk* (48), completely in the style of the 'new' age, very European and thus a somewhat alien element in the overall picture. From here there is a fine view not only over the Sea of Marmara, but also of the *Terrace Mosque* (Sofa Camii, 49), for which Abdül Mecit was also responsible.

Fountain of Ahmet III

Yıldız Saray (Çırağan Caddesi): This complex, consisting of several pavilions spread around an attractive park, dates from the late period of the sultans, when European architectural influence had made its mark in the Ottoman Empire. Şale Köşk, Yıldız Köşk and the mosques are products of historicism and date from the second half of the 19C. A small cemetery with the türbe of Yahya Effendi (16C) and some buildings associated with it are also part of this. On the other side of the street, on the shores of the Bosporus, are the ruins of Çırağan Saray (19C).

Baths

The Turkish bath (hamam) is today popular with both natives and foreigners, and has a long tradition. The Byzantines and the Ottomans built magnificent establishments, and some of them, restored of course, are still in use today. Usually a

Turkish bath consists of the câmekân, a large anteroom for dressing and undressing, a transitional room, the soğukluk (cold room) and the hararet (hot and steam room). The building includes toilets, and in some cases a swimming pool. As Islam is concerned with the separation of men and women in many areas of life, there were some baths reserved for women, combined with those for men for technical reasons such as heating and water supply, but strictly separate in the bathing areas. Such institutions are known as double baths.

Cağaloğlu Hamamı (Yerebatan Caddesi): These are charming baroque baths built under Mahmut I with spacious domed rooms. Men's and women's baths are arranged parallel to one another according to tradition, but separated by a kind of courtyard.

Çemberlitaş Hamamı (Divan Yolu):

Only the men's section of this bath built *c.*1583, and suggesting the involvement of Sinan or his pupils by its style, is still in use. The women's section was demolished as part of a road-building programme.

Çinili Hamamı (Itfaiye Caddesi): It is presumed that Sinan himself built this double bath in 1545 for the notorious admiral and corsair Cheireddin (Chair Ad Din) Barbarossa. The interior with fine tiles and faience has been well restored and offers relaxation in a uniquely oriental atmosphere.

Gedik Ahmet Paşa Hamamı (Gedik Paşa Caddesi): This well-restored bath dates from 1475. Its finest feature is the domed soğukluk with stalactite vaulting.

Küçük Mustafa Paşa Hamamı (Mektep Sokaği): This bath is now in use again after successful and thoughtful restoration. It dates from 1512, is spacious, tasteful, and lavishly decorated in parts.

Mahmut Paşa Hamamı (Mahmut Paşa Yokusu): This impressive domed building with fine portal was built in 1466 as part of the → Mahmut Paşa Camii complex, and has been much restored in the meantime. It shares the honour of being the oldest Turkish bath in İstanbul with the Gedik Ahmet Paşa Hamamı.

Bazaars

Kapalı Çarşısı (*Large* or *Covered Bazaar*, Cadircilar Caddesi): The old bedesten, a market hall with several domes, was built *c.*1460 by Mehmet Fâtih on the site where there had been trade and activity in the Byzantine period as well. The Byzantine eagle over the Gate of the Goldsmiths is a reminder of these early times. The new bedesten, additional halls with more than 20 domes, was built under Süleyman the Magnificent. Fires and earthquakes have necessitated repeated restoration.

Mısır Çarşısı (*Egyptian Bazzaar*, Harırcılar Caddesi): These L-shaped market halls were part of the → Yeni Camii complex and were commissioned by Mehmet IV's mother in 1660. As well as all kinds of general necessities spices and herbs are sold here, as they were of old. The charming restaurant is also highly recommended.

Fountains

The Koran lays down that the faithful should present themselves outwardly clean for prayer. Thus every mosque has a şadırvan, or ablution fountain, often replaced simply by taps in the walls. A city like İstanbul also needs fountains at which one may quench one's thirst and refresh oneself (sebil and çeşme). And finally Ottoman town planners and architects often used fountains as a design feature in streets, squares, gardens and even rooms.

Fountain of Ahmet III (Sakpaşa Caddesi): This is probably the most attractive Ottoman fountain in İstanbul, built in 1728 in front of the Bab-i-Hümayun, the gate to the Topkapı Saray. It has been sensitively restored. The projecting canopy roof has one large central lantern and five smaller ones at the sides. The little building has windows with charming grilles, stalactite niches, running fountains, fine relief decoration and a copperplate inscription by the poet Wehbi praising the waters of this masterpiece of Ottoman baroque.

Azapkapı fountain (Cameka Sokaği): This much restored, charming wall fountain with slightly curving arched niche, inscription panels, pretty plant and fruit decoration and small side water bowls under conch arches, was built *c.*1730 on the site of an older fountain.

German fountain (At Meydanı): Kaiser Wilhelm II presented this charming circular construction with dome supported by an open colonnade to Sultan Abdül Hamit II and the city of İstanbul on the occasion of his state visit in 1895. It was completed a few years later.

Tophane Fountain (Iskele Caddesi): Mahmut I commissioned this charming fountain house, rooted in Ottoman baroque and well restored in the meantime, with canopy roof with lantern, and walls with fine ornamentation, in 1732.

Other buildings worth seeing

Alay Köşkö (Alemdar Caddesi): This pavilion with window grilles opposite the Sublime Porte on the wall of the Topkapı Saray afforded the sultan a concealed view of who was entering and leaving the rooms of his grand vizier. The existing polygonal building on a high base (the foundations of a former tower in the wall) with cool, neutral wall articulation and a fine canopy roof dates from 1819.

Bab-i-Ali (*Sublime Porte*, Alemdar Caddesi): Sublime Porte or simply Porte was at first the designation for the sultan's palace, then from 1718–1922 it was synonymous with the grand vizier and the Ottoman Empire itself. Thus diplomats were accredited to the Porte, and decisions of the Porte were discussed in Europe. The present gate, a baroque gatehouse flanked by two small, suitably designed fountains has a projecting canopy roof and stylishly framed gate. It dates from 1843, and leads to the administrative buildings of the province of İstanbul. The fine dershane of the medrese which once stood on the site has survived.

Çinili Köşk (Gülhane Park): Mehmet Fâtih, the Conqueror, commissioned this lodge in 1472. It was later much restored and altered, but is still a fine example of early Ottoman secular architecture, showing Persian and Seljuk influences. The two-storey porch with elegant columns and arches is particularly charming. There are also remains of the original cladding with glazed tile mosaic and a copperplate inscription frieze. The inner rooms, in two storeys on an almost square ground plan with inscribed cross and protruding apse, now house, as well as remains of the old revetment in shades of blue and turquoise with gold mosaic tiles, the museum devoted the the sultan who commissioned the building, Mehmet Fâtih.

Galata Kulesi (*Galata Tower*, Galipdede Caddesi): This tower, sometimes also known as the Tower of Christ, was built in the N. section of the Genoese town fortifications. It was much altered under the Ottomans in the course of the

Pera with Galata tower

centuries, and was used among other things as a prison and a fire-watch tower. Stairs or a lift lead to the night club and restaurant, from which there is a magnificent view of the domes, roofs, towers and minarets of the parts of the city on the Golden Horn.

Main Post Office (Yeni Postahane Caddesi): This comparatively recent Ottoman building dates from the first decade of our century, and is strongly influenced by French art nouveau.

Sepetçiler Köşk (Gülhane Park): The mid-17C Basket-Weavers' Pavilion has undergone various alterations and recent restoration. Thanks to this it is a good example of the waterside pavilions which proliferated near the Topkapı Saray in the Ottoman period, some of which were also used as boathouses.

Tophane (Boğanzkesen Caddesi): This former cannon foundry with five domes, which gave its name to a whole district of the city, dates from the early 19C and replaced earlier buildings on the site: there was a cannon factory here even under Mehmet Fâtih.

University (Hürriet Meydanı): Mehmet Fâtih built his first palace in newly-conquered Constantinople here in the middle of a spacious park. This was the Eski Saray, which he abandoned on moving into Topkapı Saray. The building then erected on the site, reached via the park gate, gives the impression of being a mixture of Tudor buildings (side towers) and the Ottoman style (central section). It previously served as the Ministry of War. In the 1950s the university, founded by edict of the sultan in 1845, was provided with the monumental new buildings now known as the New University.

In 1828 Mehmet II built the *Beyazıt Tower* in white marble in the park on the site of an earlier wooden building. The 164 ft. tower with striking lantern was originally a fire-watch tower.

Yedikule (Yedikule Caddesi): The Castle of the Seven Towers, whose sturdy and imposing remains can still be seen, was the work of Mehmet Fâtih and his successors, who made small alterations from time to time. It was originally a three-sided addition to the section of the land walls (→ Byzantine Monuments) of which the Golden Gate (→ Byzantine Monuments) is also a part. The pentagonal complex with massive walls, defiant towers, extensive courtyard and remains of buildings and a little mosque looks back on a terrible history: as well as part of the state treasure, prisoners of rank and name were kept here, often tortured and even killed. They included members of the sultan's family who had fallen from grace or who were unpopular, state officials, dignitaries and the unfortunate ambassadors of all the countries with whom the Porte happened to be at war at the time. Their sufferings are documented in many languages in the numerous inscriptions on the walls of the E. tower, also known as the Tower of the Inscriptions or Tower of the Ambassadors.

Finally the Fountain of Blood, said to have been connected with the sea, was intended to receive the severed heads of all those unfortunates for whom the Yedikule was to be the final resting place.

Hans

Shortly after a caravan road had become a regularly used route, special areas (water supplies in the desert) came into being at regular intervals, so-called caravanserais, intended to supply travellers and animals with accommodation and refreshment, and in which small business transactions could be carried out.

In larger towns, alongside the pilgrims' quarters which were part of any large foundation, there developed inns (hans), founded by the ruler, officials or other wealthy citizens. These provided not only accommodation, but soon became small markets where one could buy and sell and where craftsmen worked. Often such hans were classified according to trades or skills. As a rule they consist of a spacious courtyard surrounded by buildings with several storeys opening on to the courtyard with arcades and arbours. If the han was not part of a külliye, it had a prayer room.

Balkapan Hanı (Balapan Hanı Sokağı): The Byzantine vaults in the E. section of the honey-traders' han show that even at this time there was an ergasterion, a warehouse or trading post here, and thus suggests that the Ottomans were continuing a tradition of their predecessors.

Büyük Yeni Han (Çakmakçılar Yokuşu): This han dating from 1764, now much smaller than it was, has a charming street façade.

Çuhacılar Hanı (Kılıçılar Sokağı): The han of the clothes dealers and clothmakers is a fine example of early 18C Ottoman functional architecture.

Küçük Hanı (Mahmut Paşa Yokuşu): An unusual feature of this han dating from the second half of the 18C is the little mosque on the roof.

Archaeological Museum, Alexander the Great, marble head from Pergamon ▷

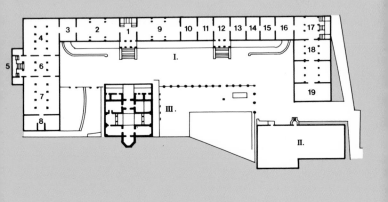

İstanbul, Archaeological Museums
I Archaeological Museum **1** Entrance. Left wing: **2** Sarcophagi of Alexander, mourning women, and others **3** Roman finds from Sidon **4** Sarcophagi from Roman imperial period **5** Storerooms (not accessible) **6** Sidamara sarcophagus and other finds from Asia Minor **7** Friezes, sculptures, mosaics, architectural items of varying origin **8** Tomb steles, sculptures, inscriptions. Right wing: **9** Sarcophagi **10** Phoenician items **11** Reliefs **12** Parts of the temple of Assos at Troy **13** Finds from Athens and Attica **14** Replicas of works by the sculptor Philiskos of Rhodes **15** Ephebos of Tralles and other sculptures from the 3C BC **16** Statues of gods and others, and reliefs of various origins **17** Statues and other items from Greek and Roman sites in Europe and Asia Minor **18** Roman room with busts and statues of emperors, gods and dignitaries **19** Finds from ancient Constantinople, especially the Galata district
II Ancient Oriental Museum
III Fâtih Museum

Kürkçu Hanı (Mahmut Paşa Yokuşu): The han of the furriers and skinners was founded together with the → Mahmut Paşa Camii *c.*1562, and is thus the oldest

han in the city, but has unfortunately fallen into disrepair.
Rüstem Paşa Hanı (Tersna Caddesi): This han built *c.*1549 on the site of the church of St.Michael for Rüstem Paşa has a narrow courtyard surrounded by two-storey buildings with arcades. At the centre is an unusual staircase giving access to all parts of the building. The fine design shows that the great Sinan understood functional buildings as well.
Simkeş Hanı (Ordu Caddesi): Road works revealed remains of the Arch of Theodosius, but at the same time spoiled the han of the silversmiths, rebuilt in 1706; it had established itself in the former mint of Mehmet Fâtih.
Valide Hanı (Çakmakçilar Yokoşu): This is the largest han in İstanbul, with three differently designed courtyards, built in the mid-17C. It was and still is the centre for the Persians living here.

Archaeological Museum, relief on Alexander sarcophagus

Museums

Arkeoloji Müzeleri (*Archaeological Museums*, Gülhane Park): The three museums known as the Archaeological Mueums of İstanbul or the Gülhane Museums are in the park at the NW extremity of the Topkapı Saray. They are the Archaeological Museum or Museum of Antiquities, the Museum of the Ancient Orient and the Fâtih or Ceramics Museum.

I. Archaeological Museum (Arkeoloji Müzesi): In 1846 an initiative of Fetih Ahmet Paşa, son-in-law of Mahmut II, set in train the bringing together of antiquities from all over the Ottoman Empire. These were catalogued, first shown in Hagia Eirene, then from 1874 in the Çinili Köşk. In 1881 Osman Hamdi Bey became director of musuems, and by the time of his death in 1910 he had made it into one

of the largest and best of its kind in the world. He set a further monument to himself by excavations in Sidon in the Lebanon (now Saida), which revealed the sarcophagi of Alexander, the Mourners and the Satraps among others. The present museum buildings date from 1896–1908, and are to be extended.

The upper storey of the museum houses a varied collection of ceramics, statues, coins, bronzes and jewellery, principally from Asia Minor. Items are always being added. However, the most important exhibits are in the lower storey. The rooms are numbered from 1 to 20, starting from the extreme left of the left wing. The excellent catalogue, available from the cash desk, follows this scheme. The sketch follows the line of the normal tour.

From the entrance (1) proceed to the left wing, and Room 1 (2). The *Sarcophagus of Alexander*, found in 1887 and made *c.*

Archaeological Museum, Ephebos of Tralles (left), relief of weather god, department of ancient Oriental cultures (right)

310 BC in the form of a Greek temple, never contained the mortal remains of Alexander the Great, but shows battle and hunting scenes involving him. Although the colours have faded or disappeared, the sarcophagus is still an extremely impressive example of early-Hellenistic art, and indisputably the finest piece in the museum. The slightly older *Sarcophagus of the Mourners*, in the form of a Greek temple with Ionic columns has reliefs of mourning women on its sides, each in a different pose. On the sides of the lid, which is in the form of a temple roof, are representations of ancient funeral processions. The room also contains 3 other sarcophagi, a bust of Hamdi Bey and plans of the Sidon necropolises. In the next room (3) are various Roman finds from Sidon and other places in the Lebanon. The sarcophagi on show in the next room (4) were

found in various places in Europe, Asia Minor and North Africa, and almost all date from the Imperial Roman Period. Outstanding are the *Garland* and the *Meleager Sarcophagi*. There are also reliefs and steles. The great *Sidamara Sarcophagus* with reliefs on various subjects and representations of the dead man and his wife comes from ancient Sidamara (near modern Konya in Anatolia). There are also various sarcophagi, tomb steles, reliefs from Sidon and other places. Outstanding among the architectural exhibits in the next room (7) are sections of the frieze from the *Temple of Artemis* in Magnesia and the *Temple of Hecate* in Lagina. The *funerary steles* dating from the 4&3CBC excavated on the 3rd and 4th hills of İstanbul merit particular attention in the last room in the wing (8). The first room in the right-hand wing (9) also con-

Archaeological Museum, ancient Oriental department, relief of a weather god

tains outstanding finds from Sidon. The *Satrap Sarcophagus* dating from the 5C BC has scenes from the life of a Persian satrap, the *Lycian Sarcophagus* hunting scenes and fighting centaurs. The 6C BC *Sarcophagus of King Tabnit* is shaped like a mummy. The mummy itself is on display in a showcase. There are also other sarcophagi shaped like human beings and showcases with finds from sarcophagi. The subsequent rooms (10–13) contain a large number of interesting architectural exhibits, statues and other finds from various sites. The sculptor Philoskos came from the island of Rhodes, and a room is devoted to his work (14). The *Ephebos of Tralles*, a statue of a youth draped in a cloak (*c.*300 BC or later), and an idealized head of the young Alexander of Macedon copied from a 3C BC original by Lysippos are the highlights of the adjacent room (15). Statues, reliefs and architectural

fragments from various sources are exhibited in the next rooms (16,17). Particularly noteworthy are the *Recumbent River-God* from Ephesus, the *Colossal Statue of Tyche* from Bolu and a representation of *Leda and the Swan*. In the next room (18) are representations of emperors and gods, outstanding among which is the *Head of the Emperor Arkadius* (reigned 395–408), found while the University of İstanbul was being built. The so-called *Prince's Sarcophagus* (*c.* 400), found in Sarıgüzel, and several steles and tombstones from Galata are the most striking exhibits in Room 19, which is devoted to important and interesting finds from the Byzantine and Genoese periods, fascinating chapters of the history of İstanbul.

II. Museum of the Ancient Orient (Eski Şark Eserleri Müzesi): This 1970s building houses an extensive collection of finds of all kinds from ancient cultural sites all over the Near East, including Egypt, the Assyrian, Babylonian and Hittite Empires and exhibits from the early Islamic period.

III. Fâtih Museum:
Mehmet Fâtih, the Conqueror of Constantinople, commissioned the Çinili Köşk, which formerly housed the whole of the archaeological museum and now houses a museum devoted to this ruler. However, much more interesting than the exhibits concerned with Mehmet Fâtih is the magnificent and valuable *Tile and Ceramics Collection*, by which title the museum is also known. It offers a good and thorough survey of the various phases and styles of the famous potteries in İznik and elsewhere.

Carpet Museum and Kelim Museum
→ Sultan Ahmet Camii

Fine Arts Museum
(Dolmabahçe Caddesi): A building next to the Dolmadahçe Palace houses a collection of sculpture and painting by modern native artists and works by important European artists.

Hagia Sophia Museum → Hagia Sophia.

Mosaic Museum → Imperial Palaces.

Municipal Museum
(*Belediye Müzesi*, Atatürk Bulvarı): This is housed in the cells of the former medrese of Gazanfer Ağa, this lovingly compiled collection gives a view of life in Ottoman İstanbul, based on old pictures, cards, engravings and vedutas, miniatures, manuscripts, decorative and applied art, craftwork, crockery, silhouette figures etc.

Museum of Turkish and Islamic Art:
This is in the Ibrahim Paşa palace on the At Maydanı (Hippodrome). Nomad tents and domestic bourgeois interiors are shown, also tiles, calligraphy, wood- and metalwork.

Naval Museum
(*Deniz Müzesi*, Beşiktaş Caddesi): This museum near the Dolmabahçe Palace gives a wide-ranging

Taksim square, monument of the republic (left), Üsküdar, Karaca Ahmet graveyard, stele (right)

and interesting view of the history of Turkish seafarers and the navy.

Topkapı Museum → Topkapı Saray.

Turkish and Islamic Museum *(Türk ve Islam Eserleri Müzesi,* Şifahane Sokağı): This museum was founded in the 19C, and houses a full and interesting collection of books and manuscripts including spiritual and secular works from various periods, e.g. the Abassid, Mameluke, Seljuk and Ottoman eras. A collection of carpets with numerous valuable and historically important pieces gives a good view of the range of this craft. Ceramics, glass, wood-and metalwork are also on show.

Also worth seeing

Atatürk Bridge: This pontoon bridge dates from 1935 and can be raised. It starts in Atatürk Bulvarı and spans the Golden Horn between Old Stamboul and the newer parts of the city. **Atatürk Monument:** This is set on the tip of the Seraglio facing the Bosporus, and commemorates the founder of the modern Turkish state.

Galata Bridge: This pontoon bridge, which can be raised, was completed in 1912 and spans the Golden Horn between Eminönü and Galata. It is the starting point for trips on the Bosporus, very busy, and always full of pedestrians and tradespeople. The fish market, which is most interesting, is held here, and the restaurants, largely specializing in fish, are a major culinary experience. **Karaköy Square** is the lively gateway to Galata. **Taksim Square:** One of the liveliest squares in İstanbul, in which the *Monument of Independence* is to be found. A stroll through the streets of this district gives a good impression of modern İstanbul.

Üsküdar—the Asian quarter of İstanbul: In the 7C BC *Chalcedon* (now Kadıköy), which soon became a flourishing town, and its suburb Chrysopolis (Golden City) came into being as the starting-point of the military and trading roads to the Asian interior. Chalcedon's star quickly set again, not least because its somewhat exposed site led to its being frequently conquered in the early centuries AD, and Chrysopolis took its place. It became Otto-

Fruit market under the Galata bridge

man a good century before Constantinople, and subsequently as Üsküdar developed into a place of retreat from the busy European quarters of the city for upper-class families and a starting point for trading caravans and pilgrimages to Mecca. Üsküdar can be reached by steamer from the Galata Bridge or by car via Ortaköy. It was certainly not untouched by Kemal Atatürk's Europeanization and modernization, but some areas have retained their original character, with typical old houses, mostly built of wood. The general impression is more oriental than that of European İstanbul, and it is certainly worth a visit, and not just to be able to say that you have set foot on another continent.

Ecclesiatical buildings

Ahmediye Camii (Doğancilar Caddesi): This is a late-classical mosque founded in 1732 with fine pulpit and marble Koran stall. The complex includes medrese, library and dershane.

Atik Valide Camii (Valide İmâret Sokağı): Sinan is named as the architect of this mosque built in 1583 for Nur Banu, wife of Selim II and mother of Murat III. The mosque has one of the finest courtyards in the country; the side sections were added later, and the sultan's loge in the course of restoration in the 18C. The interior is beautifully balanced, with fine wall decoration. The mihrab apse with wonderful İznik tiles, mihrab and minbar, all excellent works in marble, are striking features. This külliye, after the Süleymaniye the largest and most extensive in the city, is not open to the public.

Çinili Camii (Selamsiz Caddesi): Built in 1640 for the mother of Mad Ibrahim and Murat IV in the middle of a fine irregular courtyard as a plain square building with dome. The porch and minaret with charming balcony are Turkish baroque additions. The 17C İznik tiles which decorate the inner and outer walls of the mosque, which also has a fine minbar, have given it the name Tiled

Mosque. The roof of the şadırvan is striking, and typical of its period.

Karaca Ahmet Cemetery (Num Kuyusu Caddesi): This romantic and somewhat overgrown park is the last resting place of a number of high-ranking, Ottomans. The old tombstones are decorated with all kinds of inscriptions, and also artistic and imaginative reliefs. The headdresses featured on the women's tombstones suggest a high degree of inventiveness in the women who wore them, probably also dependent upon fashion and the spirit of the times. The men's headdresses show the tribe and position of the wearer. The visitor is confronted with an impressive assembly of a wide range of officials and dignitaries of the Empire.

Mihrimah Camii (*Iskele Camii*, Paşaliman Caddesi): The great Sinan built this mosque on a high platform directly by the steamer anchorage in Üsküdar in 1547&8 for the favourite daughter of Süleyman the Magnificent. The şadırvan is incorporated in the porch, an unusual feature. The mosque also includes a medrese and a primary school.

Rum Mehmet Paşa Camii (Doğancilar Caddesi): This plain mosque founded by a Byzantine Convertite in 1471 clearly shows Byzantine influence. The Convertite's türbe is adjcent.

Selimiye Camii (Kışla Caddesi): This is the last purely baroque mosque in the city, built in 1804 by Selim III in a wonderful park. Impressive features are its balanced proportions and the cool solemnity of its interior.

Semsi Ahmet Paşa Camii (Semsi Paşa Caddesi): This is small and plain, but impressive as part of a harmonious complex in a charming situation directly on the Bosporus. It was built by Sinan in 1580. As well as the little mosque with open porch there is a courtyard with arcades and a medrese. The founder's türbe is built directly on to the mosque, and separated

Üsküdar, Kiz Kulesi, the Leander or Maidens' Tower ▷

Princes' islands (Kızıl Ada), view of one of the nine islands from Büyük Ada

only by a grille, an unusual feature.
Yeni Valide Camii (Doğancilar Caddesi): This was built 1707–10 by Ahmet III in honour of his mother. The open türbe of the Sultana Mother and the drinking fountain (sebil) are particularly charming, each whimsical and excessively lavishly decorated in a style typical of the romantic tulip period. Other buildings in the külliye have survived.

Secular buildings

Çamlıca: This is the highest point in the vicinity of İstanbul (876 ft.). There is an Ottoman pavilion with a modern teahouse. Fine view of the city, environs and the Anatolian hinterland.
Kız Kulesi (Leander's Tower): This square tower with baroque lantern (1723) is set on a tiny island in the Bosporus. It had many predecessors, and like these was formerly a customs post and lighthouse.

The English name is obviously misleading, as the tragedy of Hero and Leander occurred in the Hellespont. The Turkish name means Maiden's Tower, and refers to a legend, which exists in many versions, of a beautiful maiden who flees to an island to escape her predicted fate of being killed by the bite of a poisonous snake, but dies in a shipwreck.
Selim Barracks (Çesmelkebir Sokağı): As it is still used for military purposes this massive, square complex of buildings with corner towers is not open to the public. It was built under Selim III and his 19C successors. Nearby is a cemetery for the dead of the Crimean War. Florence Nightingale (1820–1910) worked in a hospital which used to stand beside the barracks.
Üsküdar Çeşmesi (Iskele): This is a somewhat alien rococo fountain built for Ahmet III, dating from 1728.

Rumeli Hisarı fortress on the European shore of the Bosporus

Environs: Belgrade Forest (Belgrat Ormanı): This can be reached by Bosporus steamer or bus via the village of *Büyükdere*. From there you can walk or take a taxi to these beautiful woods, also popular with the people of İstanbul themselves. The *ruined settlement* to be found here is the village of *Belgrat*, in which Süleyman the Magnificent settled men and women from Belgrade as foresters and keepers of the water supply equipment. In 1898 the inhabitants of the village were expelled for failing to discharge their duties adequately, and their village fell into disrepair. As well as the forest itself the *aqueducts* and other *water supply equipment* are important features. Some of them are wonderfully adapted to the beautiful landscape, and are continuations and extensions of equipment dating from the Byzantine period. Formerly they supplied İstanbul with the water essential for its existence.

Bosporus (*Boğaziçi*): The Ford of the Cow, according to legend swum across by Zeus' beloved Io while flying from the jealous Hera. It connects the Sea of Marmara with the Black Sea and divides Europe from Asia. Since 1973 there has been a road bridge over the straits, which are 31.7 km. long. The currents are extremely treacherous in places, which have made these waters the grave of many a proud ship. The best way of gaining a general impression is by steamer trip from the Galata Bridge to the Black Sea coast. The boats call alternately on the European and Asian shores. The following sections present the principal sights, separated according to continent to simplify matters. *The European shore of the Bosporus* **Ortaköy** has an unusual hamam by Sinan, and mosque dating from 1870. **Arnavutköy** has a charming harbour

promenade and Robert College. **Bebek** has a picturesque bay, the Bosporus University and an ancient Dervish cemetery. **Rumeli Hisarı:** This fortress, built in under twelve weeks in 1452 by Mehmet Fâtih, at the narrowest point of the Bosporus, a magnificent setting, site of a bridge built by the Persian king Darius in ancient times, still greets the traveller with its sturdy towers and massive battlemented walls. **Emirgân** is a picturesque village with old houses and mosque. **Istinye** has docks and shipyards. **Yeniköy,** Greek Neapolis, has splendid villas, hotels and restaurants. **Tarabya** has a fine bay and diplomatic residences. **Büyükdere** → Belgrade Forest. **Sarıyer** has a small regional museum, fish market and good restaurants. **Rumeli Kavaği** is the last stop on the European shore, with remains of a Genoese fortress. Further along the beautiful coast is Rumeli Feneri, a lighthouse near the Symplegades, the notorious pair of rocks at the mouth of the Bosporus.

The Asian shore of the Bosporus

Beylerbey has a large, lavishly furnished 19C palace and 18C baroque mosque. **Cengelköy** is a charming village. **Kandilli** is a picturesque and popular destination for outings, where two rivers, the Sweet Waters of Asia flow into the Bosporus. **Anadolu Hisarı** is a fortress dating from 1395, opposite Rumeli Hisarı. **Kanlıca** is an attractive village with mosque and charming summer residence typical of the area. **Cubuklu** was formerly the site of the monastery of St. Alexander. The palace of the Khedive of Egypt is on the hill. **Beykoz,** on the bay of the same name, is devoted to fishing and industry, and also has charming houses and a fine 18C fountain. **Anadolu Kavagi** is the last stop on the Asian shore, with ruins of an 18C fortress. Nearby is the highest point on the shore, Yuş Tepese, which affords a wonderful panorama including the lighthouse of Anadolu Feneri.

Eyüp and the Golden Horn: Again a

steamer from the Galata Bridge presents the best way of getting to know this part of İstanbul. The Golden Horn (*Haliç*), an inlet of the Bosporus, takes its name from its shape and the formerly picturesque shores, once rich in vegetation, where the noblemen of the city had charming weekend and summer residences. The arrival of industry and the chaotic and undirected expansion of İstanbul have robbed the waterway of much of its charm. Interesting features are: the *Piyale Paşa Camii* in the *Kasımpaşa district*, an impressive and unusual classical building dating from 1573, with fine İznik tiles, and the old *cemetery* in the former Jewish quarter of *Hasköy*.

Eyüp was once a popular resort of the people of İstanbul. *Sultan Camii:* Eyub Ansara, standard-bearer in the first Islamic Wars and comrade of Mahomet, is said to have been killed during a siege of Constantinople in the 7C, and to have been buried here. His magnificent *türbe* decorated with ceramics is thus a holy place for Muslims, to be treated with respect by all visitors. The existing mosque, a cubic domed building with inner and outer courtyard, is Turkish baroque dating from 1798, replacing an earlier building commissioned by Mehmet Fâtih which fell into disrepair. The complex includes many buildings founded by Mihnşah Sultan, the mother of Selim III, and a fine cemetery in which, as the headdresses on the tombstones show, many dignitaries of the Ottoman Empire are buried. Notable features are the magnificent *türbe of Sokullu Mehmet Paşa*, designed by Sinan in 1573, and the equally lavish *türbe of Siyavus Paşa* (*c*.1600).

Princes' Isles (*Kızıl Ada*): It is an hour by boat to this archipelago of islands in the Sea of Marmara. Very little has survived of the Byzantine monasteries which used to be here. During the last century the larger islands became popular for excursions from İstanbul among citizens who could afford to flee from the brooding summer heat of the city. The boats call at:

◁ *Bosporus bridge at Ortaköy*

to the Byzantine buildings which used to exist on this island with charming reddish cliffs.

İzmir/Smyrna

İzmir   p.572□C 4

The city is beautifully sited on an inlet of the Aegean, and has a fine climate and fertile soil. There has been a settlement here since prehistoric times.

Behind the town in a hill with buildings on it, ancient name *Pagos*, now *Kadife Kale* (Velvet Castle). There is a wonderful view of the gulf, the Kara Burun hills, with twin hills (Two Brothers) on the left and behind them to the right Manisa Dağı (Sipylos), famous for the legend of Tantalus and Niobe. In the E. is Nif Dagî (Olympus). From here one can also see how the harbour has changed to the W.: the present N. coast is made up of alluvial deposit by the Gediz Çayı (Hermos), which until 1886 flowed into the gulf opposite the Two Brothers; at that time its course altered, as probably also happened in ancient times.

İzmit, head of Diocletian

Burgaz Ada: This is an island with attractive landscape, dense vegetation and remains of Byzantine buildings. There is a fine panorama from the highest point.

Büyük Ada: The largest of the Princes' Isles, this has numerous fine villas, still used as summer quarters, and pretty, secluded bays. It is still the island in the archipelago most often visited by local people and tourists, which of course produces the characteristic consequences of tourism. Parts of the monasteries of Christ and of St.George have survived, and are to some extent in use today.

Heybeli Ada: This is the third-largest of the Princes' isles, with charming landscape, and pine woods offering cool shade to the visitor who wishes to walk and to discover remains of Byzantine walls.

Kınalı Ada: Byzantines of high temporal and ecclesiastical rank were once banished

Old Smyrna/Bayraklı: The village is opposite Pagos on the N. side of the bay on a low hill, now Tepekulu, a peninsula in ancient times, excavated by English and Turkish archaeologists in 1948–51. There are 3 levels and 3 different kind of building. The foundations of a *Temple of Athene* dating from the 7C BC, Aeolian capital (various small finds in the *Archaeological Museum* in the *Kültür Parkı* in the NE of the city). On the N. side of the hill: remains of the Tomb of Tantalus, necropolises. The Hellenistic refoundation was inspired by Alexander the Great, who visited the city in 334 BC. According to Strabo it was built by Antigonos and Lysimachos. Strabo praises the site of the city, and mentions the Homereion, a rectangular hall with shrine and statue of Homer, who is said to have been born here. The Pramian wines of Homer's

İzmit, gold coin with image of Diocletian

heroes were mixed with cheese, flour and honey. Pure wine was considered to be barbaric.

Very little remains of Hellenistic and Roman Smyrna on the Pagos hill. The *Kadife Kale* (castle) dates from the late Byzantine and Ottoman periods.

On the slopes of the hill, troughs can be seen on the sites of the *theatre* and the *stadium*; they have been built on, and little remains. The *agora* of the Roman town (Marcus Aurelius, AD 178) was uncovered on the Namâzgah, visible from the Kadife Kale: square central courtyard, surrounded by colonnade, vaulted lower storey on the N. side with haut-relief (Poseidon, Demeter).

The old town of İzmir was destroyed by fire in 1922, during the Graeco-Turkish War. The character of the town was altered by the expulsion of the Greeks, and by modernization. The *bazaar* is still worth seeing (near the rear exit), with traces of the Ottoman period. The starting point is the symbol of modern İzmir, the *clock tower* (1901), and the route then passes the *Konak Camii* (1756) in Konak Square; the street leading to the bazaar is the Anafartalar Caddesi. In the bazaar are the Şadirvan Camii (built in 1636 by Bıyıklıoğlu Mehmet) and the *Hisar Camii* (former church, 1598).

Environs: Baths of Agamemnon (*Ağamemnun Kaplıcaları*): These may be found 10 km. W. outside the city, S. of the main road to Çeşme, in the direction of Inciraltı, if one turns left at the junction. They are hot sulphur springs in and around a little river. They are dry in summer.

Diana Hamamları (*Baths of Diana*): This is E. of the Basmahane station over the Kemer bridge over the little river

İznik, Nilüfer İmaret

Melez, 2 km. E. of the suburb of Tepecik, near the Olimpiat Stadı.

İzmit

İzmit-Kocaeli   p.564☐E 2

The acropolis and ruins of the citadel stand above the town, laid out as in an amphitheatre in the innermost part of the bay of the same name.

History: *Olbia* is said to have been founded here by the Megarians c.700 BC. Lysimachos of Thrace destroyed the city c.326 BC. Nicomedes I founded the capital of the kingdom of Bithynia here in 264 BC and called it **Nikomedeia**. The city flourished, and splendid public buildings and numerous temples were built. The town was famous for the many statues with which it and its buildings were decorated. Among the most beautiful was the life-size ivory statue of Nikomedes I taken by Trajan to Rome. In the year 74 BC Nikomedeia fell to Rome by testament. Pliny the Younger, the Roman writer, was governor of Bithynia here from 111–113. The Emperor Hadrian also resided here for a time. After the town had been severely damaged by the Goths in the year 259, the Emperor Diocletian (284–304) rebuilt it as capital of his section of the Roman tetrachy. Under Constantine the Great the city was as brilliant and famous as Rome and Alexandria. After changing fortunes İzmit remained in Ottoman hands from 1326.

Worth seeing: *Pertevpaşa Camii*, on the E. edge of the city, built by the famous Ottoman architect Sinan. *Orhan Camii* and acropolis with *ruins of the citadel*. In the E. part of the city is a *Roman aqueduct*. The remains of the town walls are partly Hellenistic, and were restored in the Roman, Byzantine and Ottoman periods. The ancient remains are more in evidence as spoils than as old buildings.

Environs: Gebze (48 km. W.): Parts of some interesting buildings from Gebze's Byzantine past have survived. It was then known as *Dakybiza*. Worth seeing: *Eskihisar fortress* near Gebze. This medieval citadel was a chain of fortifications intended to protect the road from the E. and the coast. The sections added under the Palaeologus emperors are in polychrome materials. *Orlan Gazi mosque* (1519), cubic single-domed building with fine İznik faience decoration. Fragment of an ancient relief in the base of the minaret. The *Coban Mustafa Paşa mosque* is also an early Ottoman single-domed building with tall drum set on the cube. Next to it is the founder's polygonal *türbe*. Ancient **Libyssa** is not far SE of Gebze, on the gulf. It was here that Hannibal escaped the vengeance of the Romans by taking poison in 183 BC, after his host King Prusias of Bithynia, whose seat was in Bursa, seemed inclined to respond to the

İznik, Aya Sofya

Romans' request for extradition.

Hereke (27 km. W.): Hereke was known in ancient times as *Charax*, and famous for its carpets. Constantine the Great died in the ruined castle of Ankyrion in 337. Sultan Mehmet II, conqueror of Constantinople, died in nearby **Hünkar Çayre** in 1481.

Şile (40 km. NW): This is a pretty little town on the Black Sea with a *Genoese castle* on a nearby rock. Ancient *Artane* is in a rugged and rocky area, unexpected in these surroundings.

İznik

Bursa   p.564□E 2

History: The past of the once famous and distinguished town of *Nicaea* has been a story of alternating rise and destruction until the present century. There were proven settlements on the site in the E. bay of Lake İznik in the first millennium BC, and according to Strabo the town was expanded in 311 BC by Antigonos, a general of Alexander the Great, and called *Antigoneia*. In 301 Antigonos was defeated by Lysimachos, also one of the Diadochi who followed Alexander, and he named the city *Nicaea*, after his wife. In 281 BC the city became the residence of the kings of Bithynia, but was succeeded in this role by Nicomedeia (İzmit). The famous Greek astromomer Hipparchos was born here in the 2C BC. In 74 BC Nicaea was taken over by Rome, and flourished again as the new capital of the Roman province of Bithynia. The historian Pliny the Younger had a gymnasium and a large theatre built in the town; the latter was subsequently cannibalized to strengthen the town walls, and only the vaults in the lower part of this building in the SW of the town have survived. The inhabitants call it Eski Saray. The city was destroyed by an earthquake in AD 120, then rebuilt more lavishly and beautifully by Hadrian in 123. The Hippodamian town plan, used when the town was founded, involving streets set at right angles, was retained. The Sodales Augustales, games dedicated to the Emperor Augustus, were held here for many centuries, and are impressively commemorated on numerous coins. In the mid-3C AD the city was laid waste by Persians and Goths. The town walls were also strengthened on this occasion. In 325 the famous First Ecumenical Council was opened in the imperial palace by the Emperor Constantine. It concluded with the condemnation of the Aryan heresy and the confirmation of the Apostolic Creed. The town was again severely damaged by earthquakes in 362 and 368. It was rapidly rebuilt under Byzantine rule, concentrating particularly on the building of the town walls. This seems to have paid off, as it was unsuccessfully stormed (on two occasions) and besieged by the Arabs in the first half of the 8C.

In 740 Nicaea was yet again ruined by a massive earthquake; it is said that only a single church remained standing (reported by Theophanes). But by 787 the Seventh Ecumenical Council (Second Council of Nicaea) was opened here, concluding in the restoration of the veneration of images and condemnation of the iconoclasts, a historic event for religion and the history of art. In 1065 another earthquake destroyed large sections of the city. In 1081 a troop of Seljuk mercenaries, summoned to assist the illegitimate ruler Nikophoros Botaniatas against the Emperor Michael VII Ducas, under their leader Süleyman Shah, declared themselves independent and established their quarters in the imperial palace in Nicaea. The city was reconquered for Byzantium by knights of the first Crusade under Geoffrey of Bouillon in 1097. After the Crusaders took Constantinople in 1204, Theodore I Lascaris fled to Nicaea, which became residence of the government in exile of the Byzantine Empire and the Ecumenical Patriarchate of Constantinople until 1281. At this time, and until the early 14C, Nicaea enjoyed a final period of great prosperity as a new centre of ecclesiastical, social and cultural life.

In 1331 Orhan and his troops took the town, which had been starved out. From this time it was called İznik. New Ottoman buildings came into being, confirming the esteem in which the new rulers held the city. In 1402 Timur-Leng (Tamerlane) and his Mongol hordes overran the city. In 1514 Selim I compulsorily resettled all artists and craftsmen from his conquered territories in İznik and Küyahya. This marked the start of two centuries of a tradition of ceramics in İznik to which mosques, palaces and museums owe their famous glazed tiles and vessels of all kinds. The removal of the İznik potteries to İstanbul was one of the events which led to the city's subsequent decline, reaching its lowest ebb in the destructive Graeco-Turkish fighting after the First World War. After the Greeks were driven out in 1922 the old ring walls filled, slowly and modestly, with the new, small life of a Turkish town.

Aya Sofya (*Hagia Sophia*): The building is at the intersection of the two main streets leading to four gates at the four points of the compass. It is presumed that the basilica with nave and two aisles was built by Justinian in the late-5C BC, and the opening session of the 7th Ecumenical Council was held here in 787. The church was frequently destroyed and rebuilt, and three different building phases can be made out. It is assumed that in the original building the nave was supported by columns. The apse was surrounded by a marble bench, parts of which have survived. The outer walls set on marble ashlar have survived, except on the portal side. After destruction by an earthquake in 1065 the rubble was flattened out and the floor level raised by more than 4 ft.

İznik, İstanbul gate

The surviving W. wall and the side walls of the nave were part of this second basilican building phase. The domed pastophories N. and S. of the bema, liturgical side rooms like prothesis and sacristy, date from the same period. Access to the aisles was through three tripartite arches on piers, the central one of which was replaced in the third phase of building by a small door with ogee arch, and the others by large arches. The floor was yet again raised by flattening rubble, caused this time by fire at the time of Orhan's invasion in 1331 or the Mongols in 1402. Mihrab and minaret were added, and the interior decorated with İznik tiles. The Christian basilica became a mosque. The marble mosaic on the floor by the W. entrance dates from the late-Byzantine period.

Koimesis church (SE of the town): Built in the early 8C. The removal of the ruins in 1955 revealed the scant remains of this once important church of the early-Byzantine crossing-dome type. The nave was cruciform. The dome square with four massive piers was extended by cruciform tunnel vaults. A tripartite arch led to the narrow aisles. Thus the optical connection of the central space with the aisles was indistinct, and the aisles had no concrete supportive function. The church was blown up in the Graeco-Turkish conflict in 1922. Details are known from a set of photos dating from the early years of this century.

Böçek Ayasma (Secret, Sacred Spring): E. of the Koimesis church a flight of steps leads to an underground vault with four niches and cisterns, inscriptions and a representation of a (Jewish) seven-branched candlestick.

Hacı Özbek Camii (on the main road half way to the Lefke Gate in the E.): This mosque contains the oldest Ottoman building inscription, dating from 1333. Along with comparable buildings in Bursa (Alaeddin Camii, 1335) and Bilecik (Orhan Gazi Camii, early 14C) the Hacı Özbek Camii belongs to the earliest group of plain Ottoman single-roomed mosques on a square ground plan. The dome over the cube is supported by a drum which is twelve-sided on the outside. In the interior a band of lozenges links the cube and the dome. The former narthex is no longer in existence. The masonry has polychrome ornamentation.

Yeşil Camii (Green Mosque): The Yeşil Camii is an interesting example of the early development of Ottoman mosque building. Here the original plain cubic building, built about 60 years after the Hacı Ösbek Camii, is varied by additional spaces and by using various architectural forms and decorative devices. The linking of porch and domed space, the differently shaped domes, the emphasis of the marble revetment and its decoration, the use of subsequently well-known forms such as stalactite capitals, lozenge bands and Turkish triangles on the drum, the inclusion of a lavishly decorated and colourfully glazed minaret in the harmonious overall pattern of the building: all these innovations were used by the architect Hacı Musa in the Yeşil Camii at the beginning of this new epoch of mosque architecture. Access to the porch is via a rectangular portal decorated with mukarnas work. The façade with three bays corresponds to the three domed areas in the interior: a high central dome flanked by mirror vaults. Seven 'Gothic' arches on piers and four ancient columns in polychrome marble dominate the spatial impression. The original screens in fine marble grille work were destroyed in the fighting in 1922. The adjacent anteroom is connected with the prayer room by a tripartite arch on two columns with fine stalactite capitals. This combination of domed cube and preceding bay creates an impression of solemn space. The mihrab is an outstanding example of very early Ottoman stone carving.

Mahmut Çelebi Camii: This mosque dates from 1444 and is comparable with the Yeşil Camii in type and condition; the interior, however, is strikingly vertical in emphasis.

Nilüfer İmaret: This medrese is the earliest example of the new post-Seljuk building technique to have survived intact. The new element is the domed porch with open arcades borrowed from Byzantine church architecture. The former main iwan opposite the entrance is drawn forward like an apse, and given a dome. The original open courtyard at a lower level becomes the domed central space, and the former side iwans, now domed, take on an independent function behind their small access portals. This impressive, well-restored building was founded in 1388 by Murat I in memory of his mother Nilüfer Hatun. The domed main room with transverse rectangular side rooms forms the wide façade side. The narrow, but

Yenişehir (İznik), janissaries' barracks

dominant loggia is built in front of this in the proportion 5:8. Five domed bays correspond with the five tall façade arches on piers and columns. The central dome with drum and tall lantern towers over lateral mirror domes. The W. iwan has two domes. This is a mosque of the Bursa type.

Museum (in the Nilüfer İmaret): Objects from all periods of Bithynian history are exhibited in the main domed space, the W. iwan and the N. side iwan. The ceramic tiles and other objects from the İznik faience kilns from the 15–17C are of particular charm and interest.

Early Christian tomb (5 km. N. of the town, guide and keys in the museum): This vaulted tomb 16 ft. deep and 9 ft. wide is completely painted with beautiful motifs. By the entrance are peacocks with open tails, on the façade wall two drinking peacocks facing each other, surrounded by flowers. On the lower walls of the tunnel vault areas decorated with geometrical patterns alternate with pictorial representations, and the ceiling is decorated with squares of flowers. A den-

ticulated cornice painted in persepctive divides the wall and ceiling vault. This painting dates from the 4C and is surprising in its artistic beauty and the freshness of its condition.

Baths: The *Hacı Hamza Hamami* (*c.* 1500) and *Ismail Bey Hamami*, dated from the Seljuk period up to the 17C, are both worth seeing. The splendid furnishings make the bath worth seeing, but it is in an unfortunate condition.

Walls and gates: These fortifications are compared with the walls of İstanbul, and make an overwhelming impression on the visitor. The original square town was enclosed by a Hellenistic wall of 16 stadia (over 3,000 yards) in length. Little has survived of this. Later extension established the present polygonal shape with almost 5,000 yards of wall. The older section of the present wall is W. of the İstanbul Gate on the inside and dates from the time of Hadrian. The larger part of the main wall was built in the 3C AD, and was over 13 ft. thick and 29 ft. tall. Until the 8C the wall was continually repaired after earthquake damage and provided with new

towers. The outer wall 6 ft. thick and over 13 ft. high, with moat, was built around the existing ring by the Emperor Theodosius in the 1st half of the 13C. This made it necessary to raise the main wall to between 33 and 43 ft. in height. The *İstanbul Kapı* (gate) in the N. is now half buried in rubble and soil washed there by floods. It consists of a Roman arched gate with with central and smaller side openings. The inscription referring to Vespasian and Titus confirms the 1C AD as the building date. The two large masks in the inner gate are later. *Lefke Kapı*, like the N. gate quadripartite, and also dating from the 1C AD. On the architrave is an inscription of gratitude to Hadrian for rebuilding the gate after the earthquake in 120. All the gates and walls have interesting spoils built into them.

The *Yenişehir Kapı* in the S. was originally tripartite in articulation and set back at each stage. It fell victim to through traffic, and very little of it remains.

Environs: Yalova (50 km. NW, on the S. shore of the Gulf of İzmit): Nearby is the ruined *Karakılise*. This brick building originally had a large crossing dome, and dates from the 6C. Its purpose is unknown. It was later used as a Byzantine church. 12 km. W. in a little valley is **Yalova Kaplıca**, famous in antiquity for its sulphur, iron and radioactive hot springs (61–65C). In the legend of the Argonauts the baths are referred to as Pythia. The Greeks built a temple dedicated to Apollo-Pythios here in the 6C BC. The emperors Constantine the Great and Hadrian and the empress Theodora used the spa facilities here. There are ruined *Byzantine baths* near the spa hotel. S. of this are Hellenistic and Roman *memorial steles*. Up the hill from the bridge over the brook are the remains of Justin II's palace. 5 km. E. of Yalova Kaplıca, near the village **Çiftlikköy**, there are more Byzantine ruins. It is suggested that this is the ancient Pylai.

Yenişehir (19 km. SW): In the early 14C this little town was Osman's fourth residence, after Söğüt, Eskişehir and Karacahisar, before he took Bursa. Today Yenişehir is the centre of the paprika trade in the region. However, the town is now developing a new sense of its early Ottoman past. The remains of an early-15C Ottoman *külliye* are being carefully restored. The former *medrese* is now a U-shaped set of buildings around a large inner courtyard. The individual square rooms have domes on octagonal drums, and are topped with fine lanterns. In between, chimneys rise to the height of the lanterns. The former arched windows now have rectangular stone frames. The Ottoman *Sinan Paşa Camii* is part of the külliye which has survived in good condition, but the han has almost completely disappeared. The medrese is traditionally known as the Janissaries' Barracks. The rooms are now occupied by external Koran students of the mosque. In the Davotoğlú Sokağı the restored 16C *Semaki Evi* is used as a museum. It is a pure Ottoman house formerly used by the Semaki family, which is still in existence. The open balcony of this magnificent house has been glazed to protect it. The divan room (men's room) attached to the balcony is similarly furnished and decorated to two other residential rooms in the upper storey, with painted wood panelling on the walls and doors, lavishly decorated and painted coffered ceilings, of which one has survived unrestored in its original condition, and decorated fireplaces with pointed hoods. In the divan room is a particulary fine carved turban medallion, with the tip hanging from the centre of the ceiling. Wall paintings and decorated niche cupboards complete the impression of a high level of domestic culture. At the W. end of the town is an old *tumulus* on which ceramics dating from the 3rd millennium BC have been found. It is now part of the Baba Sultan Parkı. At the top of it are the remains of a monastery inhabited until 1920 by Kadri Dervishes. These miracle men were worshipped as saints by the people, and Baba Sultan used their monastery mosque as his türbe.

Karaman, İbrahim Bey Imarat

Karaman

Konya   p.574☐J 5

History: Excavation finds in the immediate vicinity confirm settlement on the
S. Konya plain from the 7th millennium
BC. It is probable that Hittite Landa was
identical with **Laranda**, a town laid waste
by Perdikkas, the former general of Alexander the Great. Landa was an important
Hittite trading and military post *c.*1300
BC. Under the Byzantines Laranda,
modern Karaman, was a fortified and gar-
risoned against persistent Arab raids. Various Turkish overlords followed each other
in the first half of the 12C. After short
interruptions by Frederick Barbarossa on
his last Crusade (1190) shortly before his
death in Göksu (Salef) 140 km. S. and a
six-year occupation by Lesser Armenia
(Cilicia), Laranda became Seljuk again in
1216. In 1220 Celâleddin Rumi (known
as Mevlâna) and his parents came to Karaman as refugees from Afghanistan 'because
the town was famous for its delicate
peaches'. In 1228 his father was called to
Konya as professor of theology, and his
son Mevlâna became a famous lyricist and

mystic there, and founded the Mevlâna Order of Dancing Dervishes. The height of Seljuk power under Alaeddin Kaykobad I was quickly followed by the decline of the Seljuk state. It began to break up after 1281 under growing pressure from the Persian Ilkhane (Mongols) and became a number of principalities. The Karamanoğlu period began, and their powerful dynasty lasted for more than 200 years, until 1466. Its first prince, Kerimüddin-Karaman, also gave his name to the capital of his emirate. The timber dealer from Ermenek began to found his own Turkoman rule c.1255. He made pacts with the Mamelukes against the Mongols and their Pervans in Konya. The capital was finally moved to Konya in 1320, after several vain attempts, but Karaman remained the seat of the Karamanoğlu dynasty, who in 1356 further extended and fortified the impressive citadel on the acropolis.

The Karamanids were very conservative both in architectural style and way of life, and saw themselves as the heirs of the Seljuks in matters of art. They brought famous poets and scientists to their court. In 1277 they made Turkish the official language instead of Persian, which had been used under the Seljuks.

The emirs' buildings compare very favourably with those of the Seljuks. Karaman was an important city, and the emirate was politically stable and powerful. For 45 years the Ottomans tried to break the power of the Karamanoğlu. Their great period ended in 1466.

Yunus Emre Camii (1349): This mosque is the oldest Karamanid building in the town, and is said to contain the tomb of Yunus Emres, now considered the greatest Turkish writer (1280–1322). His poetry and prose were written in the simple language of the Turkish people, while most people were writing in the court language, Persian.

İbrahim Bey Imarat (1433): This medrese follows the Seljuk tradition for such buildings as exemplified by Anatolian-Seljuk closed medreses dating from the second half of the 13C, like the Karatay medrese and the Ince Minare medrese in Konya. There is only one iwan, placed behind the domed 'court room' opposite the entrance. It had two

Karaman, citadel

rooms on either side. Between these and the portal wall were the rows of pupils' cells. A three-bayed, open entrance hall with ogee arch, with two spoil columns in the middle, is domed to correspond with the bays and connected on its right to the fine *minaret* with glazed tiles. The large dome has a lantern with six windows. The *türbe* of the founder, Emir Ibrahim Bey, is outside on the right. Above the plain, slender portal to the tomb the cube of the tower becomes an octagon, thus preparing for the transition to the dome with pyramidic trangles. There is no cornice, but this is replaced by a slender mukarnas band in the exterior. In front of the Imarat is a magnificent *fountain*: the Ibrahim Bey Çeşmesi in the Seljuk style.

Mader i Mevlâna Camesi (also *Ak Tekke*): This monastery founded in 1371 by the emir Alaeddin Bey was a centre of the Order of Dancing Dervishes founded by Celâleddin Rumi (Mevlâna), uninterruptedly active here until its dissolution by Atatürk in 1923. It contains the tombs of Mümone Hatun, Mevlâna's mother, his elder brother, his first wife Gevher Hatun and of the Emir of Karaman, Seyfeddin Süleyman Bey. On one side of the courtyard are the dervishes' cells, in which they fasted for forty days and meditated without seeing the light of day, following the example of their master in Konya. The main hall of the mosque dates from the Seljuk period. The dome on a tall, octagonal drum towers over the centrally-planned building. The porch on three arches with one dome per bay was a later addition. Adjacent is the *Süleyman Bey hamam* dating from 1358. This Emir Bath is an interesting and characteristic building dating from the period of the Emirate.

Medrese of Nefîse Sultan (also *Hatuniye*): This foundation of the daughter of the Ottoman Sultan Osman I of Bursa, the wife of the Karamanoğlu Alaeddin Bey, was built in 1382 by the well-known architect Hoca Ahmet. The imposing *entrance portal* is in white marble to a point above the door, alternating with black marble in the door frame. The upper portal block with its tall mukarnas arch is in yellowish stone. A broad, delicate and lavishly ornamented decorative façade forms the transition to the high-arched

Binbir Kilise (Karaman), Degile: ruined monastery

door jamb, broadened to the right and left by correspondingly decorated niches, before leading through the gate arch to the entrance iwan. The portal building is set in front of almost 60% of the façade of the building as a whole and at its original height towered over the building. It is a fine specimen of Karamanid portal art in the Seljuk tradition. The main iwan is opposite the entrance, and adjacent on the right is the winter auditorium with a remarkable portal, and in the corresponding room on the left, also domed, is the *tomb of Nefîse Hatun*. The domed students' cells are on either side behind a loggia and four 'Gothic' arches on tall columns. This medrese was a famous university, in which mathematics, astronomy, medicine and theology were taught by distinguished professors.

Museum (behind the Nefise Sultan medrese): This outstanding museum has interesting and well-presented collections on the history of religion from the Turkish period back to the neolithic age in Çanhasan (full prospectus in the museum).

Alaeddin Türbesi: This is the tomb of one of the great Karaman emirs, Alaeddin Bey, son-in-law of the Ottoman sultan Murat I. He died in 1388. The massive polygonal building with comparatively delicate, elaborately decorated entrance portal narrows above an inscription from the Koran to a drum with interior dome and exterior conical tower supported over the drum sections by one and two half ribs respectively.

Hacıbeylar Camii: The mosque was built in 1358 and after falling into disrepair was restored and took on its present role as *municipal library* in 1953.

Arabzade mosque (late 14C): This is of the Kufa type, with transverse kibla wall. The ceiling is supported by ten piers and two columns (in front of the mihrab).

Citadel (on the old town hill): Surrounded by medieval houses and alleys, the massive fortress, used and restored throughout its history, this is still in excellent condition today. At the corners are 4 massive, partly rectangular and partly circular defensive and support towers connected to the walls. Directly to the E. is

Binbir Kilise (Karaman), ruins with view of the Kara Dag massif

an *ancient Ottoman house*, probably the oldest in Karaman, which is to be renovated and extended as a museum house. Also adjacent are the *Eski Camii* (early 15C), the *türbe of the Karamanoğlu Alaeddin Bey* and the *ruined city gate*.

Environs: Binbir Kilise (1,001 Churches): Turn left 24 km. N. of Karaman in the village of Dinek into the Kara Dağ massif. 9 km. of metalled road lead to *Madenşehri*, the first village with significant church ruins and remains of wall paintings. 8 km. into the hills, the little village of *Degile* is on the right, set among the ruins of churches, monasteries and tombs. One of the monasteries has been converted to a mosque by means of primitive painting. The valley between Madenşehri and Degile is known as the Valley of the 1,001 Churches. From the 3–8C ecclesiastical life flourished here, and it did not die out completely until the 11C, under the Seljuks. Since then the number of ruined churches, monasteries, fine houses, fortresses and cisterns—there were over 50 in 1914—has considerably decreased. The interesting architectural feature of the Binbir churches is the

domed basilica of the Syrian African type. Because of timber shortage a roof with a stone dome was used instead of a flat wooden roof. There are galleries above the aisles behind the upper row of columns (as in Alahan). Most of the entrances have double arches supported by a squat central column. Large ashlar blocks were used for the masonry. The apses have double-arched windows. The Binbir Kilise district is very extensive, and thus a detailed description following a plan is impossible. There are also Hellenistic, Roman and Hittite remains in the area.

Çan Hasan (13 km. NE of Karaman): Excavation undertaken by the British Archaeological Institute of Ankara 1961–70 revealed three hill cultures from various periods, called Hills I–III. On *Hill III* a 7–6 millennium BC neolithic settlement was discovered. The buildings were rectangular, with thick clay brick walls. Apparently no wood or stone was used in the buildings. Pottery was unknown. Evidence of primitive agriculture and cattle breeding can be discerned. The houses had no doors, but were entered from above by means of ladders. Obsidian, stone and bone implements are exhibited

Binbir Kilise (Karaman), ruins

Domuztepe (Karatepe)

in the museum in Karaman. Çan Hasan I dates from the chalcolithic period, between the 6–4 millennium BC. The houses had two storeys, and were entered by means of steps and ladders. The brick walls were between 15 and 23 ins. thick, without doors or windows, with storerooms and stabling for cattle (horses, sheep, goats). Models can be seen in the museum, along with ceramics, figurines and implements, but the most important finds are in the Museum of Anatolian Culture in Ankara.

Derbe (22 km. NE near the village of Kerti Höyük): The ruins of a *Byzantine church* have survived here. A text found here dating from 157 suggests that this is ancient Derbe, mentioned in the Acts of the Apostles and visited by St.Paul. In any case Derbe was important enough to enjoy the right to mint coins in the 2C AD. The square stone with text in a circular ornament is in the flower-filled garden of the museum in Karaman.

Gödet (40 km. SE): The so-called *Yabangülü Sakli* (hidden churches). A group of cave churches on various levels with rooms carved out of the rock varying from very small to a considerable size, spread over about 1 km. around the village.

Ibrala/Manazan (30 km. ESE near the village of Ibrala): The *monastery of Manazan*, one of the oldest early-Christian monasteries, is carved out of the rock. It consists of several tunnels, galleries and hundreds of rooms on three levels, reached by unusual staircases.

Isaura (*Sengibar Kalesi*; turn of to the left at Özyurt, 35 km. W. of Karaman): This is the site of the Roman district capital of Isaura. Roman and Byzantine remains can be seen near modern Sengibar Kalesi on the ancient Anemurion-Laranda (Kara-

Karatepe, late-Hittite lion sculpture (left), late-Hittite relief (right)

man)-Isaura-Ikonium road. Archaeological investigations have been under way since 1984, conducted by a team under the direction of the first director of the Karaman museum, Ilhan Temizsoy. The town was surrounded by an extensive wall, and remains of this, an interesting gatehouse at the S. gate and ruined towers to a height of 50 ft. have survived. N. of the S. gate is the acropolis with remains of the stoa and exedra. W. of this is the agora, and 100 yards to the N. an Arch of Hadrian which is still impressive. In Byzantine times there were two churches beyond this, and a third W. of the S. gate. At the northernmost point of the town wall is a centrally-planned octagonal church, with eight piers and apse. 200 yards to the NW, 500 yards SW outside the wall and S. and SE of the S. gate are necropolises with very interesting rock tombs of the temple type with lavish relief decoration featuring lions

and other animals. There are also interesting orthostatic reliefs with battle and hunting scenes. Information and details from the museum in Karaman.

Kara Dağ (via Binbir Kilise): It is well worth a trip to the highest peak of the Kara Dağ, the Mahliç Hill. At a height of 7,450 ft. are the architecturally interesting ruins of a 9C *Byzantine monastery*, and a *Hittite cult cave* with a long hieroglyphic inscription of which there is a copy in the museum in Karaman. On the W. slope of the same massif, on the rocky foothills known as Kızıl Dağ, there is a throne-like *Hittite cult site* with bas-relief. Here the late-Hittite potentate Hartapuş was worshipped, and his name was associated with the same sign, even with the winged disc of the sun above it, which was used by the kings at the time of the Hittite empire. Visitors should beware of the wild horses that live in the hills.

Karatepe

Adana   p.576□M 5

The ruins are about 25 km. SE of the regional capital, Kadirli. The site was discovered by Theodore Bossert in 1946. Excavations started a year later on the hill, which is over 1,000 ft. high, and led to the discovery of a late-8C BC Hittite city, once surrounded by a wall about 1 km. long, 7–13 ft. thick, and including defensive towers.

Excavations: The two *town gates* with several rooms which have so far been excavated are lavishly decorated with reliefs at their bases, and the openings are flanked with lion sculptures. The pictorial representations are a mixture of local late Hittite, Aramaic, Assyrian and Phoenician motifs and styles. There is also Egyptian influence in the 2 relief blocks with representations of the dwarf god Bes. The best-known is probably the banquet scene, showing the Hittite rulers feasting, with musicians and servants with fly whisks. There are also unusual representations such as a fully-rigged ship.

All this makes Karatepe the most important Hittite site after the ancient Hittite capital of Hattuşa (Boğazköy). Karatepe's greatest claim to fame is the discovery of a bilingual inscription (Hittite hieroglyphic and Phoenician) which made it possible to decipher Hittite hieroglyphics for the first time. The other Hittite writing system, cuneiform, had long been legible.

The ruins discovered date from the period of the late-Hittite king Azitawandas (8C BC) who ruled Kizzuwatna, later Cilicia, from here. His palace was at the top of the hill, where various basalt statues were also discovered. The city fell to the Assyrians c.680, but was probably settled at the time of the Hittite empire (before the 12C BC).

As excavations are still under way photography is not permitted on the site.

Environs: Domuztepe (Pig Mountain): Remains of a small *fortress* , probably an older Cilician base than the one on Karatepe, were discovered on this hill opposite the more famous site. The lowest level (C) yielded few remains, but dates

Kars, citadel

back to the 9C BC. Level B, above it, contained ceramics showing clear Cypriot influence, establishing that the place was part of the Mediterranean trade network. This second settlement was destroyed by fire. When it was rebuilt (Level A), 8C BC, and therefore contemporary with Karatepe, sculptures from an earlier building in Level B were used for the so-called Lion Gate. A small Roman citadel was later built on the site.

Hemite (also *Hamide*): The site of this *Hittite rock relief* is identifiable from a distance because of a medieval fortress (*Hemite Kale*). The acropolis hill rolls in gentle waves to the S, and the relief is at river level. It is inclined to the E, and can thus only be seen clearly in the morning light. An additional difficulty is caused by the fact that the rock is of poor quality, and thus the relief is severely weathered. It is possible to make out the figure of a king or prince with bow and lance facing left, towards the river, and a two-lined inscription on the figure's back. The relief dates from the 13C BC, and like the one in Sirkeli was probably intended to indicate a river crossing.

The site is reached by turning E. in the village Sakarçali, on the road from Osmaniye to Kadirli, between the bridge over the Ceyhan and a petrol station. After the village of Hemite and before the fortress the road turns towards the river again.

Kadırlı (25 k. NW): The present regional capital in the N. of the Adana district is almost certainly on the site of ancient **Flaviopolis**, founded by the Roman Emperor Vespasian (AD 67–79). There are no significant Roman remains, but archaeologists have made some spectacular finds such as a *tombstone* erected by a military tribune of the 6th Roman legion (Legio Ferrata), or a *bronze statue* of the Roman Emperor Hadrian (AD 117–138).

Tecırlı: NE of the village on the other side of the Ceyhan are the ruins of ancient **Hieropolis Castabala**. Between 52 BC and AD 17 this was the capital of a small independent empire ruled by Prince Tarcondimotus, who made skilful use of the power vacuum caused by the death of the Cilician king Ariobarzanes II in his own bid for independence. His successor Tarcondimotus II was installed as Roman governor in Anazarbus/Anavarza in AD 19.

Kars, Archaeological Museum, sculpture of horse

Kars

Kars   p.570□T 2

The history of the present provincial capital on the Kars Çayı mirrors the troubled history of Armenia. The first historical personality to emerge is the Bagtarid Ashot the Great, proclaimed king by the Armenian nobility, a fact confirmed by the despatch of crowns and gifts from the Caliph of Baghdad and the Byzantine emperor himself in 884. Ashot's son and successor Smbat I (the Martyr; 890–914) had to defend his kingdom against the rival Armenian principality of Vaspurakan and neighbouring emirs. Finally Emir Yusuk proclaimed Prince Gagik of Vaspurakan of the Ardschruni family (→ Hakkâri and environs) as the new King of Armenia, and had Smbat captured and crucified. Ashot the Iron (914–18) succeeded in driving the Muslims out again. Under his brother Abbas I the capital of the Bagtarid empire was transferred to Kars, where it enjoyed its period of greatest prosperity. When the rightful king Ashot III (the Merciful; 952–77) moved the capital back to Ani, his brother Mushegh (962–984) founded the rival kingdom of Vanand in Kars, which persisted under the regents Abbas and Gagik. This was a sign of the break-up of Armenia into constituent principalities, which started as early as 970. After Byzantium had conquered large areas of the Caucasus and South Georgia and the former principality of Vaspurakan under Emperor Basil II in 1021, his successor Constantine IX Monomachus (1042–55) succeeded in subduing Bagtarid Armenia. After an unsuccessful siege of Kars in 1055 by Toğrul Beğ, Muslims under Alp Arslan finally conquered the city in 1064. The Georgians under Queen Thamqr (1184–1213) took Kars in 1205, and in 1585 it fell to the Ottoman sultan Murat III. The Russians held Kars in 1807, and during the Crimean War (1854–6) and again from 1877–1920, finally as part of the Transcaucasian or Armenian SSR. Kars did not become Turkish again until 1921.

Old town and citadel: The heart of the historic town is set on a rocky peak. The settlement was protected by an encircling wall halfway up the hill. On the summit is the citadel itself (*Narin Kale*), once an

Kars, Kümbed Camii

Kaş, theatre

Armenian palace, altered and fortified by the Saltukoğulari 1145–74 and in the late 16C by Murat III. The present appearance of the fortress dates from rebuilding in the 19C, after severe damage in the Crimean War. Beneath the citadel in the heart of the old town are the *Ulu Cami*, the *Beylerbey Serayı* and the *Beşik Camii*. The latter, built as a Bagtarid church in 1045, is now used as a warehouse. The *mausoleum of Celal Baba*, a popular local saint martyred by the Mongols in 1239, is open to the public every Thursday.

Kümbed Camii: This building at the foot of the acropolis hill is of particular interest. It was built 930–7 by Abbas I of Ani (929–53) as a church of the Apostles, and Christian services were held here until the end of the last period of Russian occupation. The building was not secularized until the Turkish period. Until recently it housed the Archaeological Museum. The crude reliefs on the high drum portraying the 12 Apostles reveal the earlier dedication.

Archaeological Museum (on the Cumhuroyet Caddesi): The road to the ruined city of Ani automatically takes you past this new building. The largely 16C Armenian animal sculptures in the garden make it impossible to miss. It is usually possible to buy photographs of Ani here (photography is forbidden on the site).

Taş Köprü (Stone Bridge): This building dating from 1725 crosses the Kars Çayı in the N. of the town. Its name contrasts with the Denir Köprü (Iron Bridge) a little further to the S., which leads to the Atatürk Park on the E. bank. Two of the original three baths near the Taş Köprü are still in use (*Muradiye Hamamı* and *Topcu Hamamı*, 17&18C).

Environs: Beş Kilise (35 km. SE): The road to Diğor passes through this village, which takes its name (Five Churches) from a group of 11C churches which can be reached by a forty-five minute walk, starting 1 km. before the village on a field track branching off to the right. The path descends into a deeply incised valley in the course of which it meets a rocky spur on which stands the one still-surviving *church*, also called Karakale (Black Castle), and formerly dedicated to St.Sergius. In the

Armenian period the place was called *Chtskonk*.

Chochawank (*Gregorian church*): This church built in 985 or 989 by local monks is on the other side of the Arpa Çayı, and is an hour's walk from the monastery of Horomots. There is a relief of a lion above the gabled door.

Diğor (47 km. SE): The church of old Armenian *Tekor* dates from the 5C, and after being rebuilt twice was finally turned into a domed basilica in 986. It is one of the most important monuments in the architectural history of Armenia, as it can be said to be a 'typical' Armenian church. This makes it all the more regrettable that it was not rebuilt after its collapse in 1912. Instead the stone was carried off for building elsewhere, and only the ground plan can be made out. Not far away, at *Harabedigor*, is another church dedicated to St. Sergius.

Horomots monastery (10 km. NE): The foundation goes back to 10C Georgian monks, but most of the present buildings date from the time of King Hovhannes Smbat III (1020–42). The last kings of Ani, including Ashot IV, were buried on this site, an important Christian centre well into the 18C. The *Shepherds' Church* is a stellar building. Its conical roof is now missing. The largest church is *St. John's*, built by Smbat III. The narthex (zamatun) turned out larger than the actual church interior. The *Menas church*, a domed building with narthex and apse with 2 side rooms, dates from the 10C.

Karabağ (*Mren*; 60 km. SE): Diğor (see above) is the starting point for a trip to this domed basilica, which is in remarkably good condition. It is in the village of Karabağ, in a deeply incised valley. The *church of Mren* was built 623–40. The dome is supported on 4 sturdy central piers, and the rectangular building has a five-sided apse. There are stone carvings above the lintel of the W. gate.

Keçivan (65 km. SSW): 24 km. along the road to Erzurum a side road branches off. It leads via the village of Kötek to the Erzurum-İğdır road. The village of Pasli is on the link section before Kötek. Here a valley opens up to the right, and this leads in another 6 km. to the old Armenian town of *Artageyra*, where some Seljuk buildings have survived. The *mausoleum* (kümbet) with relief decoration over the portal is particularly charming.

Vladikars (Olgovka; 12 km. SW): On the edge of the village, which is on the way to Sarıkamış, not far from Olgovka, about 200 yards from the road are the remains of an square Armenian church with sculptural decoration.

Kaş/Antiphellos

Antalya   p.572□E 6

This is one of the most beautiful places on the S. coast, and has always been known and inhabited. Ancient Antiphellos, whose Greek name goes back to the early 4C BC, was the harbour of the town of Phellos, which was high in the mountains. At this time Antiphellos was still a tiny place, but in the Imperial Roman period it became an important economic regional centre, exporting wood and sponges. As the city was protected on the land side by the steep cliffs, it only needed to be fortified with sea walls. About 600 yards of the lower sections of these, built in fine Hellenistic ashlar, have survived in the W. of the town. Above this, on the W. side outside the town, is one of the most beautiful ancient theatres in Turkey. It has 26 rows of seats, and has survived in very good condition, although the scena is missing. To the NE is an undamaged *tomb*, hewn from a monolith (4C AD). It can be reached on foot. The entrance façade with portal over 6 ft. high is bordered by two shallow piers. The kline on the rear wall of the interior has a frieze of 20 girls dancing and holding hands. To the right of the route from the

Kekova Tersane (Kaş), Byzantine ruined church ▷

Simena (Kaş), castle hill

theatre into the town is the lower part of a 1C BC temple. N. and NE above the town are several *rock tombs*, one with a Lycian inscription. There are large numbers of *sarcophagi* in the immediate vicinity and farther afield; the finest *hyposorion sarcophagus* for miles around is right in the middle of the town. The hyposorion is just under 5 ft. high, and has a covering slab about 30 ins. thick, upon which is the sarcophagus of the person interred. The whole tomb is in the Lycian wooden house style and has a particularly finely decorated lid with pointed arch with ridge pole and jutting lions' heads used to attach the carrying ropes.

Environs: Aperlai: This is a ruined Lycian town E. of Kaş; three-quarters of an hour by boat. History: silver coins dating from the 5C BC are the earliest evidence of the existence of Aperlai. It is

first mentioned in literature by Pliny and Ptolemy. In the Imperial Roman period Aperlai was part of a league of four cities also involving Simena, Apollonia and Isinda. Aperlai is recorded as Aprillai by the Byzantine church administration. It is not clear for how long the town has been uninhabited. It is worth seeing the *ruined town* as a whole, enclosed within its original rectangular wall. This runs parallel with the coast about 100 yards away from it, and extends to the ridge of the hill. It is solidly built, and has almost all survived at its original height, with gates and towers, some of which are in good condition. There were no larger buildings such as theatres and temples. The lowering of the level of the coast over the centuries has meant that the extensive harbour installations and tombs are now more than 6 ft. below water level. This is also the explanation for the 'floating'

Kastamonu, citadel

sarcophagi, here and in numerous other places on the Mediterranean coast.

Apollonia (Kılınçlı): N. of Aperlai above the village of Kılınçlı (also Siçak) on the way to the bay of Kekova. The ruins of this Lycian, later Greek town are on a hill almost 300 ft. high. It was a member of the Aperlai-Simena -Isinda league, but also paid its own tributes as an independent city to Augustus and Tiberius. Little of its history has come down to us. Six Lycian pier tombs without inscription are evidence of the Lycian past, and there are numerous Hellenistic tombs, and a town wall in good condition to the W. The theatre has been destroyed, cisterns and a vaulted storehouse are in reasonable condition.

Kekova-Tersane: The long, narrow island of Kekova almost blocks the bay of Simena, producing peaceful harbours and anchorages for Kekova and Simena,

already valued in ancient times. Thus on Kekova and throughout the bay there are harbours and quays suggesting intensive port and shipping activity, and the Turkish name Tersane (shipyard or naval base) also indicates such activity. On a narrow section of the W. point of the island are the picturesque ruins of a *Byzantine church*: apse with polychrome arch and remains of walls. There are many ancient ruins on the extensive island of Kekova, but a somewhat wearisome sequence of inquiries is necessary to find them.

Phellos: The town associated with the harbour of Antiphellos (Kaş) is high in the hills. It is reached via the village of Çukurbag, from which Fellendağı can be climbed. Phellos is at a height of about 2,000 ft. on a small plateau measuring about 650 by 200 yards, from which the hill drops steeply. Little is known of the history of the town. Phellos is first mentioned *c.*500 BC by Hekataios, an ancient geographer. The site has many *sarcophagi*, particularly on the N. edge of the plateau, and there are remains of massive polygonal walls, probably of earlier date. There is an isolated, well-crafted house tomb in the W. of the plateau. There is only one tomb chamber, and on the rearmost of the three klines it is possible to make out a gorgon's head in the middle of the front side. Further E. is a larger tomb with rock wall, on which there is a damaged, larger-than-life-sized bas-relief of a bull. Below the town wall, and visible over long distances, is a badly damaged hyposorion sarcophagus with clear reliefs on the hyposorion and on the lid: a man on a couch, with two other people. The W. relief has been destroyed, there are two handles on the lid above it.

Simena (*Kale*): 18 km. E. of Kaş, turn right, then 30 km. on the road to Uçagiz (Teimiussa), then only accessible by boat. The ancient town of Simena on the tongue of land opposite the island of Kekova has now been completely invaded by the houses and other buildings of the village of **Kale.** This is a picturesque spot in a remote, bizarrely beautiful coastal landscape. Simena was part of the league of four cities represented by neighbouring Aperlai in the Lycian League. The village has grown up the hill and is dominated by the curtain wall, in good condition, with battlements and towers, of a medieval castle on ancient foundations. Inside the castle is an attractive theatre with seven rows of seats cut in the rock. Below the wall is a stoa. In and around the village are sarcophagi, remains of polygonal town walls, a Roman thermal bath on the shore and remains of the ancient harbour installations, parts of which are below the surface of the water.

Teimiussa (turn S. 18 km. E. of Kaş, 30 km. to the village of Üçagiz): E. of the village are the remains of ancient Teimiussa, whose history is unknown. Lycian inscriptions confirm the existence of the town in the 4C BC. Apart from a large number of sarcophagi and rock tombs there is also, on E. side, an impressive rectangular gate with posts in

Kasaba (Kastamonu), Mahmut Bey Camii

Kasaba (Kastamonu), Mahmut Bey Camii, wooden ceiling

good condition and a decorated lintel, through which the local working camels gravely stride. On the left, well outside the village, is a large, multi-storey building, presumably a provision store. Further E. up the hill on a peak are the walls of a precisely constructed ashlar building, a fortress or a large tower. In the village are two Lycian house tombs with a relief depicting boys. The rock tombs and sarcophagi of the necropolis on the E. shore are an unforgettable sight when seen from a boat. On the E. edge of the urban area is a quay cut into the rock, 100 ft. long and 30 ft. wide.

Kastamonu

History: This town on the banks of the Gök Irmak river is a Byzantine foundation, later the bishop's town of **Castamon**. The name comes from Castra Comneni (Comnenus' Citadel). These aristocratic military officers from Comne near Adrianople advanced in the imperial court and acquired large estates in Paphlagonia, where the Comneni built the fortress of Castamon as their residence in the 12C. The first Comnenus and founder of the the famous imperial dynasty in Constantinople was Manuel Eroticus, a high government official at the court of Basil II. Isaac I, as the highest military officer, became the first Comnenus emperor in 1057–9, and he was followed by 5 more from 1081–1185. In the 11C Castamon was conquered by the Seljuks, and shortly after that by their fellow-tribesmen and rivals the Danishmendids. In 1132, 1133 and 1135 the town was reconquered by the Byzantines, but at the end of that century fell to the Isfendiyaroğlu, whose second emir, Süleyman, (1300–39) conquered the whole of Paphlagonia from Kastamonu, with the connivance of the Mongols. When Tamerlane took the city from the Ottomans in 1402, it was completely destroyed, then rebuilt as capital of Paphlagonia by the Isfendiyaroğlu. In 1459 Mehmet II Fâtih finally destroyed this dynasty, and Kastamonu remained Ottoman.

Atabey Camii: This building dates from 1273, and was commissioned by

Cobanoğlu Atabey. It is the oldest mosque in the town, a conservative building of the early emirate, and was part of a külliye which has been destroyed, or simply fell into disrepair. The fine, plain roof is supported by 40 columns. The founder's türbe is in the mosque.

Ibni Neccar Camii or **Eligüzel Camii** (1353): The woodwork in this mosque is particularly fine. The door, an excellent example of Seljuk carving, is in the museum.

Ismail Bey Camii: Built in 1454 by the last Isfendiyaroğlu emir. It developed from a domed medrese with central courtyard, but without the Ottoman influence which otherwise shows in the architecture. The people of Kastamonu are considered to have been exceptionally conservative. The mosque has a remarkable portal. Beside it are the founder's tomb and a poor kitchen. The medrese is used as rent-free accommodation for old men of limited means.

Nasrulla Camii: Founded in 1506 by the kadi of the town, Nasrulla. Unusual architectural experiments have been made in the rebuilding of this mosque, involving the placing of a modern glass box in front of the portal side. The square prayer room with nine domes is still very impressive. The two beautiful şadirvans (fountains for ritual washing before prayer), formerly inside the mosque, now look rather lost in the modern square.

Yilanli Darüşşifası: One of the oldest buildings in Kasamonu, dating from 1271 in the early emirate. It is said to have been a house of healing for the mentally ill, and a hospital. The small mosque in the interior is still zealously used, and parts of the original building have been converted into flats. There are türbe in some of the old rooms on the ground floor, probably from the period of the emirate. The original *portal* on the main road gives an impression of the original beauty of this building. The original floor level has risen significantly.

Hamam of Cemaleddin Firenkşah: An Anatolian-Seljuk double bath, said to date from 1262. This is one of the oldest baths in Anatolia, and was recently excavated and restored. It is in the main square of the town, considerably below the present level of the ground.

Yakub Ağa Külliyesi: Large külliye founded in 1547 by Süleyman the Magnificent's master of the kitchens and provisions. It is a classic ensemble consisting of mosque, medrese and poor house with kitchen. The mosque is centrally-planned, with a dome, and has a lavishly decorated portal with fine wooden door.

Karanlık Bedesten: This is a bazaar built at the time of the vizier Cem (son of Sultan Mehmet II), later murdered by his brother Beyazıt II in accordance with a law passed by his father. The Karanlık Bedesten is known for its ropework.

Museum: This is housed in the building from which Atatürk proclaimed 'hat reform', officially banning the fez in Turkey. The important ethnological collection is of interest.

Citadel: Significant remains of the inner castle and large wall with massive towers have survived of this enormous fortress dating from the 12C, set over 300 ft. above the town.

Ev Kaya (Stone House): These Phrygian *tombs* with rock façades are monuments in the Greek style dating from the later Phrygian rock tomb period (4C BC). The façade pediment of one of the buildings is supported by two columns. Three entrances lead to the courtyard, from which there is access to the tomb chamber. In the centre of the pediment is a man, standing, flanked to the right and left by animals used for riding. A second building with gable has a façade with

Kaunos, cult tholos

architectural and representative relief. Ev Kaya is one of the earliest examples of this type of tomb.

Environs: Kale Kapı (turn N. about 4 km. to the W. of Taşköprü, then ask after travelling roughly 4 km. further): Kale Kapı (Castle Gate) is an impressive rock relief in the form of a building with pediment. The trapezoid anteroom to the tomb cave, hewn in the rock, is supported by two squat columns with bases and capitals. All around and on the gable are reliefs of animals and winged monsters (lion, buffalo, wolf, panther). There is a double-headed eagle in the pediment spandrel. Kale Kapı, like Ev Kaya, is a Phrygian rock tomb designed in the Greek style. It dates from the second half of the 5C BC and is the oldest known example of the type.

Kasaba (14 km. on the road to Daday, then right after 3 km. to Kasaba Köy): This building, plain on the outside, but because of its interior rightly counted amongst the most beautiful wooden mosques in Turkey, is opposite the school. The *Mahmut Bey Camii* was built in 1366 in the conservative period of the emirate, in the Seljuk tradition. A guide from the museum, generally recommended, is not necessary. The beautifully crafted wooden door, decorated using fine chip-carving technique, has a pear-shaped ornament above the lower decorative border with the round side turned to the central mandala. The same figuration above this in the upper border is decorated with carved calligraphy. The semicircular stop bar in the middle is particularly beautifully decorated. The spatial impression in the interior of the high basilica with nave and four aisles is extraordinary. The wooden ceiling, higher above the nave, with longitudinal coffers, is supported by smooth, slender columns. The columns by and behind the kibla wall support the weight of a large bolster. The two-storey gallery on the entrance side is a unique feature, reminiscent of the organ gallery in a Bavarian baroque church, and most beautifully carpentered. The beams are lightened by decoration, such as the carved wooden balustrades with round barred surfaces. In the corners under the gallery are square wooden stands with grilles around them for students of the Koran. All the wood is painted, the dominant colour being dark red.

Safranbolu (110 km. W. of Kastamonu): This well-kept little town is set in a conglomerate sinkhole washed clear of the mineral. Its buildings are largely *timber-framed*, in the Ottoman tradition. They are brightly painted, and cluster in a picturesque fashion around the mosque and an old hamam at the lowest point of the sinkhole. Mingling with modern houses, they climb the slope to the new town, where they again collect around a mosque. Halfway up is a large ruined, palace-like building in late-19C European style, perhaps the home of a rich Greek.

Many employees from the nearby Karabük coalfield live in Safranbolu.

Tasköprü, ancient **Pompeiopolis** (45 km. from Kastamonu on the way to Sinop): On the edge of the village is an old *arched bridge* about 170 yards long over the Gökirmak. There are numerous Roman *cave tombs* in the area.

Kaunos
Muğla   p.572□D 6

Near Dalyan and Lake Köyceğiz, ancient Kaunos spreads over two mountain ridges. Formerly on the sea, its position as a great trading city in ancient times was deleteriously affected by silting and malaria (stamped out in 1948). It is now in a reedy delta 2 km. from the sea. The origins of the city are difficult to trace, excavations have been fragmentary. In the centre of the town is an inscription in Carian script, but a different language. Herodotus disregarded the people of Kaunos' assertion that they were descended from the Cretans; he considered them to be natives of the region. The

Kaunos, rock tombs

fortunes of this border town between Caria and Lycia are a microcosm of the changing history of these two provinces. It did not become Greek until the time of the satrap Mausolos. He fortified it with a wall so long that the town could not possibly have filled the space created. This wall is a striking demonstration of the culture of the various peoples who repaired breaches with polygonal stones or ashlar after they had conquered the town. There is a necropolis with about 150 *tombs* in the river cliff. They include Carian pit tombs, and alongside them tomb chambers with pediments and, in the uppermost row, magnificent façades (4C BC) in the form of temples in antis with Ionic columns and rows of stylized beam ends under the pediments. These tombs (the largest is incomplete) are carved free of the rock, so that it is possible to walk round them. A short walk takes you into the ancient town. In the principal E. section of the acropolis on its 500 ft. hill are the ruins of the ashlar *fortress*, 66 by 130 ft. The towers and walls on the N. slope are medieval. The W. section was on the hill where the old wall, here from the classical period, still runs past the old harbour and from there to the

N. for a considerable length. The 5&4C BC *theatre* has diazoma and 24 rows of seats, half cut into the rock and half supported by walls. The cavea forms a semicircle, the vaulted entrances are have survived in their original form. There are also a *basilica* with lavishly decorated masonry, a late-Roman *thermal bath* and an intriguing late *building* of indeterminate function. On the excavation site above the harbour an unusual water basin was discovered in 1969. It consists of two concentric circles of wall, columns of various kinds, and a pedestal from which steps lead to an interior slab in purple stone.

Kayseri

Kayseri   p.576☐L 4

Kayseri is not far N. of Erciya Dağı, in a treeless steppe landscape. Many buildings of the Seljuk period have survived. It has always been one of the most important centres in central Anatolia, because of its position at the junction of several ancient trade routes. The growth

Kayseri, wall surrounding the citadel

of tourism has made Kayseri well-known as a carpet capital.

The settlement which preceded the present provincial capital was somewhat further to the SW. The first recorded mention of the town was in the Hellenistic period, when it was called *Mazaka* or *Eusebeia*. It suffered greatly in 77 BC in a raid by Tigranes, who deported sections of the population. In the imperial Roman period, Tiberius made the town capital of the new province of Cappadocia, and it was thenceforth known as **Caesarea**; this notion is preserved in the modern name. In the early 3C AD Kayseri was an important Christian centre, and the seat of a bishop. The Christianization of Armenia was directed from here. Under Bishop Basil, an important ecclesiastical teacher at the time of the Emperor Justinian (527–565), the town moved to its present site, and this new town was soon walled against raids by the Persian Sassanids. Despite Arab progress in the 7&8C the Ottomans held the town until 1077. In the 11C it was contested between Crusaders and Seljuks. The latter, after finally conquering it in 1082, made it the second capital after Konya, so that it had a last period of great prosperity, interrupted by Mongol raids (1243), although their princes, who had established the independent empire of Eretna, chose Kayseri as their capital in 1335. In 1397 the Ottoman sultan Beyazıt drove out the Mongols, who had survived a Mameluke raid. But under Timur-Leng (Tamerlane) the town again fell to the Mongols and subsequently (1402) to the emirs of Karaman. After another Mameluke raid in 1419 Kayseri finally became part of the Ottoman empire under Sultan Selim in 1517.

Citadel (*İç Kale*): This fortress is approximately 900 by 200 yards, and was probably established by the Byzantines in the 6C. The present building is dominated by Seljuk alterations, however. Access is from the S. The walls, almost 10 ft. thick, are armed with 19 towers, and can be climbed using narrow staircases. Some of the towers can be dated precisely. The *Yogun Burç*, (Fat Tower) was built in 1212 under İzzettin Kaykavus I, the *Hassan Bece Burç* under Pir Ahmet Bey in 1465, and the *Ok Deposu* (arrow store) was commissioned by Alaeddin Kaykobad, from whose reign several other buildings in the town date. The mosque inside the citadel was founded by Mehmet II (1468).

Hunat Hatun Külliyese: This large complex with mosque, medrese and mausoleum, founded *c.*1273 by Sultana Mahperi, wife of the Seljuk sultan Alaeddin Kaykobad, is directly to the E. of the citadel on the opposite side of the street. In the medrese, which has an iwan at the rear of the central courtyard and colonnades on the other sides, is the fine *Ethnographic Museum*. Directly adjacent is the octagonal *mausoleum* in a small walled courtyard. Inside this are the cenotaphs of the founder and two of her daughters. The *piered mosque* which is also part of the complex has a lavishly decorated portal. The minaret is a later addition.

Ulu Cami (W. of the Vizir Hanı): This house of prayer was built in 1136 by Mehmet Gazim, the vizier of the Danishmendid dynasty, and altered under Gıyasettin Kayhüsrev I (1189).

Külük Canmii (Dükkan Ömü Maydanı): This mosque, which includes a Koran school and a bath, is one of the oldest in the town. It was founded *c.*1210 by Azzız Elti Hatun, a daughter of the Seljuk vizier Muzafferettin Mahmut and thoroughly restored by Şemsettin in 1305.

Kurşunlu Camii (Lead Mosque; NW of the citadel not far E. of the Sahibiye medrese): This house of prayer dates from 1580&1 and is attributed to Sinan, Süleyman the Magnificent's great architect.

Kayseri, Döner Kümbet ▷

Kayseri, Döner Kümbet, frieze decorations (left), museum, Hittite vessel with stamp decoration (right)

Döner Kümbet (Turning Mausoleum): This is by far the most beautiful of the numerous tombs, and is on the right of the road to Talas on the way to the Archaeological Museum, about 1 km. SE of the citadel. It was built in 1267 for the Seljuk princess Şah Cihan Hatun. Its pointed roof makes it no more like a spit (döner) than other mosques of the same design.

Archaeological Museum: This fine collection is housed in a new building in the NE of the town. It is down a signposted street going off to the left from the road to Talas, a few yards beyond the Döner Kümbet. In the garden are a portal lion from Göllüdağ, an architectural site SW of Kayseri between Nevşehir and Niğde, a cast of the Firaktin rock relief (→ Develi and Environs) and other pieces

from the Hittite to Roman periods. In the museum itself are more casts of Hittite rock reliefs from the surrounding area (Immamkulu and Ivriz) and above all numerous finds from the important site of Kültepe, N. of the town (→ below). There are other individual Hittite pieces (standing figure in Hittite costume; sphinx's head with strong characteristics of the period of the Hittite Empire, actually from the late period; relief block with the cartouche of King Tudhaliyas IV) and numerous Hellenistic and Roman statues.

Also worth seeing: *Melek Gazi medrese* and *Hatuniye medrese*, both S. of the bazaar quarter, the latter medrese built 1431&2 using ancient spoils. *Vizir Hanı*: S. of the covered bazaar (bedesten), itself W. of the citadel; central courtyard with

Kayseri, archaeological museum, inscription of King Tudhalia IV

fine colonnade. *Sahibiye medrese*: N. of the citadel at the junction of Istayon Caddesi and Cumhuriyet Meydanı, built in 1267 by Kayhüsrev III. *Çifte medrese*: badly damaged early-13C Koran school, directly behind the Tourist Hotel. Numerous *baths (hamamı)*, such as the Kadi hamamı, Cafer hamamı, and Selahattin hamamı (Saladin baths).

Environs: Çifte Kümbet (4 km. N.): The Two-Domed Mausoleum is on the right-hand side of the road to Kültepe. A wife of the Seljuk ruler Alaeddin Kaykobad is buried here.

Gesi (24 km. NE): Take the road to Sivas, and after 16 km. the road to Gesi goes off to the right. This road passes two arches of a ruined bridge, some rock chambers and a few km. further on the ruins of the Armenian monastery of *Surb Karapet*. Gesi itself is on the site of the ancient town of **Nea Kassiane**. If you branch off before the village of Agirnas to the right to *Üsgübi* you will find the foundations of a *church* dedicated to the Virgin Mary built before the 9C. The name Üsgübi is said to derive from Episcopi, which suggests that this was the seat of the former bishopric of Aragena.

Incesu (35 km. SW): Just outside the far end of Incesu, which is on the road to Konya, on the right-hand side are the ruins of a *caravanserai* built *c.*1660 by Kara Mustafa Paşa.

Karatay Hanı (44 km. E.): This caravanserai was probably built in 1240&1 under Alaeddin Kaykobad. It is in the village of Karataköy, near Elbasi. There is a direct road from Kayseri to Elbasi, but it is safer to take the road to Sivas, turning right in the direction of Bünyan (11 km.) after 30 km. The han is 38 km. beyond Bünyan, directly on the line of the

Kültepe (Kayseri), Assyrian trading colony, living room with stove

road. In design it is closely connected with the two 'Sultan hans' (on the road to Sivas and the road to Konya, beyond Aksaray).
Kültepe (23 km. NE): This extensive ruined site was ancient **Kanesh** (Kaneş), centre of the numerous trading colonies set up by the Assyrians in the 19&18C BC in Anatolia. The Assyrian name for such a base was karum (smaller outstations were called wabartum), and so the entire epoch in Anatolian history is often called the Karum Period. At that time local copper was exchanged for lead, tin or textiles, with gold and silver being used to balance values if necessary.

When the Assyrians extended Kanesh as their central trading point a local population had been living here for several centuries, as deep excavation has revealed levels dating back to the early 3rd millennium BC, the early Bronze Age. It is possible that the Assyrians were not the first foreign merchants attracted by the rich metal deposits. A cylinder seal of King Ibbisin (of the so-called Ur-III period, which followed the Akkad period in Mesopotamia) was found in Kültepe itself and suggests that foreign tradesmen were present as early as 2000 BC. The oldest levels (IV and III) of the Kaneş karum could date from this period; they are puzzling as there is no written evidence from this period. This changes in Levels II and Ib, where over 12,000 cuneiform tablets, mainly business correspondence of the foreign merchants with their motherland or local trading partners, give a lively picture of the commercial life of the time.

The first of these clay tablets appeared in the hands of art dealers in 1881. Although the writing was Assyrian cuneiform, they were said to come from Cappadocia. E. Chantre excavated the Kültepe setlement mound in search of the origin of the 'Cappadocian tablets' in 1893&4, but did not find the textual material he was hoping for. The Assyrian trading colony, which at the time of its greatest prosperity occupied more than twice the area of the native settlement but lasted for a much shorter time, was in fact at the foot of the tepe, and had left no visible accumulations of rubble on the site. The Czech archaeologist and Hittite specialist B.Hrozny (who was the first person to recognize that the Hittite language was a member of the Indo-European family) investigated the fields in front of the settlement mound and finally found 930 tablets there. Thanks to systematic excavation by the Turkish husband-and-wife archaeological team of T. and N. Özgüç from 1948, the number of cuneiform texts rapidly increased. Historical evaluation of the clay tablets is made more difficult by the fact that in a large number of cases there is dispute over precisely which level they come from, and this leads to differing conclusions about the history of the settlement.

It is certain that the Assyrian merchants came across a number of independent principalities when setting up their trading colonies in the mountainous landscape of Anatolia. It is unclear, however, whether at this period the (Indo-European) Hittites were already resident in Anatolia or immigrated at that time. Nevertheless Kanesh in particular, which under the Hittites was called Neša, must have been highly significant, as the Hittites once called themselves Nešili (People from Neša) after this place. Our modern name Hittite for the Indo-European group is a misnomer, as the Nešili people called the native population of Anatolia which they found there Hatti. However, since academics have come to use the notion Hittites for the wrong people (it comes from Luther's Bible) the original population are now called Hattians or, to distinguish them more clearly from the Hittites, Proto-Hattians.

The first Assyrian trading colony can be

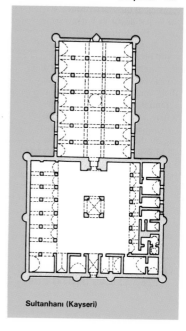

Sultanhanı (Kayseri)

dated to *c.*1950–1850 (=karum Level II), as the Assyrian king Sargon I (not to be confused with the above-mentioned Sargon of Akkad!) and his successor Puzur Assur II are mentioned in the texts. This colony came to a violent end in a fire. Many academics attribute this destruction to Prince Pithana, who at the time was gradually conquering neighbouring empires from his seat in Kuššara. His son was the famous Anitta, who not only extended Kanesh-Neša as his residence, but also continued his father's campaigns, finally succeeding in conquering and destroying Hattus, later the Hittite capital of Hattuşa (Boğazköy), where at the time there was also an Assyrian karum. Despite his new capital, in which a dagger with his name on it was found (now in the museum in Ankara) he continued to call himself Anitta of Kuššara.

Before it was removed in the course of

excavations the oval settlement mound was the largest hüyük in Turkey, between 500 and 600 yards in diameter and 60 ft. high. The Assyrian karum at its foot measured 1,100 by 760 yards. Here the foundations of closely-packed, formerly two-storey houses were discovered, with much of their contents intact. Among these the ceramics, with enormous formal variety (often in the shape of animals) deserve the most attention. The most important building on the hill was a magnificent palace of 32,290 sq. ft. which was discovered in the excavations. Another complex of buildings was discovered which may also have been a palace. A puzzling, almost square building with corner towers from Level Ib was probably a temple. A millennium later the Urartians built their temples to a similar scheme.

The finds, including ceramics from all periods (Proto-Hattian to Phrygian), and also strange disc-shaped alabaster idols with pointed heads (Proto-Hattian) and steatite lead moulds, are now in the museums in Kayseri and Ankara, along with the clay tablets with their seal stamps and cylinders, showing the influence of various styles.

Sultan Hanı (50 km. NE): This conspicuous village on the road to Sivas near the village of the same name dates from 1230–6, and is one of the largest caravanserais in Turkey, with an area of 34,265 sq. ft. In the Seljuk period, like its namesake on the road to Konya beyond Aksaray, it was a stopping place on the important trade route which crossed Kayseri from E.–W. Both of the Sultan hanıs are very similar in design (courtyard with central mosque with substructure, at the rear large domed hall with several aisles for camels etc.), with the exception that the kitchen tract is on the other longitudinal side of the courtyard. As the building was thoroughly restored in 1950 it is in an excellent state of repair. It is usually necessary to ask for the key in the village.

Talas (9 km. SE): Because of its fine view of Kayseri, Talas has become the preferred summer residence of rich Turkish families. Somewhat to the S. is the site of ancient *Zincidere*, in Roman times *Flaviana*, the residence of the archbishops of Kayseri. An *underground church* (1728) and 2 *rock chapels* have survived.

Tomarza (about 55 km. SE): Not far

Kültepe (Kayseri), excavation site, buildings used by the Assyrian trading colony

from Tomarza, which is near Develi but easier to reach from Kayseri, there are numerous *rock buildings, monasteries* and *chapels* with painting. The Panagia church in Tomarza, with crossing dome and apse, has now been destroyed. All that has survived is a *tomb* in the shape of a squat column with acanthus capital and a massive substructure.

Kırklareli

This town in Thrace, formerly *Kırık Kilise* (Ruined Church) was probably founded by the Romans and was important in the Byzantine period. It was conquered by the Ottoman Murat I in 1361. It has had a railway station since 1912.

Bayezid (Paşa) Camii (Hatice Hatun mahallesi): This was completed in 1594 by Beglerbeg Güllâbi Ahmet Paşa, whose tomb is in the garden.

Büyük (Hızır Bey) Camii (in the market, or Çarşı): This is the oldest mosque in Thrace, built by Kösenihalzade Hızır Bey for his son Abdullah Bey (1382); it has been restored many times.

Kadi (Emin Ali Çelebi) Camii (opposite the Ahmet Midhat Ilkokulu): This was built in 1577.

[C]Klaros

15 km. S. of Değirmendere, about 200 yards from the road, on the bed of the old Halesos is the shrine of Apollo, rich in legend. After the Trojan War the famous seer Calchas is said to have settled here and to have looked into the future, empowered by a spring in a cave. Homer mentions a shrine in the 7C BC in his hymn to Apollo. It did not become famous as an oracle until the Hellenistic period, and then again later under the Romans, when messengers from all over the Empire asked for advice here, and commemorated themselves in hundreds of inscriptions. It was one of the last oracles which survived into the Christian period; Hadrian had it reconsecrated. It was then completely buried by an earthquake at an unknown date. It was not until 1950 that the French managed to excavate it again despite seeping water. The entrance to the sacred grove (now full of wild tamarisks) is via the *propylon* (2C BC), and from here the sacred way, fringed with exedrae, columns and remains of statues, leads to the temple, under which are the two secret oracle chambers, into which the uninitiated were never allowed to penetrate. It was built in the late 4C in the Doric style, measures 85 by 151 ft. on a base with 5 steps, and has 6 x 11 columns over 5 ft. in diameter, of which some have survived. At the entrance two blue marble staircases lead to underground corridors, which meet only to split again to lead to the two vaulted chambers. The sacred spring flowed into a pool in the smaller one. Pliny confirms that the soothsayer needed only a sip of it in order to be able to make the most marvellous oracular pronouncements. He then immediately went through the little door and around a large stone block into the large room almost 20 ft. deep in which priests sat on stone benches around the 27 ins. long, ovoid blue Omphalos, the navel of the world, in order to versify and write down what had been revealed to him. Directly above all this Apollo kept watch in the cella in the form of a 26 ft. high statue, seated, with a laurel twig in his right hand, and with his mother Leto and sister Artemis at his side. This image is stamped on the coins of Colophon, and one of the god's arms, almost 10 ft. long, is one of the fragments among the ruins which indicate the great size of the statue. About 100 ft. in front of the temple was a *double altar*, 59 by 29 ft., which he shared with Dionysos. A little

Knidos, two harbours with cape

further on is a hollow spherical *sundial* with dial and a magnificent *seat*. By the temple is a smaller 6C BC Ionic temple with an altar of Artemis. A statue of the goddess, of the same date, has been excavated.

[C]Knidos

Muğla   p.572□C 6

Knidos is 28 km. W. of **Datça** on the W. extremity (Tekir Burnu) of the Reşadiye peninsula. Ancient Knidos (a member of the Dorian League in the 7C BC) was near Datça, and was transferred to Tekir in the 4C. It was much referred to in classical literature (Herodotus, Thucydides, Pliny etc.). The geometrician and astronomer Eudoxos (4C BC) came from Knidos. He was a pupil of Plato,

made mathematical calculations in the field of astronomy and founded an observatory in Knidos late in his turbulent life.

Ancient Knidos (N. of the Iskele from Datça): The *acropolis* is about one and a half km. from the Iskele, on a promontory. The fortifying wall extends from the summit to the sea. To the S. the remains of a harbour can be seen in the water. NW of modern Dalacak are two harbours (Körmen limanı). There is a *mosque* with archaic capital.

Modern Knidos (near Tekir): Smaller than the old town, modern Knidos is more compact; the ashlar wall on the N. side has survived, and leads to the acropolis in the E. There are square towers, with a round tower at the harbour entrance. There is a larger harbour to the S., with remains of moles under water. High on the N. side are the ruins of a large *theatre*. E. of this on the cliff is the perimeter wall of the *Temple of Demeter*, excavated by Sir Charles Newton in 1856–8. The most valuable finds are in the British Museum in London (statue of Demeter). Marble from the theatre was taken to Cairo for palace building and to İstanbul for the Dolmabahçe Palace. A *circular building* dominating the isthmus to the N. was excavated by the Americans. This is said to be the Temple of Aphrodite known from literature, with Praxiteles' statue of the goddess. The *lower theatre* has been excavated: 35 rows of seats (8,000 spectators), 2 lateral passages, vaulted access on both sides. The stage building is in poor condition. *Necropolis* outside the town wall, tombs of various kinds.

Konya

History: Konya is in the SW of the enormous central Anatolian high steppes, where extensive salt lakes have formed because of imperfect drainage through the syncline. Despite this, Konya-Ovasi is one of the most fertile regions of Turkey, and even in the 4th millennium BC, the chalcolithic period, attracted cattle breeders and arable farmers. Sample excavations on the Alaeddin Tepesi, the acropolis hill, have confirmed settlement 5,000 years before the Dancing Dervishes. Çatal Hüyük, one of the oldest Anatolian cities, 35 km. S. of Konya, had a proven settlement from 6500 BC, in the neolithic period. Hittite written sources tell us that Anitta was an important Anatolian ruler in the 2nd millennium BC, who permitted 'homage by the gift of a throne and an iron sceptre' from Purushanda (in the plain of Konya). According to a Phrygian legend their city around the Konya hill was the first after the Great Flood. The Cimmerians destroyed it again in the 7C. According to Greek mythology Konya is

the place where Perseus struck off Medusa's head and fastened it to a column.

Persian satraps and the kings of Pergamon did not bring *Iconium*, as the town was then called, quite the greatness and far-reaching fame that it later acquired under the Romans after 133 BC. The Apostles Paul and Barnabas made several missionary visits to Iconium and nearby Derbe in the 1C, althought they were driven out of the town by the Jews, and even stoned (Acts 14,1). It was also in Konya that Paul met Thecla, later St.Thecla. The Byzantine bishopric of Iconium was unable to resist the Arab storm in the 7,8&9C. After the decisive defeat of the Byzantines by the Seljuks at Malazgirt in 1071, the Seljuks conquered Konya in 1087 and in 1134 made the city the capital of the Sultanate of Rum. In May 1190 the approach of the Crusader army under Emperor Frederick Barbarossa spread horror through the capital. Sultan Kiliç Arslan had promised the emperor free passage, but he could not prevent the wild Turkoman mounted hordes from subjecting the weary, thirsty and starving Crusaders to ceaseless ambush. It was a matter of life and death for the totally powerless army to conquer the market in Konya. The unbelievable occurred, and while the sultan and his many belligerent sons sought refuge in the citadel, the Crusaders filled their stomachs and replenished their stores.

The great Seljuk sultan Alaeddin Kaykobad I (1219–37) used building material from almost all the ancient and Byzantine buildings to strengthen the fortress with 108 massive towers and a great wall, and to build palaces, medreses and mosques. We shall never know what buildings were formerly supported by the 42 ancient and Byzantine columns now holding up the flat roof of the Alaeddin Camii on the acropolis hill in Konya. Alaeddin Kaykobad I did not only conquer, found and organize a major empire in the few years before he was murdered by his own son, but intervened personally and persistently in matters of architecture, the fine arts and the sciences, and achieved a peak of unmistakably Seljuk culture which was never surpassed. A well-thought-out network of well-designed defensive caravanserais made it possible to conduct secure overland trade with caravans. In the evenings they reached secure quarters for the night, with all the comforts of oriental hospitality. Between Konya and Kayseri alone (600 km.) there were 24 caravanserais. Around Konya itself are a number of such hans, among the most remarkable evidence of this oriental branch of culture. Famous and beautiful mosques, medreses, hamams and tombs are all to be found in the Seljuk metropolis, as well as geometrical relief decoration always specific to the architecture in question, carved stone decoration, faience with powerful colour and expressive quality, and a high level of finest wood carving on the surfaces of minbars, doors and pedestals. Much of this fell victim to frequent earthquakes. Alaeddin brought famous academics, artists and architects to Konya, and his magnificent palace was a centre of academic life and poetry, with a strong

Konya, Karatay Medrese, dome tiles

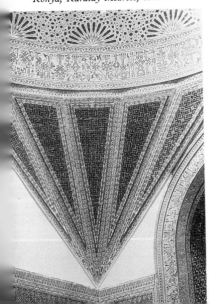

Persian influence. In 1228 Mevlâna Celâleddin Rumi moved from Karaman to Konya, where his father was given the chair of theology. This refugee from Afghanistan became a famous poet, philosopher and mystic. His Order of the Dancing Dervishes rapidly spread throughout Anatolia. The influence of this Order was finally so important that its grand masters achieved the right to hand the sword to a new sultan in Eyüp/İstanbul, a ceremony equivalent to coronation. The fascination of his original monastery in Mevlâna was also not broken by Atatürk's ban in 1925. Huge numbers of pious pilgrims, mingling with tourists, pass through the holy places of this pious and passionate Order, and the dervishes dance once a year on Mevlâna's birthday.

After Alaeddin's murder decline set in, accelerated by the Mongol victory at Erzincan in 1243. The Ilkhane (Mongols) who had ruled Persia since 1200 placed governors (pervans) in Konya. In 1308 the last member of the Seljuk dynasty was killed by the Mongols. In 1320 the emir finally succeeded in making Konya capital of the neighbouring and powerful emirate of Karaman. The tradition of magnificent building was boosted once more. After five years of Ottoman rule Timur-Leng (Tamerlane) helped the Karamanoğlu to return to Konya in 1402 by his victory over Sultan Beyazıt, but the city finally became Ottoman again from 1466. Konya was firmly locked into its tradition as an Anatolian city dominated by Seljuk culture, but its subsequent economic development has been breathtaking in both senses. In 1860 Konya had 8,000 inhabitants, in 1960 there were 120,000. The population had again expanded threefold by the time this book was written, suggesting unbroken immigration from elsewhere, and optimistic planners see unlimited possibilities of growth for the already considerable industries on the broad plain of Konya, for which preparations are being made with huge irrigation projects.

Alaeddin Camii (1150–1250): This is a unique example of the development of early-Seljuk mosque architecture, as it took 100 years to be completed. The entire complex, high on the Alaeddin hill above the city, is in the shape of an irregular trapezium.

The high entrance façade to the mosque courtyard is a magnificent 115 ft. wide. It is irregularly articulated with blind windows, a large carved star ornament, a central tall rectangular portal wall reaching up to the upper cornice of the building, and on each side of this a gallery with ten (on the right irregular) arched windows. The upper section of the 'Gothic' arched gate niche has unusual polymorph and geometrical ornamentation in alternating lighter and darker stone. A flight of six steps leads through a lavishly decorated portal to the inner courtyard. The türbe on the right, an octagonal building, is incomplete, with a dome. On the left is the towering *Kılıç Arslan türbe*, built after 1170 by the sultan of the same name. The massive tower is ten-sided, and built in smooth ashlar. This typical Anatolian-Seljuk tower tomb has a tomb chamber on the ground floor, accessible by a separate staircase on the E. side. This contains the body of the sultan. The door on the NE side leads via a double staircase to the prayer room above the tomb. This has mihrab and a lavishly decorated cenotaph, and is covered by a dome with an outer ten-sided roof like a pyramid. The portal door is set in a shallow round-arched niche. The square building inscription is above the door, which is surrounded by columns and geometrical decorative patterns. Above the niche is a tall rectangular window frame which provides light for the prayer room. The mosque was damaged by the earthquake of 1986.

The plain wooden roof of the *older mosque*, also trapezoid, to the SE is supported by six rows of pointed arches on Byzantine and ancient columns running parallel to the kibla wall. This mosque is closely related to the 7C Arab type. The adjacent SW section was built before 1225. The mihrab niche forms the S. side of a domed bay whose hemisphere is supported by a band of Turkish triangles. The wonderful faience decoration of the Turkish triangles and mihrab frame give an impression of the original appearance of the dome and mihrab niche. This domed

Konya, Mevlâna monastery

Konya, Ince Minare Medrese

used as a museum on a temporary basis. The father of Mevlâna Celâleddin Rumi taught theology and philosophy in the attached medrese in his first years in Konya. After his death Mevlâna took over his father's students and taught them his own brand of mysticism. They became his first enthusiastic supporters.

Sahib Ata Camii (S. of the Alaeddin hill, near the Archaeological Museum): This ruined mosque also dates from the period of Seljuk greatness (1259), and is well worth seeing. The decorated portal, by the same architect as the Ince Minare Medrese, is of comparable quality. The fine *mihrab* with mukarnas gable has choice faience decoration. The stucco friezes on the mihrab are exemplary specimens of this Iranian-Seljuk art. Minbar and wooden door are remarkable museum pieces. The founder, vizier Sahib Ata Faheddin Ali, also commissioned the *hamam* of the same name, a small *mesçit* (house of prayer) and the *türbe* with glazed faience for himself and his family. Sahib Ata was one of the leading figures of the Seljuk Sultanate of Rum for more than 50 years, until he was beheaded by the Mongols in 1277. He founded many major buildings in the empire, including the Ince Minare medrese in Konya and the famous Gök medrese in Sivas.

Serefeddin Camii (in the central Hükümet Meydanı): This was originally a Seljuk mosque, rebuilt after falling into ruins in 1636. The fine masonry is worth seeing. The Serefeddin Camii is a copy of Sinan's Kılıç Ali Paşa Camii in İstanbul, which in its turn is based on Hagia Sophia in İstanbul. The length of the nave is emphasized by the two half domes by the main dome in the longitiudinal axis, and this is further strengthened by the apse-like mihrab niche.

Selemiye Camii (by the Mevlâna Tekke): This mosque was completed under Selim II (1566–74), and is the high

prayer room with adjacent bay to the N. and entrance portal show a complete architectural concept which the section to the W. does not share. The minbar is a magnificent example of Seljuk wood carving. It is dated 1155&6, the earliest confirmed date on a comparable work of art. The minbar is carved in Kündekari technique, using lozenge-shaped, stellar and octagonal panels with toothed edges, filled with arabesque reliefs and joined without glue or pins by tongue and groove joints.

İplikçi Camii (between the Alaeddin hill and Hükümet Square on the right of the Alaeddin Caddesi): This mosque is one of the oldest Seljuk buildings in Konya, built in 1202 under Sultan Kılıç Arslan II. The classical Arab prayer room is rectangular with a flat ceiling supported by two rows of six columns. The mosque was badly damaged by earthquakes, abandoned, and

point of Ottoman architecture in the Seljuk capital. The design of this lucid single-roomed mosque is clear from the exterior. The walls of the main room have blind arches articulated with windows. The dome is not set immediately above the arches, but on a polygonal drum. The open porch on seven round arches with colourfully alternating levels on tall columns has a dome over each bay, and concludes in two slender minarets flush with the rear wall. The polychrome marble minbar is a striking feature of the inner room.

Mevlâna monastery (*Mevlâna Tekkesi*): This is the best-known and probably the most famous building in Konya, even though only the dominant green türbe, the symbol of the city, is all that has survived of the original monastery buildings. And if it were possible to weigh the fervour with which the millions of visitors spend their time at various places in the city, then the tomb of the 'greatest poet and deepest thinker and most pious of all men' would probably be the most important place in Konya. This monastery is not simply one of the most visited museums in Turkey, it is a venerated national shrine and one of the holiest places of Islam. Although only few have read the profound writings of the poet, philosopher and mystic Celâleddin Rumi (known as Mevlâna), the fascination with which Mevlâna kept his pupils and supporters in passionate self-immersion and boundless asceticism is still alive today. On their journey to recognition, to divine revelation and inspiration the dervishes gathered every Friday morning in the semahane, the dancing room. It is rectangular, surrounded by two-storey galleries for those who were not dancing, with a special niche for the musicians.

The ceremonial of the sacred dance is much described in ancient sources. The great master, a successor of Rumi, sits cross-legged on a skin at the edge of the room. The dervishes wear tall pointed hats in brown camel-hair, and flowing cloaks,

Konya, Karatay Medrese

and sit in a semicircle around the master. When the musicians start to play their melancholy, supernatural melodies on the ney, the Anatolian shepherds' flute, the dervishes stand up, bow to the master, circle round him in a great semicircle with solemn steps, bow as they sweep past and stand still when the sign is given. The slow transition from rest to the whirling dance is achieved, they all drop their cloaks and stand there in the pure white garments of the order: full gown, white trousers, tight upper garments which some of them remove, beginning the ritual dance with the upper part of their bodies naked. One after other other they kiss the master's hand, whilst he kisses the cheek of each. The music speeds up, supported in its rhythm by drums. Both arms are raised horizontally, the whirling dance begins. With lowered head and left hand pointing to the ground, arm fully extended, and the right arm stretched towards heaven to receive its grace, they whirl and spin on bare feet across the polished floor, following the driving music at ever-increasing speed, until their gowns stand out horizontally from the spinning motion, increasing the consciousness-removing experience of the ecstatic whirling. Turning on their own axis they move in ever-increasing circles until they stop, with foam on their blue lips, and, old men, men and boys, all sink unconscious to the ground. Servants throw cloaks over the perspiration-soaked bodies, the music dies away.

Atatürk silenced the Mevlevis' reed pipes in 1925. In 1927 the monastery became the *Islamic Museum*.

Tour: Proceed through the Dervish Gate, left in the courtyard past the şadırvan and right past the Şebi Arus (Pool of Nuptial Night) to the *Museum Portal*. The Persian inscription means: 'This is the kaaba of the devoted. Here perfection can be reached.' The next room, the dervishes' reading room, shows the rise of Seljuk art in Anatolia in a mere hundred years by the development of calligraphy at this period. The Koran verses were originally copied in heavy Kufic script, then this developed into the most beautiful calligraphy, though admittedly it later became slack and overblown. Calligraphy in the ornamental design of stone façades of ecclesiastical and secular buildings went through the same phases of development. In the next room, the Presence of the Saint, are the sarcophagi of dervishes who left their homes with Mevlâna's family and moved to Anatolia. Heads of the order after Mevlâna Celâleddin, with the exception of his immediate successor, and other relations, also found their last resting place here, close to the great master. The men's graves have dervish hats on them. The bronze April Bowl, with silver and gold ornamentation, in which the blessed rains of April were collected, was the present of a pious Eastern khan in 1333. *Mevlâna's marble sarcophagus*, screened by a silver grille dating from 1597, is in a green türbe built in its present form by Karaman emirs in the first half of the 15C. Next to Mevlâna are his son and later successor Sultan Weled and his father. The inscription means 'Do not seek us in the

Kısılören Han (Konya)

tombs, we are in the hearts of the enlightened'.

The *dancing room (semahane)* was built at the time of Süleyman the Magnificent. The musicians' gallery is in the N. The walls of the hall are hung with old Anatolian rugs. Exhibits in the showcases include the 5 musical instruments with which the orchestra accompanied the mystic dance: reed pipes, tambourines, zithers, drums and rebecs (three-stringed instrument). A finely-carved *Koran lectern* in walnut with the only surviving original Seljuk painting is the oldest (1278) and finest example of Seljuk cabinet-making. In the adjacent *mesçit* (prayer chapel) is a sacred hair of the master's beard, and also his (?) prayer mat, 12C monastery manuscripts and rosaries.

In the monastery courtyard are four 16C Ottoman *türbe*. On the left near the exit is the *kitchen pavilion*, in which the novices were prepared for 1,001 days before admission to the monastery, and on the right the *dervish halls*, in which the monks fasted and meditated in darkness for up to 40 days. The first two cells are furnished. The adjacent *carpet museum* is a treasure-house of Anatolian carpet-making technique.

Büyük Karatay Medrese (N. of the Alaeddin Camii): The medrese was exclusively an institution of advanced specialist education, in contrast with the mosque, in which elementary instruction was also given. The 'university' of philosophy, astronomy, medicine and mathematics founded in 1251 by Vizier Karatay later became a famous law school and 'administrative academy' for civil servants. It is a medrese with one iwan and a domed inner courtyard. The iwan is opposite the entrance, flanked by two domed rooms. These, like the courtyard and the iwan, were used as teaching spaces. The inner courtyard had cells for residential students on either side. In the middle of the courtyard was a pool reflecting the light from the oculus of the dome. Fanshaped pendentives make the transition from the corners of the walls to the dome. Before the building was damaged the domed room and iwan were an orgy of blue-toned tiles and faience with delicate ornamentation. All the walls, the

Konya, Alaeddin Camii, interior view

Konya, Karatay Museum, Kubadabad, relief

pendentives, the large dome, which was almost 40 ft. in diameter, the ogee arches and ogee-arched bay of the iwan, all these were covered with fine tiles from the famous Konya factory. External decoration was restricted to the gate façades and minarets of the medrese. The gatehouse was always covered with carefully-cut ashlar, despite the fact that other materials such as brick were used elsewhere in the building. The gate, the gate niche with mukarnas gable under a Gothic arch, framed with interlaced patterned bands in two colours, relief inscription strips in the centre and at the top geometrical hook patterns to the right and left of the portal niche with small twisted columns: all of them presented an imaginative profusion of Seljuk façade decoration. The Karatay medrese houses the fine *Ceramics Museum*, with exhibits ranging from finds from the early-Seljuk period on the citadel hill to modern tile manufacture.

The most important part of the collection comes from excavations at the the *summer palace of Alaeddin Kaykobad* on Lake Beyşehir, built *c.*1230. The palace buildings were surrounded by extensive fortify-ing walls. There is a reconstruction in the museum. The hall and the most important residential and harem rooms were decorated with stellar or cruciform tiles, some of which were manufactured in Kubadabad itself. The figurative motifs suggest Persian and other central Asian traditions. The eagle or double eagle which occurs frequently goes back to shamanic beliefs. Dragon shapes are Chinese in origin, the lion is a popular Sel-juk motif. The Kubadabad palace tiles are painted with all sorts of animals which can be hunted, and also fabulous creatures, usually as elements of skilful compositions, and showing graceful movement. Sphinxes, dragons, double eagles, sirens and gryphons were intended to protect the palace. Three kinds of tiles found in the Kubadabad palace can be distinguished: 1. Underglazed stellar tiles allow the use of bright colours and fine contrasts. 2. Cruciform tiles as the linking element between the stars have black, abstract ornaments under the turquoise glaze. 3. Overglaze painting is rare, but fine examples with figurative representations were found in Kubadabad. The stellar tiles are simply brown and yellow, the linking

Konya, Archaeological Museum, Roman sarcophagus

crosses violet. A characteristic feature of the Kubadabad tiles is that they were painted in two stages: the drawing in black does not quite correspond with the mingling colours. The palace also had very interesting stucco, of which there are some good examples in the museum. Opposite the Karatay medrese are interesting remains of the **Karatay mesçidi,** a house of prayer dating from 1251 (liwan and brick mosaic have survived).

Ince Minare medrese, also **Ince Minare Camii** (90 W. of the Karatay medrese around the hill): This medrese (1260–5) was founded by Vizier Sahip Ata Fahrettin Ali and is comparable with the Karatay medrese in ground plan and purpose. In this period the distinction between mosque and medrese was blurred. Prayer was part of study just as study was part of prayer. A mosque which was only a mosque was open to all the faithful, and also had a function as a Koran school, the medrese had higher educational aims and was a cadre school used for certain purposes by those in power: the training of an administrative elite, for legal decisions in agreement with the interpretation of the

Koran, or as a scientific faculty. The Medrese with the Slender Minaret was built as a theological seminar by the great architect Abdallah ibn Kelük. It differs from the neighbouring Karatay medrese in its façade decoration, which here has become more three-dimensional, indeed more baroque. The reliefs are cut more deeply into the ashlar, and run vertically from top to bottom. Dominant are the broad central inscription strips, starting over the gate arch and curling around each other twice on the way to the top. The fluted outer strips also run right up to the topmost edge. The inscriptions are in Nashi and Kufic script. New elements are leaf and architectural ornaments. The design is completed at the top by a tight hanging garland. Large sections of the medrese are built of brick, which is unusual. The fluted shaft of the minaret was two-thirds higher before lightning struck in 1901. It is covered with turquoise and violet tiles. In the domed *main room* are collections of Seljuk stone carving and ornamental stucco, and also wood carvings: reading desks, door panels, banisters, columns, capitals, window frames and consoles in walnut, apple, pear, cedar, ebony

Konya, Archaeological Museum, Roman sarcophagus

and rosewood. The stone reliefs from the citadel are also a *Seljuk rarity*; a double eagle, angel with crown, lion sculptures, fabulous creatures and human figures.

Palace of the Sultans of Rum (Alaeddin hill): Only fragments of the building remain. It was built under Kiliç Arslan, who entrenched himself there when Barabarossa took Konya for his starving Crusaders. The remains of a pavilion on a fortress tower have survived of the fortress area within the palace. Texier's travel reports suggest that in the mid-19C intact sections of the palace with lavishly painted wooden ceilings could be seen. Laborde drew the citadel *c.*1830, and *c.*1860 Texier established that the city had been rectangular in plan, with walls with 108 massive rectangular towers 46 ft. apart. Each tower was almost 33 ft. wide and 26 ft. deep. The two main towers, containing access points to the citadel, and two small fortifications with lavish ornamentation and statue decoration, were commissioned by Alaeddin Kaykobad I himself, who then encouraged notable citizens to endow towers and name them after themselves. Thus a huge system of walls came into being: the citadel wall closed around the hill as a second ring. It is hard to understand why this wall was destroyed by town planners in the last century.

Sirçali Medrese (S. of the citadel hill; now **Funerary Museum**): The medrese was founded as a theological seminary under Sultan Keyhusrev II. The entrance portal has the elegant simplicity of earlier days. The gate is set in a deep arched niche with flanking side niches, the latter only with mukarnas decoration. The niche arch with delicate trefoil ornamentation is supported by two small fluted columns with double capitals. The medallions, later hemispherical, are here attached over the decorative arch like shallow flower bowls. The ground plan is similar to that of the Karatay Medrese, but designed as a summer school with open courtyard. The

iwan still has old faience decoration with fine stellar ornamentation on the rear wall. In the domed room to its right are Seljuk tombstones, and stones associated with the emirs of Karaman. On the left are Ottoman tombs. On the left-hand side of the courtyard, a rarity in Konya, are large *Hittite funerary urns* from the surrounding area.

Hasbey Darül Hüffaz: Hospice built in 1421 during the Karamanoğlu period, near the Funerary Museum to the W. This is a rare example of architecture of the period of the Emirate; it is suggested that it may have been used as a Koran school.

Archaeological Museum (S. of the Funerary Museum by the Sahip Atta Camii): The extensive collection includes a particularly interesting sarcophagus showing the Twelve Labours of Herakles (3C AD). Outstanding are the Phrygian statues of the Mother Goddess Cybele, and Roman glass. Other items are inscriptions, steles, statues of the Roman and Byzantine periods and interesting architectural defensive items.

Ethnographic Museum: This is by the Mevlâna monastery.

There is a picturesque **bazaar** near the Hükümet Meydanı (post office).

Environs: Çatal Hüyük (35 km. S. of Konya-Karaman, left for 12 km. near Çumra): The Double Hill is on the W. bank of the Çarşamba-çay. Excavations begun in 1961 by the British Archaeological Institute in Ankara under James Mellaart produced outstanding insights and finds, suggesting that Çatal Hüyük was among the most interesting and earliest settlements in Anatolia. The double hill rises almost 60 ft. above the plain of Konya, and covers 450 by 300 yards. Although some of the excavation shafts have been partially filled in again by the weather, it is still possible to see the sequences of levels and places where the finds were made. Friendly curators provide interesting information, which together with the particular atmosphere of the place give an idea of the city, more than 8,000 years old. The character of this settlement distinguishes Çatal Hüyük from all other settlements in Asia Minor. The earliest strata at a depth of 64 ft. date from the New Stone Age, *c.* 6500 BC, the subsequent ones, up to Level X, end roughly at 5700 BC. Small houses of clay brick with flat roofs were set close together, often as terraced houses around larger courtyards. Entrance was by means of ladders through roof shafts into a house which usually had two rooms with clay floors. Stone was short on the plain, and the bricks were a mixture of air-dried clay and straw. Until Level VII houses and rooms are similarly arranged: main room 16 by 13 ft., one or two side rooms for stores, kitchen, workshop. In a corner of the living room was a raised section for sleeping and sitting, in another a cupboard or shelf, opposite this the separate fireplace in front of the baking oven, hollowed out of clay, without a chimney. The walls were covered with white or cream-coloured

rendering. Quantities of limestone filler were found. The roof was supported by painted piers around the walls. Cult rooms, temple shrines, cult niches and cult objects make it possible to come to clear conclusions about religious ideas, cult customs, the relation of the Çatal-Hüyük people to birth and death and other existential problems. The most important finds in this connection were red and black *wall paintings* in the living and cult rooms. The pictures were painted on the clay rendering, which was covered with a cream-coloured filler. The pictures are of a remarkable artistic standard, and show scenes of dancing and hunting, people moving gracefully, bulls, deer, wild boars, wild asses. The finest wall painting, also the one in the best condition was found in Level III: It is a splendid cult hunting scene showing a large auroch with 25 people dancing around it. In the hunting scenes pigs, stags, and wild asses are being hunted with clubs, axes and nets. Among the men, who wear skins, are a woman with long breasts, and a small child. The colours used in Çatal Hüyük were red, white, black, orange, light purple and yellow. The sculptures and statuettes

Konya, Archaeological Museum, detail of a Roman sarcophagus

Underglaze star-shaped tiles from Kubadabad

found are gods of both sexes, animals, and combinations of these groups. Fat goddesses, heavily pregant and with large breasts, were popular idols. Among the birth pictures in Level VI is a goddess helping with the birth of a calf. The goddess of fertility and life was particularly worshipped in Çatal Hüyük, as can be seen from the large number of pictures and statues, and also from the materials used. Painted work in terracotta, marble, stone or alabaster represent the fat goddesses giving birth, in various attitudes or surrounded by lions. Terracotta bulls' skulls with real horns, singly or in numbers, were hung on the walls of cult and living rooms. The bull was always worshipped as a sacred animal in Anatolia, as it was connected with higher powers, such as thunderstorms. A cult room has been reconstructed in the Ankara Museum: wall paintings, bulls' heads, benches or platforms on the ground, pots and pilasters all included. From the earliest times the dead were buried under the floor in Anatolia. Ceramic ware found was monochrome and undecorated. Agriculture was relatively highly developed in the neolithic period on the plain of Konya. Both equipment and the right soil conditions existed for productive field cultivation. Goats, oxen and sheep were domesticated. Meat needs, as pictures document, were met by extensive hunting. Game was plentiful. All the finds are in the Museum of Anatolian Culure (Archaeological Museum) in Ankara.

Dokuzun Derbent Han (25 km. N. of Konya on the road to Akşehir, on the left before the village of the same name): This is a crude and simple han, built according to the building inscription on the tympanum of the entrance portal by a private individual, Haci İbrahim, perhaps the sultan's vizier, in 1210. The courtyard, originally the same size as the hall, has disappeared. The central aisle with five bays is twice as wide as the 10 ft. side aisles.

Horozlu Han (turn left 6 km. N. in the modern suburb of Horozlu): This magnificent caravanserai, once on the open steppe, was built under Kaykaus II (1246−9) and is now surrounded by industrial buildings. It was beautifully restored in 1956. By this time the outer building had fallen into disrepair, and all the ashlar cladding had been cannibalized. The former semicircular side towers had to a large extent disappeared, and also the once large courtyard. It is no longer clear how the hall portal, now rebuilt, was decorated. The dimensions of this portal, 23 ft. wide and protruding more than 6 ft. from the hall, are the original ones. The Horozlu han is almost the same size as the Susuz han near Buçak, and was built at the same time, thus making comparisons possible. The pointed tunnel vault of the central aisle is raised, and runs on five arches to the rear wall. The dome at the centre of the hall is built of brick, and in good condition. A tall, octagonal drum with slit windows moves easily into the supporting brick pendentives. Between the central aisle and the side walls are five transverse aisles with pointed vault on two squat arches. Most of the vaults had collapsed.

Kadın Han (61 km. NW of Konya on the left of the road to Akşehir in the village of Kadın Han): The name means woman's han, and according to the inscription over the entrance the caravanserai was founded in 1223 by a woman named Radiya Hatun. This is the only known example of a female founder. The courtyard was considerably larger than the hall, but has disappeared with the exception of vestiges of wall to the right and left of the hall façade. The slightly pointed vaults of the three aisles run to the rear wall on six 'Gothic' arches. There are only three windows in the hall, all in the rear wall. Soil deposits have raised the floor level by about 20 ins. The hall façade contains a spoil with a relief of two women, which is in good condition.

Kısılören Han (43 km. W. of Konya in the direction of Beyşehir, left of the road): The exterior of this romantically lonely caravanserai is in better condition than the interior. The building in front of the courtyard is unusually large, 51 by 14 ft. The large surface is articulated by the great 'barn door' with basket arch, the pointed-arched openings in the left-hand section and above these the three windows in the polychrome ashlar façade. The sides of the courtyard are set back, and flanked by massive polygonal towers. This gives the courtyard façade an imposing and lavish quality unusual in a Seljuk han. The inner courtyard is 79 by 79 ft., over 8 ft. wider than the hall on either side, and has 4 iwans on the right and on the left, unconnected with each other. The hall portal is plain. The vault of the central aisle has collapsed, and so has that of the left-hand side aisle. Six arches carry the tunnel vaults to the rear wall. The vault in the right-hand aisle is supported on two wall arches. The han mosque is on the first

Konya, Karatay Museum, wall tiles

floor on the left by the 'barn door'. A well-carved mihrab niche has survived in good condition. The building on a hill just over 400 yards away is something of a mystery. It measures 49 by 69 ft., and is built using the same techniques and the same materials as the Kısılör han, and probably at the same time. It has two aisles with vaults of differing widths, and has an entrance placed off-centre and leading into the wider aisle. Opposite this, on the rear wall, is a prayer niche. This suggests a separate mosque building, but the han has its own mosque in the gatehouse, and two-aisled mosques of this kind are most unusual. On the other hand a second han near so large a first one is unlikely.

Sadeddin Han (20 km. N. of Konya, 5 km. right by the road to Ankara): This is a superb caravanserai founded in 1235 by Emir Sadeddin Köpek. Köpek (the Dog) was an influential dignitary at the court of Alaeddin Kaykobad I.

Every han has a main façade, and in this case it is the wide S. side, with the courtyard portal in the left-hand corner. The hall begins on the left of this. The rear wall of the hall, finely built in ashlar, the left transverse side, is also a show side. The courtyard portal makes its function eminently clear by its considerable size and the regularly alternating light-coloured marble and dark-grey limestone in the lintel, niche arch and gatehouse building as a whole, creating a striking zebra effect. A clearly legible building inscription has survived over the doorway. The entire complex is 282 ft. long and between 82 and 111 ft. wide. The walls are supported by thirteen towers of varying size attached to the walls. The towers at the side of the courtyard portal are slightly more than semicircular. The courtyard is more than twice as long as the hall, and more than 6 ft. wider on the N. side. At its centre it is 16 ft. wider still. The small, lavishly-decorated mosque is above the main portal, reached from the courtyard by a flight of steps. On the N. wall opposite are three smaller, closed rooms, then three

open arbours each with one bay and a closed room. After this come four arbours with vaults almost 30 ft. deep on two squat arches. Only the middle of the three vaulted rooms on the narrow side of the courtyard has an access door. The groin vaulting in brick in the left-hand corner is atypical. On the portal side of the courtyard are six shallow arbours with single vaults and three enclosed rooms. The hall portal is not unlike the entrance portal, but has additional ornamentation. Above it is a second building inscription, giving the name of the sultan, the founder and the building date, similarly to the main portal. The hall has a very narrow central aisle. Originally it had a high pointed vault running to the rear on six arches, but this has collapsed. The dome in the fourth bay is also no longer in evidence. Wall arches and decorated spandrels have survived. From the central aisle six low transverse aisles run to the side walls, supported on two pointed arches.

Sille (8 km. NW): This town is set in a fertile valley. There are remains of frescos in two old *cave churches*. This was an early Christian settlement and various generations of church buildings have been

Konya, Karatay Museum, wall tiles from Kubadabad

confirmed on the foundations of previous buildings. After a break of 400 years a new phase in church painting started with the first painting of the large, late-Byzantine *church of the Archangel* in 1708. Later stages of painting followed *c.*1830 and 1880. Byzantine wall painting fell from favour in the churches of Cappadocia (around Kayseri) and Lycaonia (around Konya) in the 13C, and a new start was not made until the early 18C, apparently under the influence of the baroque.

Halfway from Konya, some distance from the road, is the *rock monastery of St. Paul.*

Korykos

Mersin/İçel   p.574 □ K 6

The sites of Korykos, 85 km. SW of Mersin, are distributed over two areas. N. of the Mersin-Silifke coast road are, not far from the Kızkale Motel, the ruins of a necropolis and Byzantine ecclesiastical buildings.

S. of this road directly on the Mediterranean coast is the great land castle of Korykos with the island fortress of Kız Kalesi in front of it.

In ancient times Korykos was famous for the cultivation of saffron, and the present name probably comes from the Greek krokos, the word for saffron. Like Ayas (→ below), not far to the NE, decline set in in the 6&7C AD, when the frontier between the Byzantine and the Arabian empires ran only a few km. away on the River Lamos (now Lamas Çayi) and Korykos and the surrounding area were suddenly merely part of the fringe of the Byzantine empire.

Land castle (Korykos Kale): This fortress with its whitish-grey double walls with towers was probably built by the Armenian Rumenid kings in the 12C AD. In 1361 city and castle were in the hands of the Cypriot Lusignan, and the Emir of Karaman conquered the fortress in 1448.

Kız Kalesi (Maiden's Castle): This sea castle about 100 yards off shore, originally connected to the mainland by a causeway, was built by the Byzantine admiral Eustathios in 1104.

It is said to be named after a princess who

Korykos, land castle

grew up in hiding here because an oracle had predicted that she would die early from a snakebite. The prophecy was, however, fulfilled because a snake was brought to the island in a basket of fruit. After the fall of the land castle the Emir of Karaman also took the sea fortress, which became a notorious pirate base in the Middle Ages. Here Cem, the son of Mehmet II, hid from the persecution of his brother Beyazıt after his father's death in 1481, before finally having to flee to the island of Rhodes.

Necropolis: An extensive city of tombs is spread throughout the stony, overgrown site, in which rock tombs and remains of ancient sarcophagi can still be found among the ruins of early-Christian churches, mostly dating from the 6C. Five churches set strikingly close together were probably dedicated to early Christian martyrs.

Environs: Ayas (about 8 km. NE): Ayas, now on a spit in the Mediterranean, was in ancient times, when it was called *Elaissa*, set both on the mainland and an offshore island. This was the residence of Archelaos, made King of Cappadocia by Mark Antony in 41 BC, after Augustus also gave him parts of Cilicia in 20 BC. In AD 17 he was called to Rome by Tiberius to face a court of the Senate, and he finally died there. After the city fell to Antiochos IV of Commagene in AD 38, it became part of the Roman Empire, within the province of Cilicia, in AD 74. In 454, now known as *Sebaste*, it was represented by a bishop at the council of Chalcedon. The great basilica with nave and four aisles, still among the ruins on the former island, is generally held to be the first official church of this ecclesiastical dignitary.

The identification of Ayas with ancient Vilusa, mentioned in Hittite cuneiform texts in the Boğazköy/Hattusa clay tablet archives, is highly controversial.

Today the *ruins* are largely buried under sand dunes. On one slope it is possible to make out the indentation formerly occupied by the theatre, now missing its rows of stone seats. Isolated stretches of the former town walls have survived, and also sections of the aqueduct which once brought water to the settlement from Lamos, 10 km. away. The temple in the SW now appears as a gigantic heap of ruins consisting of collapsed ashlar blocks, column drums and capitals. The peripteros covered 108 x 57 ft., and had six columns on the narrow and twelve on the long side. There are two terraces of funerary buildings with sarcophagi.

Remarkable among the Byzantine remains in the former mainland part of the town is a 5C *church* which, when it was excavated in 1952, still had a mosaic with scenes of Paradise, now destroyed. The early 16C *Paşa türbe* (period of the Emirate) is a late form of the Seljuk türbe. It used to contain three sarcophagi, but these have disappeared. Access to the rectangular building in relatively crudely-cut ashlar with a pyramidal roof is via a carefully-crafted rectangular door niche. There is a crudely-cut inscription stone above the opening giving the date of the building, which is not quite clear (1505 or 1515).

The road between Ayas and Korykos, the Via Sacra, is lined with numerous *tombs*.

Kanlıdıvane (about 15 km. NE): 3 km. inland from the Mesin-Silifke coast road is ancient *Kanytelleis*, of which ruins of various buildings including 2 basilicas and a necropolis have survived.

Lamas Kalesi (about 20 km. NE): The remains of the *castle* are not far from the coast, directly S. of the mouth of the Lamas Çayi, the ancient Lamos, which in the 6&7C formed the border between the Byzantine and Arab empires.

Narlikuyu (about 6 km. SW): Narlikuyu—the modern name means Pomegranate Fountain—was formerly known as Talu Su. On a side road between the main Mersin-Silifke road and the sea, in an unassuming stone building (key in

Narlikuyu (Korykos), Roman 'Three Graces' mosaic ▷

Aisanoi (Kütahya), Temple of Jupiter

the nearby beach café) is a late-4C AD mosaic which used to decorate the floor of a Roman bath. It shows the Three Graces, with the central figure turning her back on the visitor and putting her arms round the other two at breast height. A Greek inscriptions says: 'Who drinks of this water will be wise and live long, the ugly will become beautiful'.

Another text names the governor of the island province of Poimenios as builder of the baths and discoverer of the spring which fed the pool.

These caves are about 3 km. inland from Narlikuyu. They consist of two karstic caves popularly known as Cennet ve Cehennem, (Heaven and Hell). Heaven *(Cennet Deresi)*, 218 yards long, 109 yards wide and about 65 ft. high, is the larger of the two, and may be visited. The climb down starts from the S. edge, where under a rocky vault there is a small 5C *church*

of *Mary*, of which only the outer walls without roof are still standing. An Armenian inscription has survived on the chapel lintel. In the semicircular apse, which has two sacristies, traces of painting can still be made out. The smaller cave above this can only be visited with mountaineering equipment, because of the overhang. It is called Hell *(Cehenem Deresi)* because the oxygen content is so low that deaths have occurred.

Susanoğlu (12 km. SW): The remains of ancient **Korasion**, near the modern village of Susanoğlu at the E. end of the delta of the Göksu (Blue Water), the ancient Kalykadnos, have still to be investigated. The site is promising however, as it was founded between AD 367&75 by Flavius Uranus, governor of Isauria, abandoned in the 7C and never built over. Thus it would be an example of a pure Christian-Byzantine town, unaffected by later settlement. It is possible to make out ruined churches, tombs, and large warehouses by the harbour, now silted up.

Yapilikaya and **Adamkayalar:** Leave the coast road at Korykos and strike NW in the direction of Hüseyinler. After about 7 km. on the good metalled road a signposted path goes off to the left to Adamkayalar, and a little further on is another one to Yapilikaya. In both cases a short climb—a local guide is an advantage— leads to a steep rocky valley with *tomb chambers* and splendid *rock reliefs* on the walls, showing individuals or couples standing or lying in niches.

Kütahya

Alexander the Great made his quarters in ancient **Kotaeon** on his march to Gordion. The Byzantines built a great castle on the acropolis hill, and after their defeat at Manzikert in 1071 the town was occupied by the victorious Seljuks, but they abandoned it to the army of the first Crusade. Byzantium lost Kütahya to the Germanioğlu c.1300, and they made it the capital of their emirate until 1428. The massive fortress was extended at this time; its ruins can still be seen on the acropolis. Timur-Leng (Tamerlane) chose Kütahya as his headquarters for a short period. Under Mehmet II the Conqueror (1451–81) the city finally became Ottoman. From 1514 Selim I forcibly resettled faience workers from the conquered lands of Azerbaijan in Kütahya and İznik. Since then the tile and pottery industry has flourished here, while that of İznik was transferred to İstanbul, thus deciding the 200 year rivalry in favour of Kütakya.

The faience factory which reached its peak in the 16C and decorated many Ottoman mosques now concentrates on ornamental plates and pottery in the old style. These goods are available in great quantities at all tourist centres. One of the workshops is open to show how the objects baked in white clay are painted. The original matt white, cobalt blue and green were complemented with an incomparable and mysterious tomato red. The old recipes are forgotten, and it is not difficult to distinguish the modern multicoloured wares from the clear and noble shades of the 15&16C.

Ulu Cami: Started before 1400 by Sultan Beyazıt I, continued by Mehmet Celebi on his father's behalf and completed by Mehmet II. It was later restored by Sinan itself.

İshak Fatih Camii: This is a mosque dating from 1434. Adjacent is the *medrese* of the same founder, built 6 years later, a well-known theological college.

Vahit Paşa Kütüphanesi: This is a library established in 1822 in an old mosque dating from 1440.

Vecidiye medrese: This is one of the oldest buildings in the town (1314) by Umur Bey Bin Savat, now a *museum*.

Environs: Aisanoi/Aesani: Aisonoi is reached by travelling 47 km. SW from Kütahya towards İzmir, then turning right in the direction of Emet. You cross the ancient Rhyndakos, spanned here by Roman bridges still used by local people. In the nearby village by Çavdar Hisar on a great masonry terrace is the magnificent *Temple of Jupiter* in the Ionic style, despite damage by the earthquake of 1970 still one of the best-preserved Roman buildings in Asia Minor.

Tavşanlı (50 km NW of Kütahya): The 12C *Kavaklik mosque* and some Roman *rock tombs* are worth seeing. About 18 km. NNE of Tavşanlı, on the other side of the Koca Çayyi, the ancient Ryndakos, in a side valley is a Phrygian rock monument known as **Dilikitaş** (also Delikitaş). This is ancient Phrygian rock façade architecture without the later pediment and columns influenced by the Greeks.

Labranda

Muğla   p.572□C 5

14 km. N. of Milâs is Labranda or Labraynda (from labrys = double axe). It was a central Carian cult site of Zeus Stratios, who was for a long time worshipped in the open air here. The shrine with its numerous buildings is spread over four terraces cut into the mountains and was connected with Mylasa (Milaş) from which it was governed, by a via sacra which has in part survived.

After lengthy conflict with the Persians, Mylasa and then finally Labranda were taken. 100 years later the satrap Mausolos (377–353 BC) and his brother Idrieus after him had the place rebuilt. Labranda's fame and influence grew. For a long time the Chrysorian League from Stratonikeia, a political centre of the Carians, tried to gain dominance over the shrine. On the other hand Labranda attempted to make itself independent of Mylasa. Hellenistic kings had to intervene repeatedly, and Philip V finally succeeded in restoring the old order for a long period. The via sacra, made of stone slabs 26 ft. long laid transversely, leads to the two *propylaeia*. Their foundations can be seen in the SE of the site, about 100 ft. apart. Between them are a small early-Christian *church* and an Ionic building (?treasury). The latter was incorporated in the adjacent baths by the Romans, and the fluting of the columns was smoothed off for reasons of fashion. Between the foundations of a shop and a house a flight of steps almost 40 ft. wide leads to the second terrace. About fifty yards further on are the remains of an *andron* (place of assembly for men) and behind this a *stoa*. A smaller flight of steps

Labranda, Temple of Zeus

to the E. leads to the next terrace. Opposite a somewhat heavy Roman *fountain house* has survived. W. of this is the ruined *andron* of Mausolos with extensions. Next to this a small flight of steps leading to a narrow intermediate terrace. Above the fountain house was another stoa. To the W. 2 narrow flights of steps led along the corridor and rooms of a large *shop building* (3C BC) which replaced the old one immediately to the E. (5C) and whose roof concluded with the level directly under the Temple of Zeus. *Main terrace:* In the W. is another *andron*, the only building rising to its full height. This was founded by Idreieus, and is almost the same in design as his brother's. They were used for meetings and cult purposes about which unfortunately no details are known. The design is that of an Ionic temple in antis with the two columns between the longitudinal walls, drawn forward to form the pronaos. A door led into the main room with high niche on the rear wall. A striking feature are the many lights, which could be closed with shutters (holes for hinges). The gneiss walls were clad in marble, at least on the façade, and this was decorated with a

unique set of ornaments, as can be worked out from the remains around it: columns and antes are lavishly decorated with capitals in the Ionic style, and above them is a smooth Doric architrave with royal dedicatory inscription, above this a metope frieze, framed with triglyphs and slabs decorated with drops. Sphinxes with beards were mounted at the corners. The adjacent *house* with two rooms for the priest was built at the same time. The brick dome was added later, and the building was used into the Christian period. The oldest version of the Temple of Zeus dated from the 5C BC, and was a simple building in antis with three shallow steps. It was extended in the 4C: an opisthodomos was added at the rear, a large ambulatory paved and 6 x 8 columns set up, forming a peripteros. The entabulature is pure Ionic: architrave in three layers, decorative band, denticulation. The cross cornice is simple, with a kyma (decorative strip) in the style of Lesbos, and a smooth upper gutter with lion head gargoyles. The entire temple was remarkably large, as it was built around the old one. At the N. extremity of the site are remains of a magnificent *stoa*, used for

Labranda, fountain house

numerous purposes. On the E. edge is a building of unknown function, probably the oldest stones in the shrine (*c.*600 BC). The exedra in front of it was added at a late stage. There is a striking *tomb* on the slope above the temple. Its entrance was closed with a slab weighing six tons. It contained two chambers one behind the other built of ashlar blocks almost 6 ft. thick with heavy vault with console, which contained five large sarcophagi. The upper storey is low, and roofed with stone slabs 13 ft. long. Further up the slope are remains of a *stadium*. At the top of the hill ruins of an *acropolis* which has so far not been investigated. In the SE part of the shrine, by a long wall, is an interesting two-storey building, called the washing hall. Seven monolithic granite columns form an open hall in the upper storey. An interpretation based on Aelian and Pliny is that it was a fish oracle, of the kind found in Lycia (→ Limyra).

Limyra

Antalya   p.572☐F 6

N. of Finike, E. of the large village of *Turunçova*, is the ancient Lycian metropolis of Limyra. The city extended from the edge of the fertile coastal plain, which begins here, to the acropolis at a height of almost 1,000 ft. on a foothill of the Tocak Dağ massif. According to Strabo the width of this plain must have doubled in about 2,000 years. Recent geomorphological research suggests that the alluvial strip has increased its breadth by almost 550 yards in the last 3,500 years.

History: It is not possible to imagine the size of the settlement found here by Harpagos when he conquered Lycia for Cyrus the Great *c.*545 BC. After Kimon had destroyed the Persian fleet at Aspendos for Athens in 469 BC, he later compelled the Lycian cities to join the Attic-Delian league. It is possible that a 'massive gateway' revealed by Professor

Borchardt in the 80s in the W. part of the lower town dates from the early 5C. We also owe to Borchhardt's research the knowledge of Perikles' rule in Limyra, later extended to the whole of Lycia as the king chosen by the Lycian princes. He acted as executor and co-ordinator of the interests of the highly independent cities and principalities. The defeat of Athens in the Peloponnesian War brought back the Persians as rulers of Lycia in 385. Perikles and the Lycian princes came to so skilful an accommodation with the Persian satraps that they limited their dependence to the payment of tribute and the making available of militray resources. King Perikles was the *de facto* satrap. He appears as a powerful ruler, held court in his palace, commissioned work from artists in the ancient world and presumably kept a naval and a commercial fleet in the harbour of Limyra, modern Finike.

The unbroken Ionian influence of past centuries was followed by a second 'Persian wave': a second period of high artistic activity in a mixed early Lycian-Ionian-Persian style starting *c.* 400 BC can be seen in the heroon and extended necropolises of Limyra. Purely religious portraits in the tradition of Greek coins were replaced by portraits of the ruler under Persian influence. Tissaphernes, Persian satrap in Lycia, was the first to break the divine coin privilege in 412 BC, and he was followed by Perikles. Greek influence on writing and language broke through in the late 4C at the latest, as is confirmed by inscriptions on tombs and coins. When the ambitious satrap Mausolos of Caria made emphatic claims to Lycia, Perikles organized effective resistance. His involvement in the failed satraps' revolt against the Persians in 366 caused his star to set. When Pixodares of Caria, brother of Mausolos, ruled briefly over Lycia as satrap in 358 BC, as recently proved by the

Limyra, Gaius Caesar cenotaph, with relief ▷

Trilingue of Letoon, Perikles had lost his power. The rule of the local dynasts came to an end,) and the democratic and co-operative tradition of the Lycian cities reached its height in the Lycian League, to which Limyra also belonged. The League was already in existence under Perikles, was fully active according to Strabo around the turn of the era, and remained so into the Imperial Roman period.

When Alexander's former general Ptolemy returned to conquer Limyra as king of Egypt, Perikles had probably lain for some decades in his temple tomb, which was visible over great distances. King Antiochos III of Syria, a Diadochos like Ptolemy, took Limyra and other territories from him in 197 BC. The grandson and adoptive son of the Emperor Augustus, Gaius Caesar, died in Limyra in the year AD 4, after a plot against him in Armenia. According to Pliny there was a spring oracle in Limyra, in which trout played the role of the prophetess. If they accepted food offered to them, the answer was positive. If they showed no interest, the news was bad. The ancient Limyros was clearly the river which rises from various sources below the road and then flows into the sea. An ideal place for a spring oracle. Olympic Zeus was particularly worshipped in Limyra, and games were held in his honour. Artemis and Apollo were the favoured gods elsewhere in Lycia.

Necropolises in Limyra: The first rock tombs were cut in the second half of the 6C BC, and are, in terms of their number, situation, multiplicity of type and the breadth of their decorative strips, unique in Lycia, and confirm the city's importance in the ancient world. It is advisable to hire an expert guide in the village of Yuvalilar.

Necropolis I is some distance away, beyond the Arykandos river. A large tomb house and about ten rock tombs with façades showing Persian influence suggest a border fortification. Necropolis II has about 170 rock tombs, and was probably the principal necropolis. It is about 450 yards NW of the Roman theatre, begins about 300 yards above the road, and extends for some distance between the spurs of rock. This is where most of the tomb reliefs and inscriptions are to be found. Necropolis III begins about 330

Limyra, King Perikles

yards E. of the theatre above the road, and IV is further E. of III.

Between the theatre and Necropolis III, still within the ancient, lowest castle wall, is the *tomb of Chäntabura*, who must have been close to King Perikles in rank or birth. In type it is a hyposorion sarcophagus (with a chamber in the hyposorion and a tomb space in the sarcophagus of the occupant of the tomb on a massive base above it), and its relief decoration shows a remarkable legend. The relief on the W. side shows three naked men. The excavators' interpretation leaves no doubt that this scene in far-away Lycia represents the classical Greek judgement of the dead. After particular errors of justice Zeus proclaimed that both the dead to be judged in the Underworld, portrayed here with their clothes in their hands, and also the judges, on the left Aiakos, who judged the dead of Europe, and on the right Rhadamanthys, who judged the dead of Asia, were to appear, stripped of confusing externals, naked for judgement.

Heroon: This *temple tomb* at a height of over 700 ft. is well worth the difficult climb. The mausoleum stands on a rock terrace over 4,000 sq. ft. in area on a base which already existed on the site. The lower grave chamber is 20 ft. wide, 30 ft. deep and 10 ft. high, and supported a temple of the amphiprostyle type with four caryatids instead of columns on the front and rear narrow sides. Two of the 8 ft. 6 ins. high, powerful female figures have remained on the site. The cella frieze blocks on the W. side have survived in good condition, and show the occupant of the tomb getting into his chariot, with a team of four horses which have only survived as fragments. Armed men follow on foot and on horseback. The heroon dates from the early 4C, and shows clear Greek and Persian influence, corroborated by the weapons and garments shown in the frieze. Perseus stood on the central acroterium, with the head of the Medusa in his hand, and the slain figure at his feet. Her lightly-clad sisters vainly pursue the triumphant Perseus as side acroteria (acroteria and reliefs in the museum in Antalya).

There is a ruined *Byzantine church* by the path to the upper castle. The well-preserved door and cyclopean walls,

Limyra, burial ground

parts of which have survived in good condition, are striking features.

S. of the Roman theatre, whose vaults the archaeologists use as a store, within the Roman walls, in good condition towards the road, is a cenotaph in honour of Gaius Caesar, who died here at the age of 24. E. of the middle arm of the Limyros is the *Byzantine town* within its own walls.

Environs: There is a *Roman bridge* in good condition on the direct route from Limyra to **Kumluca**.

Lüleburgaz

Kırklareli   p.564□C 1

This little Thracian town is between Edirne and İstanbul. The *Sokullu Mehmet Paşa Camii*, built in 1570 by Sinan, in the town centre is worth seeing; it was founded by Mehmet Paşa (1506–79). In the garden in front of the mosque are a *medrese* (1570) and the *türbe* of Zindan Baba, Gazi Evrenos Bey's standard bearer (14C) and a double bath (*Çifte Hamamı*).

Malatya

Malatya   p.576□O 4

Modern Malatya has only existed since about 1838, and so this provincial capital in the E. Taurus on the edge of the fertile Euphrates plain has essentially modern buildings, with no ancient monuments worth mentioning. However, older buildings have survived in the town's two predecessor settlements, first *Milid* (now Arslantepe), and later *Melitene* (now Eski Malatya). The following deals with their historical development in chronological order.

Arslantepe (7 km. NE): This was the oldest predecessor of Malatya, which appears in cuneiform texts as **Milid** as early as the 18C BC. C. Schaeffer's excavations in 1946 and 1948 on the mound, at the time topped by a ruined 16C Turkish palace, revealed that the site was occupied in the first half of the fourth millennium BC. Delaporte had uncovered strata from the period in which the settlement was most flourishing in 1932&3 and 1938&9: from the 11–9C BC this was the capital of the late- Hittite principality of Kammanu. A town wall with gates, a palace of the late-Hittite ruler that has now disappeared, and another palace built by the Assyrian king Sargon II (721–705) after conquering the city date from this period. The Assyrians had always been attracted by the region's rich metal deposits, and after the fall of the Hittite Empire (*c.*1200 BC), when a Hittite settlement (possibly called Šamuha) on the Arslantepe was destroyed, the Assyrian king Tiglatpileser I appeared for the first time to demand tribute. Tribute was also paid to Salmanassar III (859–824), in order to protect the city from violent invasion. With the rise of the Urartians (from 804 under Menua of Urartu) the town came into their sphere of influence on several occasions, interrupted by periods of political independence. When the Assyrian Tiglatpileser III (745–727) defeated the Urartians the old threat returned, and Sargon II finally conquered the town, deported the population and settled natives of the Persian Gulf here. At the same time he built the residence mentioned above. The end of the town came with destruction by the Cimmerians in the first half of the 7C BC. The relief blocks which had been placed in front of the late-Hittite town wall (11–9C) are still in the traditional Anatolian style, while a large statue of a king (late 8C BC) is strongly influenced by Italian court art. All the finds are now in the museum in Ankara.

Eski Malatya (12 km. NE): On the approach to the ruins, whose W. wall runs directly along the road to Sivas, are two small türbe surrounded by tombstones. The site itself, Roman **Melitene**, is surrounded by a trapezoid double wall with ditch in front of it. The E. wall, unlike the other three sides which are almost at right angle to each other, runs diagonally, and is additionally protected by the Dermes Su, which flows past it. The S. section of the wall is in the best condition, and the outline of the former polygonal and rectangular towers can be seen. This is also the entrance to the site, and just beyond it are the Ulu Cami on the right and on the left, diagonally behind a ruined palace, the *Adile Cami*. The latter was founded in 1373 by Hassan Ibn Abdullah, one of the Mameluke sultan Malik al Ashraf's officers. The *Ulu Cami* is now Seljuk (date 1247 over the W. gate with Hüsrev named as architect), but there was a mid-7C Arab predecessor destroyed by the Byzantine emperor Constantine V (751) and rebuilt by Al Mansur in 756. A rectangular courtyard within a rectangular area 115 x 164 ft. is surrounded by galleries on the N., E. and W. sides, has a deep iwan decorated with faience on the rear S. side, leading to the domed prayer room. The Mustafa Paşa Hanı in the NE corner of the town is badly damaged in places. It was built 1623–40 by the eponymous general of the Ottoman sultan Murat IV.

The town was founded when a Roman military camp for the XII Legion (Fulminata) was established N. of the ruins of Milid (Arslantepe), which had been destroyed by the Cimmerians, in AD 70. This small border fortress of Melitene was enlarged and additionally fortified in the 6C AD under Justinian, but despite this conquered by Persian Sassanids in 577. The Arab Habib ben Masalama, who took the place in 656, used it as a base for his campaigns. During the subsequent period

Malatya, landscape with view of Nemrut Dağı in Commagene

Manisa, Muradiye Camii

of Abbasid rule the town suffered from Byzantine attacks: the first raid in 751 led to its destruction, and it was rebuilt by Caliph Al-Mansur (754–775), then further plundered by Theophilus (829–842) in 837 and 841. From 934, when the ruined town was conquered by the Armenian John Kurkus, then rebuilt under emperor Nicephorus Phocas (963–969) and settled with Syrian Jacobites, it was firmly in Byzantine hands. After a brief Seljuk interregnum (from 1057) the emperor Constantine X Ducas (1059–1067) had the fortifications extended. The Armenian Philaretos, named governor of the region under the Byzantine emperor Romanus IV Diogenes (1076–1071), after the defeat of his overlords at Malazgirt, established an independent state with its centre in Maras and appointed city governors for Melitene, who had to negotiate a skilful course between Byzantium, the Crusaders and

the Turks. Finally it fell to the Turks, firstly the Danishmendids in 1103, then in 1178 to the Seljuks under Kiliç Arslan II. Despite encroachment by the Mongols (from 1243) the patriarch Mar Dionysos Angur was able to hold the city until 1257. In 1316 the Mamelukes took over from the Mongols, and they remained in power with interruptions by the Ottoman sultan Bayazıt I and the Mongol leader Timur-Leng (Tamerlane) in 1395, until 1515, when Sultan Selim I incorporated the region in his empire. When the Egyptian Mohammed Ali's army pitched camp here in the winter of 1838 the town was finally destroyed by the establishment of entrenchments, trenches and other defensive constructions. Today all that remains is a little village, but the houses are partially built from stones from the ruins of Melitene.

Malatya: The nucleus of the modern town is formed by summer residences built by the Ottomans, S. of the great Euphrates plain on the slopes of the Bey Daği, after conquering Melitene in 1515. This settlement was known as Aspuzu, and stood on a picturesque site between streams in a poplar grove. After Mohammed Ali extended Melitene as winter quarters for his troops the population were not allowed to return and had to stay in their summer residences. Even in 1840, when Mohammed Ali had achieved his aim of independence for Egypt from the Ottoman empire, and left Syria and SE Turkey, the former citizens of Melitene did not return, but remained in Aspuzu, which became modern Malatya. The only sight in this very young town is the Archaeological Museum, established in the municipal park in 1971 and housing exhibits from the New Stone Age to the Seljuk period.

Environs: Hekımhan (78 km. NNW): Not far from a mosque in this village on the E. road to Sivas, which runs through Sinanli and then follows the Kuru Çayı, is the *caravanserai* that gives the village its name. It was built in 1218 under the Seljuks and restored in 1660 under the Ottomans.

Şirzi (86 km. NNW): This village 8 km. N. of Hekımhan (see above for route) is reached via the road to Hasançelebi, which leaves Hekımhan in the W., but then soon turns N. and follows the course of the Kuru Çayı, which is to the left of the road, crossing the same railway line twice. After 7 km.,r. by a group of houses and a water tower, a narrow path branches off on the right to Şirzi (3 km. further). About 500 yards before the village and about 400 yards to the right is a rock with an inscription in Hittite hieroglyphics on a smoothed surface, known to the local people as 'Yazılıtaş'. The translation of the text is still disputed in some details, but it appears to be a mining inscription.

Manisa/Magnesia on Sipylos/Manisa Daği

Manisa   p.572☐C 4

The town is at the foot of the Sandık, foothills of the Manisa Daği, and looks back on a turbulent past. Manisa is said to have been founded by the Magnetes returning to Thessaly on their way back from the Trojan War (1190–1180 BC). It was later ruled by the kings of Lydia, the Achaemenids, Alexander the Great and the Seleucids. In 190 BC Antiochos III lost a decisive battle against the Roman legions here. The Romans handed the city over to the Pergamene Attalids. It flourished for a time under the name *Magnesiopolis*. It was rebuilt after an earthquake in AD 17 on the instigation of Tiberius.

Under the Byzantines Magnesia served as the residence of John III Ducas (1204–61) during the period of Latin rule in Constantinople, and became an important Byzantine citadel. Seljuk raids soon followed, and the city was conquered by Emir Saruhan in 1313, who gave the province the name which it kept until

Manisa, Işhak Çelebi Medrese, minaret

1927. The Ottoman Murat III made it his capital in the late 16C. Many monuments date from this period.

Archaeological and Ethnological Museum (E. of the Muradiye Camii): The museum is housed in the adjacent Muradiye medrese (1585) with imaret hans (public kitchens).

Çeşnegir Camii (in the market, Çarşı Mahallesi, 15th street): This was built in 1474, library on the left.

Hatuniye Camii (Hükümet Meydanı): This was built in 1490 for Şehinşah, son of Beyazıt II, for his mother Husnüşah, who founded the Kurşunlu han S. of the mosque.

Ivaz Paşa Camii (on the bank of the Çaybaşı river): The building dates from

1484, and has decoration, stained glass, wooden door and minbar.

Muradiye Camii: This is an important Ottoman mosque, built 1582–5 by Murat III.

Sultan (Mesir) Camii (İzmir Caddesi opposite the Muradiye): This was founded by Ayşe Hafza Hatun (d.1534), and built in 1522. The medrese is in front of the mosque. In the garden are a hamam (1540) and a darüşşifa (1535; hospital), now housing the Museum of Hygiene.

Ulu Cami: Built in 1366 by İshaq Bey, grandson of Saruhan, this is the oldest mosque in Manisa, situated on the Sandık hill below the Byzantine citadel. It affords a fine view of the town, and has a garden surrounded by columns and a şadırvan. To the right of the mosque is a *medrese* (1378), by the gate a short minaret with green, blue, yellow and violet ceramic tiles. Near the medrese are the *türbe* of İshak Çelebi and his wife Gülgün Hatun, and of two of their sons.

Other türbe: *Revak Sultan türbesi* (1371) in Dere Mahallesi; *Saruhan türbesi* (after 1348) in İzmir Caddesi; *Yedi Kızlar türbesi* (place of pilgrimage for Muslims and Christians since the 14C). Pieces of cloth from the dowry and bridal veil of girls and brides who died young are fastened to the coffins. Seven virgins are said to be buried here.

Environs: Cybele-Niobe relief (near Akpınar, 5 km. E. of Manisa): This is a steep mountain wall with weathered *relief* above a pool fed by a spring. There is said to be a Hittite inscription in the upper right-hand corner. The relief was identified as Niobe or Cybele even in ancient times.
Niobe rock (1 km. SW of the town in the direction of İzmir to the Çay Başı Mahallesi, on foor from there): This is a natural rock 65 ft. high at the entrance to the Ak-Baldır gorge. From a particular angle it is possible to see it as a weeping Niobe.

Manisa citadel (Manisa Kalesi): 3 km. S. of the town on the Sandık, 1,476 ft. (1 hour's climb). It is said to have been built by the Magnetes originally. According to legend Alexander the Great stored his treasure here. Later it was an internal Byzantine fortress of John II Ducas, (1254), and has been restored many times. A mosque was built in the interior of the fortress at the time of Mehmet II. The fortress walls have now fallen into disrepair.

Akhisar (52 km. NE of Manisa): Lydian foundation, called Thyatira in Macedonian, also Pelopia. It became a flourishing city under the patronage of the Roman emperor Caracalla. The early-Christian community is mentioned in Revelation. It has only been successfully excavated in recent years. The outstanding finds can be seen in the town centre.

Manyas Gölü/Lake Manyas

Balıkesir   p.564☐ CD 2

To reach Lake Manyas, turn off the Bandırma-Balıkesir road after about 16 km. Near the village of Sığırcık is a nature reserve with bird sanctuary *(Kuş Cenneti)*, in which are 250 kinds of bird, and also a *Bird Museum*. The bird sanctuary was established in 1938 by the German hydrologist and zoologist Professor Curt Cosswig.
Daskyleion (SE of Lake Manyas near Ergili): This town was founded in the early 7C BC by Daskylos, the father of the Lydian king Gyges. It was the seat of the satrap Pharnabazos *c*.400, who built a fortified palace between the lake and the city. Of this rare Persian-Greek foundations have survived by being incorporated later in the Hellenistic wall. Tomb reliefs for Persians carved by Greeks were also found here (İstanbul museum), and hundreds of imprints from Persian stone seals (Ankara museum).

Maraş/Kahramanmaraş

Maraş   p.576 □ M 5

At the foot of the Ahir Dağı (8,179 ft.), foothills of the Antitaurus, is Maraş, capital of the province of the same name, dominated by its citadel. It appears in Assyrian texts as *Markasi*, then capital of the late-Hittite kingdom of Gurkum, which flourished under the independent king Halparundaş c.800 BC. Tribute had to be paid to the Assyrian king Salmanassar V (727–721), and his successor Sargon II (721–705) finally took the town and destroyed it.

It is probable that this was the site of Roman Germaniceia in the 1C AD, extended in the Byzantine period as a fortress which constantly changed hands between Byzantines and Arabs. It was destroyed after being conquered by the Arabs in 637 and rebuilt under Harun al-Rashid, and after being reconquered by Nicephorus Phocas (962) it remained a Byzantine possession for about 100 years and increased significantly in population on the arrival of Armenians fleeing from E. Anatolia before the Seljuks. One of these Armenians, Philaretes, established as town governor of Maraş under Emperor Romanus IV Diogenes, succeeded, with the support of an army of Frankish mercenaries, in founding an independent empire here against the Muslims after the defeat of the Byzantines. It also included Malatya, Edessa and Antakya. After Philaretes' death the Seljuks took Maraş, but it was reconquered by Crusaders in 1097, who handed it over to Byzantium, then under Alexius I Comnenus. In 1104 it passed to the county of Edessa, in 1152 it was taken by Nur ed-Din, who passed it on to the Armenian prince Mlech. Maraş remained within the Armenian Cilician kingdom until Hetum II lost it to the Mamelukes, who held it despite Mongol raids. It was conquered by the Ottoman sultan Selim I in 1515&16. From 1832–40 the area was ruled by Egypt, and Maraş was administered by İbrahim Paşa,

the son of Mohammed Ali. After the First World War the region was occupied first by the English, then the French. Because of the embittered resistance which the people of Maraş showed the foreign European powers from 1918–20 the prefix Karaman (hero) was added to the town's name.

Worth seeing: *Citadel*, originally Byzantine, but with considerable Ottoman rebuilding. Sections are now laid out as a park. It also includes the **Archaeological Museum** with finds from the immediate area. The *Ulu Cami, Hatuniye Camii* and *Taş medrese* date from the late 15–early 16C. The covered *bazaar* was redesigned in the 17C.

Mardin

Mardin   p.578 □ Q 5

There is a fine view of the Syrian plain from this provincial capital, picturesquely perched on a mountain slope. Even in the Roman period Mardin, then called *Marida*, was overshadowed by the nearby centres of Amida (now Diyarbakır) and Nisibis (now Nusaybin).

The old Assyrian empire, which had the area around Mardin under its control in the second half of the 18C BC under its king Shamshi-Adad I (a fragment of a victory stele, apparently from Mardin, now in the Louvre in Paris, is attributed to this ruler) became a vassal state of the Mitanni empire c.1450 BC, and did not achieve independence again until a few decades later (middle and new Assyrian empires).

The Islamic period began in Mardin in AD 640 with the Omayids, who were replaced by the Abbasids in the 8C. The Shiite Hamdanids (from 843) were followed in 990 by the Sunni Merwanids, a local Kurdish dynasty, and by the Seljuks in 1096. The Turkoman Ortokids ruled from 1108, resisted sieges, often lasting for several years, by the Kurds in

1183, 1193 and 1202, but were defeated by the Mongol storm: the town was taken 1259&60, after a blockade of six months. Mardin was conquered a second time by a Mongol army under Timur-Leng (Tamerlane) in 1394. A revolt by his brother, whom he had appointed governor, caused Timur-Leng to reappear in 1401. In 1408 Mardin passed to the Karakoyunlu (Black Sheep), when the ruler at the time, Sultan Salih, swapped the town for Mosul. The Akkoyunlu (White Sheep), in power from 1431, were replaced by Persian Safawids under Shah Ismail in 1508, and they yielded to the Ottomans under Sultan Selim Yavuz in 1516. Mohammed Ali of Egypt, trying to free his country of the Ottomans, supported strivings for independence by the Kurds of Mardin, who risked their first revolt in 1832. A second Kurdish uprising in 1840 was preceded by a short occupation of the city by Mohammed Ali himself.

Citadel: The fortress was so large that the whole population could shelter here in case of danger. It now houses an American military base whose white radar domes can be seen for miles. For this reason parts of the complex are not open to the public. Here, at the summit of the hill, was a citadel at least from Roman times, which was constantly rebuilt and extended up to the time of the Akkoyunlu (15C). The steep climb may be started at the Sultan İsa medrese. The entrance gate has two lion reliefs.

Archaeological Museum: In a former Koran school not far to the left above the Sultan İsa medrese archaeological finds from the area and a small ethnographic collection are exhibited. The most important exhibit is a unique *fruit stand* (a modern coinage by archaeologists for broad ceramic bowls with a decorated foot or stem). It was found in the course of excavations which have been in progress since 1982 in Girnavaz near Nusaybin. The large artefact has two handles on the upper outer edge, and between these two ox heads in terracotta relief. Five more three-dimensional faces are to be found at the point of transition from the bowl to the foot, which is crafted in openwork. Above the row of faces is a frieze with geometrical patterns and stylized animals.

Mardin, town hill

Ulu Cami: This courtyard mosque, only 200 yards from the main square (Cumhuriyet Meydanı) was built in the 11C under the Ortokids. In its present form, as an inscription on the base of the minaret announces, it dates from 1176 (under Kubt et-Tin). It was badly damaged in the Kurdish revolt of 1832, and rebuilt on the old model.

Sultan İsa medrese *(İsa Bey medrese):* The most striking feature of this complex consisting of two-storey Koran school and domed mosque with two courtyards, set in the E. part of the town, is the lavishly decorated *entrance portal,* with an inscription naming the year 1385.

Latifiye Camii: This house of prayer with a remarkable *portal* directly on the main E.–W. road dates from 1371. The minaret was not added until 1845, however.

Sultan Kasim medrese *(Kasim Bey medrese):* Like the Sultan İsa medrese, this Koran school in the W. of the town has two storeys and an adjacent domed mosque.

Bishop's Palace: This is the residence of one of the Metropolitans of the Syrian Orthodox Church, which separated from the Byzantine imperial church after the Council of Chalcedon in 451 (rejection of Monophysitism, according to which Christ's nature was only divine, never human). Their first great theological teacher was Jacob Baradair, after whom this religious group were also known as Jacobites.

Also worth seeing: *Reyhaniye Camii;* Şehidye Camii (13C, but heavily restored)); *Babusor Camii* (14C) on the edge of the town, and not far from this on the other side of the road the *Sultan Hamza türbesi.*

Environs: Deir az-Zafaran (Turkish: Deyrulzaferan; 7 km. E.): This monastery dedicated to Ananias, reached via the road to Akıncı, is one of the best-preserved complexes of its kind around Tur Abdin (→ Midyat and environs). The drive up to the fortress-like, walled monastery, which is still occupied, and houses a Jacobite boarding school, affords a fine view of the hilly town of Mardin. In the

Mardin, Sultan İsa Medrese (left), ornamental portal inscription on medrese (right)

monastery, in which the patriarch of the Jacobite church has resided, with interruptions, since 1160 (the first was driven out of Antioch), there are three churches next to each other at the rear of the courtyard with its pointed arches: the *church of Mary* probably dates from the 6C; the adjacent *church of Ananias*, founded by Anastasius I (490–518), is a rectangular building with pyramidal roof; the bell tower was added later. In the *funerary chapel* the mortal remains of the Jacobite patriarchs are kept in rectangular niches in the walls.

Girmeli (about 105 km. SE): It is possible to reach the *monastery town* of **Mar Augen** on foot from this village; it is about 6 km. away. About 3 km. E. of Mar Augen is the **Mar Yohanna monastery**. The ruins of Mar Augen are spread over a hillside. In the Middle Ages they housed several hundred monks. Until 1505 the Nestorians had their seat here, followed by the Jacobites.

Istilil (92 km. SE): This is now an insignificant village on the W. link road between Nusaybin and Midyat (→ below for route to Nusaybin, then 17 km. NW), but it is on the site of the strategically

Deir az-Zafaran (Mardin), evangeliary

important town of *Dara*, in Byzantine times still called *Anastasiopolis* after its founder Anastasius, who established a border fortress against the Persian Sassanids here. Despite extension by Justinian (mid-6C AD) it was conquered by the Muslims in the 7C, and soon fell into decline.

Kızıl Tepe (*Koç Hisar*, also *Dunaysir*; 20 km. SW): This place on the road to Viranşehir and Urfa was formerly an important staging post on the trade route from Antakya and Adana to Mosul and Persia. The 13C *Ulu Cami* with fine portal and mihrab gives an idea of Kızıl Tepe's former splendour.

Nusaybin (*Nisibis*; 83 km. SE): This town on the river Djadja is an important frontier post with Syria, corresponding with Qamichliye across the border. *Nasibina* was mentioned in Assyrian texts at the beginning of the first millennium BC. It is now no longer assumed that the present town is built over its predecessor, but that it was 5 km. upstream in *Girnavaz*, where there is a settlement mound. Here, at the intersection of two ancient trade routes, excavations under H. Erkanal, in train since 1982, have revealed that the site was occupied in the early dynastic period (beginning of the 3rd millennium BC), and continuously from then onwards. It is hoped that the three tablets with cuneiform script discovered in 1984 and 1986, and another specimen which has been bought, will provide further insight into the site, to which attention was first drawn by the fact that local people offered to sell ceramics which they had found (Nineveh V ware: beginning of the early dynastic period) to the museum in Mardin. From the 3C BC Nusaybin was capital of the Parthian province of Antiochia Mygdoniae, and hotly disputed between Parthians and Romans. It was conquered by Lucullus in 68 BC, but the Romans lost the town again after Crassus' defeat at Carrhae in 53 BC. It was not until AD 115 that it became part of the Roman Empire again, under Trajan. It was capital of the Roman province of Mesopotamia from

195. The Sassanids, who replaced the Parthians in Persia, were concerned to take Nisibis, but, with the exception of an interregnum by Shahpur, ended by the Emperor Diocletian, the sieges of 338, 346 and 350 were ineffective. However, after signing a peace treaty with the Sassanids, the Emperor Jovian had to give up the town, whose Christian population had to be evacuated to Amida (now Diyarbakır, q.v.) within three days. Despite this, a Christian community under Sassanid protection again came into being here, but only because its members were of the Nestorian persuasion (central tenet: Mary is not the Mother of God, but simply the mother of Christ the human being), which was opposed to that of the official Byzantine church, which since the Council of Ephesus (431) had insisted that Mary was the Mother of God. In 640 the town fell to the Arabs, in 1260 it was completely destroyed in Mongol raids under Hulagu, and in 1515 it finally became part of the Ottoman empire.

The *Archaeological Museum* and the *church of Mar Jacub* are of interest. The latter is a 4C square building with pyramidal roof, rear apse and narthex with two aisles. It

was enlarged in 759, and contains a crypt with sarcophagus. It was restored in 1872.
Viranşehir (101 km. W.): As its name suggests (Ruined Town), the once important ancient town of *Constantina*, which used to be here, only survives as sparse ruins. The most impressive feature is the rectangular *town wall* in basalt ashlar, which once enclosed an area of 546 by 656 yards. It was built under the emperors of Western Rome, and rebuilt in the 6C under Justinian.

Mersin

İçel   p.574☐K 6

The capital of the province of İçel is 70 km. W. of Adana in a broad Mediterranean gulf. It has been deliberately extended since 1954, and is now the third-largest harbour in Turkey.

Eski Cami (old mosque): This foundation by Sultan Bezmi Alem was built in 1870, but has since been restored.

Yeni Cami (new mosque): This house of

Deir az-Zafaran (Mardin), monastery

prayer by the Gümrük park was built in 1900 by Abdül Kadir Saydani.

Environs: Karaduvar: There are ruined Roman *thermal baths* with mosaics in this place not far to the E. of the town.

Viranşehir: As a result of Mersin's rapid expansion the site is now on the E. edge of the town. Settlers from Rhodes founded a trading post here in the 7C BC. Shortly after this Attic colonizers took over the place, as the site was so favourable, and it was called **Soloi** from then onwards. In 91 BC the settlement was conquered by the Armenian king Tigranes, who deported the population. This stretch of the coast soon developed into a nest of pirates, defeated by Pompey in 64 BC, and the town was rechristened *Pompeiopolis* in his honour, and prisoners-of-war were settled here. There are sparse remains of the harbour mole, but the most impressive feature is the ruined 1C BC *colonnade*. These columns with Corinthian capitals are the remains of a via sacra formerly almost 500 yards long and leading to the harbour. It was once lined with about 200 columns.

Yümüktepe settlement mound (3 km. N.): This was excavated by the British architect J.Garstang from 1937–40 and 1946–9. The 33 strata discovered go back to the New Stone Age. At that time a characteristic greyish-black shiny ceramic ware with white incrustations was made here, and known as Mersin ware. Despite strong fortifications with casemates built in the Chalcolithic period the city was destroyed in the early Bronze Age, and replaced by Tarsus as the new centre of Cilicia. The town was fortified again under the Hittites. No evidence of this has survived.

Midas, Şehri

Midas Şehri is 25 km. SE of Seyitgazi in the direction of Kırka, near the village of

Yazılıkaya (Rock with Writing). The town is associated with Gordion (→ there for history). The landscape is characteristically Phrygian. Rock formations rise directly from gently rolling plains and valleys. Their shapes are often so fantastic that they seem as though they are man-made. It is easy to understand how the Phrygians, with their taste for mysticism and ecstatic cults, were magically attracted to them. Midas Şehri is in the middle of the high plain between Gordion, Eskişehir, Kütahya and Afyon, a popular area for Syrian settlement. Most of the great rock monuments, so common in the region, are cult sites. With the exception of a few monumental rock chamber tombs with relief façades, like the Phrygian Lion Tomb of Arslantaş or the Buffalo Tomb in Kümbet, the dead of this region were buried in rock chamber tombs or cave tombs which generally speaking had plain façades. There are no tumuli like those of Gordion. The massive Midas Şehri plateau has steep sides surrounded by cult façades, some of them very large, rock tunnels, deep caves with steep steps, cult niches and rock tombs.

So-called **Midas tomb:** This dates from the 8C BC, and is in the NW of the cliff below the plateau. It is an impressive cult façade 52 ft. wide and 56 ft. high. The shallow relief with meander patterns and an ornamental pediment is carved in the smooth, vertical tufa wall. The opening above ground level in the middle is not the tomb of Midas, as was long supposed, but a cult cave for the great mother goddess Cybele, the personification of fertility. The inscription strips on the façade are in the Phrygian alphabet, and use one of the goddess's other names: Mida, also the mother goddess of the dynasty.

Midas Town: This consisted of an upper town high on the plateau, 875 yards long and 440 yards at its widest point, and a

Viranşehir (Mardin), row of columns

Midas Şehri, cult throne

lower town to the N., at the foot of the
acropolis. Impressive fragments of the
massive *fortifying wall* with defensive
towers that surrounded the acropolis have
survived. In the E. a flight of steps leads
to the acropolis, and a ramp rises to it a
little further to the S. This area has several
altars with inscriptions, and tombs with
and without rock reliefs. In the SW of the
acropolis is the finest example of a 'step
altar' or rock throne, on which the figure
of the god was placed. A walk round the
edge of the plateau gives an impression of
the surviving buildings. A route starting
from the so-called tomb of Midas at the
foot of the hill and proceeding W. passes
interesting *cult rooms*, cave steps and
tombs, and arrives at the incomplete
monumental *rock relief* on the W. side of
the hill: Küçük Yasılıkaia.

Environs: Arslan Kaya: This is reached

via Işhaniye (N. of Afyon) and *Döger*,
where there is an interesting *caravanserai*.
Turn right at right angles out of the town
again, and keep right at points where the
road forks. Well outside the town on the
right among the rocks is an imposing
shrine of Cybele with cult niche on 5 steps,
which has been damaged by thieves using
dynamite. About 3 km. from Döger on the
right is the most imposing of all the
Phrygian cult monuments: Arslan Kaya,
the Lion Rock. It consists of an isolated,
gigantic tufa monolith with a strange
Phrygian 'pointed cap', flanked by other
bizarre rock figures. A cult relief with
pediment occupies the smooth façade to
a height of over 30 ft., of a kind familiar
from Midas Şehri. It covers the full width
of the monolith. A large rectangular gate
niche with stone jambs contains Mother
Cybele flanked by two larger-than-life
lions holding their paws protectively over

Yirlantaş (Midas Şehri), chamber tomb

her. There are two sphinx reliefs in the tympanum of the pediment, which is divided into two. The façade faces E. On the N. and S. sides are two lions rampant, as high as the top of the pediment.

Ayazin (21 km. beyond Bahşiş/Gökbahçe turn left before the petrol station in the direction of Afyon): There is a *cave church* in remarkable condition and a beautiful setting in the tufa rocks on the left just before the village. Inside is a very large early-Christian church with crossing dome completely carved out of the rock. It has transepts of equal length, tunnel vaulting and an apse that protrudes outside, a high central dome, rows of columns and finally a baptismal chapel extending deep into the rock. Windows and roofs, many individual decorative details, ornamentation and architectural elements are all carved out of the stone. There are other caves, some simple, but others with lavishly decorated

façades and skilfully carved domes.

Bahşiş (*Gökbahce Köyu*; 9 km. beyond Kümbet in the direction of Afyon): Here, as everywhere in the district, one finds friendly Karachai Caucasians who were settled here in the 19C. Behind the school, set very high on the right of the gorge, is a fine Phrygian *cult memorial* on the rock face. After returning to the metalled road, turn right by an old well after 15 km. in the direction of Afyon. After 2 km. comes **Arslantaş**, an enormous *chamber tomb* 34 ft. high and almost 20 ft. wide, guarded by two large rampant lions. About 50 yards away is **Yirlantaş**, also a rock chamber, from which a gigantic lion relief has fallen. Nearby are rock chambers with columns, and a precisely crafted room just under 10 by just over 13 ft, with a pediment. A field path leads after a further km. straight ahead to the 8C BC Mal Taş, a façade monument comparable with the

Midas Şehri, so-called Midas tomb

Ayazin (Midas Şehri), rock church

so-called Midas Tomb, with similar meander ornaments and pediment decoration. Half of the façade is below ground level.

Gerdek Kaya: Between Seyitgazi and Midas Şeri just by the village of Çukurça is a large 'classical' *rock tomb* in the form of a temple with columns and pediment carved out of the rock. There are numerous cave tombs nearby. 1 km. beyond the village in the direction of Midas Şeri on the right is the *Arezastis cult façade*, 26 ft. high, and high on the rock, with pediment and inscription strips. There are rectangular ornaments in the right- and left-hand sections of the pediment. The acroterium is in good condition.

Kümbet (between Midas Şeri and Kırka): In Kümbet is the so-called *tomb of Solon*, a Roman rock chamber tomb with pediment relief: two lions before an urn,

within the pediment with relief denticulation two small animals and a shield. Near the minaret are two *cult sites*, the more interesting of which, the 'rock throne' with pointed baldacchino, is lower, hidden behind the other one. Opposite is a Seljuk *polygonal türbe* with spoils, of which there are a lot in this beautifully sited village.

Kybele Kapıkaia: The best route to this site is via ücler Kayasi Köyü, which is reached a few km. before Döger. Charming Phrygian *cult memorial* in open countryside: there is a life-size figure of Cybele in a niche, and the rock surface, 20 ft. wide and 6 ft. 6 ins. high, to the right and left is covered with meander reliefs. Here the goddess very strikingly symbolizes the view the Phrygians had of her: she appears to man from the woods and mountains in which she lives by stepping out of the rock.

Midyat

Mardin   p.578☐R 5

This small town 68 km. NE of Mardin
is largely known for its hand-crafted
silverware (telkari). Even today the
population is still predominantly
Christian, and the town is the seat of a
Jacobite metropolitan. Since its recent
restoration the old church of Mar
Philoxenos has been called *Mar Aznoyo*.
Apart from this there is little of interest
to be seen. It is, however, the best base
for visits to the churches and monasteries
of the **Tur Abdin** (Mountain of the
Servant of God), most of which are a
greater or lesser distance from the track
leading to Kerburan (48 km. E.). The
track branches off the road to Hasankeyf
7 km. N. of Midyat.
The district known as Tur Abdin is a
karstic high plateau (2,900–4,500 ft.),
enclosed by a bend in the Tigris to the N.
and E. and extending to the Syrian border
in the S. The Byzantines, hoping to secure
their border in this way, insisted that W.
Syrian Christians settle here from the 5C.
At the peak of its powers, in the Middle
Ages, the area had over 80 monasteries,
organized   in   four   bishoprics.
Depopulation was caused by the
encroachment of the Crusaders, and later
by the Mongols. The death blow to this
Christian centre was, however, not struck
until after the First World War, when
anything reminiscent of the hated French
occupation, including Christianity as the
religion of the occupying nation, was
systematically persecuted and eradicated.
The Syrian Orthodox Christians were
driven out, but since then their numbers
have climbed back to about 20,000. Only
six monasteries are still active. The

religious head of this faith, which denies Mary's status as Mother of God, has his seat in Deir az-Safaran, near Mardin (q.v.). These Syrian Orthodox Christians are also known as Jacobites, after their first ecclesiastical teacher, Jacob Baradaeus. The dispute as to whether Christ had simultaneous divine and human nature, or was only God and never really man, was decided by the Byzantine church at the Council of Chalcedon in 451 in favour of Christ's dual nature. Those who only acknowledged one nature for Christ, the divine, split away as Monophysites. In contrast with the Byzantine emperor Justinian (527–565), who had to put forward the offical line, his wife Theodora supported the Monphysites, and so did the above-mentioned Jacob who, covered with a horse blanket (hence his name Baradaeus or Baradai = the felt one) conducted missions promoting Monophysite beliefs in N. Syria.

Environs: Arnas (15 km. E.): Not far from this village, which is 15 km. down the track leading to Kerburan, is the *monastery of Mar Kyriakos*. The W. façade of the church, which was restored in the 19C, has three windows, and a courtyard with galleries on the S. side. The choir screens in the interior date from the 8C.
Hasankeyf (*Hisn Kayfa*; 44 km. N.): Hasankeyf, which dominates a narrow stretch of the Tigris, was founded in the Roman period as a border post against the Persians. Ancient *Cephe* or *Kiphas*, an important bishopric in the Byzantine period, was conquered by the Arabs in AD 640 and renamed Hisn Kayfa. Then the city was ruled by Ortokids and Aijubids, and did not recover from plundering by the Mongols in 1260. Four arches of the old *Tigris bridge* have survived. It is not known when the bridge was built, but it was mentioned in the early 12C AD, and restored by the Ortokid Fahr ed-Din Kara Arslan in 1116.
The river narrows are dominated by the *citadel*, which contains the ruins of the 12C Ortokid palace. The steep climb to

the fortress passes three gatehouses. The ruins of three old mosques can be seen in the town. The most appealing building is the *Zeynel Bey Türbesi* (15C), a cylindrical mausoleum in alternating natural and blue-glazed brick arranged in a herring-bone pattern. The base of has been unsuitably restored with large limestone blocks, and the türbe is topped with an onion dome.
Kartmen (*Qartamin*, also *Deir el Omar*; 30 km. ESE): 5 km. NE of the village is the *Mar Gabriel monastery*, probably the most interesting of the Christian sites in Tur Abdin. It is reached via the road to the border town of Cizre. The Turkish government has recently built 3 km. of road branching off 25 km. beyond Midyat and running NE; this makes the approach considerably easier. The monastery is still active. It was founded in the 5C by a monk called Samuel, but its present name comes from a later Bishop Gabriel (593–677), who is said to have raised the dead. In the early 6C the place was so famous that the Byzantine emperor Anastasius I (491–518) founded a new monastery church in the year 512. The complex is now entered from the S., and the *church of Gabriel* (formerly church of Anastasius) is on the left. Its narthex, once part of a cloister, and nave are set transversely, the rear central apse is flanked by two rooms of equal size, and still has some remains of mosaics. On the W. edge of the monastery is the *church of Mary* with nave and two aisles, which is entered from the side. The NW section of the monastery no longer exists; this was the site of a *church of Simeon*. The complex also includes some *tombs* such as that of the Egyptian monks, which is set somewhat to the side, and the tomb of the 40 martyrs. The most important of these is the domed building on the N. side of the courtyard (rectangular outside, octagonal with 8 wall niches in the interior), said to have been founded by the Empress Theodora herself (see above).
Kefr Zek (about 25 km. E.): Not far from the village is the monastery church of *Mar*

Azaziel, in design very similar to the near-by *Mar Kyriakos* near Arnas (q.v.). A special feature here is the iconostasis with four acanthus capitals on small columns supporting an architrave.

Khakh/Chach (Hah; about 60 km. E.): In order to visit the *church of Mary* (**El Hadra**) in this village, take the road to Kerburan (48 km.) then proceed SW. The church is striking decorated with arcatures on the outside walls, and the nave (with large central and flanking side domes) is set transversely, and the apse is in the centre of the rear broad side. The reliefs on the door from the narthex to the nave are striking (*c.*700). The church of *Mar Sovo* in the village has survived only as a ruin.

Salah (about 20 km. E.): Salah is reached by walking N. for about 3 km. from a point 13 km. from the beginning of the road to Kerburan. The *monastery church* of *Mar Yakub* is worth a visit. It is a single-aisled building with three-aisled sanctuary dating from the 14C. The vaulted narthex is to the N. At the side of the entrance portal are figurative (birds) and ornamental (tendrils) reliefs.

Milâs/Mylasa

Muğla   p.572☐ C 5

Milâs, ancient *Mylasa,* is in Caria, a district ruled by Leleges, Carians and Dorians who had immigrated. In the 6C BC the sovereignty of the Persian Achaemenids extended as far as Mylasa. Herodotus mentions the tyrant Oliatos as ruler of Caria, with Mylasa as its capital. Mausolos was born here in the 4C BC. It was the seat of a bishop in the Byzantine period, and in the 13C capital of the principality of Menteşe, then Ottoman. Mosques from this period are the Ulu Cami, Orhan Bey Camii and Gök (Firuz Paşa) Camii (1397). In 1943 Milâs was accidentally bombed by the English.

All that remains of the numerous temples for which Mylasa was famous is a single *column* on the E. slope of the Hisabaşı hill in the centre of the town. It is Corinthian, with a podium almost 11 ft. high.

Baltalı Kapı (Gate of the Double Axe): N. of the town among the remains of a wall (aqueduct?). Round-arched marble gate, with a double axe (balta) over the arch on the outside.

Gümüşkesen: This is a well-preserved mausoleum in the Gümüşlük district on the W. edge of Milâs, similar to the famous Mausoleum in Bodrum. It has two storeys, an ashlar base, and grave chamber, with the entrance offset to the N. on the W. side. The upper storey is surrounded by an open colonnade with square piers at the corners, and between these on each side two fluted oval columns in the Corinthian style. The roof is pyramidal. The architrave has geometrical and plant decoration, and formerly was painted.

Rock tomb: Opposite the *Beçinkale* (ancient acropolis?, citadel of the Turkish Menteşe emirs) S. of the town is a rock tomb, cut halfway up the cliff. It is in the form of a Doric temple in antis with false

Milâs, ancient town gate

door; the entrance beneath it leads to two rooms. Local people call this tomb *Berber Ini* or *Berber Yatağı*.

Environs: Stratonikeia (now the village of **Eskihisar**, in the Muğla region, 35 km. E.): Remains of the *town wall*, a *gate* and a *Corinthian column* have survived inside the gatehouse. In the village of *Eskihisar*, which was the centre of the old town, is the so-called *Serapeum*, the Temple of Serapis (2–3C BC), with ashlar walls, garden inside. The N. wall is completely covered with Greek and Latin inscriptions, particularly on the outside. There is a gate with posts and threshold in the W. W. of the temple precinct is the *agora*, which just has marble blocks to mark the edges of the alleyways. On the N. slope of the acropolis hill is a *theatre* which has survived in good condition. The cavea is divided into nine segments by flights of steps; the horizontal passages have not survived. The theatre seated 10,000 spectators. The foundations of the stage building have survived in good condition. Above the theatre are the ruins of a small Ionic *temple*, dedicated to the cult of the Emperor with a Latin inscription. Finds

are exhibited in a small *museum* by the school on the edge of the village.

Miletos

Aydın   p.572☐C 5

Miletos and not Athens would have become the spiritual and economic centre of Greece, were it not for the fact that the city was completely destroyed in the Persian Wars in 494 BC. The site is now 10 km. from the sea, as the Meander, known to Herodotus as 'the worker', pushes the coastline into the sea at a rate of about 20 ft. per year. Miletos was the largest Greek city in W. Asia Minor (80-100,000 inhabitants), and the port had four separate harbours, and was the largest centre of W.–E. and N.–S. trade. At the same time the city had a unique combination of money and intellect, expansive commercial spirit and a cast of mind as speculative at it was empirical. The city affected the world in the following ways: *1. Scientific and philosophical:* Miletos was the home of Thales (625–545 BC), Anaximander (611–545 BC) and

Miletos view of theatre

Anaximenes (585–525 BC), the pre-Socratic philosophers. It was thus the birthplace of Greek occidental philosophy, and also science, particularly natural science. In Miletos the human mind detached itself from myth and the world of the gods and sought measurable reality and causal links. 'The gods died in Miletos. The Europeans discovered reality in Asiatic Miletos.' These are the words of the German writer G.Nebel. This science based on reality, and a generally realistic view of the world also included history, which started in Miletos with Hekataios, who published his 'Histories' in 502 BC with the introductory sentence: 'I am writing this as it appears true to me, as the narratives of the Hellenes are manifold and foolish, as I see it.' Hekataios was also associated with a third science based on reality which started in Miletos, namely geography. In his 'Journey Round the World' Hekataios attempted a description of the areas in which he had himself travelled between the Pillars of Hercules and India.

2. Cultural in the broadest sense: Miletos was the centre of the Greek colonial movement from 750–550 BC, with 90 colonies of its own, largely around the Black Sea, but with trade links extending as far as Russia (precious metals from the Urals, furs, wool, cereals and slaves were traded for Milesian products). Miletos became a centre of culture as well as trade and civilization: the Greeks' acquisition of the Phoenician alphabet took place via Miletos, as did the use of Lydian currency.

3. Political: In 500 BC Miletos initiated the uprising of the Ionian Greeks against the Persians with the raid on the lower town of Sardes. The Persian Wars ended not far from Miletos with the destruction of the Persian Fleet off Cape Mycale in 479 BC. The following points suggest that the core of the population consisted of unscrupulous men of action:

- the foundation myth (when Neleus, the son of the King of Athens, Kodros, arrived in the area of Miletos, already populated with Cretans and Carians, with his all-male group of settlers he had all the men who were already there killed, and compelled the women to marry the newcomers, whereupon the women swore never to sit at table with their husbands, nor to call them by their names),

- involvement of the Greek motherland in

Miletos, theatre

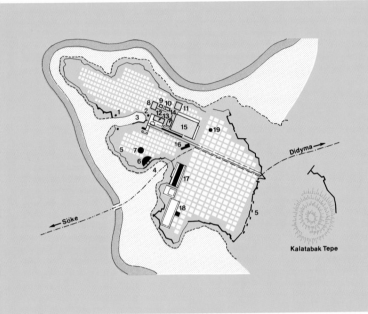

Kalatabak Tepe

Miletos 1 Lions **2** Harbour monument **3** Lion harbour **4** Theatre harbour **5** Town wall **6** Theatre **7** Castle **8** Shrine of Apollo Delphinios (Delphinion) **9** Seljuk bath (thermal bath) **10** Gymnasium **11** Nymphaeum/church **12** Ionic hall **13** N. market **14** Buleuterion **15** S. market **16** Faustina thermal bath **17** Stadium **18** Athena temple **19** Ilyas Bey Camii

the conflict with the Persians, which was in fact without prospects,
- equally prospectless resistance against the approach of Alexander the Great in 334 BC, which forced the Macedonians into a siege of several weeks' duration.

The ruins: The remains of the Roman city are worth seeing. They are placed on the chessboard of the Greek city, as designed by the 'inventor' of this pattern Hippodamos of Miletos (the Milesian architect, who also designed the Piraeus) in the 5C BC when rebuilding the city after it had been destroyed by the Persians.

The extensive site was excavated by German archaeologists: T. Wiegand from 1899 for the Königliches Museum in Berlin, from 1938 C. Weikhert and from 1955 G.Kleiner.

Theatre: The Roman theatre was a modification of an existing Greek theatre c.AD 100 under Trajan. It seated about 25,000 spectators. The lower section is set on a natural slope, and the upper is supported by masonry. Wide vaulted underground passages (ambulacri), accessible via underground steps, bring the spectators via two wide horizontal passages (diazomata) to the three sets of seats (maeniana), each with 18 rows. In the central wedge (cuneus) of the Roman semicircle (cavea) were two piers supporting the baldacchino of the *imperial box*. The seats of rows 3–6 are slightly raised in comparison with the rear section, and

Miletos, theatre

carry inscriptions showing that they were reserved for goldsmiths, Jews etc. In front of the cavea is the *stage building*, which was decorated as a palace façade with polychrome marble, columns and statues, and opened into the proscenium through three openings. The lower storey of both has survived. Dimensions: width of façade 459 ft.; height 131 ft. including surrounding gallery of 33 ft. (about 98 ft. have survived); diameter of orchestra 111 ft. At the top of the theatre hill are remains of a trapezoid *Byzantine citadel* (probably 7C), rebuilt by the Seljuks.

Baths of Faustina: These are Roman baths (2nd half of the 2C AD), founded by Marcus Aurelius' wife, who not only bore 12 children but as 'mater castorum' constantly accompanied her husband on his journeys through the Empire and on his campaigns, and also received the attribute Pia (the pious) after her death, because of her numerous foundations.

The rooms are organized in the usual way: a room with apse with ten wall niches for statues (Apollo and the Nine Muses, now in the Museum of Antiquities in İstanbul) leads into the *apodyterium*, a large, long room (about 260 ft.) with 13 changing and rest rooms on each of the long sides, and a *palaestra* (still not excavated) on the right; on the left are the cold bath (frigidarium; pool with the river god Meander and a lion), tepid bath (tepidarium), warm bath (caldarium) and hot bath (sudatorium). The rooms for heating water are E. and N. of the caldarium, and from there warmth was conveyed by hypocausts (floors on short brick columns) and tubili (pipes).

Ilyas Bey Camii: This mosque in an Islamic cemetery, a *medrese* and a *library* make up the Menteşe Emir Ilyas' foundation. The buildings were completed in 1404 and are grouped around a rectangular courtyard in the middle of which was a şadırvan (ablution fountain). The Seljuk-early Ottoman building with central dome has a transitional octagonal zone with spandrels leading to the round dome. The mihrab is designed as a gateway, and corresponds inside with the entrance façade with its stepped arches in various colours. The smooth internal and external walls have stalactite ornamentation (mukarnas), and in the interior, particularly on the lavishly decorated *mihrab*, these combine with tendrils, geometrical patterns and calligraphy. The mosque was badly damaged in the earthquake of 1955, but has been excellently restored in the meantime.

Also worth seeing: The foundations and ruins of the many large public buildings from various times in the Roman period are at various stages of excavation. A view of the former *town centre* can be obtained from the theatre hill looking E. The more open spaces working from left to right

were part of the Lion Harbour, the small N. market was directly by the harbour, with the larger S. market behind a harbour colonnade. The via sacra leads through the harbour gate to the large market gate to the S. market (now in the Pergamon Museum in Berlin), then to the via sacra to Didyma. Crowded between the N. and S. markets are the striking Ionic hall (1C AD) on a base with seven steps (used by spectators of the sacred procession), with a gymnasium and the Capito baths in front of it, the Delphinion on the left, a nymphaeum on the right. The *Delphinion* was dedicated to Apollo Delphinios; this was the starting point of the annual procession in honour of Apollo to his principal shrine in Didyma 19 km. away. A pavilion-like room was set on a round base with columns and a conical roof in the middle of the colonnaded courtyard. The three-storey *nymphaeum* had a lavishly decorated façade with columns, niches and statues. It contained the largest water reservoir in the town and was founded by Marcus Ulpius Traianus, the father of the emperor Trajan (AD 79/80). The smaller *N. market* (295 x 148 ft.) and the large *S. market* (643 x 538 ft.) were

Miletos, Faustina thermal bath

surrounded by covered colonnades, and on the N. side of the S. market was a corn warehouse 535 x 43 ft., with adjacent *Shrine of Serapis* dating from the 3C AD, a building with three aisles and Ionic columns. Between the N. and S. markets is the *council house* (buleuterion), built by the Milesian brothers Timarchos and Herakleides in honour of the Seleucid king Antiochos IV in 175–163 BC (both high officials at his court in Babylon): a propylon (gatehouse) led to a peristyle courtyard with Doric colonnades, behind which was the conference room with a semicircular tier of raised seats for the 1,200 council members.

An impression of the *Lion Harbour* (one of Miletos' four harbours) is given by the two lions with heads rising from the silt on either side of the harbour mouth; on the S. edge of the harbour basin there is still a fragment of the great *harbour monument* (1C AD), probably in commemoration of the ending of piracy in the E. Mediterranean by Pompey's sudden and unexpected action in 68&67 BC. The monument has a circular base with four steps surmounted by a plinth with triton frieze (some of which has

survived) on which stood a tripod; it was probably dedicated to Apollo. Beyond the monument are traces of the outline of the long Doric *harbour hall*. Another interesting building is the *stadium*, 754 ft. long by 243 ft. wide, opposite the theatre in the other direction from the Lion Harbour. This and the adjacent W. market give an idea of the extent of the Theatre Harbour, between the stadium and the theatre.

Among the Roman ruins there are also *Christian buildings*, such as the *bishop's palace* with adjacent 6C *church of St.Michael* with nave and two aisles. The bishop's palace (partially roofed for storage purposes) has various kinds of floor mosaic in the smaller rooms around the central hall, and so does the *galleried basilica*, also 6C, with atrium and baptistery SE of the nymphaeum.

The fact that the city lived on after the Turkish conquest is shown by the Ilyas Bey mosque and also the *late-Seljuk bath* (15C) at the N. end of the Ionic colonnade. This is a centrally planned building with dome with smaller domed bath rooms grouped around it, and finally the stable of a 15C *caravanserai* on the lower Humeitepe, the ridge on the E. side of the

Miletos, district of town near lion harbour

Lion Harbour parallel with the theatre hill.

Misis

Adana   p.576☐L 6

Misis was an important staging post on the route from Central Anatolia to Persia, and was occupied even in the Hittite period. It flourished in the Roman period, when it is said to have had about 150,000 inhabitants, and was called **Mopsuhestia**. The 4C AD Roman-Byzantine bridge with nine arches over the Ceyhan is still in use, and forms part of the Eski Yol. In the middle of the little settlement which nestles on the slope directly N. of the bridge near the bend in the road are the foundations, built of large ashlar blocks, of an ancient theatre. They have been partially built over. At the top of the hill are an underground cistern and some architectural ornament (blocks with triglyph frieze).

Caravanserais: Two have survived S. of the Roman bridge. The one to the W., formerly the larger, is of particular architectural interest despite its poor condition. It probably dates from the Seljuk period (mid 13–14C) and is of the walled fortress type, with an interior with vaulted aisles, of which the central, raised section and two flanking side aisles with groin vaulting have survived. The carefully built ashlar building looks rather like an aqueduct from a distance, as the surrounding wall is now missing from the sequence of arched constructions.

In front of the caravanserai is a badly damaged *domed mosque* with collapsed minaret.

The E. caravanserai is in better condition, and is popularly known as Kafırbina, which goes back to the fact that the han was apparently founded by 'infidel' merchants. In the 13&14C Misis certainly was an important Genoese trading settlement, but the date on the building inscription, no longer in existence, was 1542. Another text mentions restoration under Hassan Oğlu Paşa as late as 1830. This is a typical Ottoman courtyard caravanserai with groin-vaulted stables, storerooms and accommodation grouped around an arcaded courtyard. The

Misis, Roman bridge over the Ceyhan

entrance to the buildings is lavishly carved, and has survived in good condition. The decorative rosettes on both sides of the gate arch are particularly striking.

Yakpinar: In the village of Yakpinar, at the W. entrance to Misis, N. of the main road, are the famous Noah's Ark mosaics from the Martyrion basilica in Misis-Mopsuhestia.

Environs: Sirkeli (10 km. E.): Level with a quarry on a cliff by the River Ceyhan is a *Hittite rock relief*, directly after crossing a railway line and before reaching a bridge over a tributary of the Ceyhan about 110 yards off the road to Ceyhan (Eski Yol). The image has survived in good condition. It marks an old river crossing and shows a Hittite king looking to the left, in typical ruler's garments. The hieroglyphic inscription behind the figure's neck shows that he is of Muwatalli, known for his peace treaty with the pharaoh Rameses II after the Battle of Kadesh (1275 BC). The inscription by the relief also names Muwatalli's son Mursili. This image dating from the mid-13C BC, not discovered until 1934, is thus the oldest pictorial representation which can be dated with certainty from the period of the Hittite Empire, and also the oldest monumental portrait of a Hittite ruler. The Armenian fortress and Crusader castle of Yilanlikale (→ Ceyhan, Environs) can be clearly seen from the Sirkeli rock relief.

Muş

Muş   p.578□R 4

Armenian tradition has it that this provincial capital on the edge of a fertile plain (Muş Ovası) was founded in the 6C AD by Mushegh Mamikonian. It was in its early days the centre of the conflict between the founder dynasty and the Bagtarid house. Subsequently it was capital of the royal house of Tarum, and in 966 passed from the Bagtarids to the Byzantines. After their defeat at Malazgirt in 1071 Muş fell to the victorious Seljuks, who successfully resisted two Aiyubid sieges (1207 and 1228). The city was then twice victim of the Mongols (1260 and late 14C), before becoming part of the

Misis, early Christian mosaic of Noah's Ark

Sirkeli (Misis), rock relief of a Hittite king

Ottoman Empire under Selim Yavuz in 1515. During the First World War the Russians occupied the town until 1917. The earthquake of 1966 caused severe damage.

Worth seeing: *Ruined castle, Ulu Cami, Arslanhane caravanserai* and the two Seljuk mosques *Alaeddin Paşa Camii* and *Hacı Şeref Camii*.

Environs: Arak (formerly *Khorene;* 5 km. SE): It is half an hour's walk W. from this village to the *monastery of Arak Vank (Lazarus monastery)*, the only one of the many Christian sites formerly around Muş which is still worth seeing.

Bingöl (118 km. W.): Bingöl stands at a height of 3,690 ft., has 28,000 inhabitants and is the capital of one of the smallest Turkish provinces. The predecessor

settlement of Çapakçur is in the immediate vicinity. Because of severe earthquake damage, most recently in 1966 and 1971, Bingöl has no notable monuments other than the *ruined fortress*. The numerous glacial lakes in the N. Bingöl Dağlari mountains, which give the place its name (Bingöl = 1,000 lakes) are a paradise for walkers.

Çangilli (21 km. NE): Leave the road to Elâzığ, which leaves Muş in a northerly direction, but soon turns W., at the village of Yaygin, turning on to the side road N. to Zitaret. From here it is about two hours' walk NNE (it is also possible, but extremely difficult, to drive) to the *monastery of Surb Karapet* (also *Çangilli Kilise*, church of John the Baptist). The church has nave and four aisles and five irregular chapels in the E., and was founded in the 5C, supposedly on the site of the tomb of John the Baptist, in the first place just as a simple basel. The bell tower in the W. is also 8C. The building was plundered by Kurds on several occasions and finally rebuilt in the 17C. Prince Stephen and the Armenian hero Vahan Kamsarakan are buried here. As the local population persists in taking the stones away, all that survives are the foundations and two vaults used for agricultural purposes. Nor has anything survived of the once famous monastery library.

Kayalıdere Kalesi (about 45 km. N.): About 30 km. beyond the fork for Elâzığ on the road to Varto a field path goes off to the right. This path crosses the little river Abderrahman Paşa and from here it is 8 km. further to the ruined Urartian castle of Kayalıdere near the village of Tepeköy. The castle hill falls sharply to the Murat, and is visible over considerable distances. The Urartians built fortifications in the W. to protect themselves against the Assyrians. In 1965 the British Archaeological Institute in Ankara and two English universities under the direction of S.Lloyd began excavations. Inside the fortress, divided into an upper and lower castle by a once massive access gate in the W., the foundations of a typical

Urartian *tower temple* with thick walls (exterior 41 x 41 ft., interior only 16 x 16 ft.) and characteristic protruding corners; the rear façade of this cult building was cut into the rock. An impression of the feet of a three-legged sacrificial vessel had survived in the temple courtyard. Other discoveries include storerooms with large jugs, a bronze lion (*c.*700 BC) and, above a thick stratum of burnt material, several finds including bronze quivers and shields. Halfway up the SE slope is a large *tomb* with six chambers and a terraced entrance cut into the rock.

Surb Salah (about 25 km. SE): Gregory the Illuminator (d. 320) founded a group of three churches replacing a heathen temple on this site not far E. of Ziyaret (access → Çangilli). These *ecclesiastical buildings* have survived only as ruins, but were the spiritual centre of Anatolia in the 4C, and the seat of a Catholicos. They are: *Ashtishat* (church of Mary and Our Lord), *Karapet* (church of John the Baptist) and *Matnavank* (church of the Apostles).

Mut, Lal Ağa mosque

Mut

Ancient **Claudiopolis** was founded *c.*50 BC by Marcus Aurelius Polemo, high priest in Olba. Polemo had combined the wild and notorious Isaurian tribes, who lived in the Taurus mountains around Mut, into a single kingdom. The Byzantine emperor Zeno was an Isaurian.

Citadel: This fine fortress with massive round tower dominates the town. It was originally Byzantine, strengthened and expanded by the Karamanids in the 14C.

Lal Ağa mosque (2nd half of the 14C): This is an interesting emirate version of the central domed mosque. The slender minaret is adjacent to a monumental porch with five bays. In the interior the central dome has four large pendentives and dominates the prayer room. Two large arches form two side rooms, giving an effect of aisles.

Hocendi türbe (mid-14C): This is an unusual tomb from the period of the emirate. The very high pyramidal roof over the squat polygonal body of the building makes this tower-tomb look very unusual. The interior dome is also pointed.

Environs: Ermenek (89 km. W.): This is the earliest centre of the later Karaman emirate. The founder of the Karamanoğlu dynasty and its first prince, Kerimüddin Karaman was a wood dealer in Ermenek and founded his Turkoman tribal rule from there in 1255 (→ Karaman). The emirate of Karaman remained transfixed by archaic and conservative early Seljuk architecture for centuries. Four mosques of the Arabian kufa type are examples of this in Ermenek, the *Akca Mascit* (1300), the *Ulu Camii* (1302), the *Sipas mosque* (1306) and the *Meydan mosque* (1436). None has a courtyard, and they have the ground plan of a broad rectangle, with the mihrab (kibla wall) on the broad side, and montonously-placed columns. The roof of the Ulu Camii is supported by twelve piers, the mihrab is placed off the central axis to the left. An unusual feature are the six windows in the kibla wall, affording a wonderful view over the sweep of the countryside. There is a vestibule with several bays to the W., with a double-arched entrance in the extended kibla wall. The 12C *Sare Hatun mosque* has an important, because rare, example of a minbar with carved bevelled decoration.

Myra

Antalya   p.572☐EF 6

History: The acropolis of ancient Myra is in the foothills of the Alaça Dağ massif, 1 km. N. of Kale, and protected by the steep walls of the plateau and a massive fortifying wall. Myra was always one of the leading cities of Lycia, with three votes in the assembly of the Lycian League. The first historical mention is in the 1C BC, but remains of buildings and inscriptions confirm the town's importance from the 5C BC: polygonal walls on the acropolis hill and a number of important rock tombs. The large Graeco-Roman theatre, famous in the Imperial Roman period, gives an impression of Myra's size and importance at this time. The harbour of Myra, Andriake, about which the Apostle Paul wrote on his way to Rome, and where he changed ships, is 5 km. from the town in the very fertile flood plain. The harbour made a considerable contribution to Myra's prosperity. At this time there was a ferry service, confirmed by inscription, between Andriake and Limyra. The Byzantine emperor Theodosius II (408–450) made Myra the capital of Lycia. In the previous century St.Nicholas had been bishop of Lycia. Many miracles and deeds are attributed to this multifarious patron saint, but there is no doubt at all about his existence as bishop of Myra. Arabs failed to raid his tomb in 808, but merchants from Bari succeeded in April

Myra, 'painted tomb' in the burial ground in the rocks

1087, and a famous pilgrimage church was built over his mortal remains in that city. This has, however, done nothing to deter the streams of pilgrims who have made their way to Myra from the 5C to the present day.

Graeco-Roman theatre: This is below the steep S. wall of the acropolis, and supported on a fine substructure. The upper diameter of the cavea is 360 ft. With 38 rows of seats and lavish stage facilities and decoration it was considered a wonder of the world at the time. The four different mask friezes on the scenae frons and the S. façade of the stage building may have contributed to this.

Necropolises: The famous Myra *rock tombs* are concentrated at two points. In the steep W. face near the theatre one tomb follows close upon the next, making the surface look like a gigantic honeycomb. These are various versions of the mausoleum, from the most modest to tombs with many sections and storeys with inscriptions and reliefs, some of them painted. On the NE side of the hill is a second group of closely-packed rock tombs, of which one, because of its lavish relief and painting, which is still in evidence, is considered one of the finest, and was already famous in ancient times. This so-called 'painted tomb' presents the dead man and his family in 11 vivid life-size relief figures.

Church of St.Nicholas: This is W. of the village of Kale/Demre. There was already a church on the site in the 3C, destroyed by the earthquake of 529. The basilica then founded by Justinian was destroyed in the 8C. In 1043 Constantine IX extended the church as a monastery with defensive wall and towers. 19C travellers describe the church in a desolate condition with collapsed vaulting and the nave full of water and rubble. The Russians, always great venerators of St.Nicholas, began to rebuild the church but were never able to complete it. Turkish archaeologists restored it to its present condition in the 1960s. A later porch with four bays leads into the narthex. The original basilica with nave and two aisles, dome, bema and apse was later extended by the addition of an S. aisle. The two chapels S. of the bema are

Andriake (Myra), granary

part of the earlier building. The semi-circular apse, somewhat narrower than the bema, is surrounded by a synthronon with ambulatory.

Environs: Andriake: The harbour basin is now silted up, but could be closed with a chain in ancient times. N. of the Andrakos River, which flowed into the harbour by the ancient water mill, were the N. town and a large necropolis. Near the old warehouses and harbour buildings, W. of the Plakoma market is the 2C AD granarium, commissioned by the Emperor Hadrian and almost intact. Almost 8,000 cubic yards of grain could be stored in the 8 rooms of this carefully built granary. This and the identical granary in Patara, also commissioned by Hadrian and also in good condition, made this part of the coast an important food supply base for Rome and its troops. There is a small relief of Hadrian and his wife Sabina over the central gate in the W. A dedicatory relief represents Sarapis and Isis, and below this is the dedicatory inscription. In the *Andrakos valley* (near Andriake) are the picturesque ruins of a *nymphaeum* and an *aqueduct*.

Nevşehir, Kurşunlu Camii

Nevşehir

Nevşehir   p.574□K 4

Ancient *Nisa* is set on the slopes of a hill, with a Seljuk fortress later used by the Ottomans on the summit.

Nevşehir is at the W. extremity of the SW Cappadocian tufa region, famous for its weathered rock formations. Within the Nevşehir-Ürgrüp-Avonas triangle in particular, over an area of about 120 square miles, there are countless lavishly decorated cave churches and monasteries carved out of the soft rock, but the Peristrema valley to the NW (→ Aksaray) and the region to the S. as far as Soğanlı offer a similar combination of natural beauty and culturally interesting monuments.

This bizarrely weathered landscape, running down to the valley of the Kızıl Irmak (ancient Halys) in the N., was formed by eruptions of Erciyas Dağı between Kayseri and Develi (12,848 ft.). However, other volcanoes in the region, such as Hassan Dağı near Niğde (10,673 ft.) must have contributed to these huge tufa masses. The extent to which soft tufa was combined with harder, rocky volcanic stone determined the steepness of the river valleys and made it possible for wind and water to wear the material down in such a way that slender rock needles or cones, often with a stone covering the top, were left isolated in the landscape. These are the so-called 'fairy chimneys'. These are often close together in groups, or after severe erosion they are spread out more, or completely isolated on the slopes of the hills.

It is not possible to say with certainty when Christian hermits began to build their cells in this lonely countryside. In the 7&8C, however, Arab raids compelled the by now numerous Christians to move closer together. This was also the period of the iconoclastic controversy, the dispute over whether it was permissible to paint Christ or God the Father in human form. Until this dispute was finally resolved in 842, and pictorial representations of God were allowed again, the rock churches of Cappadocia were decorated only with geometrical patterns, or paintings or reliefs of the Cross. It is interesting in terms of both culture and religion to observe that here in the Nevşehir region, even before the dispute became official, i.e. in the so-called pre-iconoclastic period, there are cave churches with representations of the deity and others where this has clearly been consciously avoided.

Cappadocian cave church painting reached its peak immediately after the end of the iconoclastic controversy. This was partly because of external considerations: Cappadocia enjoyed a period of peace under the Macedonian dynasty (867–1059). These Christian churches, cut into the rock on the same scheme as their fellows built in brick or stone, were decorated down to the last corner with paintings of saints (often in medallions), and also with personified abstracts or friezes showing whole sequences from the Old or New Testament in chronological order. From time to time these absorbed Byzantine, Armenian and Syrian influences in differing degrees to form a particular Cappadocian style within the history of Byzantine art. Alien elements are also to be found in the architecture of the churches, which were by no means built to the plain basic design of a single-aisled, tunnel-vaulted hall with horseshoe apse and parclose in the typical Cappadocian manner.

Good centres for visits to these sites, some of them hard to find, are Göreme, Ürgüp and Avanos as well as Nevşehir itself.

Kurşunlu Camii: This house of prayer was founded in 1726 by Grand Vizier

Çavuş In (Nevşehir), fresco

Damat İbrahim Paşa, and is called the Lead Mosque because of its roof covering, said to be in this metal. The complex also includes a hospital and Koran school with library. The latter building now houses the little *local museum*, established in 1967, and containing valuable manuscripts.

Also worth seeing: *Citadel* and *Kaya Camii*, an Ottoman mosque.

Environs: Acıgöl (22 km. SW): This town on the road to Aksaray is thought to be the site of Hittite **Topada**, presumed to be under the hill above the little town. There is a crater lake on the left before Acıgöl.

Açık Sarayı (10 km. NW): This underground *monastery complex* on several levels in the extremely soft tufa of this area is on the way to Gülşehir. It consists of cells, kitchen, refectory and church. The walls and ceilings are decorated with reliefs rather than painting, usually representing the Cross, but also including the otherwise rare motif of two bulls facing each other in aggressive attitudes. The name means 'open palace'.

Avanos (18 km. NE): This town on the Kızıl Irmak (Red River) is known for its carpet tradition and numerous *potteries*, of which we are reminded by a modern sculpture on a fountain in the town. The workshops, most of which offer visits to their wheels, get their clay from small pits by the bank of the river.

Avcılar (7 km. E.): Half of this picturesque place, long known as *Göremeköy*, consists of cave dwellings. About 600 yards from Avcılar is a rock cone with *cave churches*. Nearby there is also a large group of *soft tufa pyramids* with harder stones on top of them. Avcılar is also the birthplace of the important Cappadocian saint, St.Jerome.

Çavuş In (also Çavuşin; 10 km. NE): Çavuş In is on the way from Avcılar to Avanos. It has numerous cave dwellings in a 200 ft. high cliff. The most important monument is the *church of St. John the Baptist*, which used to have outstanding

architectural detail. Unfortunately the columned entrance with façade arch collapsed recently, so that only the apse with throne and flanking stone benches remain. The paintings can hardly be made out any longer, which is all the more regrettable as this church is one of the oldest in the district, and probably dates from the 5C. On the edge of Çavuş In, on the Avanos side, is Çavuşin Kilise, also very early, with predominantly green and reddish-brown frescos.

Cemil (about 30 km. SE): Not far S. of Cemil in the **Gorgoli (Girgoli)** side valley is the *Archangelos monastery*, in very good condition, with refectory, cells and a church of St. Stephen, a plain, single-aisled building with horseshoe apse, but unusually not tunnel vaulted, but with a flat roof (7&8C). Whether the geometrical *paintings* in the interior date from the iconoclastic or pre-iconoclastic period is a matter of dispute. On the other hand it is certain that the figurative pictures in the *church of St.Michael*, also part of the monastery, date from the 11C. The monastery itself, by a spring and a well, is held to be one of the oldest complexes in the region.

Damsa (*Taskin Paşa Köyu*; about 35 km SE): Ancient **Tamisos** is only a few km. beyond Cemil. A mosque with two türbe at its side and a Seljuk building, probably a former medrese, with a lavishly decorated façade but otherwise in ruins, have survived. The few churches in Damsa, which did not become the seat of a bishop until the 14C, replacing Suve, 3 km. to the S., are in a state of extreme disrepair.

Derinkuyu (31 km. S.): This impressive *subterranean town* reached via the road to Niğde, passing its counterpart Kaymaklı, equally worth seeing, may well be Hittite in origin. So far eight levels have been excavated, grouped around a shaft about 280 ft. deep. They include dwellings, food and water stores and a sophisticated

Göreme (Nevşehir), landscape of tufa cones ▷

ventilation system for an estimated 15–20,000 people. There is also an underground monastery. The entrances could be closed with great stones like millstones which were rolled in front of the doors. The *dark stone church* in the middle of the modern town, now used as a mosque, was built in the last century. A large marble Roman eagle discovered here is now in the garden of the Ankara museum.

El Nazar (about 20 km. NE): This gorge, the easternmost of the three valleys that meet at Avcılar (the other two are the Göreme basin and the Kiliçlar gorge) contains the *El-Nazar chapel* (cone badly damaged by earthquakes) and the *Sakli Kilise* among others. The latter—the name means 'hidden church'—has transepts and three apses. The frescos show scenes from the life of Jesus and Mary. Monks moved into this valley and the Kiliçlar valley in the 12C, when there was no more room for monastery buildings in the Göreme basin.

Göreme (20 km. E.): The closely-packed cave churches and monasteries in the Göreme (Byzantine *Korama*) valley are probably the best known in the entire region. A little outside the area, for which an admission charge is now made, is the *Tokalı Kilise* (Church with the Shield), one of the best-preserved of all the buildings, and not restored until the 1960s, an additional advantage. The nave was originally trapezoid with tunnel vault and preceding narthex, and was then extended by the addition of a wide transept with three apses. The vault of the narrow transverse passage which precedes the apses is supported by four sturdy piers. There is another chapel with apse N. of the transept. The narthex vault and the walls of the nave have paintings whichä date from the reign of Nicephorus II Phocas (963–9), depicting scenes from the Life of Christ in chronological order. As well as a baptismal cycle and the miracles of Christ there are also various saints (Michael, George, Basil of Cappadocia among others). The apse conch shows Christ with two angels. Within the fenced area included in the visit the first feature is the *Elmalı Kilise* (Apple Church), the smallest church with crossing dome in the Göreme valley. The frescos date from the early 11C, with saints, prophets and scenes from the Life of Christ on the vaults and pendentives of the dome. The bowl of the central dome and the apsidal conches contain medallions with images of Christ and the Archangels. Immediately adjacent is the *church of St. Barbara*. The patroness herself is portrayed alongside other church patrons and Christ. These rather crude pictures, their colouring dominated by ochre, suggest that the church was painted shortly after the end of the iconoclastic controversy. In the *Yılanlı Kilise* (Snake Church) the Byzantine emperor Constantine and his wife Helena appear among the portraits. This church is directly by the *church of St. Onuphrios*, which is less important. Further to the N., also very close together, are the *refectory* (with double apse and tables and benches cut out of the rock) and the *Karanlık Kilise* (Dark Church), which is part of the same monastery complex. It is a mid-11C church with crossing dome with frescos of the Life of Christ. Similar material is to be found in the *Çarıklı Kilise* (Sandal Church, named after the footprints below the scene of the Ascension, said to be an exact copy of those in the Church of the Ascension in Jerusalem). The Four Evangelists and the Crucifixion are depicted.

Gülşehir (19 km. NW): Gülşehir is 2 km. away from the Kızıl Irmak, on the site of ancient **Zoropassos**. The *Kurşunlu Camii*, a 17C Ottoman mosque, is particularly worth seeing, and there are also a *medrese*, a *hamam* and several *fountains*. There is a fine view into the Kızıl Irmak valley from the bridge.

Güzelöz (about 45 km. SE): Güzelöz is also known as **Mavrican**, and is sited with *Ortaköy* to the W. at the head of the Soğanlı valley (→ below). 1 km. outside the village is a small *rock church* preceded by a painted narthex, and in the village itself the *dome* of a church which is now in ruins is used as an octagonal mosque.

Göreme (Nevşehir)

Göreme (Nevşehir), tufa cone with cave dwellings (left), Elmalı Kilise, frescos

Hacıbektaş (about 50 km. NW): Hacıbektaş, on the road to Kirşehir is known throughout the country as the birthplace of Hacı Bektaş Vali, who founded the notorious Bektasci Dervish Order in 1357. The *monastery* (tekke) and *türbe* of the founder of the Order may be visited. This faith, which embraces Shiite, Sunni and even Christian views, reached its peak when the Janissaries were also members of it.

Hashüyük (about 95 km. NW): Excavations of this *settlement mound* not far from Kirşehir carried out in 1931 by Delaporte established that this site was occupied from the chalcolithic period to the end of the Hittite Empire. The sequence of ceramics typical for each settlement epoch was also helpful in solving dating problems at other settlement mounds.

Karapınar (29 km. SSW): Not far from Karapınar is the *Karahüyük*, with an inscription in Hittite hieroglyphics on one of its smoothed rocks. The stone bearing the text has been strikingly cut into a rectangle. The only interesting feature in the village is a simple *mosque* dating from 1758. The road from Nevşehir first passes *Boğaz* (13 km.) at the foot of the Ertaş Dağı, and after a further 6 km. reaches **Iak**, where a small number of Roman remains were found, some of which are in the museum in Kayseri.

Karlı (about 45 km. E.): There is a *cave church* with three apses not far from Karlı, which is on the road to Kayseri 11 km. beyond Ürgüp.

Karşı Kilise (about 20 km. NW): This *double church* is 1 km. from Gülşehir, and contains some smoke-blackened paintings dating from the early 13C. The lower church is a cruciform building with short arms and apse in the E. section.

Göreme (Nevşehir), Snake Church, St. Theodosius on horseback

Kaymaklı (20 km. S.): This is the site of one of the *subterranean towns* along the road to Niğde, which have recently beome well known. They have been investigated and excavated since about 1960. Similarly to Derinkuyu (→ above) and **Çardak** (turn E. off the road to Niğde 8 km. beyond Nevşehir, 3 km. from there), Kaymaklı is estimated to have sheltered about 15–20,000 people, probably Christians seeking refuge from the Romans. Kaymaklı, with its seven levels, was considered to be the largest subterranean settlement of its kind until the discovery of *Özkonak*, 10 km. NW of Avanos. The latter site is still largely unexplored and not yet open to the public, but its capacity is estimated at about 60,000 people. The most striking feature of Kaymaklı is the *church* with two apses.

Kesik Köprü Hane: The ruins of this *caravanserai* are 18 km. from Kırşehir

about 350 yards from the right bank of the Kızıl Irmak not far from the remains of a Seljuk bridge. The building dates from 1268. The name means Caravanserai of the Destroyed Bridge, and the magnificently decorated *courtyard portal* and high central aisle are worth seeing.

Kılıçlar gorge (Gorge of the Swords; about 20 km. NE): This valley and the El-Nazar gorge (q.v.) surround the Göreme basin. This little valley contains among other things the *Aynali Kilise* (Mirror Church) and the *Kılıçlar Kilise* (Church of the Swords). The latter is a centrally planned building with magnificent frescos dating from the late 10–early 11C.

Kırşehir (96 km. NW): This capital of the province of the same name is probably on the site of ancient *Justianopolis Mokyssos*, which was granted a charter by Emperor Justinian I *c.*AD 536. The present name appears officially for the first time in the early 14C in a treaty between the Ottoman sultan Mehmet Celebi and one of the emirs of Karaman. From the 14–18C it was the centre of the Ahi sect, who also played an important role in politics. Seljuk mausoleums in the town include the *Melik Gazi Türbesi* and the *Aşik Paşa Veli Türbesi*, which are the best known. The *Alaettin Camii* was founded in the 13C by the sultan of the same name. However, the present *Cacabey Camii* was founded in the 2nd half of the 12C as a Seljuk observatory and guardhouse.

Kızıl Çukur (about 12 km. NE): Like others, this valley begins at the foot of the *Ak Tepe* (White Mountain), not far S. of Çavuş In, halfway to Ortahisar. The name means red river-bed, and refers to the pale pink colour of the local tufa, also found in the neighbouring and parallel *Göllüdere valley* (Valley of the Roses or Pink Valley). This region features particularly simple flat-roofed chapels of the pre-iconoclastic period, of which the best-known example is the *Haçılı Kilise* (Cross Church) at the end of the Kızıl Çukur valley. Here the ceiling of the single aisle carries a large relief cross. The contrasting paintings in the almost circular apse date from the 10C, and show Christ surrounded by the symbols of the Four Evangelists. The *üzümlü Church* (Grape Church) in the same valley is actually dedicated to the stylite Niketas. The most important cave church in the adjacent Göllüdere valley is the *Church of the Three Crosses*. It too dates from the pre-iconoclastic period, and is named after the three crosses surrounded by floral motifs on the ceiling.

Mazıköy (*Mataza*; about 28 km. S.): There are churches and chapels in the high cliffs of this region 8 km. N. of Kaymaklı, and also tombs, of which some are particularly striking for their decorated façades consisting of columns and gables. The subterranean town recently discovered nearby has still to be excavated and investigated.

Mustafapaşa Köyü (about 25 km. SE): This village SE of Ortahisar was known as *Sinasssos* and exclusively occupied by Greeks, who left the area after the population exchange. The village church and its frescos date from the last century. The most important of the cave churches a little outside the village is the *church of St. Basil*. Relief decoration in the iconoclastic tradition shows surprising formal variety, and can be dated to 726–80 from inscriptions. Inscriptions also make it clear that the three apse crosses are intended to symbolize the Old Testament figures Abraham, Isaac and Jacob.

Ortahisar (15 km. E.): This village not far S. of the road to Ürgüp is named (Castle of the Middle) after the gigantic rock needle containing numerous cave dwellings around which the present village huddles. In the village are the *Cambazlı Kilise*, a church with crossing dome, and also the *Harım Kilise*, which is unfortunately used for storing equipment, both lavishly painted with Old and New Testament scenes. About 1.5 km. from Ortahisar is the *Halasdere valley*, which is rarely visited, but has an old, lavishly decorated monastery built by Armenian Christians. SE of Ortahisar is the *Church of St. Theodore*, surprising for its local naïve paintings (9C), which contrast starkly with the frescos in the other churches showing strong Byzantine influence. Although it is not very easy to get to, the *Balkan Deresi valley*, 2 km. from Ortahisar and running S. of Ürgüp, is worth seeing. The walk up the usually dry river bed passes countless dovecotes with decorative façades. The frescos in the four churches in the valley are in very poor condition, but some of them go back to the 6C, and are thus among the earliest pictures in the region. In the *üzengi Dere valley*, running almost parallel to the Balkan Deresi, is the *Church of the Holy Apostles of Sinassos*, the modern Mustafa Paşa Köyü (q.v.).

Şahineffendi (about 38 km. SE): Sahineffendi, about 3 km. S. of Damsa is ancient *Suveş*, known to have been the seat of a bishop since the 10C, but replaced

Göreme, 'Sandal Church', fresco ▷

Üçhisar (Nevşehir), cave dwellings

as such by Damsa/Tamisos in the 14C. It is known for the *double church of the Forty Martyrs of Sebasteia*, where the painting dates from 1216&17, and thus, with those in the church of St.George in Belisrama, are the latest pictures in Cappadocia. At the same time they document the religious tolerance afforded to Christianity by the Seljuk sultans in power at the time.

Sarı Hanı (about 24 km. NE): The Yellow Caravanserai, a Seljuk building, is in a lonely position about 6 km. E. of Avanos on the left bank of the Kızıl Irmak not far from its confluence with the ürgüp Suyu. The entrance to the building, now in a state of severe disrepair, is in the E., and leads first of all into a courtyard with arcades to the N. and S. The large main hall with central aisle and four transverse halls is entered through a magnificent gate on the W. side of the courtyard.

Soğanlı valley (about 70 km. SE): The region of cave churches SW of the road to Yeşilhisar has hardly been opened up at all. The landscape is dominated by plateaus rather than pointed formations. A particular architectural feature are the domed churches cut out of tall tufa cones, reminscent of Armenian churches in the interior, and indeed it can be assumed that there was direct influence from Armenian Christians fleeing into the Kayseri area from the Muslims. The *Karabaş Kilise* with 11C frescos including a Last Supper scene is particularly noteworthy. Also striking are the numerous dovecotes in the rock, with the holes through which the birds fly edged in white.

Tağar (about 40 km. SE): Halfway between Ürgüp and Cemil a side road about 7 km. long leads to Tağar, which is between Avla Dağı and Hodul Dağı. It has a church with an unusual ground plan, including three conches, and surprising dimensions (45 ft. by 37 ft.).

Tavşanlı Kilise (25 km. ESE): The simple Church of the Hare (one aisle with flat ceiling and additional apse) is below the track connecting Mustafapaşa Köyu and İbrahimpaşa Köyu (ancient Babayan). The frescos of scenes from the Gospels, dated by inscription to the period of Constantine VI Porphyrogenitus (913–920), are painted over earlier iconoclastic motifs which still show weakly through in places.

Tilköy (19 km. S.): In this little village on the road to Niğde are the ruins of a Seljuk caravanserai, the **Dolay Hanı**. Nearby is the *church of St.Andrew*, a basilica with nave and several aisles, also in an extremely poor state of repair.

Üçhisar (about 12 km. E): This village halfway between Nevşehir and Ürgüp not far N. of the road between them is dominated by the ruins of a castle cut into the rock which affords a magnificent panorama. The village is surrounded by tufa peaks and has numerous buildings with sculptural decoration on their façades.

Ürgüp (23 km. E.): This village at the foot of a cliff riddled with cave dwellings is in

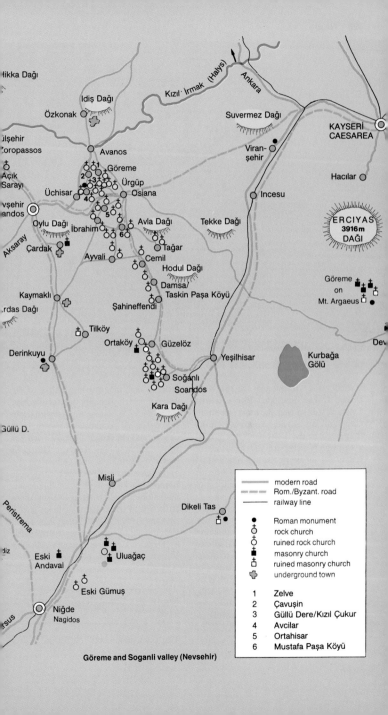

Göreme and Soganli valley (Nevşehir)

Göreme (Nevşehir), Church of St. Barbara, saints on horseback

a small valley running N. to the Kızıl Irmak. It has developed into a tourist centre as it is so near the most important Cappadocian sites. Ancient *Osiana* flourished in the 10&11C as the seat of a bishop. Nearby are the churches of *Kepez*, also including *Sarıca Kilise*, an 11C church with crossing dome with Christian symbols (fir twigs, birds) in the form of red line drawings.

Zelve (14 km. E.): Not far E. of Çavuş In is the rock face of ancient Zelve. It was not until the 1950s, when the population was moved to the newly-founded village of Yeni Zelve, that it was possible to investigate the numerous cave dwellings and churches thoroughly, and the work is by no means complete. At the foot of the cliff, riddled with numerous cells, are the ruins of two pre-iconoclastic basilicas, including the church known as *üzümlü Kilise* because of its vine decoration. The most

striking monument in the Valley of the Monks, which precedes the Zelve gorge, is the *cone of St.Simeon*, topped with triple tufa cones. At ground level it contains a chapel, and above this a hermit's cell has been hollowed out (10C). The area between Derinkuyu and Gelveri in the approaches to the Peristrema valley near Aksaray (q.v.) is to all intents and purposes unexplored, and therefore all the more attractive to interested travellers. It also contains the *Nar Gölü* (Pomegranate Lake) with mineral thermal springs, surrounded by bleak tufa cliffs into which cells and churches have again been cut.

Niğde

Niğde   p.574☐K 4

The town dominates the top of a pass

Zelve (Nevşehir), monks' valley

flanked by two volcanic cones, Melendiz Dağları (9,629 ft.) in the NW and Pozantı Dağı (8,822 ft.) in the SE. The town's present name first occurs in a text dating from AD 1188. At that time Niğde, which was certainly already in existence in the Byzantine period, was part of the Seljuk Sultanate of Rum (=Kayseri), but fell into the hands of the Mongols in the 13C. After a period of dominance by the Karamans, the Eretna princes ruled from Sivas from 1135. Another period of Karaman rule lasted until 1467, when Niğde became part of the Ottoman Empire.

Citadel: This fortress running from N. to S. is set on a rock in the middle of the town. It was probably founded by Alaeddin Kaykobad in the 1st third of the 13C. The massive octagonal tower probably also dates from this Seljuk

foundation period, even though it is sometimes ascribed to the Ottoman restoration (c.1470). There is a clock tower close by. The site to the S. of the castle hill is occupied by the *Alaeddin mosque*, founded in 1223 by the sultan who gave it its name. A portal in good condition leads to the prayer room with nave and two aisles of this domed mosque.

Bedesten: This covered bazaar, a street of shops just under 100 yards long, was established in the 17C and has a pointed tunnel vault. It is to be found at the foot of the hill in the S. section of its W. slope.

Sungur Bey Camii: This mosque built under Mongol rule in 1335, with a particularly striking *portal*, is in the SW below the castle rock, thus forming the S. end of the bedesten. The interior was completely redesigned after a fire in the 18C.

Eskiciler Çeşmesi: This fountain on the citadel hill dates from 1421.

Ak medrese: This Koran school in the S. of the town not far E. of the road to Bor, founded under the Karamanoğlu in 1409, formerly housed the small archaeological collection, which was transferred to the new *Archaeological Museum* in 1986.

Hüdavent türbe: This mausoleum built in 1312 for Princess Hüdavent Hatun (d. 1331), daughter of the Seljuk sultan Rukneddin, is on the NW edge of the town. There are two more tombs quite close by. The octagonal building has a pointed roof, with a wide transitional double octagon. The geometrical and figurative decoration on the façade shows considerable formal variety. A little further N. is the *Dört Ayak türbe* with mosque, also dating from the 1st half of the 14C.

Also worth seeing: *Diş Camii*, a little 16C Ottoman building; *Kiğli Camii* (in the S. of the town), 17C mosque with small tombs in the courtyard; a little further S. not far from the railway line is the *Tabak hane*; the *Hakki Bayab türbe* dates from 1334.

Environs: Bor (14 km. SW): Bor is a small town on the Human Cayi, with some picturesque quarters, particularly on the river bank. Not far from the town square is a small *covered bazaar* (bedesten) with a *bath* (hamam), both dating from the 16C. Notable buildings are the *Şari Camii* (1205) and the *Kale Camii* (1629), and above all the *Alaeddin mosque*, probably, as its name suggests, a Seljuk foundation, albeit rebuilt in 1410.

Eski Gümüş (9 km. NE): Somewhat to the E. of the road to Kayseri are the villages of Eski Gümüş and Yeni Gümüş, separated by a gorge. *Eski Gümüş*, with its man-made holes in the rock to the W. and S. looks rather like Zelve near Nevşehir. There is an important *rock church* to the N. with 11C frescos in good condition. These were not carefully examined and cleaned until 1962&3, as the building had been used as stables until then. A small rock tunnel, which could be

Niğde, Alaeddin Camii on castle mountain

defended against attack by an opening like a machicolation in the apex of the passage, leads to a rectangular courtyard, cut into the surrounding rock walls in the form of an imposing shaft. Its walls are articulated with arched niches, and deep holes for beams on its upper edge suggest that it was formerly wholly or partially roofed. On the left of the rear façade is the entrance to the incomplete exonarthex, and on the right a corridor leading to the tunnel-vaulted narthex of the rock church. Motifs on the frescos include Mary with the Christ Child and the large Archangels Gabriel and Michael. In the adjacent square church the hollowed-out dome is supported by four piers of rock which has been left standing. In the middle of the N. wall, on which the Annunciation and the Birth of Christ are portrayed, there is access to a large niche with two sarcophagi. The central apse at the E. end of the church is decorated with a frieze in three strips: Christ and the Mother of God twice, the Archangel Gabriel, the Four Evangelists and their symbols, the Apostles and other Church Fathers.

Kemerhisar (19 km. S.): Near here are the scant remains of ancient **Tyana**, in Roman and Byzantine times an important fortress, subsequently abandoned in favour of Bor and Niğde. The late-Hittite principality of Tuhana continued to exist here after the fall of the Hittite Empire (c.1200). Its most important ruler was Warpawalaš, who is not only depicted in the Ivriz rock relief near Ereğli, but also in a broken stele, now in İstanbul, which was found in Bor (2nd half of the 8C). It is difficult to make a clear distinction between his empire and the mighty principality of Tabal, also in this region, and so important that Sargon II of Assyria (721–705) went as far as to marry one of his daughters to a Tabal prince.

Misli (35 km. N.): Ancient *Musilia* is still in village in which half of the houses are built into the rock. From here a track goes off to the right to *Hasaköy*, where the tomb of St.Makrina is in a Greek *church* built in 1843, and now used as a mosque.

Ordu

Ordu   p.568□N 1–2

This harbour town on the Black Sea was founded in the 18C, and first called *Bucak*. There were two earlier settlements. In the 7C or 6C BC colonists from Miletos NW of the modern town established a trading post called *Kotyra* on the coast. In 401 Xenophon sailed from here with the remainder of the famous 'Ten Thousand' for Herakleia on Pontus. In the 14C AD the population moved to *Bayramli*,

Eski Gümüş (Niğde), Archangel Gabriel

modern *Eskipazar* (5 km. S. of Ordu). All that remains of this once flourishing community are the ruins of two baths and a mosque, as Eskipazar very quickly declined in importance after the harbour of Ordu came into being. The area at the E. foot of the Boztepe, just under 2,000 ft. high, and sloping steeply to the sea, was chosen as the site. On the occasion of Atatürk's hundredth birthday the harbour was thoroughly renovated, in commemoration of his stay there in September 1924. As the town has only existed for two centuries there are no ancient monuments.

Worth seeing: The *Ibrahim Paşa Camii* (also *Orta Camii*) is an older mosque which started to be used again *c.*1800. The *Hamidiye Camii* (1889), *Yali Camii* (also *Aziziye Camii*; built in 1895 on the site of the old Ahşap Mosque) are also worth seeing. Unfortunately the 18C *Armenian basilica (kilise)*, later used as a prison, high on a plateau to the W. of the town above the coast road to Samsun, has only survived as a ruin.

Environs: Giresun (46 km. E.): This coastal town with 50,000 inhabitants is the administrative centre of the province of Giresun, to the E. of the province of Ordu. It is picturesquely sited at the foot and on the slopes of a promontory which thrusts into the Black Sea like a little peninsula. The top of the hill is occupied by a *citadel*. As in the neighbouring town the Miletans established a settlement here, conquered in 183 BC by Pharnakes, the grandfather of Mithridates the Great, and called **Pharnakeia** after him. The Greeks called it *Kerasos*, and the Romans **Cerasus**. It gave its name to the first bitter cherries which Lucullus took from here to Rome after his campaigns against Mithridates, which he called 'prunus cerasus'. The Byzantine princes Alexios and David, who fled to Trapezunt/Trabzon in 1204 during the siege of Constantinople and founded the Byzantine Empire of Trebizond; they also gained control of Giresun. After the Seljuks and the Mongols, the Ottomans, under Mehmet the Conqueror, took over the city in 1461.

Worth seeing: The walls of the Byzantine *citadel* on the cliffs overlooking the sea have survived in good condition. The *Armenian domed church* (18C) by the E. harbour and the *Vakkas türbesi* (15C),

Ordu, 18C Armenian basilica

the mausoleum of a local Muslim saint who claimed to have been a direct descendent of Mahomet, are also worth seeing.

6 km. E. of the town the *island of Giresun Adazi* is just off the coast (ferry available). This is ancient *Aretias*, on which according to legend the Amazons had a Temple of Mars. The ruins still visible on the island are the remains of a 10C Byzantine monastery, however.

Tirebolu (100 km. E.): This is ancient **Tripolis**, in a sickle-shaped bay on the shores of the Black Sea. Formerly the hinterland was of economic importance because of rich deposits of silver with a lead content, mined particularly in Argyria on the Tirebolu Suyu. In the Middle Ages merchants from Genoa maintained an important trading post here, secured by three coastal fortresses around the town, Andoz Kalesi, Bedruma Kalesi and Merkez Kalesi.

Üuniye (81 km. W.): The modern harbour town (28,500 inhabitants) was probably, like many other towns on the Black Sea coast, founded in the 5C BC. In the Roman period its wines were famous, and today it is the westernmost point of the 'Hazel Nut Coast' (Findiksahili). With the exception of the 18C town hall, the town, which was part of the Ottoman Empire from the 15C, has few interesting sights. Worth seeing in the surrounding area are *Üniye Kalesi* (5 km.), a Byzantine fortress with a fine view of the surrounding hazel-nut colonies, and the *Tozkoparan caves* (7 km.), rock tombs of uncertain date, as yet still unexplored.

ancient town, and which shine from the steep cliffs far down into the plain of the Cürüksu, a tributary of the Meander. They are formed by the warm springs, at a temperature of 33 C and containing calcium bicarbonate. The waters flow out

Pamukkale, burial ground

Pamukkale/Hierapolis

Denizli   p.572 □ E 5

19 km. N. of the provincial capital Denizli are the ruins of the Graeco-Roman city of Hierapolis, about 500 ft. above the Meander on a limestone terrace. The Turkish name Pamukkale (Cotton Castle) refers to the ruins of a 11&12C fortress which has only survived in fragments by the world-famous **stalactite terraces** falling over 300 ft. from the plateau of the

of the terrace at various points (the so-called Sacred Spring, now used to feed the swimming pool of the motel in the centre of Pamukkale; the main spring, worth seeing for its colourfulness, is easy to find on driving on through the necropolis after about 5 km). The deposits are formed when the water loses its carbon dioxide and the limestone is deposited in various shapes and colours (white, grey, gold, brown; the water also contains iron, magnesium, sulphureous acid) and forms a complex system of basins, gutters, overhanging surfaces and beard-like stalactite formations.

The ancient town was founded by Pergamon in the 2C BC. King Eumenes II established a border fortress for a military colony here *c.* 190 BC at the time of the expansion of the Pergamene empire. He called it after Hiera, the wife of the mythical Pergamene founding father Telephos. When the town was taken over by the Romans in 129 BC the name of this city was mistakenly understood as Holy City, as it had many temples, and the Greek word hierós means holy. All the surviving ruins date back to the extension of the city by the Romans in the Imperial period. Only the site of the theatre and the foundations of the Temple of Apollo are evidence of the Hellenistic garrison. Hierapolis had constantly to be extended and rebuilt because of the numerous earthquakes on this geologically unstable site. Four particularly severe earthquakes are recorded in the Roman period alone: one of them (AD 60) caused Nero to rebuild Hierapolis completely.

The thermal spa was also popular in the Imperial period, and flourished in the 2&3C AD under Septimius Severus and Caracalla, whose tutor, the Sophist Antipater, came from Hierapolis. The city is on the borders of Caria, Lycia and Phrýgia. Thus its position, the original Greek population and subsequent Roman immigration meant that the population was always mixed. Its citizens tended to

Pamukkale, calcified terraces ▷

Pamukkale, monumental Roman gate

be employed in the wool industry, as shearers, washers, dyers, weavers and spinners. It was also a centre of nail-making and copper-founding, and the hot springs attracted spa visitors throughout the town's history. The strong Jewish community developed into a Christian one at an early stage, and the Apostle Philip is said to have passed his last days here, before being martyred in 87.

The whole settlement is divided into two, a town laid out on a rectangular plan in the S., and a necropolis of roughly the same size in the N. The first excavations were made under the German archaeologist Carl Humann in 1887; Italian archaeologists under P. Verzone have been working here since 1957. A colonnaded street over 1,300 yards long runs right through the town. It has 20 ft. walks at either side, separated from the street by columns. It formerly had gates at its N.

and S. extremities. The N. gateway has survived in good condition. It has three arches and two side towers, and was built in AD 84&85 by the proconsul of the province of Asia, Julius Frontinus, in honour of the Emperor Domitian.

Temple of Apollo (3C AD): The foundations are Hellenistic. The front of the temple is supported on a base over 6 ft. high, the back is built on natural rock, and reached by a flight of steps. Its forward orientation is emphasized by six unfluted Corinthian columns on the façade side, and by the pronaos in front of the cella.

Plutonium (on the S. side of the Temple of Apollo): This is a sacred precinct of Pluto, the god of the Underworld, entered by a yard-wide crack in the rock which exudes a smell of gas. Only a closed room

Pamukkale, burial ground

and a paved courtyard remain of the buildings. The Greek geographer Strabo (64 BC–23 AD) wrote of it: 'The Plutonium was a man-high, very deep opening under a gently-sloping hill. In front of this was a 50 ft. square enclosure in which the vapours were so thick that it was impossible to see the floor. Outside the enclosure the air is free of fumes when the wind is not blowing, and it is possible to approach quite close; but any living creature that enters will find death upon the instant. Bulls for example collapse and die. We let some little birds fly in, and they at once fell lifeless to the ground. The eunuchs of Cybele are resistant to the extent that they can approach close to the opening and indeed go in without having to hold their breath.'

The juxtaposition of the Temple of Apollo (a shrine to Cybele preceded it on the site) and the Plutonium means that the god of light is confronted with the dark god of death, shining order with the uncanny, the chaotic. This is the significance of ancient Hierapolis: living by the entrance to Hades, close to the realm of the dead: hence the extensive necropolis.

Theatre (*c.*AD 200 under Septimius Severus): The theatre has been painstakingly restored and completely rebuilt in sections. It is set on a natural slope. Behind the 330 ft. wide façade, once lavishly decorated, opens the auditorium with 50 rows of seats, divided into seven wedges by eight flights of steps. A horizontal passage halfway up makes a further division into two blocks. The imperial box is in the middle of the cavea. The orchestra is surrounded by a wall almost 6 ft. high. The stage is 13 ft. above the orchestra, equipped with niches towards the front. The stage building has

Pamukkale, memorial site for martyrdom of the Apostle Philip

two storeys with three rows of columns one above the other, and five doors with windows above them.

Thermal baths (2C AD, now used as a storehouse for archaeological finds): A large hall for gymnastics, a room for the emperor, a room for events, a frigidarium and a caldarium can still be discerned, also a palaestra belonging to the baths.

Also worth seeing: *Christian buildings*: Hierapolis as the seat of a bishop and from the 6C of a metropolitan had a series of churches: this is indicated by three churches which have survived as ruins. They are a large secular building near the baths converted into a vaulted church *c.* 410, then a 6C columned basilica with nave and two aisles roughly in the middle of the colonnaded street, and finally, just before the necropolis, part of a building

with three arches and points from which the vaulting sprang, a 2C AD thermal bath later used as a Christian church. *Martyrium of St. Philip the Apostle* (about 600 yards beyond the theatre): Access to eight chambers is afforded from an octagonal central space, with the core of the building enclosed by a square section containing numerous rooms accessible from the outside. This is a place of remembrance for the Apostle (whose tomb has not yet been found), with rooms to accommodate pilgrims. The apse-like niche in the octagon with a semicircular row of seats for the priests suggests a room used for worship. *Nymphaeum:* This ruin near the Temple of Apollo consists of a rear wall and two protruding side walls. It contained a pool reached by a flight of steps, and the whole building was once lavishly decorated with marble columns and decorative cornices. *Necropolis:*

Hierapolis has about 1,200 tombs, making it the largest ancient cemetery in Asia Minor. Because of its position on the fringe of many cultures there is a considerable mixture of tomb types: the large Lycian mausoleum-style sarcophagus on a high pedestal, the Lydian tumulus with vaulted, partially underground round tomb chamber, the temple-shaped house of the dead based on the magic housing of the dead.

Environs: The well-known places to visit around Hierapolis are Akhan, Kolossae and Laodiceia. Probably the most rewarding visit is to Laodiceia, although it has hardly been excavated.

Akhan (22 km. SE): Seljuk *caravanserai* built 1253&4 by Emir Karasungur, 8 km. E. of Denizli on the Denizli–Dinar road. It is rectangular, closed on the outside, with an internal arcaded courtyard and a three-aisled vaulted room beyond it.

Colossae (about 24 km. SE of Pamukkale; 15 km. E. of Laodiceia near the village of *Monaz*): No buildings, only imprints on the ground (acropolis, theatre) have survived of the third city, a Phrygian foundation, alongside Hierapolis and Laodiceia in the Lykos valley, and thus the town exists only in historical reminiscences.

Laodiceia (10 km. S., on the ancient River Lykos, now Cürüksu): 3 km. along the route from Denizli to Pamukkale, then branch off and proceed 4 km. further; with the exception of a nymphaeum no excavations have been undertaken. The Ecumenical Council of Laodiceia *c.* AD 360 forbade spells and magic, refused to accept the introduction of hymns into church services and established a canon of the Holy Scriptures. The holding of the synod here confirms the dominance of the Christians in the city. Epaphras of Colossae, Paul's 'beloved fellow-servant' had introduced Christianity to and beyond the strong Jewish community. Paul's Epistle to the Colossians mentions Laodiceia (4,13), and the Revelation of St.John the Divine threatens the

Pamukkale, theatre

community, which it describes as lukewarm, with a terrible fate. But Laodiceia bacame the seat of a bishop very early, and remained one until the 13C, and is thus one of the earliest of all Christian communities. This is due most of all to the city's position at the junction of the great road link from the W. coast to the E. via the Meander valley and the spur leading to the S. coast of Anatolia. Here Antiochos II (261–246 BC) of Syria had founded a city on a hill not far from the River Lykos (between 261 and 252 BC) in honour of his wife Laodice, who then had him murdered after his divorce. Two smaller rivers Asopos, (Gümüş Çay) and Kaproz (Ellez), defined the site. The population lived, like that of Hierapolis, from wool processing (naturally black wool from Laodiceia was famous) and cloth manufacture. The wealth thus acquired made it possible for the citizens to rebuild their city with their own means after it was destroyed by the earthquake of AD 60. After being conquered by the Seljuks the settlement was abandoned in the 13C.

The ruins between the villages of Eskihisar and Goncali are contained within a ring wall with three gates, enclosing an area of about one third of a square mile. The gates are in the N., NW and E.: in the N., the Hierapolis Gate, of which very little remains; in the NW, the Ephesus Gate, dedicated to the Emperor Domitian (AD 81–96): a tripartite arch with side towers (cf. Hierapolis); in the E. the Syrian Gate, still recognizable, and with a street lined with tombs leading away from it.

Gymnasium (opposite the stadium): Possibly this was also a thermal bath, as suggested by the 16 ft. high water tower, with vertical water pipes completely blocked by calcification. The tower also supplied parts of the town with water (→ nymphaeum). The water arrived from the S. via an aqueduct, of which fragments can be seen around the site. The water came from a vigorous spring above Denizli (Başpinar), flowed through a settling pool, and was then pumped into the water tower.

Nymphaeum (3C AD; almost in the centre of the town): This was excavated by French archaeologists in 1961–3, and consists of a 33 ft. square reservoir surrounded on two sides by columns, with two semicircular fountains on the diagonal sides, fed with water from two chambers behind them. A statue of Isis, part of the once lavish decoration, has been found. Later the square room with a pool was closed and put to another use.

Odeion or council chamber for the town council, about 100 yards N. opposite the stadium.

Stadium (in the S. of the town; AD 79): Dedicated to the Emperor Vespasian (AD 69–79) by a rich citizen. The building is extraordinarily long (1,150 x 200 ft.) and was used for athletic competitions and gladiatorial contests (cf. stadium in Aphrodisias).

Theatre: There are two theatres on the N. slope of the settlement plateau, a larger and a smaller one, recognizable by the few rows of seats which have survived in each. They face each other, but are slightly offset.

Necropolis: This is outside the town in the direction of Pamukkale.

Pamukkale, Roman thermal bath

Pergamon/Bergama

İzmir   p.564□C 3

Modern Bergama on the N. slope of the
acropolis hill running down to the plain
of the Bakir Çay (Kaikos) is a commercial
and administrative town, centre of local
fig, tobacco and cotton growing, and also
a long-standing centre for the manufacture
of carpets with geometrical patterns showing Caucasian influence, and in glowing
colours, above all red, blue and creamy
white.

The town is about 30 km. from the sea,
below ancient Pergamon, which was a
terrace town on the upper slopes of the
volcanic hill 1,092 ft. high. The town was
cut into the mountain in the 3C BC, just
after the death of Alexander the Great. It
is carved into the hillside almost
sculpturally, in a fashion reminiscent of
a plan formed by one of Alexander's
architects who wanted to make Mount
Athos into an image of Alexander, holding an entire town in one hand, with a
river pouring from the other. The
foundation myth also helps to explain the
town's self-image: Herakles wanted to
spend a night in Arcadia on his way to
Augias in Tegea. He was accommodated
by the local king, Aleus. The drunken
guest raped Auge, the king's daughter,
who was also a priestess of Athena, Auge
was driven away, gave birth to a son in
the mountains, and was sold into slavery.
The child was suckled by a hind, found
by shepherds and called Telephos. When
he grew up, Telephos went to Delphi. 'Set
sail and seek King Teuthras, the Mysian'
was the oracle's pronouncement. In Mysia
in Asia Minor he then found his mother
Auge married to Teuthras, King of Mysia.
Telephos married their daughter, and later
inherited the kingdom. Auge's tomb is to
be seen by the Kaikos in Pergamon. Thus
Pergamon is the product of violence and
reconciliation, also with Athena, whose
temple stood in the centre of the city.
Pergamon, with its central cult of Athena,
was also a centre of science and the fine
arts: thus it had the largest library of the
Hellenistic period after Alexandria, and
its artistic style represents the peak of the
entire Hellenistic period (c.225–150 BC).
In its distinctive cult of Demeter (goddess
of corn and of all growth) Pergamon saw
itself as a rural and agricultural centre,

Pergamon, gymnasium, upper terrace

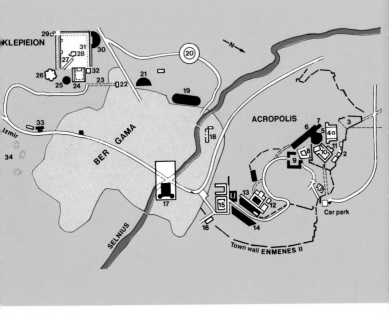

Pergamon 1 Upper acropolis gate 2 Kings' palaces 3 Stores 4 Trajan temple 5 Theatre 6 Theatre terrace 7 Dionysos temple 8 Zeus temple 9 Upper agora 10 Athena temple 11 Library 12 Upper gymnasium (neoi) 13 Middle gymnasium (epheboi) 14 Lower gymnasium (paides) 15 Lower agora 16 Lower acropolis gate 17 Kızıl Avlu (red hall) 18 Ulu Cami 19 Stadium 20 Roman amphitheatre 21 Roman theatre 22 Viran gate 23 Colonnaded road 24 Propylon 25 Temple of Zeus-Asklepios 26 Spa 27 Tunnel 28 Sacred spring 29 Toilets 30 Theatre 31 Colonnaded hall 32 Library 33 Museum 34 Burial hill

entwined in the seasonal sequence of growth and decay, enhanced by the cultic mysteries.

In the struggle of the Olympian gods of light against the giants, representing darkness, in which Herakles considerably helped the Olympians, the city, high on its hill and in the light, saw itself as standing above deadening entanglement with earth. As a centre of culture and

civilization Pergamon felt itself to be a bastion against any kind of barbarity (not only in its victory over Celts storming down from the N. in 230 BC).

Despite signs of early settlement going back to the Bronze Age, Pergamon is entirely a Hellenistic city which came into being in the 2&3C BC under the Attalids, a race of unusual parvenus comparable with the condottieres of the Italian Renaissance. For 150 years, five generations, they clung on to power, and from 281–133 BC the basis of this power was military might: when Alexander's general staff broke up after the king's death, his general Lysimachos withdrew to the safety of the already existing fortress of Pergamon, with a large proportion of the war funds, which he adminstered. He had 9,000 talents at his disposal, enough money to acquire mercenaries to strengthen his forces, builders and crafts-

Pergamon, acropolis, temple of Zeus

men to extend the fortifications, and also land around the city of Pergamon.

After the death of Lysimachos in 281 BC the pattern of events after Alexander's death was repeated: Lysimachos' treasurer and officer Philetairos succeeded him and founded a dynasty with the money. Pergamon, as can still be seen from its buildings, rose directly from the legacy of Alexander, and is a small-scale model of a state under the Diadochi, one of the smaller states which formed after the decline of the empire of Alexander alongside the three great empires ruled by the Diadochi, Macedonia, Syria and Egypt. Three generations of founders were needed to give Pergamon the status of an autonomous state: Lysimachos (323–281 BC) laid the base by selecting the site and secured it in military terms. The Temple of Athena was probably built by him (now the oldest building on the acropolis).

Philetairos (281–263 BC) stabilized the system by expanding the fortress into a settlement and founding the Attalid dynasty. Under him the Shrine of Demeter was established (now the second-oldest building in Pergamon). His nephew Eumenes I (263–241 BC) continued to extend fortress and settlement, acquired more land in the surrounding area and above all gained political recognition from outside for the new state as an independent entity. Finally his successor, Attalos I (241–197 BC) succeeded in making Pergamon the dominant power in western Asia Minor. In 230 BC he put up a successful defence against the Celts and Gauls who had attacked Asia Minor, thus maintaining freedom and Greek culture for the W. part of the country. He was celebrated as Soter, the Saviour of Asia Minor. The lords of Pergamon called themselves king from this point.

The three subsequent generations, working on this politically, economically and militarily secure basis, transformed Pergamon into the leading cultural centre on the W. coast of Asia Minor and put an end to Alexandria's monopoly as the intellectual centre of the Hellenistic world. Thus it is fair to say of Eumenes II, (197–159 BC) the successor of Attalos I, what was said of Augustus about himeslf in the context of Rome: 'I took over a city of brick and left behind a city of marble'. The majority of the buildings still to be seen on the acropolis hill date from his reign. He extended the city towards the foot of the hill by the addition of a second, the lower, agora, constructed a new town wall and built the extensive royal palace. The Altar of Zeus, the library and the three-tier gymnasium were built under him, and he also replaced the wooden stage with a stone building. He gathered a circle of scientists and poets around him and the Pergamon library began to build up its extensive collection, and became a centre of Homeric research. After Attalos II, (159–138 BC) who is historically less securely recorded, Attalos III was more a scholar than a politician, for which reason he found no difficulty in bequeathing the whole of Pergamon to the protective power in the West, Rome, a legacy which Rome accepted in 133. In his work 'Greek Cultural History' J.Burckhardt wrote of Attalos III: 'He is truculent with relations and friends, and then sinks from time to time into dark melancholy, does not cut his hair or beard, withdraws from affairs of state and occupies himself only with gardening, sculpture and metalwork'. This shy, suspicious ruler-scholar only rarely left his palace, lived for his research, produced healing and poisonous plants and tested them on criminals. He also wrote a book on agriculture.

The transfer of power to Rome after the death of Attalos III certainly did not take place smoothly. A natural son of Eumenes II, Aristonikos, refused to accept the will and tried by means of a revolt of the non-royal slaves (the royal slaves had been released by Rome) and the proletariat to found a new state with some communistic traits under the resounding name Heliopolis (Sun State). Rome had to intervene militarily to secure its inheritance, and Pergamon became the centre of the Roman province of Asia.

Germans have been excavating in Pergamon since 1864. The engineer Carl Humann, while building a road, noticed a peasant with marble reliefs on his cart. He was taking them away to be used for lime production. Investigations took him to the Altar of Zeus in Pergamon. From 1878–86 the first excavations took place under C. Humann and A. Conze. The sultan gave permission for their finds to be taken to Berlin, where they still form the core of the Pergamon Museum in East Berlin. Further digs followed under W. Dörpfeld (1900–13) and T. Wiegand (1927–38). The German Archaeological Institute of İstanbul has been working on the site since 1957. They are at present concerned with the restoration of the Temple of Trajan and the excavation of the residential area.

The best place at which to start a tour of Pergamon is the acropolis at the top of the hill, progressing down the mountain terraces to modern Bergama and concluding with a visit to the Asklepion about 1 km. outside Bergama.

Acropolis (ancient Pergamon):
Agora, Lower: This square paved with stone slabs is 112 by 210 ft. It was formerly surrounded on all four sides by two-storey Doric halls. The stone spheres piled up here are from the magazines of the Byzantine fortress at the top of the hill.
Agora, Upper: This is an open space S. of the Altar of Zeus and about 45 ft. below it, with Doric colonnades on three sides and a small Ionic-Doric temple perhaps dedicated to Hermes, the god of merchants and dating from the first half of the 2C AD on the fourth (the valley side). The whole agora was surrounded by a second

Pergamon, Asklepieion, colonnaded hall ▷

wall. The tomb of C.Humann, under a granite slab, is E. of the agora below the guard house.

Altar of Zeus: The famous Pergamon altar, called 'Satan's seat' in Revelation (2,13), was built *c.*180–160 BC by Eumenes II in honour of Zeus and in gratitude for the king's victory over the Galatians in 183 BC. The building is now flanked by two pines and stood on an almost square terrace 226 by 253 ft., with a base 119 by 112 ft. The substructure had five tiers, and supported by a plinth with an upper and a lower section, on which stood a double covered columned hall with interior wall and a total of 90 Ionic columns (height of columns 8 ft. 6 ins.). The fourth, open side was taken up by a 65 ft. wide flight of broad, gently-rising steps, leading through a tripartite building to an inner courtyard surrounded by piers and half columns, with the sacrificial altar in the middle. The upper, 7 ft. 6 ins. high base of the plinth was surrounded by a frieze almost 400 ft. long (with the Parthenon frieze the most elaborate relief of antiquity) showing the struggle of the Olympian gods of light with the giants,

Pergamon, colonnaded road to Asklepieion

the untamed earth forces, and also the foundation legend and the life of the founding father Telephos. The Pergamon Altar was thus not an altar, but the festive frame for an altar. A fragment of the core of the building in trachyte tufa remains on site, and the parts of the step section which were recovered are in the Pergamon Museum in East Berlin.

Gates: The *Acropolis Gate*, above the upper car park behind the modern approach ramp, leads through the acropolis wall directly into the palace precinct behind it on the right. It was built under Eumenes II (197—159 BC) and so was the *main gate* of the city below the lower agora, a courtyard with two gate openings.

Gymnasia: These were built under Eumenes II for physical and mental education, and were among the most beautiful in the Greek world. There were three sections in descending tiers on the slope, and each terrace was devoted to a particular age group: the paides (children under 15) were trained and taught on the lowest terrace, the ephebes (youths, 15–18 years) on the middle terrace, and on the upper terrace the neoi (men, 18 and above). The upper terrace was surrounded on three sides by a two-storey Corinthian covered colonnade; on the N. side set into the slope were, from E. to W., a thermal bath, a room with two apses for for imperial statues, the imperial chamber with inscription, a large hall, the epheion, and a room with semicircular rows of seats, the auditorium. Opposite on the S. side was a covered stadium 695 by 23 ft. The middle gymnasium lay 46 ft. deeper. Two parallel buildings ran its full length to the N. and S., and between them at the E. end was a small temple of Herakles and Hermes with an altar in front of it. In the middle of the S. building a vaulted staircase led to the lower gymnasium, crushed in between the supporting walls of the middle gymnasium and the road to the upper acropolis. It was cleared in the 8C AD to make way for the Byzantine fortifying wall.

Heroon: On the way from the gate to the upper acropolis to the Altar of Zeus on the left are the remains of a peristyle building with residential section and a colonnaded courtyard, extended by the addition of a columned hall with cult room behind it, a heroon, a place for the worship of the ruling house.

Houses: Contemporary German digs are concentrating on the area above the Shrine of Demeter, where a Roman residential area is being revealed. So far excavations have uncovered a small *gymnasium with baths*, an *odeion* with raked seats, a *marble hall* and *kitchens*, all built over on many occasions, indicating the cramped conditions on the acropolis.

Library: This was associated with the Temple of Athena, and is a sequence of rooms behind the hall surrounding the temple to the N. It is still possible to see from the easternmost room that a bench about 3 ft. high ran round three sides with a space of about 17 ins. between the bench and the wall. This was filled with wooden shelving for 70,000 volumes and rolls. As the library had a total of 200,000 titles there must have been additional rooms. On the fourth side of each room was a door, and opposite the door of the middle room a statue of Athena, a copy of the statue by Phidias in the Parthenon. The Attalids, and Eumenes II in particular, were passionate book collectors, and they sent buyers and copiers all over the then known world (Galen avers that false manuscripts were prepared for them). The Ptolemys, responsible for the rival library in Alexandria, then forbade the export of papyrus to Pergamon. The Pergamenes replied by using skins to write on. These, unlike papyrus, could not be rolled up, but had to be placed with one page on top of another and bound, and thus the codex (block) came into being, essentially the shape we now know as a book. Antony took the enormous stock of books to Alexandria as a wedding present for Cleopatra, where they were destroyed by the caliph Omar after the fall of Egypt (7C AD).

Palaces: Just beyond the acropolis gate are the foundations of the royal palaces in a confusing, long-drawn-out sequence. They were essentially peristyle buildings, with the palace of Eumenes II in the centre (opposite the library). It has a floor mosaic, and also a cistern.

Shrine of Hera: Above the gymnasia is

Pergamon, Asklepieion

a tripartite temenos with a small Doric temple in the middle, flanked by a semi-circular room and a small hall. According to a dedicatory inscription the shrine was built under Attalos II (159–138 BC) for Hera Basileia, patroness and protectress of marriage.

Storehouses: On the highest plateau of the acropolis hill are stone foundations for four large storehouses, probably used to ensure supplies for the acropolis.

Temple of Athena: This is the oldest building, (late 4C) and the core from which the city developed: a Doric peripteros with 6 x 10 columns on a stylobate of 39 by 72 ft. (according to an Attic custom the principal temple of the town had to be Doric). The slender columns around the pronaos with its two columns between the antae and around the double cella without rear chamber (opisthodomos) are slender and placed very far apart, replacing closed architecture with the illusion of a hall-like space. The precinct was surrounded by two-storey colonnades (the N. colonnade on the library side had two aisles) with Doric columns in the lower and Ionic in the upper storey. Between the upper columns were relief slabs with representations of weapons commemorating Attalos' victory over the Gauls. A monument to Attalos I and sculptures of Gauls (Dying Gaul) in the square were further memorials of this nature (the remainder of a tower near the temple is part of the Byzantine fortress, which held out against the Seljuks until 1302).

Temple of Demeter: The shrine was devoted to mysteries similar to the Eleusine rite, purification ceremonies by means of which the faithful hoped for a better place in the next world. The complex built by Philetairos and Eumenes I in the 3C BC included a *Temple of Demeter* at the W. end, a megaron 21 by 42 ft. in trachyte with two columns between in antis and a bucranium frieze above the wall architrave, in front of this an altar (23 by 8 ft.) with horns forming volutes. The square in front of the temple is 66 ft. wide, (used for mystery plays and processions) and had a long hall on the N. side, in the W. part of which was a colonnade (141 ft.), and the E. section of this had ten steps for 800 worshippers. The narrow set of buildings ended in a *colonnade* 279 ft. long on the valley side. Finally, the *propylaeum*, which gave access to the temenos, was built under Eumenes II.

Temple of Trajan: Trajan's (AD 98–117) temple is on an artificial terrace 223 by 190 ft. formed by vaulted substructures. It was begun under Trajan and completed by Hadrian (AD 117–138), and its cella contained statues of both emperors. The Corinthian temple was freestanding in the square, and the peripteros with 6 x 10 columns was in the middle of an open space 193 by 216 ft., surrounded on three sides by Ionic covered colonnades.

Theatre: This is the most impressive building in Pergamon, and at the same time the steepest theatre in the Greek world. Its rise and fall are a powerful architectural demonstration of the dramatic counterplay of hubris and downfall manifested by the protagonist. The cavea accommodated about 10,000 spectators. It covered an area of 45,208 sq. ft., and rose through 121 ft., with 2 horizontal passages splitting the 87 rows of seats into three ranks divided into six wedges by narrow flights of steps. Facing the spectators was a terrace 807 ft. long by 49–56 ft. wide, supported on 39 ft. high walls, above which there was a three-storey hall on the valley side. In front of this the square stone bases for anchoring the posts for a wooden stage can still be seen. It is probable that the whole complex was not cut out of the cliff until the late 3C BC, probably under Eumenes II; after Pergamon was taken over by the Romans in 133 BC the stage house was rebuilt as a marble showpiece. The 2C BC *Temple of Dionysos* at the end of the terrace is part of the theatre. It stood on a podium 15 ft. high reached by a flight of 25 steps. The stylobate was 39 by 66 ft., and supported a cella and a porch with four

Ionic columns. It was rebuilt under Trajan, and completely redesigned under Caracalla in the 3C AD.

Bergama (modern Pergamon): The centre is dominated as ever by a long red-brick building with a broad square in front of it and a round building on the rear wall at each side. This is the so-called *Red Hall*, Kızıl Avlu, a Roman place of worship probably dating from the 2C AD, perhaps a Shrine of Serapis, as suggested by statues which have been found and by the water: the 853 by 360 ft. square is built out over the Selinus, which flows under it in a double tunnel. The hall is 190 by 85 ft., its walls were once marble-clad and rose to a height of 62 ft., and it had a shallow pool of water; behind this was a cult statue over 30 ft. high on a base with sides measuring 15 by 15 ft. on a podium 33 ft. wide and almost 5 ft.high. In the Byzantine period a basilica with nave and two aisles, apse on the E. side and arches, the church of St. John or St. Paul, was built inside the hall. Pergamon was one of the seven Asian apocalyptic churches. The building had open courtyards on its long sides, and outer halls with fountains. There was also a covered colonnade in the temple square in front of the building.

Museum: The museum on the road to İzmir contains Archaic, Hellenistic, Roman and Byzantine finds from the area around Pergamon, and also has a good ethnographic department. The ceramics, inscriptions, statuettes and portraits of Roman emperors are particularly worth a visit.

Ulu Cami: The great Friday mosque was built by Beyazıt I in 1398&9. It is almost square in plan, with three aisles and three domes over the central one. It is well worth seeing, and so are the old bridges in the town: they are based on Hellenistic and Roman constructions.

Ancient Buildings in the Environs

Amphitheatre: W. of Bergama, in a trough, are the remains of a Roman amphitheatre above a brook which could be diverted into the arena for naumachiae (naval battles). The oval building had an arena 446 ft. long by 56 ft. wide; the surrounding tiers of seats held about 50,000 spectators for animal and gladiatorial contests.

Pergamon, view of foundations of altar of Zeus

Asklepieion: This shrine of the god of healing Asklepios is about 2.5 km. from the acropolis hill in the SW of Bergama. It is linked with Pergamon by a straight road which in the Imperial period was lined on both sides with colonnades and shops (one section has been excavated). This self-contained religious precinct combined cult and therapy for the sick and under the Romans (evidence exists for the 2C AD) was for a time a fashionable spa and meeting place for high society. It is said to have been founded in the late 4C BC, but was extended in the 2C BC, particularly under Hadrian (AD 117–138) and Antoninus Pius (AD 138–161), and also by private subscription. It functioned until the 6C AD under Justinian. It was founded by the Pergamene Aristarchus, who was cured of a broken leg in the Asklepieion in Epidauros, and in his gratitude brought the cult to Pergamon. He was thus involved in the rapid spread of the cult of Asklepios, which as well as central cult sites in Epidauros, Kos and Pergamon had more then 200 shrines in the ancient world (then the Roman Empire). In Homer's 'Iliad' Asklepios was still a human doctor, by the 5C BC he was already a god, whose cult spread from Epidauros to the Pelopponese. The special feature of the therapy practised in Pergamon in the context of his cult was that it was based on psychosomatic connections, a combination of medicine and psychotherapy. Sleep was part of the treatment, used to provide dreams as a basis for diagnosis during incubation, followed by sleep in the temple and healing sleep. The regime included diet, cold and hot baths, sporting exercises (running a distance barefoot) and gymnastics for the sick. Pergamon was sometimes also a medical research station, as is shown by the fact that Galen (AD 131–210), after Hippocrates the most famous doctor of ancient times, practised, taught, researched and wrote here. An Asklepieion was directed by priests, supported by temple slaves. They were freed from taxes, permitted to till land belonging to the Asklepieion and given an honorary share of the sacrificial animals. A team of doctors worked under their supervision. Citizens of the town formed lodge-like cult societies in close association with the shrine. The following buildings are within the rectangular open space 302 by 394 ft. The starting-point is by a slightly radioactive spring.

Library: This is on the right just beyond the propylaeum, recognizable by the rectangular niches for books and the apse on the façade side for the imperial statue.

Incubation rooms: These are rooms near the spring and the temple entrance in the middle of the square in which newly-admitted patients slept after purification and sacrifice, at first in order to find information from their dreams, and later to be healed.

Latrine: This was a public lavatory with seats for 40 people over a water channel.

Spring: Three small *temples* (to Asklepios Soter, Asklepios the Redeemer, Hygeia the goddess of health, and Apollo, as father of Asklepios) and several *fountain houses* were gradually built around the spring, which rises from a cleft in the rock near the theatre.

Propylaeum: Gateway to the whole complex, with staircase leading to a square courtyardwith access to the actual propylon with four columns via another flight of steps leading to the Asklepieion square.

Circular building: On the left of the entrance in the SE corner of the Asklepieion, the building had at least two storeys and a tunnel-vaulted ambulatory in the basement with basins and fountains on the walls and a circular room on the ground floor with six additional rooms like an exedra. The building was certainly vaulted, and probably the main hospital.

Stoa: Hadrian had covered Ionic colonnades built around the great square on the S., W. and N. sides. The N. colonnade has been partially re-erected.

Temple: The circular temple directly to the left of the propylon originally had four columns and is approached by a flight of

Pergamon, theatre in Asklepieion

steps. It was dedicated to Zeus-Asklepios in association with the cult. It is a small-scale replica of the Pantheon in Rome (144 ft. diameter reduced to 79 ft.) and its exterior had a sequence of round and angled niches for statues.

Theatre: The little theatre in the NW corner accommodated 3,500 spectators and had five flights of steps, diazoma and three-storey stage building. It was restored for a visit by Atatürk in 1935.

Tunnel: A vaulted tunnel runs diagonally under the square from the circular hospital building to the central spring. Its purpose has been interpreted in many different ways, from a water-carrying channel to cultic ceremonial way for patients, from incubation room to treatment area.

Environs: Ägä (45 km. S. of Bergama, 45 minutes' walk from the village of Köseler): The remains of the Aeolian city of Ägä are on the plateau of a steep mountain ridge ascended from the N. Ägä was mentioned by Herodotus, but was never important, because of its isolated situation. The summit plateau is surrounded by a wall 1.5 km. long, on the E. edge the ruins of a three-storey *market hall* rise to a height of 36 ft. This dates from the Hellenistic period, the upper section was rebuilt by the Romans, and the whole building is 269 ft. long. Interesting details of the construction are easily seen. Otherwise the site is strewn with large quantities of unsorted rubble from the theatre and two temples, among other things. A hour's walk to the E. on the N. bank of the stream which flows round the acropolis to the N. was an important shrine of Apollo. The 20 ft. high *portal frame* made up of three monoliths still towers up from the ruins of a 1C BC peripteral temple.

Maltepe (S. of Bergama E. of the main road): This is a tumulus 66 ft. high with a diameter of 558 ft. and an internal passageway 230 ft. long, 10 ft. wide and 15 ft. high., leading via a transverse tunnel to three tomb chambers. The tomb has carefully-crafted vaults, and probably dates from the Roman period (2–3C AD). About 900 yards further SE is a second tumulus, **Yiğma Tepe**, with a surviving ring wall (lost in the case of Maltepe), which is thought to have been a royal tomb for one of the Attalids.

Perge

Antalys   p.574 □ F 5

Like Aspendos, Perge was founded in the period of Greek immigration under the seers Kalchas and Mopsos after the Trojan War. Historically Perge is first mentioned in reports of Alexander the Great's campaigns. The city willingly opened its doors to him, as it was unfortified. After this Perge was a Seleucid garrison, and enjoyed rights of minting and considerable freedom under the Pergamene kings. The popularity of Artemis of Perge made her the dominant motif on coins and in art. Even in the Christian period the people of Perge continued to worship their Artemis, though now as the Virgin Mary, and saw their Apollo in Christ. The shrine of Artemis, known in the local language as Vanassa Preiia, was of the highest divine order, and the votive gifts were of corresponding quality. They were administered by a caste of priests and priestesses, who were expressly not to be virgins. These priests and priestesses also supervised the cult of Artemis, and had a highly respected position in the social hierarchy. Local sources also confirm that among Anatolian deities the goddesses were in the majority. The notorious quaestor of Cilicia, Gaius Verres quite openly plundered the Temple of Artemis in Perge to swell his personal coffers. Perge also suffered in the anarchy of the Civil War, but the city flourished under the emperors, and expanded considerably. Most of the surviving Roman buildings date from this period. Perge was one of the first cities to be converted to Christianity, which was certainly not unconnected with its famous cult of Artemis. On their first visit in AD 46 Paul and Barnabus were taken for Hermes and Zeus, and hospitably received as such.

Theatre: This follows the Greek design, which means that the auditorium is larger than a semicircle. Access was at two points between the stage building, some of which has survived to its full height, and the auditorium. The attraction of this theatre, which could seat up to 14,000, is that its ruins are in relatively good condition, which makes its original design and decoration extremely clear. The surviving artefacts in the lower part of the stage make it easy to imagine the marble reliefs and friezes, portal and wall covering, the plinths and niches with statues which formerly decorated the stage façade. The surviving elements date from the second half of the 2C AD. There is a fine view over the ruins of the ancient town from the uppermost of the 48 rows of seats. Originally the upper arcaded gallery was closed to the outside. Later the outer façade had a 40 ft. high nymphaeum placed in front of it, a particularly striking feature, of which five fountain niches have survived.

Stadium (opposite the theatre): Only the stadium in Aphrodisias is in better condition than this one. All the rows of seats in the arena have survived with the exception of those on the S. curve. The arena held 15,000 spectators. The diagonally placed tunnel vaults in carefully crafted ashlar—there are about 50 of them—under the rows of seats were used partly for access, partly, presumably on the W. side, as shops.

Perge, theatre and ancient town ▷

Town precinct: Access is via the S. *main Roman gate* in the great wall. The Hellenistic inner section of the *wall* was built around the centre of the lower town in the 3C BC. The larger wall was proably completed in the early 4C AD. 60 paces away is the second, *Hellenistic gateway* with round towers survivng to their full height and excellent ashlar masonry. The round wall towers are a characteristic of the town. The plinths on walls and towers were used for dedicatory and honorific statues of gods, dignitaries or great sportsmen. Many of the inscriptions which have been discovered are of historical interest. In the area of the S. gate numerous dedicatory statues were found, 22 of them in the town as a whole, set up by the city in honour of Plancia Magna, or by Plancia Magna in honour of members of the Roman Imperial family. They all mention Plancia Magna, however, who was chief priestess of Artemis *c.*AD 120, and held the 'office of Demiurgos', the highest in the city. Her tomb is SE of the S. gate. The town plan is typically Roman. The N.–S. road is not quite straight and leads from a long way outside the S. gate to the nymphaeum below the acropolis. From

there to the gate it was 0.6 km. long. A system of heavily calcified channels runs alongside it, and also to the side of the E.–W. colonnade. This crosses the N.–S. axis just below the nymphaeum and leads to the town gates in the E. and W. Colonnades and shops lined the show streets. The *Roman agora* E. of the S. gate is surrounded by a stoa, and at its centre is the round temple of Tyche, goddess of luck. Towards the centre of the town are impressive ruins of palaces from the imperial period. Between the *nymphaeum* and the W. gate is the great *palaestra*, traditionally part of a larger gymnasium complex. This building is the oldest outside the original town wall. By the W. gate is a Roman *thermal bath*. The *main necropolis* is outside the W. gate. The finest sarcophagi, reliefs, statues and inscriptions are in the museum in Antalya. There has been discussion since the last century about the most probable site of the famous Temple of Artemis in Perge, documented in various literary sources. Strabo not only praised its size and fame, he also provided an exhaustive description of its site 'on a hill near the town'. Polemo spoke of a 'miracle of siting, beauty and execution'.

Perge, stadium

An image of the temple, albeit simplified, appears on many coins of Perge. Searches within the town precinct were consistently unsuccessful.

Phaselis

Antalya   p.574 ☐ F 6

History: Phaselis is said to have been founded by Rhodes, and had proven trade links with Egypt in the mid-6C BC. Wood from the forests of Lycia and cosmetics, especially attar of roses, were much sought after. Expanding commercial and military shipping activity led to the extension of Phaselis' three natural harbours, which was one of the most important ports in the Mediterranean.

Good relations with Persia brought advantages and disadvantages. When Kimon marched against the Persians in 466 BC the people of Phaselis made difficulties for him. After his victory over the Persians he extorted a horrendous contribution for compulsory membership of the Delian League from them. When Perikles of Limyra was defending Lycia against Mausolos of Caria, Phaselis sided with Mausolos. Phaselis was never accepted as a Lycian town. Alexander the Great was invited to take the town with a golden crown as a gift of welcome. Membership of the Lycian League was not achieved until the mid-2C, and was interrupted by 30 years' dominance of Phaselis by pirates. After this Phaselis went over completely to Lycia, and even abandoned its Greek name. Phaselis also gained from the general upsurge of the cities of Asia Minor in the Imperial Roman period. In the 7&8C it flourished as a fleet base under Byzantium. The town's first silver coins, struck before 466 BC, showed the bow of a ship, and the favoured gods, Athena and Apollo, are to be found on most of the coins from this long minting tradition.

Town: The town centre and acropolis are on a spit between the small town harbour and the large S. harbour. The ancient link road between the two starts in the S. with the *Gate of Hadrian*, N. of the *Byzantine agora*. Adjacent to the NE is the *Domitianian agora* and the *Tetragonos agora*. All of these are on the ancient road. SE of the road is the *theatre*, and above this the *acropolis*, which is difficult to reach. The use of most of the buildings is unknown. Around the spit and the central harbour are the *fortifications*, and N. of the 'rectangular agora' is a section of the *aqueduct*.

The N. harbour was the key point in terms of defence, and for this reason the *defensive walls*, still visible, are to be found here. They were part of an effective defensive complex. There is a way up to them NE of the N. harbour.

Environs: Olympos (about 10 km. S.): The site is hidden away on a circular plain. This was once an important Lycian city, one of the six with the privilege of three votes in the federal assembly. Little is known of its early history. For centuries Olympos suffered a great deal from pirates, who brought the Mithras cult

Phaselis, agora road

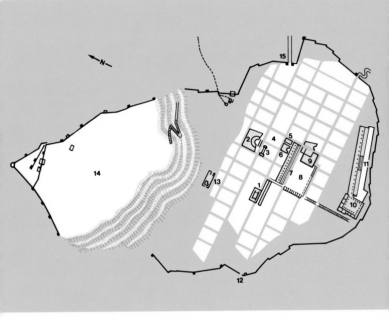

Priene 1 Athena temple **2** Theatre **3** Byzantine church (episcopal church) **4** Upper gymnasium **5** Prytaneion **6** Buleuterion **7** Colonnaded hall **8** Agora **9** Zeus temple **10** Lower gymnasium **11** Stadium **12** W. gate **13** Shrine of Demeter and Persephone **14** Acropolis **15** E. gate

here. The town is not yet excavated, and it is possible either to relax into its Sleeping Beauty atmosphere, or to take a guide. About an hour's walk to the NW of the town on a mountain slope 820 ft. high is the Chimera Fire, Yanar in Turkish.

Priene

Aydın   p.572 □ C 5

130 km. S. of İzmir, 15 km. from Söke, are the ruins of this Hellenistic terrace city, dropping over 300 ft. towards the flood plain of the Büyük Mendere, the Great Meander. The site is halfway up a 1,200 ft. marble cliff, part of the Mykale mountains. Originally Priene, along with Miletos, Herakleia and Myus was one of the ring of Greek harbour towns around the Gulf of Latmia. This silted up (the Meander washes 20 ft. of alluvial land into the sea per year), compelling the citizens of Priene to refound their city on the secure heights of a rocky plateau almost 300 ft. high, protected by a limestone massif which supported the acropolis (the earlier city of Priene, deep in the alluvial deposits of the Meander, has not yet been rediscovered). The German archaeologist Theodor Wiegand wrote, on his arrival in 1895: 'Above the terrace of the ancient city of Priene is a rust-red mass of rock with bluish tints, a hundred feet high, with eagles constantly circling round it'. Because of its proximity to Panionion (shrine of the sea-god Poseidon on the N.

Priene, castle hill (left), Temple of Athena (right)

slope of the Mykale mountains, the central cult site of the Delian League) Priene was at the centre of the maritime trading towns, linked more by cult than politics. The town had 5,000 inhabitants and was never of great political significance. In 334 BC Alexander the Great assigned it the task of watching unreliable Miletos. He lived in the city and paid for the building of the Temple of Athena. In the Byzantine period the city was the seat of a bishop for a time, with the Meander as symbol on its coins, in the 13C it fell to the Seljuks as they pressed W.

Ancient town: Priene is an early example of town planning under limiting topographical conditions. The chess-board layout follows the colonial planning system of Hippodamos of Miletos. The outer defence is a town wall 2.5 km. long, irregular, as it has to fit the site, 20 ft. high and over 6 ft. wide. It was constructed as an ashlar shell filled with rubble and clay, with a small number of towers set in front of it, battlements running the whole way round, with a W. and two E. gates. The overall pattern of the walls is saw-toothed, making it possible for archers to protect the long sides from attack from the short ones. From the W. to the E. gate five longitudinal streets run parallel to the 23 ft. wide main street along the agora, intersected at right angles by fifteen transverse streets only 13 ft. wide. Within this pattern the town is organized in four districts: a religious one (including the Temple of Athena) and opposite this the political area (with town administration) as the central axis, and by the cultural district (with theatre) in the N.. The commercial area (including the agora) in the S. Looking at the plan in greater detail, the streets enclose 90 'insulae' 156 by

Priene, Buleuterion

116 ft. in area, each containing a block of four to six private houses or a public building. The peristyle type of building occurs most frequently: a two-storey building with no windows on the street side set around a courtyard, built in clay brick on a stone base, with a colonnade opposite the entrance. The city was excavated 1895–9 by Carl Humann and Theodor Wiegand, and because of its good condition is often referred to as the Pompeii of Asia Minor.

Agora: The commercial centre covers more than two insulae. It was surrounded on three sides by a colonnade, originally decorated with statues, and had the precinct of the Temple of Zeus Olympos at its E. extremity. On the N. side is the *Sacred Hall* built *c.*150 BC, 380 ft. long. It contained a cult room for the Dea Roma and Augustus. The hall was reached by

six steps, and the saddleback roof was supported by 49 outer Doric columns and 24 Ionic inner columns. In the centre of the agora was a rectangular *altar* of Hermes, the god of trade.

Acropolis: This is a fortress nearly 300 ft. above the city plateau, which can be reached by an arduous climb up a flight of stone steps. Fragments of some of the walls and towers built in the Byzantine period can still be seen.

Temple of Athena: Temple of the goddess of Priene, Athena Polias (Protectress of the City), built 350–330 BC as the religious centre of Priene. The proportions of this temple set the classic pattern for the Ionic peripteral temple, taken as authoritative by the Roman architect Vitruvius in his 'De Architectura'. Through him it became a

Priene, theatre, seat of honour

model for Renaissance architects (6 x 11 columns; stylobate 122 by 64 ft.; the rest of the dimensions are in Attic feet: overall axes 120 x 60, stylobate 100, cella 50, pronaos 30, opisthodomos 12, height of sides 50, height of columns 10 times their diameter). The architect was Pytheos, who was also responsible for the Mausoleum in Halikarnassos. Funds were provided by Alexander the Great. The inscription on the S. anta of the temple reads 'King Alexander presented this temple to Athena Polias'. The temple stands on a plateau extended by means of supporting walls, since the 2C BC concluding on the S. side in a colonnade opening to the S. The entrance to the sacred precinct in the E. is through a propylon: four Ionic columns with a porch on either side. Behind this is the *main altar*, like the Altar of Zeus in Pergamon a tiered structure within a horseshoe-shaped colonnade, with sculptural representations of the battle of the gods and giants on the base and statues of females in long robes between the columns. Behind this is the *temple* proper, opening to the E., with the following sequence or rooms: pronaos, cella with 13 ft. wide doorway and doors 26 ft. high, opisthodomos. The rooms had coffered ceilings. The *cult image* was on a plinth 10 ft. high in the cella: it was a copy reduced by one third of Phidias' gold and ivory Athena in the Parthenon in Athens: the goddess is portrayed with helmet, aegis, shield and spear, and the statue stands 21 ft. high. The temple was built of marble from the Mykale mountains. Five columns were set up again in 1964.

Buleuterion: This and the adjacent *Prytaneion* were the political centre of the city. It was used for meetings of the town council, which met frequently to debate public matters, advised and supervised the town administrators and prepared the people's assembly. It was also responsible for criminal justice and the police. The assembly room held 640 people, had rows of seats on three sides and was covered with a 48 ft. wide wooden roof. On the fourth side were two doors, with a niche for the chairman between them. In front of him were an altar with bulls' heads and laurel, and bowls with busts of Asklepios and Apollo, the place for sacrifice at the beginning of the meeting, and also a place for the speaker. The Buleuterion in Priene and the one in Miletos are the best-preserved in the whole of ancient Greece.

Prytaneion (adjacent to the Buleuterion): The council house was the seat of the elected city administration and housed official receptions. The official rooms were set around its colonnaded courtyard.

Shrine of the Egyptian Gods (on the left by the entrance to the town): This is an altar in a courtyard (no temple) for Isis, Serapis and Anubis, a relic of the short rule of the Egyptian king Ptolemy III

Priene, Temple of Athena, column

Euergetes over Ionia in the mid-3C BC. Egyptian priests performed the rites here.

Shrine of Demeter and Persephone: This is the oldest temple in the town, high on the cliff 130 ft. above the town plateau and only accessible by an arduous climb up a rocky path. At the end of a long court-yard is a temple with porch and sacrificial pit for the gods of the Underworld (Persephone).

Sports facilities: Gymnasium and stadium on the lower terrace.

Gymnasium: Surviving features are a *palaestra*, a square courtyard surrounded by columns, a *teaching building* with at least five rooms, including a large central room for teaching with some inscriptions by pupils on the walls which have survived in good condition, and a washroom with lion-head basin.

Stadium: This running track next to the gymnasium was built in the late 2C BC. It is 208 yards long and 66 ft. wide, with starting facilities. Spectators could only sit on the N. side, on stone seats in the central section, and on wooden ones at the sides. All the races ended at the E. end.

Theatre: The path from the Temple of Athena leads NE through the 6C *episcopal church* (basilica with nave and two aisles, narthex and apse) and then through the stage building into the theatre, which extends over two insulae. It is of the Greek type, and was built in the 3C BC to accommodate about 5,000 spectators, then rebuilt by the Romans in the 2C BC. The auditorium (cavea) had about 50 rows of seats with a wide horizontal passage half-way up, and divided into five wedges by six flights of steps. Five marble seats with arms were provided for priests and magistrates. There were two access points between the supporting wall and the stage; there was a water clock at the W. entrance, and its base has survived. The stage building had two storeys and was nearly 60 ft. long. Fragments of the original painting have survived. In front of this is a proscenium with twelve piers, with ten Doric half columns in front of them.

Residential area: There were paved streets between the houses, which were up to 20 ft. high. In the NE was Alexander's house, restored for 1,000 drachmas in 130 BC. Water came from a stream in the E. of the town just under the cliff in clay pipes through the E. town wall, and was distributed from there down into the houses and many fountains.

Environs: The *Panionion* found on the N. side of the Mykale mountains near the village of Güzelcamli, the central cult site of the Delian League, administered from Priene, is not worth a visit from the point of view of excavations. The only evidence of the former importance of the site are remains of a relatively large surrounding wall, rows of seats on the slope and possibly the large cave nearby.

Samsun

Despite having been devastated several times, Samsun has maintained its position as the chief Turkish port on the Black Sea. In the 7C BC, the Milesians, coming from Sinope, founded a trading colony here, ancient **Amisos,** which is 3 km. NW of the present town and known as Kara Samsun. Sparse surface finds have been made on this site, which has so far hardly been investigated archaeologically.

After being conquered by Alexander the Great, the town fell to the kingdom of Pontus, and Mithridates IV Eupator (132–163) expanded it into a residence. During the period of Roman occupation, the town was barely able to recover from severe damage in battles between this ruler and the Roman general Lucullus in the Third Mithridatic War. The neighbouring harbour town of Sinope was a powerful rival to Samsun in the Byzantine period, and this was one reason why Samsun, then known as *Amynsos*, did not see an improvement in its fortunes at that time, even though it was a bishop's seat. Looting by the Arab emir of Malatya (863) weakened the town still further. It was not given its present name of Samsun until the subsequent Seljuk period. A local dynasty came to power and enabled Genoese merchants to set up trading posts here. The town then underwent a period of rapid economic growth, scarcely lessened by Mongol invasions and an interregnum by the Ottoman ruler Beyazıt I (1393–95), who was replaced by Timur-Leng (Tamerlane) after its defeat by the Mongols in 1402. The Ottomans occupied the town again in 1425, then the Genoese reduced it to rubble. Samsun was not completely incorporated into the Ottoman Empire until 1470. There was a revolt, after which the Turkish navy subjected the town to heavy bombardment. The national liberation movement led by Atatürk began here on 19 May 1919. This is commemorated by the equestrian statue of the 'father of modern Turkey' in the park outside the tourist information office. The house in which Atatürk lived at that time is a popular memorial.

Frequent and severe damage over the centuries has meant that hardly any old buildings survive in the town. But the Hacı Hatun Camii and the Pazar Camii (Market Mosque) should be noted (14C). The *Site Camii*, not completed until 1986, is an example of contemporary Islamic architecture.

There are some ruined sites nearby which, like ancient Amisos (Kara Samsun), have not yet been excavated, but the few sites which have been investigated have yielded interesting results. Thus the *Dündar Tepe* is evidence that the area around Samsun was populated in the early Bronze Age, and excavations at *Akalan* were very productive as regards the Phrygian period (1st millennium BC).

Environs: Bafra (51 km. NW): This town, which today numbers some 50,000 inhabitants, was once on the Black Sea coast, but is now inland because of alluvial deposits from the Kızıl Irmak, at whose mouth it lies. Today the town is known as a centre of tobacco-growing. Surviving old buildings include a 13C *bath*, a complex consisting of a *mosque, türbe* and *medrese* (15C), the *Büyük Cami* (18C) and, a few km. outside, two *mausoleums*.

In the ancient Hittite period, the town of *Zalpa* lay on the mouth of the Kızıl Irmak. Legend has it that it was founded by 40 sons and 40 daughters, all born at the same time. After their birth they were exposed by their mother in rush baskets on the Yeşil Irmak.

Cakallı Hanı (35 km. SW): This little town near the road to Merzifon and Çorum is reached after winding down into a valley. The eponymous 13C *caravanserai* has sculptures on the façade of its main hall.

Terme (55 km. E.): This small harbour town on the coast between Çarşamba and Ünye is probably identical with the ancient town of **Themiskyra**, which Lucullus was obliged to besiege in 73 BC during the Third Mithridatic War against the kingdom of Pontus. This would make the Termes Suyu, the river on which the town lies, the ancient Thermodon. Legend has it that Hippolyta, queen of the Amazons, lived here. Herakles had to carry her girdle to Argos as the ninth of his twelve Labours.

Sardes/Sart

Manisa   p.572□D 4

Sardes was the capital of the Lydian empire and lay centrally, in the Gediz

House of Oman Pasha in Bolaman (environs of Samsun)

valley (ancient name: Hermos), some 100 km. from the Aegean. Its site is immediately adjacent to the small town of Sart, founded in the present century. The Lydian empire, while varying in size, dominated central western Asia Minor between Halys (E.) and the Aegean coast (W.) for some 150 years. From *c.*700−547 BC it was an expanding monarchy with an army of mercenaries; socially speaking it was a feudal state, with large landowners, serfs, and horse-breeders. The alluvial land meant that the wide Gediz valley was a fertile area, centred around the two towns Sardes and Magnesia. There is still agricultural variety today: cereal, grapes/currants, wine, olives, figs and cattle-breeding. Wholesalers, retailers and craftsmen were dominant in the two towns, and these merchants' main products were wool, textiles and leather. One particular trade was gold processing, based on the gold mines around Sardes and on the Paktolos which flows past Sardes and is gold-bearing. Sheepskins were used to filter gold dust from the river. One of the cultural achievements of the Lydians was the invention of coins (which the Greeks then adopted and passed on to the Romans). The coins were first made of electrum, an alloy of silver and gold, during the reign of Croesus, and after this there were gold and silver coins (300 smelting pits dating from the 6C were discovered by the Paktolos in 1968). The Lydians are also said to have invented inns and the game of dice. There was a lively cultural exchange between them and the Greeks. The matriarchal Lydian religion was based around the cult of Cybele. Finally, the Lydians may be the ancestors of the Etruscans who emigrated westwards. Alkman (7C), the first Greek choric lyricist known to us, came from Sardes. The finds in Sardes date back to the 2nd millennium. The Lydian dynasty proper was the Mermnad family who ruled from *c.*700−547 BC. The best-known of the five kings are Gyges, who founded the dynasty in *c.*680 BC, and Croesus, the last Lydian king, known from legend and saga. Herakles had to serve the Lydian queen Omphale for three years as the penalty for committing murder. He had to sit at the distaff wearing women's clothes while the queen wore his lion-skin and club. The dynasty of the Heraclidaeè sprang from their union. This dynasty was overthrown

Sardes, Temple of Artemis

by the Mermnads in the early 7C, and they in their turn fell when the Persians defeated them. After this, from 547/546 onwards, Sardes was the residence of the Persian satraps and at the western end of the Persian royal road from Susa.

In 499 BC, the lower town was destroyed in the Ionian revolt of the Greeks, led by Miletos, against the Persians. Alexander the Great conquered the town in 334 BC and founded a temple to Zeus Olympios on the site of the residence. Sardes was part of the Seleucid empire until 190, and at that time Antiochos III rebuilt the town which had been destroyed when the Persians were expelled. Antiochos settled 2,000 Jewish veterans from Mesopotamia here. They formed the basic stock of the powerful Jewish community in Sardes, which was itself the basis of the early Christian community: Sardes is one of the seven churches in Asia Minor referred to in Revelation. Sardes was Pergamene until 133 BC, and after that it was part of the Roman province of Asia. In AD 17, Tiberius rebuilt the town, which had been destroyed in an earthquake. In the 5C AD there were new fortifications, showing that the town experienced a renewed if short-lived revival in the early-Byzantine period, when it became an episcopal seat. In the late 11C it fell for the first time into the hands of Turkish conquerors, but was liberated by John Ducas in 1098. It was finally incorporated into the Ottoman Empire in 1390, but in 1402 Timur-Leng devastated the town and expelled the population. From that time on Sardes was no longer a large populated area, although it had been a centre of continuous urban culture and civilization for over 2,000 years.

The Lydian town lay below an impregnable acropolis (of which almost nothing survives because the rocks have eroded) at the foot of the Tmolos mountains (6,750 ft.). According to Herodotus, its clay houses with reed roofs covered the low hills below the acropolis and spread out towards the Gediz plain.

Temple of Artemis: This is in the valley of the Paktolos (a tributary of the Gediz) at the foot of the acropolis. Two complete Ionic columns survive, along with parts of thirteen others. This large building from the Seleucid period is an Ionic pseudo-dipteros with 8 x 20 columns

Sardes, gymnasium, courtyard hall

(there is no second, inner row of columns; cf. the Ionic dipteros at Didyma, with 10 x 21 columns and a double stoa). Building took 500 years, from the late 4C BC to the 2C AD. This large, initially Hellenistic temple was never completed, and its design was altered three times. The core of the Artemis temple precinct, built above an old shrine of Cybele, is the altar in the W., erected in *c.*400 BC and surrounded by Persian votive sites. Behind it, the first temple in antis, reached by seven steps, was erected *c.*300–250 BC. There were six columns between the projecting antae, two columns in the short opisthodomos, and twelve columns in the cella, in the middle of which the goddess's statue stood (naos: 75 x 221.7 ft., pronaos: 55 ft., opisthodomos: 20 ft.). In the 2C BC, the Pergamene king Eumenes II (197–159 BC) built a peristasis around the temple (Sardes was in the hands of the Pergamenes from 190 onwards). A stoa about 330 ft. long and 33 ft. wide was constructed; for this purpose the seven steps were built over, and the columns between the antae were removed and set up in front of the antae in order to form a hall on both sides of the temple façade (4 x 2 columns in both cases). The incomplete building was altered by Antoninus Pius in the 2C AD: two columns were added to the cella in the W. (so that the size of the pronaos was reduced to that of the opisthodomos), and the cella was divided in two by a central wall, so that a second shrine was formed in the E. part of the temple, in addition to the previous shrine to Artemis in the W. This second shrine was dedicated to Faustina, the wife of Antoninus Pius. She died in AD 141 and was later deified (the head of her cult image was found). Only the E. façade was completed.

Gymnasion: This is a complex in four parts on the edge of Sardes, N. of the İzmir-Ankara road, which corresponds to the Persian royal road and the Roman main road. The gymnasion was uncovered and reconstructed by American archaeologists (since 1958, the American School of Oriental Research has been in charge of this work). The gymnasion was completed in AD 211. The central part is a palaestra, which is a courtyard for wrestlers, surrounded by colonnaded halls. On the front side there is another courtyard area, with several storeys, separated off by a row of columns and partly roofed over. It has a splendid, richly decorated and articulated façade. Behind it there are thermal baths with a long pool in the centre.

Synagogue (S. courtyard section of gymnasion; built in AD 230–250, rebuilt in the 4C): This complex rebuilt in 1965–73 consists of an atrium with surrounding columns and a main room divided in three by pillars, with seats for the elders in the apse, shrines for the Tora scrolls, and a pulpit in the entrance wall. The remains of floral *floor mosaics* and *marble inlay work* on the walls give an idea of the colourful former decorations. There is a row of *Byzantine shops* on the long S. side opening towards the road. Opposite them on the other side of the road is the *house of bronzes* (*c.*AD 550), where many

Sardes, gymnasium, restored façade

bronze figures have been found. Remains of houses, a stadium and a theatre are to be seen on the site between the road and the Roman acropolis.

Environs: Bin Tepe (100 Hills; about 12 km. NW): This is an area of burial mounds between Gediz and Lake Gyges, with the *tumulus tombs* of the kings, the great and the wealthy of Lydia. The largest mound (225 ft. high, 1165 ft. wide) contains the tomb of Alyattes (607–560 BC), the penultimate Lydian king, with a burial chamber lined with masonry.

Selge

Antalya   p.574□G 5

The traveller driving along the coast road should branch off to the N. some 10 km. E. of the turning for Aspendos, and follow the ancient river Eurymedon upstream through Taşağil and Beskonak. This drive through delightful countryside crosses the ancient paved road several times, and also a beautiful little Roman bridge without a parapet over the emerald-green River

Selge, Roman bridge

Eurymedon. It has a single arch 100–115 ft. high, depending on the water level. After reaching the other side of this steep, vertical canyon, more than half of the difference in altitude between the coast and Selge still has to be negotiated. The steep ascent passes between bizarre rock formations alternating with pine forest, and climbs to the ancient town, which is located in the middle of the village, on a broad, fertile plain.

History: What can have induced Calchas to have settled in this high spot along with his troops left over from the Trojan War? This arid region with its rugged climate was more suited to the Spartans, who later also settled here. Strabo—it must have been in summer—felt 'enthusiastic about the wild, precipitous countryside,' but also about the communal achievements of the citizens and their urban government. It is reported that Selge was consistently free, safe and independent until the Romans assumed power.

The interest which people took in the warm and fertile Pamphylian plain is the common thread running through the history of the Pisidian town. Good relations were maintained with neighbouring Aspendos, and the two towns had a common coinage, probably in the 5C BC. The silver coins of the two towns scarcely differed from one another in their motifs and inscriptions. The Selgians sent a delegation to Alexander the Great while he was besieging far-off Termessos, and this fact throws light on the traditionally hostile relations between the two towns of Selge and Termessos. Alexander announced that he was not interested in a joint siege of Termessos, and then the Selgians pointed out to him that a better way of reaching Susa, which lay on the imperial road, was to pass through Sagalossos, with which the Selgians were on similarly bad terms as with Termessos. Arrianus gives a detailed report on the subject. The Selgians also held peaceful negotiations with the Romans. They were thus able to expand their trade, which was already dominant over a wide area. Their merchandise included wine, olives, a fragrant massage ointment which was much in demand, and an anti-superstition incense obtained from the styrax tree depicted on Selgian coins. The resinous wood of that tree is so hard and elastic that it was a favourite material for spear manufacture. Thus Selge exported a wide range of useful and vitally necessary products. As can be seen from the ruins distributed over a wide area, Selge was a large and prosperous town in the Imperial Roman period, with up to 20,000 inhabitants (according to Strabo).

Tour on foot: The visitor proceeds from the village of Zerkl to the Roman *theatre*, the largest and best-preserved building in the town. The Greek design, with an auditorium taking up more than a semi-circle, is often found in S. Anatolia. The theatre is very large, with 45 tiers and 10,000 seats. The Roman stage building is in ruins, but its components are interesting. All the seats are reached via the diazoma, to which four entrances lead. Crushes like those in Aspendos could not occur here. The town was active in sports,

and local sporting events were held in the town's own *stadium* beside the theatre. The main hill (called Kesbedion in ancient times), about 1 km. SW, is the site of the town's chief temples. They are a *temple of Zeus* (probably), and a smaller *temple* which is thought to have been dedicated to Artemis because an inscription in the town refers to the existence of a priestess of Artemis. The enormous *round container* behind the hill is 25 ft. deep and held about 134,200 cu.ft. of water, which was brought from the NW by canal. The *tower* in the S. was adjoined by a *town wall* which led to the main gate of the town, with a guard-house. The wall surrounded all three hills of the town, and its line can be traced. The *agora*, formerly surrounded on three sides by shops and buildings, is just over 500 yards E. of the Kesbedion hill. The ruins of a Byzantine *basilica* are nearby.

Seyitgazi

Eskişehir   p.566□F 3

The name is derived from Şehit, a Muslim

Selge, agora and theatre

martyr who fell in battle. A gazi is one who fights for the faith. Şehit Battal Gazi, leader of an Arab army group, fell at the siege of Afyon in the 8C. He was buried in Seyitgazi, and beside him a Byzantine princess who, out of love for him, had followed him into death. The mother of Kaykobad I learned of this romantic story and ordered a türbe to be built for him. According to Prof. Erdmann, this was linked to a medrese. The tomb of this hero and his loved one became the most popular pilgrimage goal of the Anatolian Muslims, and this induced Haçi Bektaş, the founder of the Bektaşi order, to build a *dervish monastery* here in the 13C. The türbe and monastery were liberally restored and enlarged in the time of Sultan Selim I (1512–26). The sarcophagus is over 23 ft. long, and is said to date from this period. It is a symbol of the martyr's greatness. The princess's sarcophagus is next to the hero's, and gazi and princess both receive devout affection from innumerable pilgrims. Selim also built a new *mosque* with a large *kitchen for the poor.* The U-shaped complex is open towards the mountain, and has a large courtyard. At the upper entrance is a large Byzantine *church,* and beside this the Sel-juk mosque with its tomb. The Ottoman mosque is to the rear. The building set transversely to the valley, with a large fountain, was evidently a monks' common room, and affords a splendid view of the town and the surrounding countryside. The arm of the U on the valley side begins with a large kitchen with typical Ottoman fireplaces. The following hall-like rooms are in the best Ottoman architectural style with large fireplaces. They were probably refectories and rooms for spiritual exercises.

Side

Antalya   p.574☐G 6

History: A language appearing on coins in Side from 500 BC and on inscriptions until 300 BC seems to have been written by the original indigenous population. This language was not deciphered until recent times. It is unique as regards both words and script, has some Greek elements, and can probably be designated ancient Anatolian/Pamphylian. It can be assumed that Greek colonists from Kyme to the N. of Smyrna settled here later than the 8C BC, but their language made no impact upon the region until the time of Alexander the Great, when Greek became the official language. Greek inscriptions on coins did not appear in Side until the 2C BC. However, the pomegranate, called 'side' in Anatolian, is found on coins dating from the earliest times to the Roman period. After the sea battle off Side in 190 BC, in which Hannibal's navy was beaten and driven off by the Rhodians, in alliance with Rome, Side increasingly came under the influence of pirates. Side provided a naval base for them, and also had a large and internationally renowned slave market in which the pirates auctioned off their prisoners, making the town much talked about. The town had a dubious reputation in earlier years.

Seyitgazi, Şehit tomb and dervish monastery

When asked who the biggest rascals were, Stratonikos, an ancient wit, replied: 'The Phaselians are the biggest rascals in Pamphylia, but the biggest rascals in the world are the citizens of Side.' A peak in early imperial Roman times was followed by decline and impoverishment. A general upsurge began in the late-Roman/Byzantine period around 500, and Side became the seat of a metropolitan bishop. Definitive decline set in when the Arabs invaded, and in the 10C the remainder of the population migrated to Antalya.

The best parts of the **main gate** and **town wall** are at the point where the traveller arrives by car. They give an accurate impression of an ancient fortification. The Hellenistic wall which runs transversely across the peninsula survives at its original height. The wall of smoothly-fitting ashlars, with a decorative cornice, had no external projections which might have assisted an enemy. From the inside, the enemy was attacked from two storeys, the casemates and the parapet on the third storey. Towers increased the wall's solidity and defensive power. The formerly massive gate fortification, flanked by two towers in the wall, was both unusual and effective. Outside the gate was a monumental, three-storeyed marble *nymphaeum* 165 ft. long, larger and more splendid than similar buildings in neighbouring towns.

Town centre: The old processional road led through the later town gate with monument to Vespasian, which survives up to a height of 40 ft. This monument gave this quarter of the town the name of 'quadriga district', because of the statue of Vespasian and his team of four horses on top of it. Around it are grouped the theatre, the agora with the Tyche temple, two nymphaea, the Roman latrine, a propylon and a temple. The *museum* is in a large 5C bath. All the finds made in Side are to be seen in it, ranging from coins to large statues from the 'imperial hall' and the nymphaeum by the E. gate. Richly decorated Roman sarcophagi (sarcophagus with cupids), artistic reliefs and friezes (nereid frieze), statuettes, decorations and architectural elements all combine to make this collection definitely worth seeing. *Agora:* The slave market, which was known far and wide, was held in this

square, over 86,000 sq.ft. in area and surrounded by halls of columns, shops, exedrae and a latrine with a fountain. Unimaginable numbers of prisoners are said to have been sold here.

Theatre: This is a charming building on level ground by the sea. The absence of a natural slope brought about a labyrinth of supporting arches, tunnel passageways, and stairs, to underpin the cavea. This Greek-style auditorium is larger than a semicircle and is one of the largest on the S. coast. It had almost fifty tiers of seats, and thus held almost as many spectators as the auditorium in Aspendos. As in Perge, the frieze on the façade of the stage has been systematically destroyed, probably for religious reasons by Christians who later held divine service in the theatre. The path turns left after the theatre, passes the late-Roman Dionysos temple, and peters out near the old harbour. The remains of the *Athena temple,* which was the main shrine of the town, and next to it the elegant column bases of the *Apollo temple,* stand behind the ruins of the Byzantine basilica with nave and two aisles, to the W. of the temple of Men and a Byzantine

Side, town gate, Vespasian monument

nymphaeum. The sacred precinct was evidently always here, on the site of the Athena temple, just near the old harbour which has now silted up. A possible way back leads along the wall up to the *state agora.* This square (230 x 295 ft.) is surrounded by broad Ionic colonnades and was used mainly for show purposes. On the E. side is the imperial hall, so called because 20 Roman copies of Greek statues were found here, including one of Antonius Pius.

Environs: Manavgat (4 km. E.): A fine Roman-Seljuk *bridge* spans the Manavgat Çay to the N. of this town and its waterfalls. Remains of the *aqueduct* of Side are further E., by the asphalt road. Shortly after this, take the first earth-covered path left to Köy Şihlar. Up in the pine wood 1.5 km. beyond Şihlar is the well-preserved ancient ruined town of **Seleucia in Pamphylia.** Its history is unknown. Its excellent strategic location makes access possible only from the S. On the other sides the hillside falls away steeply. Gates and associated buildings point the way through the wood to the *agora,* which measures 100 x 100 ft. It was surrounded by colonnades, and there are stretches where remains of the columns survive in situ. In the E. of the agora, there is a row of buildings 150 ft. long surviving to a height of more than two storeys. These are the eight *market halls.* At their N. end, a *gatehouse* with a large round arch leads out of the agora. The market halls are adjoined by a semicircular building (odeion?) in the S. In the N. is a well-preserved building in precise ashlar, and next to it is a vaulted passageway. On the steep W. slope, the square was supported by a cellar two storeys deep. The side walls of the cellar can be reached through rows of arches starting from the central passage. A small, well-preserved *temple,* with a cella which has some spacious internal niches, stands outside the agora to the N. of the market halls. External evidence suggests that these niches were fitted with grilles, and intended for votive gifts or the like.

Silifke

Mersin (İçel)   p.574 □ J 6

History: Ancient **Seleucia on Kalykadnos** (the river is now known as the Göksu) was founded in the 3C BC by Seleucus, previously one of Alexander's generals. As the founder of the Seleucid dynasty, he called himself Seleucus I Nicator (312–281 BC). The main reason for founding the town was to build a barrier against the wild Tauros tribes who repeatedly advanced through the Göksu valley into the plain. These tribes included the Isaurians, who later gave the cognomen 'the Isaurian' to the emperor Zeno (AD 474–491), their tribal chief. He built the massive basilica of Meriamlık, dedicated to St.Thecla.

On 10 June 1190, Barbarossa drowned in the Göksu, 10 km. outside Silifke/Seleucia. Seleucia, like all the harbour towns on the coast of Asia Minor, flourished greatly in Roman imperial times. In addition to travellers on trade and military routes, there were also streams of pilgrims travelling to the nearby shrines of the priests' dynasty in Olba/Diocaesarea (near modern Uzuncaburç to the NE of Silifke) and to the famous oracle and temple of Apollo in Seleucia. The few remains of large buildings in modern Silifke date from that period. The Byzantines enlarged Seleucia to form a bulwark against the Arabs who mounted raids from the 7C on. In 1098 the Crusaders occupied the castle and added extra buildings. The Armenians, whom the Seljuks had driven out of the N., founded their new homeland of Lesser Armenia, with its centre in Cilicia. They were responsible for most of the surviving towers and bulwarks in the castle. Seleucia too had various rulers because of all the movements of peoples in this troubled connecting link between E. and W., until the Ottomans replaced the Karamanids in 1471.

Worth seeing: The ancient acropolis on the conical hilltop (605 ft.) includes the ruined *citadel*. Most of the buildings are Byzantine. Ancient remains consist of 23 towers and bulwarks, battlemented walls, a ruined palace, a mosque from the emirate period, a dungeon in a cellar hewn from the rock, a storeroom measuring 15 x 15

Seleuceia (Side), market hall in the agora

x 60 ft., and a large cistern. Scant remains of a formerly large theatre and a stadium are found on the E. side of the castle hill. An upright column with a Corinthian capital indicates the site of the once-famous *temple of Apollo Sarpedonios*. Around it are column bases, fallen columns, and remains of buildings. The temple was a peripteros with 8 x 14 Corinthian columns. It was built in the 2C AD. There are large *burial grounds* on the road to Mut and near Dimircili on the road to Olba. The large *bridge* over the Göksu in the S. was later rebuilt on the model of the old Roman bridge on whose remains it stands. Ancient spoils are to be found all over the town. The small *Reşadiye Cami* (1328) had 21 ancient columns supporting its portico. The large new *museum* stands to the left of the town's main exit road, leading to Antalya.

Environs: Liman Kalesi (10 km. W., on the road to Antalya): The picturesque ruins of a medieval marine fortress stand on a peninsula in the sea. **Tokmar Kalesi** is a massive fortress in a splendid mountain setting. It is reached by turning right a few km. W. of Liman Kalesi

and continuing 3 km. uphill on a new road. The polygonal castle wall is supported by massive round towers. The use of bossed ashlars is reminiscent of European architecture in the Hohenstaufen period, possibly under the influence of the Crusaders, who established many fortified bases on the Mediterranean coast.

Meriamlık (2 km. S.): An early Christian pilgrimage site for St.Thecla, linked to Silifke by a staircase in the rock, stands amidst an early Christian burial ground. In *c.*480, the Byzantine emperor Zeno the Isaurian built a *basilica* (130 ft. long, 85 ft. wide) on the site of an older church of St.Thecla. Only parts of the apse survive, but ground plan and superstructure can mostly be reconstructed. St. Thecla is regarded as the oldest domed basilica which can be dated with any certainty. The basilica had a rectangular narthex in its W., and an atrium-like forecourt, some 130 ft. long and jutting beyond the width of the church's façade. The nave, which included the apse, was divided by two massive pillars into two bays of equal size. The W. bay either had a flat ceiling or a conventional tunnel vault, and the E. main

Silifke, Göksu, scene of Barbarossa's accident

bay was probably domed. But a pyramidal wooden dome would also have accorded with the centralized design indicated by the four sturdy piers of the square main room. This new style of basilica is continued in Alahan Monastiri nearby. It is said that St. Thecla, in the 1C, was a beautiful virgin of good family who met the apostle Paul in Ikonion in the 1C and was baptized by him. Thecla refused to marry the man to whom she was betrothed. He sent persecutors of Christians in pursuit of her, but she always miraculously escaped their torments, sometimes dressed in man's attire in which she followed Paul who had been whipped and driven out of Ikonion. But he 'took fright' and sent her back. According to one of the many versions of the story, Thecla, who lived in caves, was drawn underground to escape her persecutors.

Sillyon

Antalya   p.574□F 5

Sillyon was one of the five main towns of ancient Pamphylia, the others being Attalaeya, Perge, Aspendos and Side. This is one of the towns whose foundation is attributed to Mopsos and the Greeks returning from Troy. The geographer Skylax is the first to mention Sillyon, in the mid-4C BC. This town on its tall plateau is visible from far away in the plain, and cannot be missed by a traveller turning off towards Eski Yürük and Asar Köyü at a point 22 km. E. of Antalya. The flat-topped mountain falls away steeply on all sides, but slightly more gently in the W. Earthquakes, and the enormous pear-shaped vaulted cisterns cut deep into the rock, have caused great masses of rock to break away from the edges of the rocky plateau.

The site is impressive. The visitor starts from the horseshoe-shaped *gatehouse* with two towers, and continues along an enormous *ramp* to the *upper gate* at the edge of the plateau. The ramp is supported by a Hellenistic wall with high towers. The road on the ramp is 16 ft. wide. Part of the upper section of this ramp is now missing. A wall ran from the lower gate to the large and well-preserved rectangular tower N. of the gate. This wall was built later, to protect the section of the lower

Tokmar Kalesi (Silifke), fortress

town enlarged for citizens who had a lot of business in the plain. The ancient town centre was in the SW tip of the plateau. A *large Byzantine building*, surviving to its full height, stands S. of the upper gate. Diagonally to the S. of this is a *Hellenistic building* of finely cut stone, probably a gymnasium, and surviving to a height of 20 ft. Ten windows of different sizes, with fine jambs and grooves for the shutters, are still in a perfectly perpendicular position. E. of this is a *smaller Hellenistic building* with a good inscription on the doorpost in a local Pamphylian dialect. The length of the text is of great importance both for identification and for many details of the language, as it is otherwise known only in the shorthand used on tombs and pedestals. The basic language is Greek, as is the alphabet. From the steps surviving from the large *theatre* in the S. there is a view of the neighbouring town of Perge, whose large Artemis temple may have been visible. Further E. on the plateau are terraces and steps which were part of the town's residential area. The remains of *houses*, whose walls are still standing, have been found here. The stairs led from one residential level to another.

Remains of walls and foundations of a *temple* whose exact function remains undefined, are seen at the end of this area.

Sinop

Sinop   p.566□L 1

This town was founded by Greek Milesians, and some 200 years after this Diogenes was born here in 413 BC. The birth of Mithridates VII, king of Pontus, took place here about another 280 years later. Xenophon's troops embarked here on their return journey in 401 BC. In 63 BC the town became Roman and was called *Colonia Julia Felix*. After the Byzantine Comnenus emperors had lost Sinop to the Seljuks in 1214, the emirs of Kastamonu took over the town in 1301. They granted extensive trading monopolies to the Genoese, and town and harbour flourished. Sinop became Ottoman in 1458. In 1853, the Russians destroyed the town along with the Turkish fleet which was anchored there. The Crimean war was the result.

Sillyon, gatehouse tower and ramp up to acropolis

Büyük Cami (Great Mosque): This is a late example of the transverse type (1270), with the mihrab on the wider side of the prayer room. There are three domed bays on the kibla wall. Three *türbe* in the mosque courtyard.

Seyit Bilal Camii: This is an Ottoman mosque with glazed tiles.

Süleyman Pervane Medrese (also called *Alaieye Medrese*): Originally a theological seminar, this is a classical courtyard medrese with two iwans, an entrance iwan with the main iwan opposite. The rows of cells are between the two iwans, on the right and left sides of the courtyard.

Citadel: Notable remains of this are to be found on the way to the harbour.

Old town wall: Ancient spoils were used to build the massive towers near the sea.

Museum (in the Seljuk mosque): Good collections from the surrounding area are exhibited here.

Serapis temple: Remains of this Hellenistic building are to be found in the municipal park.

Sivas

Sivas   p.568□N 3

The origins of today's provincial capital on the Murdar Irmak, a tributary of the Kızıl Irmak, are obscure. The town was granted civic rights as *Megalopolis* by Pompey (106–48 BC). Under Augustus it was called **Sebasteia** and had a wall built around it. The old settlement is probably all underneath the modern buildings, and only a few stretches of wall in the outer part of the town are sometimes considered to date from this early phase of the town's history. The local early Christian community was persecuted by the Romans. The '40 martyrs of Sebasteia',

all soldiers of the Legio XII Fulminata, became famous and are often found as motifs on icons. They died for their faith naked in an ice-cold river c.AD 320. When the empire was reformed under Diocletian (284–305), Sebasteia became the capital of the province of Armenia, and continued as such even after the territories E. of Erzurum were ceded to the Persian Sassanids in 387. The fortifications were reinforced by Justinian (527–565), but despite this the Sassanids finally succeeded in capturing the town, by then an episcopal seat. The Arabs briefly occupied the town in 712. The Byzantines were in a better position to defend the endangered E. border against the Seljuks. For this reason an exchange of territories took place in 1021: the Armenian king Senekerim Hovhannes, along with some 40,000 followers, abandoned his kingdom around Lake Van, and the Byzantine emperor Basileios II assigned Sebasteia and the area around it to the Armenians as a new area for settlement. Thus this town once again became the capital of a kingdom. The Seljuks defeated Byzantium at Malazgirt in 1071, and after this the Seljuks were also able to overrun the Armenian kingdom. The town was probably given its present name of Sivas during that period. An interregnum by the Danishmendid dynasty (c.1080 onwards) was followed by another period of Seljuk rule initiated by Kiliç Arslan, who rebuilt the town walls. The Mongols occupied Sivas, and governors were then installed there. One of them, Eretna, became independent and founded a dynasty which maintained itself in Sivas until 1380. After this, the Wesir Kadi Burhaneddin ruled here. After his death in 1396, the inhabitants requested the Ottoman Sultan Beyazıt I to assist them in opposing the encroachments of the Turkoman Akkoyunlu (White Sheep). But four years later the Mongol leader Timur-Leng (Tamerlane) conquered Sivas and ordered the Christian inhabitants to be killed and the town walls to be razed.

In more recent Turkish history, Sivas is

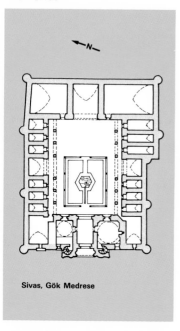

Sivas, Gök Medrese

Sivas, Cifte Minare Medrese

important as the venue of the national congress headed by Atatürk (4–11 September 1919) which gave the country its independence. All the Christians, most of whom were Armenians, had to leave the town in 1923.

Ulu Cami: This early-12C mosque stands on the Cemal Gürsel Caddesi in the town centre. The minaret in its SE corner, with a ring of stalactites, was added in the 13C. Three portals lead into the mosque courtyard, which is adjoined by the prayer hall with its 11 aisles.

Gök Medrese (Blue Koran School): The vizier Fahr ed-Din Ali ben Hussein commissioned the Greek architect Kaloyan to design this typical Seljuk building in *c.*1271. Entrance is via a passage in the W., flanked by brick minarets, leading into the courtyard with central fountain,

Sivas, Muzafer Bürüciye Medresesi

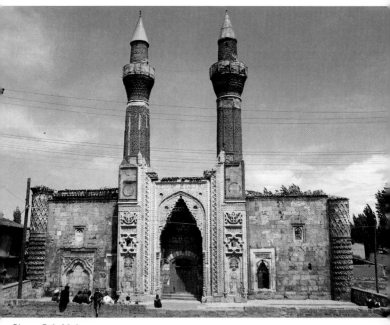

Sivas, Gök Medrese

surrounded by teaching rooms. This broad access area includes the entrance to a small domed mosque with splendid *decorative tiles*. There are small iwans in the middle of the wider sides of the courtyard, which is lined by a row of columns with Byantine and Seljuk capitals. A larger but less well-preserved iwan occupies the centre of the rear façade.

Several Koran schools stand close together in the centre of Konak square:
Cifte Minate Medrese (Double-Minaret Medrese): This building (1271) took its name from its two tall round minarets. But only the façade with its rich decorative architecture survives.
Muzafer Bürüciye Medresesi: Inside this Koran school (1271) founded by Muzafer the Mongol are a mosque and, on the left, the türbe of the founder. Today the *archaeological collection* is housed in this building with its sumptuously decorated façade. Opposite it is the *Mehmet Paşa Camii*, a domed Ottoman mosque (*c.* 1580).
Sifahdiye Medrese: The Seljuk sultan Kaykavus I founded this building as a hospital in 1217. The sultan's tomb is in the S. iwan below a brick structure with a pyramidal roof.

Also worth seeing are: the building known as *Güdük Minare* in the NE of the town is the tomb monument of Sheikh Hassan (1347); *Abdulyahap Gazi Türbesi* (1233); *Kadi Burhaneddin Türbesi* (1399); *Kale Camii* (Castle Mosque), *Ali Ağa Camii* and *Sehram Paşa Hani*, three Ottoman buildings.

Environs: Boğaz Köprü (10 km. E.): This 'bridge over the gorge' not far from the road to Erzurum had seven arches and formerly spanned the Kızıl Irmak (now in ruins).

Eğri Köprü (3 km. S.): This bridge crosses the Kızıl Irmak on the way to Kangal. It takes its name (Bent Bridge) from the bend with which this eighteen-arched structure braces itself against the river.

Tavro (3 km. NW): A little way from this suburb of Sivas there is a rocky hill with numerous cave tombs.

Sivrihisar

Eskişehir   p.566□G 3

Ancient *Justiniapolis* lies at the foot of the precipitous and jagged Çal Dağı mountains (5540 ft.) and is overlooked by the ruins of a Byzantine castle.

Ulu Cami: This is one of the older Seljuk mosques (1274) built to the Kufa scheme, but the forecourt, which contained a şcadırvan and was originally at the centre of the mosque, is no longer there. This form exists only in Anatolia. This Kufa type of mosque (also known as the transept type) derives from the Arab style of house with an open arcaded courtyard, and has a *transverse* prayer hall. The mihrab is on the wider side of the mosque. The timber ceiling is supported by five rows of wooden columns, with 13 columns in each row (against the rear wall there are only 11). Further peculiarities are rich carving on all wooden parts, colourful painting with Turkoman tent motifs, and many ancient spoil capitals. The Seljuks were fond of using such capitals in the mosques they built.

Gazi Alemşah-Türbe (1308): This is a tower tomb in the Seljuk tradition, from the emirate period. 'Turkish triangles' join the main body of the tower to the drum of the dome.

Environs: Amorion (40 km. SW): Amorion is documented as populated in

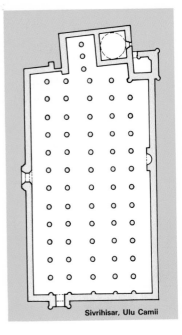

Sivrihisar, Ulu Camii

Hittite and Phrygian times. It became known both as a border fortress and as the capital of the military district of Anatolikon, created for defence against the Arabs. Captured in 716 by the Umayad caliph Sulaiman during his campaign against Constantinople, it was liberated by Leo II shortly thereafter. In 838 it fell to the Arabs after a long siege led by the caliph Al-Mutasim. The Arabs massacred most of the inhabitants, completely destroyed the town and deported the highest-ranking officers to Samarra. After seven years of captivity they were killed for their steadfastness of their faith. Since then the Greek Orthodox church has venerated them as the 42 martyrs of Amorion. Amorion fell into decline in the time of the emperor Theophilos, who was a member of the Amorian dynasty in Byzantium (820–867). *Ruins* of several buildings survive.

main cult symbol of Cybele, had to be transported to Rome. King Attalos of Pergamon maintained good relations with the priests, and in 205 BC he was able to obtain their agreement that the holy stone of the Magna Mater should be transported elsewhere. 16 years later the Roman consul Manlius Vulso inflicted a crushing defeat on the Galatians. The kings of Pergamon then ruled in Pessinus from 183 BC on, and erected splendid buildings in the town. All heathen cults were prohibited by the Eastern Roman emperor Theodosius in the late 4C AD. The consequence was that the town fell into decline and abandoned.

The *temple of Cybele*, dating from Hellenistic times, was excavated by archaeologists in the mid-1970s. The cella measures 25 x 25 ft. Further down the slope is a well-preserved *odeion*. The remains of the town, with parts of a theatre and tombs, were below the remains of the acropolis. On the river bed there is a processional road with statue bases. The town has a small *museum*.

Balhisar (Sivrihisar), Temple of Cybele

Balhisar/Pessinus (13 km. S.): Ancient *Pessinus* was founded by the Phrygians in the early 1C BC. They built a temple to the matriarchal goddess Cybele. Pessinus was famous for many centuries as a result. Later the town was the centre of a priests' state. After the Galatians invaded Anatolia in 277–244, Pessinus became the capital of the Galatian Tolistoagians, who continued to observe the priestly temple cult but introduced some variations. Great wealth accrued to the town over the centuries as a result of they pilgrimages that came from far and near. Roman generals also visited this cult site, wreathed in legend, of the matriarchal goddess of Asia Minor and her young lover Attis, who had emasculated himself under tragic circumstances. Emasculated priests also had a part to play in this gruesome cult. According to the Sibylline books, the Baitylos, a black meteorite which was the

Tarsus

Mersin — İçel   p.574☐K 6

There was a settlement in this strategically favourable location in the neolithic period. It was excavated in Gözlükule Hüyük in the present town centre. It was then populated continuously until the end of the late-Bronze Age. Hetty Goldmann investigated the archaeological sites in 1934–39 and 1947–49. This brought to light a large number of inscribed Hittite document seals. They date from the two periods mentioned, and underline Tarsus' importance as a trading post at that time. In *c.* 1200 BC, the town was destroyed by the seafaring peoples who also laid waste the Hittite empire in central Anatolia. The Assyrian king Sanherib finally conquered the town in 696 BC.

After the death of Alexander, the town became part of the Seleucid empire. It was later renamed *Antiochaia,* in honour of Antiochos IV. From 64 BC onwards Tarsus was the capital of the Roman province of Cilicia. This began in the time of Cicero, who resided here as governor. Antony and Cleopatra spent their honeymoon here. Tarsus was the birthplace of the Apostle Paul, who worked here as a tent-maker (Acts 21,39).

In AD 260, the Sassanid king Shahpur occupied the town, which shortly thereafter (in 276) also fell victim to a looting campaign conducted by the Goths. The late-Roman emperor Julian the Apostate (361–363) was buried in Tarsus. The town was in Turkish hands when the Crusaders occupied it shortly before 1100. On 6 January 1199, the Armenian count Leon Rubenian was crowned king of Cilicia in the cathedral of Tarsus. This was the birth of the kingdom of Lesser Armenia.

Cilicia flourished under the regency of this Armenian ruler, known as King Leo I (1199–1219). Lucrative trade agreements were concluded with Genoa and Venice, and secular buildings, as well as several churches, were built here by Italian merchants.

The royal palace and the large cathedral were destroyed when Tarsus, at the time under the Armenian King Leo II (1270–89), fell to the Turkish Mamelukes. King Oshin, the fourth son of Leo II and next but one in line of succession (1308–20), recaptured Tarsus and had himself crowned king there, as the founder of the kingdom had done before him. Half a century later, Tarsus once again fell into Mameluke hands, and in 1515 it finally became Ottoman under Selim I.

The ancient level of settlement is now several yards below the alluvial depositsts

Tarsus, Cleopatra's Gate

of the Tarsus Çayi. The result is that hardly any classical or ancient Armenian monuments survive in the town, despite its rich past, but most of those which do are located close together in the town centre.

Cleopatra's Gate *(Cleopatra Kapisi):* Today the Roman town gate stands in isolation on a broad, green central reservation in the town centre on the Mersin road. At the other end of this traffic island there is a memorial stone with the *independence inscription* (Özgürlük Yaziti). The text, which dates back to the Roman emperor Severus Alexander (222–235), grants a large measure of freedom of action to the provincial government of Cilicia, and gives the unusual ruling that Roman civil law should apply in Tarsus.

Gözlükule Hüyük: A theatre, of which only scant remains survive, was built into the slope of this hill a little to the E. of Cleopatra's gate. The oldest remains in the town were discovered in this hill.

Local museum *(Müze):* A small archaeological collection has been assembled in the former Kubatpaşa medrese in the town centre. A Roman sarcophagus, surrounded by the bases, capitals and fragments of column shafts, stands in the central courtyard which has a domed iwan with pointed arch on its rear side. The small rooms containing the exhibits open on to both the long sides of the courtyard. There are numerous small *marble and limestone statuettes* from the Graeco-Roman period, also a small collection of *glasses* from the same period.

Kilisesi: A former church, later converted into a mosque, stands on the opposite side of the road to the museum. This basilica, with its plain Gothic portal, is characterized by a small polygonal superstructure on the ridge of the tiled, and rather flat, saddleback roof. Light enters the building through this superstructure. Apart from this, only a few very small windows assist in lighting the church, which therefore, when looked at from the outside, makes a massive impression like that of a fortified church. The minaret to the right of the old entrance can clearly be seen to be a later addition.

Tarsus, courtyard of Kubatpaşa Medrese, now the local museum

Roma Hamami: Sparse remains of Roman *thermal springs and baths* are to be seen a little to the N. of the museum. Some of the arches and vaults, built of coarsely cut ashlar, still survive.

Ulu Cami (Great Mosque): This complex in the town centre is surrounded by a wall with corner towers. Apart from the prayer hall, there is also a Koran school (medrese). The wings of the school building are supported by granite columns and stand around the central courtyard. The mosque has three aisles with pillars alternating with columns. The inscription relating to the foundation of the mosque states that it was established by Ibrahim Ramazan Oğlu in 1579. However, the projecting arched buttresses on the outside of the carefully worked masonry between the peak-arched windows are evidence that the building is of earlier date, perhaps even 15C.

Donukatş (also *Dönik Taş):* The foundations of an enormous *temple*, with a surface area of 355 x 170 ft. and 10 x 21 surrounding columns, are to be found in this quarter in the very E. of the town, on the right bank of the Tarsus Çayi. This site is popularly known as the 'tomb of Sardanapal'.

St.Paul's fountain *(Saint Paul Kuyusu):* The house in which St.Paul was born is considered to have stood on this site in the NW part of the town centre. The second surviving gate of the six former Roman town gates *(Kancik Kapi)* is also named after Paul the Apostle. (The other surviving gate is Cleopatra's Gate.)

Justinian bridge *(Justinianus Köprüsü):* Some remains of the curving stone bridge which dates back to the Roman Emperor Justinian (mid-6C AD) survive at the entrance of the town, just N. of the turn-off which leads from the Adana-Mersin road into the centre of Tarsus.

Environs: Selale: Alexander the Great is thought to have bathed at the Tarsus Çayi waterfalls to the N. of the town. They are now a popular place for an outing.

Cave of the Seven Sleepers *(Eshab-i Kehf):* 14 km. NW): A few steps lead into this approximately square rock chamber near the village of *Dedeler Köyü.* The early Christians are said to have hidden here from the persecutions of the Roman governor Dacianus. They are reported to have stayed so long that upon their return to the town they attracted attention because their clothes had in the meantime gone out of fashion.

Teos

İzmir   p.572☐B 4

Teos was one of the richest towns in the Ionian League. The acropolis was in the middle of an isthmus, hence the two harbours. The lyric poet Anakreon lived here in the 6C BC. The town later became famous because the 'Technites of Dionysos' settled here in the late 3C after many wanderings. This was the name given to a group of artists who enjoyed privileges such as freedom from taxes, but were also notorious for their debauched life-style. On the acropolis there are polygonal remains of walls, ruins of a *gymnasion* with inscriptions relating to administrative matters, and the ground plan of the Roman *stage* of the *theatre* which is Hellenistic in design. To the S. are the remains of the *classical settlement*, and 655 ft. W. are those of a Roman *odeion*. These are adjoined by a rectangular *wall*, of which some impressive blocks, together with a paved road, have been uncovered beside the temple. Most of the shrine of Dionysos 'Setaneios' was sold in the 18C in the form of bluish marble blocks. Hermogines of Priene built the temple in the Ionic order on a pedestal. (The Attic column bases and the frieze are in a museum in İzmir.) Hadrian had the shrine rebuilt.

Tercan
Erzincan   p.568☐Q 3

Tercan is noteworthy for its Seljuk buildings.

Mama Hâtun Kümbet: A Seljuk princess who used her troops to support Saladin's campaign of conquest in this region is buried in this gorgeous *tomb building.* The mausoleum (1192) built of ashlars is the work of Sesi Muffada (the Squinter), a prince from Ahlat on Lake Van. It consists of the tomb proper (türbe) and a round surrounding wall.

The conical roof of the tomb is divided into eight segments. The interior of the tomb has two storeys. The burial chamber with the *sarcophagus* is in the vault. The room above this is a little above ground level, and contains the prayer room with the mihrab. Niches, located side by side and almost semicircular in shape, form a ground plan in the shape of a rosette with eight blossoms. Articulation using eight segments of a circle is repeated on the outer façade, but here the flat convex curves in the rising masonry are separated from one another by ribs.

The tomb building is surrounded by a circular outer wall a short distance away. The top of this wall can be reached from the inside by stairs to the right of the entrance. The small niche to the left of the entrance is a prayer niche.

Caravanserai: The caravanserai dates from the same period as the tomb, and is reached via its richly-decorated door. The smooth exterior walls of this rectangular building are today articulated only by identical pencil-shaped towers (there were formerly also some windows). Inside, there are undecorated galleries at an extraordinarily high elevation. The camels were kept in the high stables, the horses and mules in the lower ones. The large kitchen also survives.

Mama-Hâtun bridge: This is named

Tercan, Mama Hâtun Kümbet

after the same princess as the two buildings just described, which suggests that the bridge dates from the late 12C.

Termessos
Antalya   p.574☐F 6

This ruined Roman town is among the most charming and best-preserved towns in southern Turkey. The original inhabitants called themselves Solymers after Solymos, the local mountain. Homer refers to them as 'warlike Solymers', whom Bellerophon (→ Tlos under Fethiye, Environs) was obliged to fight. This skill in warfare also led to a failure for Alexander the Great, who was unable to conquer the town. The citizens of Termessos were also in conflict with many of the neighbouring towns, and *c.*200 BC they were in dispute with the entire Lycian League. The town was much Hellenized in the three last centuries BC, and flourished under the Romans. The splendid buildings and tombs are evidence of this. The inhabitants of Termessos did not support Mithridates against Rome, and this gained them Rome's friendship and a guarantee of independence.

Tour of the town: This begins on the right of the Street of the King, at the monumental portal of the Ionic propylon which is part of the *Temple of Hadrian*. Then continue to the lower fortifying wall with its main gate, and 400 yards further along the Street of the King is the *upper wall*, still at almost its original height. The turning to the left leads to the *gymnasium*. The astonishingly well-preserved *theatre*, 330 ft. to the S., is an example of wealth and elegant architecture. The cavea is Greek and larger than a semicircle. The 24 rows of seats held some 5,000 spectators. There is some neat ashlar work in the Hellenistic auditorium, while the stage building is later, dating from the Roman period when the five doors leading into the orchestra were required for circuses and animal-baiting. The *odeion*, a short distance to the S., is excellently preserved. The splendid masonry survives to a height of 30 ft. The fine ruins (almost 20 ft. high) just nearby are part of an unknown *temple* (Zeus Solymeos?). The portal of the small 3C temple S. of the odeion survives in its entirety.

A *heroon* by the agora stands on a block of rock with arch-shaped niches for cult figures. The two market halls were founded by Attalos II of Pergamon in 145 BC, and by the unknown Osbaras 300 years later. The *'founder's house'* to the W. of the stoa of Attalos is a large Roman house with an enormous portal 20 ft. tall. Some 330 ft. to the N., just at the beginning of the colonnaded street, formerly lined with colonnaded halls and

Termessos, Roman theatre ▷

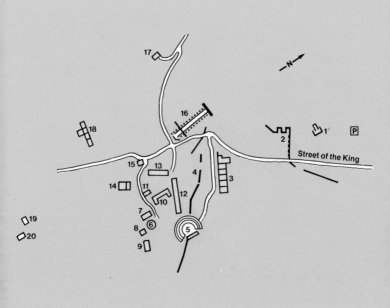

Termessos 1 Propylon of Hadrian temple **2** Lower fortifying wall **3** Gymnasium **4** Upper fortifying wall **5** Theatre **6** Odeion **7** Temple **8** Artemis temple **9** Large Artemis temple **10** Agora **11** Heroon **12** Stoa of Osbaras **13** Stoa of Attalos **14** Founder's house **15** Small Artemis temple **16** Colonnaded street **17** Tomb of Alketas **18** Dwelling houses **19** Burial temple with lion sarcophagus **20** Sarcophagus of Agathemeros

shops, a path on the left branches off to the W. and leads to the *tomb of Alketas,* the most prominent tomb in Termessos. Diodoros relates its story which dates from the time of the conflicts between the Diadochi in 319 BC, four years after Alexander's death. Perdikkas, the highest-ranking general, was appointed regent by Alexander, and was the brother of Alketas, the infantry general. Alketas and Attalos slew Meleager the Macedonian and his supporters. After the Macedonian officers of Perdikkas murdered him by the Nile, Alketas and others were outlawed. Alketas had fled to Termessos with an army, and Antigonos demanded that Alketas be extradited. The older citizens wanted to extradite him, but the younger ones opposed this. The older citizens devised a stratagem to extradite Alketas and end the siege, but before this could be done, Alketas killed himself. Antigonos defiled his body, which was nevertheless brought back into the town by younger citizens, who gave him a magnificent funeral on a rock. There is a larger-than-life relief showing a horseman galloping uphill. His head was destroyed by gold prospectors as recently as the 1960s. Under the head there are infantry weapons: helmet, greaves, round shield, and sword. The original state of the tomb just to the right is difficult to reconstruct. The sarcophagus of the main tomb was probably in the right-hand part of the double niche; the whole structure has been badly damaged

Termessos, gymnasium

by looters. The bas relief on the rear wall depicts what may be an imitation of the wooden lattice work of a folding screen, an eagle flying with a snake in its claws and, on the right, Hermes and Aphrodite. This building is one of the earliest in Termessos. All round the outside of the town are groups of *tombs*, ranging from the simplest type of coffin to sumptuous burial houses and Lycian rock tombs of all kinds, some with fine reliefs.

Environs: Evdir Han: About 7 km. from the Antalya to Burdur road in the direction of Termessos and just over 100 yards E. of the bridge over the river is a small path leading N. to the Seljuk caravanserai (1217) of Sultan Kaykaus I (near the village of *Yeşilbayir* or *Uzumkuyu*). This is a Syrian-type han with courtyard and surrounding rooms, without roofs in this case. The iwans which accentuate the middle of all four sides are also Syrian. The courtyard portal, with its well-preserved niche with pointed arch, still looks majestic, but large parts of the han have fallen into ruin.

Kirkgöz Han (near the Antalya-Burdur road, before it begins to climb into the Çibuk gorge): This han built 1236–46 is similar in type to the older Evdir han, but its manner of construction is rough, as are the materials of which it is built. The gigantic unadorned building, with its 16 rectangular supporting towers, looks menacing rather than inviting. The portal which is fitted in simple style into a porch 25 ft. wide leads into the courtyard which measures 80 x 140 ft. and has six successive pergolas on the left and six on the right. Their tunnel vaults run to the side wall along two squat arcades. The Kirkgöz han differs from the Evdir han in that it has a single room 35 ft. deep and 150 ft.

wide running transversely to the rear wall, across the entire width of the building. This room has six broad wall arches.

Tokat

This town has in large part preseved its medieval appearance. It stands on the Tokat Suyu on the S. flank of the Pontic coastal mountains.

Overlooking the town in the N. there is a ruined Ottoman fortress on a two-peaked mountain which is difficult to climb. The present citadel was probably preceded by another dating from the Hittite period. The town was known as *Dazimon* in ancient times. In the 4C AD, during the Byzantine period, it gradually began to outshine the neighbouring town of 'Comana Pontica' (→ Gümenek: Environs).

The local Danishmendid dynasty, founded by Melik Gazi, ruled here in the 11C, followed by the Seljuks from the 12C. It was briefly taken over by the emirate of Eretna the Mongol in 1335, and in 1392 it became part of the Ottoman Empire under Sultan Beyazıt I. Uzan Hassan, leader of the White Sheep, plundered the settlement in 1471. At that time it was an important staging post for caravans, because it was on a N. fork of the silk route which, coming from Persia, passed through Syria to the Black Sea coast. Numerous fortresses protecting the trade route survive along this road, as do many caravanserais. Most of these date from the 17C&18C, when the town was enjoying the prosperity which the silk trade brought to it.

The main square (Meydan) to the E. of the citadel hill has several good buildings grouped around it:

Gök Medrese (Blue Koran School; on the W. side of the Meydan): This building completed in 1271 was used as a Koran school until 1811. Today it houses the *Archaeological Museum* with excavation finds from the surrounding area, mostly from Comana Pontica, and a good *collection of icons*.

Voyvoda Han: This is a caravanserai built in 1630 a little to the S. of the Gök

Termessos, tomb of Alketas

Medrese. Its rectangular courtyard is surrounded by two-storeyed buildings.

Horozoğlu Han: This small caravanserai to the S. of the Meydan is probably 18C.

Hatuniye Camii: This mosque (1485) diagonally opposite the Horozoğlu han in the SE corner of the Meydan was built by Sultan Beyazıt II in honour of his mother Gülbahar Hâtun. This domed mosque with vaulted portico contains inappropriate classical columns.

Halef Gazi Tekkesi: This is a small dervish monastery (1291) in the N. of the Meydan on the road to Amasya.

Solu Sokağı: This street with its bazaar has many shops selling copper goods. It stands to the S. of the citadel and runs in an approximately E.-W. direction. Other buildings, such as caravanserais, mosques, baths and türbes, stand in groups in the adjoining districts of town. To the E. is Paşa Hamam, a bath house in the bazaar street. A little to the W. of this is Ali Paşa Camii (16C).

Also worth seeing: are the *Sünbül Baba Zaviyesi,* a small dervish monastery (1292) a little to the W. of Halef Gazi Tekkesi, the *Nur ed-Din Sentimur Türbesi,* a tomb monument (1314) to the W., on the road to Amasya and the 12C *Seljuk bridge,* over the Yeşilirmak.

Environs: Çiftlik Hani (Country-estate Caravanserai; 22 km. S.): The traveller proceeding S. towards Sivas will first cross the Kizilinişgeçidi Pass (5,740 ft.). The Çiftlik Hani, of which only the dilapidated main hall survives, stands to the right of the steeply sloping road 10 km. before it crosses the Çekerek river (also known as Değirmen-Dere) at Camlibel.
Ezinepazarı (70 km. NW): This was formerly the last stopping-point for caravans before they reached Amasya, a day's journey away. Ezinepazarı has a 12C Seljuk *caravanserai.* The town is reached via Turhal, from which it is 25-km further north. The modern tarmac road follows the old caravan route.
Gümenek (10 km. NE): The ruins of the Pontic town of **Comana Pontica,** for a long time the main town in the region until it was outstripped by Tokat, are to be found near this village. They are on the road to Niksar, not far from the Tokat castle rock. The excavation finds discovered here are now on display in the Tokat museum (Gök Medrese).
Horos Tepesi (9 km. S.): The ruins of an ancient and medieval *citadel* are on the steep hill to the left of the Tokat-Sivas road. Two rock tombs survive, and so does a tunnel with a staircase. To the E. of this, at the *Keşlik* excavation site, there is another cave tomb, later converted into a Byzantine chapel.
Maşat Hüyük (90 km. SW): Ruins extend across several terraces on a natural rocky elevation of crystalline limestone. Excavations have shown that these are the ruins of a Hittite palace inside a citadel wall. The hill takes its name from a village located 1.5 km. to the E., but now called Yalinyazi. The site is best approached via Zile, 20 km. to the N. of Yalinyazi.
The *excavation site* is at the confluence of two E. tributaries of the Çekerek, which is referred to in Hittite texts as the Zuliya river, and itself flows into the Yeşilirmak. A Hittite clay tablet was found on the hill in 1943. A brief excavation, carried out in 1945 in conjunction with the publication of the text on the tablet, did not lead to any results worthy of mention. Success was not achieved until the works performed in 1973 and supervised by T.Özgüç. Three Iron Age strata, and below them three Hittite strata, were discovered on the hill which measures 1475 ft. from E. to W. and 740 ft. from N. to S.
The lowest stratum of human settlement (stratum III) proved to be the most significant. It contained the large *palace* of a Hittite governor who was responsible for safeguarding the frontier. Two wings of this building were excavated. They are

grouped in typical Hittite style around a large courtyard which was surrounded on all sides by a colonnade of pillars. The square bases of the pillars correspond to rectangular projections on the façade of the palace walls facing the courtyard. Ten bases survive on the N. side along its length of 140 ft., while on the E. side, which is 130 ft. long, eight bases still stand. The whole palace had well over 40 rooms and occupied an area of at least 260 x 330 ft. To build the palace, it must have been necessary to level some of the terrain artificially, and to support and terrace it by constructing protective walls on the slope.

The best find inside the palace was the *palace archive*, discovered in 1975, with 130 clay tablets inscribed solely in the Hittite language. Most of these tablets are letters sent direct from Hattuşa (Boğazköy), the capital, some 115 km. away. In these letters, reference was made to Tapigga, the Hittite name of the place. The fact that the governor and the Hittite king corresponded directly with one another is evidence that Maşat Hüyük/Tapigga was important.

In *c.*1400 BC, during the time of King Tudhaliya II, the palace burned down in one of the Kashkaean raids, in which Hattuşa, the capital, also suffered. But Tapigga was quickly rebuilt: one generation after Tudhaliya, whose state seal was found on two letters inscribed on clay tablets in the palace archive, there was another large administrative building on the citadel hill (stratum II). This latter building dates from the time of Suppiluliuma I (mid-14C BC). This is proved by an impression, found in the building, of that ruler's seal. This building stood above the NW corner of the old residence, and like that residence it was built in a kind of timber-frame style consisting of wood and clay bricks resting on low stone foundations. Large mosaic stones in four different colours, polished on their upper sides, probably once decorated some of the walls. This building was itself devastated, possibly in

another Kashkaean raid led by King Muwatalli (*c.*1300 BC) and again continued as far as the Hittite capital.

The last Hittite buildings (stratum I) were erected above this. Many foreign ceramic fragments (Mycenaean III-B ware and Cypriot 'milk bowls') have been discovered in these last-mentioned buildings, which were themselves destroyed in the late 13C BC. The small Phrygian settlement, built in the 6C BC on the Hittite ruins, only took up a small area on the hilltop. Some of the old walls which were still standing were used for this settlement. The conflagration had fired their clay bricks and made them durable. The stone blocks of the Hittite foundations were also reused at this time. This modest settlement, in which three phases of construction have been ascertained, even had a drainage system. The most recent of these Iron Age strata, all of which date from the 2nd half of the 1st millennium BC, may even have been built by the Scythians. After this there was never again a human settlement on this site.

Niksar (57 km. NE): Like Tokat, this town on the bank of the Kelkit Çayi has a *ruined fortress* on a natural rocky projection. The present appearance of the fort derives from conversions and reconstructions performed in Byzantine and Ottoman times. It was probably preceded by older buildings on the same site because this town, known in ancient times as *Cabeira* or *Neo Caesarea*, was among the most important fortifications in the Kingdom of Pontus, which was finally incorporated into the Roman Empire in 64 BC under Pompey.

One of the decisive battles in the Third Mithridatic War between Rome and the Kingdom of Pontus was fought not far from the ancient settlement, when L. Licinius Lucullus gained a victory over Mithridates VI Eupator in 71 BC. But after his army mutinied, the victorious campaigner was recalled to Rome in 68 BC. The town enjoyed another peak period in the Middle Ages under the local Danishmend dynasty, whose main town

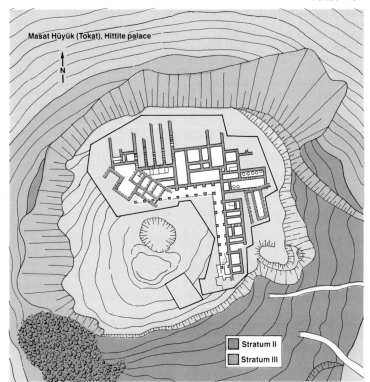

Masat Hüyük (Tokat), Hittite palace

N

Stratum II
Stratum III

was here from 1071 onwards. Melik Gazi, founder of the dynasty, was buried here. The *Yagbasan Medrese* is 12C. There is also the large *principal mosque* (Ulu Cami). **Pazar** (32 km. W.): The chief sight in this town is the *Hâtun Hani*, a 13C caravanserai. The site is reached by the road to Turhal, off which, after 26 km., there is a left-hand turning towards Pazar (then it is another 6 km.).
Turhal (45 km.): The ruins of a *citadel* stand on the rock overlooking the town, as is also the case in Tokat and Niksar. Again, as in the two towns just mentioned, the fortification dates back to the Pontic Kingdom.
Zile (69 km. W.): The origins of this little town date back at least as far as the Hittite

period, when there was a border fortress here against the hostile Kashkaeans to the N.
It is though certain that the present name of the town derives from the name which the site had in Roman times, namely **Zela.** It was here that the famous battle between Caesar and Pharnaces of Pontus was fought in 47 BC. Pharnaces was the son of Mithridates VI Eupator. After his father's defeat at the hands of Pompey, Pompey appointed him as governor. Rome was passing through a period of weakness, due to the civil war. Pharnaces tried to exploit this in a bid for independence, but failed. Just under three weeks after Pharnaces landed in Antioch, Caesar reported to the Roman Senate his victory

over Pharnaces, using the words 'veni, vidi, vici' ('I came, I saw, I conquered'). The defeated Pharnaces was able to flee to the Bosporus, but was murdered shortly afterwards.

A *ruined citadel* on a natural rocky elevation overlooks the town, and today still houses a military observation post.

Trabzon

Trabzon, formerly **Trapezunt**, and long known as Trebizond, is today the third largst Turkish town on the Black Sea. The earliest traces of the town's history date from the early 6C BC, when Milesian merchants established another trading post here from Sinope. But the coastal region was certainly populated earlier than this. The name of the settlement may relate to the fact that many of its inhabitants were originally immigrants from Trapezos in Arcadia. The Greek mercenary leader Xenophon was in the town in *c.*400 BC, along with the soldiers remaining from his former 'Ten Thousand', who had taken part in the battles between the Persian brothers Cyrus II and Artaxerxes II, who were mutually hostile. In the 1C BC, the Romans succeeded in capturing Trapezunt in the Third Mithridatic War against Mithridates VI Eupator. Hadrian (117–138) had the town enlarged, and this included the construction of a new harbour. Roman domination was only briefly interrupted by an invasion of the Goths in AD 257.

The princes David and Alexius fled to Trapezunt in 1204 in order to escape the Crusader armies coming from Byzantium. These two princes founded the Byzantine Empire of Trapezunt when Alexius ascended the throne as Emperor Alexius I Megas Comnenus. Trapezunt was the capital. Eighteen emperors and three empresses ruled the empire for some 250 years, but riots and civil wars were a constant danger to them. The empire could only maintain its independence towards the outside world by making payments to the surrounding great powers. These were the Seljuks, and later the Mongols and Ottomans.

A colony of Genoese merchants brought about an economic upturn in 1204. They

Trabzon, Hagia Sophia from the S.

later established further trading posts in Samsun (Amiso, 1289) and Sinope (1301), but in Trapezunt they faced stiff competition from the Venetians in 1319. In 1295, Marco Polo left from here on his famous voyage to China. David, last emperor of the Byzantine Empire of Trapezunt, handed the town over in 1462 to the Ottoman Mehmet Fâtih, who deported some sections of the population to Constantinople, and enlisted others into his armies. David, a nephew and six of his sons were murdered in Constantinople the following year. In the period that followed, the Ottoman crown princes (Beyazıt II, Selim I and Süleyman) were prepared for their future task as rulers by each serving as governor of Trapezunt. Until World War I, caravans starting from here proceeded to Persia via Erzurum. The town was occupied by Russia from 1916–18. After it became Turkish again, the Greek population of the Black Sea area was expelled in 1923.

Fortifications of the old town: The elongated walled area stretching from N. to S. in the middle of the modern town may almost be regarded as a town wall where its dimensions are concerned, but on the inside it is a fortress, divided like a citadel into three sections: a lower section (Aşağıhisar), a middle (Ortahisar) and an inner (Kulehisar). Almost nothing survives of the palace buildings described in late-medieval texts, because this area was severely damaged by civil war in the 17C. It is not clear when the wall was built around the old Trapezunt. All that is certain is that 1324 was the date when extensions under Emperor Alexius II (1279–1330) were completed. In the middle ring of the fortification is the *Ortahisar Camii,* the former Christian cathedral of Panaghia Chrysokephalos (Virgin of the Golden Head), converted into a mosque in 1468. This house of prayer, designed as a basilica with a nave and two aisles, was converted into a cruciform domed structure in the 13C. Its copper roof is said once to have been gold-plated.

Boz Tepe (Grey Hill): This eminence (740 ft. high) to the S. of the town provides the best view of the historic core of Trapezunt. There was a temple of Mithras here in the early period of the town's

Trabzon, Hagia Sophia, S. portal, Fall of Man

history. Today, during the fasting month of Ramadan, a cannon shot proclaims the end of the day, and thus also the end of the prescribed period of fasting. The **Ahi Evren Dede Camii** on the hill occupies the site of a former temple of Apollo, which in the early Christian period was itself replaced by a church dedicated to Eugenios, the town's patron. The first mosque here was built by the later sultan Selim for his father Beyazıt II while Selim was town governor. The present appearance of the building derives from a Persian dervish who, in 1809, provided the finance for extensive restoration and rebuilding.

Çarsı Camii: This mosque (1839) not far from the bazaar (bedesten) in the N. of the town was built by Haznedarzade Osman Paşa, who was town governor at that time. With its central dome supported by six pillars, it is the largest house of prayer in the town.

Gülbahar Hatun Camii (*Büyük Imaret Camii*): This mosque (1507–14) below and to the W. of the citadel was constructed by Selim I Yavuz for his mother

who is also buried here, and is thus the oldest building in the town always to have functioned as a Muslim house of prayer, whereas in other cases Christian churches were converted.

Hagia Sophia: This, the best church in Trabzon, is in the middle of a plateau surrounded by a wall and lies on the shore of the Black Sea on the NW edge of the town. Signs refer to the site as **Aya Sofıa Müzesi.** Today it is fitted up as an open-air museum. The sparse foundations of a Byzantine church, which had three semicircular apses and survived at least until 1850, are to be found on the N. side of this area, which is the side facing the sea. There is a free-standing bell tower in the NW corner. The main church in the centre of the precinct dates back to the beginnings of the Byzantine Empire of Trapezunt. Its *frescos* now again shine in their former splendour, thanks to uncovering and restoration by Russia (1917) and England (1957–62). The basilica originally had a nave and two aisles, and was converted into a cruciform domed structure, as was also the case with many other churches in the town. The church has

Trabzon, Hagia Sophia, fresco

retained to the present day the form which it was given under Emperor Manuel I (1238–63), with a narthex and three porticos. Its frescos date from shortly after 1250. The church was first restored in 1486 and 1547, and in the early 17C it was converted into a mosque, which the Christians were initially also permitted to use. However, when the paintings were whitewashed out in c.1880, it became a purely Muslim place of prayer, and so it remained until 1959, when it became a museum.

Today the main scenes depicted in the frescos are explained by notices. Apart from the frescos, there are also decorative sculptures on the outside of the building. The Miraculous Draught of Fish and Doubting Thomas are depicted in frescos in the N. of the main apse, and on the rear wall is the Virgin Mary with Gabriel and Michael. Above this are the Ascension and the Assumption, and adjoining these to the S. is the Mission of the Apostles. The two side apses have frescos showing Anne and Joachim, the parents of the Virgin Mary, in various scenes. A ring of hovering angels is seen in the dome above the

Apostles and Prophets who occupy the space between the windows of the drum. The Four Evangelists appear in the pendentive arches in scenes from the New Testament: St. Luke and the Nativity, St. Mark and the Baptism of Christ, St. Matthew and the Crucifixion, and St. John and the Resurrection. In the part of the nave vault near the narthex: Last Supper, Washing of the Feet, Garden of Gethsemane. The arch panel in the following section shows the Annunciation above Christ (right) and the Virgin Mary (left). The symbols of the Four Evangelists, and also angels and disembodied wings, are grouped around the hand of God, relatively small, on the ceiling of the narthex. The walls are decorated with Christ's miracles (Feeding of the Five Thousand, Calming the Storm and Walking on the Water, Raising the Dead, Healing the Sick, Marriage at Cana, etc.). The visitor entering the portico sees above him an Eastern Church variation on the motif of the Sudarium of Veronica. Scenes from the Last Judgement are then seen on the walls and ceiling. The frescos in the N. portico depict Old Testament motifs, such as the

Trabzon, Hagia Sophia, symbols of the Evangelistic

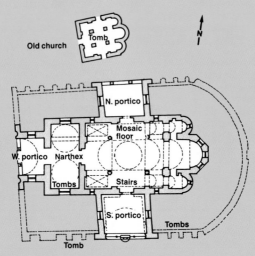

Trabzon, Hagia Sophia

Burning Bush, Jacob's Dream, Jacob Wrestling with the Angel, Job, and the Three Angels Visiting Abraham.

Iskender Paşa Camii: This mosque stands behind the town hall (Belediye Binasi), not far from the municipal park. It was founded in 1529 by the then town governor (1512–33), and bears his name.

Kudrettin Camii: The church of St.Philip, converted into a mosque in 1665, stands in the E. of the town, not far from the road to the airport. Founded by Anna Komnenos in 1341/2, it was converted and enlarged when the then bishop transferred his official seat from the Panaghia-Chrisokephalos church to here.

Küçük Ayvasil Kilisesi (St.Anne's church): This church standing to the E.

of the citadel, in the old part of town, is probably the oldest Christian house of prayer in Trabzon. The date of its building is unknown, but the inscription on the S. portal states that the church was restored as long ago as 884/885.

Nakip Camii: This place of prayer to the NW of the citadel is now ruined. It was probably formerly the church dedicated to St. Andrew, the first missionary in Trapezunt. It is said to have been built by the daughter of Emperor Alexius III in the 2nd half of the 14C, but in that case one would have expected a cruciform domed basilica. The design of the church, with a nave and two aisles, means that in fact probably dates from the 10C or 11C.

Panaghia-Theokephastos convent: Until 1923, this building on the N. side of Boz Tepe was occupied by Greek nuns.

Empress Irene, the mother of Alexius III, is said to have founded it out of gratitude for the victory over the Mongols at Paipert (Baiburt). At any rate, Andronikos, the son of Alexius III, is interred in a monument with a baldachin in the E. garden of the convent. The wall paintings of this 14C convent were still well preserved last century, but are barely discernible today. The cave church contains a spring said to have miraculous powers.

Yeni Cuma Camii: This former Christian church of Eugenios stands to the SE of the citadel, in the first of the three equal sections of the way to Boz Tepe. The original building suffered a fire in 1340, and a new cruciform domed church was then built here.

Also worth seeing: *Erdoğdu Bey Camii:* A 16C Ottoman mosque on the way to Atatürk's country house outside and to the SW of the town. *Musa Paşa Camii:* Small 17C Ottoman mosque in the E., inside the town fortifications. *Alacahan* (18C) and *Taşan* (16C) are two inns located respectively E. and S. of the bedesten (bazaar). Taşan was built under Iskender Paşa, but is today much restored. *Sekis Direkli Hamamı:* This bath is the town's oldest, and stands near the sea, NW of the outer town wall. It is no longer in use today. Its name (Bath of Eight Columns) derives from the dome supports of the hot-water channel.

Environs: Akçaabat (13 km. W.): Ancient **Hermonassa** and **Platana/ Polathane** are on the coast road to Giresun. The single-aisled *church of St.Michael* (13/14C) stands in the W. of the town. 8 km. further on is the White Castle *(Ağçakale),* the place where Kalo-Johannes landed in 1429 to seize power and become John IV, the penultimate emperor of the Byzantine Empire of Trapezunt.

Çamlihemşin and **Ayder** (about 170 km. E.): These two villages are located one after the other on a road leading from the

Trabzon, Hagia Sophia, fresco

small coastal town of Ardesen into the interior. This road is still under construction; it is a good road for vehicles as far as Çamlihemşin (23 km.). The two villages are here given as an example of the many mountain villages in the Kaçkar mountains (Kaçkar Daği: 12,900 ft.), which form the hinterland beyond the Black Sea coast E. of Trabzon. Ayder, with its thermal springs, also offers some modest overnight acommodation (such as the Hilton Oteli!). After the coast has been left behind, the numerous tea plantations on the mountain slopes gradually give way to a landscape of mountain pastures in which the peasant houses remind the traveller of Central European mountain regions. The road follows the River Fırtına upstream for a while. Stone bridges, consisting of a single vaulted arch with no parapet and fantastically overgrown with hanging plants, span this river, which is rich in trout. Above Çamlihemşin, the fortress of *Zil Kalesi* dominates the Firtina Vadisi (Storm Valley).

Eynesil (about 70 km. W.): The scant remains of a *coastal fortress* built of large ashlars are seen at the entrance to this town, immediately after the end of the road tunnel.

Fetoka (about 90 km. SE): The *monastery* which here survives only as a ruin is only one of the many monks' refuges built and maintained by the Greeks who resided in the hinterland of the Black Sea until 1923. These refuges included the Seno, Oma and Charweti monasteries.

Gümüşhane (115 km. SW): This is today the capital of the province, and is located at the N. foot of the mountain chain (up to 10,850 ft.) after which it is named. The town stands at a height of 4,100 ft. on the road to Erzurum. Its name (silver works) refers to the formerly rich silver deposits which were exploited in ancient and medieval times.

Kap Yeros (*Ferner Burnu;* 31 km. W.): In 1309, Emperor Alexius II built a castle by the shore of the small isthmus on the coast road to Giresun. The aim was to safeguard Trapezunt. Justinian is also said to have founded the St. Foca monastery, of which however nothing survives.

Kaymaklı (5 km. S.): A steep path climbs upwards from the road to Erzurum, passes the ruins of Roman aqueducts (3 km.) and leads to the *monastery,* where Armenian monks lived until World War 1. Today the main building with its two-storeyed arcaded façade survives, and so do the ruins of a bell tower, as well as two chapels standing close together (built in 1424 and 1622).

Kiremitli (about 55 km. S.): A road leads through Maçka (31 km.) to Küçük Konak (46 km.), from where it is a three hours' walk to the village of Kiremitli on the left bank of the Değin Mendere (Pyxites). The *monastery of St. John Vazelon* stands on a rock overlooking the village. This monastery is the best in Pontus after Sumela, and was built by Justinian as a signal station (cf. St. George in Peristera), but was converted and enlarged several times. The core structure ends in a cave. The remains of a chapel (1410) of John the Baptist, built by Manuel III and still containing a few paintings, stand beyond the monastery terrace.

Rize (79 km. E.): The capital of the

Trabzon, Hagia Sophia, fresco

province was formerly called *Rhizus/Risso*, and stands on the Black Sea coast. With its population of some 37,000, it has developed into a tea-growing centre, although the first plantations were not laid out until 1938. The *tea institute (Çayi Institüsü)* on a steep slope in the S. of the town gives a fine view of Rize and the surrounding tea plantations. Attached to the institute there is a collection of teaching materials on the subject of tea, together with a small botanical garden. The export of tea was expanding, but suffered a severe setback due to the nuclear accident at Chernobyl in 1986, and the same happened to this region's export of hazelnuts (cf. Üniye at Ordu). The town became part of the Ottoman Empire under Mehmet Fâtih in 1461, and Murat III then had to put down an insurrection by the Laz.

St. George in Peristera (*Hizit Ilys;* some 28 km. S.): Like the Sumela monastery and the monastery of St. John of Vazelon (see above: Kiremitli), this complex also contained a signal station for giving the Byzantine Trabzon timely warning of attacks launched by hostile mountain tribes coming from the hinterland. These stations were probably established under Justinian in AD 532. The monastery was destroyed in 1906 in a major fire, in which the famous collection of manuscripts also perished. The building was evacuated in 1923. It is reached via the village of Esiroğlu on the route towards Maçka and Sumela (19 km.). From here a walk of about three hours, undertaken in the company of someone who knows the area, leads E. through the villages of Liboda (4 km.) and Kostul as far as the rock on which the monastery stands, and from here 93 steps lead up to the destination.

Sumela Monastery (about 62 km. S.): This monastery, today officially known as *Meryem ana manastiri*, derives its traditional name from the Greek Hagia Maria tou Mela (St. Maria of Mount Mela). The safest way of reaching the town is in the 6-passenger public taxi which departs from the tourist information office in Trabzon and, on the road to Erzurum, passes through the villages of Esiroğlu (19 km.) and Maçka (another 11 km.), where a side road follows a small river upstream for 23 km. Here the four-storeyed façade is seen on a steeply rising rock wall 820 ft. high. Looking at

Rize (Trabzon), tea bush

Sumela monastery (Trabzon), exterior view

the façade, one would hardly suppose that the monastery buildings behind it are badly damaged. The best view of the complex is obtained from the slope opposite, where there is a lookout point with a park bench. After about half an hour's climb up a narrow zigzagging path, one comes upon 67 steps which end at the entrance gate at the S. of the monastery. Before entering the building, the visitor sees the remains of aqueduct arches on the rock wall. Looking down from the gate, one sees the monastery courtyard at a lower level, and one's eye is immediately caught by the chapel, which is painted on its outside walls and stands directly next to steeply rising rock wall to the left.

To the left of the chapel is the fountain with its miraculous water which was consecrated every month by a relic of the Cross donated by Emperor Manuel III in 1390 on the occasion of his coronation here in the monastery. His father, Alexius III, was probably himself crowned here in 1349. The monastery was first abandoned in 1916 when the Russian troops were approaching. It was burned out in 1920/22 during the Graeco-Turkish war. When the monks, who had returned, finally relinquished it in 1923, the relic of the Cross and the monastery's main icon were buried in the church of St. Barbara which is located away to the S. and now ruined. This icon is said to have been a portrait of the Virgin Mary which St. Luke the Evangelist painted and always carried with him. It is alleged that the two hermits Barnabas and Sophronios brought this portrait from Athens to the Pontic mountains in the early 5C. It then found a resting-place in the oldest monastery (probably built under Emperor Anastasios, 491–518, but burned down in 640). When the Turkomen devastated the rebuilt

Sumela monastery (Trabzon), view from entrance into monastery courtyard

monastery in the 12C, the icon is said not to have been destroyed in spite of attempts to hack it to pieces. In 1931, the Virgin Mary portait, the relic of the Cross, and a four-volume evangeliary written on gazelle leather belonging to Abbot Fazelon and dating from 644, were salvaged from their underground hiding-place in the St. Barbara chapel by an Athenian monk who transferred them to the Benaki Museum in Athens. The monastery library formerly took up two storeys. Manuscripts from the St.Catherine monastery in Sinai were donated to the library by Sultan Selim II (1566–74). Its ruins can be seen on the valley side of the monastery courtyard, opposite the painted apse chapel. Since 1952, the successors of the Sumela monks have lived in a flourishing monastery on Mount Vermion near Kastanea, 95 km. WSW of Saloniki in Greece.

Sürmene (41 km. E.): This village formerly known as *Hamurgan* or *Susarmia* appears in the report of the military expedition conducted by the 'Ten Thousand' mercenaries led by Xenophon, and is there described as the place where many soldiers were poisoned by the 'mad honey' growing by the River Kora. 5 km. outside the town is *Sürmene Kastili* with *Derebeyili Castle,* a noble early-19C property on an eminence just by the coast road. The interior decorations are worth seeing.

Troy/Truva

The hill of Hisarlık (the name of the present village is *Tevfıkye*) is 30 km. S. of Çanakkale. The hill is associated with the sagas of the Trojan War and its description by Homer (c.750 BC) in his two epic poems 'The Iliad' and 'The Odyssey'. It is also linked with the German excavator Heinrich Schliemann, who discovered Troy here by using the topographical data found in Homer. When he discovered golden, silver and bronze vessels, cups, diadems and earrings, it was the sensation of the age. He believed these items to be 'Priam's treasure'. The hill stands on the edge of the plain of Skamandros (today Küçük Menderes). The visitor who is in a hurry will find it difficult to understand the meaning of the hill, because it is at the same time the result not only of the history of human settlement here, but also of the history of its excavations. At the very least it affords a view to the NW across the wide Scamander plain towards the Dardanelles (on a clear day, the islands of Tenedos, today Bozcaada, and Imbros, today Gökceada, can also be seen), as well as a view to the S. towards the Ida mountains (today Kaz Dağ). In this way we can obtain a concrete geographical idea of the scene of the warlike events described in Homer. The hill is 720 ft. in diameter at its base,

and was originally 85 ft. high, but the ruins left behind by civilization over 4,000 years of history caused its height to rise to 130 ft. It was initially thought that there were nine strata of human settlement, but research work has now differentiated 46 strata. The place's long and varied history can be explained by its exposed geographical location. It is open to both the Aegean and Black Seas, in the area connecting the two. It is protected in the E. by the Yida mountains, 5,550 ft. high, from which the River Scamander flows, converting the plain around Troy into a fertile landscape with abundant water, while the mountains are rich in metal. All this favoured a mercantile town which maintained itself autonomously and was well fortified. It probably originated in the transitional period between the Stone and Bronze Ages. The names of three founding fathers are known: Dardanos, Tros and Ilios. They may have been representatives of the tribes who came together when founding the settlement. The last two appear in the names 'Troja' and 'Ilion' which were given to the town, while 'Dardanians', which derives from the first name 'Dardanos', is the name of the

Sumela monastery (Trabzon), Annunciation

inhabitants. The hill of Hisarlık contains a succession of human settlements making it an important site showing the development of urban culture.

T.I (3000–2400 BC): This period includes the first ten strata of settlement in a cultural layer 13 ft. thick. The fortified town which stood here in the neolithic period or early Bronze Age had a diameter of 295 ft. and was encircled by a wall of herringbone design, with two towers securing the entrance gate. The clay-brick houses followed the pattern of the Indo-Germanic megaron house: a rectangle with projecting side walls (antae). The articles of daily use included black polished ceramics. There are indications that this settlement perished in a disastrous fire.

T.II (2400–2200 BC): Seven Bronze Age settlement strata were discovered in a layer

Troy 1 E. gate (VI) **2** Rectangular room (VI) **3** Room with supports (VI) **4** Megaron (VI) **5** Foundations with storage vessels (VII) **6** NE corner tower **7** Athena temple (IX) **8** Propylon (II) **9** Megaron houses (II) **10** Megaron (VI) **11** Ramp (II) **12** Foundations (VI) **13** Castle wall (VI) **14** Odeum (IX) **15** S. gate **16** Buleuterion/theatre (IX) **17** Gates and castle wall (II)

Troy

The nine settlement strata in Hisarlık hill

T IX: from 334 BC
Hellenistic-Roman building work

T VIII: 700–334 BC: New population: Aeolians; from 546 BC Persian

T VIIb: 1260–1100 BC: New population: Phrygians

T VIIa: 1300–1260 BC: Homeric Troy

T VI: 1800–1265 BC: The best-fortified town, similar to Tiryns

T III-V: 2200–1800 BC: Succession of small villages

T II: 2400–2200 BC: 1st peak period: Enlarged settlement behind massive wall; 'Priam's treasure'

T I: 3000–2400 BC: Beginning of human settlement: walled village; early Bronze Age.

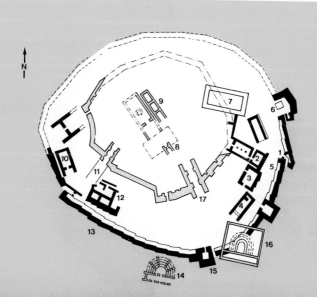

of rubble 10 ft. thick. They belonged to a town which was laid out in terraces, was 360 ft. in diameter (larger than T.I), and had a wall of clay bricks on a stone foundation, with two town gates and a paved ramp up which carts could be driven. The buildings were once again megaron houses, and there is also a row of megaron houses which may have been the palace. There are ceramic finds which are evidence that the potter's wheel was used here, and the metal-working craftsmanship reveals a Mesopotamian influence, indicating that relations existed at an early stage between this mercantile town and Mesopotamia. It was in this stratum that H. Schliemann discovered the so-called *Priam's treasure* in 1873: 'I found all the above-mentioned objects in a square heap. They were either lying together or were packed inside one another, and on the encircling wall. It therefore seems certain that they were in a wooden case like those mentioned in the Iliad (XXIV, 228) in Priam's palace...' (H. Schliemann, 17 June 1873). Schliemann unearthed gold, silver, pearls, bronze, diamonds, bracelets, bands, earrings, vessels, cups, royal axes in jade, lapis lazuli objects, rock crystal, and vases. He donated these objects to the Museum of Prehistory and Early History in Berlin. Priam's treasure was lost during World War Two and has not been found. Some ceramic objects were evacuated, but in 1945 village boys broke them by using them at a party held on the night before a German wedding, at which dishes are traditionally smashed. T.II, like T.I, was destroyed in a major fire, and this was one reason why Schliemann imagined that he was in Priam's city when he made this find.

T.III–V (2200–1800 BC): Each stratum is 6.5 ft. thick and indicates village settlements about which little detail has been established.

T.VI (1800–1265 BC): A stratum 20 ft. thick, made up of eight layers of human settlement. This stratum, reminiscent of Tiryns in many respects, was the largest and best-fortified town, with a town wall 1,150 ft. long and 15 ft. wide, built of stone ashlar outside and unfired brick inside. The wall has towers up to 30 ft. in height, and slopes towards the outside. The individual stretches of wall overlap at the gates to allow effective defence of the entrances to the town. The wall still

The famous Trojan wall (left), E. wall of Troy (right)

stands to a height of 13 ft. The houses were arranged concentrically around the acropolis, and the megaron type of house was enlarged by adding a hall supported by pillars and probably two storeys high. There is said to have been a shrine of Athena on the acropolis. The palace precinct was demolished by Schliemann's excavations which ran from N. to S. T.VI was destroyed by an earthquake.

T.VIIa (1300–1260 BC): This is 'Homeric' Troy, reduced to ashes at the end of the Trojan War. The initial cause of the war was the Judgement of Paris. Paris, the Trojan prince, the son of Priam and Hecuba, was appointed to judge the most beautiful of the three goddesses Hera, Athena and Aphrodite. The most beautiful woman was promised to him, and in exchange for this Paris decided in favour of Aphrodite. On a journey to Greece, he abducted Helen, the wife of Menelaus, king of Sparta. Menelaus, together with Ajax, Achilles, Agamemnon, Odysseus and a large navy, set off for Troy to wage the war, which was to last ten years. They constructed a large camp by drawing their ships on land on plain of the Scamander.

T.VIIb (1260–1100): Modest settlements occupied by Phrygians, and not comparable with T.VIIa. The same applies to:

T.VIII (700–334 BC): Aeolians now settled on the acropolis. Troy became Persian from 546 BC onwards. The influence of Homer's writing shows in the fact that Xerxes also visited Troy on his expedition to Greece and, according to Herodotus, stayed in the temple of Athena on the acropolis, sacrificing over 1,000 cattle (480 BC). Homer's work also had its effect on:

T.IX (334 BC onwards): Alexander the Great came to Troy in 334 BC. Believing himself to be the descendant of Achilles, he visited the tombs of Achilles and Patroclus, sacrificed to the spirit of Priam and took with him some weapons from Troy which he ordered his bodyguards to bear before him as talismans. He also commissioned a large temple of Athena, actually built by Lysimachos, his Pergamene successor. Outside this Doric building, Schliemann found a metope depicting the sun god. The town was held in particular regard under the Romans, who pursued intense building activities

Troy, excavation site

here. The Romans believed that Aeneas, who escaped westwards from Troy when it was burning, was their ancestor, and they thus considered Troy to be their place of origin.

The special features of this historic site are also seen in the sagas associated with it. Thus, Apollo and Poseidon wanted to depose Zeus, and by way of punishment were obliged to serve King Laomedon of Troy for one year. Apollo, the god of shepherds, tended the sheep on the Ida mountains, and built the town walls together with Poseidon. When Laomedon refused to pay them their wages, Apollo spread plague in the town, and Poseidon sent a sea monster to which Hesione, the king's daughter, was to be sacrificed. Heracles killed the monster and freed Hesione. When he too was not paid for this, he raised an army in Greece, conquered Troy and exterminated Laomedon's tribe, except for Priam, whom Hesione ransomed with her jewellery.

The search for Troy: Other prominent scholars pursued excavations in the Scamander plain in the 18&19C. Heinrich Schliemann, accompanied by his Greek wife Sophia, began digging in 1870. In 1873, he discovered what is known as Priam's treasure. Further excavations followed in 1878&9 (with Virchow) and 1882 (with Dörpfeld). Schliemann faced much animosity. He therefore invited international scholars to his last excavation in 1890. Virchow also arranged for Schliemann to become an honorary member of the Anthropological Society and an honorary citizen of Berlin, and also induced him to donate the excavation finds to the Berlin Museum.

After H. Schliemann, Carl William Blegen of Cincinnati University conducted excavations in 1932–8 and arrived at a better insight into the complex arrangement of differing settlements, and also at a more exact dating. This made it possible to discern 46 layers of settlement rather than the traditional number of nine.

Worth seeing: The hill as a whole is a document of our historical development. The visitor looking at it is advised to follow the excellently signposted path going around the hill. Foundations, surviving items, and other indications, can then be used to identify the following:

Temple of Athena: Nothing survives of its final appearance in the 3C BC. Remains of columns, capitals and beams, strewn about the site, indicate a Doric peripteros. Only traces remain as tangible evidence of the Roman design of the central sanctuary (colonnaded halls around the temple forecourt).

Gymnasium: This Roman structure is in the S. of the acropolis, with remains of mosaics.

Sanctuaries: Two terraced sanctuaries with several altars stand in the SW corner of the acropolis. The upper structure has a round altar from T.VIII, and two Hellenistic altars. This structure was then entirely covered over and a Roman marble altar stands on top of it.

Megaron: The existing foundations from houses of this type date from different periods. A megaron house, some 70 ft. long and belonging to T.VI, stands on the path surrounding the hill, behind and to the left of the E. gate. There is a series of megaron houses from T.II in the NW of the acropolis, and in the SW, between a ramp and some sanctuaries, there is a megaron (T.VI) where various Mycenaean ceramics have been found. Finally, behind the odeion, there is a house with pillars (also T.VI).

Museum: A museum documenting ceramic finds in Troy is to be found in the garden outside the excavation site.

Odeion: A semicircular building at the S. end of the acropolis, near the end of the path surrounding the hill. It has ascending rows of seats, and a recitation room dating from the Roman period.

Rooms: Just behind the E. gate and to its left, there are two rooms from T.VI: a plain rectangular room, and next to it a rather elongated room with two rows, each of five pillar bases, and in the middle are two larger stone abutments. Foundations from T.VIIa, with a fountain and three vessels for provisions, are found between these two sets of room foundations and the E. wall.

Ramp: A steep stone ramp, 18 ft. wide and in the SW of the acropolis, leads to T.II. It must have been a road for carts going up to the acropolis.

Town walls: The E. wall is at the beginning of the circular corridor belonging to T.VI. It is a sloping wall of ashlars, is articulated by vertical benches about 30 ft. apart, and is reinforced by a tower. The corner tower in the NE of the acropolis points in the same direction as this wall and is part of it. The remaining foundations of a gatehouse tower belonging to T.I are found on the N. side between the Athena temple and a group of megaron houses (T.II). To the S. of this, two gates from T.II stand next to one another. The S. tower, belonging to T.VI, is to the S., between the odeion and the theatre. It is thus possible to gain a good overall idea of the surrounding wall, fortified with towers, from T.VI (1800–1300), with a few remains from the smaller circles which are T.II and T.I.

Theatre: This is a semicircular structure to the right of the S. gate and near the Odeion. It has a row of seats surviving from Roman times. It is more likely to have been an assembly room for the town council (Boulé/Senatus) than a theatre.

Environs: Three more ancient towns can be included in a journey from Troy to Assos in the S. of Troas. They are: **Alexandria Troas, Chryse** and **Neandria.** This is the route to follow: On the Çanakkale-Edremit road, turn right (to the W.) in Ezine. After about 8 km., take the left-hand turning towards Ilıca. After about 15 km. along this stretch, Kayacik is reached at the foot of Ciğri Dağ. On the upper plateau of this mountain, it is about half-an-hour's walk to the city wall of the Aeolian settlement of **Neandria** (1700 ft.), with a splendid panoramic view across the Troas. The foundation walls of an Ionic

temple are also seen here. The road leads back from Neandria to a turning 15 km. away, and from there it continues to the left, passes through Geyekli and arrives at the ancient coastal town of **Alexandria Troas,** a Hellenistic foundation dating from the late 4C BC, with the remains of Roman buildings (theatre, temple, thermal baths). From here the road runs southwards along the coast to **Chryse,** which is 47 km. away from Geyekli and contains the temple of Apollon Smintheus below the village of Gülpinar which stands on the mountain slope. The temple has 8 x 14 Ionic columns on an area measuring about 70 x 130 ft. It has now been uncovered again, and dates from the mid-3C BC.

Urfa

This town was formerly known as **Edessa.** It has had a troubled history, but little evidence of its earliest history has survived. Prefixes are sometimes added to Turkish place names. Thus, Antep was given the prefix Gazi, and Maraş had Kahraman added to its name. Similarly, Urfa was given the attribute Şanlı (worthy) because of its resistance to the French occupation after the end of World War One, so that the official name of the town is now Şanlıurfa.

The modern town probably stands on the site of ancient *Uršu*, which is mentioned in Sumerian, Akkadian and Hittite cuneiform texts and was an important centre in the Hurrian empire of Hanigbalbat. Its rulers tried to curb Hittite expansion by maintaining close contacts with Egypt, but the Hittite king Suppiluliuma managed to conquer and destroy Uršu *c.*1370 BC. After the downfall of the Hittite kingdom *c.*1200 BC, the town was part of the small state of Karkemish, and in the 4C BC it is referred to as *Orhai*. Seleukos I, one of Alexander the Great's generals, tried to reinforce his claims as Alexander's successor by refounding the town and calling it Edessa, after the ancient capital of the Macedonian kingdom. Under Antiochos IV, the town was for a time called *Antiochea epi Kallirhoe*, and after the Parthian Wars with the Romans (145–129), the tribal prince Agu founded a small independent kingdom here which held its own for three centuries against the Armenians, Parthians and Romans.

The town was besieged by Trajan in AD 115&116 without success, but in AD 165 Lucius Verus finally succeeded in conquering Edessa, which was a Roman province from 214 onwards. When Abgar VIII (the Great) was converted to Christianity, the town rapidly developed into a Christian centre which produced numerous theologians. The Roman emperor Caracalla was murdered not far from the town in April 217. Edessa still remained part of the Roman Empire after Mesopotamia was lost to the Persians (AD 244). It is unclear whether the siege by the Persian Sassanid king Shahpur I was successful, but the Roman emperor Valerian was taken into Persian captivity. During the period of Byzantine domination, the bones of St. Thomas were transferred to the cathedral of Edessa, before the Sassanids once again conquered and plundered the town in 502–505. The town was rebuilt under Justinian and soon became a centre for the Monophysite Christians. In 609 it fell victim to another Sassanid attack under Khosroes II, but was recaptured by Herakleios in 628. The Marwanids functioned as the town's governors appointed by the Arabs, who ruled the town after their victory at Yarmuk in 637. The Marwanids were followed by the Numairids, who in 1030 sold Edessa to the Byzantine governor of Samosata. A siege by Alp Arslan the Seljuk was unsuccessful, but Smbat the Armenian managed to capture the town in 1083. When his successor Thoros called upon the Crusaders to assist him against the Turkmenians, the Franks entrenched themselves here, and Balduin of Bouillon (brother of the famous Gottfried) founded the county of Edessa in 1098. The town was then at the height of its powers, but declined when it was conquered by Zengi, governor of Mosul, in 1144. Some of the inhabitants were deported at this time. Count Jocelyn of Edessa tried to recapture the empire after Zengi was murdered in 1146. The final result of this attempt was that the town was completely destroyed by Nur ed-Din of Aleppo, with 30,000 people being killed and 16,000 enslaved. The Christian churches were either torn down or desecrated and used as stables.

Urfa, Makam İbrahim

It proved impossible to recapture Edessa in the Second Crusade, initiated by Pope Eugene III together with Bernard of Clairvaux. In 1182, Saladin began the period of Aiyubid rule. This was briefly interrupted by the Seljuk Alaeddin Kaykobad in 1234. Between the two Mongol periods (first Hulagu, then Timur-Leng), the Mamelukes ruled the town, most of which was in ruins. The Ottomans under Sultan Selim had Urfa in their possession after defeating the Mamelukes in 1516, but they lost it to Persia in 1623–37. Under Murat IV, they finally incorporated it into their empire. Apart from the French occupation in 1918–20, the only interruption to Ottoman rule was when the rebel Mohammed Ali occupied the town with Egyptian troops in 1837.

Today Urfa gives its name to what is at present the largest tunnelling project in the world. This is part of the East Anatolia Project (official abbreviation: GAP). The plan is that two concrete pipes, each 25 ft. in diameter and about 100 km. long, will pass underneath the S. foothills of the Taurus mountains and transport water from the Euphrates into the fertile but dry Harran basin to the S. of Urfa. 1,564,000 acres of land could be irrigated in this way. This underground water pipe begins in the artificial lake created by the Atatürk dam which is still under construction (545 ft. high, 2 km. long at the top), and ends a little to the E. of Urfa. From here the water is to be channelled to the fields. Up to now the Harran plain has only been scantily irrigated with wells 230 ft. deep, which often means a harvest only once every three years. This ambitious project is aimed at securing regular agricultural production, and further objectives are to increase the cotton quota fivefold and, in particular, to reverse the tide of emigration. The planners intend that the region's population, which is at present 4.5 million and declining, should double again.

Citadel: This badly damaged Crusaders' castle is in the S. of the town, on a spur of Top Dağı. The outer ring of walls has three gates, the inner ring 25 towers. The two conspicuous columns with Corinthian chapels from the early Christian period are popularly known as the *throne of Nemrud.* The mosaic from the 1st half of the 3C

Urfa, citadel

AD, found in a grotto on the S. slope, is now in the local *Archaelogical Museum.*

Hali Rahman Camii *(Yeşil Kilise):* The mosque probably stands on the site of an old church of the Virgin Mary, and is at the S. end of Birket Ibrahim. This rectangular basin measuring 100 x 490 ft., and the associated small pool of Ain Zeliha (Zulihe Gölü), are both fed by the Roha spring which has its source at the foot of the citadel. Ain Zeliha is thought to be where Abraham camped when on his way from Ur of the Chaldaeans to the Promised Land. The Birket İbrahim (also known as Hali Rahman Gölü) is said to have been created by God in order to allow Abraham a gentle landing after being miraculously blown away from a pyre which had been built to execute him.

Ulu Cami: This late-12C building with its characteristic octagonal minaret probably stands on the site of the former church of St. Stephen which may have itself replaced a synagogue.

Dersa Camii (also *Makam İbrahim Mevlud Halil Camii*): This mosque E. of the fish pond stands on the site of the hermitage of the prophet Halil İbrahim, and has a spring with curative powers.

Tomb of the Prophet Eyüb: Steps lead down to this underground room in the S. of the town.

Crusaders' church: This is the only building in the town to survive from the peak period of the county of Edessa. It had previously at times been used as a prison, is now being restored (work not completed in 1986), and will later probably be used as a mosque.

Environs: Harran (*Altınbaşak;* 45 km. S.): This is now an out-of-the-way and insignificant village, but it was formerly one of the most important towns between the Mediterranean and the upper Tigris. It is even mentioned in the Old Testament

(Genesis 11,31 and 12) as being the place where Abraham resided for several years on his way from Ur of the Chaldaeans to the Promised Land. Harran was probably already of some importance at this time in about the 18C BC. It must though be remembered that large parts of the Old Testament were not written down until the time of Babylonian Captivity. The episodes had previously only been passed on by word of mouth. The Babylonian King Nebuchadnezzar II (Nabucco; 604–562) took the people of Israel into captivity in 587/586 after Jerusalem had been conquered and destroyed. Captivity was finally brought to an end by the Persian king Cyrus II in 538. This was long after the heyday of the ancient Harran, where the 'cedar temple' of the moon god Sin had been a major cult site in the Assyrian empire. Assurbanipal, the last great Assyrian king, even seems to have moved his capital town to Harran in 635. Previously, only an Assyrian governor had been in residence here. Assuruballit II, the last ruler of this former empire, entrenched himself in Harran after the downfall of the old imperial capitals Assur (616/614 BC, conquered by the Medes) and Nineveh (612 BC, conquered by the Medes and Babylonians). Harran did not fall until 608 or 606 BC. The Assyrian empire was thus brought to a close.

The cult of the moon god Sin of Harran survived the downfall of Assyria. This is because the Babylonian king Nabonid, successor to the great Nebuchadnezzar, ordered the temple to this god to be rebuilt in *c.*550 BC, allegedly in response to a divine instruction received in a dream. This is reported in a cuneiform text on a block of stone which was found in 1956, along with two more inscribed steles of the same ruler. They had been been used as building materials in the main mosque in Harran. This is a good reason for believing that the old temple to the god Sin was probably not very far from the modern Ulu Cami, even though one stela bearing the moon god's emblem came to light in

Aşagi Yarimca (6 km. NE of Harran). The moon god Sin was also worshipped in the Hellenistic period, when the town was called *Karrai,* and in imperial Roman times, when there must even have been a ruler's palace in the town, then known as *Carrhae.* The reason for this is that the Roman Emperor Caracalla, probably at the instigation of an officer, was murdered here in AD 217 when on his way back from the temple to his residence. A more famous event is the battle of Carrhae, fought some 30 km. S. of Harran on 28 May 53. The Roman general Crassus, triumvir together with Pompey and Caesar, was annihilated by his opponents in this battle when attempting to conquer the Parthian empire.

Christianity was making advances, and the temple of the god Sin was demolished under Emperor Theodosius in 382. A new town wall was built in the 6C under Justinian, but the Arabs still captured Harran in 639. The town had its last period of splendour when Sultan Merwan II (744–750) enlarged it to form his residence. The Numairids ruled the town in 990–1081. The Crusaders, led by Bohemund of Antioch and Balduin of Edessa, were defeated by the emir of Diyarbakır and the Atabeg of Mosul in 1104 in a battle outside the town gates. After Nur ed-Din (1149) and Saladin came the town's devastation by the Mongols in 1260. The damage resulting from this had not been repaired even in 1516, when Hurran became an Ottoman town under Sultan Selim.

Today the town is characterized by the beehive-shaped *Trulli houses* of crushed clay. Their domed style of architecture is optimally adapted to the climatic conditions prevailing there. The *town wall* is in extremely poor condition, but its line can still be discerned. There were formerly seven gates on the wall, and five of them still survive: the Aleppo Gate (W.; restored by Saladin in 1192), the Lion Gate (N.), Mosul Gate (E.), Raqqa Gate (S.) and the Bab er-Rum (Roman Gate). A *citadel,* which stood to the SE of the old town and

Harran (Urfa)

was formerly surrounded by a deep ditch, can be proved to have existed since 1032. Today only three of its polygonal towers survive. A *church* with a nave, two aisles and an apse survives from the Christian period. The best Islamic building is the *Ulu Cami.* This court mosque in the N. of Harran was probably built by the Umayads, enlarged in 830 and restored in 1171–84 under Saladin. The three steles of the Babylonian king Nabonid are now preserved in the museum in Urfa. They were unearthed here during the excavations which, with some interruptions, were performed by English archaeologists in the period from 1950–9. Today the site is reached via the town of Akçakale on the Syrian border (53 km.). Harran is NNE of here.

Sultantepe (16 km. SE): A Turko-English team carried out researches here in the 1950s in parallel with the excavations in Harran. The result was the uncovering of an Assyrian citadel inside the hill of ruins, with ivory works, a stele with the symbols of the moon god Sin, and a library of clay tablets which an old Babylonian named Qurdi Nergal had collected in his house between 650 and 612. Mythological texts were discovered (describing the epic of the Flood, Gilgamesh and the Creation), along with texts on magical medicine and astrology, and prayers. Some 15 km. along the road to Akçakale, a track leads off to the left to the hill on which there was a human settlement. The road towards Sumatar traverses the left side of this hill.

Sumatar (58 km. S.): It is advisable to use a cross-country vehicle for this trip, because it involves such hazards as driving through an irrigation ditch some 20 inches deep shortly after passing Sultantepe (route described above). First comes the village of Sumatar, some 29 km. beyond Urfa. It can also be reached from Urfa on the road to Mardin and Nusaybin. A well-signposted side road leads southwards from this road. Starting from Sumatar, another stretch of some 30 km. along a stony track to the rocky waste of the Tektek mountains then has to be covered (only possible if accompanied by a guide from Sumatar) before *Eski Sumatar* is reached, with its remains of the mysterious *star temple of the Sabians.* The Koran attributes monotheistic tendencies to this unique religious community, which even carried out human sacrifices. But the chief role in this cult was played by the planets, which they held to have been created by God as rulers of fate and the worlds and were thought of as spiritual beings. These ideas had been adopted from Babylonian astrology, but the cult also included Western influences in the shape of Neoplatonic philosophy. Like many Beduin tribes in Arabia, the Sabians worshipped their chief god Marilaha in the form of a stone monument (Betyl). Prayers were held three times a day, at sunrise, sunset and high noon, with the worshipper facing N. Until at least the 14C AD, and

possibly up until the 17C, there were adherents of the Sabian faith living in nearby Harran, which was the centre of the moon cult in ancient times. Each of the constellations had a characteristic emblem assigned to it: a square for the Sun (Helois), an octagon for the Moon (Sin), a triangle for Mercury (Nabuq) or Venus (Balti), a hexagram for Saturn (Kronos). It is not clear which emblems were assigned to Jupiter (Bel) and Mars (Ares). All these heavenly bodies are now represented in the extensive cult complex at Eski Sumatar, where there is a shrine. The fulcrum and pivotal point, in the truest sense of those words, is the 'central hill', a bare rock some 165 ft. high in the SE of the area. The N. side of this rock is decorated with two reliefs (standing figure and bust, the latter having an inscription stating that it was carved in honour of the moon god Sin in *c.*AD 165). The temples of the individual planets, beginning with Saturn, then Jupiter, the Moon, Mercury and finally Mars (here a statue depicting a torso with trousers and sword) stand in a row along the imaginary arc of a circle which begins to the W. of the central hill (which is the centre of the circle), has a radius more than 1 km. long, and covers an angle of a little over 60. The cultic sites of the Sun and Venus, and finally two grottoes with reliefs and inscriptions on the inside (2nd half of 2C AD), are to be found along a smaller segment of a circle, about half a km. in radius and running parallel to the above. So far as can be ascertained (only four of the cult sites survive in good condition), six of the temples had crypts, and the entrances to the cult sites were all oriented on the central hill.

Uzuncaburç

Mersin/İçel   p.574–J 6

This town 30 km. N. of Silifke contains the ruins of the old **Olba Diocaisareia,** which are numbered among the best-preserved ancient sites in Turkey and mostly go back to the 2C BC. It was from here that the dynasty of Teucrid priests ruled western Cilicia until Vespasian integrated the area into the Roman province of Cilicia.

Long Tower *(Uzuncaburç):* The ruined site takes its name from this five-storeyed building (74 ft. high, 50 ft. long, 40 ft. wide) in the N. of the site. In ancient times, the tower was a motif on the coins of Olba and thus became the town's ancient landmark. It was formerly the tomb of one of the local ruling priests (*c.*200 BC).

Temple of Zeus-Olbios: This large religious building was probably erected under Seleukos I Nikator in the early 3C BC. The peristyle (the surrounding colonnade) survives from the main temple, with about 30 columns more than 39 ft. high. It was converted into a church in Christian times by removing the cella (formerly dedicated to Zeus, the father of the gods), building walls between the surrounding columns, and adding an apse. The sacred precinct comprised not only the temple itself, but also a large area divided into four parts by two splendid streets intersecting at right angles, were lined with columns, built in their surviving form in the 1C AD.

Theatre: This dates from AD 160, and is directly beside one of the former colonnaded streets.

Temple of Tyche: A temple (1C AD) to Tyche, the goddess of fortune, to the W. of the temple of Zeus. Five granite columns still stand. They have Corinthian capitals connected by monumental architraves bearing the dedicatory inscription.

Town gate: This entrance gate NW of the Zeus temple has three openings. The central gate is tall, while those on both sides are smaller. The temple precinct had a wall around it in the Hellenistic-Seleucid period, but this entrance passage was not built until Roman times.

Environs: Demircili (20 km. S.): This burial ground is on the road from Uzuncaburç to Silifke. Numerous stone

Uzuncaburç, Diocaisareia, temple of Zeus-Olbios

burial towers and *burial houses* with pedimented roofs mostly 2C AD) survive. **Ura** (4 km. E.): An ancient paved road, lined with tombs, leads past the Long Tower to the *ancient residential town*, which is near the place called Ura and belonged to the Olba-Diocaisarea temple precinct (some 50 min. on foot). The impressive ruined site includes the remains of churches and houses, and remains of a *nymphaeum* and of the *aqueduct* from the time of Emperor Pertinax (AD 193). This aqueduct formerly supplied the town with water from the upper Lamos. A similarity in the names has led scholars to believe that the place called Ura in Hittite cuneiform texts was located here. At that time the merchants of this town were involved in one of the earliest trade disputes in history. Prince Niqmepa of Ungarit on the Mediterranean coast, not far from modern Lazkiye or El Ladhaqiye in Syria, had complained to his superior, the Hittite king Hattusili III, that foreign merchants from Ura, who were also subjects of the Hittite king, would place a great strain upon the economy of his small principality. The Hittite king then decided

that the foreign merchants could only trade in Ugarit in summer, and that in winter they would have to return to their home town in Cilicia.

Van

The modern capital of the province stands not far from the E. shore of the lake named after it (in Turkish: Van Gölü) between the hills of Vankale (5,965 ft.) and

Van, Vankale

Toprakkale (6,010 ft.). But the lakeside towns Erçis and Ahlat occasionally also give their names to this body of water which has an area of about 3,764 sq.km. and is thus more than six times the size of Lake Constance. The lake now only has water flowing into it, and there is no longer any flowing out of it (it was blocked some 100,000 years ago due to an eruption of the Nemrud Daği at Tatvan).

The Urartians had a large empire on Lake Van in the first half of the 1C BC. For a time this empire was Assyria's most powerful enemy. The Urartian lanaguage is closely related to that of the Hurri, so that it is thought that it was initially the Hurri who from *c.*1800 formed small principalities located around Lake Van, referred to as the Nairi countries in Mesopotamian cuneiform texts. The Assyrian king Salmanassar I (1274–45) mentions a small state called Urnatru, from which the original Urartian empire was formed in the early 9C BC by uniting the parts of the empire. It may have been King Arame who united them. He was a contemporary of the Assyrian ruler Salmanassar III. A temporary period of Assyrian weakness was cleverly exploited

to achieve this unification. Sardur I (*c.*835–825) is often regarded as the first genuine king of Urartu. There is evidence that Van, then known as **Tushpa,** was the capital of the kingdom during his reign. Starting from here, a large empire was gradually created. At the time of its furthest expansion, under Argishti I (785–753), it stretched from Lake Sevan (now in the USSR) and Lake Urmia (now in Iran) in the E. as far as the Euphrates in the W. But an Urartian advance across the Euphrates and Tigris, led by Sardur II and aimed against Assyria, was repulsed by Tiglatpileser III (745–727), and Assyria itself prepared to hit back. Sargon II (722–705) conquered Tushpa/Van, inducing its king, Rusa I, to commit suicide. The Urartian town of Musasir (cf. Hakkâri) was razed to the ground in the same campaign. This setback was quickly followed by a period of Urartian consolidation, but the gradually advancing Cimmerians posed a constant threat. Rusa's successor Argishti II was obliged to fight them. It was during his period of rule that the Assyrian king Sanherib was murdered in 681 BC, and if the Old Testament (2 Kings 19, 37) is to be

Van, Vankale, E. half seen from old town of Van

believed, the murderers fled to Urartu. Under Rusa II, the next king, the residence was evidently moved from Vankale at the W. end of present-day Van to Toprakkale at the E. end of the town. The new capital was called Rusahinili (Built by Rusa).

There is only scanty source material relating to the late-Urartian rulers. Assyrian reports of military expeditions are silent on this subject, although otherwise they are the most reliable sources of information on the history of the empire on Lake Van. The arrangement of the kings' names appearing on votive gifts found in Urartu is in dispute. The last ruler seems to have been a certain Rusa, son of Rusa, who would accordingly have to be counted as Rusa IV. His name appears on the impression of a seal in Karmir Blur (now in the USSR), the old Teişebaini which, under Rusa II, replaced the fortress of Irebuni (now Erivan/Yerevan) as the E. residence of the Urartian empire. It is though doubted whether this Rusa IV ever ascended the throne, because Urartu came to a rapid end in c.585 BC when Karmir Blur was stormed by the Scythians and the Medes overran Toprakkale near Van. The Lake Van region was part of the satrapy of Armenia in the Persian period, and after the decline of Alexander's empire it belonged to the kingdom of Pontos. The Armenian king Tigranes the Great (95–54) enlarged Van into a centre of his empire, and in the period that followed the Romans and Parthians were in dispute over it. The Persian Sassanids incorporated it into their kingdom in the 4C AD. The rule of the Reštuni dynasty under King Theodoros was brought to an end by the Arab invasion in 634. The Bagratids were replaced as rulers of the Lake Van area by the Ardsruni (from 722 on) and the dynasty of Vaspurakan (from 908 on). The latter formed the kingdom of Vaspurakan (908). Gagik I Ardsruni (908–943) selected Van as his capital, but this was later moved first to Vastan (Gevaş) and then to the island of Akhtamar. Attempts were made to counter the Arab raids by forming a close alliance with the caliphate of Baghdad, but under the pressure of a threat from the Seljuks the last king ceded his kingdom to the Byzantines and, in exchange, was awarded Sivas (q.v.) and the area surrounding it.

Van, Vankale, detail of Argishti inscription

When Byzantium was defeated at Malazgirt (1071), Van first fell to the Marwanids, and then to the Karakoyunlu. When Van was laid waste by the Mongols under Timur-Leng (Tamerlane; 1387), Persians and Ottomans disputed the town, with the Ottomans finally prevailing. The Russians occupied Van in 1915–17, and when they withdrew they destroyed the old town (Eski Van), which extended southwards at the foot of Vankale. It was then decided that when the town was rebuilt it was to stand on a new site, that of today's town. Thus there are no sights to be found inside the area populated today. The visitor should though see the *Archaeological Museum,* set up in 1972. The first exhibits are found in the garden. They are mostly stones carved with Urartian cuneiform inscriptions or reliefs, including a reassembled figure of a bull from Adılcevaz near Ahlat (q.v.). Inside the building, there is an ethnographical department on the storey above the archaeological department proper, which includes Urartian finds from Toprakkale, Vankale, Cavuştepe, Giyimli and Patnos.

Old Van *(Eski Van):* Before being destroyed by the Russians in 1917, the town of Van was about 2 km. W. of the large modern town. It stood at the S. foot of Vankale, the castle hill. The lake formerly extended as far as the settlement, which is completely surrounded by a wall. The Germans were the last to reside in the settlement, and even maintained an orphanage and a technical high school there. Until last century, the town frequently suffered from earthquakes, the most severe of which was in 1648. Today all that remains is ruined buildings in the meadows, which are marshy in parts. The best view of the ruins is from the castle hill. The Armenian churches of *Surb Paulus* (c.960) and *Surb Petrus* (badly damaged) stand close together, and are often also referred to as Çifte Kilise (Double Church). The most conspicuous building on the site is the *Ulu Cami* (11C or 12C), a brick building close by the steeply ascending castle rock. Here there is a stairway in the rock (not accessible today). Built under the Seljuk ruler Kiliç Arslan, it has nearly 1,000 steps, and covers the distance in height, amounting to about 300 ft., between the town and the citadel.

Van, Vankale, Xerxes inscription

Vankale: A limestone ridge about 350 ft. in height descends steeply to the S. and somewhat more gently to the N., extends for about 1 km. in the E.-W. direction, and formerly harboured the citadel of the Urartian residence of Tushpa with the rulers' tombs. It is not clear if the fortress built here under Sardur I had predecessors. What is certain is that earlier settlers lived on the hill, owing to its favourable location. The Urartian castle only occupied the W. part of the rise, but the Seljuks and Ottomans later enlarged it to its present size, occupying the entire ridge. For topographical reasons, the N. flank is not so well protected and was therefore given special attention. Thus several walls running along the slope in parallel to one another are to be found on this side; they have sturdy semicircular towers. A *necropolis* with burial urns has been uncovered at the foot of this lengthy section. Step-like structures, hewn from the rock, are to be found everywhere. They are usually interpreted as being the underground foundations of the immense Urartian defensive walls. The traveller approaching from Vankale comes first to the E. tip of the castle rock where, only a few yards above ground level, there is an Urartian inscription, much damaged, dating from the period of coregency between Ispuini and Menua. The traveller going along the N. flank (from here the most convenient way of ascending to the castle is along the NW edge of the rock) passes the two conspicuous round-arched niches, each 18 ft. high and 6.5 ft. wide, half way up the rock. In front of these niches is a flattened courtyard with stone benches. This place, popularly known as Hazine Kapisi (Treasure Gate), was probably a cult site. One of the niches contains fragments of basalt blocks bearing Urartian cuneiform writing, giving an appreciation of nine of the 22 years for which King Sardur II reigned, in honour of Haldi, the principal Urartian god. Urartian stone blocks with cuneiform inscriptions were again used to help build the succession of walls on the slope. The visitor passing by these walls finally arrives at the square platform known as Madir Burçu, where there is a small rest house. The platform survives as an L-shape, and was built of colossal blocks (up to 20 ft. long) piled one above the other. Scholars refer to this building of unknown function (theories range from water reservoir to audience hall to temple foundations) as *Sardur's castle*, because six identically worded inscriptions of this king (the best-preserved of these is at the NW corner) have now been found here.

A feature of greater interest is the steep S. flank of the castle hill above Eski Van. There are innumerable inaccessible holes in the rock, and also the *rock tombs*, mostly accessible, of the Urartian kings. The name of the king concerned has been established with certainty for some of these tombs, but other tombs have been only conjecturally assigned to particular kings. The tombs are carefully hewn from the rock and each one has several chambers. Their inner walls are often decorated at eye level with rectangular recesses whose edges run inwards and which have a hole in the middle, probably designed to receive the colourful peg-shaped tiles known as zigati. Such tiles are otherwise only known in the palaces of the Assyrian kings, such as those in Assur, the traditional capital. The Argishti tomb, in the extreme W. of the S. flank, can be inspected from above. It is attributed to that ruler (*c.*790–765), because the rock walls, smoothed by man, outside the tomb entrance are covered with a long text in Urartian cuneiform writing concerning this ruler (the so-called Horhor chronicle). Visitors have unfortunately repeatedly attempted to break off parts of the text as souvenirs, so that the entrance is frequently barred (inquire at the museum for opening times). Some way to the E. of this (further E. than the Xerxes inscription) there is a man-made rock platform half way up the steep S. slope. From here two sets of rock chambers lead into the

Ahtamar (Van), Holy Cross church ▷

smoothed rock (possibly prepared for inscription): the Neftkuyu chambers lead to the N., and the other set (the Içkala chambers) leads W. It is not certain that Ispuini (815–807) and Menua (804–790) were really interred here. A broad open-air staircase leads down to the E. tomb complex, assigned to Sardur II (765–733). An inscription on the right states that the Menua hall in between was used as a stable. The hall of rock, some 1,940 sq.ft. in area, is concealed behind an entrance (about 25 ft. wide), which is now largely filled up with rock and blocked with drifts. The inscription of the Persian king Xerxes (486–465) is cut into the steeply rising S. wall of the castle mountain. It is inaccessibly located at a great height above the minaret of Ulu Cami, and dates from the period of Persian domination when an Achaemenid governor ruled in Tushpa. In a rectangular niche in the rock, the same text is reproduced in three columns in Ancient Persian, Elamite and Babylonian, the three official languages of the Achaemid empire.

Environs: Ahtamar (42 km. W.): This is the largest island in Lake Van, and is famous for the unique church which stands at its E. end and is decorated with reliefs. It is reached by a 15-min. boat trip from a jetty located directly by the road to Tatvan outside a small restaurant 42 km. beyond Van and a little way past the second turning-off to Gevaş. Armenian legends report that there was formerly a town on this island about 2.5 km from the mainland, but of this nothing has survived. Only the remains of a monastery can be identified (in 1911 it still survived as a ruin to the S. and SW of the church; it has now disappeared). The royal palace probably stood here before this holy site was built, because Ahtamar was the last residence of the kingdom of Vaspurakan. Not only were the domes of the palace allegedly gilded, but the ruler is said to have had a throne of pure gold. This may be merely a legend, as is shown by reports concerning the reliefs on the outside of today's church, which are also said to have been formerly gilded and decorated with precious stones; the nature of the 'precious stones' is clear from the traces of glass paste in the eye sockets of some of the figures.

Ahtamar was the seat of the Armenian

Ahtamar (Van), Holy Cross church, relief on exterior wall

catholicos in 913–992 and 1113–1464, but the island patriarch maintained his title up until 1895, which was after the Armenian empire had come to an end and the official seat of its spiritual head had moved to Echmiadsin.

The outside of the *church of the Holy Cross* is decorated with reliefs in three horizontal strips running around the building (upper strip: vine-leaf frieze with many small genre scenes; below this: large figures; finally, about 10 ft. above the ground: a strip of vine tendrils). The church was founded by the Vaspurakan king Gagik Ardsruni (908–943), and Manuel, a monk and architect, built it in 915–921 of red sandstone quarried not far from Diyarbakır. More churches and annexes were later grouped around this church. The first of these was the originally free-standing N. chapel (1316) to the NE; later a room connected it to the N. portal of the main church. When the large W. portal was added in 1763, the main entrance, also in the W., had to be moved to the S., where a bell tower was erected c.1900. The church of the Holy Cross is a cruciform domed structure with four conches, and stands on a two-storeyed foundation. Inside the church, the remains of wall paintings can still be discerned under the whitewash; dating from 921, they are the oldest Armenian frescos so far discovered. These and the outdoor reliefs were restored in 1963, this work being funded by the Gulbenkian foundation, set up by a well-to-do Armenian businessman. The motifs of the surrounding series of images are sometimes immediately recognizable (Adam and Eve, David and Goliath, etc.) and are sometimes identifiable by the inscriptions (Prophets, the founding king Gagik and his family, etc.), but often defy interpretation.

Anzaf (*Hurdur;* about 16 km. NE): The street beyond Toprakkale runs through Erçek and Ölzalp, and at the village of Anzaf, shortly before reaching Lake Erkek, it passes two Urartian *fortresses,* possibly to be identified with the town of Hundur mentioned in the report of the expedition conducted by the Assyrian king Sargon II. The larger fortress on the right side of the road is rectangular, with 13-ft.-thick walls reinforced by semicircular bastions at intervals of about 35 ft.

Aparank (about 150 km. SW): A trip to this site will require at least three days,

Çavuştepe (Van), masonry in lower castle

and almost takes on the character of an expedition. A cross-country vehicle is required for the drive to the village of Bahçesaray (after 32 km. along the road to Bitlis/Tatvan, turn off to the S. towards Çatak and, after 31 km. along this track, turn off to the W., after which it is another 45 km.). After this, mules or similar transport must be organized for the ride to Aparank, which takes about 10 hours. A guide who knows the area is of course indispensable. The destination is the Kurdish village of Vatâs (Aparank) at a height of 6,170 ft., where there are a 17C monastery and five Armenian churches. The oldest building is the church (943–952) dedicated to John the Baptist, centrally planned, with three apses. The church of the Virgin Mary dates from 983, and that of St. Stephen is also from the last third of the 10C. The former parish church (1664) is today a barn.

Çavuştepe (26 km. SE): This archaeological mound stands only half a km. to the right of the road to Hakkâri. It is easy to obtain a view of its low surrounding wall. The Urartians set up a bipartite *fortress* on the long limestone rock which dominates the Hoşap valley and falls away steeply on all sides. The upper castle has a few remains of a temple precinct, and stands on the considerably higher left-hand section, while the lower castle is on the lengthy right wing. The latter castle has buildings standing outside a transverse wall with a passageway through it. Previously there were storerooms behind this wall. Some of the monumental storage vessels found there had cuneiform inscriptions on their edges, describing the contents. These vessels are now in the museum in Van. The basalt block foundations of the temple behind the storerooms still survive. The temple has a typical Urartian ground plan (cf. Altıntepe, under Erzincan), with thick walls and corner projections. Its entrance is on the front side and has shallow stairways. On the left side of the entrance is a cuneiform inscription, the last few lines of which survive. But the basalt block above, which belongs to the side of the door, has been lost and replaced by a modern composition stone with speckles. Last of all, after the temple complex, comes the residential section with an ingenious sewage system. The utensils found in the individual rooms enabled the

Erçis (Van), main mosque

excavating scientist to identify the rooms of the former harem, or at any rate the women's chambers. The summit of the rock on which the palace stands was protected by a transverse ditch in front of it. The ditch is today largely filled up with earth, but is still readily discernible, and today, as in the past, it still provides a good panoramic view which includes the old irrigation channel running along the S. flank of the rock. It is very probable that this is the castle of Sardurihurda mentioned in the report of Sargon II's military expedition. As its name indicates, it was built by the Urartian king Sardur III (c.765–733). The work of uncovering this castle on the mountain plateau made it necessary first to remove a medieval cemetery and, below that, a small 4C BC settlement, before the two Urartian strata underneath were reached.

Deveboynu (about 60 km. W.): This triangular peninsula is to the W. of Ahtamar and projects into the S. of Lake Van. On its shore are *monasteries* which can be reached by boat from the Ahtamar jetty. They are the badly-damaged monastery of the Miracles of Chakhur, and the 10C monastery of the Mother of

God and, at the tip of the peninsula, the Resurrection monastery (mentioned in the 13C, but certainly older) with fragments of paintings.

Further inland (it is first one hour to the village of Ganzak, then two more hours to Mezir) is the 10C St. Thomas monastery which formerly held a relic of its patron Saint. The church, with its pyramidal roof, and some monastery buildings still survive.

Erçis (24 km. N.): Today's little town at the NE tip of Lake Van was preceded by two earlier settlements. The Urartian town of *Arzaskani*, a few km. to the NE, was captured and destroyed by the Assyrian king Salmanassar III in 857 BC. King Argishti rebuilt it a little nearer the lake, and it was named *Argishtihinili* after him. This town fell to the Assyrian king Sargon II in 714 BC. The sound of the town's old name may have lingered on in its post-Christian Arabic name of *Arjesh*. In 996, David of Taik added this town as well as Manzikert to his Armenian province of Erzurum. The Seljuks arrived in 1055, and were replaced in the 14C by the Karakoyunlu (Black Sheep), whose Turkoman emirs sometimes even had

Gevaş (Van), Halim Hatun Türbesi

their residence in Erçis. Last century, the water level in the lake rose and the land by the lake shore subsided, compelling the inhabitants to move 3 km. to the N. and found the modern town there. Some ruins of the old settlement still stand in the marshy terrain by the lake.

Gevaş (41 km. W.): Two turnings to Gevaş (after 35 and 41 km.) are passed on the way to the Ahtamar jetty. From there it is another 6 and 2 km. respectively. *Vastankalesi* castle at the edge of Gevaş has a name reminiscent of the village's Armenian name *Vastan*. Inside the village, the *Izdişar Camii* is worth seeing. The *Halim Hatun Türbesi* is in the fork between the lakeside road and the road leading to the village, a little way past a petrol station on the side of the lakeside road nearer the lake. This *Halim* is a tomb building, polygonal on the outside, with a chamber for sarcophagi in the cellar and, above this, a prayer room covered by a stone roof with a stalactite frieze running along its lower edge (1322). This building is in a small cemetery with several tomb steles which have fallen over.

Hoşap (Güzelsu; 58 km. SE): This village is reached on the road to Hakkâri. The traveller approaching it first leaves the Çavuştepe hill on his right, and after about another 20 km. he passes the most recently completed stage of the reservoir on the River Hoşap (still under construction in 1987). In Hoşap, the *Mahmudiye castle,* with its massive round towers, stands upon a steep rock on the other side of the river. It is being restored at present, and as it is unsafe it will not be open for visitors until the work is completed (otherwise access is from the W.). The visitor approaching the village sees the castle hill, which is part of a fortification enclosing a large surrounding area. Some towers and stretches of wall still survive, dotted about the open country. The present castle dates from 1643, when it was built by a Kurdish bey of whom almost nothing else is known. He made use of the remains of a 14C Seljuk castle. The three rings of surrounding walls formerly contained 360 rooms, two mosques, three baths, granaries, storerooms and a prison. The bridge over the Hoşap Su is also from the Kurdish period. It was built by Zurnel Bey, a member of the Mahmudiye dynasty.

Kamrak Vank (*Karmir Vank;* Red Monastery; about 60 km. W.): Unlike the other monasteries on the Deveboynu peninsula (q.v.), this site, now known as *Göründü Kilisesi,* is not reached by boat, but by land: 2 km. after the jetty for Ahtamar, a turning leads off the lakeside road and proceeds N. towards Göründü (10 km.). From here it is another one and a half hours' walk into the mountains. The monastery in the village is said to have been founded by King Gagil Ardshruni in the early 10C, but the two surviving churches are of later date.

Keçanis: The scant remains of the small Urartian *castle* are on the road to Özalp (see under Anzaf for route), a few km. beyond Erçek. This may be the Urartian castle of Bubuzi, and the fertile valley along which the road proceeds after Erçek may be Armarili. Both these names appear in the report of the Assyrian king Sargon II's military expedition.

Hoşap (Van), castle mountain

Körzüt Kalesi (about 100 km. NE): This fortress 20 km. SE of Muradiye has a *wall,* some sections of which survive in very good condition (up to 25 ft. high in the SE). The wall is reinforced by turrets standing at regular intervals of about 35 ft.

Muradiye (about 80 km. NE): It was on this site on the road to Çaldiran (q.v. for the approach route) that the Urartians built a fortress to defend the plain. But Shah Ismail I of Persia built on top of this fortress in the late 15C and early 16C. In 1514, that Shah was defeated by the Ottomans in a battle fought not far from here.

Narek (about 60 km. W.): Some 4 km. to the S., off the lakeside road to Tatvan/Bitlis, there is a village in the hinterland between Ahtamar and Deveboynu. Formerly a famous 10C monastery stood nearby. It has now been pulled down but countless *spoils* from it featuring decorative carving (signs of the Cross, etc.) still survive because they were used for domestic building. The Armenian mystic Gregor of Narek was born here in *c.*945. He was acquainted with Greek and Arab philosophy. His best-known work is the 'Book of Laments', with 95 laments and poems.

Şamiram Suyu (Semiramis canal; S. of Van): For some unfathomable reason, this artificial waterway is popularly attributed to Semiramis/Shammuramat, the legendary Assyrian queen who was the mother of Adadnirari III (809–782). It was actually built by the Urartian ruler Menua (804–790), who ordered his inscription (mostly removed today) to be carved in several places along the canal route on the immense lower sections. The canal formerly supplied Van with drinking water from a spring about 50 km. away at the village of Minciyer, and then proceeded from E. to W., running approximately parallel to the valley of Hoşap Su. This canal is still used for irrigation today. Much of its original appearance has unfortunately disappeared because the canal bed has been concreted over. When the residence was moved from Vankale to Toprakkale, a branch was added to the Menua canal. in order to supply the new capital with water. Later, when the water level in the lake sank, the canal had to be lengthened. This section is the most impressive part of the canal.

It is reached 18 km. beyond Van on the road towards Bitlis and Tatvan. 2 km. before this, at Gümüşdere, this road crosses the Hoşap Su shortly before the latter flows into Lake Van.

Toprakkale (Clay Mountain; 4 km. NE): Until c.585 BC, when the Medes laid it waste, this area included Rusahinili, the last capital town of the Urartian empire. Today there is a military camp here, and the area can therefore only be visited by special permission (which is practically unobtainable). Unauthorized excavation performed in the last quarter of the last century brought Urartian finds on to the art market (in this process, a splendid throne, with bronze decorations, was divided up among at least five different museums). Only then were more exact investigations carried out, and the items uncovered included the foundations of a typically Urartian temple (cf. Altıntepe, Çavuştepe, Kayalıdere). Its exterior length along one of its sides was 45 ft. A palace was also discovered, in which a decorative effect had been attempted by alternating bright limestone with dark basalt. It is not clear what purpose was served by a shaft in the rock, fitted with a spiral staircase and leading into a subterranean room measuring 165 x 80 ft. The most likely theory is that it was a cistern. The greatest archaeological difficulty is the question of determining which of the Rusa kings it was that founded the town named Rusahinili after him, and/or transferred the capital from Vankale to here. Before Rusa first appeared as a king's name in the genealogy, the successive rulers Ishpuini and Menua ordered a cuneiform text to be inscribed in a niche in the rock on Meher Kapısı in the immediate vicinity of Toprakkale proper (6,010 ft.). This inscription listed 79 Urartian gods and the sacrifices prescribed for them. It should be realised that the 'clay mountain' was only the citadel hill of a much larger urban region. The remains of clay bricks surviving in this region have given the whole area its name.

Yedi Kilise (Varak Vank; 20 km. ESE): This town took its name from the seven churches which formerly stood here. Partly due to several earthquakes, not many of these buildings still stand, and those which do survive have been

Yedi Kilise (Van), portal between Genekerim and Yor church

Yedi Kilise (Van), ornament

incorporated into a farm and are now used as barns. The last stretch of road leading to these former churches, which stand on a foothill of the Warak mountains, is in very poor condition. There were formerly some more monasteries in this remote region, such as Surb Grigor in the N. and Karmivor in the W. near the village of Susan, which gave its name to Susan Dağı, the highest peak (9,020 ft.) in the Warak mountains. The *Yedi Kilise* monastery was probably founded in the 8C. It harboured a 'genuine' relic of the Cross, and in its peak period 300 monks are said to have lived here. Documents show that it was the residence of the patriarch Anania de Moks from 943–967. The two oldest church buildings (8C) are in the extreme S. One of them is almost completely devastated, while the other (the choir (now a barn) still survives. A little to the N. there is a *cruciform domed church* dedicated to the Virgin Mary. King Senekerim built it in the 11C before making an exchange of territory with Byzantium (see Sivas). It is the best building here, even though the dome and its drum are missing today. Most of the architectural decorations and paintings are

in the square *porch* (150 x 150 sq.ft.), which has eight flat domes supported by four pillars and was built in front of the Senekerim church in the 17C. The best feature is the portal with pointed arch which stands between the porch and the main church.

Xanthos

Antalya   p.572☐E 6

This town stands on a rocky plateau high

above the largest and fullest river in Lycia. This is the most fertile part of the Xanthos valley and formed the basis for the prosperity and importance of this town, which was always the largest in Lycia. French archaeologists who excavated in Xanthos from 1950 onwards did not discover any signs of settlement on the acropolis earlier than the 7C. At that time the peasants lived in the plain. When the Persian campaigner Hapergos marched down the valley in 540 BC, plundering the area, the Xanthians, unaccustomed to warfare, had to withdraw to the acropolis. Herodotus relates the tragedy of the freedom-loving men who transported their wives, children and belongings up to the castle and set fire to them, before hurling themselves into the hopeless battle. 80 families returned from their summer quarters in the mountains and rebuilt the town.

Appian describes the details of a similar act of self-destruction in 42 BC. The Xanthians armed to defend themselves against Brutus' plans to seize the town, but the Romans finally succeeded in capturing it. The men then slaughtered their families and afterwards themselves died in the flames of their household goods, which had been set on fire. Only 150 Xanthians survived to rebuild the town. But Xanthos once again became a leading town in Lycia during the Roman imperial period, and new large buildings were erected, including a theatre. Coins minted in Xanthos were evidently used all over Lycia. Xanthos appears on its own coins from the Hellenistic period onwards. In the Byzantine period, the town wall surrounding the acropolis was rebuilt, and large quantities of ancient spoils, including many art works, were used in this building work. The high rear wall (scena) was included in this fortification. The English archaeologist G. Bean reports that Bacon and Spratt and their sailors broke down the Byzantine wall in 1842 when Xanthos was plundered for the last time, and that they packed up the precious objects, including spoils consisting of sculptures demonstrably deriving from tomb temples dating from *c.*470 BC, when Kimon of Athens devastated the Lycian towns.

Worth seeing: The overall layout of the town is of interest, but few major details remain. The route from the village of

Xanthos, relief on a sarcophagus lid

Kınık up to the Lycian agora leads past the Hellenistic *town gate,* built of massive ashlar with a dedicatory inscription by Antiochos III. Next to it is Vespasian's Doric *triumphal arch,* surviving as an imposing structure. To the E. of it is the base of the famous Ionic temple known as the *Nereid monument,* which was a heap of ruins when Fellows discovered it in 1838. Today it can be seen in its original form in the British Museum in London. In the 5C BC the Lycian acropolis was surrounded with a *polygonal wall,* some remains of which survive in the E., S. and W. The N. wall dates from the Byzantine period. Beside the theatre there is a tall sarcophagus, and next to this again is a Lycian monolithic tomb 25 ft. high, with its burial area and covering slab intact. This early Lycian *pillar tomb* (5C) is important because of it is in good condition, and there are few tombs of this kind in Lycia. The relief plaster casts around the burial area—the originals are in London—depict dynastic scenes and suggest that a prominent person was buried in the tomb; this is also indicated by the exposed location. According to Graeco-Lycian ideas, the function of the mystic bird-women—wrongly referred to as Harpies—was to escort the souls of the departed into heaven. The site of the tombs was piously respected when the later Roman theatre was built. At the NE corner of the Roman agora, which adjoins the theatre in the N., there is another good tomb monument. This is the *inscription pillar,* unfortunately much damaged. It has some 250 lines and is the oldest surviving Lycian inscription. The Greek text on the N. side suggests that this is the tomb of Kerei, son of Harpagos, who ruled in Xanthos in the late 5C. He seems to be bragging of his heroic feats. This text is illustrated in the relief. The burial chamber was faced with relief slabs. *Reliefs* are seen on the remains of tombs at the E. edge of the Hellenistic and Roman residential town which extended to the E. of the Roman agora.

Environs: Letoon (4 km. NW): This sacred precinct dedicated to the goddess Leto was the shrine of the Lycian Confederacy. The highest priests of the Confederacy observed the cult of the national goddess here. According to mythology, Leto was a lover of Zeus and,

Xanthos, pillar sarcophagus and harpies' tomb

to avoid Hera's revenge and jealousy, fled from Delos, where she had given birth to Apollo and Artemis, and escaped to Lycia. She intended to wash herself and quench her thirst at a spring. The inhabitants drove her away, whereupon Lycia turned them into frogs. Wolves escorted the thirsty goddess to the River Xanthos. In memory of this, the Termilae called themselves Lycians (from the Greek lykos = wolf) and founded Letoon. The traces of this settlement, which is known to date back to the 8C BC, are in the marsh below the temple foundations, which are still visible. When it rains, the foundations of the nymphaeum and stoa (both from the period of Hadrian) sink below the water table, which has considerably impeded excavation work. The remains of the three *temples* of Leto and her children Artemis and Apollo are at a slightly higher level. The temples are identified by a Lycian inscription 'Ertemi' (= Artemis) on the N. foundation. The floor mosaic in the cella of the next temple depicts a bow, quiver and cithara, and indicates that this is the shrine of Apollo. The final temple is the Ionic peripteros in the W., which has 6 x 11 columns and is dedicated to

Leto. The Letoon was a general cultural centre, where musical, theatrical and sporting events were also held. The fine Hellenistic theatre is reached through a tunnel whose entrance arch is decorated by a gable façade. The *museum* is well-designed and tastefully laid out by the French archaeologists who worked on the site. The best find in Letoon is the *stele*, inscribed on three sides. This trilingual monument was discovered in 1973 and has 27 lines in the Aramaic court language of the Persians, 35 lines in Greek, and 41 lines in Lycian. The three texts are almost identical. Where research into the language of Lycia is concerned, this is the find of the century.

Patara (6 km. SW): One of the six Lycian cities, with the privilege of casting three votes in the Lycian Confederacy. The importance and prosperity of this early Lycian foundation derive from its favourably located harbour and from an old oracle tradition. It is said that Patara was for a time the next most important oracle after Delphi. Alexander the Great, his Diadochi, Rhodians and Romans successively made use of the advantages of this harbour. In the course of these

Letoon (Xanthos), nymphaeum

eventful centuries, Patara escaped more lightly that the less flexible Xanthians. This was also seen under Brutus, who contented himself with the town's gold and silver. Patara was famous in Byzantine times as the birthplace of St. Nicholas of Myra. The town is entered through a three-arched *gateway* (AD 100) which survives in good condition. The traveller passes the remains of an ancient *building* of indeterminate function in the S., while 660 ft. further along the N.-S. axis are the ruins of a Byzantine *basilica*. 820 ft. away is a small temple of the Corinthian order, surviving in good condition (2C AD), with a portal 20 ft. high. The ruins of the *Vespasian thermal bath* (980 ft. SE) are an imposing sight. The way to the W. around the harbour, which has filled up due to sedimentation, leads past the well-preserved *theatre* (c. AD 15) to the *granarium,* which is beyond the old harbour, about 750 yards W. of the town gate as the crow flies. This granary is attributed to Hadrian and was an important base for supplying not only Rome but also the emperor's troops, as was the case in Andriake too.

Pinara: A path branches off the road from Xanthos to Fethiye and leads to a rocky hill, 1,480 ft. high, on the steep slope of which there is a honeycomb-like arrangement of over 900 *tombs.* There is no normal means of access to these tombs. The work of carving them out of the rock wall was done from platforms let down on ropes. This is a unique burial ground for Lycia. The long climb up the S. side to the acropolis is steep and strenuous. On top, there are only cisterns and rock foundations to be seen. This is an extensive area with much vegetation, and the traveller is advised to ask a villager who knows the sites to take him to the best buildings, especially the tombs. These tombs—they include the king's tomb and the tomb with an acroterion of ox's horns—are on the E. slope of the lower hill, which is the second and later acropolis and has fortifying walls, an odeion and remains of various buildings.

Yazılıkaya

Çorum   p.566☐K 2

Near the village of Boğazköy (today Boğazkale), 3 km. NE of the former Hittite capital of Hattuşa, there is a rock shrine dating largely from the time of King Tudhaliya IV, the last Hittite ruler but two (mid-13C BC). There are two pictorial depictions of him here. The two rocky gullies of this shrine are decorated with reliefs, as is also indicated by the site's present name of Yazılıkaya (Inscribed

Pinara (Xanthos), monolithic house tomb

Rock). In front of these decorated chambers there was formerly a complex of buildings designed like a typical Hittite temple (today only the foundations survive). It was similar to the temples in Boğazköy (q.v.) in that it initially consisted of a gatehouse (portico or propylon) in the SW. This was adjoined by a section at a higher level, reached by flights of stairs. This terrace-like section took the shape of a courtyard, which had halls of pillars and was surrounded by small adjoining rooms. From here the route continued into the sanctuary, as was normal in such buildings. In the present temple, the route took a small bend to the N. before continuing to the decorated rock chambers.

Ceramics finds suggest that there was a Hittite cult site here in *c.*1500 BC. At that time there was only a wall blocking the two adjoining gullies, which were not yet decorated with reliefs. It was not until the 13C BC that the rock walls were given their pictorial decorations and the buildings erected. After the buildings was destroyed, the temple was rebuilt, but to a different ground plan which had fewer rooms and was more strongly oriented on secondary chamber B.

Yazılıkaya, relief chamber B

Rock shrine: This is on the left-hand side. It is some 100 ft. deep and is thus the larger *(main chamber A)* of the two rooms cut out of the rock and decorated with reliefs. On the steep walls there is a total of 66 figures, all of which, with one exception, are depictions of gods. The scenes can be mainly divided into two *pictorial friezes,* each about 33 in. long, along both sides of the gully, and a large image, about 7 ft. 2 in. high, on the rear wall. In front of the face of most of the figures, and above their outstretched arm, there are inscriptions in Hittite hieroglyphs which make it possible to identify the gods by name. To the archaeologists great surprise, the names turned out to be not Hittite, but Hurrian. This foreign influence was also seen at the Hittite royal court at that time, where the princesses and queens had Hurrian names. This also applies to Tešub and Hepat, the pair of gods who are the principal protagonists in the scene on the rear wall. They are facing one another, and Tešub the weather god has each foot standing on a mountain god, while his wife Hepat is standing on a panther. Their son Šarruma, also on a panther, stands behind his mother. Behind him are twin goddesses whose feet are touching the outstretched wing-tips of a double-headed eagle.

Along both sides of the valley section there are two rows of gods and goddesses oriented towards the group of seven large figures described above. The row of male gods is on the left, behind Tešub, whle the goddesses are on the opposite rock wall, behind Hepat. The exception is the war goddess Šaušga who, along with her maidservants Ninatta and Kulitta, is placed among the male gods. The procession of goddesses consists of 19 figures of fairly uniform appearance. They all wear the same vertically pleated skirt, a broad belt and cylindrical headgear (known as a polos). The row is interrupted at one point by a fracture, which is probably the original site of the relief block that now stands alone outside the entrance to the rock chamber.

The weather god of Hattuşa, the capital, is seen standing on mountains. He leads the procession of male gods, and is followed by the cereal god, the Mesopotamian weather god Ea, and the above-mentioned war goddess Šaušga with her maidservants. There follow two conspicuous figures: the moon god Kusuh with the crescent moon, and the sun god with the winged disc of the sun on his head.

After four more deities, there follow two figures with human bodies and bulls' heads (so-called 'bull-men') standing on the hieroglyphic sign for earth and carrying sky hieroglyphs in their raised arms. Then follow 11 more gods and four mountain gods.

At the end is what is probably the best-known individual motif in Yazılıkaya: this is the succession of 12 armed war gods in a close echelon formation. They are depicted in what is thought to be a walking position. Exactly the same scene is repeated in subsidiary chamber B, also on the W. wall.

Another relief, not directly related to the procession of gods, is seen opposite the main relief in chamber A, on a rocky projection near the entrance. This is the only relief to portray not a god, but a king, as can be seen from his clothing and the rod, the top of which is rolled up, in his left hand. There is an inscription stating the name, with hieroglyphic signs and the winged disc of the sun. This identifies the king as Tudhaliya IV, who is presumed to have built the rock shrine. The king stands on two mountain tops. The scenes in the main chamber A are evidently connected with one another, but the *secondary chamber B* displays isolated reliefs which at first glance do not appear to be interrelated. The entrance is guarded by winged demons with lions' heads and raised paws. On the E. wall are two depictions: in one of them, Šarruma, the personal tutelary god of King Tudhaliya IV, is using his left arm to protect the ruler, a smaller figure. In the larger scene adjoining this, the mysterious 'sword god' appears in the shape of a sword blade which reaches to the ground and is flanked by lions couchant. The upper part of a human body is seen where the sword handle should be. Instead of arms, lions' heads project from the shoulders. A Hittite ritual text has been discovered, mention-

Yazılıkaya, chamber A, procession of male gods

Yazılıkaya, chamber A: detail of procession of goddesses (left), sun god (right)

ing the 'bronze swords of Nergal' and the 'twelve gods of the road fork'. Since its discovery, this 'sword god' image has been interpreted as being a depiction of Nergal, the god of the underworld. This idea is supported by the fact that twelve more deities, in a close echelon formation, are found on the rock wall opposite the 'sword god' (this is a repetition of the scene at the entrance to the main chamber A). Remnants of cremations have been found in niches in the rock beside this row of gods. It is not clear whether these niches were carved at the same time as the reliefs. If they were, then secondary chamber B is intended for the death cult of Tudhaliya IV, who is also depicted here. There are tomb niches and also images of the god of the underworld and his followers.

The neighbouring chamber A was probably used once a year for the New Year festivities, which coincided with the beginning of spring. Hittite texts on clay tablets mention that such festivities were held in the open air not far from the capital. Yazılıkaya would have been a good place for this. Hattusa and the rocky shrine were also linked by a processional path which, for the most part, is also the route followed by today's paved access road. The path led away from the N. edge of the capital and then turned NE, where it crossed a small stream and passed a rocky graveyard area with funeral urns from the Hittite period.

The rows of reliefs were themselves always visible and never had to be excavated. Nevertheless, excavations performed in 1937, 1939 and 1966 contributed much to our understanding of the site. A third chamber was found: the small *rock chamber C*, a rear extension of secondary chamber B. It ended in a wall of huge blocks and contained in its centre the foundations of an altar, near to which many remnants of the ashes of burnt offerings have been discovered. On the rock wall on the way up to chamber C there is an isolated Hittite hieroglyphic inscription of the name Tudhaliya IV. It is disputed whether this means that a figure of that ruler once stood against the rear wall as a symbol receiving the sacrifices offered for the dead king. If so, this last room, probably intended for the death cult of Tudhaliya, can only have been constructed under one of his successors, Arnuwanda or Suppiluliuma.

Yozgat

This capital of the province, half way between Ankara and Sivas, was founded by the Ottomans in the mid-18C. Its recent date means that it has few good buildings. But the visitor should see the Çapanoglu Mustafa Paşa Camii, a typical Ottman mosque (1779) and, just near the latter, the *Süleyman Bey Camii*. The *Nizamoğlu palace* from last century today has an *ethnographical collection*.

Environs: Alişar Hüyük (55 km. SE): This *hill* was investigated by the Oriental Institute of Chicago in 1927–32 (the excavations were led by F. Schmidt and H.H. v. der Osten). It is reached by the road to Sivas, from which there is a turning to the right 5 km. after Sorgun (and then it is another 28 km.). The crater-shaped depression on the plateau on which the hill stands results from the excavations which continued right down to the natural soil. The lowest strata go back to the 4th millennium BC. The chalcolithic village, which was not fortified, had rectangular houses that were also used for burying the dead. A surrounding rampart was built in the subsequent early Bronze Age (from *c.* 2500 BC onwards). The ceramics were hand-made at that time. The potter's wheel did not appear until the next period, when the town wall was reinforced. Assyrian merchants set up a trading post (karum; see Kültepe under Kayseri, and Boğazköy) in the stratum above. A cuneiform text from this period, inscribed on a clay tablet, has been discovered. It mentions the mighty prince Anitta of Kuššara and his son Beruwa. The karum on Alişar Hüyük came to a violent end, as did the other trading colonies. As regards the following period of Hittite rule, it is disputed whether Ališar is identical to the town of Ankuwa, which occurs in Hittite descriptions of routes and was three days' journey from Hattuşa, the capital. In any event, the distance of 70 km. from there to the modern Boğazköy would fit in well with this idea. The Hittite kings used to spend winter in Ankuwa in times of peace. After the end of the Hittite empire (*c.* 1200 BC), there was a small Phrygian successor colony, defended by a citadel.

Çınçınlı Sultan Hanı (about 73 km. E.): The ruins of the Seljuk *caravanserai* (1239/40) not far from Karamağara are reached on the road to Sivas, from which, after 67 km., a side road leads off to the N. (it is then another 6 km.).

Kerkenes (40 km. SE): The remains of a post-Hittite *fortification* were uncovered at Kerkenes Daği, 15 km. S. of the road to Sivas (the turning-off is 25 km. after Yozgat). It is disputed whether it was built by the Phrygians, or whether the previous Luwian-speaking population constructed it as a defence against Phrygians expansion.

Yoğun Hisar (76 km. S.): A little way from the road to Kayseri, after Osmanpaşa (30 km.) and Yenipazar have been left behind, there is a hill with the remnants of an ancient *wall* which cannot be dated with any accuracy.

Chronological table

BC

before 8000: Palaeolithic and mesolithic eras. Cave painting and artefacts in Antalya (Beldibi, Karain), Isparta, Antakya.

8000–5000: Neolithic era. Settlements at Çayönü, Çatal Hüyük, Beyşçesultan, Haçılar.

5500–3200: Settlements at Alaca Hüyük, Alhisçar, Kuruçayhöyüyü, Çanhasan, Haçılar, Norsçuntepe, Fekirtepe.

3200–1800: Early Bronze Age. Settlements throughout Anatolia.

2500–2000: Hatti culture.

c.2000: Immigration of Hittites and Hurri.

from 2000: Greeks on the western coasts of Asia Minor.

1950–1750: Assyrian trading settlements (first writing in Anatolia).

1700–1200: Hittites: Old Kingdom and Empire.

1700–1350: Hurrite Mitanni Empire.

c.1200: Fall of Troy, increased Greek immigration, destruction of Hattusça.

1200–700: Late Hittite city states in south-eastern Anatolia.

855–585: Urartian empire in eastern Anatolia.

from 800: Phrygian, Lydian, Carian and Lycian empires in western Asia Minor. Rise of the Greek cities on the west coast of Asia Minor.

c.700: Cimmerians destroyed many cities in western Anatolia and broke the power of the Phrygians.

c.700–600: Miletans colonized the Marmara and Black Sea coasts.

c.650: Scythians broke through into Syria.

585: Medes conquered Asia Minor to the River Halys.

546–540: Persians under Cyrus the Great destroyed the Lydian empire and subjugated the cities of Ionia.

521: Armenian rebellion suppressed by Persia. The empire was divided into satrapies by Darius I.

499: Ionian revolt against the Persians.

494: Ionian revolt suppressed and Miletos destroyed by the Persians.

490–478: Persians defeated in various battles in Greece. The cities of Ionia joined the Delian League.

386: After decades of internal strife amongst the Greeks Ionia came under Persian rule again.

334–333: Alexander the Great conquered Asia Minor and defeated the Persians.

from 323: Start of the struggles between Alexander's successors (Diadochi). Foundation of the Hellenistic kingdoms: they included Egypt (Ptolemaic dynasty), Syria (Seleucids), Macedonia.

from 278: Conflict with immigrating Galatians.

233: Pergamon became a Hellenistic kingdom (Attalids).

190: Romans gained increasing influence in Asia Minor as intermediaries or allies.

163: Kingdom of Commagene.

133: Attalos III of Pergamon bequeathed his kingdom to the Romans. Continuing extension of the Roman provincial system in Asia Minor.

88–64: King Mithridates VI of Pontus' vain struggle against Rome.

AD

45–60: Apostle Paul's missionary journeys. The first Christian communities came into being.

c.300: Gregory the Illuminator established Christianity as the state religion in Armenia under King Trdat III.

325: First Ecumenical Council of Nicaea (Christ's divinity).

330: Constantine the Great made Byzantium the capital of the Roman Empire, and promoted the Christian religion.

391: Christianity became the official state religion under Theodosius I. Heathen cults were forbidden.

395: Final division of the Roman Empire into Eastern and Western Rome.

523–537: Hagia Sophia was built in Constantinople under Justinian I.

534: Codification of Roman law by Justinian I.

622: Mahomet fled to Mecca. First year of Islamic calendar. Islam spreads.

c.630: Greek became the adminstrative and military language of Eastern Rome under Heraclius.

636: Arabs won the first great battle against Byzantium in Syria.

674–740: Repeated dangerous threats from Arabs in southern and western Asia Minor. The four-year siege of Constantinople was unsuccessful.

from 700: Islam reached the eastern parts of the Byzantine empire.

730–787: Iconoclastic controversy shook Byzantium and deepened the gulf between the eastern and western church.

from 1048: The eastern territories of Asia Minor were threatened by Seljuks.

1054: Final break between the Greek Orthodox and Roman Catholic churches.

1071: Byzantines defeated by Seljuks at the Battle of Manzikirt. Seljuks continued to conquer and settle in Anatolia.

1081: Sultanate of Rum in Nicaea.

1095: First Crusade passed through Anatolia.

1134: Konya became the capital of the Rum Seljuks.

1176: Byzantines under Manuel I again defeated by Seljuks, at Myriokephalon.

1190: Barbarossa drowned in the Göksu (Saleph) on the Third Crusade.

1204: Constantinople conquered during the Fourth Crusade. Foundation of the Latin Empire (until 1261). Byzantine exile empires formed in Nicaea and Trapezunt.

1243: Gradual decline of the empire of the Rum Seljuks as a result of Mongol victories. Ertogul, leader of the Turks, later known as 'Osmans' or 'Ottomans', hitherto liegeman of the Seljuks, became independent.

1299: Ertogul's successor Osman declared himself sultan.

1326: Sultan Orhan founds the Janissaries.

1365: Adrianople (Edirne) became Ottoman capital under Murat I with the aim of expanding into eastern Europe.

1402: Sultan Beyazıt I was defeated and taken prisoner by the Mongol Timur-Leng (Tamerlane) at Ankara.

1413: Mehmet I re-established the Ottoman Empire after ten years of fraternal strife.

1453: Mehmet II Fâtih conquered Constantinople.

1517: Selim I took over the caliphate (spiritual leadership of Islam) after conquering Mesopotamia, Syria and Lower Egypt, including Mecca and Medina.

1520–66: Süleyman II, the Magnificent, conquered Baghdad, Belgrade, Rhodes, almost all of Hungary, Georgia, Aserbaijan and parts of North Africa.

1529: First Turkish siege of Vienna.

1550: Sinan built the Süleymaniye.

1683: Second unsuccessful siege of Vienna (Grand Vizier Kara Mustafa). Ottoman empire at its largest. Change of policy to defence and retreat.

1699: Loss of the Polish territories, Dalmatia, Hungary and parts of southern Russia.

1718: Further territorial losses in the Balkans as a result of victories by Prince Eugène.

1730: Bloody uprising of the Janissaries against Ahmet III's attempted reforms.

1768–1812: Russo-Turkish War.

1826: Extermination of the Janissaries and, shortly afterwards, of the Bektasçi dervishes. Army reforms, later assisted by Prussian officers (Moltke).

1829: End of the successful Greek struggle for independence with the assistance of philhellenic Europe. Eastern Armenia fell to Russia.

1839: Beginning of legal and administrative reform (tanzimat) by Grand Vizier Resçit Pasça.

1853–6: Turkey fought on the side of the Western powers against the Russians in the Crimean War. Russia lost territory as a result of the Treaty of Paris.

1876: First Ottoman constitution, soon rescinded again.

1878: Peace of St.Stefano and Congress of Berlin: the European powers reduced Turkish territory considerably after another Russo-Turkish War.

1897: Greeks declared war on Turkey over

Crete. Turkey lost after intervention by the Great Powers.

1903–18: Baghdad railway built under German direction and with German personnel.

1908: Revolution of the Young Turks. Officers insisted on the reinstatement of the 1876 constitution (Enver Paşca).

1911–12: Libya and the Dodecanese (Rhodes) fell to Italy almost without fighting.

1913: The Peace of London ended the Balkan War, and took away all Turkey's European possessions (only Adrianople/Edirne was later returned).

1914: Turkey's entry in the First World War on the side of Germany meant that it had to fight in four theatres.

1915–16: Successful defence of the Dardanelles with German assistance.

1916–17: Russians conquered Erzurum.

1919–20: Treaty of Sèvres with unacceptable, provocative conditions (Greeks to occupy Smyrna). Treaty accepted by the İstanbul government (Mehmet IV), but not by Nationalists under Mustafa Kemal.

1921–2: Victorious fight under Mustafa Kemal against the Greeks; Sultanate abolished.

1923: Treaty of Lausanne regulated population exchange with Greece. Mustafa Kemal Atatürk elected State President, Ankara declared capital.

1925–38: Abolition of the caliphate. Many reforms in the years following, intended to bring Turkey closer to Europe.

1938: Death of Atatürk.

1945: Turkey declared war on Germany. Founder member of UNO. Progressive democratization.

1950: Victory of the Democratic Party under Celal Bayar.

1952: Turkey joined Nato.

1960/71/80: Repeated corrective military intervention against dangerous internal political tensions. The process of democratization continued on each occasion.

Asia Minor
melting pot of the peoples

Akkadians: Semitic tribes from Arabia settled in Mesopotamia from 3000 BC. The old Sumerian written language was displaced by Akkadian, written in Sumerian cuneiform. In 2400 a state ruled by an Akkadian dynasty extended as far as Anatolia. In the 2nd millennium BC Akkadian was the international diplomatic language of the Near East, replaced by Aramaic in the 1st millennium.

Arabs: Before Mahomet, Semitic tribes in central and northern Arabia lived in rival nomadic groups on the edge of the desert, without forming a state. Most of them worshipped ancient Arabian deities and the Kaaba, the holy place. Mahomet's proclamation of Allah as the one god brought religious and political unity to the Arabs, leading to violent and belligerent expansion. They invaded Byzantine imperial territory under Kalif Omar in AD 634, and reached Kayseri in 646. For more than two centuries they mounted raids into the interior, occupied territory and besieged the capital, Constantinople, from the sea. The consequences of these 'Saracen' raids were impoverishment of rich villages, destruction of fertile agricultural land, fortification of cities and abandonment of large monasteries in favour of cave and rock churches. The general population and monks emigrated to the West. Shortly after Mahomet's death the Arabs' old tribal way of thinking reasserted itself. Disputes over succession split adherents. The caliphate, the Islamic leadership, passed from Arabian Omayids to Arabian Abbasids in 750. These soon absorbed Iranian civilization and were removed from power by Turkish mercenaries in the 9C. Other independent Islamic states soon followed, with the Arabian element remaining as the religious basis. Islam now bore the stamp of stronger, older cultures. Mahomet's revelations were presented in lofty poetic Arabic shaped by him. As it was not permitted to translate the Koran for services, the non-Arab faithful were compelled to learn Arabic, with Arabianisms appearing in other languages as a consequence. Arabic remained the language of administrators and scholars. In this connection Arabic script was used in calligraphy as a decorative element (abolished in 1928 in Turkey). Despite 'purification of the language' there are many Arabic words in everyday use in Turkey. Half a million Arabs live in south-eastern Turkey.

Aramaeans: Semitic nomads from Arabia invaded Mesopotamia c.1200 BC and settled around the central Euphrates and in North Syria. They took over late-Hittite cities such as Charran, Karkemish and Sam'al (south-eastern Turkey) despite opposition from the Assyrians. The Aramaic language spread throughout the Near East and beyond to become an international language. Aramaic, which was written in the Phoenician alphabet, replaced cuneiform Akkadian in the 1st millennium. Persians also adopted Aramaic as the language of the chancelleries.

Armenians: Their origin is uncertain. Herodotus maintained that they were related to the Phrygians (similar clothing and weapons) and came to Asia Minor with them in the 2nd millennium BC. They settled in the Eastern highlands, in Urartian territory, where they learned to work metal and to build in stone. The Armenian language is Indo-European with oriental elements, which suggests assimilation of the native population. Xenophon described (Anabasis, 401 BC) the Armenians as rich peasants who hid provisions underground to protect them against raids by poorer mountain peoples (Kurds). Land-hungry hordes streamed through Armenian territory, it was occupied by great states from East and West, but local kings usually maintained independent rule. The extent of their territories changed and so did the site of their capitals, according to which principality happened to have the space

and the opportunity to expand (→ Ani, Farkin, Kars, Van). In the 11C AD Armenia was abandoned under Seljuk pressure. Some of the population fled to Cilicia, where Lesser Armenia came into being (until 1375, → Tarsus, Namrun). Today Armenia is divided under Russian and Turkish rule (ASSR in Russia, Armenian Museum in Jerewan, close links maintained abroad). See chronological table from 1829. About 80,000 Armenians live in İstanbul, with their own churches. In the pre-Christian period the Persian god Ahura Mazda was worshipped wherever the political situation permitted. The Great Temple of Garni (ASSR) was Roman in design. Christianity was adopted at an early stage in Armenia, becoming the state religion in AD 300 under the influence of Gregory the Illuminator (national saint). The monk Mesrob developed a script for the Armenian language, used for an early translation of the Bible. For centuries the national church was the basis of national unity. Armenian literature included epics, novels, heathen hymns and songs and interesting scientific works. Particular treasures were notation of old hymns, miniature painting, gold and silver work (museum in Jerewan). Some churches and monasteries have survived in Turkey. Armenian church architecture developed its own style, influenced by late Roman, Syrian and Persian design. Ashlar cut from red and black lava formed the outer and inner masonry shell, even in domes and roofs, giving rise to the thick walls typical of Armenian churches. After the basilica the most popular form is a central plan with dome, of which the best example is the church at Zwarthnotz (AD 650, foundation walls survive in the ASSR).

Arzawans: Few records of this people exist. Their territory was in southern to south-western Asia Minor, near Lycia. The central towns may have been Afyon and Burdur. Hattusili, an Old Hittite king, marched against Arzawa before 1600 BC. This was essentially a raid, but war followed. In the archives in Amarna (Egypt) is a copy of a letter from Amenophis III (1413–1375 BC) to Prince Tarkundaraba of Arzawa in the Hittite language. At the time of the Hittite Empire, Suppiluliuma (1370) made the king of Arzawa his son-in-law. The country resisted at first, but became a faithful vassal within 200 years. It is possible that a race of Hittite-Luwian lords became dominant. Texts from Hattuşça suggest Luwian adminstration of southern Anatolia. In the Battle of Kadesh in 1299 Arzawans fought on the Hittite side (Muwatilli) against Egypt (Rameses II). Under the last of the Hittite Great Kings vassals became treacherous.

Assyrians: Less is known about the old Mesopotamian city state of Assur and its Akkadian successor states than about their trading colonies which came to light in Turkey. From 2000 independent rulers appeared in the 'lists of kings'. They built temples and conquered cities. Old Assyrian cuneiform tablets and cylinder seals dating from the subsequent ten centuries were excavated at a site over 1,000 km. away (Kültepe near Kayseri). They show the Assyrians in another perspective: private trading houses in harmony with their state, host states and the countries through which they passed and to whom they paid taxes, founded a network of trading posts centred outside Kanesh (Kültepe). They used black asses for transport. The traders used their own techniques for the manufacture of ceramics and small artefacts, thus exerting an influence on central Anatolian culture. Commercial contracts and letters provide information about conditions in Anatolia before the Hittite Empire. These trade links were broken in the late 18C BC. The middle and new Assyrian empires (1400–700 BC) also had points of contact with Asia Minor. The Assyrians freed themselves from the Mitanni yoke c.1400 and conquered their territories in modern eastern Turkey. This led to conflict with the Hittites and later the Urartians. The Sumerian and Hurrite traditions enabled an Assyrian style to develop in masterpieces of cylinder seal art and, in the 1st millennium, in the monumental wall reliefs in the capitals, representing military success. Late-Hittite orthostatic reliefs still carry a faint glimmer of this style.

Byzantines: This is a problematical expression because of the blurred transition from Rome to Byzantium. Byzantium had a heterogeneous population of differing origins and ideas. The political basis for Byzantium was Constantine the Great's transfer of the Roman capital to the East in AD 330. The old Thracian-Greek city of Byzantion was transformed by planning on an expansive Roman scale: 'Deutera Rhome', Constantinople. Eastern Roman detached itself from ancient cults and philosophical schools, and the language, ancient art and architecture of Rome. Hellenism dissolved into the Christian era. The splendour of cities and culture exerted a considerable attraction. Nomadic peoples, armies and hordes, competing traders and pirates appeared on every frontier. Eastern Roman provinces were lost, then won back again. The greatest single loss of power was to the Crusaders, who plundered Constantinople at the behest of Venice in 1204 and reigned for 60 years. Byzantium never recovered. In a thousand years the empire had shrunk to a tiny fragment. The capital survived alone for 100 years, until 1453.

The architecture was a serious of masterly variations on basic late-Roman forms. The transparency of classical temples gave way to a closed, complex accumulation of walls and domes as a protective shell for the sacred space, and the faithful within it. The interiors were magnificently and skilfully decorated in terms of both design and material. Ancient stone mosaic gave way to glass mosaic underlaid with colours and gold, and late-Roman portraits painted on wood developed into icon painting. Church walls were covered in frescos. In contrast with the naturalism of the Romans, figurative art was expressively abstract, even in pictorial cycles of saints. The most refined form of expression was book illumination, which continued to be pursued uninterruptedly and universally for 1,000 years. Byzantine art had many currents, stylistic trends, schools, peaks and periods of stagnation, but was always unmistakably Byzantine. Ornate court ceremonial was echoed by the lavish and technically elaborate refinement of decoration in the imperial palaces. Valuable art and craft products (silk and gold brocade, gold vessels and jewellery, shrines with enamel and ivory work etc.) made money for the state until its fall in 1453.

Galatians: Eastern Celtic tribes, for years forced back to the Danube by Alexander the Great and Lysimachos, attacked

Macedonia in 279 BC. Antigones Gonatas, the Macedonian ruler, defeated the Galatians, one of the Celtic tribes, on the Hellespont. Nikomedes of Bithynia brought the rest of the hordes to Asia against Antiochos I (Seleucid). Tolistoagians, Tektosages and Trokmen settled in eastern Phrygia from 277, and conducted raids against the cities of Asia Minor. Antiochos I defeated them in the 'Elephant Battle' of 275. Galatians were used as mercenaries by Hellenistic kings. There were soon further raids, until Attalos I defeated the plunderers in 230 (victory monument in Pergamon). Tolistoagians took over the Phrygian shrine of Cybele in Pessinus, the Tektosages fortified Ankara; certain tribes formed the Galatian League, finally defeated by Gnaeus Manlius Vulso in 189. Galatia became a Roman province in 25 BC; Paul the Apostle wrote his Epistle to the Galatians in AD 50.

Georgians: In the classical period and the Middle Ages, Georgia included the eastern shore of the Black Sea, Achaean Kolchis (with Greek settlers) and the territory of the Caucasian Iberians. Their beginnings are known from Greek mythology. In 750 BC Urartu declared a kingdom in Kolchis. Georgia was a satrapy under the Persians. In the 1C BC Mithridates occupied Georgia, and after his defeat his kingdom of Pontus and Georgia became a Roman province. Georgia often shared the fate of Armenia—both were sometimes victorious. Both were always bastions against the peoples of the East and North-East. In AD 330 Georgia declared itself Christian under St. Nino. This was supported by local kings, as in Armenia, and the country resisted violent missions by Neozoroastrian Persians and Islamic forces. When Armenia could no longer hold out, in the 11C, Georgia, protected by its northerly position, remained the only Christian nation in the East. King David the Builder (1089) succeeded in extending his territory. Subsequent centuries saw an upswing in both state and art, until the country was laid waste by the Mongols in 1386. After this there was partially autonomous administration independent of Russia, Persia and the Ottomans. Full independence was granted in 1918. In 1921 the Red Army invaded, and the Grusinian SSR was established in 1936. Part of Georgia was in eastern Turkey. The Armenian monk Mesrop gave the Georgians their alphabet. The literature consisted of epics, stories and legends of saints in extraordinary versions, translations of Biblical and liturgical texts. Separation from the Armenian church

Mosaic, c.1050, Constantine IX

Byzantine stone inlay work, St.Eudoxia

took place in 607, in favour of the Byzantine Orthodox Church. Georgian monks founded monasteries and libraries throughout the region of the Eastern Church (on Mount Athos, for example). In the Middle Ages, in the reign of Queen Tamar in 1184, a philosophy independent of the church, and belles-lettres of the highest order developed. Georgian architecture derives much from the Armenians, but there are differences: in Georgian churches the thickness of the walls in comparison with the space occupied is less. The interior is often more heavily articulated by the use of free-standing piers. In façades, blind arches are more conspicuous and deeper, breaking up the wall surfaces more. Iconostases, often made of carved stone slabs, were needed in Georgian churches for the Byzantine rite. External architectural ornament was more refined and rounded than under the Armenians. Icons and book covers were mounted in finely-wrought metal inlaid with semi-precious stones. Later (1200) painting detached itself from the iconographic austerity of Byzantine convention, showing vigour and naturalistic tendencies.

Goths: The Goths were on the move in Europe from the beginning of the AD era, and by AD 200 they had reached the Black Sea Coast. A few decades later they were enlisted by the Romans. When they were not paid, they raided Asia Minor, and in the mid-3C destroyed holy cities such as Ephesus, Pessinus and other places on their way to Cappadocia. They also struck in eastern Asia Minor. From 270 they were divided into Ostrogoths (eastern) and Visigoths (western). Visigoths and Sarmatians were settled north of the Danube to defend the Roman Empire. Adjacent to the east was Ermanarich's Ostrogoth kingdom, stetching from the Baltic to the Black Sea. The Goths were driven out by the Huns in 375, and recommenced their warlike wanderings. Later the Visigoth kingdom was established in Gaul, with the Ostrogoths in Northern Italy. The Goths learned to forge metal from the Iranian Sarmatians, as well as horseback tactics and clothing styles. Gothic runes were used to encode information and as magic signs. As border-dwellers, mercenaries, Roman generals and hostages the Goths became familiar

with Graeco-Roman culture and Aryan Christianity (Christ not God). The bishopric of Gothia was represented at the Council of Nicaea in 325.

Greeks: The lords of Troy VI (1800–1300 BC) were immigrants at least related to the Greeks, and later traded with Greece. From the middle of the 2nd millennium BC Mycenaean ceramics appeared in large quantities on the west coast of Asia Minor. Despite written evidence of Greeks on the south coast, so far only very few Mycaenean shards have been found there. From 1200 BC culture was extinguished on both sides of the Aegean. Signs of a new period of cultural development appeared in the 11C BC, in the form of protogeometric vessels. Pressure from the Dorians led to increased Greek settlement in Asia Minor. The settlers sought out bays with long peninsulas to protect their territory, or hills for acropolises. Greeks were rarely found in the interior. The Greek cities formed alliances according to tribal patterns: the Aeolian Laegue from the southern Troas to the Bay of Smyrna, the Ionian League from there to Miletos. 100 years later Dorian Hexapolis was in the extreme south-west. They all shared Greek language and Greek gods in various versions. Cretan-Mycaenean syllabic script was lost c.1200. Because of trade contacts with the Syrian coast, the Phoenician alphabet was adopted, with the addition of vowels. The oldest written finds date from the 8C BC. The polis was independent within the league. Political systems swung between democracy and oligarchy. Kings were elected or self-selected; there were no dynasties. From the 8–6C BC eastern Greek cities, Miletos in particular, founded colonies on trade routes to the eastern Black Sea. Greek cities which for years had been in danger from the East developed splendidly. Much was destroyed by the Cimmerians c.700. The Lydians turned an acquisitive eye on the west coast, but the cities came to an arrangement with Croesus in the 6C. The Persians conquered Asia Minor in 546–540 BC. Greek cities paid high taxes, levied by their own kings as Persian governors. In 499 the Ionians, incited by Miletos and supported by Athens, dared to rebel, and destroyed the seat of the Chief satrap in Sardes. Darius mounted a punitive expedition in 494, resulting in complete defeat of the Ionians. Darius' and Xerxes' campaigns of vengeance against Athens brought the Persians a series of defeats and meant retreat from Greece. Cities under the protection of Athens paid for or provided ships for the Delian-Attic League. Freedom lasted for 100 years, then the Persians were strong enough to attack the Greeks, weakened by the Peloponnesian War. All the cities on the coast of Asia Minor became Persian again almost without a struggle in 386 BC. 50 years of peace under the Persians followed. In 334 Alexander the Great entered Asia Minor to unite the Greeks and conquer the Persian empire in 331. Alexander died in 331, and his generals, the Diadochi, divided the empire between them. There were conflicts among the Diadochi, and finally three empires emerged: Ptolemaic in Egypt, Seleucid in Syria and Macedonian in Greece, under various dynasties. There were older kingdoms in the North: Bithynia and Pontus. The 3C saw the kingdom of Pergamon, the 2C that of Commagene, in northern Syria. For decades there were raids by the Galatians. Hellenistic kings ruled for 300 years; some cities were autonomous. Despite turbulence success and prosperity increased.

Greek culture in Asia Minor developed rather differently from that in Greece. At first protogeometric and geometric styles were taken over from the motherland, and connections remained. Trade with peoples in the hinterland and the Eastern Mediterranean led to orientalization of form and motifs, and a separate Eastern Greek style evolved. Ionian cities increased in size, prosperity and importance, and developed the full spectrum of their superior Greek culture. Links with the motherland and the Orient were maintained, and both were influenced in return. This Greek phenomenon remained the strongest element amongst the multiplicity of cultures for over 2,000 years. The Hellenization of the Orient had begun even before Alexander. Hellenistic notions of empire and autocracy were far from those of the actual Greeks (megalomania on Nemrut Daği in Commagene). Little archaic art and architecture has survived in Asia Minor, and little more from the classical period. The late-classical period in the 4C was under Persian supremacy, and art flourished particularly in Caria and Lycia because of the presence of Greek artists. Town walls and public buildings were built on the Greek pattern even in non-Greek cities. Imposing ruins have survived from this period.

Eastern Greek terracotta, 6C, Archaeological Museum, İstanbul

Hattians or Protohattians: In ancient oriental texts Hittites and Hatti were both used to describe the people of the Hattiland, c.2500–700 BC. In order to make a distinction the later people (from 2000 BC) are known as Hittites, the ancient population of Central Anatolia Hattians, or more clearly Protohattians. Hattians are first referred to in old Mesopotamian texts of 2300. On the written tablets of the Hittites, their successors, the Hatti language is used for cult and court ceremony, names and the names of gods. It belongs to no known linguistic group. Hattians had no script, only scratched seal stamps. There were many settlements with lavish grave goods from central to southern Anatolia from 2500–2000, with a common Bronze Age culture. Small principalities had fortified towns with tightly-packed houses. In Alaca, Hüyük, Alişçar, Horoztepe, Mahmatla among others a surprising wealth of objects and forms abounded. This was a generally peaceful court society, with lavish decoration, ceremonies and cult as the most important aspects of life. Particularly striking were metal standards with three-dimensional representations of animals. They had a highly developed metal-founding technique for bronze (copper and tin), gold, silver and lead. Gold vessels had parallel grooves like Bronze Age ceramics. As well as jewellery, stylized female double idols in gold plate and three-dimensional statuettes with naturalistic detail have been found. Hatti culture was taken over by the Hittite conquerors.

Hittites: The people later known as the Hittites moved from the East to central Anatolia c.2000 BC. Layers of burnt material in Hatti settlements suggest periods of war. Assyrian trading posts brought Mesopotamian influences to the country from 1950–1750 BC. Ceramics were refined, and the potter's wheel adopted. Highly-polished monochrome and reddish-brown patterned pottery was made. Stamp seals existed alongside cylinder seals with scenic representations. Among the 18C BC cuneiform texts found in Kültepe was a letter from King Anitta, son of Pithana, who claimed to have conquered and unified principalities. The Hittite Empire did not come into being until the 17C BC under Hattusili I, with its capital in Hattuşça. Mursili I extended it as far as Babylon. Under his successors some ground was lost and some gained, until Suppiluliuma found the New Hittite Empire in 1350. He secured the Northern border, and waged war against the Hurri in Northern Syria, making the Hittites the third great power alongside Egypt and Assyria.

The Hittite language is Indo-Germanic. As conquerors they took over Hattian cult institutions, and also names of places and gods, and the cult language. Hittite texts are written mainly in an otherwise unknown ancient Mesopotamian cuneiform script. The second script was hieroglyphic, used for seals and inscriptions in the Luwian language, long used in the late-Hittite states. The existence of '1,000 gods' suggests religious tolerance. Deities were subject to change, but the principal weather-god Tešub maintained his position. Myth in Hittite epics was Hattian, Hurrite and Mesopotamian. Despite many influences, essential Hittite features were maintained. Among the nobility the king was primus inter pares, in vassal states a theocrat. In comparison with their oriental neighbours, Hittite law was essentially humane, with a higher regard for the individual (no punishment by maiming). They were warlike, but there is no evidence of cruelty of the kind found among the Assyrians. Hattuşça provides the best examples of Hittite architecture: there are remains of massive town walls in cyclopean stone blocks with defensive refinements and brilliant harmonization with the landscape. There are monumental rectangular temples (foundations have survived) dominated more by the functionality of a number of rooms for complicated rites than the will to demonstrative form. Large terraces and courtyards with open piered halls make an impressive framework for dynastic buildings. A particular cultural achievement was the establishment of the 'magazines' (library) for clay tablets on wooden shelves with catalogues of contents and stocks. Large-scale sculpture was produced under the Empire (1500–1200): gate sphinxes and lions in Hattuşça, carved almost in three dimensions from the rock.

Hurri (Churri): The Hurri settled in eastern Anatolia, where a Bronze Age culture has been proved to have existed *c.*2300. The language is unclassifiable. In the early years of the 2nd millennium the area was conquered by Indo-Aryans using two-wheeled chariots (spoked wheels) drawn by horses. The Hurri language was soon enriched with Indian names, gods, concepts involved in horse-breeding and chariot-building. The new overlords formed a dominating noble caste, the Marjanni (Indian Marja = young hero) and small, feudal states. They expanded to the South; from 1530–1350 BC the Hurrite Mitanni empire existed in North Mesopotamia and Syria, kept the Assyrians in check and traded with Egypt. The capital, Waššukanni has still not been discovered. In Alalach (northern Syria) and Nuzi (Iraqi Kurdistan) texts in poor Akkadian with Hurrite and Aryan words have been discovered. The list of kings is incomplete: Barratna (*c.*1500), Saushshata (1470–40) took a door with golden furnishings as booty from Assur. Aratama (1440–15) and Shutarna (1415–1390) exchanged embassies with Egypt, and sent daughters to the Pharaoh after some hesitation. Tushrata (1390–52) presided over the state's declining fortunes. Despite some warlike clashes there were also friendly exchanges with the Hittites. The Hurri passed on the Sumerian-Akkadian language, cuneiform script (for international relations) and Babylonian epics.

Carians and Leleges: These tribes lived in south-western Asia Minor, between the Meander and Lake Köyceğiz. According to ancient writers the Carians were early pre-Greek seafarers to the Aegean islands. Herodotus considered the Carians and the Leleges to be the same people. Homer, 300 years before, knew Leleges from the southern Troas (near Assos) and Carians from Miletos. It is assumed that the Greeks drove the Leleges from the North and the Carians from the islands and coast near Miletos: both tribes moved to modern Caria. Lelege settlements have been found on the Halikarnassos peninsula: garrisons with citadels, fortified farms, tumuli built of layers of stone with some cyclopean blocks, circular buildings with vaulting. The Leleges had no script, and their economy was based on cattle. The Dorians founded Knidos and Halikarnassos on the coast. Carians lived in villages throughout the land, and in some cities such as

Mylasa, Alinda and Alabanda. Federations were formed along old tribal lines. There was a common temple of Carian Zeus in Mylasa and a shrine of Zeus Stratios in Labranda. In the late 7C Caria was under Lydian rule. That of the Persians in the 6C was more severe. In 499 BC the Carians were involved in the Ionian revolt, and recklessly defended themselves when the Persians struck back. Soon many Carian cities joined the Delian League. In the 4C Caria was again part of the Persian empire, ruled by a satrap dynasty, with Mausolos in the third generation. Diplomacy secured him Carian sovereignty and the execution of ambitious plans: the Hellenization of Caria, building programmes in the cities, extension of the territory governed. Mausolos founded a new capital in Halikarnassos. He introduced the Greek language and alphabet, against the will of many Carians. After 334 there was conflict between the Diadochi in Caria as elsewhere, involving Rhodes, and ending in 129 with the establishment of the Roman province of Asia. In the Imperial Roman period there were 220 years of peace and prosperity from 27 BC, and many major buildings date from this period. Despite the existence of numerous inscriptions the script is still not legible, and the language cannot be classified.

Cimmerians: These were nomadic Iranian-speaking Indo-Europeans who had pastures in the 1st millennium BC in the steppes of south-western Asia and southern Russia. The names of their rulers are Iranian: Teushpa, Tugdamme, Sandochsatra. According to Herodotus the Scythians drove the Cimmerians out of southern Russia in the 8C (Cimmerik is in the Crimea). A large number of Cimmerians crossed the Caucasus *c.*750, and invaded Urartu, burning and murdering. Rusa I lost a battle against them in 714, and killed himself. The Cimmerians defeated his son Argishto II in 707. The Assyrian king Sargon II fell in the conflict with them. In 700 Sinope on the Black Sea was attacked, and Phrygian Gordion destroyed in 696 (675). King Midas committed suicide. The Cimmerians plundered Sardes in 652, and the Lydian king Gyges died. In 640 the Cimmerians reappeared in the South-East, where they were defeated by the Assyrians.

After defeat by the Lydians, their urge for expansion was halted. Because of their martial skills they were feared like other mounted peoples, and valued as mercenaries. After 100 years of wandering around Asia Minor they are said to have settled in Cappadocia.

Kurds: The Kurds lived largely in eastern and south-eastern Turkey (Persia, Iraq). They shared peripheral territory with others. They emigrated to large Turkish cities. The Kurds are an old people; Xenophon described them in 401 BC as a freedom-loving mountain people, not subdued by the Persian Great King. The Kurdish language is Indo-European, related to Iranian-Medic. It is assumed that Medes fled to the eastern Taurus in 600 BC and mingled with Hurrite mountain peoples. No overall Kurdish state was ever formed, only striven for. Earlier there were indpendent clans and feudal principalities. National independence was fiercely defended, with additional protection from the high mountains. The Kurds resisted civilization because they equated it with administration, linguistic compulsion and classification. Rural Kurds were Shiite Alevi with different religious customs (no village mosque). They led a hard life as farmers or semi-nomads: winters are very severe in eastern Turkey.

Latins: (Crusaders, Franks, Italian Maritime Republics): The Byzantines called Christians of the Roman Catholic faith Latins. Because of lack of money and need for weapons the Byzantines had to sell important privileges to to the Italian trading powers (Venice, Genoa, Pisa) between 1000 and 1450. These cities dominated the Eastern Mediterranean with many bases and large fleets. Anger over this dependence welled up in a massacre of Italian merchants in a large quarter in Constantinople, in 1182. Disinclination for Latins turned into fear when the Crusaders were seen. It is true that the Byzantines had asked for military aid against Islam, but the emotional masses of pilgrims and knights who appeared at the gates of Constantinople in 1096 were different from the usual European soldier-mercenaries and passing pilgrim tourists. Because of the large numbers of French-speaking knights the Crusaders were called Franks in the Orthodox East. In 1204 the Franks, incited by Venice, attacked the richest city in the world, destroying and plundering, and founded a Latin empire there, ruled by Frankish nobles. When the Byzantines reconquered their city in 1261, its magnificence lay in ruins. In the Islamic east of the Byzantine republic French knights on the First Crusade established their own states in 1097, such as the kingdoms of Antioch, Jerusalem, Edessa, which lasted for 50–200 years.

Luwians: From 2000 BC Indo-Germanic nations related to the Luwians as well as the Hittites immigrated to Asia Minor. Palaeans settled to the north, Luwians to the south of the Hittites. Only their language has survived. Hattusça produced many Luwian texts in cuneiform and hieroglyphs. Religious ritual is described in Palaeic, Hurrite, Hattian and Luwic. Luwians took over the administration of the southern states: Arzawa, Lycia, Kizzuwatna. It is clear from texts that they adopted gods from the old-established cultures. such as the stag-god Rundas and the weather-god Dattas. After the fall of the Hittite empire in 1200 BC Luwian was written for a further 500 years in 'pictorial Hittite', also as an accompanying text to pictorial work; it was later displaced by Aramaic.

Lydians: The kingdom of the Lydians came into being in the 8C BC in the hinterland of the Ionian states on the West coast of Asia Minor, with Sardes as its capital. When King Gyges came to power in Lydia he pursued ambitious expansionist policies. But the Cimmerian storm which destroyed neighbouring Phrygia c.700 also raged over Sardes. Ardys, son of Gyges, succeeded in liberating his country again and expanded in the direction of Phrygia and the coast. Alyattes and Croesus continued this policy and took over the Ionian cities (with the exception of Miletos) that did not consider the Lydians as barbarians. Lydia protected them to the East and because of their proverbial wealth its people were excellent trading partners. Croesus made generous investment in Greek cult sites. In 585 a peace treaty was signed between Alyattes and the Medes, until Cyrus overthrew this dynasty in 550. Croesus was encouraged to attack the Persians by a pronouncement from the Delphic oracle saying 'If you cross the Halys (Kızıl Irmak) you will destroy a great empire', but this campaign was Lydia's downfall. Sardes became the principal seat of Persian satrapies. The Lydian language has survived in inscriptions. It is Indo-Germanic, related to Hittite. The script is like that of Eastern Greek. Little Lydian art has survived. In its early stages it was modelled on Greek works, later Persian. The Lydian court was rich in finely-crafted luxury articles. The palace has not yet been discovered. Alyattes' tomb in the great tumulus and other large-scale tombs have been plundered.

Lycians: Lycia thrusts its high mountain chains into the Mediterranean between Fethiye and Antalya. Herodotus said that the Lycians came from Crete as Termiles under Sarpedon c.1400 BC. The Hittites noted that Suppiluliuma conquered Lycia in 1350, and that it revolted. The Lycians fought and drove off Rameses II at the battle of Kardesç c.1300, alongside Hittites, Arzawans and Pisidians. Strabo recorded that the Lycians built cyclopean Tiryns for the Achaeans in the 13C. Homer portrayed the Lycians as allies of Troy in the late 13C. The pharoah Merenpta reported that people of the sea such as Achaeans, Lycians etc. unsuccessfully attacked Egypt from the west in 1230. Nothing was heard from the southwest or central Anatolia from 1200 BC. In 545 the Persian conquered Lycia after Lydia and the west coast. Lycia put up desperate resistance despite the enemy's overwhelming superiority. It then had to pay tribute like other cities, and was administered by its own dynasties with the right to strike coins. Lycia had to provide 50 ships for the Greek campaign. After the Greek victory in 480, Lycia was briefly a member of the Delian League, then under Persian rule again in 385. This period was noted for considerable building activity with artistic design under local dynasties. After the failure of the satrap uprising, Mausolos of Caria laid claim to the whole of Lycia c.360. In 334 it was taken by Alexander the Great. His Ptolomaic successors ruled in Lycia for 100 years. In 190 BC Rome presented Lycia to Rhodes for services rendered. The Lycians resisted violently and successfully. In 167 a decree of the Roman senate set Lycia free again. Under the Roman Republic freedom and dependence alternated. In the IC AD Lycia and Pamphylia formed a single administrative unit. For a good 200 years Lycia enjoyed peace and prosperity under the Roman emperors. In the late 3C AD economic decline set in, and the area was Christianized. So far in Lycia no traces have been found of feudal lords like those of Mycenae or Troy. It is certain that the Lycians were deeply freedom-loving and defended some cities to the point of self-immolation. The Lycian League lasted until the Imperial Roman period. The cities sent up to three delegates, according to population size, to the League Assembly to elect the Lyciarch. Jurors were used at the League court, and communal decisions were taken about internal security. At times of political freedom, decisions were also made about matters of foreign policy and the deployment of League troops. According to older 4C inscriptions there was an earlier League of Termiles, a predecessor or contemporary of the Lycian League. The Lycian language appears in 5&4C BC inscriptions. The script is an early Greek alphabet with characters for Lycian sounds. Fragments can now be translated. The language is related to Hittite-Luwian, and was not used after the 3C BC. So far

Heroon of Limyra, Lycian phalanx

there is archaeological evidence of pre-historic settlement only in Elmali in northern Lycia. Ancient buildings in Lycian towns are no older than the 6C BC, and most date from the Roman period. The many tomb reliefs show Ionian influence in their design, and also the involvement of Attic artists. In content and the organization of images the Persian overlords were respected. There is a bewildering profusion of tomb forms. Combinations of independent basic design with Greek elements predominate, the purest being the pillar tomb (original probably in clay brick). Another is the wooden building recreated in stone, and a third is a sarcophagus with pointed-arched roof (derivation uncertain); this is known as the Lycian sarcophagus, popular in a simplified form as a lid for stone trough tombs until the Roman period. The triangular pediments and temple in antis designs are Greek. These basic forms, with the exception of the pillar design, are varied and combined in the densely-packed tomb façades cut into the cliffs. The pillars were free-standing monoliths on a tiered base, hollowed out at the top as a tomb chamber with a stepped lid. Various mausoleum types are also placed one on top of the other. The sarcophagus or mausoleum may also be raised by an orthostat or hyposorium (plain lower tomb chambers). A particular combination of the three pre-Greek basic forms was a lower building in the wooden design, a pillar-like base on a flat roof, continuing as a sarchophagus with pointed-arched roof.

Mamelukes: The nomad rulers on the caravan routes of Central Asia had an inexhaustible supply of an extremely valuable commodity at their disposal: slaves from hostile or alien races. From the 8C BC the centres of Islamic power in Damascus, Baghdad and Cairo bought in large quantities. Turks and Circassians from the Northern steppes were bought as heathens, then converted to Islam, given a stiff military training and later their freedom, with the possibility of advancement to become officers, civil servants, emirs or even sultans. This military oligarchy itself trained slaves (Turkish: mamluk) as faithful members of their retinue, and became a power in the state, for more than 1,000 years in the case of Egypt. Turkish and Kirghiz Mamelukes reigned there as sultans from 1250–1517 and maintained a show caliphate as a mark of their legitimacy. Mameluke sultans included outstanding generals and politicians.

The Mamelukes wiped out Mongol garrisons in Elbistan, reduced Crusader bases to ashes (the Franks were enslaved or murdered, except in Cyprus); they attacked the cities of Cilicia for more than 100 years. The Ottomans under Beyazıt II fought the Mamelukes in Asia Minor from 1485–91, and seized power in Cairo under Sultan Selim in 1516. Tribute and booty had made possible a luxurious life for the Mamelukes. Their mosques and tombs are furnished with the most refined and valuable objects.

Mongols: This was originally the name of a small nomadic tribe in Central Asia to the North-West of China, ruled feudally by a tribal chieftain. Temüdshin, later Genghis Khan, a Mongol aristocrat born in AD 1155, assured that his following consisted of men of equal rank. Many tribes joined together, and adopted the name Mongol. Their most powerful enemies were overrun and plundered. Their military tactic was to attack in many waves, shoot, then wheel; this required a high degree of discipline. The troop was undefeatable. An enormous empire grew up under Genghis Khan and his successors: Russia, eastern Turkey, Mesopotamia, northern India, China and the whole of Central Asia with residence in Karakoram. Control and organization were achieved by unqualified obedience and extreme brutality. The empire was split up under successors in 1227. Under the influence of Chinese and Iranian culture, cosmopolitan states with a thin upper layer of Mongol culture and magnificent courts were established. Caravan trade was encouraged, and duties were levied. This was the pax mongolica, 80 years of secure exchange between the Far East and the Occident. Seljuks from Asia Minor were defeated by the Mongols in 1243. The Sultanate of Rum was a vassal state paying tribute. Streams of nomads poured into the country from Central Asia. The Mongols were converted to Islam c.1300, and the power of the Mongol empire collapsed. Asia Minor was reduced to anarchy: Seljuks, Turkoman and Mongol emirates fought among themselves. Mongol princes in Persia, the Ilkhane, promoted scholarship and art with an outstanding centre in Tabris. The state in Central Asia lasted for longer than the others, but by the 14C Genghis Khan's successors were simply marionettes of Turkish emirs. Timur-Leng (Tamerlane), the son of one of these emirs, botn in 1336 south of Samarkand, acquired a military following and ruthlessly stamped out rivals. Samarkand became the capital, with extravagant buildings in the style of the Islamic-Iranian overlords.

Ottomans: Before the great Central Asian migration they were Oghusen, Turkish nomads living east of Lake Aral. In the 10C they streamed across the Oxus before the Mongols to Horasan in northern Persia. There they were converted to Islam by the 11C. This process was repeated over the centuries. The Kayi, later Osman, tribe came to Asia Minor under Prince Süleyman, apparently with 400 families. His son Ertogrul received a fief near Bileçil from the Seljuk sultan Kaichosrau II c.1240. From here he made inroads into Byzantine territory. Ertogrul was buried in 1289 near the first residence in Sögüt. His son Osman pursued his expansionist policies, and 30 years later was retrospectively named the first sultan of the dynasty. The Seljuk Sultanate of Rum fell c.1300. The Ottomans were only one among several princely families. The Karamanids had now taken the place of the Seljuks. Osman succeeded in expanding his territory by a policy of alliances. He used experienced men of other nationalities as administrators. Newly-conquered cities were made capitals. The much-desired city of Prusa (Bursa) was besieged for ten years, and Osman's son Orhan took it in 1326. Prusa was extended as residence, and later became the magnificent seat of their old age. Here they built their baths and their tombs. Internal consolidation occurred under Orhan: legislation, cultural and social centres and a permanent army were established. The later famous troop of Janissaries was founded, firstly consisting of prisoners-of-war. In 1354 the first step towards Europe was taken at the Dardanelles. Further progress was made under Murat I, who made Adrianople (Edirne) capital and a great military camp in 1365. Constantinople was in a pincer grip. Serbia and its allies were beaten at the battle of Kossova in 1389. The victor, Murat, was stabbed to death in his tent by a Serbian officer disguised as a turn-coat. Beyazıt I Yilderim (Lightning) advanced as far as Styria, Greece was taken. Preparations were made for the taking of Constantinople, by building great citadels on the Bosporus, for example, but Mongol raids under Tamerlane demanded a march to the East. Beyazıt was defeated at Ankara in 1402 and taken prisoner by Tamerlane. After Beyazıt's death in 1403 and Tamerlane's sudden withdrawal, a fraternal war broke out among the sons of the sultan. Süleyman I was the first victim after three years. The second was Musa, a supporter of sheikh Bedreddin, who tried to achieve 'freedom and equality for all' with a people's army. Supported by the army and the administration Mehmet I, the third son, succeeded in restoring order 1413–21. A good relationship with Byzantium was established, and Mehmet was received with honour as a visitor. Murat II consolidated his power without major conquests. In the meantime the Janissaries had become an important instrument of war: strong youths from Christian families were gathered by devşcirme (boy harvest) in the conquered Balkan countries, taken to barracks, and trained in Islam and military skills. They were not allowed to marry, formed the sultan's bodyguard and were his most powerful fighting troops. They had the opportunity of promotion to the highest office. In later centuries they had so much power and independence that they deposed and enthroned sultans. They revolted against reforms, particularly in the 18&19C, and thus were violently abolished by Mahmut II in 1826 (by beheading). Constantinople was taken under Mehmet II Fâtih (the Conqueror) in 1453. Hagia Sophia was turned into a mosque, but Christians were permitted patriarchates. Military campaigns were mounted against the North, to consolidate power in the Balkans. The last Byzantine ruler in Trapezunt and the principality of Karaman were removed. The Genoese had to leave the Black Sea, and the Venetians were forced to sign a humiliating peace treaty. In Italy Mehmet attacked Byzantine Otranto. The Ottoman Empire was now an important factor in European politics. Despite numerous wars, Mehmet II extended his new capital, using some European artists. Beyazıt II was more interested in diplomatic intrigue than military campaigns, and only marched against the Mamelukes in Anatolia 1485–91. His son Selim I pushed his father into the background, and waged war in Asia on a large scale. Persian Sayawids threatened to take on political influence in the East, particularly as Shiites. Selim drove all the Shiities out of the country, turned against the Mamelukes, conquered Syria, Egypt, the holy city of Mecca and brought the last of the false Abbasid caliphs from Cairo to İstanbul, and had the caliphate transferred to himself: making him 'leader of all the world's Muslims', in fact a mere title. The Ottoman empire reached the peak of its power under Süleyman the Magnificent, for Europeans the prototypical Islamic-oriental ruler, admired and feared. Under him the Turks first reached the gates of Vienna in 1529, Hungary was defeated, Belgrade taken, the Knights of St. John driven from Rhodes and Baghdad taken. The former pirate admiral Cheireddin

Ottoman military music, 17/18C miniature

Barbarossa dominated the Mediterranean on the Ottomans' behalf. Süleyman, also Kanuni-Sultan (Lawgiver), extended and systematized Mehmet Fâtih's Islamic laws, and reformed the civil service and the army, advised by excellent viziers. Building flourished on an extraordinary scale in the 16C. The splendour of these sultan-heroes was never again achieved, although the empire grew larger in later years. State business was now in the hands of the viziers. The administrative apparatus, with an enormous army of civil servants, ran without the sultans' direct involvement (→ Chronological Table from 1683). By now the sultans hardly had Turkish blood because of marriage with the daughters of foreign princes. The choice of civil servants was determined not by race and religion, but by ability and loyalty to the Ottoman state. The Wakf, a religious foundation for the general good, had a precedent under Byzantines, Seljuks and emirates. The large-scale külliye was a major feature of the Ottoman period. This was a complex of buildings set around the founder's mosque and tomb, arranged both functionally and aesthetically (medrese, library, poor kitchen, hospital with school of medicine, old people's home, baths, well, toilets). It sometimes also included hostels and markets etc. as a source of income to support the külliye as a whole in the future. The pursuit of the Islamic notion of empire based on the Islamic jihad (holy war) had created a spatial freedom which needed to be shaped. It was open to ideas and forms from exisiting cultures which could be imposed on Islamic institutions. Artists, technicians, craftsmen were trained or imported to fulfil this need. Models and influences finally led to Ottoman art in its own right. The rise to political power was accompanied beyond its zenith by cultural achievements. In the sultans' workshops many craftsmen worked on the decoration of seraglio buildings and to produce luxury objects as gifts and rewards. Ottoman architecture adopted the traditional piered hall as a multidomed mosque, but in the early 14C moved to the plain domed cube. Variations and developments soon began to appear, such as small domes over the narthex, side rooms or mihrab room. The Bursa type of mosque has two domed rooms leading into each other on the long axis. The breakthrough to the large central room was made in Edirne in 1445 in the Üç Şcerefeli Camii with dome on two massive supports, flanked by four small domes, thus giving a dome over a hexagon, incorporating the side rooms. In İstanbul the thousand-year-old former church of Hagia Sophia was the model. In early-Ottoman mosques the central dome was combined with one or two half domes. They were a transition to the spatial creations of Ottoman classicism, by the great architect Sinan. Sinan was a Janissary and pioneer, and was thus involved in numerous military campaigns before becoming court architect under Süleyman in 1539 at the age of 50. As well as the famous sultans' mosques Sinan built many smaller ones for Istanbul and other towns, and also hundreds of functional buildings: bridges, dams, aqueducts and külliye. His mosque designs favour a central domed space, stamped with the Byzantine architecture with which he came to terms. He experimented with various possibilities, placing the dome on squares, hexagons and octagons, formed by half domes, screen walls or a combination of both. Following Islamic tradition (wide kibla wall) Sinan's main room is a transversely-placed rectangle, achieved by means of high-arched openings between the side piers and the inclusion of the other piers in the entrance and kibla walls; it was rare for him to stress the longitudinal axis. Sinan's individual variations on old schemes are seen in the transition from one horizontal zone to another and the articulation of the walls and piers. The pinnacle of his achievement, his last monumental work, was the Selimiye in Edirne. Some of the most brilliant achievements of Ottoman architecture were luxury buildings such as kiosks, summerhouses, fountains and baths. Ottoman buildings are unthinkable without supplementary decoration such as mukarnas (stalactites) or other ornaments in carved stone or wood, ornamental wall and dome painting, calligraphic Koran texts, marquetry on tables and wood panels, windows with grilles in pastel shades, carpets covering all the floors (the best specimens from 400 years ago are now in the museums), wall tiles, which sometimes dominate the spatial impression, a Persian tradition taken over by the Seljuks and passed on to the Ottomans.

Parthians: In the early 3C BC the Sarmates, a nomadic people related to the Scythians, succeeded in striking down from the North to Horasan in Persia. The were called Parthians after the area South of the Caspian Sea. Mithridates I, an Arsakid, founded a Parthian empire in 171 BC. He fought Scythians in the North and Seleucids in the South, and succeeded in conquering large areas of Persia and, in 139, Greek Bactria. In 53 BC the Parthians struck a severe blow against the Romans. The next 250 years were dominated by the struggle against them, and they succeeded only in reconquering territory for a short period. Armenia was incorporated in the Parthian empire, and a Parthian Arsakid, Thiridates, became king of Armenia (AD 66). The Parthians were also related by marriage to the kings of Commagene and Pontus. They remained essentially nomadic. Armed horsemen were raised to a state of fighting ecstasy by drumming. Kings are portrayed in riding garments. Small *objets d'art* were made in animal shapes. Their palaces were the first with iwans, tunnel-vaulted rooms opening on to a courtyard.

Persians and Medes: These were among the Indo-Germanic peoples who emigrated to Northern Iran from the Southern Russian steppes in the second millennium BC. Archaeological finds show that they were castle builders and mounted warriors with bow, sword, bronze helmet and armour. They were mentioned by the Assyrians in the 9C as fellow-fighters in eastern Asia Minor. They achieved military success by shooting with bows from horseback, which made them much more fast and flexible than warriors in chariots. The Medes were famous for Medean riding breeches, horse-breeding and their courage in attacking Assyria c.700. After Cimmeria and Scythia the Mede king Kyaxares destroyed the Assyrian empire with the assistance of Babylon in 616. In 585 a peace treaty was concluded with Lydia. His son Astyages enjoyed riches and the life of the court until his vassal Cyrus II, king of Persia rose in 550 and made the Medes his vassals in their turn. Cyrus smashed the Lydian empire and subjugated Western

Asia Minor in 546. Darius I of the Persian Achaemenid line took over the Great Kingdom. In 494 he suppressed the Ionian rebellion and destroyed Miletos. Defeat in Greece awaited Darius in 490 and Xerxes I in 480&79. Thus western Asia Minor was free, until Artaxerxes II subdued it again in 387. The Ionian cities of Lycia and Caria flourished economically and culturally under Persian satraps, mainly drawn from local dynasties. Achaemenid Persia was destroyed by Alexander the Great 50 years later.

As barbarians, the Persians were confronted with the ancient cultures of Asia Minor. Cyrus spared Babylon. For the administration of this state of many peoples the language of the Elamites, a people long resident in Asia Minor, was adopted, then Akkadian after the fall of Babylon, and Aramaic c.500 BC. The Persian Great Kings were isolated from their fellow-countryman by their unlimited power. The Syrians and Jews were administered by bureaucrats. 20 satraps were responsible for military matters, taxes and legislation. Other religions were tolerated, and laws established according to their precepts. The imperial postal system and the royal road from Susa to Sardes made administration of the far-flung empire possible. Financial matters were regulated by means of taxes, levies, work controls, a unified coinage. Persian art, reliefs on rocks and palaces, was subject to the notion of empire and the demonstration of power; stylized animal portraits were also a demonstration of power. Some of the traditional models date from the 3rd millennium BC: large terraces, brick building, Babylonian enamelling techniques for brick reliefs. Columned rooms, colossal guardians of gates and reliefs are similar to those of New Assyria. Artists were drawn from throughout the empire, including Ionian Greeks. A different development occurred in north-eastern Persia. The nomadic warriors became sedentary cattle-breeders and lords of castles, and defended their territory against invaders alongside the local peasants. Contrast, the notion of civilization as opposed to lawlessness, settlers as opposed to nomads, forms the background to the prophecies of Zarathustra (Zoroaster; 599–522 BC),

consisting of prayers and sayings (Gathas) and forceful verse in the eastern Persian language (Avesta). Ahura Mazda was God in nobility and greatness. Traditional gods became qualities of the one god: wisdom, truth, humility. Personal responsibility before God was required. He had an apocalyptic idea of the day on which the saviour of the world will hold judgement. Zarathustra opposed ecstasy, hero-worship, haoma drinking (the horsemen's drug). He praised the ox (the basis of the cattle-breeding culture), which is 'of good sense', and particularly condemned orgies involving ox blood, as found in the cult of Mithras, later popular among Roman soldiers. Darius, like his son Xerxes, accepted the teaching of Zarathustra, but they both abused it as political propaganda. Artaxerxes II also admitted other gods in the 4C. When the Macedonians conquered Persia in 331 BC they found a decadent civilization in the South, sinful Babel, in contrast with the North-East, where they found a Persia still dedicated to the old knightly qualities and the teaching of Zarathustra. Alexander built his policy of unification on this military élite and expressed it in mutual cult ceremonies, the wearing of Persian clothing and marriages to Persian women. His successors took a rather more military view of Persia (Seleucids). The Achaemenids left traces in Anatolia: oriental courtly traditions in the architectural and relief art of the Carian and Lydian dynasties, the Persian palace remains in Daskyleion (400 BC), tomb reliefs, numerous Persian fire altars.

Ardasha, grandson of Sasan, a Persian priest and nobleman, saw himself as liberator and successor of the Achaemenids after 550 years of foreign domination (Seleucids and Parthians) in AD226. His son Shapur I succeeded in defeating and taking prisoner the emperor Valerian. This was the beginning of a long struggle between Eastern Rome and the Sassanids. Christian Armenians were persecuted and murdered by the Sassanids. The Nestorians fled from the Byzantines, and were given guests' rights in Persia. Shortlived peace treaties were signed. The emperor Heraclitus delivered Asia Minor from Persian Sassanids in AD 627, shortly before the capital, Ktesiphon, was conquered by Arabs. The cult of Zarathustra saw a Renaissance under the Sassanids, and became the state religion. The sacred writings were gathered together in the Avesta. Other religions were not tolerated. A social revolt by the Mazdakits shook the powerful nobility. Chosrau I reorganized the nobility, at the same time reinforcing the king's centralized power. Byzantium served as the model. Sassanid literature and art were dominated by horse and rider. Captured craftsmen were housed in barracks and forced to work there. Kings were represented on three-dimensional rock reliefs as large-than-life horsemen with armour and visor, and the god Azura Mazda was also portrayed on horseback. The concept was developed by Roman artists. Iwans dominated palace design, and the throne-room was domed with squinches over the corners of a square. The walls were covered in ornamental coloured stucco. Hunting scenes on stone reliefs and silver vessels were delicate and dynamic. The life of the court was enhanced by astrology, polo, the playing of stringed instruments, chess and literature. Behaviour, food and perfumes were refined. Sassanid culture exercized an influence from China to Byzantium and in the future Islamic centres of Damascus, Baghdad and Cairo. After defeat by the Arabs, Persia was the scene of Islamic con-

flict over the prophet's successors. Although under Islam and the administration of the Islamic caliphate, Persian culture and the native ruling houses maintained their influence. Under the Grand Seljuks from 1000–1200 science and art flourished again, and did not succumb to Mongol raids and empire-building from 1220–1450, or to the rule of the Turkomen. After 200 years of splintering into small principalities an Iranian state under the Safawids came into being c.1500. It reached its brilliant peak in Isfahan with superb buildings under Shah Abbas. Political continuity was interrupted by Afghans and Ottomans. Iranian cultural traditions made a considerable contribution to Islamic artistic creativity, which crystallized around the residences of changing, rival dynasties. Artists and craftsmen, summoned or captured, created new variants from old motifs, transferred them to new materials, brought together what was profoundly separate. The old was transformed by new functions. Persian iwans and domed buildings stood alongside Arabian courtyard mosques. Brick building and brick mosaic were skilfully applied in the Seljuk-Iranian mosque. Portal and mihrab were highlighted with filigree stone or stucco reliefs in the language of

Alexander fighting the Persians, Alexander sarcophagus, İstanbul

Hellenistic-Sassanid design. The Seljuks brought models from Iran to Asia Minor and passed them on to the Ottomans, who found new stimulus from their Persian conquests in the early 16C.

Phrygians: The Phrygian empire came into being at a period in Central Anatolia which is ill-documented, as Hattuşça, the source of information, was completely destroyed c.1200. The Phrygians invaded via Thrace, and were presumably the cause of this catastrophe. The principal Phrygian settlements were on the Anatolian high plain around the capitals, Gordion and Midas. Greek myth tells of the Gordian Knot as the symbol of the problem of controlling Asia, later solved by the sword of Alexander. According to legend the kings of Phrygia were called Gordios and Midas alternately. The first Midas immigrated from Macedonia and was adopted by Gordios. In the late 8C the Assyrians referred to a King Mita of Mushki as an opponent whose cities stretched as far as Cilicia. The earliest archaeological finds also date from this period. By about 750 the Phrygians had established and secured an empire stretching from the cities of Ionia in the West and Urartu and the late-Hittite states in the East. The Cimmerians attacked in 696 or 675. King Midas committed suicide. The culture survived until the country was conquered by the Persians, when its individuality was lost. The surviving town walls in Gordion with massive gate and foundation walls of buildings give an impression of Phrygian architecture. In cities like Midasşçehri, set on steep rocky plateaus, the walls have fallen into the valley. The way in which the surrounding rock has been worked shows with what skill they were erected. Other constructional achievements are wooden and stone chambers in the tumuli on Gordion and Ankara. The principal grave goods are bronze objects: cast dishes in omphalos form, large clasps for clothing with a 'patent fastening', large vessels on stands with bulls' or human heads around their rims, as found in Urartu, Olympia and Etruria. The question of whether technique, vessel or craftsmen came from the East is unanswered. This is also true of the fine beechwood and ivory carvings in late-Hittite animal shapes. The patterning on late-8C BC megaron pebble

mosaics is astonishing: a large number of geometrical patterns, deliberately arranged off a symmetrical axis. Otherwise Phrygian art is characterized by a strong sense of symmetry, as in marquetry in wood and in the form and painting of ceramics (even in animal shapes). Vessels are covered with a dense net of geometrical patterns, framing the painted figures. Another kind is monochrome and polished, rather like the metal vessels. Next to nothing of the 'legendary' gold has been discovered, not even in the otherwise lavishly-provided tumulus. Perhaps the sense of the myth of Midas, who was able to cleanse himself of the gift that everything he touched turned to gold in the Lydian River Paktolos, is that the Lydians succeeded in siezing Phrygian gold and themselves became 'fabulously' rich. In the open countryside near Midas are monumental demonstrations of Phrygian artistic creativity: areas of rock face carved like the gables of buildings with niches and false door for movable cult images. The gables are reminiscent of wooden constructions, and the geometrical patterns of the wall surfaces of brick mosaic. In some of the niches a female figure is cut out of the rock, alone or accompanied by lions. There were rock thrones, niches and steps for cult purposes. These were centres of Cybele worship, the 'Great Mother of Asia Minor' (a variation on Kubaba in the South-East). Her cult was orgiastic, whipped up by music, with wild dances and conditions of intoxication which could lead to self-castration (the priests were eunuchs). The legend of the beautiful Attis, who dies in such worship, formed the mythological background to the games and processions (→ Pessinus). The Cybele cult had reached Rome by c.200 BC.

Romans: In the late 3C BC the Romans' political attention was drawn to the East by Philip V of Macedon, who sided against them with Hannibal. At this time the Romans had no imperial ambitions as far as the East was concerned, but they were sensitive to concentrations of power if they disturbed the balance formed by the Hellenistic states after 100 years of warlike squabbling. The Ptolemaic empire in Egypt was disintegrating. Macedon and the Seleucids (Syria) took the opportunity of sharing out Egyptian possessions in Asia Minor and the Aegean between them.

Pergamon had been a friend of Rome since 211 BC, and together with Rhodes was able to convince the Romans of the danger. The Romans for a long time indulged in long-winded and fruitless diplomatic negotiations, but then defeated the Macedonians, and then Antiochos III (of Syria) at Magnesia on Sipylos in 189 BC. The Roman general Manlius Vulso took it upon himself to free Greek Asia Minor from the Galatians, who had been a thorn in the flesh for 90 years. When called upon in the case of disputes, Rome weighed up its commitment to the parties concerned and used diplomatic means to compensate for power differences. Heirs to thrones were brought to Rome as hostages and trained to be friends of Rome, but were not accepted on returning home. All Rome's efforts failed, as the Hellenistic kings' dreams of power could not be checked. Rome began to doubt its own policy, and changed to one of suspicion and severity, crippling for the politics and economies of the states concerned. Although it had been bequeathed to them by Attalos III, the Romans hesitated before making the Pergamene empire into the province of Asia in 129 BC. Roman governers exploited it brutally. Roman merchants moved into the cities in large numbers and turned fear of the power of Rome to their advantage. Mithridates VI of Pontus (an Anatolian-Greek state with a Hellenistic-Iranian ruling house) appealed to the Greeks to fight against Rome. Accumulated hatred reached its peak in the murder of 80,000 Romans in the province of Asia in 88 BC. Western Anatolia was at war for twenty years, probably against the will of Mithridates. After Sulla and Lucullus Pompey succeeded in putting an end to the war in 63 BC and placed matters on a different footing.

Bithynia, inherited with Pontus in 74, also became a province: in the South-East Syria, after the last Seleucid, in the South Cilicia, where Pompey dealt with the pirates in a special foray in 67 BC. They had been the terror of the Eastern Mediterranean since the fall of the Ptolemaic dynasty. Smaller dependent principalities were Cappadocia, Paphlagonia, Galatia, Eastern Cilicia, Armenia, Commagene. Pompey collected fabulous wealth from the Asian princes,

but improved the situation by the reduction of taxes and cancellation of debts, and also founded new towns as well as camps for the legions. Thirty years later this development was considered in the Imperial period under Augustus. The number of provinces increased. Many placed themselves voluntarily under the protection of Rome. The 'pax romana' lasted for more than 200 years, disturbed only in Armenia and Parthia, where the problems were not open to diplomatic solution. The Roman administration continued to function despite some less than efficient emperors.

Greece and things Greek were much admired in Rome, and educated Romans spoke Greek, Hellenism also brought oriental influencs into the Romans' austere and simple lives, which concerned conservatives like Cato. Admiration was not unmingled with contempt, though there was greater tolerance in the imperial period. Early Christianity grew out of Judaism and Hellenism, a new attitude of mind which was able to spread quickly because of security and the road system. The Imperial Roman period allowed Asia Minor a seamless pursuit of Hellenism. Urban culture developed to an extraordinary extent in the 1&2C. New towns as markets in agrarian provinces opened up out-of-the-way parts of the country. Magnificent new buildings were built in the old towns, some of them founded by rich merchants. Town centres shifted from the acropolis to the plain, where monumental façades and colonnades lined the market streets. Theatres were semicircular, with closed scena façade. There were colossal buildings using the technique of ashlar shells filled with rubble, and brick buildings clad in marble. Roads, aqueducts and baths (with mosaic floors) improved living conditions even in the smaller towns. Temples for emperor worship, victory columns, triumphal arches represented the idea of empire. Long rows of statues of people held in high public esteem were set up. Many Roman scultures were copies of Greek originals. In contemporary portraits the mastery of Roman sculptures is shown in their lifelike and sharply-focussed quality. The Romans' greatest achievements were in the spheres of functional building, civil and military organization, legislation and the writing of history.

Seljuks: Seljuk, a prince of the Turkish Oghusen who had immigrated from Central Asia, converted to Islam c.1000. His successors placed themselves and their people in the service of the Ghaznawids (a dynasty of former military slaves). In 1040 the Seljuks put their masters to flight. The Seljuk Toğrul-beğ of the Sunni faith delivered the Abbasid caliph from his Shiite masters in 1057, and gained legitimization for the conquering of Transoxania as far as Syria. His successors Arp Arslan and Melik Şah enlarged the empire in 1063 and 1072 respectively, and adopted the style of the Iranian court. Their adviser and vizier was Nizam al Mulk, an Iranian statesman and scholar. Alp Arslan resettled related nomadic tribes in Eastern Anatolia, where they were able to graze their cattle and undertake raids, thus challenging the Byzantines. Arp Arslan defeated the emperor Romanus at Malazgirt in 1071, and the Byzantine frontier collapsed.

Turkish tribes which had been converted to Islam moved westwards, some forming principalities like the Danishmendids in the North. Süleyman, son of a hostile relation of the Great Seljuks, was the founder of the Rum Seljuks (Rum = on Roman territory). As a fellow-fighter in disputes about the throne of Byzantium he succeeded in acquiring Nicaea in 1081 and pronounced himself sultan. In extending his power towards Syria he fell in 1086 in a conflict with the Great Seljuks. His son Kılıç Arslan was taken prisoner, and was unable to enter into his inheritance in Nicaea until 1092, which was reconquered by Crusaders for Byzantium. He consolidated his position by fighting, alliances and matrimonial policy. His son Masud made Konya the capital in 1134, enlarged the empire, secured frontiers and re-established ravaged towns and villages. His son Kılıç Arslan II had again to fight on all fronts in 1156. In 1175 he finally destroyed the Danishmendids. Now his principal opponent was Byzantium under Manuel I Comnenus. Byzantine armies were almost completely destroyed in two battles at Niksar and Myriokephalon (Sultandağı). In 1186 Kılıç divided his empire between eleven sons, and they quarrelled until

1204. Kaikosrau I sought protection in Byzantium, found friends there, married a Greek and established himself as sole ruler in Konya. In 1210 he fell in a battle with the Franks. The Seljuk empire was at its most flourishing and extensive under Kaikaus I and Alaeddin Kaykobad I (1219–36).

The Seljuks undertook extensive building programmes: Greek, Armenian and Persian artists and craftsmen were heavily involved in this new architecture. The style of the Rum Seljuks was supported by the spirit and architectural ideas of those giving the commissions. As well as bridges, which were built all over the country, the caravanserais, or hans, are particularly impressive. There were formerly 90 of these large, fortress-like buildings, placed roughly every 30 km. along the main trading routes. Most of them were built in ashlar, and fortified with towers. They had vaulted halls with several aisles and drum domes for goods and beasts of burden; additionally there was almost always an extensive courtyard with arbours on the long sides for bedrooms, kitchens, baths or workshops, with a mescit in the entrance building. The most magnificent of the hans had a mosque on four arches in the courtyard. Courtyard and hall portals were emphasized, and often lavishly decorated. The Seljuk mosque showed considerable variety of design. Models from other Islamic lands were transformed with reference to local climate and the materials available. Stone buildings existed, as well as Persian-Seljuk brick mosques. The most common design was a vaulted hall with piers. Flat wooden ceilings were rarer, and ancient columns or wooden columns as supports rarer still. The number of bays tended to be reduced. The influence of the Christian basilica led to emphasis of the centre by means of raised and broadened central aisles, or similar treatment of the dome above the prayer room in front of the mihrab. Medreses and hospitals had longitudinally extended open courtyards leading to an iwan, or a domed central room with fans of triangles between the square room and the dome. By the iwan were the tombs of the founders, and cells for students or the sick along the side walls. Free-standing türbe had pyramidal roofs set on a polygonal building. In the period of the emirate from the 14C round türbe with conical roofs appeared. All buildings had portals similar to mihrab niches in front of them, arches with mukarnas (stalactites), broad strip decoration framed by geometrical patterns, stylized inscription borders, leaf ornamentation or plant tendrils with Eurasian animal motifs. Stone relief varied from extremely shallow to high, sometimes almost baroque, with bulbous, boss-like design. Lavish decoration also spread to façades and minarets. Many minarets show ancient Persian-Seljuk brick mosaic technique with patterns of turquoise glazed and unglazed bricks. Many patterns were transferred to wood-carving or marble on the sides of the minbar. The mihrab often had stucco ornamentation, often combined with glazed tile revetment. Sometimes entire domes are covered with wall tiles. The favoured colour combinations were black with dark blue, turquoise and white or dark brown with beige and yellow (gold). Faience decoration of the palaces was more lively: tiles with human or animal figures and ornaments were mounted in stellar patterns. Tile mosaic was used to decorate niches and vaults: fragments of monochrome tiles were set in patterns with broad mortar joints. Brocades and carpets were the splendid textiles of the sultan's court. The culture of the emirates did not quite achieve the brilliance and style of its models, but encouraged national elements.

Scythians: The Scythians were among the Indo-European peoples who forced their way from the Eurasian steppes towards the South to countries with old-established cultures in the first millennium BC. Herodotus provides detailed information about the lives of these mounted warriors and their burial ritual, which involved human and animal sacrifices. They drove the Cimmerians, a related tribe, out of Russia, and in the 8C swept through Urartu, leaving scorched earth behind them. In the early 6C they were driven out by the Medes, and returned to Russia after their 100 year adventure. Scythian arrowheads from the period of destruction have been found in Urartian castles, and 7C horses' bits in typical early-Scythian style, which survived in southern Russia alongside the Graeco-Scythian style until the 5C. The extraordinarily decorative forms showed stylized realism.

Turkomen: A large group of nomadic Turkic peoples appeared between the Altai and the Oxus from AD 500. Most of them remained within the inner Asian steppe belt. Some founded empires in the South, the Seljuks, for example. Countless of them made their way to Anatolia as individual clans, where Byzantine border protection broke down in 1071, or c. 1300, when the Mongols and the Seljuks lost their power. Islam, often handed down in unorthodox form, gave them the right to present themselves to infidels as Gazi (Fighters for Faith). These Turkomen were mainly responsible for the Turkification of Anatolia. They formed into new principalities, or emirates. The mutually hostile Turkomen princes of the Ak Kojunlu and Kara Kojunlu (White Sheep and Black Sheep) show their nomadic origins in their names. Their short-lived empires left behind interesting buildings in eastern Anatolia and Persia. Nomadic tribes were welcomed by Islamic and Christian potentates as accomplished horsemen and warriors, but feared by town-dwellers and farmers because they destroyed cultures and lived by pillage. They did not feel themselves bound by state laws, nor the precepts of Islam, but the rules of the clan were respected and enforced. The Turkomen offered some products in the marketplace: animals, dairy produce, craft work, densely knotted and woven carpets in gleaming wool, with geometrical patterns and finely-matched colours. The number of Yürüks (Wanderers) has dropped to a few thousand in modern Turkey. Intensive agriculture and forestry are not compatible with extensive grazing. There are now hardly any dromedaries and Yürük tents in black goat-hair on the yaila.

Urartians: The Urartian empire came into being in the 9C BC in the Van-Urmia-Lake Sevan area. There was continuous prehistoric, early-Hurrite settlement here from the third to the middle of the second millennium BC. From 1550–1350 the Hurrite Mitanni empire lay to the south, towards northern Mesopotamia and Syria. The Urartian language is very similar to Hurrite, which suggests they might have been late successors of the Hurri. So far few traces of the period 1350–900 have been discovered. The annals of the Assyrians that King Arame of Urartu's capital was plundered in 856. The Assyrians were the great opponents throughout Urartu's 200 most successful years. Even before the Urartian empire was formed the Assyrians fought against '60 kings of Nairi or Urartri'. The reason for this was the trade routes from eastern Asia to the Black Sea and from Syria to Asia Minor. Iron came down from the North, and horses from the Manaeans, Persians and Medes. Arame drew together the lords of smaller kingdoms. The first king mentioned in Urartian inscriptions, Sardur I (844), ruled over a large region, and built a massive fortress on the cliffs at Van. His capital was Tuspa. His successors Ispuini (828), Menua (810) and Argisti I (785) subjugated new lands, punished traitors, and and secured conquered territory with fortresses. Under Sardu II (765) Urartu was at its largest, and extended from the Mediterranean to the Caspian Sea. Then came the first great defeat by the Assyrians. Rusa I founded the new residence of Toprakkale in 733 and won back some territory. In 714 the Assyrian Sargon II described how he had again destroyed flourishing cultures. The Cimmerians ravaged the remainder of the empire between 717 and 707. Rusa committed suicide. Urartu continued to exist on a modest scale. Kings with traditional names undertook rebuilding, achieved economic success, and entered into an alliance with the Assyrians under pressure from new enemies, the Scythians and Medes, to whose attacks both nations succumbed c.600. There were many gods in the Urartian pantheon, with the national deity Haldi to the fore. The kings ruled on his behalf. The ancient Hurrite demigod Tešub appears as Tesheba, still connected with bull cult and tree oracle. Urartian inscriptions in the Assyrian langauge and in cuneiform script were chiselled into stone, sometimes in two languages (Urartian and Assyrian). They document conquests objectively, and also record the laying of foundation stones. There were also hieroglyphic inscriptions which so far have not been deciphered. The oldest sites show what a high standard Urartian architecture had already reached. They built fortresses, usually on high sites,

on the rocks of their capitals and also at many strategically important points (40 in the Van region). The network of castles was so dense that news could be transmitted by beacon fires. Rocky sites were sweepingly terraced for cult places and buildings, and steps cut for the building of defensive walls. These were 13–19 ft. thick and 40–50 ft. high, stabilized with stone towers and supporting piers. Palaces were several storeys high with battlements and arrow slits. Many buildings were precisely rusticated, and some were patterned with light limestone and dark basalt ashlar. The temple was at the highest point, usually square with a pedimented roof and throne for the god. The walls were decorated with painted hunting or cult scenes with pale blue backgrounds. The palace in Altıntepe had a porch with many columns, a predecessor of the Apanada in Persia. Rural fortresses served as bases for governors and their staff, as centres for collecting tribute and storing provisions, and there were rooms with long rows of clay vessels, each holding 600 litres. They built an irrigation system of stone canals, often with aqueducts over the mountains, up to 70 km. in length, admired even by their enemies. Some of them still function. Barren highland valleys were made into orchards and vineyards, plateau groves, artificial lakes, paddocks for horses. Urartian architects had no difficulty in driving shafts into the rock for tunnels, cisterns and impressive tomb chambers for their kings. Objects made by Urartian metalworkers, now spread around the museums of the world, were in demand even in antiquity. Large bronze sacrificial bowls with human, gryphon and bulls' heads were also found in Etruria, Greece and Phrygia. Helmets, shields, belts and quivers in bronze with friezes of figures, despite their similarity with Mesopotamian-Assyrian designs, also show qualities of their own: length of lions' legs, the shape of the human nose, snakes on helmets, eight spokes on the wheels of war chariots, not found in Assyrian chariots until decades later. A dominant concern with horses is reflected in naturalistic hunting scenes almost 100 years older than the famous Niniveh hunting reliefs. Urartian culture lived on and could be recognized in its successors.

Index of places referred to in the guide

The place names printed in bold are the towns listed in alphabetical sequence in the main text, and the other place names are those listed under 'Environs'.

A   26°   B   27°   C   Burgas

BULGARIA

Plovdiv

Ardas

Edirne

Kırklareli

1

Havsa

Babaeski

Lüleburgaz

Saray

GREECE

Meriç N.

Ergene N.

Çorlu

Thessaloníki

Tekirdağ

Alexandroúpolis

Keşan

2

Marmara
Adası

Samothráki

Gelibolu /
Gallipoli

Kapıdağı Yarımad

Erdek

Kyzik

Aegean Sea

Dardanelles

Bandırm

Gökçeada

Manyas Gö
Lake Many

40°

Çanakkale

Çan

Límnos

3

Troy/
Truva

Bozcaada

Alexandria
Troas

Neandria

Balıkesir

Key

Antandros

Edremit

Chryse

Town described under
main heading in text

Assos /
Behramkale

Town described under
Environs in text

Ayvalık

Motorway

Main road

Secondary road

Railway

Lesbos

Pergamon /
Bergama

Airport

Maltepe

Frontier

Scale 1 : 2 000 000

0   20   40km

Continued p.572

B   27°   C   Akhisar

BLACK SEA

1

Belgrade
Forest
İSTANBUL
Eyüp
Üsküdar

Şile

Karasu
41°

Sea of Marmara

Princes' Isles

Gebze
Libyssa
Hereke
İzmit
Adapazarı

2

Yalova
Çiftlikköy
Yalova
Kapliça

İznik Gölü
İznik

Geyve
Sakarya N.

Mudanya

Yenişehir

Osmaneli
Vesirhan

Bursa

Uluabat Gölü
Apollonia /
Apolyont

Bileçik

eion
Mustafakemalpaşa

İnegöl

Söğüt

Continued p.566

Simav C.

Eskişehir

Tavşanlı

3

Kütahya

Aisanoi /
Aesani

Arslan
Kaya

Kybele
Kapıkaia
39°

Simav

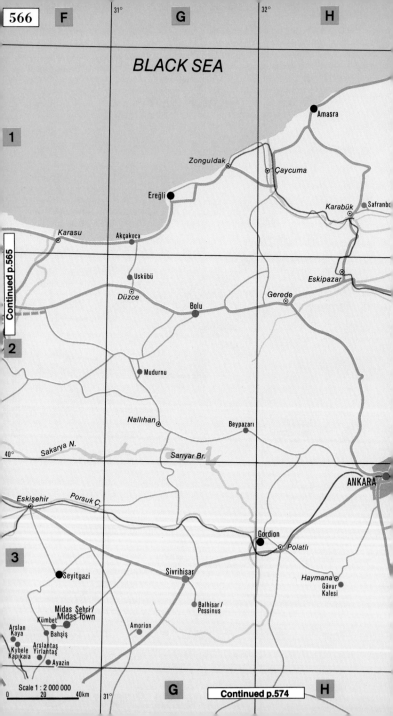

F

31° G 32° H

BLACK SEA

Amasra

Zonguldak
Çaycuma

Ereğli
Karabük
Safranbo

Continued p.565

Karasu
Akçakoca

Uskübü
Eskipazar

Düzce
Gerede

Bolu

Mudurnu

Nallıhan
Beypazarı

40°
Sakarya N.

Sarıyar Br.

ANKARA

Eskişehir
Porsuk Ç.

Gordion

Polatlı

Seyitgazi
Sivrihisar

Haymana
Gâvur
Kalesi

Midas Şehri /
Midas Town
Kümbet
Balhisar /
Pessinus

Arslan
Kaya
Bahşiş
Amorion

Kybele
Kapıkaia
Arslantaş
Yilantaş

Ayazin

Scale 1 : 2 000 000
0   20   40km
31°

G Continued p.574 H

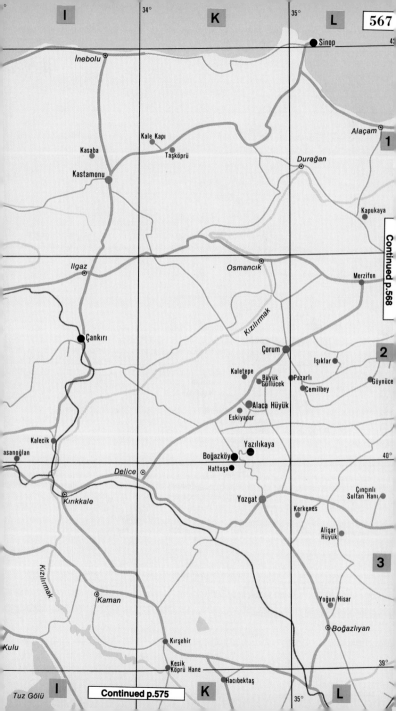

Sinop

İnebolu

Alaçam

Kale Kapı

Kasaba

Taşköprü

Durağan

Kastamonu

Kapukaya

Ilgaz

Osmancık

Merzifon

Continued p.568

Kızılırmak

Çankırı

Çorum

Işıklar

Kaletepe

Büyük
Güllücek

Pazarlı

Cemilbey

Göynüce

Alaca Hüyük

Eskiyapar

Yazılıkaya

Kalecik

asanoğlan

Boğazköy

Hattuşa

Delice

40°

Kırıkkale

Yozgat

Çınçınlı
Sultan Hanı

Kerkenes

Alişar
Hüyük

Kızılırmak

Kaman

Yoğun Hisar

Boğazlıyan

Kulu

Kırşehir

Kesik
Köprü Hane

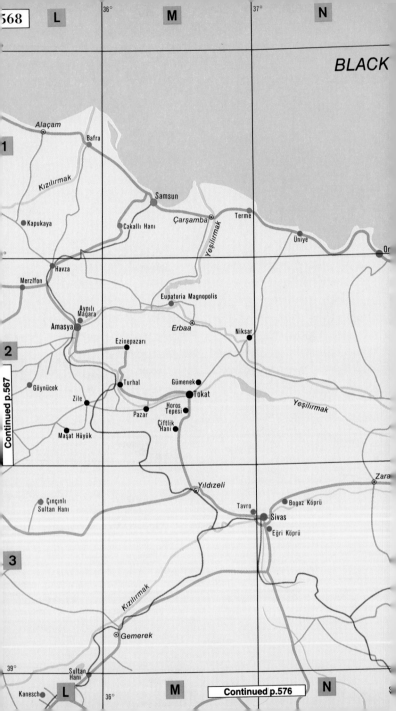

L 36° M 37° N

BLACK

1

Alaçam

Bafra

Kızılırmak

Kapukaya

Samsun

Çakallı Hanı

Çarşamba

Terme

Yeşilırmak

Üniye

Or

Havza

Merzifon

Eupatoria Magnopolis

Aynılı
Mağara

Amasya

Erbaa

Niksar

2

Ezinepazarı

Göynücek

Turhal

Gümenek

Yeşilırmak

Zile

Tokat

Horos
Tepesi

Pazar

Çiftlik
Hanı

Maşat Hüyük

Continued p.567

Yıldızeli

Çınçınlı
Sultan Hanı

Tavro

Boğaz Köprü

Sivas

Zara

Eğri Köprü

3

Kızılırmak

Gemerek

39°

Sultan
Hanı

Kanesch

L 36° Continued p.576 N

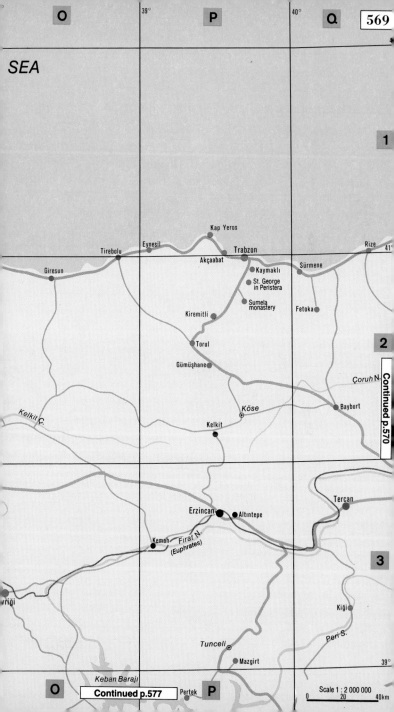

SEA

O | 39° | P | 40° | Q

1

Kap Yeros

Eynesil

Tirebolu

Akçaabat

Trabzon

Rize

41°

Giresun

Kaymaklı

Sürmene

St. George
in Peristera

Kiremitli

Sumela
monastery

Fetoka

Torul

2

Gümüşhane

Çoruh N.

Continued p.570

Köse

Bayburt

Kelkit Ç.

Kelkit

Tercan

Erzincan

Altıntepe

Kemah

Fırat N.
(Euphrates)

3

rüği

Kiği

Peri S.

Tunceli

Mazgirt

39°

Keban Barajı

O

Continued p.577

Pertek

P

Scale 1 : 2 000 000

0   20   40km

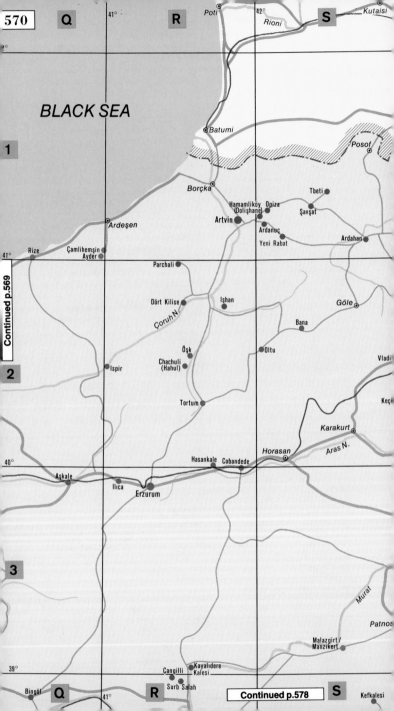

Q

R

S

42°

Poti

Rioni

Kutaisi

BLACK SEA

Continued p.569

1

⊙ Batumi

Posof

Borçka ⊙

Hamamliköy Opiza
(Dolişhane)

Tbeti

Ardeşen ⊙

Artvin

Şavşat

Ardanuç

Ardahan

Yeni Rabat

41°

Rize

Çamlihemşin

Ayder

Parchali

2

Dört Kilise

İşhan

Göle

Çoruh N.

Bana

Öşk

Oltu

Vladi

Ispir

Chachuli
(Hahul)

Keç

Tortum

Karakurt

Aras N.

40°

Hasankale Cobandede

Horasan

Aşkale

Ilıca

Erzurum

3

Murat

Patnos

Malazgirt /
Manzikert

39°

Çangilli

Kayalıdere
Kalesi

Bingöl

Q

R

Surb Salah

Continued p.578

S

Kefkalesi

41°

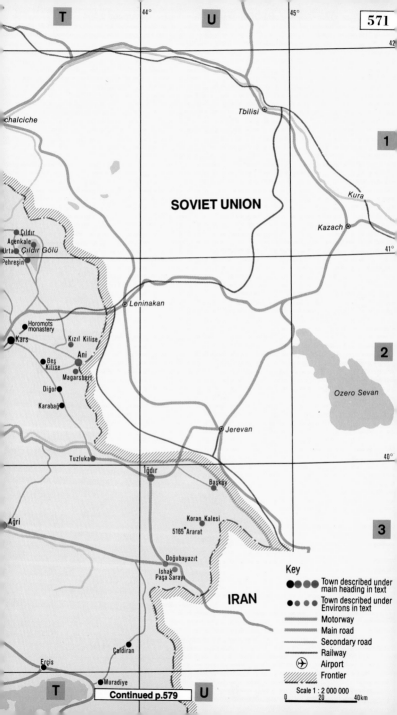

T
U
U

chalciche

Tbilisi ⊙

SOVIET UNION

Kura

Kazach ⊙

Çıldır
Agenkale
Urta Çıldır Gölü
Pehreşin

Leninakan ⊙

Horomots
monastery
Kızıl Kilise
Kars
Ani
Beş
Kilise
Magarshert

Diğor

Karabağ

Ozero Sevan

Jerevan ⊙

Tuzluka

Iğdır

Başköy

Ağri

Koran Kalesi
5165● Ararat

Doğubayazıt
Ishak
Paşa Sarayı

IRAN

Çaldiran

Erçis

T
U

Muradiye

Continued p.579

Key

●●●● Town described under
main heading in text

●●●● Town described under
Environs in text

━━ Motorway
━━ Main road
━━ Secondary road
━━ Railway
⊕ Airport
▨ Frontier

Scale 1 : 2 000 000
0   20   40km

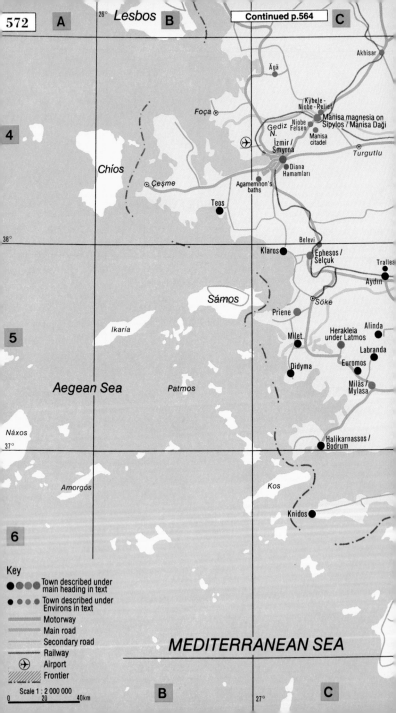

572

Continued p.564

Lesbos

Akhisar

Ağa

Kybele -
Niobe - Relief

Foça

Gediz
N.

Niobe
Felsen

Manisa magnesia on
Sipylos / Manisa Daği

4

Chíos

İzmir /
Smyrna

Manisa
citadel

Turgutlu

Çeşme

Diana
Hamamları

Agamemnon's
baths

Teos

Belevi

Klaros

Ephesos /
Selçuk

Tralles

Aydın

Sámos

Söke

Priene

Ikaria

Milet

Herakleia
under Latmos

Alinda

5

Didyma

Labranda

Euromos

Aegean Sea

Patmos

Milâs /
Mylasa

Náxos

Halikarnassos /
Bodrum

Amorgós

Kos

6

Knidos

Key

● ●●● Town described under
main heading in text

● ● ● ● Town described under
Environs in text

Motorway

Main road

Secondary road

Railway

✈ Airport

▨ Frontier

MEDITERRANEAN SEA

Scale 1 : 2 000 000

0   20   40km

Continued p.574

4

5

6

Afyon

Uşak

Sardes / Sart

Birgi

Beyşesultan / Çivril   Işıklı

Dınar

Nysa

Büyük Menderes N.

Pamukkale / Hierapolis

Laodikeia   Akhan

Kolossae

Çardak Han

Acıgöl

Burdur Gölü   Isparta

Burdur

Kuruçay-Höyüğü

Haçılar

Aphrodisias / Geyre

Denizli

Alabanda / Araphisar

Acıpayam

atonikeia kihisar)

Muğla

Tefenni

Dalaman Ç.

Korkuteli

37°

Termessos

Marmaris

Kaunos

Kadyanda

Elmalı

Kizilbel

Karataş-Semayük

Arykanda

Fethiye

Kaya

Tlos

Pinara

Limyra

Kumluca

Letoon

Xantos

dos

Patara

Phellos

Andriake

Apollonia

Myra

Kaş / Antiphellos

Teimussa

Simena

Aperlai

Kekova-Tersane

Megisti

36°

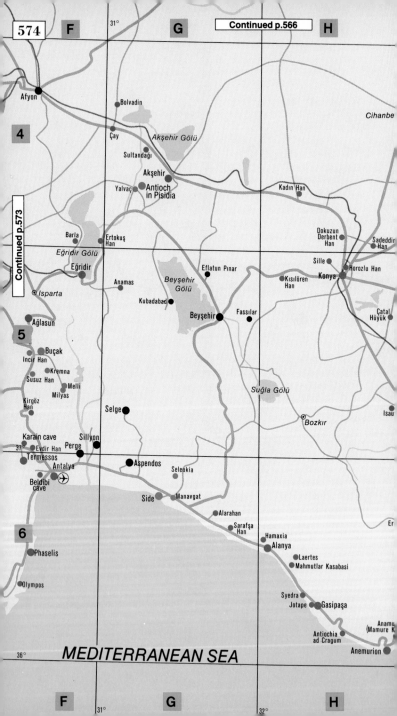

Continued p.566

Continued p.573

F G H

4

5

6

Cihanbe

Afyon
Bolvadin
Çay
Akşehir Gölü
Sultandağı
Akşehir
Yalvaç
Antioch
in Pisidia
Kadın Han
Dokuzun
Derbent
Han
Sadeddir
Han
Barla
Ertokuş
Han
Eğridir Gölü
Eğridir
Sille
Horozlu Han
Kısılören
Han
Konya
⊙ *Isparta*
Anamas
*Beyşehir
Gölü*
Eflatun Pınar
Çatal
Hüyük
Ağlasun
Kubadabad
Beyşehir
Fassılar
Buçak
İncir Han
Kremna
Susuz Han
Melli
Milyas
Suğla Gölü
Kirgöz
Han
Selge
⊙ *Bozkır*
Isau
Karain cave
Sillyon
37
Evdir Han
Perge
Termessos
Antalya ✈
Aspendos
Seleukia
Beldibi
cave
Side
Manavgat
Alarahan
Sarafşa
Han
Hamaxia
Alanya
Er
Phaselis
Laertes
Mahmutlar Kasabasi
Olympos
Syedra
Jotape
Gasipaşa
Anamu
(Mamure K
Antiochia
ad Cragum
Anemurion
31° 32°

MEDITERRANEAN SEA

36°

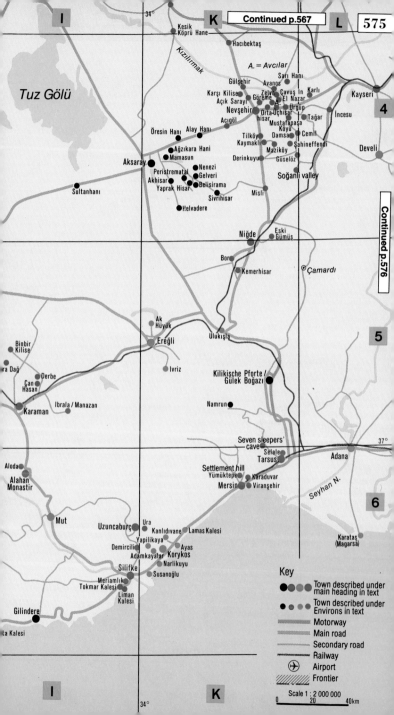

Kesik
Köprü Hane

Hacıbektaş

Kızılırmak

A. = Avcılar

Sarı Hanı

Gülşehir

Avanos

Karlı

Kayseri

Karşı Kilise
Açık Sarayı

Zelve
Göreme

Çavuş in
A. El Nazar

İncesu

Nevşehir

Ürgüp

Acıgöl

Orta-Uçhisar
hisar

Tağar

4

Mustafapaşa
Köyü

Öresin Hanı

Alay Hanı

Tilköy
Kaymaklı

Damsa

Cemil

Ağzıkara Hani

Mamasun

Maziköy

Şahineffendi

Aksaray

Peristremata

Nenezi

Derinkuyu

Güselöz

Akhisar

Gelveri

Develi

Yaprak Hisar

Belişirama

Sivrihisar

Misli

Soğanlı valley

Sultanhanı

Helvadere

Niğde

Eski
Gümüş

Bor

Kemerhisar

○ Çamardı

Continued p.576

Ak
Hüyük

Ereğli

Ulukışla

5

Binbir
Kilise

ra Dağ

Derbe

İvriz

Kilikische Pforte /
Gülek Boğazı

Çan
Hasan

İbrala / Manazan

Namrun

Karaman

Seven sleepers'
cave

37°

Aloda

Şelale
Tarsus

Adana

Alahan
Monastir

Settlement hill
Yümüktepe

Karaduvar

Mersin

Viranşehir

Seyhan N.

6

Mut

Uzuncaburç

Ura

Kanlıdıvane

Lamas Kalesi

Yapilikaya

Ayas

Demircili

Adamkayalar

Korykos

Karataş
(Magarsa)

Silifke

Narlıkuyu

Meriamlık

Susanoğlu

Tokmar Kalesi

Liman
Kalesi

Gilindere

ta Kalesi

Key

● ●●● Town described under
main heading in text

● ●●● Town described under
Environs in text

Motorway

Main road

Secondary road

Railway

⊕ Airport

Frontier

Tuz Gölü

Scale 1 : 2 000 000

0   20   40km

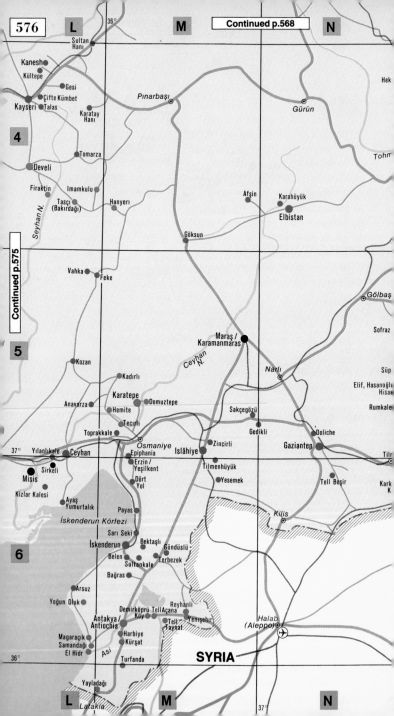

Continued p.568

Continued p.575

L   M   N

36°

Sultan
Hanı

Kanesh
Kültepe
Gesi
Çifte Kümbet
Kayseri Talas
Karatay
Hanı

Pınarbaşı

Gürün

Hek

4

Tomarza

Develi

Firaktin
Imamkulu
Tasçı
(Bakırdağı)
Hanyeri

Afşin
Karahüyük

Elbistan

Göksun

Tohm

Continued p.575

Vahka Feke

Gölbaş

Sofraz

5

Maraş /
Karamanmaraş

Narlı

Süp

Elif, Hasanoğlu
Hisar

Rumkale

Kozan

Kadırlı

Karatepe
Hemite
Anavarza   Domuztepe
Tecirli
Toprakkale
Yılanlıkale Ceyhan
37°

Ceyhan
N.

Sakçegözü

Gedikli

Doliche

Gaziantep

Tilr

Osmaniye
Epiphania
Erzin /
Yeşilkent
Dört
Yol

Zincirli
Islâhiye

Tilmenhüyük

Yesemek

Tell Beşir

Kark
K

Sirkeli
Misis
Kızlar Kalesi

Ayaş
Yumurtalık

Payas

İskenderun Körfezi

Kilis

6

Sarı Seki
İskenderun Bektaşlı
Belen   Gündüslü
Sultankale Terbezek
Bağras

Arsuz

Yoğun Oluk

Demirköprü Tell Açana
Köy
Reyhanlı

Antakya /
Antiochia
Magaracık
Samandağı
El Hıdır

Harbiye
Kürşat
Asi
Turfanda

Tell
Taynat
Yenişehir

*Halab
(Aleppo)*

SYRIA

Yayladağı

Latakia

36°

L   M   37°   N

Continued p.578

40°

Mazgirt

Peri

Bingö

Keban Barajı

Pertek

Keban

Palu

Elâzığ　Harput

İçme

4

Habibursaği

Nazar Gölü

Malatya

Ergani

Eğil

Arsameia
on Euphrates

Nemrut Dağı

Diyarbakır

Yeni Kale
(Eski Kâhta)

Chabinas-
Brücke　Arsameia
on Nymphaios

Pirin
(Perre)　Karakuş

Siverek

Adıyaman

Horis Kale

Fırat
(Euphrates)

5

Samsat
(Samosata)

Sesönk

Viranşehir

Urfa

Sultantepe

meia

Sumatar

37°

ecik

Harran

Akçakale

6

Al Furat
(Euphrates)

SYRIA

Ar-Raqqa

Key

- ●●●● Town described under main heading in text
- •••• Town described under Environs in text
- ▬▬ Motorway
- ▬▬ Main road
- ── Secondary road
- ── Railway
- ✈ Airport
- ▨ Frontier

Scale 1 : 2 000 000
0　20　40km

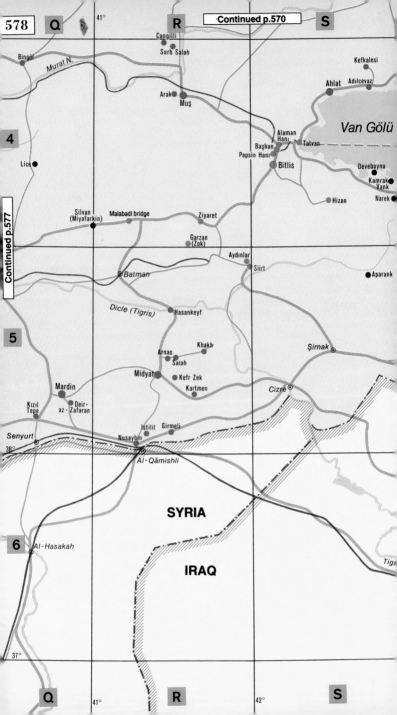

Continued p.570
Continued p.577

Q
R
S

Cangilli
Surb Salah

Bingöl

Murat N.

Kefkalesi

Ahlat
Adılcevaz

Arak
Muş

Van Gölü

4

Alaman
Hanı
Başhan
Papsin Hanı
Bitlis
Tatvan

Lice

Deveboynu
Kamrak
Vank

Hizan

Narek

Silvan
(Miyafarkin)
Malabadi bridge
Ziyaret

Garzan
(Zok)

Aydınlar

Batman
Siirt

Aparank

Dicle (Tigris)
Hasankeyf

5

Khakh
Arnas
Salah

Şirnak

Midyat
Kefr Zek
Kartmen

Cizre

Mardin

Kızıl
Tepe
Deir-
az-Zafaran

İstilil
Girmeli

Senyurt
Nusaybin

38°

Al-Qāmishli

SYRIA

6
Al-Hasakah

IRAQ

Tig

37°

Q
41°
R
42°
S

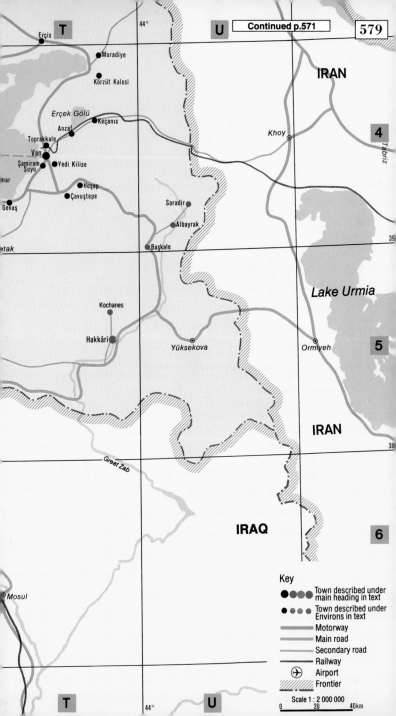

T

U

44°

Erçiş

Muradiye

Körzüt Kalesi

IRAN

Erçek Gölü

Keçaniş

Anzaf

Khoy

Toprakkale

4

Van

Tabriz

Şamiram
Suyu

Yedi Kilise

nar

Hoşap

Gevaş

Çavuştepe

Soradir

Albayrak

39

tak

Başkale

Lake Urmia

Kochanes

Hakkâri

5

Yüksekova

Ormiyeh

IRAN

38

Great Zab

IRAQ

6

Mosul

T

U

44°

Key

● ● ● ● Town described under
main heading in text

● ● ● ● Town described under
Environs in text

Motorway

Main road

Secondary road

Railway

⊕ Airport

Frontier

Scale 1 : 2 000 000
0   20   40km

Important Turkish and Arabic Terms

avlu	courtyard, mosque forecourt
bahçe	garden
bayram	festival, holiday
bedesten	covered bazaar
bend	dam
çayhan	tea house
cami	mosque
çeşme	spring, fountain
dağ	mountain
ders-hane	Koran reading school
eski	old
hamam	bath
han	guest house, inn
hane	house
hisar	castle, fortress
imam	Islamic clergyman
iwan, liwan	vaulted hall opening towards courtyard
kale	castle, fortress
kapı	gate, door
kibla	direction of prayer
kilise	church
köprü	bridge
köy	village
kufi	former Arabic style of calligraphy
külliye	complex of buildings around a mosque
kütüphane	library
mahalle	district of town
manastir	Christian monastery
medrese	Islamic school
mesçit	small mosque
mihrab, mihrap	prayer niche
minare	minaret
minbar, mimber	pulpit seat
müezzin	caller to prayer
mukarnas	stalactite ornament
oda	room
ramazan	month of fasting
şadırvan	mosque fountain
saray	castle, palace
sebil	drinking fountain
şehir	town, place
sokak	street
tekke	Islamic monastery
tepe	hill (with human settlements)
türbe	mausoleum
yeni	new
yol	way